# RESEARCH HANDBOOK ON BRAND CO-CREATION

*For Aleksandra, Bobi, Boki, Darko, Dino, Ilias, Jovana, Marin, and Marko V., with gratitude for all the years of friendship in Copenhagen — Stefan*

*For the team here at CBS and our efforts to bring international colleagues together to push the boundaries of branding research; and to Dorte, for keeping me sane — Richard*

*For Boris, with gratitude for his support in all my endeavors — Sylvia*

*For Mum (1938–2021) — Adam*

# Research Handbook on Brand Co-Creation

## Theory, Practice and Ethical Implications

*Edited by*

**Stefan Markovic**

*Associate Professor, Copenhagen Business School, Denmark*

**Richard Gyrd-Jones**

*Professor MSO, Copenhagen Business School, Denmark*

**Sylvia von Wallpach**

*Professor MSO, Copenhagen Business School, Denmark*

**Adam Lindgreen**

*Professor, Copenhagen Business School, Denmark and Extraordinary Professor, Gordon Institute of Business Science, University of Pretoria, South Africa*

**EE** Edward Elgar
PUBLISHING

Cheltenham, UK • Northampton, MA, USA

Published by
Edward Elgar Publishing Limited
The Lypiatts
15 Lansdown Road
Cheltenham
Glos GL50 2JA
UK

Edward Elgar Publishing, Inc.
William Pratt House
9 Dewey Court
Northampton
Massachusetts 01060
USA

Paperback edition 2023

A catalogue record for this book
is available from the British Library

Library of Congress Control Number: 2022931355

This book is available electronically in the **Elgar**online
Business subject collection
http://dx.doi.org/10.4337/9781839105425

ISBN 978 1 83910 541 8 (cased)
ISBN 978 1 0353 2368 5 (paperback)
ISBN 978 1 83910 542 5 (eBook)

Printed and bound by CPI Group (UK) Ltd, Croydon, CR0 4

# Contents

*v*

# Figures

# About the editors

**Stefan Markovic**

Dr. Stefan Markovic holds a Ph.D. in Management Sciences (*cum laude*), a Master of Research in Management Sciences, and a Bachelor and Master in Business Administration from ESADE Business School, Universitat Ramon Llull, Spain. He is currently an associate professor in the Department of Marketing at Copenhagen Business School (CBS), Denmark. In addition, he is the Chair of the Marketing Ethics Research Cluster, a Co-chair of the Advances in Branding Research Cluster, and a member of the Consumer Research Cluster at CBS.

Apart from his involvement at CBS, Markovic is also the National Representative of Denmark, the Chair of the Special Interest Group on Branding, and an Executive Committee Member at the European Marketing Academy (EMAC). Moreover, he is Co-Editor-in-Chief of *Business Ethics, the Environment & Responsibility* (formerly, *Business Ethics: A European Review*) and Associate Editor for Interdisciplinary Research with *Industrial Marketing Management*. Markovic is a member of the editorial advisory boards of *European Business Review* and *Industrial Marketing Management*, as well as an ad hoc reviewer for many top-tier international academic journals (e.g., *Journal of Business Ethics*, *Journal of Business Research*, *IEEE Transactions on Engineering Management*, *Technovation*) and renowned international academic conferences (e.g., European Marketing Academy Conference, American Marketing Association Conference).

Markovic's research addresses various intersections among brand management, marketing, innovation, business ethics, corporate social responsibility, and sustainability. He has published in well-established international academic journals, including *Journal of Business Ethics*, *Journal of Business Research*, *Journal of Brand Management*, *Industrial Marketing Management*, *Technological Forecasting & Social Change*, and *IEEE Transactions on Engineering Management*. With his doctoral thesis, entitled "21st-Century Brands: An Innovation Opportunity and an Ethical Challenge," Markovic won third prize in the 2017 International Doctoral Thesis Competition held by the European Doctoral Association in Management and Business Administration (EDAMBA).

**Richard Gyrd-Jones**

Dr. Richard Gyrd-Jones is Professor MSO at Copenhagen Business School (CBS) and Docent at Oulu Business School, Finland. He earned his Ph.D. at the University of Southern Denmark and has international experience as a senior lecturer at Griffith University in Australia; visiting scholar at Texas A&M, College Station, USA, and University of Technology, Sydney; and visiting professor at University of Hertfordshire, UK, IAE Paris (Sorbonne), and University of Turku (Pori). He is co-founder of the Brand Meaning Network, which brings together top international scholars on brand meaning co-creation topics; co-chair of the Advances in

Branding Research Cluster at CBS; and co-initiator of the Special Interest Group in Branding at European Marketing Academy.

His research focuses on challenges to managing brands in the context of the multiple stakeholders. He is particularly focused on how for-profit and not-for-profit organizations manage their brands in their stakeholder ecosystems. Gyrd-Jones also investigates brand identity co-creation and issues around the implementation of branding strategies at a managerial level. His most recent research marks a significant theoretical progression, moving beyond a focus on the actors involved in brand co-creation to the performative acts they adopt to co-create brands. His work has been published in journals such as *Journal of Business Research, Industrial Marketing Management,* and *European Journal of Marketing.* He also is extensively involved in teaching and teaching administration, including a recently approved project to develop and implement value co-creating pedagogy.

### Sylvia von Wallpach

Dr. Sylvia von Wallpach, SFHEA, is Professor with special responsibilities in Branding and Marketing Management at the Department of Marketing of Copenhagen Business School (Denmark). She achieved her doctoral degree at the University of Innsbruck (Austria), where she also held different academic positions between 2006 and 2014. She gained international experience as visiting scholar at Boston College (MA, USA), as Erwin Schrödinger Post-Doctoral Fellow at Copenhagen Business School (Denmark), and as visiting teaching faculty at the University of Zagreb (Croatia) and the University of Bayreuth (Germany).

von Wallpach engages actively with the international academic community, as Associate Editor for Marketing at *European Management Journal,* organizer/chair of the EMAC Climber Community (https://www.emac-online.org/intrest-groups/emac-climber-community), co-chair of the French Austrian German Workshop on Consumer Behavior, and regular reviewer for various top-tier international academic journals and conferences.

von Wallpach's main research interests are in the fields of branding, interpretative consumer research, and qualitative method development. In her branding research, she focuses on multi-stakeholder branding and brands as social processes, with a particular interest in the negotiation and co-creation of brand meaning and brand identity in stakeholder networks. Her publications have appeared in renowned academic journals such as *Tourism Management, Journal of Business Ethics, Journal of Business Research, Psychology & Marketing, International Marketing Review,* and *Nonprofit and Voluntary Sector Quarterly,* among others. Von Wallpach's research has been awarded several international prices (e.g., Social Science Space Impact Contest winner 2020; Young Researcher Award 2013 of the "Wissenschaftliche Kommission Marketing im Verband der Hochschullehrer für Betriebswirtschaft e. V."; German Market Research Award 2012).

### Adam Lindgreen

After studies in chemistry (Copenhagen University), engineering (the Engineering Academy of Denmark), and physics (Copenhagen University), Professor Adam Lindgreen completed an MSc in food science and technology at the Technical University of Denmark. He also finished an MBA at the University of Leicester. He received his Ph.D. in marketing from Cranfield University. His first appointments were with the Catholique University of Louvain (2000–2001) and Eindhoven University of Technology (2002–2007). Subsequently, he served as Professor of Marketing at Hull University's Business School (2007–2010); University of Birmingham's Business School (2010), where he also was the research director in the Department of Marketing; and University of Cardiff's Business School (2011–2016). Under his leadership, the Department of Marketing and Strategy at Cardiff Business School ranked first among all marketing departments in Australia, Canada, New Zealand, the United Kingdom, and the United States, based on the hg indices of senior faculty. Since 2016, Lindgreen has been Professor of Marketing at Copenhagen Business School, where he also heads the Department of Marketing. Since 2018, he also has been Extraordinary Professor with University of Pretoria's Gordon Institute of Business Science.

As a visiting professor, Lindgreen has worked with various institutions including Georgia State University, HEC Paris, and Melbourne University. His publications have appeared in *California Management Review, Entrepreneurship and Regional Development, Industrial Marketing Management, International Journal of Management Reviews, Journal of Advertising, Journal of Business Ethics, European Journal of Marketing, Journal of Marketing Management, Journal of the Academy of Marketing Science, Journal of Product Innovation Management, Journal of World Business, Organization Studies, Psychology & Marketing,* and *Supply Chain Management: An International Journal,* among others. His scores of books in business and economics include *A Stakeholder Approach to Corporate Social Responsibility* (with Kotler, Vanhamme, and Maon), *Managing Market Relationships, Memorable Customer Experiences* (with Vanhamme and Beverland), *Not All Claps and Cheers* (with Maon, Vanhamme, Angell, and Memery), *Public Value* (with Koenig-Lewis, Kitchener, Brewer, Moore, and Meynhardt), and *Sustainable Value Chain Management* (with Maon, Vanhamme, and Sen).

The recipient of the "Outstanding Article 2005" award from *Industrial Marketing Management* and the runner-up for the same award in 2016, he serves on the board of several scientific journals; he is Co-Editor-in-Chief of *Industrial Marketing Management.* His research interests include business and industrial marketing management, corporate social responsibility, and sustainability. He has received the Dean's Award for Excellence in Executive Teaching. Furthermore, he has served as an examiner (for dissertations, modules, and programs) at a wide variety of institutions around the world. Lindgreen is a member of the International Scientific Advisory Panel of the New Zealand Food Safety Science and Research Centre (a partnership among government, industry organizations, and research institutions), as well as of the Chartered Association of Business Schools' Academic Journal Guide (AJG) Scientific Committee in the field of marketing.

Beyond these academic contributions to marketing, Lindgreen has discovered and excavated settlements from the Stone Age in Denmark, including the only major kitchen midden – Sparregård – in the south-east of Denmark; because of its importance, the kitchen midden was later excavated by the National Museum and then protected as a historical monument for future generations. He is also an avid genealogist, having traced his family back to 1390 and published widely including eight books and numerous articles in scientific journals (*Personalhistorisk Tidsskrift, The Genealogist,* and *Slægt & Data*) related to methodological issues in genealogy, accounts of population development, and particular family lineages.

# About the contributors

**Ulf Aagerup** has a Ph.D. in business administration from Gothenburg School of Business, Economics and Law. He is currently Associate Professor of Marketing and the director of the International Marketing Program at Halmstad University (Sweden). Aagerup has an extensive business background in consumer marketing, business development, and sales with several multinational corporations. His research focuses mainly on experimental research pertaining to branding and consumer behavior.

**Feyza Ağlargöz** is Assistant Professor of Marketing in the Department of Business Administration at Anadolu University (Turkey). She received her doctoral degree from Anadolu University. She has been a guest post-doctoral researcher at the School of Economics and Management, Lund University. She teaches marketing management, marketing strategy, global marketing, and retail management at undergraduate and graduate levels. She has published book chapters, journal articles, and abstracts at international conferences. She is currently working on collaborative consumption, videography, and sustainable consumption topics; her research interests include arts marketing, consumer culture, social marketing, and critical marketing studies.

**Yun Mi Antorini** is a strategist and digital business owner at the LEGO Group. Her work focuses on digital consumer engagement with the global community of adult LEGO fans. She received her Ph.D. in user communities and innovation from Copenhagen Business School in 2007. Her research interests include user communities, user innovation, digital engagement, multisided platforms, and new governance and business models that emerge in the space between companies and external user communities. She serves as a doctoral mentor at Aarhus University (Denmark) and advisory board member at University of Southern University (Denmark). Her work has been published in journals such as *MIT Sloan Management Review*, *International Journal of Innovation Management*, and *Journal of the Association for Consumer Research*. She collaborates with research teams from Aarhus University, Copenhagen Business School, and UCL University College to develop actionable insights regarding user engagement and innovation management.

**Maja Arslanagić-Kalajdžić** is Associate Professor of Marketing at the School of Economics and Business, University of Sarajevo (Bosnia and Herzegovina), as well as Head of the Centre for Research and Development at the University of Sarajevo. She received her doctoral degree from the Faculty of Economics, University of Ljubljana (Slovenia) in 2015. Her research focuses on business relationships, accountability, branding, and international marketing. She currently serves as an Associate Editor for Special Issues at *Industrial Marketing Management* and has published in *Journal of Business Ethics*, *Industrial Marketing Management*, *Journal of Business and Industrial Marketing*, *Journal of Business Research*, *Journal of International Marketing*, *International Marketing Review*, *Journal of Macromarketing*, *British Food Journal*, and *Total Quality Management & Business Excellence*.

**Vesna Babić-Hodović** received a Ph.D. (*cum laude*) in marketing sciences from the School of Economics and Business, University of Sarajevo (Bosnia and Herzegovina), in 2001. She is currently a Full Professor of Marketing Management, Services Marketing and Strategic Brand Management, as well as the Chair of the Marketing Department and Vice Dean for the Scientific Research and Doctoral program. Her research interests include services marketing, brand and product management, and marketing management. Babić-Hodović is an associate editor of *South East Europe Journal of Economics and Business* and has published articles in *Tourism and Hospitality Management, SEE Journal of Economics and Business*, and *Emerging Markets Finance and Trade*. She also published several books pertaining to marketing, such as *Services Marketing, Marketing in Banking, Marketing Management*, and *Principles of Marketing* (co-authored).

**Fabian Bartsch** is Associate Professor of Marketing at Montpellier Business School (France). His research interests include cross-cultural consumer behavior, global branding, and global consumer culture(s). He serves as associate editor of *International Marketing Review*. To date, his work has been published in *Journal of the Academy of Marketing Science, Journal of International Business Studies, Journal of International Marketing, International Marketing Review*, and *Journal of Business Research*.

**Adele Berndt** is an associate professor at Jönköping International Business School (Sweden) and an affiliated researcher at Gordon Institute of Business Science at the University of Pretoria. Her research focuses on the intersection of consumers and branding in diverse product and service contexts. She has authored articles appearing in various marketing journals. She has lectured extensively in service marketing and consumer behavior, as well as presented international conference papers and edited books on these topics. Berndt is a member of the Academy of Marketing Science and serves on the boards of various academic journals.

**Roderick J. Brodie** is Professor Emeritus at the University of Auckland Business School. He is a leading international scholar in the areas of service relationships, branding, and customer engagement. He has authored more than 120 articles, many published in leading international journals such as *Journal of Marketing, Journal of Marketing Research, International Journal of Research in Marketing, Management Science*, and *Journal of Service Research*. He is an associate editor of *Journal of Service Research* and former associate editor for *Marketing Theory*. He has served on the editorial boards of *Journal of Marketing, International Journal of Research in Marketing*, and *Journal of Academy of Marketing Science*. He is listed among the 2020 most Highly Cited Researchers from Clarivate™ (top 0.1 percent in Business and Economics worldwide).

**Teresa Brugger**, M.Sc., recently graduated from the University of Innsbruck (Austria), with a thesis on "The Iconization of Greta Thunberg: The Role of Myths in Co-Creating a Person Brand." Her research addresses person branding, cultural branding, and the co-creation of brands. Currently, she is gathering practical experience in brand management.

**Cecilia Cassinger** is Associate Professor of Strategic Communication at Lund University (Sweden). She holds a Ph.D. in business administration with a focus on marketing. Her current research concerns social sustainability in cities and the transformative potential of branding and communication strategies to mitigate conflicts in places. She has published articles in journals such as *Place Branding and Public Diplomacy, Place Management and*

*Development, International Journal of Tourism Cities*, and *European Journal of Cultural Studies*; she co-edited *The Nordic Wave in Place Branding* and *The Routledge Companion to Media and Tourism*. She is a member of the editorial board of *Journal of Place Management and Development*.

**Bart Claus** is Assistant Professor of Marketing at IESEG School of Management (France). His research interests include consumer identities, social influences on consumer behavior, and consumer behavior related to ownership and sharing. To date, his work has been published in *International Journal of Research in Marketing* and *Journal of Services Management Research*.

**Catherine da Silveira** is an assistant professor at Nova School of Business & Economics (Portugal). She holds a Ph.D. in strategy and marketing from the Open University Business School (UK). Her fields of research encompass several branding areas, such as brand co-creation, brand identity management, branding for sustainability, and luxury branding. She has published in *Journal of Business Research* and various practitioner-oriented publications. In addition to serving as the Academic Director of the Global CEMS Master's in International Management at Nova School of Business & Economics and as a board member of a Portuguese luxury company, she coordinates consulting projects for branding and marketing for sustainability. Before joining the academic world, she worked for the L'Oréal Group as a marketing executive, across multiple divisions, brands, and countries.

**Christian Dam** is a doctoral student in marketing at the University of Gothenburg. His research crosses the fields of consumption and culture. In his doctoral research project, he is employing an interpretive lens to explore how nostalgia permeates the marketplace and how consumers interact with the past, through the mediation of consumption. Moreover, he has a keen interest in research areas involving globalization and branding. In addition to his research interests, he finds inspiration in teaching classes on globalization and consumer behavior.

**Andreas Aldogan Eklund** has a Ph.D. from the School of Business and Economics, Linnaeus University (Sweden). He is currently an Associate Lecturer in Marketing at the College of Business Administration, University of Wisconsin-La Crosse (United States) and an Assistant Professor at the School of Business and Administration, Linnaeus University (Sweden). His research addresses various intersections among sensory marketing, branding, consumer psychology, and the service-dominant logic. He recently has extended his research into digitalization and gamification. His work has been published in *Journal of Product & Brand Management*.

**Peter Espersen** is an internationally recognized pioneer in digital business models and consumer co-creation. Most recently, he was CEO and co-founder of eVote, a next-generation electronic voting and feedback company. Previously, Espersen was Head of Digital Innovation and Co-Creation for the LEGO Group, where he spearheaded the Digital Innovation team to engage fans of all ages to co-create unique products and experiences, including the Webbie-honored ReBrick LEGO Mindstorms EV3 and the LEGO Ideas site. Prior to LEGO, Espersen was GM for Sulake Corp. in Scandinavia, running Habbo Hotel, an MMMOG with almost 250 million users worldwide. He has also worked on business development and media/digital strategy for a variety of clients throughout his career, including Sony PlayStation, Disney, Amazon, and Ford. Espersen served as a board member for jovoto, an open innovation platform connecting brands with a global community of creatives, and is a Senior Advisor to Urban. Us, a venture fund investing in seed and early-stage startups that solve urban-focused problems. He is a regular speaker at tech, social media, and gaming conferences around the world and is a featured lecturer at University of Copenhagen, the ESCP Master's Program in London and Paris, and Fordham University in New York.

**Praveen Goyal**, Ph.D., is Assistant Professor of Management at the Department of Management, Birla Institute of Technology & Science (BITS), Pilani. He has published papers pertaining to CSR and corporate sustainability in *Journal of Global Information Management, Management Decision, Journal of Non-Profit and Public Sector Marketing, Benchmarking: An International Journal, Journal of Modelling in Management,* and *Sustainable Production and Consumption,* among others. He is the recipient of an Emerald Literati Network Award for Excellence 2016. He has guest edited special issues on evidence-based processes in business and systems in *International Journal of Business and Systems Research* and evidence-based management practices in accounting and finance in *International Journal of Management Practice.*

**Andrea Hemetsberger** is Professor of Branding at the University of Innsbruck, Academic Director of the Brand Research Laboratory, and Speaker of the Research Area EPoS (Economy, Politics & Society). Her research focuses on branding and interpretive consumer research with a focus on CCT and social media. Her research has been published in, for example, *Journal of Consumer Research, Organization Studies, Consumption, Markets & Culture, Journal of Business Research, Journal of Macromarketing, Journal of Marketing Management, Entrepreneurship & Regional Development,* and *Management Learning.* Hemetsberger won the Shelby Hunt Award in 2012 and the Literati Award in 2017 and is a member of several review boards.

**Linda D. Hollebeek**, Ph.D., is Senior Associate Professor of Marketing at Montpellier Business School and Full Professor of Marketing at Tallinn University of Technology. Her research centers on customer/consumer engagement and interactive consumer–brand relationships. Her work has been published in *Journal of the Academy of Marketing Science, Journal of Service Research, Journal of Interactive Marketing,* and *Journal of Business Research,* among others. She was named a Clarivate Highly Cited Researcher (2020), is the recipient of the 2020 SERVSIG Emerging Scholar Award, serves as associate editor for *European Journal of Marketing,* and has co-edited *The Handbook of Research on Customer Engagement* (Edward Elgar).

**Gry Høngsmark Knudsen** received a doctoral degree in digital marketing from the Department of Marketing and Management at University of Southern Denmark in 2012. She is currently Director of Research for applied research in business and technology at UCL University College, Denmark. Her research interests are situated at the intersection of digital marketing, gender, and consumer communities. She is part of the national reference group for Digital, Industry & Space. She has published in international academic journals such as *Journal of the Association for Consumer Research, Westminster Papers for Culture and Communication,* and *MedieKultur.* She collaborates extensively with companies such as the LEGO Group to implement and develop current knowledge in business practice.

**Oriol Iglesias** is Associate Professor and Head of the Marketing Department at Ramon Llull University, ESADE Business School. Previously he was Director of the ESADE Brand Institute and Chair of the Research Group on Brand Management. He is a member of the Scientific Committee of the Global Brand Conference and the Scientific Committee of the Special Interest Group on Brand, Identity, and Corporate Reputation of the Academy of Marketing. He is a member of the editorial board of *Journal of Brand Management* and the editorial review board of *Journal of Product & Brand Management*. He has been a member of the executive committee of the European Marketing Academy. He has published articles in *California Management Review, Journal of Business Ethics, Industrial Marketing Management, Journal of Business Research*, and *European Journal of Marketing*. Iglesias is a member of the Medinge Group.

**Nicholas Ind** is a Professor at Kristiania University College, Oslo, and a Visiting Professor at ESADE Business School (Spain), and Edinburgh Napier University. Ind has a Ph.D. in media philosophy (*magna cum laude*) from the European Graduate School (Switzerland). He is a member of the advisory board of *Corporate Reputation Review*, the editorial board of *Journal of Brand Management*, and the editorial review board of *Journal of Product & Brand Management*. Ind is the author of 13 books, published in nine languages; he also has published articles in *Journal of Brand Management, California Management Review, Business Horizons, European Business Review*, and *Industrial Marketing Management*. He was a founding member of the Medinge Group, an international think tank focused on conscientious brands.

**Ingo O. Karpen** is Full Professor of Business and Design at Karlstad University (Sweden) and the University of Adelaide Business School (Australia). As a leading international expert in strategic and service design, Karpen draws on and integrates various disciplines towards design-driven innovation. Karpen has won various (inter)national research and teaching awards, including an Australian Research Council Discovery Grant. His research has appeared in leading journals such as *Journal of Service Research, Journal of Travel Research, Journal of Retailing, Journal of Service Management, Journal of Business Research*, and *Marketing Theory*. He serves as an editorial review board member for several journals and has co-edited special issues across disciplines, as well as a book on (strategic) design. As a practicing strategic designer, Karpen consults with businesses and government institutions across sectors to lead strategic transformation projects that can foster individual and systemic well-being.

**Dannie Kjeldgaard** is Professor of Marketing at the University of Southern Denmark, in the research group Consumption, Culture and Commerce. Published in international journals and books, Kjeldgaard's work analyzes change processes involving market-based glocalization in domains such as place branding, branding, media and identity construction, global consumer segments, ethnicity, and qualitative methodology. His research has been published in *Journal of Consumer Research, Journal of Consumer Behaviour, Consumption, Markets and Culture, Marketing Theory, Journal of Macromarketing*, and several anthologies. He is the Editor-in-Chief of the journal *Consumption, Markets and Culture*. His current research interests lie at the cross-sections of climate change, responsibilization, and consumer culture.

**Oliver Koll** is a marketing scholar, researcher, and consultant. He is a marketing professor at the University of Innsbruck, where his research and teaching focus on stakeholder marketing, brand management, and retailing. Koll's research has been published in journals such as *Journal of the Academy of Marketing Science, Journal of Business Research*, and *Psychology*

*& Marketing* and presented at conferences. For the past 20 years, he has held a position as a Strategic Insights Consultant with Europanel, a joint venture of GfK and Kantar Worldpanel, the world's leading source of consumer panel insights. He also is the founder and partner of two consulting agencies in Innsbruck, IMARK Strategy Advisors and IMARK Market Intelligence.

**Monika Koller** is an associate professor in the Department of Marketing, WU Vienna University of Economics and Business (Austria). Within marketing management domains, her research focuses on perceived value in relation to products and services from consumers' perspective, by investigating relevant consequences and implications for applied marketing. Her main research interests in consumer behavior and consumer neuroscience relate to sensory perception and alternative methods to measure psychophysiological processes.

**Maria Kreuzer** is an associate professor at the International University of Monaco, lecturer at the Management Center Innsbruck, and brand consultant at IMARK. She teaches in international doctoral and master's programs and has extensive experience in executive education. As a passionate qualitative researcher, Kreuzer loves conducting research in the field on branding, consumer experiences, and qualitative research methods. Her research has been published in *Journal of Business Research*, *Journal of Marketing Management*, and *Psychology & Marketing*.

**Philip Lechner** completed his bachelor's degree in business administration in autumn 2020 at the University of Applied Sciences Salzburg (Austria), where he is continuing his master's degree. He focuses on marketing and relationship management, as well as human resources, and gained expertise by participating in the Interreg project "CE Responsible" (https://www.interreg-central.eu/Content.Node/CE-RESPONSIBLE.html). Before and during his studies, he worked in the trading industry and has practical experience in relationship and personnel management.

**Andrea Lucarelli** is an associate professor at Stockholm University (Sweden). He holds a Ph.D. in business administration with a focus on marketing. His main research interests relate to the geographical, political, and historical dimensions of consumption; advertising and marketing; the politics of marketing; and the role of techno-digital culture in the construction of market and sports phenomena. He has published articles in journals such as *Journal of Place Management and Development*, *Cities*, *Marketing Theory*, *European Journal of Marketing*, and *Annals of Tourism*. He is a member of the editorial board of *Journal of Place Management and Development*.

**Venkatesh Mani** is an associate professor in the Department of Strategy and Entrepreneurship, Montpellier Business School (France). He holds a Ph.D. from Indian Institute of Technology, and a Post Doctorate from Faculty of Economics, University of Porto, which was supported by a prestigious Erasmus Fellowship. He has more than 21 years of academic and industrial experience, along with more than a decade of experience working with Fortune 500 companies in various senior management roles. He has contributed many research articles to journals such as *International Journal of Production Economics*, *Transportation Research Part A: Policy and Practice*, *Supply Chain Management: An International Journal*, *Annals of Operations Research*, *Technological Forecasting and Social Change*, *Production Planning and Control*, and *Business Strategy and the Environment*. He also serves as an editorial advisory board member of *Management Decision*.

**Géraldine Michel** is Professor of Marketing and Director of the Brands & Values Chair at the Sorbonne Business School, University Paris 1 Panthéon-Sorbonne. In addition, she is the co-editor-in-chief of *Décisions Marketing* and a member of the editorial board of *Journal of Business Research*. She is the author of several books, including *The Art of Successful Brand Collaborations* (Routledge), and articles in renowned international academic journals, such as *Journal of Business Research*, *Psychology & Marketing*, *Journal of Advertising Research*, *Qualitative Market Research*, *Journal of Personal Selling and Sales Management*, *Journal of Brand Management*, and *Recherche et Applications en Marketing*. Her current research interests include brand management, social representation, values, and co-creation.

**Hans Mühlbacher** is Professor em. of Marketing at the International University of Monaco. He held visiting positions at universities in Austria, France, Switzerland, and the United States and has published widely in academic journals, including *International Journal of Research in Marketing*, *Journal of Management Information Systems*, *Journal of Product Innovation Management*, *Journal of Business Research*, and *European Journal of Marketing*. Having served as President of the European Marketing Academy, he is an honorary fellow of the Academy. Mühlbacher has been the longtime Associate Editor for International Business of *Journal of Business Research* and the editor of *Marketing – ZFP*. He has taught in many international doctoral, MBA, master's and bachelor programs and has extensive experience in executive education. His research interests focus on brands as social processes, open innovation, and marketing strategy formation.

**Anu Norrgrann** received her Ph.D. in marketing from University of Vaasa and has worked as Assistant Professor of Marketing at Hanken School of Economics (Finland). Currently she works at Design Centre Muova (Vaasa, Finland) with market-oriented design projects. Her research interests pertain to culturally informed consumer research, business networks, and branding and retailing, with themes in which symbols and meanings are in focus. Her current research deals with industrial service design socio-material consumption practices, consumer roles and agency, brands and other symbolic resources in business networks, and interactive learning in online marketing education. Norrgrann also has a special methodological interest in netnography and autoethnography. She has published in, among others, *Nordic Journal of Business*, *Kulutustutkimus.nyt*, and *International Journal of Entrepreneurial Venturing* and contributed book chapters to various texts, such as the *Consumer Culture Theory* anthology and the *Advances in Consumer Research* series.

**Jacob Östberg** is Professor of Advertising and PR at Stockholm Business School, Stockholm University (Sweden). He earned his Ph.D. in 2003 at Lund University (Sweden). His research focuses on consumer culture and on how meaning is created at the intersection of marketing, popular culture, and consumers' lived lives. In particular, Östberg has been interested in questions around gender and masculinity in a Nordic setting. His work has appeared in outlets such as *European Journal of Marketing*, *Journal of Consumer Culture*, *Journal of Global Fashion Marketing*, *Journal of Marketing Management*, *Research in Consumer Behavior*, and *Marketing Theory*, as well as in several books and book chapters.

**Kerimcan Ozcan** is Associate Professor of Marketing at the School of Business and Global Innovation, Marywood University (USA). His current research efforts pertain to the intersection of co-creation, interactive platforms, and digitalization, as applied to value, offerings, branding, service, experience, engagement, events, sociotechnicality, and entrepreneurship. He is the co-author of *The Co-Creation Paradigm* (Stanford University Press; translated into Turkish and Portuguese). His research also appears in *Journal of Marketing, International Journal of Research in Marketing, Journal of Business Research, Journal of Business and Industrial Marketing, Strategy and Leadership, Marketing Intelligence Review*, and *Harvard Business Review*. Ozcan holds a Ph.D. (marketing) and MA (applied economics) from University of Michigan, an MS (management) from Georgia Institute of Technology, and a BS (electrical engineering) from Bogazici University.

**Mai T. Pham** is a doctoral researcher at the University of Auckland Business School. Her Ph.D. research revolves around branding and value co-creation theories, with a particular focus to the context of nation branding. Prior to joining the University of Auckland Business School, she worked in different positions in the policy consulting industry. Her general research interests are situated within branding, place branding, regional development, and mindful consumption.

**Monica Porzionato** is a doctoral candidate in the Department of Strategic Communication, Lund University (Sweden), addressing *Rethinking Urban Tourism Development: Dealing with Sustainability in the Age of Over-Tourism*. Her current research explores the possibility of a material-semiotic approach to sustainability communication in the tourism sector of Venice. She holds a BA in communications, a master's degree in semiotics, and an Erasmus Mundus Master's Degree in women's and gender studies.

**Ahmed Rageh Ismail** received a Ph.D. in management studies (marketing) from the Brunel Business School of Brunel University (UK), in 2010. He is currently an Associate Professor of Management/Marketing at Othman Yeop Abdullah Graduate School of Business (OYAGSB), Universiti Utara Malaysia, Kuala Lumpur, Malaysia. His main research and teaching interests refer to branding, sustainability, cross-cultural marketing, consumer behavior, value, and ethics. He has published in *Qualitative Marketing Research: An International Journal, Journal of Fashion Marketing and Management, Asia-Pacific Journal of Marketing and Logistics*, and *Young Consumers,* among others.

**Venkat Ramaswamy** is a professor in the Ross School of Business, University of Michigan, Ann Arbor (USA). He is a globally recognized thought leader, idea practitioner, and eclectic scholar with wide-ranging interests in the theory and practices of value creation, innovation, strategy, marketing, branding, IT, operations, and the human side of organizations.

**Clarinda Rodrigues** received her doctoral degree in business studies (specialization in marketing) from Oporto University (Portugal) in 2014. She is currently an associate professor at the School of Business and Economics, Linnaeus University (Sweden). Her research reflects the intersection of consumer–brand relationships, brand experiences, and sensory marketing. She has published articles in renowned international academic journals such as *Journal of Product and Brand Management, International Review of Retail, Distribution and Consumer Research, Journal of Place Management and Development, European Business Review*, and *Journal of Customer Behavior*.

**Victor Saha** an assistant professor of marketing at the Jindal Global Business School, O. P. Jindal Global University (JGU). He completed his PhD and his MBA in marketing at the Birla Institute of Technology & Science (BITS), Pilani. He has published in journals such as *Journal of Retailing & Consumer Services, Journal of Product & Brand Management, International Journal of Consumer Studies, Journal of Global Information Management,* and *Journal of Business & Industrial Marketing.* His areas of interest include services marketing, consumer behavior, and brand management.

**Susanne Sandberg** is an associate professor at the School of Business and Economics, Linnaeus University (Sweden). Her research spans international marketing and entrepreneurship topics, focusing on the internationalization processes of SMEs entering and originating in emerging markets. Her current research interests include migrant entrepreneurship and the resilience of SMEs. Her publications appear in *International Business Review, International Marketing Review, International Journal of Entrepreneurship and Small Business,* and *Journal of Business Research.*

**Saila Saraniemi** is Professor of Brand Marketing at Oulu Business School, University of Oulu (Finland). Her research interests include dynamic and networked perspectives of branding, brands as transformative phenomena, and service research. In turn, her research covers topics such as co-creative branding, place and public sector branding, sustainable brands, and topics at the intersection of digitalization and value creation. She has published in *European Journal of Marketing, Industrial Marketing Management, International Journal of Information Management, Journal of Product & Brand Management, Corporate Reputation Review,* and *International Journal of Corporate Communications.*

**Cláudia Simões** is Professor of Management (Marketing and Strategy area) at the School of Economics and Management at the University of Minho (Portugal). She holds a Ph.D. in industrial and business studies from the University of Warwick (UK). Her research interests and publications primarily pertain to strategic marketing, corporate marketing (corporate identity, image, brand, reputation), service management, and customer experience. She has published in *Journal of Marketing, Journal of the Academy of Marketing Science, Journal of Business Research, European Journal of Marketing, Industrial Marketing Management, Business Ethics Quarterly, Studies in Higher Education,* and others. She is associate editor of the *European Journal of Marketing* and a member of the editorial board of *Journal of Services Marketing.*

**Sumire Stanislawski** is currently Associate Professor of Marketing at the Institute for International Strategy at Tokyo International University. Her primary research interest is in the area of sustainability in consumption and marketing. Current research topics include the following: ethical consumers, ethical brands, cause-related marketing, inclusive business, and marketing ethics. She has presented at the Association of Consumer Research in the United States and at various marketing conferences in Japan. She has published articles in *Advances in Consumer Research, Asia-Pacific Advances in Consumer Research,* and *Journal of Marketing & Distribution.* She is currently co-editing a book on inclusive business case studies.

**Kati Suomi**, D.Sc. (Econ. and Bus. Adm.) works as a lecturer in Marketing at the University of Turku, Turku School of Economics (Finland). She is a docent (adjunct professor) at Tampere

University, Faculty of Management and Business (Finland). Her current research interests include brand co-creation and extreme brand relationships, as well as branding in non-profit sectors. Her research has been published in *Journal of Business Research*, *International Journal of Public Sector Management*, and *Tourism Management*, among others.

**Jaana Tähtinen** is Professor of Marketing at the University of Turku, Turku School of Economics (Finland). Her current research interests relate to the management and recovery of business relationships, emotions in business, corporate branding, and conceptual and qualitative research in theory development. She has been published in, among others, *European Journal of Marketing*, *Industrial Marketing Management*, *Journal of Business Research*, *Journal of Service Management*, and *Marketing Theory*.

**Kieran D. Tierney** is Program Manager for the Undergraduate Marketing Programs and Lecturer in Marketing at RMIT University (Australia). His research interests refer to the intersection of consumer engagement, services branding, and brand strategy, with a particular focus on the co-creation of service brand meaning. He is a founding member of the eSports Research Network and member of the market-shaping special interest group of the Australia New Zealand Marketing Academy. His research has won international awards and been published in internationally renowned journals such as *Journal of Service Theory and Practice*, *Journal of Business and Industrial Marketing*, and *International Journal on Media Management*.

**Sofia Ulver** received her Ph.D. in 2008 from the School of Economics and Management at Lund University (Sweden), where she is currently Associate Professor of Marketing and director of the Master's Program in International Marketing & Brand Management Track 2 ("International Consumer Trends, Brands and Innovation"). She is active in the research clusters Consumer Culture Theory (CCT) (internationally) and NCCT (CCT in the Nordics) "Market, Politics and Culture" (in Lund). Ulver has published several book chapters in international anthologies and articles in international academic journals such as *Journal of Public Policy & Marketing*, *Journal of European Marketing*, *Journal of Consumer Culture*, *Journal of Macromarketing*, and *Journal of Marketing Management*. She frequently and actively communicates her research insights to the public through interviews, public speeches, and debate articles in international and national media.

**Christine Vallaster** is a professor at the University of Applied Sciences Salzburg (Austria) and heads the Department of Marketing and Relationship (www.mymarketingworld.at). Her mostly qualitative research pertains to strategic corporate brand management and social responsibility/sustainability in entrepreneurial contexts. She has published in internationally ranked journals such as *Organization Studies*, *Journal of World Business*, *Tourism Management*, *Journal of Business Research*, *Industrial Marketing Management*, and *California Management Review*, amongst others. She speaks on sustainability and circular business models and consults with businesses in their path toward more sustainability.

**Peter Walla** has been a full professor since 2009, first at Newcastle University (Australia), then at Webster Vienna Private University (Austria), and now at Sigmund Freud University (Austria). He holds two habilitations, in cognitive neurobiology at the Medical University in Vienna and in biological psychology at the Vienna University. His work focuses mainly on discrepancies between conscious and non-conscious brain processes within the frame of basic research, as well as applied research such as consumer neuroscience, together with clinical implications. He argues that the brain knows more than it admits to consciousness, and only a multi-method approach can demonstrate that. His "emotion" model promises to help the science community avoid the persistent confusion around emotions. Beyond his academic work, Walla offers neuroconsulting services to industry partners.

**Kate Westberg** is Professor of Marketing and the leader of the Consumer Wellbeing Research Group at RMIT University (Australia). She is an award-winning marketing educator and Fellow of the Higher Education Academy (UK). Westberg's research interests include branding, social marketing, consumer wellbeing, and sport marketing. She has undertaken research with a range of industry and community organizations including the Victorian Health Promotion Foundation, Special Broadcasting Services, the Foundation for Alcohol Research and Education, and Football Victoria. Her research has been widely published in international journals including *European Journal of Marketing, Journal of Business Research, Industrial Marketing Management, Sport Management Review*, and *Journal of Macromarketing*. She also co-authored the book *Brand Fans*, which examines the world's greatest sport brands to provide insight into how brands can cultivate customer engagement, cocreate value, and build brand equity.

**Verena E. Wieser** is Assistant Professor of Branding at the University of Innsbruck (Austria). She is passionate about research in the areas of branding and consumer culture theory and received her doctorate at the University of Innsbruck with a thesis on "Marketing and Moralism: Conceptual and Empirical Advances." Wieser also has several years of practical management experience in international sports events. Her main research interests lie in the areas of person branding, ethical branding, and sports branding. Wieser has published several articles in renowned international academic journals, including *Journal of Business Research, Research in the Sociology of Organizations*, and *European Sports Management Quarterly*.

**Valérie Zeitoun** received her Ph.D. in Management Sciences from the Sorbonne Business School, University Paris 1 Panthéon-Sorbonne in 2016. She is currently an Associate Professor in Marketing at the Sorbonne Business School and deputy director of the Brands & Values Chair. In addition, she is a member of the editorial board of *Décisions Marketing*. She has published several articles in renowned international academic journals, including *Psychology & Marketing, Qualitative Market Research, Recherche et Applications en Marketing*, and *Décisons Marketing*. Her research spans various intersections among marketing, brand management, creativity, and innovation, focused on qualitative methodological questions as well.

# Preface

In interconnected business environments, emerging notions of brand construction suggest that brands are co-created through the collaborative efforts of multiple stakeholders (Ind et al., 2017; Markovic & Bagherzadeh, 2018). This view challenges an existing hegemony in brand management literature, in which brands remain the prerogative of managers or agencies. That is, traditional brand management literature proposes that brand building is a consequence of managerial tactics and planning. But brands are not singular or stable concepts; they exist in continuous multiplicity, developing dynamically through ongoing processes and multi-stakeholder interactions (Berthon et al., 2009; Hillebrand et al., 2015; Mühlbacher & Hemetsberger, 2008; Wider et al., 2018). In turn, brand co-creation occurs through interactive processes within a stakeholder ecosystem (Gyrd-Jones & Kornum, 2013; Ind et al., 2017; Jones, 2005). Such co-creation approaches thus require new conceptualizations and analyses of brands as multi-actor, multi-dimensional, process phenomena, for which the role of brand managers also needs to be reconsidered (da Silveira et al., 2013; Iglesias et al., 2020a).

Emergent brand co-creation literature proposes a wide range of different, not always consistent definitions and conceptualizations though, with links to various brand-related concepts. In this sense, brand co-creation offers relevance and applicability to various brand-oriented topics, including the co-creation of brand value (Merz et al., 2009; Ramaswamy & Ozcan, 2016), offerings (Ind et al., 2017; Santos-Vijande et al., 2016), identity (Iglesias et al., 2020a; Kornum et al., 2017; von Wallpach et al., 2017a, b), meaning (Berthon et al., 2009; Tierney et al., 2016; Vallaster & von Wallpach, 2013), experience (Payne et al., 2009), strategy (Vallaster & von Wallpach, 2018), and authenticity (Beverland et al., 2008). Furthermore, studies of brand co-creation refer to a vast range of contexts, such as brand communities (Hajli et al., 2017; Schau et al., 2009), tourist destinations (Saraniemi & Kylänen, 2011; Vallaster et al., 2017), public relations (Madhavaram et al., 2005), brand capabilities and leadership (Beverland et al., 2007; Lindgreen et al., 2012), internal branding (Dean et al., 2016), corporate social responsibility and sustainability (Iglesias et al., 2020b; Vallaster & Lindgreen, 2013; Vallaster et al., 2012), and business-to-business (B2B) networks (Lindgreen et al., 2010; Mäläskä et al., 2011; Vallaster & Lindgreen, 2011; Walley et al., 2007).

This book brings together multiple theoretical perspectives on brand co-creation to consider their practical applicability and ethical implications. Accordingly, we organize the 27 chapters into six parts, designed to (1) clarify the ontological and epistemological assumptions underlying brand co-creation; (2) gain deeper insights into the co-creation of intangible and (3) tangible brand assets; (4) establish the ethical implications of brand co-creation; (5) foreshadow and critically reflect on future developments related to brand co-creation; and (6) illustrate practical applications of brand co-creation with case studies.

# PART I: THE ONTOLOGY AND EPISTEMOLOGY OF BRAND CO-CREATION

Brand co-creation is a widely used term, but the assumptions that tend to be embraced, regarding the nature of co-creation, seldom are addressed or challenged. But ultimately, what is being co-created? How is it co-created? Which stakeholders are involved in co-creation processes? What terminology should we use to describe these phenomena—for example, how does brand co-creation differ from value co-creation, co-creation, and collaboration in general? As these questions emphasize, understanding brand co-creation requires understanding the very nature of the brand and branding, together with fundamental approaches to co-creation. The chapters in this section explore ontological and epistemological phenomena associated with brand co-creation, seeking to define its limits, as well as establish underlying logics and terminology that can distinguish it as an academic field of enquiry. Furthermore, this section offers integrative insights into brand co-creation as a complex social process that is experienced as lived ecosystems at the individual level but as assemblages and power relations at the societal level.

To start this discussion, we turn to Jaana Tähtinen and Kati Suomi's effort to understand the theoretical foundation for research on brand co-creation on the basis of the conceptual language used to discuss it. In "A conceptual analysis of labels referring to brand co-creation" (Chapter 1) they examine both definitions of key concepts and descriptions of widely used terminology, seeking to identify, distinguish, and clarify any conceptual confusion or overlaps. Their application of conceptual analysis methods also advances insights into this methodology, which in turn produces conceptual maps of five frequently used brand co-creation concepts. Not only do these maps reveal the complexity of these concepts, but they also strongly encourage continued efforts to bolster multi-vocal theory.

Catherine da Silveira and Cláudia Simões (Chapter 2) also recognize confusion about the concept of brand co-creation, as demonstrated by its blurry boundaries with other types of collaboration or engagement. Reflecting their goal of "Establishing the boundaries of brand co-creation," they propose some fundamental conditions of brand co-creation, based in foundational theories such as the service-dominant logic, value co-creation logic, and service logic. By integrating these multiple streams of literature, they can reframe existing assumptions into a structured framework that establishes clear boundaries for co-creation in branding. The resulting insights into the actual theoretical and practical scope of brand co-creation can help answer an essential question: To what extent can a brand be considered co-created?

Another framework, presented in "Brands as co-creational lived experience ecosystems: an integrative theoretical framework of interactional creation" (Chapter 3), acknowledges how interactions on digital engagement platforms are transforming brand co-creation into an interactive, lived experience. Venkat Ramaswamy and Kerimcan Ozcan therefore introduce the concept of a "co-creational lived experience ecosystem," in which brands are agencial assemblages and co-creational lived experience ecosystems that possess intrinsic assemblage characteristics. Brands are in constant flux in interactive system environments; they always and already include experiencers. The experiential agencial relations of such brands are constituted in and constitutive of enacted practices stemming from interactive, lived experiences. Accordingly, the authors call for moving past goods and services categorizations to highlight practices and (digital) experiences involving interactive agencing and structuring. They propose that co-creational lived experience ecosystems require brand creation to enact the co-creation of environments featuring emergent brand experiences together with the embodied, lived brand experiences stemming from interactional creation in those environments. This theorizing can contribute to co-creation paradigms, especially related to service-dominant logics for brand value co-creation.

Andrea Lucarelli, Cecilia Cassinger, and Jacob Östberg (Chapter 4) instead take a critical performativity approach to brand co-creation in their pursuit of "Reassessing brand co-creation: towards a critical performativity approach." Rather than conventional critiques of brand co-creation, they call for a genuine critique that can reimagine its potential, within and beyond marketing. In turn, they derive a research agenda for critical, performativity-based studies of brand co-creation that offers a more constructively critical approach to adapting brand co-creation theory and practice. This chapter outlines some of the ramifications, such as for brand assemblages, brand activism, and brand ecology.

# PART II: CO-CREATION OF INTANGIBLE BRAND ASSETS

Brand stakeholders participate in dynamic processes and interconnected structures for brand development, which enables them to shape intangible brand assets (e.g., heritage, identity, experience, knowledge, meaning, value, culture, strategy) together with the company and other stakeholders. In support of a dynamic re-conceptualization of static brand-related concepts, the chapters in this part shed new light on continuous co-creation processes, involving a variety of intangible brand assets.

For example, in "Co-creation of intangible brand assets: an integrative S-D logic/organic view of brand-based conceptual framework" (Chapter 5), Victor Saha, Venkatesh Mani, Praveen Goyal, and Linda D. Hollebeek integrate the service-dominant (S-D) logic with an organic view of the brand, in line with a conceptualization of brands as experiential processes, to detail how strategic deployment of value co-creation can produce intangible brand assets. They specify different actors' resource contributions to value co-creation and thereby derive a conceptual framework that depicts how service system actors can contribute to co-creating intangible brand assets, such as heritage, identity, and meaning.

But co-creation is not the only possibility; Andrea Hemetsberger, Maria Kreuzer, and Hans Mühlbacher (Chapter 6) highlight the need for more research into the potential for value co-destruction. With a multi-stakeholder perspective, "Co-creation or co-destruction? Value-based brand formation" investigates value creation at the societal level by positing that brand co-creation that accords with some particular value order can be both creative and destructive, depending on the perspective adopted. The authors also caution against reducing concepts of creation or destruction of value to value-in-use and recommend broad-based brand value assessments that incorporate the perspectives of multiple stakeholders, consistent with notions of "value in society."

Anu Norrgrann and Saila Saraniemi (Chapter 7) also recognize the potential for both co-creation and co-destruction, which they believe depends on interaction processes in networks. In their chapter, entitled "Dealing with discrepancies of a brand in change: recomposition of value and meanings in the network," they investigate brand discrepancies, defined as disruptions or inconsistencies that can result in both brand co-destruction and reconfigured meanings of value in the ecosystem. With a process-oriented multiple stakeholder view and a longitudinal case study, this chapter outlines the ever-changing reality that surrounds brands and offers the nuanced argument that brand co-destruction does not have to be negative.

In particular, reconfigured, recomposed, and reorchestrated brand meanings and value can be positive outcomes of brand discrepancies. From this view, brand management demands orchestration of multiple stakeholders, not unilateral governance.

The next chapter accounts for divergence too, in this case between community and organizational institutions, and predicts that when brand meaning co-creation is undertaken by brand-facing actors, it can facilitate for institutional (re)shaping. These propositions reflect the institutional theory lens that Kieran D. Tierney, Ingo O. Karpen, and Kate Westberg adopt in "The role of brand-facing actors in shaping institutions through brand meaning co-creation" (Chapter 8). By arguing and demonstrating, in three illustrative vignettes, how brand-facing actors establish brand legitimacy and behaviors, in ways that shape meaning-making efforts and institutions, these authors aim to explore the nature of brand meaning co-creation and specifically how brand-facing actors might transform institutions by undertaking it, which entails a reciprocal process.

In addition to multiple stakeholders and perspectives, brand co-creation research might benefit from considerations of multi-sensory experiences. As Clarinda Rodrigues, Andreas Aldogan Eklund, Adele Berndt, and Susanne Sandberg (Chapter 9) suggest, using the luxury car segment as their research context, stakeholders in the value co-creation process might contribute to define the multi-sensory experiences available within luxury cars. They find that a brand heritage theme is critical, and they further delineate the contributions of different actors: suppliers offer competence, knowledge, and skills; consumers reveal which factors define an outstanding multi-sensory experience for them. Thus, with "Co-creation of multi-sensory brand experiences: a manufacturer perspective," they establish a framework of multi-sensory brand experience co-creation.

With another industry perspective, Christian Dam and Dannie Kjeldgaard (Chapter 10) explore how B2B brands can establish their global brand meanings, using a Danish B2B firm struggling with disrupted brand meanings as it expands globally as an exemplar. In studying the firm, they find that its brand meanings had been co-created by various brand stakeholders, who drew on different mythologies circulating throughout about global commodity networks, including globalization and global production. Such mythologies interfere with customers' perceptions of brand meanings. Therefore, the case study in "B2B branding in global commodity networks: a cultural branding analysis of a Danish company going global" offers insights regarding the need for firms to conduct cultural branding analyses of their B2B brands and for researchers to develop cultural branding approaches.

## PART III: CO-CREATION OF BRAND OFFERINGS

In the current socioeconomic environment, brands that aim to gain and maintain competitive advantages need to develop and launch relevant product and service innovations (Bagherzadeh et al., 2019), which in turn prompts them to consider opportunities for the co-creation of brand offerings. From this perspective, co-creation is a dynamic, social process based on interactions and relationships between brands and external stakeholders, oriented toward the generation of new products and services (Markovic & Bagherzadeh, 2018). In this section, the contributors address the types of interactions and relationships that brands need to establish with external stakeholders to co-create new products or services effectively. Other chapters deal with the antecedents and conditions required for successful co-creation, and then the advantages and disadvantages that co-created new products and services offer to brands.

For Nicholas Ind and Oriol Iglesias, purpose and ownership are the central determinants of "Freedom and control in brand co-creation communities" (Chapter 11). They argue that if firms initiate brand co-creation communities, those communities tend to focus on specific goals, whereas if fans create the communities, they are more organic. Then they apply a philosophy introduced by Isaiah Berlin that differentiates positive freedom, as the ability to make one's own choices and achieve self-realization, from negative freedom, involving the space for freedom. In reference to brand co-creation community typologies, each form has different management requirements, so the authors offer precise recommendations for how to manage both types of freedom in brand co-creation communities.

In an effort to add more nuanced detail to descriptions of the link between co-creation and performance, the next chapter, "Exploring the brand co-creation–brand performance linkage and the roles of innovation and firm age: resource-based and dynamic capabilities views" (Chapter 12) includes innovation and firm age as potential moderators. With an online survey of representatives of Egyptian firms, Ahmed Rageh Ismail establishes an important role of innovation but no significant effect of firm age in the link between brand co-creation and brand performance.

Beyond product and service settings, brand co-creation also can refer to locations, as suggested by "Toward a co-creation approach to nation branding: an integrative framework" (Chapter 13). Mai T. Pham and Roderick J. Brodie consider nation branding, which uses co-creation to generate knowledge and expertise and thereby create new value propositions. In proposing a novel, conceptual framework for brand co-creation pertaining to nation branding, these authors take an integrative approach and predict that nation brands form through collective marketing interactions among relevant actors within a nation branding network. These stakeholders' interactions in turn rely critically on knowledge exchanges, resource integration, and carefully negotiated value propositions. The authors offer a case study to illustrate this conceptual framework and establish theoretical and managerial recommendations.

The conceptual framework in "The dark side of brand co-creation: a psychological ownership perspective" (Chapter 14) instead highlights the potentially disruptive outcomes of brand co-creation, in line with psychological ownership theory. That is, customer co-creators might perceive themselves as owners of the outcome, because they have developed more knowledge about, control over, and investments in that co-creation. If other stakeholders then attempt to join the co-creation effort, it may appear intrusive and prompt the co-creators to exhibit territorial behavior, resist change, or spread negative word of mouth. Fabian Bartsch and Bart Claus predict that the likelihood and strength of such problematic consequences depends on several boundary conditions, including product types, brand community strength, and product consumption settings. Finally, they offer some potential strategies to mitigate the risk of negative consequences.

## PART IV: ETHICAL IMPLICATIONS OF BRAND CO-CREATION

Online communities, decentralized organizations, fast and flexible new production facilities, the rapid evolution of information technologies (Markovic, 2016)—all these trends can enhance brand–stakeholder connections and increase stakeholders' involvement in diverse co-creation processes (e.g., of brand knowledge, brand meaning, brand offerings). But they also lead to greater transparency that can give rise to a host of ethical issues related to co-creation, as addressed by the chapters in this section.

By applying Schwartz's universal moral standards to corporate codes of ethics (trustworthiness, respect, responsibility, fairness, caring, and citizenship), Sumire Stanislawski (Chapter 15) attempts to help brands manage the unique ethical challenges of brand co-creation, especially involving the blurred boundaries between producers and consumers. In "The universal moral standards and the ethics of co-creation" the author frames her investigation of the ethics of co-creation by studying digital platforms that attract substantial consumer participation. The results identify ethically questionable conduct by both brands and consumers; this chapter also offers recommendations for how to navigate brand co-creation complexities in an ethical way.

Some firms' efforts to behave ethically have led to their designation as conscientious brands. Christine Vallaster and Philip Lechner (Chapter 16) attempt to understand whether and how corporate brands that embrace an ethical brand identity actually implement societal transformations that produce greater sustainability overall. The structured literature analysis presented in "Co-creation of conscientious corporate brands – facilitating societal change towards sustainability: a structured literature analysis" integrates hybrid organizational, social entrepreneurship, and political organizational theories in an effort to describe multiple co-creation processes, including communicating, internalizing, contesting, and elucidating. The combined evidence indicates that conscientious brands can facilitate a sustainable society, but the challenges they face, in terms of balancing potential "greenwashing" against their authentic brand identity, are substantial.

Focusing on a specific universal moral principle, "Organizational citizenship behavior principles: a guide for employees and customers in the brand value co-creation journey" (Chapter 17) relies on a bibliometric literature review to establish a theoretical foundation for organizational citizenship behaviors (OCB). Maja Arslanagić-Kalajdžić and Vesna Babić-Hodović find that emergent theoretical principles reveal potential benefits of OCB for employees and customers. As a means to implement an ethical corporate culture, OCB encompasses both norms of reciprocity, which can spill over to brand value co-creation interactions, and organizational justice considerations, which can inform strategic brand value co-creation process decisions.

In an explicit effort to challenge common assumptions, Monica Porzionato and Cecilia Cassinger (Chapter 18) next propose a non-violent, ethical approach to brand co-creation in "'We look within … so we can look up': towards a nonviolent ethics of human brand co-creation." Their analysis centers on influencer brands, such as goop and Yoga Girl, and reveals how these brands develop relationships with followers that are non-oppositional, which means that brand co-creation does not need to exploit followers to succeed. The human brands, rather than being autonomous, reflect the surrounding institutional arrangements and structural conditions. Accordingly, this chapter recommends that they avoid unthinking reproductions of success norms and instead embrace market-mediated approaches to tolerance and interdependency. With a non-violent approach, human brands and followers enter into relationships defined by their institutional responsibilities toward one another and toward society.

Whereas the previous chapter seeks insights into ethical links between brands and consumers, Ulf Aagerup (Chapter 19) cautions that the increasing volume of customer-to-customer brand-related communications can create conditions ripe for conspicuous virtue signaling (CVS). That is, consumers sometimes issue criticisms on social media to establish a certain image for themselves, rather than out of sincere concern about a moral issue. As "The ethics of conspicuous virtue signaling: when brand co-creation on social media turns negative" establishes, CVS is unethical, whether viewed from a virtue or a consequentialist perspective. When virtue signalers and social media platforms combine to promote online outrage, which provides benefits for them, the detriment to brands and brand users can be extreme.

## PART V: CRITICAL REFLECTIONS ON THE FUTURE OF BRAND CO-CREATION

As any research field, including brand co-creation, gains theoretical and empirical foundations, critical perspectives emerge, reflecting questions about what brands are, how they become, and what impacts they have. The chapters in this section all take a future-oriented perspective, seeking to assess processes and outcomes of brand co-creation in multiple contexts. As sociocultural sites of meaning, cultural consumption, and production, brands reflect and affect cultural and social issues and movements. Those social movements and issues then become assimilated into brand narratives, such that brand identities, spanning multiple stakeholders, become more fluid, complex, and potentially paradoxical. The technical developments that alter extant views of brands and branding as a managerial task also provide means to reflect critically on brands' involvement in material and immaterial co-creation, including their potential functions as positive, native forces for social and material change.

To bridge the gap between the concepts of degrowth, as a sustainability option, and consumer support, as a necessary prerequisite for its influence, Feyza Ağlargöz (Chapter 20) proposes brand co-creation as a foundation. Because it requires empowered consumers, brand co-creation offers a constructive, collaborative method to leverage consumer power. Therefore, "Brand co-creation and degrowth: merging the odd couple" applies insights about empowered consumer discourse from brand co-creation literature to a degrowth domain, highlighting some global macroscale conditions that allow for sustainability and brand co-creation. It thus argues that society can achieve degrowth outcomes through brand co-creation efforts, using various alternative tactics.

Géraldine Michel and Valérie Zeitoun (Chapter 21) carefully define brand co-creation as the integration of stakeholders' brand appropriations, which can enrich the brand and complete the brand's identity, but which also might trigger a loss of brand identity. In "Brand co-creation management in the light of the social-materiality approach" they focus explicitly on the immaterial value that stakeholders, including consumers, co-create, as well as how. They thus suggest some improved managerial methods to ensure constructive co-creation processes. From a social materiality perspective, brand materiality also provides a framework for constructive brand co-creation.

The last chapter in this part, by Sofia Ulver (Chapter 22), questions how brand co-creation might allow for systemically violent relations, as exploited by populist far right groups in Western political landscapes. She asks, in "Violent brands: from neoliberal vessels to far-right fantasies," about the implications of anti-capitalist brand co-creation critiques, which traditionally have targeted neoliberal fantasies of free markets and responsible consumers, when the systemic relations assembled into brands represent far right fantasies about authoritarianism. That is, critiques of neoliberal brand co-creation as a depoliticizing distraction rely on a particular premise that, in the current era, appears to be disappearing. Ulver predicts that authoritarian far right movements increasingly will organize their systemic relations into brands, co-created through mainstream consumer culture. Such developments would challenge critical perspectives that describe brands as vessels of neoliberal relations; in turn, these critiques would need to expand to include other political ideologies.

## PART VI: CASE STUDIES ON BRAND CO-CREATION

This final part aims to extend beyond predominantly academic contributions, by presenting several practical examples and case studies about diverse types of brand co-creation.

First, by detailing how various psychophysiological methods can reveal affective processing efforts during brand co-creation, Monika Koller and Peter Walla (Chapter 23) describe emotions and affective processing from an evolutionary perspective. In outlining "Alternative methods to study affective information processing in brand co-creation," they review other consumer neuroscience methods that can clarify and inform measures of affective processing, using two empirical examples to showcase these applications for investigations of brand attitudes, as well as attitudes toward brand co-creation.

Second, Chapter 24, "Prolonging the shared project value of surplus co-creation," arises from a broader study of consumer co-creation on the LEGO Ideas platform. As Yun Mi Antorini and Gry Høngsmark Knudsen show, consumers support and work with one another on the platform, seeking to convince LEGO to review their projects, in a process that creates greater shared understanding of the project and its value. Even co-creation projects that do not enter a production phase can encourage surplus co-creation efforts by engaged consumers. However, considering the rarity of successful co-creation projects, it also is necessary to recognize how and why a lack of success may undermine shared project value or surplus co-creation. The authors adopt a view of ethics as a value to propose using surplus co-creation as a measure of consumer engagement, in that it implies a sustained "afterlife" even for rejected projects, in the form of care for consumers' shared values.

Third, citing the global climate change activist Greta Thunberg as an iconic person brand, Teresa Brugger and Verena E. Wieser (Chapter 25) conduct a case study, according to a cultural branding perspective. Through an interpretive analysis of Instagram posts and news articles about Thunberg's activist campaigns in 2019, "The iconization of Greta Thunberg: the role of myths in co-creating a person brand" details co-creation efforts by Thunberg herself, consumers, and the media to establish three mythic narratives. Those narratives include both communication myths (The Heroic Greta Thunberg, The End of the World, Demystification) and action myths (The Discovery Trip, Revolution). The resulting cultural branding is a form of myth-making, which establishes the iconic person brand, but as this chapter demonstrates, multiple stakeholders participate in co-creating these myths and the ultimate person brand.

Fourth, Oliver Koll (Chapter 26) gives an account of a B2B manufacturer that established a new scrum-type approach to uncover new product ideas, in which employees with relatively little market experience or customer interactions are prioritized as potential sources of unconventional, bolder ideas. This rapid, continuous process effectively motivated the participants, prompting four specific product ideas that currently are being developed. As "Finding new product ideas at Eisenbeiss: integrating non-frontline employees into co-creation processes" clarifies, it also initiated employee relationships across functional areas that traditionally had been siloed.

Fifth, Peter Espersen (Chapter 27) leverages his own professional experience and brand and value creation attempts by three companies to describe how to "Turning lead into gold: from weighty consumer feedback to co-creation." In their distinct business contexts, Habbo Hotel, Pixable, and jovoto each developed relevant methods and processes to uncover co-creation opportunities. This chapter also outlines some key challenges these brands faced. Together, these findings and the author's involvement in various co-creation projects offer some general lessons.

Stefan Markovic, Copenhagen, Denmark
Richard Gyrd-Jones, Copenhagen, Denmark
Sylvia von Wallpach, Copenhagen, Denmark
Adam Lindgreen, Copenhagen, Denmark, and Pretoria, South Africa

## REFERENCES

Bagherzadeh, M., Markovic, S., Cheng, J., & Vanhaverbeke, W. (2019). How does outside-in open innovation influence innovation performance? Analyzing the mediating roles of knowledge sharing and innovation strategy. *IEEE Transactions on Engineering Management*, *67*(3), 740–753.

Berthon, P., Pitt, L. F., & Campbell, C. (2009). Does brand meaning exist in similarity or singularity? *Journal of Business Research*, *62*(3), 356–361.

Beverland, M. B., Lindgreen, A., & Vink, M. W. (2008). Projecting authenticity through advertising: Consumer judgments of advertisers' claims. *Journal of Advertising*, *37*(1), 5–15.

Beverland, M., Napoli, J., & Lindgreen, A. (2007). Industrial global brand leadership: A capabilities view. *Industrial Marketing Management*, *36*(8), 1082–1093.

da Silveira, C., Lages, C., & Simões, C. (2013). Reconceptualizing brand identity in a dynamic environment. *Journal of Business Research*, *66*(1), 28–36.

Dean, D., Arroyo-Gamez, R. E., Punjaisri, K., & Pich, C. (2016). Internal brand co-creation: The experiential brand meaning cycle in higher education. *Journal of Business Research*, *69*(8), 3041–3048.

Gyrd-Jones, R. I., & Kornum, N. (2013). Managing the co-created brand: Value and cultural complementarity in online and offline multi-stakeholder ecosystems. *Journal of Business Research*, *66*(9), 1484–1493.

Hajli, N., Shanmugam, M., Papagiannidis, S., Zahay, D., & Richard, M. O. (2017). Branding co-creation with members of online brand communities. *Journal of Business Research*, *70*, 136–144.

Hillebrand, B., Driessen, P., & Koll, O. (2015). Stakeholder marketing: Theoretical foundations and consequences for marketing capabilities. *Journal of the Academy of Marketing Science*, *43*(4), 411–428.

Iglesias, O., Landgraf, P., Ind, N., Markovic, S., & Koporcic, N. (2020a). Corporate brand identity co-creation in business-to-business contexts. *Industrial Marketing Management*, *85*, 32–43.

Iglesias, O., Markovic, S., Bagherzadeh, M., & Singh, J. J. (2020b). Co-creation: A key link between corporate social responsibility, customer trust, and customer loyalty. *Journal of Business Ethics*, *163*(1), 151–166.

Ind, N., Iglesias, O., & Markovic, S. (2017). The co-creation continuum: From tactical market research tool to strategic collaborative innovation method. *Journal of Brand Management*, *24*(4), 310–321.

Jones, R. (2005). Finding sources of brand value: Developing a stakeholder model of brand equity. *Journal of Brand Management*, *13*(1), 10–32.

Kornum, N., Gyrd-Jones, R., Al Zagir, N., & Brandis, K. A. (2017). Interplay between intended brand identity and identities in a Nike related brand community: Co-existing synergies and tensions in a nested system. *Journal of Business Research*, *70*, 432–440.

Lindgreen, A., Beverland, M. B., & Farrelly, F. (2010). From strategy to tactics: Building, implementing, and managing brand equity in business markets. *Industrial Marketing Management*, *39*(8), 1223–1225.

Lindgreen, A., Xu, Y., Maon, F., & Wilcock, J. (2012). Corporate social responsibility brand leadership: A multiple case study. *European Journal of Marketing*, *46*(7/8), 965–993.

Madhavaram, S., Badrinarayanan, V., & McDonald, R. E. (2005). Integrated marketing communication (IMC) and brand identity as critical components of brand equity strategy: A conceptual framework and research propositions. *Journal of Advertising, 34*(4), 69–80.

Mäläskä, M., Saraniemi, S., & Tähtinen, J. (2011). Network actors' participation in B2B SME branding. *Industrial Marketing Management, 40*(7), 1144–1152.

Markovic, S. M. (2016). *21st-Century Brands: An Innovation Opportunity and an Ethical Challenge.* PhD dissertation. Universitat Ramon Llull, Barcelona, Spain.

Markovic, S., & Bagherzadeh, M. (2018). How does breadth of external stakeholder co-creation influence innovation performance? Analyzing the mediating roles of knowledge sharing and product innovation. *Journal of Business Research, 88*, 173–186.

Merz, M. A., He, Y., & Vargo, S. L. (2009). The evolving brand logic: A service-dominant logic perspective. *Journal of the Academy of Marketing Science, 37*(3), 328–344.

Mühlbacher, H., & Hemetsberger, A. (2008). Cosa diamine è un brand? Un tentativo di integrazione e le sue conseguenze per la ricerca e il management. *Micro & Macro Marketing, 17*(2), 271–292.

Payne, A., Storbacka, K., Frow, P., & Knox, S. (2009). Co-creating brands: Diagnosing and designing the relationship experience. *Journal of Business Research, 62*(3), 379–389.

Ramaswamy, V., & Ozcan, K. (2016). Brand value co-creation in a digitalized world: An integrative framework and research implications. *International Journal of Research in Marketing, 33*(1), 93–106.

Santos-Vijande, M. L., López-Sánchez, J. Á., & Rudd, J. (2016). Frontline employees' collaboration in industrial service innovation: Routes of co-creation's effects on new service performance. *Journal of the Academy of Marketing Science, 44*(3), 350–375.

Saraniemi, S., & Kylänen, M. (2011). Problematizing the concept of tourism destination: An analysis of different theoretical approaches. *Journal of Travel Research, 50*(2), 133–143.

Schau, H. J., Muñiz Jr., A. M., & Arnould, E. J. (2009). How brand community practices create value. *Journal of Marketing, 73*(5), 30–51.

Tierney, K. D., Karpen, I. O., & Westberg, K. (2016). Brand meaning cocreation: Toward a conceptualization and research implications. *Journal of Service Theory and Practice, 26*(6), 911–932.

Vallaster, C., & Lindgreen, A. (2011). Corporate brand strategy formation: Brand actors and the situational context for a business-to-business brand. *Industrial Marketing Management, 40*(7), 1133–1143.

Vallaster, C., & Lindgreen, A. (2013). The role of social interactions in building internal corporate brands: Implications for sustainability. *Journal of World Business, 48*(3), 297–310.

Vallaster, C., & von Wallpach, S. (2013). An online discursive inquiry into the social dynamics of multi-stakeholder brand meaning co-creation. *Journal of Business Research, 66*(9), 1505–1515.

Vallaster, C., & von Wallpach, S. (2018). Brand strategy co-creation in a nonprofit context: A strategy-as-practice approach. *Nonprofit and Voluntary Sector Quarterly, 47*(5), 984–1006.

Vallaster, C., Lindgreen, A., & Maon, F. (2012). Strategically leveraging corporate social responsibility to the benefit of company and society: A corporate branding perspective. *California Management Review, 54*(3), 34–60.

Vallaster, C., von Wallpach, S., & Zenker, S. (2017). The interplay between urban policies and grassroots city brand co-creation and co-destruction during the refugee crisis: Insights from the city brand Munich (Germany). *Cities,* 24.7.2017, 1–8.

von Wallpach, S., Hemetsberger, A., & Espersen, P. (2017a). Performing identities: Processes of brand and stakeholder identity co-construction. *Journal of Business Research, 70*C, 443–452.

von Wallpach, S., Voyer, B., Kastanakis, M., & Mühlbacher, H. (2017b). Co-creating stakeholder and brand identities: Introduction to the special section. *Journal of Business Research, 70*C, 395–398.

Walley, K., Custance, P., Taylor, S., Lindgreen, A., & Hingley, M. K. (2007). The importance of brand in the industrial purchase decision: A case study of United Kingdom tractor market. *Journal of Business and Industrial Marketing, 22*(6), 383–393.

Wider, S., von Wallpach, S., & Mühlbacher, H. (2018). Brand management: Unveiling the delusion of control. *European Management Journal, 36*(3), 301–305.

# PART I

# THE ONTOLOGY AND EPISTEMOLOGY OF BRAND CO-CREATION

# 1. A conceptual analysis of labels referring to brand co-creation

*Jaana Tähtinen and Kati Suomi*

## 1. INTRODUCTION

This chapter examines the definitions of the concepts and descriptions of the terms used to refer to brand co-creation. Brand co-creation is an emerging field of research, thus, it is apt to conduct a conceptual analysis on the theoretical language used, and to reveal and clarify instances of conceptual confusion. Our aim is restricted to illustrating the issues, we will not suggest *the* definition to be used, nor suggest an integrated form. The current chapter opens up the current conceptual language on brand co-creation so that scholars can make informed decisions on what concepts to use based on the aspects the concepts reveal about the complex phenomenon.

Concepts are scholars' tools of the trade; unless we use concepts and explain what they refer to, it is impossible to create, develop, or test a theory (Bagozzi, 1984; Suddaby, 2010; Griffin & Barczak, 2020). As Vargo and Koskela-Huotari (2020, p. 2) put it, "all scholarly articles are, necessarily, conceptual". Concepts carry basic assumptions on what the world is about and how to study it; they are also abstract, reflexive, and bound in time. A new conceptualisation allows us to "see" and understand a new aspect or view of the world in which we live and thus advance our knowledge of the world (MacInnis, 2011). The reflexive nature of concepts means that alongside world views, concepts influence both researchers' and practitioners' understanding of phenomena and the future behaviour of those working with such concepts (Giddens, 1987). Hence, the notion that concepts are critical tools is not limited to the work of researchers, concepts are also important for practitioners (MacInnis, 2011). However, ontological assumptions differ at any point in time and change over time, as is reflected, for example, in the works of Blumer and of Bartels. Blumer (1954, p. 7) treats concepts in social science as sensitising; "offering the researcher a general sense of reference and guidance in approaching empirical instances" and Bartels (1970, pp. 5–6) views *a clearly defined concept* as the first step in theory development.

We take a middle road here, and support multivocality; that involves each researcher following her/his ontological perspective and attempting to offer their audience clear definitions or descriptions of how they and those they studied understand the key concepts in a piece of research. A phenomenon may be conceptualised differently in different domains and by different participants in the study, but it is important that readers can understand how the concept is used. Unless the use is consistent, the field may use several different labels for a similar phenomenon (synonymy), or a single concept or term for different phenomena (homonymy) (Sartori, 2009, p. 111). Ambiguity in defining and using concepts (Tähtinen & Havila, 2019) makes it difficult to compare and build upon existing research.

Conceptual confusion hinders the development of knowledge in the field, so we start with the bedrock of research, the key concepts, and their meanings. Following MacKenzie (2003), we begin the journey assuming that some authors in this field underestimate the importance of presenting explicit definitions. Viewed separately, the concepts of *brand* and *co-creation* do not differ from most concepts in marketing; both are currently defined in multiple ways and from multiple angles (for branding, see Brown, 2005; De Chernatony & Dall'Olmo Riley, 1998 and for co-creation see Ramaswamy & Ozcan, 2018). Combining the concepts into "brand co-creation" could thus either increase or decrease conceptual ambiguity. This chapter aims to disclose the extent of conceptual ambiguity in the field of "brand co-creation" and to deconstruct the concept combinations used to bolster theory development.

The task will be executed by using the Conceptual Analysis Method (CAM) developed by Tähtinen and Havila (2019) and inspired by Sartori (2009) to scrutinise the definitions and terms used in articles on brand co-creation.

The results of this examination reveal the ambiguity within the discussion and clarify the theoretical state by unravelling the current assigned meanings. The meanings scrutinised can be either dominant or rare and the focus of the investigation also encompasses the direct theoretical underpinnings of the concepts and terms used. The study shows that conceptual confusion could be clarified if each study defined the main concept of interest and avoided conceptual ambiguity. A total of ten different concepts are found and dissected, half of which feature quite regularly in research on brand co-creation. Of the five, two concepts stand out as the most applied, another two distinguish certain aspects of the brand as being co-created, and one adopts a consumer perspective. Disentangling the five most-used concepts to create conceptual maps illuminates several aspects of the phenomenon and its complexity. Some of the aspects are well studied while others remain rather opaque. The analysis will aid future research to clarify conceptual choices, balance the focus of research, and direct it to less understood, but relevant aspects of the phenomenon.

The chapter is organised according to the steps of the CAM; we first describe the method and its execution and thereafter present the results of the analysis. The results section first discusses the conceptual status of the field, then outlines the dominant and rare meanings, the theoretical underpinnings of the concepts, and then presents conceptual maps. The chapter ends with a discussion of the findings and conclusions, which include suggestions to develop the CAM.

## 2.    THE APPLICATION OF CAM

The CAM consists of five consecutive tasks of (1) collecting the definitions of the concepts and descriptions of the terms used in existing studies, (2) evaluating the conceptual status of the field, (3) categorising the meanings and boundaries of the concepts and terms, (4) tracing their theoretical roots, and (5) outlining conceptual maps (Tähtinen & Havila, 2019). The data collection for the concept review was conducted systematically applying predefined selection criteria (i.e. keywords and search terms, see Tähtinen & Havila, 2019). We used the Web of Science electronic database that covers established peer-reviewed journals (see Podsakoff et al., 2005). The aim was to collect a representative sample of the discussion instead of finding all publications on brand co-creation. The discussion subject is still new and appears in a range of journals; both general marketing journals and those dedicated to branding, general management, and tourism journals.

The data collection took place on May 5, 2020, using an advanced search of articles written in English, without restricting the timespan. We used the following search sentence: TI=(brand* AND co-creation) changing the last word to cocreation (the two first combinations resulted in 86 hits), co-production & coproduction (1 hit), and co-development & codevelopment (1 hit). The search produced 88 articles and books. The only hit on brand co-production was a book chapter on film co-production, so we decided to omit that. The only hit on brand co-development was also a book chapter, but unfortunately, we could not access the book. In addition, we failed to access three articles, resulting in a sample of 83 papers.

We applied the above-mentioned search criteria systematically but as CAM (Tähtinen & Havila, 2019) aims to provide a fairly simple and manageable method, the search was not comprehensive. However, it appears to be typical of conceptual analyses and systematic reviews that some widely cited, and thus relevant studies to the field, are not returned in the search hits (see e.g. Blomberg et al., 2017). Hence, we would advise readers to add their main references into the sample to be studied when applying CAM.

To limit the data to research focusing on brand co-creation/production/development, both authors read the abstracts of all 83 studies and categorised the articles into consideration pools of "yes", "maybe" and "no" before reviewing the selections together. After discussion, our final data set consists of 47 studies focusing on brand co-creation. Examples of studies excluded are those on customer co-creation of *value* that did use the focal concept of the brand, although their empirical settings were brands or brand communities (e.g. Pongsakornrungsilp & Schroeder, 2011; Kunja & Acharyulu, 2018; Zhao et al., 2019).

At this point, after comparing the size of our sample to the example of 42 studies presented in Tähtinen and Havila (2019), we decided that a cohort of 47 studies represented a sufficient number to analyse the conceptual status of the brand co-creation discussion. Moreover, as the various streams (e.g. critical tradition, city/place branding, corporate branding) of the branding discussion were represented in the sample, we did not add studies from the *maybe* categories.

The vast majority of studies, 46, were published between 2010–2020, that of Boyle (2007) being the earliest. Further, as many as 41 articles were published in the period 2015–2020 indicating that research interest in brand co-creation has recently increased rapidly. Our sample shows that a particularly influential study is that of Merz et al. (2009) suggesting that branding research has entered a new era of *stakeholder focus*, which started with the emergence of research into brand communities such as that of Muniz and O'Guinn (2001) and McAlexander et al. (2002). Accordingly, the stakeholder focus era "parallels and reflects the new evolving service-dominant logic in marketing" (Merz et al., 2009, p. 338).

The next step in the CAM was to start evaluating the conceptual status of the field. This included a search for the key concepts, their definitions or descriptions from the articles and comparing those against each other. At this point, each author took half of the papers and ran the definition search with the help of a "find" navigation tool and using the CAM suggested key phrases (refer, define, concept, conceptualis/ze, construct). If the search failed to find a definition, we looked for any descriptions of the concepts of co-create and co-creation. The process produced a table of all concepts (Table 1.1) and we next categorised the studies in ten tables focusing on the ten different concepts the studies utilise. Those ten tables form the basis for the further steps in the CAM analysis that were conducted by both authors. Those steps are the evaluating the conceptual status, categorising the meanings and boundaries of the concepts, and tracing the theoretical underpinnings of the conceptualisations, and finally constructing the conceptual maps (Tähtinen & Havila, 2019).

At this point, however, we would like to offer an update to CAM's task of detecting conceptual ambiguity. Instead of using homonymy as CAM suggests, we will apply a more recent linguistics[1] approach where homonymy and polysemy are viewed as two categories of conceptual ambiguity, although their differences seem to be nuances. Nevertheless, in most definitions, polysemy is considered to represent a situation where a concept is used in (at least) two meanings, and homonymy applies when those two meanings are distinct and unrelated (Pethö, 2001; Klepousniotou, 2002). As the different meanings found in our sample are indeed related, we considered it best to label the ambiguity as polysemy instead of homonymy. However, the task itself, namely evaluating the conceptual ambiguity remains unchanged.

## 3.    RESULTS OF THE ANALYSIS

### 3.1    Conceptual Status of the Field: Synonymy

To evaluate the conceptual status of the field, in other words, whether the studies reveal synonymy (they employ more than one term to convey a single meaning) or polysemy (one term is used with more than one meaning), we studied the concepts used and how they were defined and/or described. Table 1.1 demonstrates the conceptual confusion in the field as it lists the ten different labels used to refer to the phenomenon, two of which stand out as the most widely used: "brand value co-creation" (16 pcs) and "brand(ing) co-creation" (13 pcs). The first article in our data, Boyle (2007) uses *brand co-creation*, and the concept remained in use through to the latest article reviewed that was published in 2020. The most-used concept in our data, *brand value co-creation*, has been in use since 2012. Several concepts first appeared quite recently, from 2016 onwards: "consumer–brand engagement", "brand co-destruction", "brand identity co-creation", "brand image co-creation", "brand strategy co-creation", and "co-creation for brand innovation". This usage pattern can imply that the field has progressed and is able to categorise different facets of brand co-creation, connected to the facets of brands themselves, the contexts, and the ontological preferences of the researchers.

Although ten different concepts were used, we found ten studies that used two or more of the concepts in the same study when defining or describing the phenomenon. As this is around 21 percent of the total 47 studies, we assessed that although the field contains synonymy, only some individual studies contain ambiguity owing to synonymy. However, some instances of synonymy seem likely to create quite severe doubts among readers as to which phenomenon the particular study focuses on. An example is the study of Hsieh and Chang (2016, p. 13) stating in its first sentence "co-creation for brand innovation (referred to hereafter as brand co-creation)", but the remaining paper uses "brand co-creation" without even mentioning the focus on brand *innovation*. Moreover, the study defines "brand co-creation engagement" in the context of "firm-sponsored co-creation, where co-creation is conducted on behalf of a firm" (Hsieh & Chang, 2016, p. 15). Such use of multiple concepts is inevitably puzzling.

### 3.2    Conceptual Status of the Field: Polysemy

Our next step – the search for definitions to check if the field contains polysemy – produced only a few explicit definitions of all ten different concepts. Hence, the vast majority of the studies do not explicitly define the concept(s) used, but those that do either build their own

*Table 1.1        Concepts and terms applied in brand co-creation articles*

| Concept/term (and variations) | Appears in // total number |
|---|---|
| Brand value co-creation | Biraghi and Gambetti (2017); Cheung et al. (2020); Choi et al. (2016); Cova et al. (2015); Foroudi et al. (2019); Fujita et al. (2017); Gambetti and Graffigna (2015); Hajli et al. (2017); Iglesias et al. (2013); Juntunen et al. (2012); Merz et al. (2018); Mingione and Leoni (2020); Nguyen et al. (2016); Nobre and Ferreira (2017); Ramaswamy and Ozcan (2016); Zhang and He (2014) // 16 |
| Brand(ing) co-creation (without specifying any facets of the brand) | Boyle (2007); Casais and Monteiro (2019); France et al. (2015, 2018, 2020); Hatch and Schultz (2010); Juntunen et al. (2012); Kamboj et al. (2018); Kaufmann et al. (2016); Lucarelli (2019); Oliveira and Panyik (2015); Schmeltz and Kjeldsen (2019); Vallaster et al. (2018) // 13 |
| Brand meaning co-creation | Bertschy et al. (2020); Dean et al. (2016); Fujita et al. (2017); Gonzalez and Lester (2018); Rosenthal and Zamith Brito (2017); Stach (2019); Suomi et al. (2020); Tierney et al. (2016); Vallaster and von Wallpach (2013) // 9 |
| Consumer–brand engagement | Cheung et al. (2020); Hajli et al. (2017); Hsieh and Chang (2016); Kamboj et al.(2018); Lin et al. (2018); Mingione and Leoni (2020); Nobre and Ferreira (2017); Seifert and Kwon (2020) // 8 |
| Brand identity co-creation | Black and Veloutsou (2017); Centeno and Wang (2017); Dean et al. (2016); Gonzalez and Lester (2018); Kennedy and Guzman (2016); Suomi et al. (2020) // 6 |
| Brand image co-creation | Hughes et al. (2016), Törmälä and Saraniemi (2018) // 2 |
| Brand value/meaning co-destruction | Kristal et al. (2018); Rossolatos (2019) // 2 |
| Co-creation for brand innovation | Hsieh and Chang (2016) //1 |
| Brand co-producing | Juntunen et al. (2012) //1 |
| Brand strategy co-creation | Vallaster and von Wallpach (2018) //1 |

definition or refer to existing definition(s); but rarely the same ones. No single definition has been used extensively by researchers.

**Brand value co-creation and polysemy**

We start the evaluation of polysemy with the largest group of studies. From the studies using the brand value co-creation concept, we found that nine of the total of 16 offer a definition. However, Table 1.2 shows that four papers do not define *brand/ing* value co-creation, but instead address value co-creation as a more general concept. In addition, none of the nine papers shares a definition. The definitions do share similarities, but "a similar meaning is not the same meaning" as Sartori (2009, p. 112) puts it. Moreover, Ramaswamy and Ozcan (2016, p. 95), sharpen the concept into "joint agencial experiencial [sic] creation of brand value", replacing co-creation by joint creation.

We conclude that the studies using brand value co-creation as their main concept do contain conceptual ambiguity caused by polysemy.

**Brand(ing) co-creation and polysemy**

Table 1.3 presents definitions of brand(ing) co-creation, the second largest group of studies in our data. This category contains only studies that did not specify any facets of the co-created brand or branding (e.g. identity, image, value). Among the 13 articles on brand(ing) co-creation, seven offer explicit definition(s), each study, however, relies on a different definition. France et al. (2015, 2018, 2020) all define exactly the same concept; customer brand co-creation behaviour (CBCB), but with slight differences. Notably, the latest article, France et al. (2020, p. 466), adds a notion of what customer brand co-creation means for a firm, in

*Table 1.2*    *Definitions of brand value co-creation*

| Article | Definition of brand(ing) value co-creation |
| --- | --- |
| Foroudi et al. (2019) | p. 219: Yi and Gong's (2013) research identifies two types of customer value co-creation behaviour: customer participation behaviour and customer citizenship behaviour. |
| | p. 225: Value co-creation behaviour: Customer value co-creation behaviour literature has argued that customers are not only the receivers of marketing information, they can also respond to the information as value creators. It can also refer to their interactive behaviour online via the website, leading to further navigation, sharing or repurchase (Tarafdar and Zhang, 2008). |
| | p. 225: Customer participation behaviour: Customer participation behaviour refers to customers' in-role behaviour so that they co-create the products or the service together with the company (Yi and Gong, 2013). |
| | p. 225: Customer citizenship behaviour: Customer citizenship behaviour refers to customers' extra-role behaviour that leads to their extra effort to interact with the organisation to contribute to the organisation's performance (Yi and Gong, 2013). |
| Choi et al. (2016) | p. 5828: Value co-creation means that customer emotional, cognitive, and behavioral experiences are the basis of the value, impressions, recognition, and internalization they accord to the brand. |
| Fujita et al. (2017) | p. 150: The brand community literature, aligned with consumer culture theory, has long discussed the co-creation concept or 'consumer collectives' as the social processes that construct brand meanings and cultural capital (Arnould & Thompson, 2005). |
| Gambetti and Graffigna (2015) | p. 157: In line with this concept of value, we contend that value co-creation, recently defined as the process by which value is co-generated, delivered and assessed in the simultaneous processes of production and consumption (Echeverri and Skålén, 2011), … |
| Hajli et al. (2017) | p. 137:…, co-creation is a process of engaging customers in creating value (Prahalad & Ramaswamy, 2004) as customers are transformed from passive customers to active players (Vargo & Lusch, 2004). |
| Merz et al. (2018) | p. 80: … we define brand value co-creation as the process of creating perceived use value for a brand through network relationships and social interactions among all the actors in the ecosystem (Merz et al., 2009; Vargo & Lusch, 2016). …Taken together, firms and customers contribute to a brand's value proposition, thereby co-creating brand value. |
| Mingione and Leoni (2020) | p. 76: … brand value co-creation can be considered as the process of brand building through network relationships and social interactions in a multi-stakeholder ecosystem (Gyrd-Jones & Kornum, 2013; Ind & Coates, 2013; Merz et al., 2009), in a way that improves the brand perception as well as its performance (Zhang & He, 2014). |

| Article | Definition of brand(ing) value co-creation |
| --- | --- |
| Nguyen et al. (2016) | p. 43: Value co-creation branding is a process of value co-creation in both daily life and research activities based on real experiences in the research laboratories of both professors and students. They can then expand research laboratory brands through viral marketing and social media. |
| Ramaswamy and Ozcan (2016) | p. 95: Joint agencial experiencial creation of brand value: Agency entails the capacity to act and actions that generate outcomes, by virtue of engagement by individuals that both reproduces and transforms structural environments in interactive response (Emirbayer & Mische, 1998). … we define "joint agencial experiencial creation" as a joint creation through agencial assemblages, oriented in its "virtual" capacity toward the future, informed in its "repetition" aspect by the past, summoned as "intensive" actions in the present, to "actualize" experiencial outcomes within the contingencies of exteriority of relations. … [Footnote:] This definition captures joint creation as a process of becoming that is simultaneously a "joint agencial creation" and a "joint experiencial creation". |

*Note:* The references used in the original definitions are not listed in the references of this study.

incorporating that CBCB "provides value to the firm". The three studies can be thought of as refining the definition of CBCB and thus do not represent polysemy as such.

Kamboj et al. (2018, p. 176) refer to Hajli et al. (2017) to define branding co-creation as "the process of branding with customers in an online environment". This definition is somewhat confusing, as Hajli et al. (2017) do not explicitly suggest such a definition. Nevertheless, the definition is contextual as it refers to online settings alone, ignores other potential platforms of brand co-creation, and offers little content other than to confirm the process is undertaken "with customers". Hence, it is difficult to determine that the phenomenon is the same as that referred to in the first-mentioned three studies.

Kaufmann et al. (2016) employ "brand co-creation" in the title and keywords, but the text actually discusses value co-creation. The two remaining articles, Lucarelli (2019) and Vallaster et al. (2018) both focus on city branding and, although the papers present slightly different contextual definitions, both refer to Vallaster and von Wallpach (2013). In summary, as a group, brand(ing) co-creation studies offer a conceptually unclear picture of brand(ing) co-creation owing to the influence of polysemy.

*Table 1.3    Definitions of brand(ing) co-creation*

| Article | Definition of brand(ing) co-creation |
|---|---|
| France et al. (2020) | p. 466: Customer brand co-creation behaviour is an active form of customer–brand interaction which provides value to the firm and, thus, becomes a useful focus of co-creation research. |
| France et al. (2018) | p. 335: Customer brand co-creation behaviour (CBCB): CBCB is appropriately defined as the voluntary, active and interactive customer actions associated with the customer–brand relationship. |
| France et al. (2015) | p. 852: Customer brand co-creation behaviours are the customer-led interactions between the customer and the brand. |
| Kamboj et al. (2018) | p, 173: Brand co-creation behaviours of customers are the customer-led interactions between the brand and customer (France et al., 2015). |
| | p. 176: Hajli et al. (2017) define branding co-creation as, "the process of branding with customers in an online environment". |
| Kaufmann et al. (2016) | p. 518: On the other hand, adopting a more collaborative approach, Ind et al. (2013), supported by Brakus et al. (2009) and the authors of this article, define co-creation as an active, creative and social process based on collaboration between organizations and participants that generate mutual benefits for all stakeholders (Ind et al., 2013, p. 9), as reflected by an active participation in a brand community (Kaufmann et al., 2012b) and influenced by the brand community principles (Muniz and O'Guinn, 2001). |
| Lucarelli (2019) | p. 227: brand co-creation is a socio-processual, multi-temporal and multi-layered involvement of different stakeholders (Vallaster and von Wallpach, 2013, 2018), featuring an uncontrollable process of branding (Wider et al., 2018). |
| Vallaster et al. (2018) | p. 55: City brand co-creation is "a discursive social process in which salient stakeholders may directly or indirectly, purposefully or coincidentally interact" online or offline, thereby shaping a brand's social reality and meaning through exchange and participation (Vallaster & von Wallpach, 2013, p. 1506). |

*Note:* The references used in the original definitions are not listed in the references of this study.

**Polysemy and the brand meaning co-creation concept**

Table 1.4 shows that of the nine studies adopting brand meaning co-creation as their main concept, a majority (six) provide definitions of the concept. However, only two of the six use the same definition; the Vallaster and von Wallpach (2013) study that initially presents the

*Table 1.4*    *Definitions of brand meaning co-creation*

| Article | Definition of brand meaning co-creation |
| --- | --- |
| Bertschy et al. (2020) | p. 48: Interested stakeholders of a sport brand cocreate brand meaning in an ongoing discourse concerning partly co-generated brand manifestations (Stieler, Weismann, & Germelmann, 2014; Uhrich, 2014; Woratschek, Horbel, & Popp, 2014) |
| Rosenthal and Zamith Brito (2017) | p. 924: Brand meaning co-creation is "a discursive social process in which salient stakeholders may directly or indirectly, purposefully or coincidentally, interact via text to shape certain aspects of a brand's social reality" (Vallaster and von Wallpach, 2013, p. 1506). |
| Stach (2019) | p. 327: By definition, research on brand meaning co-creation stresses how brand meaning is increasingly created outside of the control of marketers through interaction with multiple different stakeholders and different touchpoints (Berthon et al. 2009; Hatch and Schultz 2010; Iglesias and Bonet 2012; Michel 2017; see also Langner et al. 2016). |
| Suomi et al. (2020) | p. 212: When referring to brand co-creation, we are guided by Coupland, Iacobucci, and Arnould (2005, p. 107), who stated: 'the consumer is an active partner with the marketer in brand-meaning formation'. |
| Tierney et al. (2016) | p. 918: Thus, we introduce and define the concept of BMCC [brand meaning cocreation] as a process that encompasses brand-related, resource-integrating activities and interactions among multiple market actors within service ecosystems, leading to a socially negotiated and idiosyncratically determined brand meaning. This conceptual understanding acknowledges the reciprocal, reticular interactions between multiple market actors as key elements in BMCC. |
| Vallaster and von Wallpach (2013) | p. 1506: In line with recent views on co-creation (e.g., Vargo & Lusch, 2008), this article perceives online brand meaning co-creation as a discursive social process in which salient stakeholders may directly or indirectly, purposefully, or coincidentally interact via written text to shape certain aspects of a brand's social reality (cf. Muehlbacher & Hemetsberger, 2008). |

*Note:* The references used in the original definitions are not listed in the references of this study.

definition and the study by Rosenthal and Zamith Brito (2017) that refers to Vallaster and von Wallpach (2013). As all the other articles defining brand meaning co-creation are more recent than the Vallaster and von Wallpach (2013) one, the authors could have used the 2013 definition but chose not to. To sum up, the group of studies studying brand meaning co-creation also exhibit polysemy.

**Polysemy and consumer–brand engagement**
Of the eight studies referencing consumer–brand engagement in our data, half present detailed definitions, albeit each article employs a different definition (see Table 1.5). Engagement refers to actions, but also to attitude and emotions of the consumer. Two of the articles – Kamboj et al. (2018), and Seifert and Kwon (2020) – relate engagement specifically to the co-creation of value for a brand, and thus seem to have their theoretical roots in the literature of value co-creation. Cheung et al. (2020) draw on the literature on consumer–brand relationships and consumer–brand engagement, whereas Hsieh and Chang (2016) employ the literature on employee engagement. It is therefore apparent that studies within the consumer–brand engagement category contain polysemy.

*Table 1.5*      *Definitions of consumer–brand engagement*

| Article | Definition of consumer–brand engagement |
| --- | --- |
| Cheung et al. (2020) | p. 524: Consumer–brand engagement (CBE) refers to "consumers' brand-related cognitive, emotional and behavioural activity related to focal brand interactions" (Hollebeek et al., 2014, p. 149). |
| | p. 524: CBE is conceptualized as a psychological state that involves consumers' passion for the brand, arising from the strength of consumer–brand interactions (Brodie et al., 2011). |
| Hsieh and Chang (2016) | p. 15: This study expands the definition of engagement by Schaufeli, Bakker, and Salanova (2006), to define brand co-creation engagement as a "persistent, positive affective-motivational state of fulfillment that is characterized by vigor, dedication, and absorption toward brand co-creation". |
| Kamboj et al. (2018) | p. 173: Brand co-creation behaviours of customers are the customer-led interactions between the brand and customer (France et al., 2015). |
| | p. 173: Thus, co-creation is the process of customer's engagement in value creation (Prahalad and Ramaswamy, 2004) as online customers are changed from inactive to active consumers (Vargo and Lusch, 2004). |
| Seifert and Kwon (2020) | p. 92: Brand value co-creation engagement behavior refers to the degree to which a consumer demonstrates the participation and citizenship behavior (Yi and Gong, 2013) toward the brand on SNSs [social networking sites] by sharing his or her knowledge, experience, and opinion about the brand through interactions with the brand and other consumers on SNSs; while brand value co-creation engagement attitude represents the favorable or unfavorable disposition toward the brand with which the consumer exerts this value co-creation behavior on SNSs. |

*Note:* The references used in the original definitions are not listed in the references of this study.

**Polysemy and brand identity co-creation**

Of the six studies focusing on brand identity co-creation, only two present definitions we recognise. As with all the previous concepts, this one is also defined differently and Table 1.6 again illustrates the presence of polysemy. Even if we exclude the definition of Centeno and Wang (2017), which is restricted to personal brand identity co-creation, the remainder of the definitions differ. Suomi et al. (2020) advocate the view of da Silveira et al. (2013) that brand identity itself is a process, not an end state or static entity, and the other parts of the definition share some core features of the many co-creation definitions discussed so far.

*Table 1.6*      *Definitions of brand identity co-creation*

| Article | Definition of brand identity co-creation |
| --- | --- |
| Centeno and Wang (2017) | p. 134: … celebrity human brand identity co-creation is a social assemblage of a web of actors … both humans (i.e., celebrities, consumers, fans, and other spectators) and "non-humans" including organizations and service entities (i.e., media outfits and commercial firms). |
| Suomi et al. (2020) | p. 212: This study applies the definition of brand identity devised by da Silveira, Lages, and Simões (2013, p. 35), that is: "a dynamic process developing over time through mutually influencing inputs from brand managers and other social constituents (e.g., consumers)". |

**Polysemy and brand co-destruction and other concepts**

Although our search was restricted to co-creation, it also captured an emerging stream on the dark side of co-creation, namely brand co-destruction. Interestingly, Kristal et al. (2018) parallelise non-collaborative brand co-creation with the collaborative co-destruction of brand value (see Table 1.7). Further, the study finds two particular types of non-collaborative brand co-creation: brand play (e.g. parody) and the more aggressive subversion of a brand: brand attack. Rossolatos (2019, p. 1260), in turn, defines co-destruction as "negatively valenced comments and brand image dilution". Although there are some similarities between the definitions, the studies do not share the same meaning (Sartori, 2009, p. 112), and thus illustrate polysemy.

*Table 1.7    Definitions of brand value/meaning co-destruction*

| Article | Definition of brand value/meaning co-destruction |
| --- | --- |
| Kristal et al. (2018) | p. 336: Drawing upon the notion of "devaluation of value" (Plé and Chumpitaz Cáceres, 2010), we can characterise non-collaborative brand co-creation as the collaborative co-destruction of brand value. |
| | p. 341: … we conceptualised two forms of co-creation: brand play as the playful parodying of brand meanings, as suggested by Fournier and Avery (2011), and brand attack as the expression of negative emotions or even hate for the brand, as identified by Demirbag-Kaplan et al. (2015) and Hegner et al. (2017). |
| Rossolatos (2019) | p. 1260: … co-destruction refers to negatively valenced comments and brand image dilution, coindifference designates the utter dissolution of brand meaning by dint of being trajectorized in totally random ways (with regard to the thematic contours of specific brand initiated posts). |

*Note:* The references used in the original definitions are not listed in the references of this study.

Of the remaining concepts – brand image co-creation, co-creation for brand innovation, brand co-producing, and brand strategy co-creation – only the last is meticulously defined through employing multiple references. Vallaster and von Wallpach (2018, p. 987) define brand strategy co-creation as follows:

> these interactive branding processes are (a) "co-creative," in the sense that they consist of ongoing discourses among multiple stakeholders that require access to and transparency of information on company-internal processes and structures (Hatch & Schultz, 2010; Prahalad & Ramaswamy, 2004) and provide involved stakeholders with "actualized value" that "is subjective and varies as a function of individualized experiences" (Ramaswamy & Ozcan, 2014, p. 16), and (b) "strategic," in the sense that they shape a brand's mission, vision, goals, and objectives (Bhattacharya, Korschun, & Sen, 2009), allowing organisations and their stakeholders to jointly decide what they want to achieve and how (Biraghi & Gambetti, 2013).

As Vallaster and von Wallpach (2018) provide the only study using the brand strategy co-creation concept, it is free from polysemy.

To summarise, the discussions on the phenomenon seem to contain less synonymy, although are not free from it, and are to a large extent influenced by polysemy. In other words, the same concept when defined, seems to refer to different understandings of the phenomenon. The current situation offers scope to clarify the conceptual confusion, a task we begin in the next section.

**3.3     The Dominant Meanings and Boundaries of the Concepts and their Descriptions**

The current study aims to clarify the conceptual discussion by applying interpretative content analysis (Neuendorf, 2002) to both the above-presented definitions and the descriptions presented in those articles lacking definitions. Interpretative analysis encourages the meanings and boundaries of the concepts to emerge from the data, without applying pre-determined categories (Neuendorf, 2002). The analysis commenced with a repeat reading of the definitions and descriptions to identify the essential features that were important to their authors (see Sartori, 2009, p. 107). The number of different concepts used meant that we performed the analysis only on those concepts used in more than two studies. The analysis aimed to find out if the most commonly used facets of the concepts differ from each other. The categories that emerged from the sample were as follows: participating actors (e.g. consumers/travellers/stakeholders); characterisation of co-creation (e.g. process/activities/interaction/communication); type of co-creation (direct/indirect); and beneficiary (brand/others). Some of the feature categories proved important in all the concept descriptions, but a few emerged only in some.

Since we found variation in the meanings and boundaries, the next step in the CAM process was to tabulate the concept descriptions to isolate the most dominant ones (Tähtinen & Havila, 2019) (Table 1.8 on consumer–brand engagement will be presented as an example, Tables 1A.1–1A.4 are in the Appendix). Rather than listing the articles alphabetically, the tables order them chronologically to show any changes that occurred over time.

The value co-creation concept shows no trend in how its major features have appeared in definitions and descriptions of the concept (Table 1A.1 in the Appendix). It is also difficult to detect the dominant meanings as, for the first feature, the participating actors, all options are present from the earliest writings to the latest. Hence, the concept covers two views; one where only customers or consumers and the brand owners are active in co-creation, and the second where all stakeholders are considered parties to the co-creation. However, in general, the articles seem to characterise co-creation predominantly as a *process* of interaction between the actors, as a few studies use *activities*, a less interactive term. A few studies categorise co-creation as either direct or indirect and a few draw attention to the beneficiary of the value co-creation. Accordingly, the dominant use of the brand value co-creation concept refers to interaction processes between either customers or all stakeholders and the brand (or brand owner). The interaction may be direct or indirect, but it mainly benefits the brand.

The brand(ing) co-creation concept has also been used in place- and city branding, where the participants would include tourists and residents (Table 1A.2 in the Appendix). The brand(ing) co-creation concept encompasses all stakeholders, including consumers, residents, and tourists as active participants in the interaction processes. However, the concept has also been used in the more focused context of the consumer–brand relationship, which excludes the brand owner, but focuses on the brand itself as the interacting party. Brand(ing) co-creation is viewed as both direct and indirect. None of the above features show any changes occurring between 2007–2020.

Likewise, the brand-meaning co-creation concept shows no clear changes in its main features that set the meaning and boundaries of the concept. However, this is the first concept that clearly considers all stakeholders as playing a part in the interaction processes. Moreover, the interaction processes are more geared to indirect or direct communication than to interaction in general. As the brand meaning is co-created, the benefits flow to the brand.

We next examine the brand identity co-creation concept, to help the reader to connect it to the closely related branding and BMCC concepts. Brand identity appears only in our data published 2016–2020, and no trends are visible. Following the brand-meaning concept, brand identity co-creation is also a stakeholders' process, however, there is no dominant view of the specific nature of the process, as it is described both in terms of action and communication. However, for the first time, beneficiaries of the process other than the brand are also mentioned. This implies that the parties co-creating the brand identity might also co-create their identities.

The remaining concept that has been used in more than a single study is consumer–brand engagement. The concept is clearly focused on consumers alone, and engagement is seen as both an interaction process (in other words, behaviour), and an emotional state or attitude of the consumer, the latter leading to the actual process of co-creation (see Table 1.8). The question of who benefits does not seem to be deemed important, as only Hsieh and Chang (2016) directly address it.

In summary, the different concepts are surprisingly similar in their dominant meanings and with little changes occurring over time. However, there are some less-noted features that appear in just a few studies. This group offers interesting new perspectives on the phenomenon that could trigger future research and expand how co-creation in the context of brands is viewed.

### 3.4    The Rare Meanings and Boundaries of the Concepts

Looking at the rare meanings and boundaries set reveals some interesting aspects to the phenomenon. We start with thoughts on its fairness to consumers and overall novelty.

The debate on "prosumers" and "prosumption" involves co-creation and views the concept in (at least) two lights. First, it is argued that prosumption provides consumers with the power of agency – especially if they join forces – and shifts the power from producers to customers (Toffler, 1980; Prahalad & Ramaswamy, 2004). This shift considerably reduces the opportunities of brand managers to influence co-creation. Lucarelli (2019, p. 227) referencing Wider et al. (2018) defines the process as "uncontrollable". The alternative, a critical view highlights the questions of agency, control, and power (Lucarelli, 2019) and refers to co-creation by customers as unpaid work. In our sample, Cova et al. (2015), Black and Veloutsou (2017), and Lucarelli (2019) represent this view.

Is co-creation or prosumption a novel phenomenon? Sociologist Ritzer (2015, p. 414) argues that "pure" production (without any consumption) and "pure" consumption (without any production) are not empirically possible, as "the two processes always interpenetrate". Indeed, consumers have always been part of the value-in-use production, whenever they use a product, for example, when they drive a car (Comor, 2011). However, Ritzer (2015) argues that prosumers, for example using a self-service option, are being exploited; they perform the work without getting paid (as workers are), or being compensated *via* lower prices, and remain blissfully unaware of this injustice. When the prosumers' work contributes to *exchange* values or profits, the prosumer is being exploited (Comor, 2011).

There is certainly room for a critical discussion on whether marketers are exploiting customers and other stakeholders when trying to involve them in various brand co-creation behaviour. The question is how ready the customers and other stakeholders are to be persistent (as defined by Hsieh & Chang, 2016), passionate, and active co-creators (as defined by

*Table 1.8     The meaning and boundaries of the consumer–brand engagement concept*

| Consumer–brand engagement articles | Participating actors | | Characterisation of the engagement | | | Types of engagement | | Beneficiary | |
|---|---|---|---|---|---|---|---|---|---|
| | Consumer(s)/ customers | Stakeholders | Process | Interactions | State/Attitude | Emotional | Behavioural | The brand | Others |
| Hsieh and Chang (2016) | ✓ | | | | ✓ | ✓ | | ✓ | |
| Hajli et al. (2017) | | | | | | | | | |
| Nobre and Ferreira (2017) | | | | | ✓ | | | | |
| Kamboj et al. (2018) | ✓ | | ✓ | | | | ✓ | | |
| Lin et al. (2018) | ✓ | | | ✓ | ✓ | | | | |
| Cheung et al. (2020) | ✓ | | | ✓ | ✓ | ✓ | ✓ | | |
| Mingione and Leoni (2020) | ✓ | | | | ✓ | ✓ | | | |
| Seifert and Kwon (2020) | ✓ | | | ✓ | ✓ | | ✓ | | |

Cheung et al., 2020). That is a lot to ask. Are the actors behaving wholly voluntarily, or do the marketers' efforts engage them in co-creation without providing them their share of the value? A view of co-creation as a management tool that turns passive customers into active ones is exemplified in Hajli et al. (2017) and Kamboj et al. (2018). The definition used by Tierney et al. (2016) highlights how co-creation is *reciprocal*, indicating that both actors are aware of the other's efforts. On the other hand, other conceptualisations refer to *coincidental* co-creation (Vallaster & von Wallpach, 2013), which we assume does not require willingness, passion, or reciprocity. Finally, Centeno and Wang (2017) include not only human actors among the parties to co-creation but also non-humans, although the examples offered are companies and the media. Nevertheless, in an era of artificial intelligence and automation, non-humans are a feature that will increasingly be part of life.

To conclude the discussion on the rare meanings attributed to brand co-creation, we discuss a fairly recent notion that co-creation refers to communication between the stakeholders. This facet is present in the definitions or descriptions used by Foroudi et al. (2019), Casais and Moteiro (2019), Bertschy et al. (2020), Cheung et al. (2020), and Seifert and Kwon (2020). The communication addition expands co-creation beyond the dyadic relationships between the brand or the brand owner and the stakeholder into networks of stakeholders. This also means that the marketers' influence on what happens outside the dyad is, as is often stated, limited when co-creation happens between stakeholders and excludes the brand owner.

The limited role of brand owners brings us to the negatives of co-creation. Those negative aspects have been labelled collaborative co-destruction of brand value by Kristal et al. (2018) and co-destruction by Rossolatos (2019).[2] If we consider brand value co-creation as originating with customers, co-destruction might refer to a situation where both the marketer and the stakeholder unite to destroy brand value. We are unsure of this reading, as the examples offered focus on only the stakeholders' negative actions. In addition, brand co-destruction can involve a group of stakeholders that may collaborate with each other and for example attack a brand via social media (Kristal et al., 2018; Rossolatos, 2019).

### 3.5    Theoretical Underpinnings of the Concepts

The theoretical underpinnings of the concepts were elicited by checking the sources referred to in the definitions or descriptions of the concepts. Hence, following the CAM we did not plunge into the complete list of references of the articles, but kept the investigation on the level of the definitions and their direct theoretical bases. However, when constructing the conceptual maps, we looked more closely at the two major theoretical bases of the definitions, namely branding and value co-creation research, as both have their offshoots.

The first theoretical discussion underpinning the studied concepts is branding research and its various streams and sub-streams. To detect the streams, we used a recent categorisation by Heding et al. (2020) of brand management literature into positivist and interpretive paradigms. As the positivist paradigm views brands mainly as outcomes of companies' marketing activities, the stream remains unused as a theoretical basis. Thus, it is the identity approach that is applied as a theoretical basis. The approach incorporates an understanding of identity as being context-dependent and negotiated between all the stakeholders.

The concepts of BMCC and brand image co-creation specifically refer to the interpretative paradigm of branding research in their definitions and descriptions. The interpretative paradigm (Heding et al., 2020) was already noted in 2000, although Allen et al. (2008) label it an alternative. The paradigm views the brand as a result of the interaction between the brand's creator and active consumers and other stakeholders. Heding et al. (2020) further categorise the interpretative paradigm into relational, community, and cultural approaches to brand management. The relational approach focuses on the brand–consumer dyadic exchange process where both actors contribute equally and brand value is co-created. The community approach adds third actors, namely other consumers as a group into the interaction process, which is likely to go on even without the brand owner. Heding et al. (2020) connect this approach to the service-dominant logic (e.g. Vargo & Lusch, 2004). Finally, the cultural approach builds upon Consumer Culture Theory (CCT) (Arnould & Thompson, 2005) but also includes a macro-level focus where brands are seen as significant political and financial powers.

The second clear theoretical underpinning of the co-creation definitions is the service-logic or service-dominant logic literature (e.g. Grönroos, 2011; Grönroos & Gummerus, 2014; Merz et al., 2009; Prahalad & Ramaswamy, 2004; Vargo & Lusch, 2004) both of which have discussed value co-creation. The influence of SDL is particularly clear in the conceptualisations of brand value co-creation, customer–brand engagement, and brand(ing) co-creation but, to a certain extent, also in brand identity co-creation. However, none of the brand co-creation definitions refer to the fresh conceptualisation of co-creation by Ramaswamy and Ozcan (2018, p. 96) as "enactment of interactional creation across interactive system-environments entailing agencing engagements and structuring organizations". There could be two reasons: first, Ramaswamy and Ozcan (2018) is a recent one so is only cited in a few studies; second, it does not examine brand co-creation, although some of the study's references do relate to branding.

To summarise, definitions of the phenomenon, although described in different concepts, are largely combinations of streams of branding and value co-creation. This somewhat unified grounding explains the small differences in the dominant features of the definitions and descriptions discussed in the previous section.

Nevertheless, we also found interesting exceptions, both in theoretical backgrounds and in research approaches that have enriched the understanding of the phenomenon. Schmeltz and Kjeldsen (2019) investigate internal brand co-creation and combine the corporate branding discussion with organisation and management research. Discussions of place branding as a co-creative process stemming from tourism and city branding are used by Gonzalez and Lester (2018), Casais and Monteiro (2019), Vallaster et al. (2018), and Lucarelli (2019) when defining or describing the main concept. The place branding discussion in particular, views branding as a process emerging from the identity of the place and the stakeholders' dialogues (e.g. Kavaratzis and Hatch, 2013).

A strategy-as-practice approach is applied to study brand strategy co-creation by Vallaster and von Wallpach (2018). Earlier, Vallaster and von Wallpach (2013) had applied stakeholder theory and adopted a linguistic and hermeneutic approach to studying BMCC. Centeno and Wang (2017) reference actor-network theory stemming from sociology to discuss the co-creation of celebrity brand identities as do Ramaswamy and Ozcan (2016), where sociological assemblage theory is also applied to stress the customers' agency instead of mere actions.

Cova et al. (2015) use the multidisciplinary field of research on consumer volunteering to reveal the unpaid but planned work consumers do for brands. Consumer culture theory is represented as a background in studies where co-creation takes place in brand communities (Black & Veloutsou, 2017; Fujita et al., 2017). Two so-called hot keywords from the fields of marketing and strategy also show up in co-creation studies; brand experiences (Juntunen et al.,

2012; Choi et al., 2016; Nobre & Ferreira, 2017; Stach, 2019) and ecosystems (Tierney et al., 2016; Törmälä & Saraniemi, 2018; Mingione & Leoni, 2020). The two buzz words work in opposite directions; brand experience narrows the focus and the ecosystem extends the sphere of stakeholders to involve those who are indirectly related.

In addition to reviewing the direct references mentioned in the definitions or descriptions of the focal concept, we investigated the work of a few influential scholars in the field of branding whose work had not appeared up until that point. For example, although sociologist Adam Arvidsson is a widely cited scholar, only seven of the 47 articles refer to one or more of his authored or co-authored works (Arvidsson, 2005, 2006, 2008; Arvidsson & Caliandro, 2016; Arvidsson et al., 2008). None of the studies in our sample, however, rely on Arvidsson's texts when presenting definitions and descriptions, and thus it seems that his works do not offer a direct theoretical basis for their definitions.

## 3.6    Conceptual Maps

Although it seemed that the concepts applied in co-creation research on branding and brands are quite similar, drawing the conceptual maps of the dominant features unearths three different groups. Here, again we describe only those concepts applied in more than two studies.

The first group consists of two concepts: brand value co-creation and brand(ing) co-creation (see Figure 1.1). They both share views on the actors and the nature and type of co-creation. The phenomenon is viewed as customers and/or stakeholders interacting directly or indirectly. What seems to differentiate the two concepts is that brand value co-creation research has considered co-creation producing value for the brand and/or its owner to be an important feature. Of course, the same notion can be implicit in brand(ing) co-creation studies, but it has not been commonly stressed in the definitions or descriptions of the concept. Brand(ing) co-creation studies are more varied in the focal contexts; hence actors also include tourists and residents. In addition, the brand itself is considered an actor.

The concepts also share the rarer meanings, the critical view of unpaid work and the managerial view of co-creation as a tool; perhaps the latter is the reason for the former. Co-creation taking place between the stakeholders, without the marketer, remains a rare meaning in both concepts.

The same theoretical underpinnings; service or service-dominant logic and the community approach to branding research, could explain the similarities. Similarly, the different actors could be explained with context-related studies and roots in tourism or city/place branding, where customers are labelled tourists, visitors, and residents.

Brand-meaning co-creation and brand identity co-creation form the second group (Figure 1.2). They share a view of co-creation as a communication process driven by marketers and stakeholders that benefits the brand. The nature of the process is specified as a form of communication instead of any kind of interaction, and this separates these two concepts from the first pair. The differences in the dominant features are the type of co-creation, BMCC having a greater influence in separating direct and indirect co-creation, and the nature of co-creation (where brand identity co-creation also includes actions). Moreover, the brand identity co-creation concept stresses that all stakeholders benefit from co-creation.

The rare meanings of the two concepts are quite different. The reciprocal nature of BMCC that resides between the stakeholders remains a rare feature of that concept alone. The rare

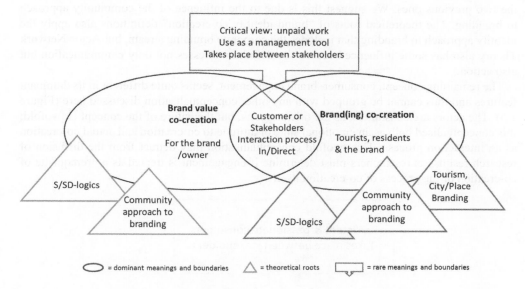

Figure 1.1    Conceptual maps of brand value co-creation and brand(ing) co-creation concepts

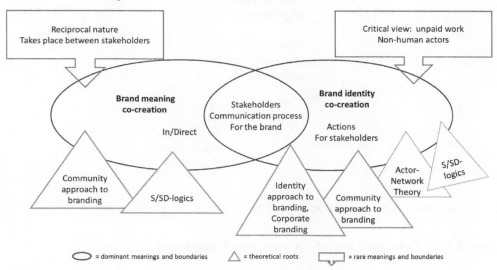

Figure 1.2    Conceptual maps of brand-meaning co-creation and brand identity co-creation

conceptualisations of brand identity co-creation include the critical view of unpaid work and a novel view of non-humans being able to participate in the process.

Looking at the theoretical influences, BMCC definitions use service or service-dominant logic as a theoretical background, however, that does not seem to connect the concept with the two previous ones. We suggest this is due to the influence of the community approach to branding. The theoretical roots of "brand identity co-creation" definitions also apply the identity approach to branding that includes the corporate branding stream, but Actor-Network Theory also has some influence because the definition stresses not only communication but also action.

The remaining concept, consumer–brand engagement, seems quite different in its dominant features and thus cannot be grouped with any other conceptualisation discussed here (Figure 1.3). The actors are consumers, as the title suggests, but the nature of the concept is twofold; it is conceptualised both as an emotional state or attitude to co-creation and actual co-creation as an interaction process. This twofold conceptualisation may detract from the diffusion of research results, as researchers must determine if engagement is treated as a prerequisite of co-creation or the process of co-creation itself.

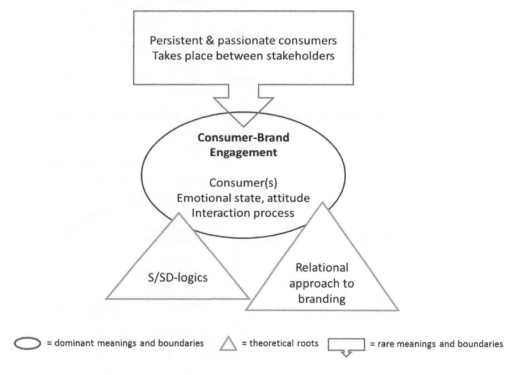

*Figure 1.3*    *Conceptual map of consumer–brand engagement*

The rare descriptions of persistent, and passionate consumers can be connected to the focus on emotional states and attitudes of the co-creating consumers. Nevertheless, the theoretical discussions used to define the concept do not differ greatly from the other concepts. Hence, the defining features seem to stem from wider theoretical backgrounds of the articles the study as a whole refers and/or contributes to, which in this case would be consumer behaviour and CCT.

## 4.     CONCLUSIONS AND DISCUSSION

This chapter reflects upon the definitions of the concepts and descriptions of the terms that research uses to refer to co-creation in the context of branding, to reveal and clarify any conceptual confusion. It confirmed the experiences of MacKenzie (2003) that many studies underestimate the value of presenting explicit conceptual definitions. By applying CAM (Tähtinen & Havila, 2019) the results showed that co-creation in branding contains conceptual ambiguity. Of the two forms causing ambiguity, the field is somewhat affected by synonymy and, to a greater extent, polysemy; hence, the task was worth undertaking.

This study found ten different brand co-creation concepts and deconstructed the most often used to show their dominant and rare features, direct theoretical underpinnings, and how they differ from each other. The concepts of "brand value co-creation" and "brand(ing) co-creation" stand out as the most applied, "BMCC" and "brand identity co-creation" both distinguish the co-created aspect of a brand, and "consumer–brand engagement" highlights the consumer's view. The unravelling of the five most-used concepts to form conceptual maps brought to light several aspects of the phenomenon and its complexity. Some of the aspects are well studied while others remain in the shadows. The analysis can help future researchers to clarify their own conceptual choices, balance the focus of their research, and direct it at relevant aspects of the phenomenon that are insufficiently studied.

Moreover, the chapter discussed interesting exceptions in the literature, explored theoretical backgrounds not often investigated, and unearthed features revealing the less studied aspects of the phenomenon and its complexity. Finally, the CAM was developed by using recent linguistics research and explicating not only the dominant features but also the rare ones, as well as looking a little more closely at the myriad theoretical underpinnings of the concepts.

This chapter does not suggest that a certain concept or definition would be better than others, or that a particular concept should be used only in its dominant meaning or to study brand co-creation in a particular context. The choice is always made by each individual researcher. It does suggest that in making the choice, researchers should be aware of which terms and concepts have been used and in what way. By exploring the meanings and boundaries of the concepts, scholars can choose to apply one or several concepts, and the theories that underpin them. Choosing several concepts makes it possible to present multiple perspectives on a complex phenomenon and enrich the understanding of it. Nevertheless, this requires that the studies explicitly define the different meanings and boundaries, in other words, present their definitions so as to avoid conceptual ambiguity.

However, we suggest two aspects to be taken into consideration when choosing the concept or concepts for a study. First, studies could build on the conceptual understanding that is firmly grounded in the branding discussions. Specifying exactly what is being co-created (e.g. identity, meaning, image, or strategy) and focusing on each facet would expand the understanding of the phenomenon as a whole. Second, studies using the concept of *value* (e.g. "brand *value* co-creation") require the user to carefully state how value is to be understood in this context and how it relates to, for example, brand equity. After all, only the constructionist stream of research on customer (perceived) value views value as co-created (i.e. value-as-process) (Zeithaml et al., 2020). Brand could be seen as a subset of value (hedonic value, status value, or expressive value), as an entity or as a process remaining outside any social constructionist definitions or categorisations of value (see Zeithaml et al., 2020). Hence, research based upon the ontological choices is in place.

Co-creation must be included in branding concepts to forestall a potential decline into thinking of brand(ing) as a process performed and controlled mainly by managers. Referring back to early definitions of brand image by Gardner and Levy (1955, p. 35) as, "The set of ideas, feelings and attitudes that consumers have about brands" and Herzog (1963, p. 82) "Brand image is the sum total of impressions the consumer receives from many sources" it becomes obvious that managers were never considered the only active actors in branding. Nevertheless, the nature of the branding process, or all the actors involved were long denied specific research attention as research wished to provide tools for brand managers.

Methodologically, it seems that following the CAM process until the final task – the conceptual maps – is a useful way to reveal differences and similarities in the conceptualisation used. Accordingly, this study serves not only as an example of how to use the CAM, but also offers a limited evaluation of the method and how it could be improved, although that was not the main goal of this chapter. We add the recently acknowledged aspect of polysemy to the early step of CAM that investigates the conceptual ambiguity of the particular research field. In addition, we include an investigation of rare features of the definitions, to unlock interesting and also somewhat contradictory aspects that only some definitions see as important to the phenomenon. We also suggest that the rare features can be visualised as a part of the conceptual maps.

The most challenging aspect of applying the CAM is distinguishing the theoretical underpinnings of the definitions. Restricting the search for those underpinnings to the definitions/ descriptions obviously shows only a proportion of them, and more careful examination would require extending CAM to search all the references cited in the articles.

As the CAM aims to study only the conceptual state of any field, one of the limitations of this study is its lack of discussion on the methodology or the findings of the studies. Further, the data set was not a full collection of all the studies in the field but the CAM protocol and this example indicates it provided a sufficient sample for the task. A deeper analysis of the theoretical progress of the field would require a fully-fledged systematic literature review. Nevertheless, the results of this study show that the different concepts, definitions, and descriptions used to refer to the phenomenon use elements that offer future research tools to categorise different facets of brand co-creation; namely who participates, who has agency and power, how is the co-creation viewed (e.g. as a process or attitude, direct and indirect), and who benefits. Moreover, the more explicitly a conceptual definition encompasses those elements, the clearer and more useful it will be for the reader.

We hope that the conceptual maps herein provide useful guidelines for future research on how to both read existing studies and to how to conceptualise co-creation when studying it in the branding context. It will be beneficial if the research stream extends its traditional management-oriented focus towards a more stakeholder-oriented approach. Before researchers could offer managerial advice, they would have to have access to more research focusing on stakeholders. Such research would probably have determined the various stakeholders' views on co-creation; whether it is a form of exploitation, or whether it offers them value, and if so, what kind of value. Further research efforts might then examine how that value might be enhanced and whether co-creation is a dyadic process between the brand and the stakeholder or if the conceptualisation and research should include a network approach or a multi-actor view where all stakeholder interactions are viewed as essential. Researchers of the topic should also consider whether to adopt a macro view and include ecosystems, or, in contrast to focus more closely on the individual stakeholders, their experiences, and their individual traits that influence willingness and engagement in the context of co-creation. Belk (2020) suggests that an abductive strategy and ethnographic, netnographic, and autoethnographic research using (participant) observation, depth interviews, and projective data collection methods, for example, could reignite marketing research. Such methods could also shed light on aspects of brand co-creation that remain very much in the shadows.

## NOTES

1. We are grateful to an anonymous reviewer for pointing this out.
2. Value co-destruction has been discussed outside the branding context in e.g. Plé and Chumpitaz Cáceres (2010) and Echeverri and Skålén (2011).

## REFERENCES

Allen, C. T., Fournier, S., & Miller, F. (2008). Brands and their meaning makers. In C. P. Haugtvedt, P. M. Herr, & F. R. Kardes (Eds.), *Handbook of Consumer Psychology* (pp. 781–822). Mahwah, NJ: Erlbaum.

Arnould, E. J., & Thompson, J. (2005). Consumer culture theory (CCT): Twenty years of research. *Journal of Consumer Research, 31*, 868–882.

Arvidsson, A. (2005). Brands: A critical perspective. *Journal of Consumer Culture, 5*(2), 235–258.

Arvidsson, A. (2006). *Brands: Meaning and Value in Media Culture.* London, UK: Routledge.

Arvidsson, A. (2008). The ethical economy of customer coproduction. *Journal of Macromarketing, 28*(4), 326–338.

Arvidsson, A., & Caliandro, A. (2016). Brand public. *Journal of Consumer Research, 42*(5), 727–748.

Arvidsson, A., Bauwens, M., & Peitersen, N. (2008). The crisis of value and the ethical economy. *Journal of Futures Studies, 12*(4), 9–20.

Bagozzi, R. P. (1984). A prospectus for theory construction in marketing. *Journal of Marketing, 48*(1), 11–29.

Bartels, R. (1970). *Marketing Theory and Metatheory.* Homewood, IL: Richard D. Irwin.

Belk, R. (2020). Resurrecting marketing. *AMS Review,* 1–4. https://doi.org/10.1007/s13162-020-00182 -9

Bertschy, M., Muhlbacher, H., & Desbordes, M. (2020). Esports extension of a football brand: Stakeholder co-creation in action? *European Sport Management Quarterly, 20*(1), 47–68.

Bhattacharya, C. B., Korschun, D., & Sen, S. (2009). Strengthening stakeholder–company relationships through mutually-beneficial corporate social responsibility initiatives. *Journal of Business Ethics, 85*, 257–272.

Biraghi, S., & Gambetti, R. C. (2013). Corporate branding: Where are we? A systematic communication-based inquiry. *Journal of Marketing Communications, 21*, 260–283.

Biraghi, S., & Gambetti, R. C. (2017). Is brand value co-creation actionable? A facilitation perspective. *Management Decision, 55*(7), 1476–1488.

Black, I., & Veloutsou, C. (2017). Working consumers: Co-creation of brand identity, consumer identity and brand community identity. *Journal of Business Research, 70*, 416–429.

Blomberg, A., Kallio, T. J., & Pohjanpää, H. (2017). Antecedents of organizational creativity: Drivers, barriers or both? *Journal of Innovation Management, 5*(1), 78–104.

Blumer, H. (1954). What is wrong with social theory? *American Sociological Review, 19*(1), 3–10.

Boyle, E. (2007). A process model of brand cocreation: Brand management and research implications. *Journal of Product and Brand Management, 16*(2), 122–131.

Brown, S. (2005). Ambi-brand culture: On a wing and a swear with Ryanair. In J. Schroeder & M. Salzer Mörling (Eds.), *Brand Culture* (pp. 50–66). London, UK: Routledge.

Casais, B., & Monteiro, P. (2019). Residents' involvement in city brand co-creation and their perceptions of city brand identity: A case study in Porto. *Place Branding and Public Diplomacy, 15*(4), 229–237.

Centeno, D., & Wang, J. J. (2017). Celebrities as human brands: An inquiry on stakeholder–actor co-creation of brand identities. *Journal of Business Research, 74*, 133–138.

Cheung, M. L., Pires, G. D., Rosenberger, P. J. III, & De Oliveira, M. J. (2020). Driving consumer–brand engagement and co-creation by brand interactivity. *Marketing Intelligence & Planning, 38*(4), 523–541.

Choi, E., Ko, E., & Kim, A. J. (2016). Explaining and predicting purchase intentions following luxury-fashion brand value co-creation encounters. *Journal of Business Research, 69*(12), 5827–5832.

Comor, E. (2011). Contextualizing and critiquing the fantastic prosumer: Power, alienation and hegemony. *Critical Sociology, 37*(3), 309–327.

Cova, B., Pace, S., & Skålen, P. (2015). Brand volunteering: Value co-creation with unpaid consumers. *Marketing Theory, 15*(4), 465–485.

da Silveira, C., Lages, C., & Simões, C. (2013). Reconceptualizing brand identity in a dynamic environment. *Journal of Business Research, 66*(1), 28–36.

De Chernatony, L., & Dall'Olmo Riley, F. (1998). Defining a "brand": Beyond the literature with experts' interpretations. *Journal of Marketing Management, 14*(5), 417–443.

Dean, D., Arroyo-Gamez, R. E., Punjaisri, K., & Pich, C. (2016). Internal brand co-creation: The experiential brand meaning cycle in higher education. *Journal of Business Research, 69*(8), 3041–3048.

Echeverri, P., & Skålen, P. (2011). Co-creation and co-destruction: A practice-theory based study of interactive value formation. *Marketing Theory, 11*(3), 351–373.

Foroudi, P., Yu, Q., Gupta, S., & Foroudi, M. M. (2019). Enhancing university brand image and reputation through customer value co-creation behaviour. *Technological Forecasting and Social Change, 138*, 218–227.

France, C., Grace, D., Lo Iacono, J., & Carlini, J. (2020). Exploring the interplay between customer perceived brand value and customer brand co-creation behaviour dimensions. *Journal of Brand Management, 27*, 466–480.

France, C., Grace, D., Merrilees, B., & Miller, D. (2018). Customer brand co-creation behavior: Conceptualization and empirical validation. *Marketing Intelligence & Planning, 36*(3), 334–348.

France, C., Merrilees, B., & Miller, D. (2015). Customer brand co-creation: A conceptual model. *Marketing Intelligence & Planning, 33*(6), 848–864.

Fujita, M., Harrigan, P., & Soutar, G. (2017). A netnography of a university's social media brand community: Exploring collaborative co-creation tactics. *Journal of Global Scholars of Marketing Science, 27*(2), 148–164.

Gambetti, R. C., & Graffigna, G. (2015). Value co-creation between the "inside" and the "outside" of a company: Insights from a brand community failure. *Marketing Theory, 15*(2), 155–178.

Gardner, B. G., and Levy, S. J. (1955). The product and the brand. *Harvard Business Review*, March–April, 33–39.

Giddens, A. (1987). *Social Theory and Modern Sociology*. Cambridge, UK: Polity Press.

Gonzalez, L. R., & Lester, L. (2018). "All for one, one for all": Communicative processes of co-creation of place brands through inclusive and horizontal stakeholder collaborative networks. *Communication & Society, 31*(4), 59–78.

Griffin, A., & Barczak, G. (2020). Effective reviewing for conceptual journal submissions. *AMS Review, 10*(1–2), 36–48.

Grönroos, C. (2011). Value co-creation in service logic: A critical analysis. *Marketing Theory, 11*(3), 279–301.

Grönroos, C., & Gummerus, J. (2014). The service revolution and its marketing implications: Service logic vs service-dominant logic. *Managing Service Quality, 24*(3), 206–229.

Hajli, N., Shanmugam, M., Papagiannidis, S., Zahay, D., & Richard, M. (2017). Branding co-creation with members of online brand communities. *Journal of Business Research, 70*, 136–144.

Hatch, M., & Schultz, M. (2010). Toward a theory of brand co-creation with implications for brand governance. *Journal of Brand Management, 17*(8), 590–604.

Heding, T., Knudtzen, C. F., & Bjerre, M. (2020). *Brand Management: Mastering Research, Theory and Practice* (3rd ed.). Abingdon, UK: Routledge.

Herzog, H. (1963). Behavioral science concepts for analyzing the consumer. In P. Bliss (Ed.), *Marketing and the Behavioral Sciences* (pp. 76–86). Boston, MA: Allyn & Bacon.

Hsieh, S. H., & Chang, A. (2016). The psychological mechanism of brand co-creation engagement. *Journal of Interactive Marketing, 33*, 13–26.

Hughes, M. U., Bendoni, W. K., & Pehlivan, E. (2016). Storygiving as a co-creation tool for luxury brands in the age of the internet: A love story by Tiffany and thousands of lovers. *Journal of Product and Brand Management, 25*(4), 357–364.

Iglesias, O., Ind, N., & Alfaro, M. (2013). The organic view of the brand: A brand value co-creation model. *Journal of Brand Management, 20*(8), 670–688.

Juntunen, M., Juntunen, J., & Autere, V. (2012). Recruits' corporate brand co-creation experiences of the Finnish military forces. *Corporate Reputation Review, 15*(2), 88–104.

Kamboj, S., Sarmah, B., Gupta, S., & Dwivedi, Y. (2018). Examining branding co-creation in brand communities on social media: Applying the paradigm of stimulus-organism-response. *International Journal of Information Management, 39*, 169–185.

Kaufmann, H. R., Correia Loureiro, S. M., & Manarioti, A. (2016). Exploring behavioural branding, brand love and brand co-creation. *Journal of Product and Brand Management, 25*(6), 516–526.

Kavaratzis, M., & Hatch, M. J. (2013). The dynamics of place brands: An identity-based approach to place branding theory. *Marketing Theory, 13*(1), 69–86.

Kennedy, E., & Guzman, F. (2016). Co-creation of brand identities: Consumer and industry influence and motivations. *Journal of Consumer Marketing, 33*(5), 313–323.

Klepousniotou, E. (2002). The processing of lexical ambiguity: Homonymy and polysemy in the mental lexicon. *Brain and Language, 81*(1–3), 205–223.

Kristal, S., Baumgarth, C., & Henseler, J. (2018). "Brand play" versus "brand attack": The subversion of brand meaning in non-collaborative co-creation by professional artists and consumer activists. *Journal of Product and Brand Management, 27*(3), 334–347.

Kunja, S. R., & Acharyulu, G. V. R. K. (2018). Examining the effect of eWOM on the customer purchase intention through value co-creation (VCC) in social networking sites (SNSs): A study of select Facebook fan pages of smartphone brands in India. *Management Research Review, 43*(3), 245–269.

Lin, S., Yang, S., Ma, M., & Huang, J. (2018). Value co-creation on social media examining the relationship between brand engagement and display advertising effectiveness for Chinese hotels. *International Journal of Contemporary Hospitality Management, 30*(4), 2153–2174.

Lucarelli, A. (2019). Constructing a typology of virtual city brand co-creation practices: An ecological approach. *Journal of Place Management and Development, 12*(2), 227–247.

MacInnis, D. J. (2011). A framework for conceptual contributions in marketing. *Journal of Marketing, 75*(4), 136–154.

MacKenzie, S. B. (2003). The dangers of poor construct conceptualization. *Journal of the Academy of Marketing Science, 31*(3), 323–326.

McAlexander, J. H., Schouten, J. W., & Koenig, H. F. (2002). Building brand community. *Journal of Marketing, 66*(1), 38–54.

Merz, M. A., He, Y., & Vargo, S. L. (2009). The evolving brand logic: A service-dominant logic perspective. *Journal of the Academy of Marketing Science, 37*(3), 328–344.

Merz, M. A., Zarantonello, L., & Grappi, S. (2018). How valuable are your customers in the brand value co-creation process? The development of a customer co-creation value (CCCV) scale. *Journal of Business Research, 82*, 79–89.

Mingione, M., & Leoni, L. (2020). Blurring B2C and B2B boundaries: Corporate brand value co-creation in B2B2C markets. *Journal of Marketing Management, 36*(1–2), 72–99.

Muniz, A. M. Jr., & O'Guinn, T. C. (2001). Brand community. *Journal of Consumer Research, 27*(4), 412–432.

Neuendorf, K. A. (2002). *The Content Analysis Guide Book.* Thousand Oaks, CA: Sage Publications.

Nguyen, D. T., Shirahada, K., & Kosaka, M. (2016). A consideration of value co-creation in branding of university research-laboratories. *International Journal of Knowledge and Systems Science, 7*(2), 40–57.

Nobre, H., & Ferreira, A. (2017). Gamification as a platform for brand co-creation experiences. *Journal of Brand Management, 24*(4), 349–361.

Oliveira, E., & Panyik, E. (2015). Content, context and co-creation: Digital challenges in destination branding with references to Portugal as a tourist destination. *Journal of Vacation Marketing, 21*(1), 53–74.

Pethö, G. (2001). What is polysemy? A survey of current research and results. In E. Nemeth & K. Bibok (Eds.), *Pragmatics and the Flexibility of Word Meaning* (pp. 175–224). Amsterdam, the Netherlands: Elsevier.

Plé, L., & Chumpitaz Cáceres, R. (2010). Not always co-creation: Introducing interactional co-destruction of value in service-dominant logic. *Journal of Services Marketing, 24*(6), 430–437.

Podsakoff, P. M., MacKenzie, S. B., Bachrach, D. G., & Podsakoff, N. P. (2005). The influence of management journals in the 1980s and 1990s. *Strategic Management Journal, 26*(5), 473–488.

Pongsakornrungsilp, S., & Schroeder, J. (2011). Understanding value co-creation in a co-consuming brand community. *Marketing Theory, 11*(3), 303–324.

Prahalad, C. K., & Ramaswamy, V. (2004). Co-creation experiences: The next practice in value creation. *Journal of Interactive Marketing, 18*(3), 5–14.

Ramaswamy, V., & Ozcan, K. (2014). *The Co-Creation Paradigm*. Redwood City, CA: Stanford University Press.

Ramaswamy, V., & Ozcan, K. (2016). Brand value co-creation in a digitalized world: An integrative framework and research implications. *International Journal of Research in Marketing, 33*(1), 93–106.

Ramaswamy, V., & Ozcan, K. (2018). What is co-creation? An interactional creation framework and its implications for value creation. *Journal of Business Research, 84*, 196–205.

Ritzer, G. (2015). Prosumer capitalism. *Sociological Quarterly, 56*(3), 413–445.

Rosenthal, B., & Zamith Brito, E. P. (2017). The brand meaning co-creation process on Facebook. *Marketing Intelligence & Planning, 35*(7), 923–936.

Rossolatos, G. (2019). Negative brand meaning co-creation in social media brand communities: A laddering approach using NVivo. *Psychology & Marketing, 36*(12), 1249–1266.

Sartori, G. (2009). Guidelines for concept analysis. In D. Collier & J. Gerring (Eds.), *Concepts and Method in Social Science: The Tradition of Giovanni Sartori* (pp. 97–150). New York, NY: Routledge.

Schmeltz, L., & Kjeldsen, A. K. (2019). Co-creating polyphony or cacophony? A case study of a public organization's brand co-creation process and the challenge of orchestrating multiple internal voices. *Journal of Brand Management, 26*(3), 304–316.

Seifert, C., & Kwon, W. (2020). SNS eWOM sentiment: Impacts on brand value co-creation and trust. *Marketing Intelligence & Planning, 38*(1), 89–102.

Stach, J. (2019). Meaningful experiences: An embodied cognition perspective on brand meaning co-creation. *Journal of Brand Management, 26*(3), 317–331.

Suddaby, R. (2010). Editor's comments: Construct clarity in theories of management and organization. *Academy of Management Review, 35*(3), 346–357.

Suomi, K., Luonila, M., & Tähtinen, J. (2020). Ironic festival brand co-creation. *Journal of Business Research, 106*, 211–220.

Tähtinen, J., & Havila, V. (2019). Conceptually confused, but on a field level? A method for conceptual analysis and its application. *Marketing Theory, 19*(4), 533–557.

Tierney, K. D., Karpen, I. O., & Westberg, K. (2016). Brand meaning cocreation: Toward a conceptualization and research implications. *Journal of Service Theory and Practice, 26*(6), 911–932.

Toffler, A. (1980). *The Third Wave*. New York, NY: William Morrow.

Törmälä, M., & Saraniemi, S. (2018). The roles of business partners in corporate brand image co-creation. *Journal of Product and Brand Management, 27*(1), 29–40.

Vallaster, C., & von Wallpach, S. (2013). An online discursive inquiry into the social dynamics of multi-stakeholder brand meaning co-creation. *Journal of Business Research, 66*(9), 1505–1515.

Vallaster, C., & von Wallpach, S. (2018). Brand strategy co-creation in a nonprofit context: A strategy-as-practice approach. *Nonprofit and Voluntary Sector Quarterly, 47*(5), 984–1006.

Vallaster, C., von Wallpach, S., & Zenker, S. (2018). The interplay between urban policies and grassroots city brand co-creation and co-destruction during the refugee crisis: Insights from the city brand Munich (Germany). *Cities, 80*, 53–60.

Vargo, S. L., & Koskela-Huotari, K. (2020). Advancing conceptual-only articles in marketing. *AMS Review, 10*(1–2), 1–5.

Vargo, S. L., & Lusch, R. F. (2004). Evolving to a new dominant logic for marketing. *Journal of Marketing, 68*(1), 1–17.

Wider, S., von Wallpach, S., & Mühlbacher, H. (2018). Brand management: Unveiling the delusion of control. *European Management Journal, 36*(3), 301–305.

Zeithaml, V. A., Verleye, K., Hatak, I., Koller, M., & Zauner, A. (2020). Three decades of customer value research: Paradigmatic roots and future research avenues. *Journal of Service Research, 23*(4), 409–432.

Zhang, J., & He, Y. (2014). Key dimensions of brand value co-creation and its impacts upon customer perception and brand performance an empirical research in the context of industrial service. *Nankai Business Review International, 5*(1), 43–69.

Zhao, J., Tao, J., & Xiong, G. (2019). Online brand community climate, psychological capital, and customer value cocreation. *Social Behavior and Personality: An International Journal, 47*(3), 1–14.

# APPENDIX: CONCEPT DESCRIPTION TABLES

*Table 14.1*   *The meaning and boundaries of the brand value co-creation concept*

| Brand value co-creation articles | Participating actors | | Characterisation of the co-creation | | | Types of co-creation | | Beneficiary | |
|---|---|---|---|---|---|---|---|---|---|
| | Consumer/customers | Stakeholders | Process | Activities | Interactions | Direct | Indirect | The brand | Others |
| Juntunen et al. (2012) | | ✓ | ✓ | | | | | | |
| Iglesias et al. (2013) | ✓ | ✓ | ✓ | | ✓ | | | | |
| Zhang and He (2014) | | ✓ | | | ✓ | | | | |
| Gambetti and Graffigna (2015) | ✓ | ✓ | ✓ | ✓ | | | | | |
| Cova et al. (2015) | ✓ | ✓ | ✓ | | ✓ | ✓ | | ✓ | |
| Choi et al. (2016) | ✓ | ✓ | ✓ | | ✓ | | | | |
| Nguyen et al. (2016) | | ✓ | ✓ | | ✓ | ✓ | | | ✓ |
| Ramaswamy and Ozcan (2016) | | ✓ | ✓ | ✓ | ✓ | | ✓ | | |
| Biraghi and Gambetti (2017) | | ✓ | ✓ | ✓ | ✓ | | | | |
| Fujita et al. (2017) | ✓ | | ✓ | | | | | | |
| Hajli et al. (2017) | ✓ | | ✓ | | | | | | |
| Nobre and Ferreira (2017) | ✓ | | | ✓ | ✓ | | | | |
| Merz et al. (2018) | | ✓ | ✓ | | ✓ | | | ✓ | |
| Foroudi et al. (2019) | ✓ | | | | ✓ | | | | |
| Cheung et al. (2020) | ✓ | | | | ✓ | | ✓ | | |
| Mingione and Leoni (2020) | | ✓ | ✓ | | | ✓ | | ✓ | |

*Table 1A.2*  *The meaning and boundaries of brand(ing) co-creation concept*

| Brand(ing) co-creation articles | Participating actors | | | Characterisation of the engagement | | | Type of co-creation | | Beneficiary | |
|---|---|---|---|---|---|---|---|---|---|---|
| | Consumer/ Residents/ Tourists | Stakeholders | Brand (consumer–brand relationship) | The brand | Others | Process | Interactions | Activities/ Actions | Direct | Indirect |
| Boyle (2007) | ✓ | ✓ | | | | ✓ | | | | |
| Hatch and Schultz (2010) | | ✓ | | | | | ✓ | | | |
| Juntunen et al. (2012) | | ✓ | | | | ✓ | | | | |
| France et al. (2015) | ✓ | | ✓ | | | | ✓ | | | |
| Oliveira and Panyik (2015) | ✓ | | | | | | | | | |
| Kaufmann et al. (2016) | | ✓ | | | | ✓ | ✓ | | ✓ | ✓ |
| France et al. (2018) | ✓ | | ✓ | | | | ✓ | ✓ | | |
| Kamboj et al. (2018) | ✓ | | | | | ✓ | ✓ | | | |
| Vallaster et al. (2018) | | | | | | ✓ | ✓ | | ✓ | ✓ |
| Casais and Monteiro (2019) | ✓ | | | | | | | | | |
| Lucarelli (2019) | | ✓ | | | | ✓ | | | | |
| Schmeltz and Kjeldsen (2019) | | ✓ | | | | ✓ | ✓ | | ✓ | |
| France et al. (2020) | ✓ | ✓ | ✓ | | ✓ | | ✓ | ✓ | | |

*Table 1A.3*   *The meaning and boundaries of the brand-meaning co-creation concept*

| Brand-meaning co-creation articles | Participating actors | | Characterisation of co-creation | | | Type of co-creation | | Beneficiary | |
|---|---|---|---|---|---|---|---|---|---|
| | Consumers/ Customers | Stakeholders | Process | Interactions | Discourse/ Communication/ Negotiation/ Conversation | Direct | Indirect | The brand | Others |
| Vallaster and von Wallpach (2013) | | ✓ | | | ✓ | ✓ | ✓ | ✓ | |
| Dean et al. (2016) | | ✓ | | | ✓ | | ✓ | ✓ | |
| Tierney et al. (2016) | | ✓ | ✓ | ✓ | | | | ✓ | |
| Fujita et al. (2017) | ✓ | | ✓ | | | | | ✓ | |
| Rosenthal and Zamith Brito (2017) | | ✓ | ✓ | ✓ | ✓ | ✓ | ✓ | | |
| Gonzalez and Lester (2018) | | ✓ | ✓ | | | | | ✓ | |
| Stach (2019) | | ✓ | | ✓ | | | | ✓ | |
| Bertschy et al. (2020) | | ✓ | | | ✓ | | | ✓ | |
| Suomi et al. (2020) | | ✓ | | | | | | ✓ | |

*Table 1A.4   The meaning and boundaries of the brand identity co-creation concept*

| Brand identity co-creation articles | Participating actors | Characterisation of co-creation | | | | Beneficiary | |
|---|---|---|---|---|---|---|---|
| | Consumers/customers | Stakeholders | Process | Actions | Communication/dialogue | The brand | Others |
| Dean et al. (2016) | ✓ | | | | ✓ | ✓ | |
| Kennedy and Guzman (2016) | ✓ | ✓ | | | | ✓ | ✓ |
| Black and Veloutsou (2017) | | ✓ | | ✓ | | ✓ | |
| Centeno and Wang (2017) | | ✓ | ✓ | | ✓ | ✓ | |
| Gonzalez and Lester (2018) | | ✓ | ✓ | ✓ | | ✓ | |
| Suomi et al. (2020) | | ✓ | ✓ | | | ✓ | ✓ |

# 2. Establishing the boundaries of brand co-creation

*Catherine da Silveira and Cláudia Simões*

## 1. INTRODUCTION

Literature presents a wide range of views on co-creation conceptual boundaries. Such boundaries vary between extremes, from market research, a "simple" and "distant" form of co-creation to understand customer needs (Ranjan & Read, 2016, p.291), to a more comprehensive view, proposing that co-creation only occurs if managers and customers act together in a merged, coordinated, dialogical, and interactive process that generates mutual value (Grönroos, 2012). Between these two poles, there are intermediary forms of co-creation that include activities such as self-service, do-it-yourself (Merz et al., 2018), engaging customers in an experience shaped by the brand (Bendapudi & Leone, 2003) or car sharing (Payne et al., 2009). In parallel, the rise of virtual networks and digital platforms has led to an environment where customers and other actors (e.g., digital influencers) co-create brand meanings aside from traditional brand owners (Fournier & Avery, 2011; Swaminathan et al., 2020). Under such circumstances, the interpretation of co-creation stretches into a notion that might not necessarily involve managers and other brand internal stakeholders. This wide range of perspectives leads to an equivocal understanding of co-creation when transposing the concept to the branding arena. The question then arises: to what extent can a brand be considered co-created? There are common grounds sustaining the multiplicity of approaches regarding brand co-creation. Influential studies converge to the principle that co-creation in branding only occurs given certain conditions (e.g., Cova & Dalli, 2009; Ind et al., 2013). Yet, theoretical evidence is disparate and conditions are incongruent.

The objective of this chapter is to address the limitations in the literature by discussing the concept and nature of co-creation, and develop a framework aiming at defining the prerequisites to assume co-creation in branding. We propose a set of fundamental conditions that apply across brands and settings. The framework establishes the boundaries of brand co-creation and leads to practical reflections for the management of co-creation.

We begin with the review of the foundational pillars of co-creation, from which we extract preliminary assumptions about core conditions to posit co-creation in branding. We then delve into the understanding of co-creation in several streams of knowledge to adjust core conditions and derive additional insights, which culminate in a framework of the proposed requisites for co-creation in branding. Finally, we suggest implications for theory and practitioners.

## 2. GROUNDING THE NOTION OF CO-CREATION

Three main "logics" emerge as central for grounding and substantiating the idea of co-creation in the literature on brand co-creation: (2.1) service-dominant logic (Vargo & Lusch, 2006,

2008, 2011); (2.2) value co-creation logic (Prahalad & Ramaswamy, 2004a, b); and (2.3) service logic (Grönroos, 2008, 2011; Grönroos & Ravald, 2011). These logics have been used over the last decades, combined or individually, to ground the development of the concept of co-creation (Payne et al., 2009; Cova et al., 2011; Ind et al., 2013; Ranjan & Read, 2016; Merz et al., 2018). We hereafter analyze each of the key co-creation "logics" in more detail.

## 2.1 Service-Dominant Logic

Vargo (2011, p.218) defines the service-dominant logic as a "pre-theoretic lens or perspective for viewing the economic (and social) world differently" to the traditional exchange of goods approach commonly used in marketing over the 20th century. To capture the essence of this emerging logic, Vargo and Lusch initially identified eight foundational premises (FPs) (2006), later expanded to ten (2008) and then to 11 principles structured in five axioms (2016). One of the original premises is that "the customer is always a co-creator of value (FP6)" (2006), which subsequently changed to "value is co-created by multiple actors, always including the beneficiary" (2016).

Two main meanings of value reflect the different understandings of the notion of value developed over time: value-in-exchange and value-in-use (Vargo et al., 2008). Value-in-exchange refers to value as created by the firm and realized in the market mainly through the exchange of goods/services and money. Value-in-use means that value emerges only when the customer makes use of the goods/services. The service-dominant logic draws to value under a value-in-use perspective, whereas the traditional goods-dominant logic relates to the term of value-in-exchange. The notion of value used in the service-dominant logic depicts "a joint function of the actions of the provider(s) and the customer(s) but is always determined by the customer" (Vargo & Lusch, 2006, p.44). The firm cannot create and/or deliver value alone. Value creation is an integrative process. Under such a perspective, the process by which co-creation occurs can be summarized as follows: first, suppliers (e.g., firms) propose value to the market; then, customers and potential customers accept, or not, the value proposition. Customers must integrate the value proposition before value is realized. Consequently, value is created only if customers make use of the value offer. This logic makes the customer, the firm, and the value co-created inseparable, and assumes the existence of an evolving process of exchange, driven by the customer perceived benefits of the company's offers.

Value creation has been extended to consider the perspective of configurations of social actors interacting and exchanging across networks (Vargo & Lusch, 2011, 2016). All actors (e.g., firms, individuals, households, suppliers, distributors, non-profit or government organizations, and other stakeholders) are resource integrators and service-provider enterprises tied together in shared systems of exchange – services ecosystems or markets. Value is co-created across the joint efforts of all economic actors. Such insight led to the notions of exchange and exchange systems in terms of actor-to-actor interactions.

The service-dominant logic characterizes value co-creation as the reciprocity of exchange between actors. The customer is an actor indirectly providing service to the firm and other stakeholders. As service beneficiary, the customer is also an enterprise resource integrator who attempts to increase value for himself. As such, customers create value throughout relationships established with firms and other actors. Managers produce inputs into customers' processes of value creation and benefit from the outputs. By maximizing customers' involvement in the process of co-creation, managers might increase the outputs.

A first pre-condition for co-creation derives from the value-in-use concept. Value for social, economic or institutional actors emerges during usage. Moreover, "the beneficiary is always a party to its own value creation" (Vargo & Lusch, 2016, p.9). Hence, a fundamental condition for co-creation is the actor's active participation in the process of value creation, whether he/she is a customer, a manager or another stakeholder.

## 2.2   Value Co-Creation Logic

Prahalad and Ramaswamy (2004a, b) oppose value co-creation to forms of consumer participation such as the co-creation of experience i.e., "the staging of an experience in which the firm constructs the context and the consumer is part of it (e.g., Disney World)" (Prahalad, 2004, p.23). Although there is consumer engagement, the context in this form of consumer experience is firm-driven and does not consist of value co-creation. The co-creation of value emerges from consumers and suppliers combining resource integration with a service-providing role: "[c]onsumers have work, service, and risks transferred from the firm, and both the consumer and the firm benefit" (Prahalad, 2004, p.23).

Prahalad and Ramaswamy (2004a) suggest four "building blocks" to ensure co-creation of value as a basis for consumer–company interaction: (i) dialogue; (ii) access (to information); (iii) risk assessment; and (iv) transparency.

(i)     *Dialogue* emerges as opposite to the traditional top-down communication process between managers and customers. Dialogue implies communication between "two equal problem solvers" (Prahalad & Ramaswamy, 2004a, p.6).
(ii)    Managers should ensure that customers have *access* to information and provide the tools to allow for a fruitful dialogue.
(iii)   *Risk assessment* supports the idea that, by participating in the co-creation of value, customers can take risks of being harmed. In order to make the risk "acceptable" (Prahalad & Ramaswamy, 2004a), firms should provide customers with information for assessing the "personal and societal risk" associated with the co-creation process and outcome.
(iv)    Managers should further ensure *transparency* of information to consumers "to avoid and eliminate the asymmetry of information" (Prahalad, 2004, p.23), contrasting with the exchange of goods' perspective.

These four building blocks – labeled "the DART model of value co-creation" (Prahalad & Ramaswamy, 2004a, b) – have been extensively investigated (e.g., Mazur & Zaborek, 2014; Albinsson et al., 2016). A frequent appraisal derived from these investigations is the conceptual overlap of the "blocks". Prahalad and Ramaswamy (2004a, b) assume the intertwining of the proposed conditions as inherent to the process of co-creation. As the authors explain, "access [to information] and transparency are critical to have a meaningful dialogue" and "dialogue, access, and transparency can lead to a clear assessment by the consumer of the risk-benefits of a course of action and decision" (Prahalad & Ramaswamy, 2004b, p.9). The four building blocks may act as indicators to the examination of the required manager–customer interactions to achieve co-creation. They further establish a grounding exploration of the conditions to realize co-creation between managers and customers.

## 2.3    Service Logic

In the service logic (Grönroos, 2008, 2011; Grönroos & Ravald, 2011), value co-creation is contingent upon direct interactions. Interactions entail "mutual or reciprocal action[s] where two or more parties have an effect upon one another" (Grönroos, 2011, p.289). Interactions take place in encounters that can be face-to-face or online/voice-based exchanges (e.g., call center services, online-based platforms). According to Grönroos, the concept of value co-creation entails a specific phase within the overall range of value-formation processes. Such a phase emerges when "the firm and the customer act together in a merged, coordinated, dialogical, and interactive process that creates value for the customer, and for the firm as well – using the strictly analytical meaning of the expression they co-create value" (Grönroos, 2012, p.1523). Interactions between internal actors and customers have a focal role in the process of value co-creation because "without interactions, the possibilities for the supplier to actively become a salient co-creator of value in the customer's process of value creation are limited" (Grönroos & Ravald, 2011, p.12). Within this context, co-creation develops from "joint collaborative activities by parties involved in direct interactions, aiming to contribute to the value that emerges for one or both parties" (Grönroos, 2012, p.1523).

The outcome of value co-creation may not always be positive both for the firm and for the customer. For the firm, a positive outcome of value co-creation is contingent upon the fact that the firm effectively makes use of the opportunity of the interaction to engage in the process of joint value creation. That is "the existence of interactions is only a platform for favorably influencing the customers' usage processes and value creation, which in order to become a value creator the firm must manage to make use of" (Grönroos, 2011, p.290). For the customer, the firm co-creation process may have both positive ("value creation") and negative ("value destruction") impacts on the customers' value creation. Nonetheless, value is typically conceptualized as having some form of benefits, and value creation as a process through which "the user becomes better off in some respect" (Grönroos, 2011, p.282).

According to the service logic, co-creation does not apply "outside direct interactions" between the firm and the customers (Grönroos, 2011, p.290). "Outside direct interactions", customers create value for themselves out of the support provided by the managers. Within this context, managers do not co-create value. Instead, they act as value proposition providers and facilitators, assisting customers in the creation of value for themselves. In sum, the service logic brings a fundamental insight into the exploration of the pre-conditions to assume the occurrence of co-creation: co-creation requires direct, joint and collaborative interactions between managers and customers.

## 3.    TOWARDS A FRAMEWORK OF THE CONDITIONS FOR CO-CREATION IN BRANDING

The fundamental value co-creation logics pave the way for the exploration of the notion of value co-creation and its pre-conditions to assist co-creation in branding. Table 2.1 presents our study's process. First, we begin by depicting the preliminary assumptions about core conditions for co-creation extracted from the three foundational logics of value co-creation (Table 2.1, Column 2). In a second step, we critically analyze those assumptions and derive key aspects that require further investigation (Table 2.1, Column 3). Then, we address each of those aspects under the lenses of significant research related to co-creation in several streams of knowledge (Table 2.1, Column 4). This exploration leads us to propose adjusted core conditions and additional insights into the co-creation process (Table 2.1, Columns 5 and 6).

## 3.1   Exploring the "Actor's Active Participation in the Process of Co-Creation" Preliminary Assumption

A first pre-condition, depicted in the service-dominant logic, is the need for the actor's *active participation in the process of value creation*, whether he/she is a customer, a manager or another stakeholder. The notion of participation requires reflection, in particular concerning the customers. Key underlying questions are: can co-creation occur when customers are given the opportunity to participate, or does it only apply when they take the initiative to participate? Why do they participate?

### Endogenous customers

Research in stakeholder participation in value co-creation confirms that customer participation is fundamental to value co-creation (e.g., Chan et al., 2010; Ind et al., 2013; Smith, 2013; Ranjan & Read, 2016; von Wallpach et al., 2017). Customer participation is "a behavioral construct that measures the extent to which customers provide/share information, make suggestions, and become involved in decision making during the service co-creation and delivery process" (Chan et al., 2010, p.49). Customer participation entails "the actions and resources supplied by customers, for example, mental (information and effort), physical (customers' own tangibles and efforts), emotional inputs, financial (monetary costs), temporal (time spent), behavioral (interpersonal interaction) and relational inputs" (Smith, 2013, p.1890). Co-creation cannot occur without "endogenous" participative customers. In fact, co-creation is only fully captured when research considers customers as endogenous to the process of value co-creation. In other words, endogenous customers constitute an intrinsic characteristic to co-creation (Merz et al., 2009; Ind et al., 2013; Ranjan & Read, 2016). Lusch and Vargo (2014) had brought this idea into light when contrasting the service-dominant logic and the goods-dominant logic by delineating the terms of endogenous vs. exogenous customers. This discussion leads us to propose that customers must be endogenous to the process of value creation, which complements the fundamental *participation* condition for co-creation.

### Customers' willingness to participate in the co-creation process

There is a debate in the literature on whether co-creation originates from the company or from the customer's initiative. Do organizations instigate co-creation by developing a favorable organizational environment to enable participants' engagement in co-creation (Ind et al., 2017)? Or does co-creation only occur when consumers voluntarily take the initiative to participate (Cova & Dalli, 2009)? Merz et al.'s (2018, p.81) "Customers Co-Creation Value" framework has two premises: (i) customers' ability to co-create brand value, capturing the "customers' voluntary resource contribution to a firm's brand building activities"; and (ii) customers' willingness to co-create brand value related to "customers' motivation to participate actively in the process of brand value co-creation". These premises confirm the voluntary nature of customers' participation. Participation is voluntary and depends on the customers' willingness and motivation to add value to the brand. In this line of thought, co-creation cannot be determined by the managers' actions but merely be influenced by them.

*Table 2.1* Study's process

| 1 | 2 | 3 | 4 | 5 | 6 |
|---|---|---|---|---|---|
| Foundational pillars of co-creation | Preliminary conditions for co-creation | Aspects to address | Literature | Outcome (i.e., conditions to ensure co-creation in branding) | Additional Insights |
| Service-dominant logic (Vargo & Lusch, 2006, 2008, 2011, 2016) | Actor active participation in the process of co-creation | Participation | Customer value creation (Chan et al., 2010; Smith, 2013) Value co-creation (Ranjan & Read, 2016) Customer Culture Theory (Sartre, 1943; Belk, 1988; Fournier, 1998; Muñiz & O'Guinn, 2001) Co-production (Cova & Dalli, 2009) Co-creation in branding (Ind et al., 2013, 2017; Black & Veloutsou, 2017; Kornum et al., 2017; von Wallpach et al., 2017) Branding in the age of online interactions (Swaminathan et al., 2020) | Endogenous consumers Customers' willingness to participate in the co-creation process Customers' belief that the co-created outcome (i.e., the brand) is affecting their personal lives as an individual and/or as a community member Humble, honest and transparent approach to brand management | This condition is moderated by the perceived *risks* of engaging in co-creation |
| Value co-creation logic (Prahalad & Ramaswamy, 2004a, b) | Dialogue between managers and consumers Access to information from managers to consumers | Knowledge sharing | Co-creation and knowledge sharing (Markovic & Bagherzadeh, 2018) Value co-creation (Ranjan & Read, 2016) Co-creation in branding (Ind et al., 2013, 2017) | Evidence of *knowledge sharing* between the actors involved in brand co-creation | |
| | Risk assessment provided by the managers to consumers Firm perceived risks of sharing knowledge with other stakeholders | Asymmetry between risk assumed by the organization and risk transferred to consumers | Co-production (Cova & Dalli, 2009) Organizational studies (Mael & Ashforth, 1992; Lam et al., 2010) Branding in the age of online interactions (Fournier & Avery, 2011; Ramaswamy & Ozan, 2018; Swaminathan et al., 2020) Co-creation in branding (Ind et al., 2017) | Collective acceptance/recognition by managers, consumers, and other brand stakeholders of the risks intrinsic to the co-creation process and outcome | |
| | Transparency of information from managers to consumers | Which level of transparency should be ensured? | Co-production (Cova & Dalli, 2009; Cova et al., 2011) Co-creation in branding (Ind et al., 2013, 2017) | The level of transparency provided by the brand should be the level that addresses the firm's needs in terms of confidentiality of shared knowledge and the customers' requirements to engage in the co-creation process | |
| Service logic (Grönroos 2008, 2011, 2012; Grönroos & Ravald, 2011) | Direct, joint and collaborative interactions between involved parties | Participants and nature of the interactions | Branding in the age of online interactions (Ramaswamy & Ozcan, 2018; Swaminathan et al., 2020) | Evidence of *interactions*, defined as value creation processes occurring across multiple interactive networks, platforms, devices and other online and offline settings, that enable the co-creation of brand experiences and brand meanings between brand stakeholders | |

Extant research and practitioner-oriented studies aim at encouraging firms to involve customers in new product development and technology improvement (e.g., McKinsey & Company, 2020). Yet, "assuming an active role for the individual consumer in value creation is different from allowing customers access to a company's technology base or seeking their help in product development" (Prahalad & Ramaswamy, 2003, p.13). Co-creation is about consumers freely taking the initiative to assume an active role in the process of brand management, and not about companies giving consumers the opportunity to customize or use products and services their own way. Practices widely used in the market, such as demand-based innovation, product personalization and customer solution may not be within the scope of co-creation. These insights concur to the idea that co-creation should rely on the customers' willingness to voluntarily participate in the process, although the firm needs to create a favorable environment for such participation. The firm cannot unilaterally decide to co-create with customers nor constrain customers to participate, yet it can develop a trustable context for co-creation.

### Customers' belief that the co-created outcome is affecting their personal lives as an individual and/or as a community member

Customers participate motivated by personal and social reasons. On a personal level, customer co-creation is triggered by a search for intrinsic enjoyment, self-satisfaction, personal gratification, pride, and social recognition (Berthon et al., 2008; Cova & Dalli, 2009). Customers actively co-produce and participate when the outcome of their participation may affect their personal lives (Sartre, 1943; Belk, 1988; Fournier, 1998). Ultimately, customers actively participate in what they believe will affect them. Inferred from this critical insight is the fact that, for co-creation to occur, customers must perceive the co-created outcome (e.g., brand) as affecting their personal lives.

Customer participation further emerges from social interaction (Muñiz & O'Guinn, 2001; Cova & Dalli, 2009; Black & Veloutsou, 2017). Communities develop as "a group of people who have a common interest in a specific activity or object and who create a parallel social universe (subculture) ripe with its own myths, value, rituals, vocabulary and hierarchy" (Cova & Dalli, 2009, p.322). Communities empower customer participation, whether the community is shaped by the brand or by individuals. Community memberships boost self-expressive and recognition mechanisms (Kornum et al., 2017). Co-creation may emerge from network flows between the individuals, the (brand) communities and the brand. When joining a brand-related group, "both the brand identity and the identity of the group need to help individuals express values and portray personality traits to which they aspire" (Black & Veloutsou, 2017, p.426). Personal purposes and social motivations intertwine as a process to drive customers' participation in co-creation.

### Humble, honest and transparent approach to brand management

Customer participation in branding can be associated with the notion of appropriation: "consumers express the sense that they 'made' the brand. [They] increasingly regard brands as shared cultural property rather than as privately owned intellectual property. Familiarity breeds ownership: brands 'belong to us' and not to the companies that own them" (Cova & Dalli, 2009, p.317). Digital interconnectivity is accelerating the shift from brand internal single ownership to shared ownership (Swaminathan et al., 2020). From a practical perspective, the typical distinction between the roles of managers and stakeholders no longer applies (von Wallpach et al., 2017), challenging existing forms of management and leadership (Ind et al., 2017). Managers need to assume customers as "living the brand" (Ind et al., 2013, p.23). Trust (Ind et al., 2013) and humility (von Wallpach et al., 2017) are essential to develop this sense of brand intimacy. Managers generate trust by being receptive to and by sharing knowledge with customers in a transparent way. Brand managers' performativity needs to be humble to give the front stage to other participants' (e.g., customers, fans) creativity, innovation, "showcasing" or "missionizing" (von Wallpach et al., 2017). Such approach to brand management – humble, honest and transparent – is only possible if managers and all participants in the co-creation process believe that their performance will bring benefits to the brand and to themselves (Ind et al., 2013; Kennedy & Guzmán, 2016).

## 3.2　Exploring Dialogue, Access to Information, Risk Assessment and Transparency

We derive grounding bases for exploring the conditions that underpin the occurrence of co-creation in branding from the fundamental building blocks – dialogue, access (to information), risk assessment and transparency – stated by the value co-creation logic (Prahalad & Ramaswamy, 2004a, b).

**From dialogue and access to information to knowledge sharing**
Dialogue is a fundamental determinant for interactivity and mutual resource integration into value (Grönroos, 2012; Ranjan & Read, 2016). Nonetheless, without the necessary knowledge and access to information, dialogue is not fruitful (Ballantyne & Varey, 2008; Merz et al., 2018). Productive dialogue is therefore contingent upon the second building block, that is, access to information. Moreover, as the literature in co-creation progresses, the one-direction process of "giving access of information to consumers" expanded into a reciprocal process of knowledge sharing (Ranjan & Read, 2016; Markovic & Bagherzadeh, 2018). Participants in co-creation give more of themselves. They consequently expect organizations not only to provide information but also to engage in a dialogue, by listening and responding (Ind et al., 2013). Each part gives and receives information from each other. This dialogical process is embedded in a process of knowledge sharing. Hence, a second pre-condition, drawn from the value co-creation logic, relies on the evidence of *knowledge sharing* between the actors involved in co-creation.

The risks in sharing knowledge are different for the firms and for the customers. In practice, *knowledge sharing* is a strong obstacle for firms to engage in co-creation. An important concern is the perceived risk in disclosing confidential information to customers (Ind et al., 2017). We expand the scope of the risks intrinsic to the co-creation process from customers (cf. Prahalad and Ramaswamy's third building block) to other brand stakeholders, in particular internal stakeholders. We further establish the condition of *knowledge sharing* as a variable moderated by the perceived *risks* of engaging in co-creation.

**Risk assessment**
Risk assessment initially emerged as a corollary to the idea that, by engaging in co-creation with customers, firms transfer part of the risk related to the co-created outcome to the customers (Prahalad & Ramaswamy, 2004a). This idea reflects the notion of equity, entailing "a firm's willingness to share control in favor of consumer empowerment" (Ranjan & Read,

2016, p.292). Firms can benefit from sharing brand control with customers. The process can bring a positive outcome to the brand and to the organization and, by extension, to managers' self-perceived success. Brand managers assess their success through the attainment of organizational goals (Kennedy & Guzmán, 2016). However, the process raises concerns on the asymmetry between the value consumers who engage in co-creation attribute to companies, and the "rare practice of returning at least part of the market value that these consumers have produced" (Cova & Dalli, 2009, p.326). By acknowledging the tangibility of a possible risk for the consumers engaging in co-creation, expectations are that companies provide customers with information for better assessing the risk (Prahalad & Ramaswamy, 2004a).

These views might not reflect the magnitude of the co-creation implications for risk. Establishing who takes the risk and the types of risks involved deserves a deeper analysis. Organizational studies suggest that the individual identifies with an organization when he/she experiences the organization's successes and failures as his/her own (Mael & Ashforth, 1992; Lam et al., 2010). Such a position implies the recognition and acceptance of a risk. Research on brand co-creation traditionally associates willingness to co-create with "stakeholders' commitment to work for the brand and its success" (Merz et al., 2018, p.81). Yet, risk can also be associated with the possible failure of the co-created outcome. To the best of our knowledge, there is little evidence in the branding literature on customers' acceptance of the risk of failure when they commit to co-creation. As Mael and Ashforth (1992, p.117) note, "individuals who identify with [an] organization are apt to support the organization in various ways", including its failures.

From the brand owners' (e.g., founders, managers) perspective, literature highlights risks in several ways. Firms perceive a risk in engaging in brand co-creation, as this might imply sharing confidential information with customers (Ind et al., 2017). We propose to address this concern in terms of the required level of transparency to ensure co-creation (see the following section). A second type of risk considered by firms is the reduction of influence over brand meanings. Brand managers involved in co-creation processes can ultimately lose control over the brand meanings. This is especially prevalent in the current context of proliferation of virtual networks and platforms. For example, consumer-generated contents may diverge from the firm-generated communication and brand identity (Fournier & Avery, 2011; Swaminathan et al., 2020). Overall, many firms consider the uncertainty regarding the final co-created outcome (i.e., the brand) as a risk within online and offline contexts.

This discussion brings a more balanced perspective to the risk asymmetry in the perceived value retrieved by customers and managers engaging in brand co-creation. We accordingly propose to reframe Prahalad and Ramaswamy's (2004a) building block – *risk assessment* – as the *collective acceptance/recognition by managers, consumers, and other brand stakeholders, of the risks intrinsic to the co-creation process and outcome*. Accepting these risks is the ultimate and most demanding level of engagement.

**Transparency of information**
An active dialogue and the development of a shared solution between the firm and the consumers are only possible if managers demonstrate willingness for *transparency* (Prahalad & Ramaswamy, 2004b). Taken to the extreme, ensuring transparency could lead to a situation where customers and managers have access to the same information. Yet, an overview of the market context suggests that such scenario, although a valuable objective, is impracticable for most firms, unable or not willing to disclose certain information (e.g., financial margins).

Hence, if defined as giving access (to consumers) to all information, transparency would restrict the boundary of co-creation. Acknowledging this challenge, Prahalad and Ramaswamy (2004a) introduced the notion of "levels of transparency". Lower levels of transparency might consist in sharing information commonly considered as less "sensitive", such as data related to products, ingredients and supply processes. Higher levels of transparency might involve disclosing records not published in annual reports or patented formulations and innovations. High levels are difficult to reach in current competitive market contexts as "sensitive" information shared with consumers might also become accessible to competitors.

However, transparency is essential. Customers and other key brand stakeholders (e.g., brand influencers) set transparency (of information from the firm) as a key return from their personal engagement in co-creation. Research suggests that customers' participation in co-creation can be limited if they perceive not to get sufficient return (Cova & Dalli, 2009; Cova et al., 2011; Ind et al., 2013, 2017). Although return can be independent from the organization (e.g., intrinsic enjoyment, self-promotion and social recognition – Berthon et al., 2008), it might be more rewarding if reciprocally raised with the organization (e.g., knowledge sharing and mutual giving – Ind et al., 2017). Providing a higher level of transparency fosters higher returns to customers. Aligned with this discussion, there seems to be a tension on the notion of transparency. Ensuring some *transparency* between the actors involved in co-creation is a condition for (customer) participation in the process of co-creation, but "full transparency" (of information provided by the organization) is impracticable. The question emerging is *which level of transparency firms and brands should realistically ensure*? We propose to conceptualize the required level of transparency as a dynamic variable. The level of transparency provided by the brand should be the level that addresses the firm's needs in terms of confidentiality of shared knowledge and the customers' requirements to engage in the co-creation process. The necessary level of transparency might be different for each brand. For example, in the fashion market, brands positioned as fully sustainable (e.g., Everlane, Patagonia) are expected to commit towards total transparency to keep their customers and other stakeholders engaged in co-creation (*New York Times*, 2020). Yet, brands such as Zara, positioned as delivering "the latest fashion trends" (Zara, 2021) might not provide such a high level of transparency.

### 3.3    Exploring Direct, Joint and Collaborative Interactions

A third pre-condition to assume the occurrence of co-creation in branding, retained from the analysis of the service logic, is the evidence of direct, joint and collaborative interactions between managers and consumers (Grönroos, 2011). The new hyperconnected market context makes information easily accessible through digital and mobile channels and turns brand owners (e.g., founders, managers) into a less relevant source of information about brands. Such context challenges the initial perspectives on brand co-creation (Ramaswamy & Ozcan, 2018; Swaminathan et al., 2020). Customers and other key brand stakeholders exchange their thoughts about brands across their networks. By doing so, they collectively create brand meanings, sometimes counteracting the brand messages generated by the firm. Should this practice be considered an advanced form of co-creation where those who market the brand are not necessarily part of the process? Or should we assume that internal stakeholders are still participating, although indirectly, in the co-creation of brand meanings?

The dominant perspective to date is that co-creation is indissociable from firm participation. Customer development of brand meanings in digitalized interactive platforms is the contin-uation of value co-creation in a "joint space of interactional value creation" (Ramaswamy & Ozcan, 2018, p.19). In such a context, value is created through interactions, and not through the mere exchange of offerings between the organization and its customers. Individuals create value through their interactive engagement with digitalized interactive platform offerings enabled by organizations and other market actors. The firm's ecosystem initiates and/or provides the environment for value production (Ramaswamy & Ozcan, 2018). Hence, the firm participates in the process of co-creation, although the scope of co-creation expands. By engaging in online platforms and networks, organizations keep connecting with the actual co-creation experiences of customers and other brand stakeholders. This discussion suggests that co-creation emerges from a process of interactions where the internal stakeholders engage in a joint space of value creation, such as the one provided by online platforms and networks.

We build on this approach of co-creation in branding to suggest that the inseparability of the brand internal stakeholders (e.g., firm, managers) with the process of brand co-creation should take a contemporary form to reflect the current market context. Interactions cannot be restricted to direct dyadic encounters (cf. Grönroos, 2011). The hyperconnected environment calls for a refocus of the initial condition of "direct, joint and collaborative interactions (between managers and consumers)" (Grönroos, 2011) to assume co-creation in branding. "Joint" and "collaborative" entail *managers, consumers and other brand stakeholders acting together* but not necessary directly. Brand meaning co-creation in the online domain does not require participants to interact face-to-face or to react to each other because an indirectly engaged participant (e.g., text/post reader or listener) is considered as equally active as a directly engaged participant (e.g., post author) (Vallaster & von Wallpach, 2013). Interactions occur across a multiplicity of interactive networks, platforms, devices and other online and offline settings and not only via direct dyadic encounters between managers and consumers. Those interactions enable consumers to co-create brand experiences and brand meanings directly or indirectly with the firm (Ramaswamy & Ozcan, 2018).

### 3.4    Framework

We develop a framework that expresses the requisites to assume co-creation in branding.

As a *first requisite*, we propose to conceptualize brand co-creation as a space that directly or indirectly *involves brand owners* (e.g., firm, managers).

The *second requisite* to assume co-creation in branding aligns with the service-dominant logic and states the brand stakeholder's *active participation in the process of value creation*, whether he/she is a customer, a manager or other stakeholder. Regarding customers, their active participation in value co-creation is contingent upon: (i) their willingness to participate in the process; and (ii) their belief that the co-created outcome (e.g., brand) can affect their personal lives as an individual and/or as a community member.

In order to make these conditions possible, brand managers need to assume customers as endogenous to the process of value creation. Such a position implies a participative and humble approach to brand management, sharing knowledge with customers and ensuring the right level of transparency. That is, the level of transparency that addresses the firm's needs in terms of confidentiality of shared knowledge and the customers' requirements to engage in the co-creation process.

A *third requisite* is the evidence of *interactions*, defined as value creation processes occurring across multiple interactive networks, platforms, devices and other online and offline settings, that enable the co-creation of brand experiences and brand meanings between brand stakeholders.

A *fourth requisite* is the *collective acceptance/recognition by managers, consumers, and other brand stakeholders, of the risks intrinsic to the co-creation process and outcome.*

Figure 2.1 presents our framework.

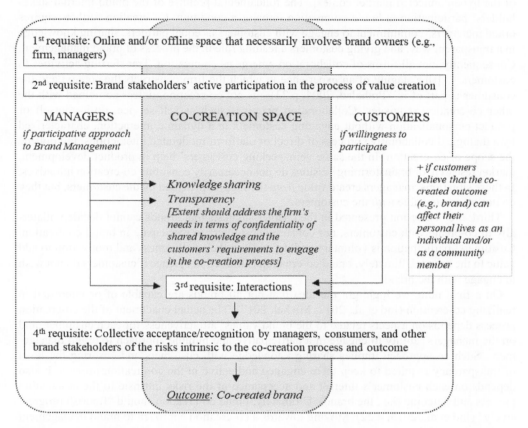

*Figure 2.1      Requisites to assume co-creation in branding*

## 4.      IMPLICATIONS

Insights from this research have important implications for both scholars and managers. First, this study establishes the boundaries of brand co-creation. Based on an interdisciplinary analysis of the literature on value co-creation, brand co-creation, consumer research, organizational identity and digital branding, we provide a framework of the fundamental conditions to assume co-creation in branding. The four main intertwined conditions are: (i) *internal stakeholders' involvement*; (ii) brand stakeholders' *active participation in the process of value creation*; (iii) evidence of interactions *between brand stakeholders*; and (iv) *collective accept-*

*ance/recognition by managers, consumers and other brand stakeholders, of the risks intrinsic to the co-creation process and outcome.*

Second, as a corollary of the framework, the study identifies the practical frontiers between co-creation in branding and other forms of stakeholder collaboration and engagement. We believe that any brand co-creation setting ought to include the managers, despite the challenges of the hyperconnected market context. The fundamental premise of the brand internal stakeholders' participation in brand co-creation remains a condition. Co-creation further requires brand managers' commitment to engage with customers as equal partners, sharing knowledge in a transparent way, and giving customers a leading role in the process of brand management. Consequently, not all forms of collaboration emerge as co-creation. Transferring activities to customers – "[t]he staging of an experience in which the firm constructs the context and the consumer is part of it" (Prahalad, 2004, p.23) – is not co-creation, unless combined with the other co-creation requisites. Collaboration practices such as self-service, do-it-yourself or product personalization without engaging customers in a dynamic interaction, characterized by a dialogical collaborative process of direct or platform-moderated interactions, fall outside the scope of co-creation. In the same vein, seeking customers' help in product development, market research, or brainstorming sessions do not necessarily constitute co-creation initiatives. In these situations, managers create value *from* the support provided by the customers, but they do not co-create value *with* the customers.

Third, the discussion presented in the chapter suggests that brands cannot decide unilaterally to co-create with customers, nor constrain customers to participate in brand co-creation. Customers' participation is voluntary and depends on their willingness and motivation to add value to the brand. Ultimately, brand co-creation is limited in essence if customers do not wish to engage with the brand.

On a final note, we highlight the idea that not all brands are capable of or interested in realizing co-creation (Ind et al., 2017; Michel, 2017). The actual enactment of the co-creation process depends on aspects related to the brand values' attractiveness for each customer, and on the managers' ability to engage in a participative and humble approach to brand management. Such an approach implies sharing knowledge with customers and ensuring the level of transparency required to keep them engaged and active in the co-creation process. It also depends on each customer's interest and acceptance of the risks intrinsic to the co-creation process and outcome (i.e., the brand). Ultimately, brand co-creation should "flourish progressively" (Ind et al., 2013, p.22). Moving towards a co-creation approach to brand management is a long but worthy process.

## ACKNOWLEDGMENTS

The first author is grateful to Fundação para a Ciência e a Tecnologia (UID/ECO/00124/2019, UIDB/00124/2020 and Social Sciences DataLab, PINFRA/22209/2016), POR Lisboa and POR Norte (Social Sciences DataLab, PINFRA/22209/2016); the second author is grateful to FCT, the Portuguese Foundation for Science and Technology (UIDB/03182/2020).

# REFERENCES

Albinsson, P. A., Perera, B. Y., and Sautter, P. T. (2016). DART scale development: Diagnosing a firm's readiness for strategic value co-creation, *Journal of Marketing Theory and Practice*, 24(1), 42–58.

Ballantyne, D. and Varey, R. J. (2008). The service-dominant logic and the future of marketing, *Journal of the Academy of Marketing Science*, 36, 11–14.

Belk, R. W. (1988). Possessions and the extended self, *Journal of Consumer Research*, 15(2), 139–168.

Bendapudi, N. and Leone, R. P. (2003). Psychological implications of customer participation in co-production, *Journal of Marketing*, 67 (January), 14–28.

Berthon, P., Pitt, L., and Campbell, C. (2008). Ad lib: When customers create the ad, *Californian Management Review*, 50(4).

Black, I. and Veloutsou, C. (2017). Working consumers: Co-creation of brand identity, consumer identity and brand community identity, *Journal of Business Research*, 70, 416–429.

Chan, K. W., Yim, C. Y., and Lam, S. S. K. (2010). Is customer participation in value creation a double-edged sword? Evidence from professional financial services across cultures, *Journal of Marketing*, 74(3), 48–64.

Cova, B. and Dalli, D. (2009). Working consumers: The next step in marketing theory? *Marketing Theory*, 9(3), 315–339.

Cova, B., Dalli, D., and Zwick, D. (2011). Critical perspectives on consumers' role as "producers": Broadening the debate on value co-creation in marketing processes, *Marketing Theory*, 11(3), 231–241.

Fournier, S. (1998). Consumers and their brands: Developing relationship theory in consumer research, *Journal of Consumer Research*, 24(4), 343–373.

Fournier, S. and Avery, J. (2011). The uninvited brand, *Business Horizons, Special Issue on Web 2.0, Consumer-Generated Content, and Social Media*, 54, 193–207.

Grönroos, C. (2008). Service logic revisited: Who creates value? And who co-creates? *European Business Review*, 20(4), 298–314.

Grönroos, C. (2011). Value co-creation in service logic: A critical analysis, *Marketing Theory*, 11(3), 279–301.

Grönroos, C. (2012). Conceptualising value co-creation: A journey to the 1970s and back to the future, *Journal of Marketing Management*, 28(13–14), 1520–1534.

Grönroos, C. and Ravald, A. (2011). Service as business logic: Implications for value creation and marketing, *Journal of Service Management*, 22(1), 5–22.

Ind, N., Iglesias, O., and Markovic, S. (2017). The co-creation continuum: From tactical market research tool to strategic collaborative innovation method, *Journal of Brand Management*, 24(4), 310–321.

Ind, N., Iglesias, O., and Schultz, M. (2013). Building brands together: Emergence and outcomes of co-creation, *California Management Review*, 55(3), 5–26.

Kennedy, E. and Guzmán, F. (2016). Co-creation of brand identities: Consumer and industry influence and motivations, *Journal of Consumer Marketing*, 33(5), 313–323.

Kornum, N., Gyrd-Jones, R., Al Zagir, N., and Brandis, K. A. (2017). Interplay between intended brand identity and identities in a Nike related brand community: Co-existing synergies and tensions in a nested system, *Journal of Business Research*, 70, 432–440.

Lam, S. K., Ahearne, M., Hu, Y., and Schillewaert, N. (2010). Resistance to brand switching when a radically new brand is introduced: A social identity theory perspective, *Journal of Marketing*, 74 (November), 128–146.

Lusch, R. F. and Vargo, S. L. (2014). *Service-Dominant Logic: Premises, Perspectives, Possibilities*, Cambridge, UK: Cambridge University Press.

Mael, F. and Ashforth, B. E. (1992). Alumni and their alma mater: A partial test of the reformulated model of organizational identification, *Journal of Organizational Behavior*, 13(2), 103–123.

Markovic, S. and Bagherzadeh, M. (2018). How does breadth of external stakeholder co-creation influence innovation performance? Analyzing the mediating roles of knowledge sharing and product innovation, *Journal of Business Research*, 88, 173–186.

Mazur, J. and Zaborek, P. (2014). Validating DART model, *International Journal of Management and Economics*, 44 (Oct–Dec), 106–125.

McKinsey & Company (2020). Completing a transformation in the consumer-goods industry. *Consumer Packaged Goods Practice*, (March).

Merz, M., He, Y., and Vargo, S. L. (2009). The evolving brand logic: A service-dominant logic perspective, *Journal of the Academy of Marketing Science*, 36(1), 1–10.

Merz, M. A., Zarantonello, L., and Grappi, S. (2018). How valuable are your customers in the brand value co-creation process? The development of a customer co-creation value (CCCV) scale, *Journal of Business Research*, 82, 79–89.

Michel, G. (2017). From brand identity to polysemous brands: Commentary on "Performing identities: Processes of brand and stakeholder identity co-construction", *Journal of Business Research*, 70, 453–455.

Muñiz, A. and O'Guinn, T. C. (2001). Brand community, *Journal of Consumer Research*, 27 (March), 412–432.

*New York Times* (2020). Everlane's Promise of "Radical Transparency" Unravels. Retrieved on January 2021 from https://www.nytimes.com/2020/07/26/fashion/everlane-employees-ethical-clothing.html.

Payne, A., Storbacka, K., Frow, P., and Knox, S. (2009). Co-creating brands: Diagnosing and designing the relationship experience, *Journal of Business Research*, 62(3), 379–389.

Prahalad, C. K. (2004). The co-creation of value. In: Invited commentaries on "Evolving to a new dominant logic for marketing", *Journal of Marketing*, 68(1), 18–27.

Prahalad, C. K. and Ramaswamy, V. (2003). The new frontier of experience innovation, *MIT Sloan Management Review*, 44(4), 12–18.

Prahalad, C. K. and Ramaswamy, V. (2004a). Co-creating unique value with customers, *Strategy & Leadership*, 3(3), 4–9.

Prahalad, C. K. and Ramaswamy, V. (2004b). Co-creation experiences: The next practice in value creation, *Journal of Interactive Marketing*, 18(3), 5–14.

Ramaswamy, V. and Ozcan, K. (2018). Offerings as digitalized interactive platforms: A conceptual framework and implications, *Journal of Marketing*, 82(4), 19–31.

Ranjan, K. R. and Read, S. (2016). Value co-creation: Concept and measurement, *Journal of the Academy of Marketing Science*, 44, 290–315.

Sartre, J. P. (1943). *Being and Nothingness: A Phenomenological Essay on Ontology*, New York: Philosophical Library.

Smith, A. M. (2013). The value co-destruction process: A customer resource perspective, *European Journal of Marketing*, 47(11/12), 1889–1909.

Swaminathan, V., Sorescu, A., Steenkamp, J.-B. E. M., O'Guinn T. C. G., and Schmitt, B. (2020). Branding in a hyperconnected world: Refocusing theories and rethinking boundaries, *Journal of Marketing*, 84(2), 24–46.

Vallaster, C. and von Wallpach, S. (2013). An online discursive inquiry into the social dynamics of multi-stakeholder brand meaning co-creation, *Journal of Business Research*, 66(9), 1505–1515.

Vargo, S. L. (2011). Market systems, stakeholders and value propositions. Toward a service-dominant logic-based theory of the market. *European Journal of Marketing*, 45(1/2), 217–222.

Vargo, S. L. and Lusch, R. F. (2006). Service-dominant logic: What it is, what it is not, what it might be. In: R. F. Lusch and S. L. Vargo (Eds), *The Service-Dominant Logic of Marketing: Dialog, Debate, and Directions* (pp.43–56). Armonk, NY: ME Sharpe.

Vargo, S. L. and Lusch, R. F. (2008). Service-dominant logic: Continuing the evolution, *Journal of the Academy of Marketing Science*, 36(1), 1–10.

Vargo, S. L. and Lusch, R. F. (2011). It's all B2B...and beyond: Toward a systems perspective of the market, *Industrial Marketing Management*, 40(2), 181–187.

Vargo, S. L. and Lusch, R. F. (2016). Institutions and axioms: An extension and update of service-dominant logic, *Journal of the Academy of Marketing Science*, 36(1), 1–10.

Vargo, S. L., Maglio, P. P., and Akaka, A. M. (2008). On value and value co-creation: A service systems and service logic perspective, *European Management Journal*, 26, 145–152.

von Wallpach, S., Hemetsberger, A., and Espersen, P. (2017). Performing identities: Processes of brand and stakeholder identity co-construction, *Journal of Business Research*, 70C, 443–452.

Zara (2021). International website. Retrieved on January 2021 from https://www.zara.com/pt/en/woman-new-in-l1180.html?v1=1712675.

# 3. Brands as co-creational lived experience ecosystems: an integrative theoretical framework of interactional creation

*Venkat Ramaswamy and Kerimcan Ozcan*

## 1. INTRODUCTION

The brand literature has increasingly recognized the active participation of stakeholding individuals in creating brands together (see for instance, Arvidsson, 2006; da Silveira et al., 2013; Gyrd-Jones & Kornum, 2013; Iglesias & Bonet, 2012; Iglesias et al., 2020; Ind, 2003; Ind & Bjerke, 2007; Ind & Schmidt, 2020; Ind et al., 2013, 2017; Lury, 2004; Markovic & Bagherzadeh, 2018; Merz et al., 2009; Payne et al., 2009; Price & Coulter, 2019; Ramaswamy & Ozcan, 2016; Schembri, 2009; Stach, 2019; Swaminathan et al., 2020; Wider et al., 2018). The COVID-19 pandemic accelerated the digitalized transformation of offerings with an enhanced logic of value creation centered on flows of interactive experiences powered by software (McKinsey, 2020). As engaging actors (whether customers, employees, managers, suppliers, partners, or citizens) interact more intensively with offerings through digitized services and digital engagement platforms in an Internetworked experience economy, the co-creation of brand value is accelerating toward interactive lived experiences.

Following the "service-dominant logic (SDL)" of marketing (Lusch & Vargo, 2014; Vargo & Lusch, 2004, 2008), Merz et al. (2009) discussed a service-dominant brand logic which views brand in terms of collaborative value co-creation activities of firms and all of their stakeholders and brand value in terms of the stakeholders' collectively perceived value-in-use. This logic

> (1) considers service to be the common denominator of exchange, (2) embraces a process orientation ("service"), rather than an output orientation ("goods and services"), and (3) makes the customer endogenous to value creation by arguing that value is always co-created with customers (and others), rather than unilaterally created by the firm and then distributed.

Their third point was the basis of a series of writings between 2000 and 2004 by Prahalad and Ramaswamy (2000, 2002, 2003, 2004a, 2004b), which introduced and discussed the concept of "co-creation" of unique value with customers (and other stakeholders). They discussed both the *de-centering* of brands toward the subjective experiences of individuals on the one hand, and its *democratization* toward the inclusion of individuals in the process of brand creation on the other hand (see also Ramaswamy, 2011). They saw interactive experiences as the basis of value co-creation in the economy (and society); one in which increasingly empowered individuals co-constructed their contextual experiences through environments of interactions facilitated by networks of firms and communities of individuals. However, this emphasis on interactive experience has not received adequate attention in the value co-creation literature, which has tended to disproportionately emphasize the "co" more than "creation" around interactive experiences (Ramaswamy & Ozcan, 2018b), by isolating human actors from practices entailing digital technology (and nonhuman actors in general) in which they are entangled, and that affects interactivity and formation of experiences.

Merz et al. (2009) mapped the evolution of the branding literature to identify (overlapping) brand eras of "Individual Goods-Focus" (1900s–1930s), Value-Focus (1930s–1990s), Relationship-Focus (1990s–2000), and Stakeholder-Focus Brand Era (2000+). The Stakeholder-Focus Brand Era (p. 337) ushered in *"collective and dynamic* processes" wherein "(1) brand value is co-created within stakeholder-based ecosystems, (2) stakeholders form network, rather than only dyadic, relationships with brands, and (3) brand value is dynamically constructed through social interactions among different stakeholders". The "Interactive Lived Experience" Brand Era (2010+) that we are in now entails a further evolution of brands, as connected smart offerings amplify personal agency in creating interactive lived experiences together with stakeholding individuals. Fully theorizing such interactive lived brand experience, however, requires overcoming the "goods- versus Service-Dominant Logic (SDL)" characterization (Lusch & Vargo, 2014; Vargo & Lusch, 2004, 2008), to instead seeing brands as *"assemblages"* in ongoing and complex processes of constant flux (Wider et al., 2018), whose relations are both constituted in and constitutive of enacted practices of interactive experiences.

In a critique of SDL, Orlikowski and Scott (2015, pp. 203–4) discuss how "services (and goods) are constituted in practice". They note that both the

> goods and service-dominant logics overlook the ways in which producing and consuming outputs—at the level of practices—are relatively similar, in the sense that they entail a range of activities, bodies, and artifacts … From a practice perspective, goods and services both require the coordination of activities, bodies, and artifacts to be produced and consumed.

The concept of the "co-creational lived experience ecosystem" introduced in this chapter transcends goods and services in this vein of practices, while simultaneously calling attention to the need to pay attention to (increasingly digitalized) flows of interactive "agencing–structuring" experiences (Ramaswamy & Ozcan, 2018b). This goes beyond the service (eco)systems of SDL that aggregate exchanges, wherein from the get-go the exchange paradigm of SDL conceptually isolates beneficiaries (and actors) from the process of service exchange. While SDL made a significant contribution in going underneath "goods and services" to unmask the "process" of service provision by actors, it remained tethered to an exchange paradigm of value creation, contrasting itself with the output orientation of a goods-dominant logic. Our theorization of co-creational lived experience ecosystems, instead, builds on the interactional creation framework of co-creation discussed by Ramaswamy and Ozcan (2014, 2016, 2018b, 2020), which they have come to call a co-creation paradigm (CCP) for short. In contrast to SDL, the CCP follows a relational creational philosophy that explicitly recognizes assemblages of experience and interactive agencing–structuring, and thereby (nonhuman in addition to human) actors, activities, and resources, as being "interactively defined" (Ramaswamy & Ozcan, 2020). As the creational and interactional relational logics are applicable at varying levels of scale, the conceptualization of brands as co-creational lived experience ecosystems can be applied at both the individual and enterprise levels, or more generally at any level of agglomeration of offerings, organizations, places–spaces, and stakeholder engagements.

In the next section, we explicitly theorize brands as co-creational lived experience ecosystems as units of inquiry, with their intrinsic assemblage characteristics, and which always-already includes experiencers. We articulate the theoretical development of our integrative framework, elucidating its various aspects, as shown stylistically in the schematic of Figure 3.1. We discuss how, in co-creational lived experience ecosystems, brand creation always entails both the co-creation of environments of emergent brand experiences and the lived brand experiences of interactional creation through those environments. We then discuss the contributions that follow from our theorization, especially in light of the SDL of brand value co-creation (Merz et al., 2009), and conclude by discussing some key brand management implications.

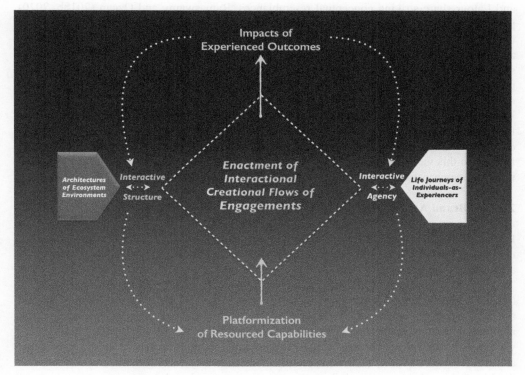

*Figure 3.1*     *Co-creational lived experience ecosystem*

## 2.     THEORETICAL DEVELOPMENT

Our conceptualization of brands as co-creational lived experience ecosystems can be seen as building on Lury's (2009) original work of accounting for "brands as assemblages". Lury (2004) has argued eloquently about seeing brands as "objects" of information and of the artificial sciences (Simon, [1969] 1996). In this view, brands are "both a response to the embedding of the logics of information in the economy and a diagram of production of further information for the economy" (Lury, 2004, p. 126). From this perspective "one of the most significant characteristics of the brand is that it is an object that is designed so that it may be otherwise; that is, that it may be quite other—in particular ways—than it is."

Brand as an assemblage (Lury, 2004) implies a site and diagram for managing the response time of interactivity between a set of products/services as manifestations of, and through, consumers' own creativity. The assemblage concept has since been adopted in brand research to signify the performative effectuation of brand subjects and objects with changing capabilities through actions, interactions, and associations in overlapping networks of heterogeneous material and expressive components (Bajde, 2013; Canniford & Bajde, 2015; Lucarelli & Hallin, 2015; Price & Coulter, 2019; Rokka & Canniford, 2016). As the concepts of agencement, assemblage, and actor-network found in the works of Deleuze and Guattari, DeLanda, and Latour share striking conceptual resemblances, Ramaswamy and Ozcan (2018b, 2020) proposed "agencial assemblage" as a better term to refer to this "rhizomatic" arrangement of heterogeneous and self-subsistent components (see Wider et al., 2018, for a discussion of "rhizomatic" processual philosophy of brands), with constitutional roles of content and expression. Brands as such assemblages of interactive agencing–structuring have a "virtual" capacity to interact (Ramaswamy & Ozcan, 2016) via semiotic sociomaterial flows, for example flows of data, goods, people, capital, ideas, signs, images, narratives, and so on, in variably emergent and recurrent processes of destabilization and stabilization. This formulation puts the spotlight on the substance and form of interactions, which are central to explaining the relational dynamics within and between assemblages that constitute brands and their environments. Brands, in this view are always in a process of becoming (Wider et al., 2018) and co-created in experience ecosystems.

## 2.1   Brand Assemblages as Interactive System-Environments

Following Ramaswamy and Ozcan (2018b, 2020), brand assemblages can be seen as human/nonhuman system-environment hybrids, that act upon interactional flows with other agencial assemblages, and hence, are also affected by their agencies (Ramaswamy & Ozcan, 2020). This view of brand assemblages as interactive system-environments accommodates interactional flows of agencial assemblages in discrete and interacting nested networks of market actors, associations, and meanings (Preece et al., 2019) in other agencial assemblages across market space–time. In their role of market-shaping devices, brands enact their performative visions within and alongside their worlds (Onyas & Ryan, 2015). In their efforts to enact interactional creation of value, marketers, and the audiences they enroll, stabilize and destabilize the brand through interactional flows between the material and expressive components of interactive system-environments (Parmentier & Fischer, 2015).

Hence, brands as interactive system-environments not only considers the ability of brands to "object-ify", but also "subject-ify". Brands are "objects that multiply realities, with 'more or less inventive consequences'", which are "performative" in contingent ways (Callon, 1998b). Brands as interactive system-environments allows us to recognize the dynamic nature of the enactment of interactive brand experiences, unfolding not only over temporal episodes but spatially (Lucarelli & Hallin, 2015), as well as contextually (e.g., assembling culture, Arnould & Thompson, 2005; Bajde, 2013; Canniford & Bajde, 2015; Cochoy & Mallard, 2018; Price & Coulter, 2019). As digitalization accelerates a new frontier of interactive brand experience innovation (Prahalad & Ramaswamy, 2004b), it foregrounds brand assemblages as interactive ecosystems of experiences that connect a multiplicity of interactive system-environments (Ramaswamy & Ozcan, 2020).

Ramaswamy and Ozcan (2020) formally discuss the interplay of the concepts of interactive agency and interactive structure in the enactment of interactive brand experiences via interactive system-environments. They define interactive agency as the agencing engagement of an interactive system-environment in acting upon interactional flows, and the accompanying concept of interactive structure as the structuring organization of interactive system-environments enabled/constrained by interactional flows. Every interactive system-environment entails a combination of acting subjects and objects acted upon. Hence, brand, as an interactive system-environment, has an objective character as immaterial, informational, and contextual capital that construct system-environments in which communication is pre-structured to unfold in particular directions to reproduce a particular brand identity (Arvidsson, 2006). Seen from the brand orchestrator's objectifying perspective, the managerial activity and function of brand*ing*, then, is a structuring organization, or networked relations of an interactive system-environment, both in terms of "what it can create" and "what creates it". As Lury (2009) elaborates, branding has to do with marking, naming, mapping, and engendering of relations of variations in a marketing possibility space for adequacy, continuity, and extension, in a reflexive manner, via experimentation and statistical testing. For the brand orchestrator, seen objectively, the brand is an interactive structure, that is, a special arrangement of interactional flows enabled and constrained by the managerial activity and function of branding, which result in emergent properties that not only cannot be reduced to, but also act back on the material and expressive components of the agencial assemblage (Ramaswamy & Ozcan, 2020).

As an interactive system-environment, brand also implies subjects, subjectivity, and subjectification, when experienced and acted on by consumers, communities, employees, and other stakeholders (Wider et al., 2018). A consumer re-interpreting perceived brand meaning at each touchpoint (Iglesias et al., 2013), a brand community member co-constructing the brand experience as part of a collective social act (Schembri, 2009), an employee engaging in brand work by negotiating assemblages of the brand in situated and gendered practices (Kivinen & Hunter, 2019), and stakeholders interacting with a brand's stable core set of elements while negotiating the periphery (Gyrd-Jones & Kornum, 2013), all indicate a particular agencing engagement with the brand, that is, embodied experiential becomings of an agencial assemblage, where the latter refers to the pertinent subjectivity itself. Therefore, seen from the brand experiencer's perspective, since brands as interactive system-environments are not closed systems, that is, their parts are open to new components becoming attached to them with the potential to engender new creational interactions, the brand has interactive agency in virtue of the agencing engagements in acting upon interactional flows.

## 2.2     Enactment of Interactive Lived Brand Experiences

Brand experience defined as sensations, feelings, cognitions, and behavioral responses evoked by brand stimuli (Brakus et al., 2009), and as bodily interactions of a consumer, product, and stakeholders the consumer deems relevant for the experience (Stach, 2019), emerges as an assemblage of interactive experiences via semiotic sociomaterial interactional flows from hybrid consumption assemblages combining cultural scripts with material and technological resources (Canniford & Shankar, 2013). Thus, a multitude of overlapping and nested experiential agencial assemblages constitute a brand experience ecosystem, that is, an interactive system-environment composed of heterogeneous networked relations of emergent brand experiences. The combination of a community of heterogeneous agencies, the environments with which the agencies interact, and the metastable symbiotic dissipative structures that facilitate active and passive circulations of energy, materials, and information between agencies and environments, engender flows that affect experienced outcomes of brand value. They can confer selective advantage on the brand as a whole, or even lead to decay and dissolution in its entirety (Peacock, 2008).

Throughout an interactive brand experiencer journey, energetic flows of desiring actor-networks mobilize flows of data, representation, and meaning (Kozinets et al., 2017), leading to connections and concomitant disconnections of flows of agencing–structuring interactions that enact interactional creation of brand meanings, images, and identities. In managing the response gap of interactivity of agencing–structuring interactions, the assemblage of brand elements can either communicate identity or difference of brand meanings to coordinate a constantly shifting series of offerings and multiple temporalities into a flow (Lury, 2004). In the context of a series of events in which brand experiencer journeys take place, brand meanings connect experiencers' involvements in brand assemblages (Batey, 2008; Berthon et al., 2009; Kärreman & Rylander, 2008; Keller, 2003) with recognizable articulations and actions afforded by them (Ramaswamy & Ozcan, 2016). Since every brand constitutes a portfolio of meanings (Iglesias & Bonet, 2012), that vary according to the mental structures built by embodied experiences (Stach, 2019), the brand as an interactive system-environment also implicates a multitude of assemblages of interactive experiences with specific properties, capacities, and expressive roles (Hoffman & Novak, 2018) for all interactive agencing–structurings mobilized around the brand.

In the enactment of interactive lived brand experiences as sociomaterial practices (Orlikowski, 2007), assemblage components can serve to focus and integrate the rays of sense-making emanating from experiencers while also gathering and energizing differential events in the brand experience ecosystem (Lury, 2004). Brand orchestrators have to therefore engage in dynamic configuration of semiotic and sociomaterial interactional flows that affect interactivity and interdependencies in brand interactions of lived journeys of experiencers. The enactment of interactive lived brand experiences via digitalized brand experience ecosystems entails organizing and engaging actors coming together in a process of joint creation of lived brand experience ecosystems that hold the promise of "interactive structures" of potentially valuable emergent experiences where "interactive agencies" are exercised through the activation of environments afforded by those offerings.

## 2.3   Engendering Experienced Outcomes through Creational Interactions

Experienced outcomes emerge from a "constellation of interactions" (Gummesson & Mele, 2010) through a process of creative differentiation in a brand experience ecosystem (Ramaswamy & Ozcan, 2016). Prahalad and Ramaswamy (2004b), in discussing the "individual and experience-centric view" of innovation and value creation, used the notion of "individual-to-network-to-individual" (I2N2I) to refer to the increasingly pervasive pathways of interactional flows from the individual to the network, and back to the individual (note the contrast to conventional "B2B" and "B2C" activity notions, see also Ramaswamy, 2011). Accordingly, interactive agencies of individuals form environments of emergent experiences subject to interactive structures, by acting upon interactional flows of brand assemblage components. The interactive agencies of experiencers pertain to the site of focal interactive experiences as well as the distributed agency implicated in the site from elsewhere in the brand value creational actor-network, either indirectly or directly. Interactive structures of brand value creation emerge from and act back on interactional flows (Thomas et al., 2013). In framing actor-networked I2N2I flows, brand orchestrators need to address the heterogeneous intentionalities of all relevant brand stakeholders, enhance the creativity of actor-networks, and the integrativity and transformativity in I2N2I flows for more valuable outcomes. From the perspective of digitalized experience ecosystem innovation, brand orchestrators can consider, among other things, giving individuals appropriate creative tools in light of their intentionalities as they exercise their interactional agency, designing platforms to integrate both lived experiences and imaginative skills, and deploying visualization, simulation, and prototyping tools to augment the quality of agencing engagement design (Ramaswamy & Ozcan, 2016).

Although brand experience ecosystems afford patterned pathways of event-based flows by which potentially valuable experienced brand outcomes can be actualized from resourced capabilities through creational interactions, it is up to the interactive agencies of individuals to make meaning from events of lived brand experiences, while interpreting and contributing to the brand context in which they exist and have experiences, and valorize their experienced brand outcomes in iterative and differential articulations of value over temporal scales of duration. Such an individuated spatiotemporal stratum of events, contexts, involvements, and meanings, which in the widest sense, contributes to the individual's narrative self (Mackenzie, 2008) implies a brand experience domain (Ramaswamy & Ozcan, 2016), that is, the brand "environment" of an experiencer's interactive system-environment or brand lifeworld, definitely a part of but not identical to the larger milieu or habitus of the experiencer (Bourdieu, 1984).

Actual domains of brand experiences from the individual side do not have a one-to-one correspondence with the environments afforded by agencial assemblages as conceived from the brand orchestrator side through its resourced capabilities (Ramaswamy & Ozcan, 2014). The latter implies a brand territory with changing relations among a multitude of material and expressive assemblage components such as consumers, retailers, packaging, advertising, media placements, social media communities, and so on (Price & Coulter, 2019), that can attach with the potential to engender new creational interactions, just as they can detach and plug into other agencial assemblages in new heterogeneous relations across the porous boundaries of the brand as an interactive system-environment. From the vantage point of the brand orchestrator, the brand territory is the "environment" of its brand as an interactive system-environment, the objective of which is surrounding brand experiencers in agencial assemblages of affordances (Gibson, 1979), manifesting some things that persist and some that do not in the brand experience domain of that particular individual. Because there is never one-to-one alignment and synchronicity between brand experience domains and a brand territory, brand orchestrators as structuring organizations need to configure brand experiences with their stakeholders by enhancing explicit dialogue, transparency, and accessibility of information, tools, expertise, and skills in actualizing valuable experienced outcomes, all the while ensuring reflexivity in the enactment of interactional creation (Ramaswamy & Ozcan, 2014).

## 2.4   Impact Valuation in Lived Brand Experience Ecosystems

Individuals' agencing engagements with brands entail their involvements in contexts of brand events from which they expect to derive meaningful outcomes. Brand meaning lies in the expressive consequences triggered by an event, in the encounter of semiotic sociomaterial flows between the components of an agencial brand assemblage (Williams, 2008). The meanings of a brand assemblage become manifest in the set of contexts into which interactive agencies place them (Chandler & Vargo, 2011; Edvardsson et al., 2011) and, for those agencies actively involved, the recognizable articulations and actions it affords them, for example narratives in which that brand assemblage can occur, which are conceivable and realistic to agents. When actor-networked flows in an interactive system-environment of a brand engender experienced outcomes of interactional creation over repeated interactions with minute differences, the cumulative impact could be enabling or constraining for the interactive agency of the experiencing individual (Hoffman & Novak, 2018). This impact is established immanently in the experience ecosystem, whenever a difference obtains between here and there, or before and after, in a relational and contextual manner (Lury, 2009).

Going beyond "exchange value" and "use value", emergence of subjective experiences implies "experience value", which provides a sense and direction to individuals' enactments (Weick, 1995) and conditions the way they valorize outcomes as interactive agencies from particularized interests in specific "regimes of value" (Appadurai, 1988). Brand orchestrators need to understand and manage the value complementarities with stakeholders who subscribe to particular regimes of value as the motivating and organizing framework in their engagement with and experience of a brand assemblage (Gyrd-Jones & Kornum, 2013). Essential to this is the realization that processes of "valorization", or "giving worth to", wherein a "performation" (Callon, 2007b; Kjellberg & Helgesson, 2006, 2007) is implied, as is an "evaluation" (Vatin, 2013), are implicated and structured in practices of interactive agencies–structures during all stages of the creational process (Ind et al., 2017), in other words, a "valorization-in-interactional creation" (Ramaswamy & Ozcan, 2020).

Brand as an interactive experience ecosystem affords an "empty diagram" (Bratton, 2015) of a multiplicity of interactive system-environments through which actor engagement is mediated with a potential increase in the value of that engagement to experiencers, however it is valorized. As loose performative assemblages of actions, interactions, and relations, brands perform actions (Lucarelli & Hallin, 2015) and reconstitute the agencial assemblage in contingent ways, engendering a multiplicity of realities with novel consequences (Callon, 1998b). By organizing the response time of interactivity, and thereby the time interval between brand experiences (Lury, 2004), the brand becomes the fulcrum that synchronizes and calibrates the enactment events of interactional creation of experiences so as to transform entire market activity performatively (Nakassis, 2012).

## 2.5   Configuration of Value Creation via Interactive Platformization of Lived Experiences

Ramaswamy and Ozcan (2016) discuss how platforms of brand engagements can be embedded anywhere in the brand value creation system, and through which a wide variety of agencing–structuring interactions can occur. Through interactive platforms, enterprise actors act upon interdependencies of engagements and create new ones (Ramaswamy & Ozcan, 2014) with the "intention of creating specific outcomes of value" (Freytag et al., 2017). As Ramaswamy and Ozcan (2018a, 2018b) have shown, the experiences of enactment of interactional creation of individuals through interactive offerings both affect, and are affected by, the relational effects of interactions and outcomes, whose impacts can evolve beyond an immediate set of interacting entities over space–time. As defined by Ramaswamy and Ozcan (2020), interactive platformization is the framing of interactional flows across instantiations of socio-technical agencial assemblages composed of artifacts, persons, processes, and interfaces (APPI), entailing interactive structures–agencies. Ramaswamy and Ozcan (2018a) refer to offerings with increasing digitalization of APPI interactions as digitalized interactive platforms (DIPs). While every framing of interactional flows produces overflows in the enactment of interactional creation through DIP brand offerings (and consequently affects valuation of outcomes), reconfiguration of heterogeneous relations between components of DIPs results in a reconfiguration of the objectives, interests, and identities of actors (Callon, 1998a), while also building assemblage capacities of lived brand experience ecosystems (Ramaswamy & Ozcan, 2014).

As platformization takes place via digital technology and can be inserted anywhere in the activity chain to include any enterprise stakeholder activity, interactive structures can both stabilize heterogeneous relations among the assemblage components and allow for experimentation and exploration, depending upon the configuration of interactive platformization. Brand as an interactively platformed experienced ecosystem patterns the spatiotemporality of networks of experiences with heterogeneous allies so as to extend offerings across wider assemblages of experience ecosystems (Canniford & Bajde, 2015; Lury, 2004). Configuring interactive platformization from a perspective of co-creational brand experiences therefore starts with understanding how brand agencing engagements intensify the formation of experienced brand outcomes from resourced brand capabilities implied by the framing (i.e., relating brand developmental capacities to the enactment of interactional creation to co-created brand impacts), a process of actualization from virtual potentials (DeLanda, 2006; Deleuze, 1994). In this figuring together, or *con*figuring, of the material and the social, representations and their contexts are mutually negotiated and temporarily stabilized, implying a reconfiguration and emergence of new brand assemblages (Mazmanian et al., 2014). This, then, implies a re-virtualization of co-created brand impacts into brand developmental capacities (DeLanda, 2016; Deleuze & Guattari, 1987) as a process of re-framing, that is, co-evolving the brand architecture. When strict rule-following is superseded by value-sensitive practices based on discourses of mutual success, communication, efficient management of partnership, commitment to fair cooperation, and principle of equality, a virtuous cycle of brand co-creation potential ensues whereby relational capital and tendency to renounce safeguards strengthen each other and economize on governance costs (Huber et al., 2017). Therefore, discursive elements, procedures, organizational forms, and incentives are critical to the configuration of heterogenous brand relations so as to "agence" assemblages as "interactive diagrams" around brand experiencers as co-creators, who can intend, anticipate, react, calculate and control their own actions (Callon, 2008).

## 3.    DISCUSSION

Applying our theorization of brands as co-creational lived experience ecosystems, consider, for instance, the example of wound care as discussed by Lawer (2020) who reframes health as ecosystems of experience and capacity emergence by positing two premises: (1) diverse experiences with health, illness and disease are by-products of socio-cultural, material-spatial, bodily-motor, and perceptual-cognitive interactions in the world; and (2) interactions that shape experience with health contain forces found in real social and other structures. Actors (as "affectors") have varying capacities to affect these forces or be affected by them (as "affectees"). In this framing of health, therefore, the unit of inquiry is not only the "patient" but also the sub-ecosystem as an agencial assemblage of health having a certain affective capacity and engendering a particular quality of experienced outcomes, wherein health is an emergent adaptive process of experience and capacity formation formed from relational events of affects, forces and encounters in places over time (Duff, 2014).

While suboptimal wound care and inappropriate use of wound treatments can lead to delayed healing, and increased infection and pain, all of which impact a patient's quality of life, it can suffer from ineffective orchestration of means, and lacking clear ownership as such. Patient-centered wound care management entails a complex adaptive health experience ecosystem of multiple stakeholders ranging from home care family and community organizations to care providers (from nurses and physicians to clinics and hospitals) and medical device and pharmaceutical companies, to payers and insurers, and investors, government organizations, and research and academic entities. Wound care requires multiple interactions among stakeholders to even understand the situation of a specific wound of a particular patient. Multiply this by several wound factors, multiple wounds on a patient, and multiple patients in a healthcare enterprise, not to mention other actors engaged directly or indirectly, and its management becomes exponentially challenging. Central to the varied interactions is the strategic need for a unified platform of wound-based data and multi-factorial information management that can engender better impacts of experienced outcomes from the perspective of care providers (e.g., patient, nurse, and physician interactions). The COVID-19 crisis only accelerated this strategic need with "telehealth" wound care arrangements, given about seven million people living with chronic wounds in the US, with industry leaders coming together in a Telewound coalition to address care delivery and health system capacity challenges.

Consider Swift Medical, one of the nodal entities in this Telewound coalition, and a world leader in digitalized wound care management for healthcare enterprises. Swift Medical's vision is to "alleviate the global prevalence of chronic wounds and the challenge of treating wounds effectively". Its Swift Skin and Wound (SSW) is an interactive brand offering for organizations across the healthcare continuum, which can transform interactions associated with every aspect of healing in the wound management experience ecosystem, from point of wound care to assessment, diagnosis, and administration by engaging actors in a focal healthcare enterprise ecosystem. The Swift brand offering consists of the smartphone Swift App, which captures wound images and measurements, and healing-related data without touching the wound. It uses an FDA-registered adhesive marker that calibrates wound images for size, color and lighting. Swift Dashboards provide real-time views of critical data such as patients at risk of deteriorating or developing new wounds, caregiver compliance to wound care protocols, and effectiveness of care improvement initiatives. By concretely visualizing outcomes for the patient and care providers and embedding connected supporting communication environments to share experiences, it facilitates new types of workflow interactions and enactment of brands in a "continuous becoming" toward enhancing wellbeing risk management and realizing better impacts for all.

The Swift Medical wound care example calls attention to how the CCP goes beyond SDL in conceiving brand relations in the "Interactive Lived Experience-Focus" Brand Era we are in. Table 3.1 contrasts brands as co-creational lived experience ecosystems through the CCP with that of an SDL perspective. First and foremost, in the CCP, co-creation is explicitly seen as a function of interactions with the very act of creation of experiences being modified through forces of interactional flows (Ramaswamy & Ozcan, 2018b). Following our discussion from the previous section, our theorization of co-creation experience ecosystems ventures beyond the process orientation of service exchange of SDL (Axiom 1) to interactive experience value creation by problematizing sociomaterial practices in the enactment of experience creation through flows of interactive "agencing–structuring" experiences as its fundamental basis. Individuals are interceptors as well as originators of material and energy flows, termed desire by Deleuze (Smith, 2012), which mobilize flows of contagious ideas, physical performances, suggestions, emotions, and beliefs across individuals in processes of invention, imitation, and opposition at the micro-level (Sampson, 2012; Tonkonoff, 2017), as well as of people, technologies, capital, data, representation, meaning, narratives, and other cultural resources at the macro-level (Appadurai, 1990; Kozinets et al., 2017). From an ecological perspective, individuals are technological bodies as interactive system-environments immersed in fields of mutual flows, data transfer, and transformations (Braidotti, 2006). From a socio-cultural perspective, individuals enact, through their perceptions, thoughts, affects, and actions, their habitus and social positions with their particular patterns of human and nonhuman flows of signification and subjectification in purposeful, repetitive, programmable sequences of inter-actions (Castells, 2010; Lorraine, 2011). From a technological perspective, individuals interact with current events, effects, and actions of others, not as much with network as the form of coordination but rather with flow as the form of observation and projection in an infinite suc-cession of heterogenous matter projected on changing interfaces while being performed and analyzed reflexively (Cetina, 2003; Thrift, 2008). By explicitly problematizing co-creation in this manner, the CCP goes beyond mere "exchange" of service (application of competence) to theorize the actualization of interactive brand experiences. It also provides a theoretically grounded integrative framework that accommodates disparate but related manifestations such as brand offerings co-creation (Ind et al., 2017; Santos-Vijande et al., 2015), brand identity co-creation (Iglesias et al., 2020; Kornum et al., 2017; von Wallpach et al., 2017a, b), brand experience co-creation (Payne et al., 2009), brand meaning co-creation (Tierney et al., 2016; Vallaster & von Wallpach, 2013), brand authenticity co-creation (Beverland et al., 2008), and brand value co-creation (Merz et al., 2009).

Furthermore, in SDL, while resources are seen as "operant" (going beyond the "operand" resource-based view of value creation), all social and economic actors are, however, seen as mere resource integrators (Axiom 3). Vargo and Lusch (2016, p. 7) state that "all actors fundamentally do the same things: integrate resources and engage in service exchange, all in the process of cocreating value". However, since resource integration and service exchange cannot completely exhaust the conceptual and practical possibilities of "creation" of experi-ences and "co", respectively, the interactional dynamics by which "experience" value gets "co"-created have remained underspecified. The CCP goes beyond operant resources to expli-cating *how* outcomes emerge from "event-sensed" interactions of experiencers in environ-ments of experience ecosystems and affects and the relations they entail. Hence, all actors are creational experiencers that enact the emergence and embodiment of interactive lived brand experiences through actor-networked flows framed by increasingly digitally platformized resourced capabilities.

Service-dominant brand logic does not explicitly problematize how lived brand experiences emerge from resource integration by actors, other than axiomatically stating that "value is always uniquely and phenomenologically determined by the beneficiary" (Axiom 4). In con-trast, by virtue of the CCP, unique "experience" value in our theorization of brands as lived

*Table 3.1　Co-creation paradigm of lived brand experience ecosystems: beyond service-dominant logic*

| Co-Creation Paradigm (CCP) | Service-Dominant Logic (SDL) | Remarks |
|---|---|---|
| Enactment of creation via flows of interactive agencing–structuring experiences is the fundamental basis of co-creation | Service is the fundamental basis of exchange (Axiom 1) | CCP transcends the "the sacred cow of exchange theory" (Sheth & Parvatiyar, 1995, p. 414) and the process orientation of service exchange of SDL, to problematizing creation through interactional flows and thereby co-creation directly. |
| Interactional creation occurs via experience ecosystems always including the experiencer | Value is co-created by multiple actors, always including the beneficiary (Axiom 2) | In the CCP, co-creation is explicitly seen as a function of interactions with the very act of "creation" being modified through forces of interactions, with explicit problematization of interactive agency in the enactment of interactional creation. |
| Actor-networked flows engender experienced outcomes of interactional creation | All social and economic actors are resource integrators (Axiom 3) | CCP goes beyond operant resources to explicating how outcomes emerge from interactional encounters of experiencers in environments of experience ecosystems, with interactional flows at the core, and the events, affects, and relations they entail. |
| Valuation is a function of impacts of lived experienced outcomes | Value is always uniquely and phenomenologically determined by the beneficiary (Axiom 4) | In the CCP, lived experience outcomes embodied through socio-technical assemblages of agencies that always includes the experiencer, with the nature and quality of their impacts determining value. Value through interactional creation, thus, transcends "exchange"-based characterizations. |
| Interactional value creation is dynamically configured via interactive platformization of lived experience ecosystems | Value co-creation is coordinated through actor-generated institutions and institutional arrangements (Axiom 5) | In the CCP, interactional creation of value is seen as becoming possible through intensification of interactional creation of networked actors. The CCP problematizes the configurational dynamics of impacts of co-creational lived experiences in terms of both framing and re-framing, as organizing actors orchestrate and strategically architect multiple interactive system-environments via interactive platformization of experience ecosystems in the lived journeys of experiencers. Institutions and institutional arrangements are, thus, emergent and themselves co-created. |

experience ecosystems is produced through socio-technical assemblages of agencies that goes beyond conventional "utility and preference" differences among actors in conventional analytical characterizations of valuations, which transcends "exchange" value (Akaka et al., 2015; Brodie et al., 2011; Chandler & Vargo, 2011). As value is expressed through interactive agencing, we have to recognize that the coming together of a multitude of individuals in a dynamic structuration of differential realities means that a multiplicity of values are at play, some based on objective properties, some based on subjective affects, derived intrinsically or extrinsically.

In short, we account for a pluralistic view of brand values in co-creational lived brand experience ecosystems. Valorization of experienced outcomes in co-creational lived brand experience ecosystems is the iterative and differential articulation of value (i.e., through difference, Deleuze, 1994), and is determined by heterogeneous agencies of experiencers as co-creators over temporal scales of duration that constitute a dynamic of ongoing interactive experience value creation through interactive offerings.

Finally, Vargo and Lusch (2016) discuss the role of institutions and institutional arrangements in "co-ordination" of value co-creation. The endogeneity of such co-ordination however remains underspecified, for the very same reason that the "creational" mechanism is unspecified in SDL. In contrast, in the CCP, interactional creation of brand value is seen as becoming possible through intensive (mechanisms of) interactional creation of networked actors. Actions and interactions of engaging actors through DIP offerings have to be enabled and constrained through framing of devices and discourses (Callon, 1998a), via the "con-*figuration*" (Mazmanian et al., 2014) of assemblages of interactive agencing–structuring by organizing actors (Callon, 2007a), despite irrepressible and productive overflows of agencing engagements. Ultimately, organizing actors have to orchestrate digitalized offering interactions in a recurrent dynamic of re-framings and overflows by connecting with actual experiences of engaging actors, as components of an interactive offering co-function in ad-hoc and shifting heterogeneous relations in a process of constant breakdowns, feedback, and self-construction.

## 4.     CONCLUSION

With the increasingly digitalized "platformization" of networked interactions in society (Couldry & Hepp, 2017; Van Dijck et al., 2018) seeing brands as co-creational experience ecosystems becomes increasingly important from a brand "management" perspective. As noted by Wider et al. (2018) brand "managers" become more like "orchestrators" of brands, less in control of pre-formatted excursions than co-shaping meaningful brand experiences and co-evolving identities together with individuals in a joint relationship journey. Following this view, managers in co-creational lived brand experience ecosystems can be seen as orchestrators framing interactional flows of interactivities across socio-technical agencial assemblages of devices, discourses, organizations, and stakeholders in various sites of interactional creation entailing "interacted" actors (Ramaswamy & Ozcan, 2020). Since every framing of interactional flows through interactive platformization of resourced capabilities produces irrepressible and productive overflows (Callon, 1998a) affecting the valuation of outcomes, heterogeneous relations between components of interactive platforms are constantly reconfigured, thereby recursively changing the objectives, interests, and identities of actors.

While a European processual philosophy of "brands as processes of continuous becoming is a perspective widely unknown to brand research and management" according to Wider et al. (2018, p. 304), we believe it will become increasingly relevant in a hyperconnected digitalized world of lived brand experience ecosystems, where brands are increasingly co-created through interactive experiences. This perspective of "creation as a co" that puts the emphasis on creative differentiation of brands through interactional flows of experiences is at the heart of the CCP. It goes beyond a mere "exchange" of service (as in a brand SDL perspective of co-creation) to emergence and embodiment of brand experiences through enacted practices via increasingly digitalized platforms of agencing engagements and structuring organizations.

As we discussed, co-creational lived brand experience ecosystems entail networked arrangements of interactive structures–agencies, framing interactional flows across its assemblage components that both "object-ify" and "subject-ify" environments of experiences. On the one hand, this is consistent with assemblage theory and "object-oriented ontology", as in the conceptualization of Hoffman and Novak's Internet of Things (IoT)-based experiences (Hoffman & Novak, 2018, p. 1178), wherein the "traditional, human-centric conceptualization of consumer experience as consumers' internal subjective responses to branded objects may not be sufficient to conceptualize consumer experience in the IoT". On the other hand, brands are "interacted actors" (Ramaswamy & Ozcan, 2020) in the sense of their being constituted in interactions, wherein the subjectivity of experience of engaging actors is also emergent from interactional creation between an individual and a brand offering (Ramaswamy & Ozcan, 2020) and embodied in lived experiences (Ramaswamy & Ozcan, 2016) through meaningful involvement in (spatiotemporal and contextual) events.

Individuals, as co-creating experiencers, can be seen as engaged in the enactment of interactional brand creation across a multiplicity of environments in co-creational lived brand experience ecosystems (Ramaswamy, 2020; Ramaswamy & Ozcan, 2020). These can span consumer communities of practice, customers/stakeholders engaged with enterprises, managers engaged with customers/stakeholders, or more generally, human actors engaged with other human actors as well as participatory nonhuman actors. In any particular site of enactment of interactional creation in a co-creational lived brand experience ecosystem, experienced outcomes emerge from enactment of creation through interactional flows.

As individuals and enterprises become ever more inextricably linked in a hyperconnected, interdependent, world of open and social resources of stakeholding experiencers on the one hand, and enterprises' own extended network resources on the other, we hope the broadened view of interactional creation of lived brand experience ecosystems will motivate further thinking and research on interactive brand experience value creation through digitally platformed offerings, and organizational co-creation of valuable impacts in lived brand experience ecosystems.

## REFERENCES

Akaka, M. A., Vargo, S. L., & Schau, H. J. (2015). The context of experience. *Journal of Service Management, 26*(2), 206–223.
Appadurai, A. (1988). *The social life of things: Commodities in cultural perspective.* Cambridge, UK: Cambridge University Press.
Appadurai, A. (1990). Disjuncture and difference in the global cultural economy. *Theory, Culture & Society, 7*(2–3), 295–310.
Arnould, E. J., & Thompson, C. J. (2005). Consumer Culture Theory (cct): Twenty years of research. *Journal of Consumer Research, 31*(4), 868–882.
Arvidsson, A. (2006). *Brands: Meaning and value in media culture.* Hove, UK: Psychology Press.

Bajde, D. (2013). Consumer culture theory (re)visits actor–network theory: Flattening consumption studies. *Marketing Theory*, *13*(2), 227–242.

Batey, M. (2008). *Brand meaning*. New York: Routledge.

Berthon, P., Pitt, L. F., & Campbell, C. (2009). Does brand meaning exist in similarity or singularity? *Journal of Business Research*, *62*(3), 356–361.

Beverland, M. B., Lindgreen, A., & Vink, M. W. (2008). Projecting authenticity through advertising – consumer judgments of advertisers' claims. *Journal of Advertising*, *37*(1), 5–15.

Bourdieu, P. (1984). *Distinction: A social critique of the judgement of taste*. Cambridge, MA: Harvard University Press.

Braidotti, R. (2006). *Transpositions: On nomadic ethics*. Cambridge, UK: Polity Press.

Brakus, J. J., Schmitt, B. H., & Zarantonello, L. (2009). Brand experience: What is it? How is it measured? Does it affect loyalty? *Journal of Marketing*, *73*(3), 52–68.

Bratton, B. H. (2015). *The stack: On software and sovereignty*. Cambridge, MA: MIT Press.

Brodie, R. J., Hollebeek, L. D., Juric, B., & Ilic, A. (2011). Customer engagement: Conceptual domain, fundamental propositions, and implications for research. *Journal of Service Research*, *14*(3), 252–271.

Callon, M. (1998a). An essay on framing and overflowing: Economic externalities revisited by sociology. In M. Callon (Ed.), *The laws of the markets* (pp. 244–269). Oxford; Malden, MA: Blackwell Publishers/Sociological Review.

Callon, M. (1998b). Introduction: The embeddedness of economic markets in economics. *The Sociological Review*, *46*(S1), 1–57.

Callon, M. (2007a). An essay on the growing contribution of economic markets to the proliferation of the social. *Theory, Culture & Society*, *24*(7–8), 139–163.

Callon, M. (2007b). What does it mean to say that economics is performative? In D. MacKenzie, F. Muniesa, & L. Siu (Eds.), *Do economists make markets? On the performativity of economics* (pp. 310–357). Princeton, NJ: Princeton University Press.

Callon, M. (2008). Economic markets and the rise of interactive agencements: From prosthetic agencies to habilitated agencies. In T. Pinch & R. Swedberg (Eds.), *Living in a material world: Economic sociology meets science and technology studies* (pp. 29–56). Cambridge: MIT Press.

Canniford, R., & Bajde, D. (2015). *Assembling consumption: Researching actors, networks and markets*. Abingdon, UK: Routledge.

Canniford, R., & Shankar, A. (2013). Purifying practices: How consumers assemble romantic experiences of nature. *Journal of Consumer Research*, *39*(5), 1051–1069.

Castells, M. (2010). *The rise of the network society* (2nd ed.). Chichester, UK: Wiley-Blackwell.

Cetina, K. K. (2003). From pipes to scopes: The flow architecture of financial markets. *Distinktion: Journal of Social Theory*, *4*(2), 7–23.

Chandler, J. D., & Vargo, S. L. (2011). Contextualization and value-in-context: How context frames exchange. *Marketing Theory*, *11*(1), 35–49.

Cochoy, F., & Mallard, A. (2018). Another consumer culture theory. An ANT look at consumption, or how "market-things" help "cultivate" consumers. In Olga Kravets, Pauline Maclaran, Steven Miles & Alladi Venkatesh City of Publication (Eds.) *The SAGE handbook of consumer culture*, London, UK: 384–403.

Couldry, N., & Hepp, A. (2017). *The mediated construction of reality*. Cambridge: Polity Press.

da Silveira, C., Lages, C., & Simoes, C. (2013). Reconceptualizing brand identity in a dynamic environment. *Journal of Business Research*, *66*(1), 28–36.

DeLanda, M. (2006). *A new philosophy of society: Assemblage theory and social complexity*. London, UK: Bloomsbury Academic.

DeLanda, M. (2016). *Assemblage theory*. Edinburgh, UK: Edinburgh University Press.

Deleuze, G. (1994). *Difference and repetition*. New York: Columbia University Press.

Deleuze, G., & Guattari, F. (1987). *A thousand plateaus: Capitalism and schizophrenia*. Minneapolis: University of Minnesota Press.

Duff, C. (2014). *Assemblages of health: Deleuze's empiricism and the ethology of life*. New York: Springer.

Edvardsson, B., Tronvoll, B., & Gruber, T. (2011). Expanding understanding of service exchange and value co-creation: A social construction approach. *Journal of the Academy of Marketing Science*, *39*(2), 327–339.

Freytag, P. V., Gadde, L.-E., & Harrison, D. (2017). Interdependencies—blessings and curses. In H. k. Håkansson & I. Snehota (Eds.), *No business is an island: Making sense of the interactive business world* (First ed., pp. 235–252). Bingley, UK: Emerald Publishing Limited.

Gibson, J. J. (1979). *The ecological approach to visual perception.* Boston: Houghton Mifflin.

Gummesson, E., & Mele, C. (2010). Marketing as value co-creation through network interaction and resource integration. *Journal of Business Market Management, 4*(4), 181–198.

Gyrd-Jones, R. I., & Kornum, N. (2013). Managing the co-created brand: Value and cultural complementarity in online and offline multi-stakeholder ecosystems. *Journal of Business Research, 66*(9), 1484–1493.

Hoffman, D. L., & Novak, T. P. (2018). Consumer and object experience in the internet of things: An assemblage theory approach. *Journal of Consumer Research, 44*(6), 1178–1204.

Huber, T. L., Kude, T., & Dibbern, J. (2017). Governance practices in platform ecosystems: Navigating tensions between cocreated value and governance costs. *Information Systems Research, 28*(3), 563–584.

Iglesias, O., & Bonet, E. (2012). Persuasive brand management how managers can influence brand meaning when they are losing control over it. *Journal of Organizational Change Management, 25*(2), 251–264.

Iglesias, O., Ind, N., & Alfaro, M. (2013). The organic view of the brand: A brand value co-creation model. *Journal of Brand Management, 20*(8), 670–688.

Iglesias, O., Landgraf, P., Ind, N., Markovic, S., & Koporcic, N. (2020). Corporate brand identity co-creation in business-to-business contexts. *Industrial Marketing Management, 85*, 32–43.

Ind, N. (2003). *Beyond branding.* London: Kogan Page Publishers.

Ind, N., & Bjerke, R. (2007). *Branding governance: A participatory approach to the brand building process.* New York: John Wiley & Sons.

Ind, N., & Schmidt, H. (2020). *Co-creating brands: Brand management from a co-creative perspective.* London, UK: Bloombsury Business.

Ind, N., Iglesias, O., & Markovic, S. (2017). The co-creation continuum: From tactical market research tool to strategic collaborative innovation method. *Journal of Brand Management, 24*(4), 310–321.

Ind, N., Iglesias, O., & Schultz, M. (2013). Building brands together: Emergence and outcomes of co-creation. *California Management Review, 55*(3), 5–26.

Kärreman, D., & Rylander, A. (2008). Managing meaning through branding—the case of a consulting firm. *Organization Studies, 29*(1), 103–125.

Keller, K. L. (2003). Brand synthesis: The multidimensionality of brand knowledge. *Journal of Consumer Research, 29*(4), 595–600.

Kivinen, N. H., & Hunter, C. (2019). "Brand work": Constructing assemblages in gendered creative labour. *Human Relations, 72*(5), 910–931.

Kjellberg, H., & Helgesson, C.-F. (2006). Multiple versions of markets: Multiplicity and performativity in market practice. *Industrial Marketing Management, 35*(7), 839–855.

Kjellberg, H., & Helgesson, C.-F. (2007). On the nature of markets and their practices. *Marketing Theory, 7*(2), 137–162.

Kornum, N., Gyrd-Jones, R., Al Zagir, N., & Brandis, K. A. (2017). Interplay between intended brand identity and identities in a Nike related brand community: Co-existing synergies and tensions in a nested system. *Journal of Business Research, 70*, 432–440.

Kozinets, R., Patterson, A., & Ashman, R. (2017). Networks of desire: How technology increases our passion to consume. *Journal of Consumer Research, 43*(5), 659–682.

Lawer, C. (2020). Health ecosystem value design toolkit 2.0. Retrieved from https://www.umio.io/#homepage.

Lorraine, T. E. (2011). *Deleuze and Guattari's immanent ethics: Theory, subjectivity, and duration.* Albany: State University of New York Press.

Lucarelli, A., & Hallin, A. (2015). Brand transformation: A performative approach to brand regeneration. *Journal of Marketing Management, 31*(1–2), 84–106.

Lury, C. (2004). *Brands: The logos of the global economy.* London: Routledge.

Lury, C. (2009). Brand as assemblage: Assembling culture. *Journal of Cultural Economy, 2*(1–2), 67–82.

Lusch, R. F., & Vargo, S. L. (2014). *Service-dominant logic: Premises, perspectives, possibilities.* New York: Cambridge University Press.

Mackenzie, C. (2008). Introduction: Practical identity and narrative agency. In C. Mackenzie & K. Atkins (Eds.), *Practical identity and narrative agency* (pp. 1–28). New York: Routledge.

Markovic, S., & Bagherzadeh, M. (2018). How does breadth of external stakeholder co-creation influence innovation performance? Analyzing the mediating roles of knowledge sharing and product innovation. *Journal of Business Research, 88*, 173–186.

Mazmanian, M., Cohn, M., & Dourish, P. (2014). Dynamic reconfiguration in planetary exploration: A sociomaterial ethnography. *MIS Quarterly, 38*(3), 831–848.

McKinsey (2020). How Covid-19 has pushed companies over the technology tipping point—and transformed business forever. Retrieved from https://www.mckinsey.com/business-functions/strategy-and-corporate-finance/our-insights/how-covid-19-has-pushed-companies-over-the-technology-tipping-point-and-transformed-business-forever.

Merz, M. A., He, Y., & Vargo, S. L. (2009). The evolving brand logic: A service-dominant logic perspective. *Journal of the Academy of Marketing Science, 37*(3), 328–344.

Nakassis, C. V. (2012). Brand, citationality, performativity. *American Anthropologist, 114*(4), 624–638.

Onyas, W. I., & Ryan, A. (2015). Exploring the brand's world-as-assemblage: The brand as a market shaping device. *Journal of Marketing Management, 31*(1–2), 141–166.

Orlikowski, W. J. (2007). Sociomaterial practices: Exploring technology at work. *Organization Studies, 28*(9), 1435–1448.

Orlikowski, W. J., & Scott, S. V. (2015). The algorithm and the crowd: Considering the materiality of service innovation. *MIS Quarterly, 39*(1), 201–216.

Parmentier, M. A., & Fischer, E. (2015). Things fall apart: The dynamics of brand audience dissipation. *Journal of Consumer Research, 41*(5), 1228–1251.

Payne, A., Storbacka, K., Frow, P., & Knox, S. (2009). Co-creating brands: Diagnosing and designing the relationship experience. *Journal of Business Research, 62*(3), 379–389.

Peacock, K. A. (2008). Ecosystems. In S. Sarkar & A. Plutynski (Eds.), *A companion to the philosophy of biology* (pp. 351–367). Oxford: Blackwell Publishing.

Prahalad, C. K., & Ramaswamy, V. (2000). Co-opting customer competence. *Harvard Business Review, 78*(1), 79–87.

Prahalad, C. K., & Ramaswamy, V. (2002). The co-creation connection. *Strategy and Business, (27)*, 50–61.

Prahalad, C. K., & Ramaswamy, V. (2003). The new frontier of experience innovation. *MIT Sloan Management Review, 44*(4), 12–18.

Prahalad, C. K., & Ramaswamy, V. (2004a). Co-creation experiences: The next practice in value creation. *Journal of Interactive Marketing, 18*(3), 5–14.

Prahalad, C. K., & Ramaswamy, V. (2004b). *The future of competition: Co-creating unique value with customers*. Boston: Harvard Business School Press.

Preece, C., Kerrigan, F., & O'Reilly, D. (2019). License to assemble: Theorizing brand longevity. *Journal of Consumer Research, 46*(2), 330–350.

Price, L. L., & Coulter, R. A. (2019). Crossing bridges: Assembling culture into brands and brands into consumers' global local cultural lives. *Journal of Consumer Psychology, 29*(3), 547–554.

Ramaswamy, V. (2011). It's about human experiences... And beyond, to co-creation. *Industrial Marketing Management, 40*(2), 195–196.

Ramaswamy, V. (2020). Leading the experience ecosystem revolution—innovating offerings as interactive platforms. *Strategy & Leadership, 48*(3), 3–9.

Ramaswamy, V., & Ozcan, K. (2014). *The co-creation paradigm*. Stanford, CA: Stanford University Press.

Ramaswamy, V., & Ozcan, K. (2016). Brand value co-creation in a digitalized world: An integrative framework and research implications. *International Journal of Research in Marketing, 33*(1), 93–106.

Ramaswamy, V., & Ozcan, K. (2018a). Offerings as digitalized interactive platforms: A conceptual framework and implications. *Journal of Marketing, 82*(4), 19–31.

Ramaswamy, V., & Ozcan, K. (2018b). What is co-creation? An interactional creation framework and its implications for value creation. *Journal of Business Research, 84*(March), 196–205.

Ramaswamy, V., & Ozcan, K. (2020). The "interacted" actor in platformed networks: Theorizing practices of managerial experience value co-creation. *Journal of Business & Industrial Marketing, 35*(7), 1165–1178.

Rokka, J., & Canniford, R. (2016). Heterotopian selfies: How social media destabilizes brand assemblages. *European Journal of Marketing*, *50*(9–10), 1789–1813.

Sampson, T. D. (2012). *Virality: Contagion theory in the age of networks*. Minneapolis: University of Minnesota Press.

Santos-Vijande, M. L., López-Sánchez, J. Á., & Rudd, J. (2015). Frontline employees' collaboration in industrial service innovation: Routes of co-creation's effects on new service performance. *Journal of the Academy of Marketing Science*, *44*(3), 350–375.

Schembri, S. (2009). Reframing brand experience: The experiential meaning of Harley-Davidson. *Journal of Business Research*, *62*(12), 1299–1310.

Sheth, J. N., & Parvatiyar, A. (1995). The evolution of relationship marketing. *International Business Review*, *4*(4), 397–418.

Simon, H. A. ([1969] 1996). *The sciences of the artificial* (3rd ed.). Cambridge, MA: MIT Press.

Smith, D. W. (2012). *Essays on Deleuze*. Edinburgh: Edinburgh University Press.

Stach, J. (2019). Meaningful experiences: An embodied cognition perspective on brand meaning co-creation. *Journal of Brand Management*, *26*(3), 317–331.

Swaminathan, V., Sorescu, A., Steenkamp, J.-B. E. M., O'Guinn, T. C. G., & Schmitt, B. (2020). Branding in a hyperconnected world: Refocusing theories and rethinking boundaries. *Journal of Marketing*, *84*(2), 1–23.

Thomas, T. C., Price, L. L., & Schau, H. J. (2013). When differences unite: Resource dependence in heterogeneous consumption communities. *Journal of Consumer Research*, *39*(5), 1010–1033.

Thrift, N. J. (2008). *Non-representational theory: Space, politics, affect*. London: Routledge.

Tierney, K. D., Karpen, I. O., & Westberg, K. (2016). Brand meaning cocreation: Toward a conceptualization and research implications. *Journal of Service Theory and Practice*, *26*(6), 911–932.

Tonkonoff, S. (2017). Sociology of infinitesimal difference: Gabriel Tarde's heritage. In F. Depelteau (Ed.), *The Palgrave handbook of relational sociology* (1st ed., pp. 63–82). New York, NY: Springer Science+Business Media.

Vallaster, C., & von Wallpach, S. (2013). An online discursive inquiry into the social dynamics of multi-stakeholder brand meaning co-creation. *Journal of Business Research*, *66*(9), 1505–1515.

Van Dijck, J., Poell, T., & De Waal, M. (2018). *The platform society: Public values in a connective world*. Oxford: Oxford University Press.

Vargo, S. L., & Lusch, R. F. (2004). Evolving to a new dominant logic for marketing. *Journal of Marketing*, *68*(1), 1–17.

Vargo, S. L., & Lusch, R. F. (2008). Service-dominant logic: Continuing the evolution. *Journal of the Academy of Marketing Science*, *36*(1), 1–10.

Vargo, S. L., & Lusch, R. F. (2016). Institutions and axioms: An extension and update of service-dominant logic. *Journal of the Academy of Marketing Science*, *44*(1), 5–23.

Vatin, F. (2013). Valuation as evaluating and valorizing. *Valuation Studies*, *1*(1), 31–50.

von Wallpach, S., Hemetsberger, A., & Espersen, P. (2017a). Performing identities: Processes of brand and stakeholder identity co-construction. *Journal of Business Research*, *70*, 443–452.

von Wallpach, S., Voyer, B., Kastanakis, M., & Muhlbacher, H. (2017b). Co-creating stakeholder and brand identities: Introduction to the special section. *Journal of Business Research*, *70*, 395–398.

Weick, K. E. (1995). *Sensemaking in organizations*. Thousand Oaks, CA: Sage Publications.

Wider, S., von Wallpach, S., & Muhlbacher, H. (2018). Brand management: Unveiling the delusion of control. *European Management Journal*, *36*(3), 301–305.

Williams, J. (2008). *Gilles Deleuze's logic of sense: A critical introduction and guide*. Edinburgh: Edinburgh University Press.

# 4. Reassessing brand co-creation: towards a critical performativity approach

*Andrea Lucarelli, Cecilia Cassinger and Jacob Östberg*

## 1. INTRODUCTION

The present chapter outlines a critical performativity approach to brand co-creation. We will both unpack the foundation of such a critical perspective and assess the utility in regards to the specific concept of brand co-creation. In doing so, we merge the scattered accounts of what may be labelled "critical branding studies" (e.g. Arvidsson, 2006; O'Reilly, 2006; Bertilsson & Tarnovskaya, 2017) – a smaller stream of critical marketing studies (Tadajewski, 2010; Zwick, 2013; Zwick & Cayla, 2011) – with the increasing focus on *performativity* in branding studies. In fact, while performativity is increasingly applied to branding (see Nakassis, 2012; Lucarelli & Hallin, 2015; Onyas & Ryan, 2015; Stevens et al., 2015; Törmälä & Gyrd-Jones, 2017; Von Wallpach et al., 2017a), its critical potential has neither been explored nor exploited. Critical performativity refers here to a relational and embodied form of *doing critique* that gives attention to the capability of material-discursive practices to constitute the worldly phenomena they refer to. In other words, critical performativity is here understood as the scrutiny of constitutive features of language, body and materiality and its inseparability from action while ontologically not merely focusing on practices; performative actions are thereby not understood as intentional, but rather as material, embodied and practised.

In its capacity as a concept that has caught the imagination and been popularized by academics and managers alike, we suggest that brand co-creation is an ideal concept through which to critically scrutinize contemporary processes of value creation and their productive capacities. Brand co-creation implies the blurring of boundaries between branding and consumption processes. Value does not reside in brands, but emerges when brands are used by consumers (Iglesias et al., 2017). This idea – that consumption is a value-producing activity and not merely an activity whereby the value created in production is devoured – is one of the core features of marketing scholarship building on anthropology (McCracken, 1986) which has found a permanent place in marketing as consumer culture theory (Arnould & Thompson, 2005). Despite the long tradition of marketing scholarship building on anthropology and thus stressing co-creation of value, the proponents of a service-dominant logic (Vargo & Lusch, 2004) have tended to neglect this theoretical background and claim brand value co-creation as a conceptual innovation in marketing (Arnould, 2006).

Furthermore, the concept brings together two of the most important, and perhaps debated theories in marketing research, namely *branding* and *co-creation*. Although these theories singularly are objects of critical scrutiny (see e.g. Arvidsson, 2006 for branding and Hietanen et al., 2018 for co-creation), the critique has not yet concerned the joint form of "brand co-creation". While these types of critiques are highly insightful they tend to stay at a fairly abstract level and can be characterized as "armchair" critique. The utility and viability of the learnings, outcomes and consequences of these studies can thus be questioned. In order to develop a more performative critique the chapter develops some new pathways, which, as pointed out by Tadajewski (2010, p. 213), "involve [an] active and subversive intervention into managerial discourses" (Spicer et al., 2009, p. 538). Such intervention involves a more constructive endeavour where scholars do not only "deconstruct" the taken-for-granted nature of marketing concepts, but try to revitalize them. In advocating a performativity perspective in critical management studies, Spicer et al. (2009, p. 548) argue for an affirmative critical approach that scrutinizes "forms of social domination encouraging emancipation/resistance", whilst at the same time caring for and respecting the lived experiences and struggles of those working within management. Theory and practice, then, is understood as performed and as "in becoming", which opens up a space for more action-based and experimental critical research. To conduct critical research means to be open for unexpected results and a readiness to challenge one's own assumptions accordingly.

In this chapter, we take inspiration from the critical performativity perspective in revisiting brand co-creation. To this end, we first outline some of the problems with the previous critiques levelled against brand co-creation. We then make an argument for why a performative critique is needed to reimagine the potential of brand co-creation beyond the realm of marketing. Subsequently, we outline three ways of performing critiques that reassess the concept of brand co-creation: brand assemblage, brand activism, and brand ecology. We end the chapter by proposing some directions of a research agenda for critically performativity studies of brand co-creation.

## 2.    CRITIQUES OF BRAND CO-CREATION: A BRIEF REVIEW

In this section we unpack the foundations of the previous critiques directed towards branding and co-creation within critical marketing research (e.g. Eckhardt et al., 2018; Marion, 2006). Three streams of critical research are identified on the basis of a close reading of the literature: brand co-creation as *exploitation*, *governmentality*, and *social fantasy*. These streams may be understood as different views of the agency of brands and consumers in processes of co-creation. The first stream views co-creation as the control and manipulation of consumers; the second stream views co-creation as providing means by which consumers can govern themselves; the third stream views co-creation as an ideological fantasy that consumers choose to identify with. In the following we seek to disclose the ideologies and assumptions embedded in the critical knowledge of brand co-creation and demonstrate the lack of a "performative intent" of this type of critique, in other words, the absence of real effects on brand co-creation practice and discourse (Spicer et al., 2009, pp. 554).

### 2.1    Brand Co-Creation as Exploitation

The first critical research stream mainly deals with brand co-creation as the exploitation of consumers' labour. Scholars belonging to this research stream typically approach consumption as a type of immaterial labour that produces brand value (Arvidsson, 2006, 2008). The concept of immaterial labour is used to denote "labour that produces the informational and cultural content of the commodity" (Lazzarato, 1996, p. 133). Arvidsson (2006), for instance, views the brand as an expression of a communicative logic of capitalism arguing that value is generated by forms of immaterial labour that are autonomous in that they are not directly controlled by capital. Such labour is defined by its capacity to produce things such as brand community, social relations, and shared experiences and meaning among consumers.

The concern in this critical stream of research is consumers' well-being and the social consequences of participating in co-creation processes. For example, Cova and Dalli (2009) argue that consumers may feel exploited because their social and cultural engagements with brands are not recognized by organizations. Consumers are also charged a premium price for branded goods, in which they have invested time and energy adding to their experiences of exploitation (Zwick et al., 2008). How then should we understand the consumers' motivations of engaging with brands? The critical scholarship in this stream primarily attributes the ongoing exploitation of consumers' labour to their false consciousness of social reality (Eckhardt et al., 2018). Consequently, research is also often criticized for reducing consumer agency in co-creation processes (Pongsakornrungsilp & Schroeder, 2011) as well as overemphasizing the productive capacities of consumption (Zwick, 2013).

## 2.2    Brand Co-Creation as Governmentality

The second stream of research concerns a critique towards the neoliberal ideology that underpins brand co-creation. For example, Zwick et al. (2008), drawing on Foucauldian thought, present the main argument that "co-creation" as a marketing strategy represents a neoliberal form of governmentality typical for advanced capitalist societies (see also Cova et al., 2011). In a broad sense, for scholars in the second stream, governmentality includes any programme, discourse or strategy that attempts to shape human conduct and the ways in which we act upon ourselves. Governmentality involves an understanding of power as being de-centralized and mobilized through discourse; power works through the capacity of individual subjects to govern themselves in a way that benefits capital rather than the subjects themselves (Arvidsson, 2006). In a critical note, Cova et al. (2011) argue that successful co-creation relies on "ambiences that program consumer freedom to evolve in ways that permit the harnessing of consumers' newly liberated, productive capabilities" (p. 233). Understood as governmentality, co-creation is conceived of as a construct mainly operating in and through discourse.

The second stream underscores the question of regulating power in processes of co-creation. Consumer agency is considered to be temporal, and the consumer is not viewed to be on equal terms with the organization in the co-creation process. Lury (2004), for instance, points towards the asymmetrical relationship of exchange where the brand serves as a site of interactivity – not of interaction. In a similar vein Zwick et al. (2008) argue that co-creation is yet another form of (neoliberal) marketing strategy to bring about particular forms of life in which consumers voluntarily supply unwaged, exploited, yet enjoyed labour to create value for firms that the consumers themselves are excluded from. The brand is here viewed as a frame restricting and directing what can be created, when and where it can be created, and by whom. This way of interpreting brands as platforms of action reveals the unsettled side of co-creation, where these platforms can become battlefields for dominance, control and ownership (Lessig, 2005). Thus, to sum up, the second wave emphasizes brands as agentic objects and control mechanisms in processes of co-creation, especially on digital platforms.

## 2.3    Brand Co-Creation as Social Fantasy

The third critical research stream is informed by a fusion of psychoanalysis and Marxism in the work of Žižek (1989), and suggests that branding works on the level of ideological fantasy (Carah, 2010; Murtola, 2012; Zwick & Bradshaw, 2016). This form of ideology critique implies that consumers in brand co-creation processes are aware that they may be manipulated, but for different reasons let it happen. They may enjoy it or cannot be bothered to change their habits. Hence, here agency is mainly ascribed to the consumer and the social context in which she or he is embedded. A way of explaining why consumers engage in co-creation is that it is the most rational thing they can do in view of the neoliberal ideological fantasy that currently structures their social reality, which holds that brands have become ubiquitous to everyday life and that we must engage with them. We are perhaps even able to cynically comment on or joke about engaging in brand co-creation, while continuing such practices. Critical scholarship, then, seeks to unmask "the production of ideology in the social world" (Carah, 2010, p. 165). One example of unmasking and resisting such fantasy is by overidentifying with its message (Murtola, 2012; Žižek, 1989). In the context of brand co-creation this may involve expressing an enthusiastic loyalty with brand values and visions. Overidentification with the "obscene underside of power" is believed to lead to political transformation by dismantling ideology and revealing the dark side of powers that are keen on representing themselves in a pleasant manner (Bryar, 2018, p. 5). In the context of branding, such obscene powers have been observed in nation-branding campaigns that promote dictatorial countries by glossing over violations of human rights. Overidentification also involves parody and comedy in order to reveal the absurdities of branding (Harold, 2004). Examples of studies on this topic include the impersonations of Borat by Sacha Baron Cohen, the anti-capitalist activism of Reverend Billy and the Church of Stop Shopping, and cultural jamming activities performed by collectives, such as Adbusters (Carducci, 2006; Murtola, 2012; Sandlin & Callahan, 2009).

## 3.    CRITICAL "PERFORMATIVE" BRAND CO-CREATION

The brief overview of the three streams of critical research demonstrate that there has already been an in-depth critical engagement with the ideological assumptions underpinning brand co-creation. Much has thus been done, but we still suggest that a more networked, embodied, and lived account of the process of brand co-creation and its critical implications and consequences for stakeholders is needed. Networked in this context implies a reticular, omnipresent way to approach and criticize co-creation; embodied here implies not only a bodily but also an actively practised way to rethink co-creation; and finally lived here implies not only a type of scholarship that is engaged and personal but also a more mundane attitude towards the way co-creation is practised and researched. Building on the previous critiques of brand co-creation summarized above, this part turns to performativity as a relational and embodied form of *doing critique*. Adding a *performative* dimension to critical branding studies helps capture the productive and processual qualities of brand co-creation. Performativity is commonly associated with the works of Butler (1993) on the performative constitution of identities, which she developed from Austin's (1962) writings on the performativity of language and Derrida's (1986) work on iteration. The core assumption in theories on performativity is the constitutive features of language and its inseparability from action. Actions are not understood as intentional, but most of the time, embodied and practised in other than purely linguistic forms as presented in the work of science and technology scholars, such as Barad (2007) and Haraway (1988) (see Thrift, 2008 for an account of the genealogy of performativity). This means that the focus of performativity studies is on the conditions that enable the production of a phenomenon, in this case, brand co-creation.

A critical performative perspective on branding means to embark on a "different relationship between concept, theory and practices" (Gibson-Graham, 2008, p. 618). It implies acknowledging that a concept or a theory, such as brand co-creation, is not neutral. Rather, it has been shaped according to certain ideas, knowledges, and interests. Approaching brand co-creation in a critical performative manner consequently means unpacking such a knowledge apparatus in a way that could help practitioners and academics to gain understanding for how the enactment of brand co-creation could result in domination and oppression (see Cova et al., 2015), or how the concept may be used in an affirmative manner, to enable us to "see openings, to provide a space of freedom and possibility" (Gibson-Graham, 2008, p. 619). The adoption of a critical performative approach to brand co-creation is not predicated on a specific view taken by an individual author, but rather on the way in which performativity emerges as assembled perspectives (see Thrift, 2008) that scholars can adopt when dealing with theory, concepts, methods, as well as empirical phenomena.

# 4.    RAMIFICATIONS

The present section accounts for three specific ramifications of the critical performative approach to brand co-creation, all sharing the same onto-epistemological and axiological premises, being genealogically interlinked to performativity. Each ramification more specifically gives a more detailed and concrete illustration of the implications for brand co-creation. These ramifications are not exhaustive nor exclusionary, but should be understood as different materializations of performativity. This is because critical performativity has a Janus face insofar as it can be used to critically examine performances of the brand co-creation discourse, while at the same time doing critique by subversively intervening in performativity of brand co-creation to push for change in the field of knowledge (Spicer et al., 2009). What we thus aim to contribute with is not merely academic viewpoints aimed to criticize scholarship on brand co-creation, but also more constructive, yet critical, viewpoints enabling an adaptation of a brand co-creation theory and practice.

## 4.1    Brand Assemblage

The first ramification of the critical performative approach to brand co-creation stems from recent theoretical advances in marketing influenced by "relation-centric" perspectives (Hill et al., 2014) that draw inspiration mainly from actor network theory and assemblage theory. Conventional branding has typically been either firm-centric, implying that brand value stems from company activities (e.g. Aaker, 1991), or consumer-centric, implying that brand value stems from consumer activities, such as creating "linking value" (Cova, 1997) or "identity value" (Elliott & Wattanasuwan, 1998). The concept of brand co-creation, then, represents a blurring of these two distinct spheres and a suggestion that value might be better conceptualized as happening in the intersection between the two. The relation-centric perspective goes beyond this rather dichotomous view of firms and consumers as the two primary nodes relevant for creating brand meaning and infusing a brand with value. Rather than attributing power to either firms or consumers, or the two of them together as implied in the co-creation perspective, the relation-centric perspective – especially the assemblage perspective that has been applied specifically to brands (Lury, 2009; Rokka & Canniford, 2016) – views a brand as an entity distinguished by the *relations* between the components that make up the assemblage.

The brand assemblage perspective thus aims to embrace relations between components as ontologically more salient than the components themselves by stipulating that phenomena take on form and meaning through their relations with other things (Hill et al., 2014). Of particular importance in the assemblage perspective is the questioning of the primacy of the individual, whether these individuals are consumers or managers, by not taking the subject–object hierarchy for granted (Bajde, 2013; Cluley and Brown, 2015; Hill et al., 2014). Rather, attention is expanded to how the relations within the assemblage are enacted and re-enacted by actors, whether they are subjects, objects, or institutions, to better understand the dynamics of the connections among the actors (Canniford & Shankar, 2013).

While the assemblage perspective, at least given the way it has been adopted in marketing, is not overtly critical, the brand assemblage perspective has the potential to start undermining some of the naive ideological underpinnings of marketing scholarship (Hackley, 2003). Both the firm-centric and the consumer-centric approach, as well as the conventional co-creation perspective which blurs the two, is marred by an implicit understanding that value is produced by intentional action. Managers, consumers, or a mix of the two, are seen as agents with an implicit agenda leading them to produce value. Value, furthermore, is construed as something solely positive and the mere fact that a brand has market success is seen as an implicit proof that value has indeed been produced. In the brand assemblage perspective brands are instead conceptualized as heterogeneous, co-creational and evolving configurations, involving multiple authors that not only include firms and consumers, but also other heterogeneous and evolving sets of components with varying capacities (Lucarelli & Hallin, 2015; Parmentier & Fischer, 2015; Rokka & Canniford, 2016).

By theorizing brands from an assemblage perspective rather than the more essentialist conceptions underlying the conventional co-creation perspective, three things are accomplished. First, by emphasizing the multiple and heterogeneous aspects of brand assemblages, firms and consumers are dethroned from the center stage and instead seen as part of a larger web of components generating brand value. Second, these components have certain capacities based on what they are able to do when interacting with one another. Of particular importance here are material capacities since they have been curiously absent from conventional branding theories. The material capacities refers to the physical capacities of components and might be exemplified with the way in which a high-heeled shoe interacts with a wearer and makes him/her stand and walk in a particular way (see Parmentier, 2016). The other broad category of components' capacities are expressive and involve communication and can only be activated in relation to interpretive beings. Staying with the example of high-heeled shoes, such objects have been coded as "feminine" and "sexy" in many contexts and will be interpreted as such by individuals' knowledge of these cultural codes. Third, the brand assemblage perspective emphasizes that brand assemblages are not fixed, but involved in dynamic and emergent processes as they move in time and space and to different degrees integrate and/or detach components. The productive and processual qualities of brand co-creation are thus highlighted.

## 4.2    Brand Activism

The second ramification revisits the co-creation process of brands engaged in activism and deals with the performative conditions and production of the relation between brand activism and publics. Brand activism is an increasingly common marketing strategy by which corporations seek to position themselves in the marketplace by "taking public stances on social and political issues" (Vredenburg et al., 2020, p. 444). Moorman (2020, pp. 388–389) similarly defines brand activism as "public speech or actions focused on partisan issues made by or on behalf of a company using its corporate or individual brand name". Brand activism may be further understood as incorporating the social and environmental critique directed at corporations into marketing actions aimed at accomplishing social change (Aronczyk, 2013; Klein, 2000). The performativity approach to how meanings of activist brands are co-created may be understood as resting on two premises. First, brand meanings are shaped by embodied actions in the public sphere. Second, meanings are related to the vulnerable condition of resistance in brand activism, which inserts a critical ethical potential into the co-creation process.

Corporate brand actors, like Patagonia, Nike, and Lush, nowadays adopt the tactics of activism, resistance, and protest to support political views and actions. Patagonia's chief storyteller Vincent Stanley (2020, p. 394) narrates the company's shift to becoming an activist brand through its interventions in environmentalist struggles: "We have sued the Trump Administration when it reversed protections for Bears Ears Monument. We have called out climate deniers in Congress." The brand-led activism Stanley refers to is based on direct actions in the public sphere that in various ways embodies the brand's activist spirit, such as petition writing, demonstrations, and physical interventions (e.g. blocking a road). Actions are jointly carried out by employees, who take on the role as social activists and campaigners, and by consumers, who can access the activist experience through the brand story, or perform as activists through participating in protests organized by their local brand activist group (Aronczyk, 2013). The collective actions that make up activist brands do not fit neatly within commonly used concepts in the brand co-creation literature, like brand community, brand public, or crowd (see e.g. Arvidsson & Caliandro, 2016 for a review), which tend to neglect the performative dimension of brand co-creation. The organization of brand co-creation of activist brands has more resemblance with the flat hierarchy and networked communication of social movements, such as the Occupy Movement. From a critical performativity perspective, Butler (2015, 2016) understands social movements as public assemblies, which she describes as "deliberate exposures to power" by people who come together and make embodied political claims in public space. Assemblies are performed in and through democratic deliberations and exposures of the self before others in order to contest and resist given norms in the public space. Public assemblies are furthermore characterized by vulnerability as a mode of resistance. In resistance, the vulnerable confront the dominant order and in so doing make themselves vulnerable to both violence and loss (Butler, 2016). Activists become vulnerable to violence in confrontations with the police or counter-protestors, while at the same time risk losing their identity and relationships in taking a political stance.

Hence, the co-creation process of the meaning of activist brands is tied to embodied public action (not only by consumers but anyone who is committed to the activist cause) and a condition of vulnerability. Embodied political enactments, in which something is at risk and therefore vulnerable, seems necessary in brand activism to prevent political standpoints from becoming free floating signifiers and reduced to mere symbolism. For example, Hoffman et al. (2020, p. 172) demonstrate how political antagonism is replaced with "affirmative consent" and consensus in Nike's 2018 Dream Crazier campaign, featuring the football player Colin Kaepernick who initiated a protest movement against racial injustice by kneeling during the American National Anthem before the start of the games. Because the campaign does not show the protest, its message is detached from the political act. Kaepernick becomes yet another representative of Nike's ethos "Just do it" (Hoffmann et al., 2020), rather than the face of radical political change.

The mode of resistance that underpins the Dream Crazier campaign recapitulates the critical performativity approach to the co-creation of activist brand meanings. First, Kaepernick's resistance is not an autonomous individual performance. He is not the first, nor the last, to protest against racial discrimination; his act is inserted into a North American history of civil right protests. Second, Kaepernick cannot control the Black Lives Matter movement in which his protest is situated, but rather he is being performed by its collective enactment. The protest exposes his and many other black people's vulnerable condition manifested in the loss of his contract and sponsorships and the violence that they confront in the shape of angry spectators and politicians. It demonstrates the ethical potential of brand activism in exposing the vulnerable conditions of marginalized groups as a way of revealing the material conditions of their existence and thereby challenging injustice.

## 4.3    Brand Ecology

The third application of a critical brand performative perspective entails an ecological view on brands (Giovanardi et al., 2013) where co-creation is more specifically the place of interaction inhabited by stakeholder practices. Such practices are seen as both the materialization of the functional and the representational aspects of brands. It is an approach that helps analyse the "living" condition that is usually analysed in brand co-creation (such as questions of value, substance, and appearance) while at the same time allowing for consideration of the ideological condition in which brand co-creation emerges. It posits that brand co-creation is a neoliberal-managerial practice, and for this reason it should be rather seen as a biopolitical apparatus, that is as a system controlling and ordering stakeholders involved in branding practices. Such a biopolitical apparatus and the subsequent brand co-creation is not, however, necessarily "negative" as per previous critical branding studies (see Arvidsson, 2006). Instead brand co-creation as a concept must be viewed as alive, and as such is "affirmative". It is affirmative because it keeps at the centre politics and biological life in their ecological complexity, featuring a mode of being which is based on immunitarian mutuality (see Esposito, 2011). In the case of the present chapter it means that the mutual determination of the "brand" on one side and "co-creation" on the other, results in the "brand co-creation", as practical mundane responses or actions performed by companies, institutions, consumers, and legislators in co-existence.

Based on this perspective, ecology can be seen as the "modus operandi" of brand co-creation, recognizing the multiple connections that contribute to making brand co-creation more alive, and thus visible. Brand co-creation should be recognized as a circular process of "translation" where the practices of translation should be analysed as ecology of practice (Stengers, 2005), by being attentive to how branding as a form of biopolitical language transforms everyday life practices. One example would be the progressive biopolitical transformation of individuals from human beings into living brands by the action of different branding practices as they are materialized by media, companies, consultants, and peers. Furthermore, brand co-creation should not be seen as a sort of social contract among actors whereby these come to an agreement about certain social conditions for co-creation; instead it should be seen as an epistemic co-evolution, as an area of political agonism (see also Mouffe, 1999, 2005). This is linked to the idea that such political agonism contains "change" understood as spatio-temporal analysis in which brand co-creation should be considered as a place where different relationships among different stakeholders are in a state of ecological (in)balance and transformation.

Accordingly, since brand co-creation is a matter of an "inhabited place" and therefore a site for political agonism, the researchers' role here is crucial as they have to pay attention in sketching articulations and differences in relation to various political implications. Brand ecology is therefore an epistemological project whereby ecology features as the study of the brand co-creation as performative habitats in which different stakeholders can potentially synergistically act together and the ethos and habitus enacted in the customs, social organizations, and creative-regulative principles by which they strive or fail to achieve this end. In this way, it can be affirmative as it looks backward in attempting to understand how certain states of affairs (i.e. processes as the institution of brand identity), situations (i.e. effect and events as the highlighting of brand equity), and living things (i.e. brand logos and symbols) came to be nurtured. It can also look forward by mapping the existence of epistemic political terrains to analyse the promises and problems for transforming in different ways products, companies, institutions, and places that are co-creatively branded. This is potentially transformative of the neoliberal status quo in which branding ideology, according to traditional brand management thought, resides.

The implications of this perspective are important to highlight. The locus of brand co-creation moves from the company–advertising–consumer nexus to the multiple-stakeholders nexus (i.e. ecology), where the process of co-construction is performative thus creating brand performances (Von Wallpach et al., 2017b). However, this does not mean to look at the ecology understood as an ecosystem in service studies (Vargo et al., 2017), thus closed, or as pointed out by Hietanen et al. (2018) ideologically neoliberal. Rather it should be understood as an "ecosophy", thus open, or biopolitical (Lucarelli, 2019), as it should not underestimate the important political "agency" ecology since it might be less democratic in terms of stakeholder participations and more indicative of an apparently invisible and less explicit political dimension. Further this means a focus on action as a repository of expression (see Hietanen et al., 2014) as brand co-creation could be analysed as "affective" power relationships between expression, practice and technologies of production in a constant process of transformation situated within networks, hierarchies and discourses of power, being shaped through political practices at various scales. Such an approach analytically focuses on practices (i.e. what people do with things) and points out the entanglement of processes, embodied practices and technologies in which brand co-creation process analysis should not be based on singularity (i.e. singular, sequential observations as relationships), but on multiplicity (i.e. multiple, parallel observations as practices). Analytically, where practices unfold is where the consequences of those practices (i.e. what is made visible in those practices, what is rendered invisible, how is it made visible) are more visible and able to be changed and modified by researchers and engaged practitioners.

## 5.      TOWARDS A CRITICAL PERFORMATIVITY APPROACH

In this chapter we aimed to offer a critical performative approach to analyse and assess brand co-creation with the aim of arriving at a future research agenda where we sketch some pathways to be adopted for critical studies in brand co-creation specifically, and branding more generally. Towards this aim, we have taken account of the present status of critical branding studies and have attempted to build a bridge to focus on *performativity* as a way to infuse branding studies with a critical edge. In the section above we laid out three ramifications that all, in different ways, build on this idea. While all the three are different, they rest on some common denominators that could be presented as characterizing a critical performative perspective on brand co-creation. On an overarching level they all attempt to reassess the concept of brand co-creation from a non-representational perspective. Such critique is part of an emergent stream of marketing research anchored in relational ontologies and non-representational theory (e.g. Hill et al., 2014; Medway & Warnaby, 2017). Hill et al. (2014, p. 377) describe relational ontologies in marketing as "a set of approaches that understand 'things in the world' as taking on form and meaning through their relations with other things, rather than possessing any essential substance." They suggest that non-representationalism enables researchers to "'grow their ontologies' and make inventive use of relational theories" (p. 384) to direct attention towards new and marginalized (non)human actors that are not part of the mainstream accounts (see also Thrift, 2008). This entails widening the concept of brand co-creation to encompass an ongoing performance dispersed among different actors. It is argued that such an approach is particularly apt to critically scrutinize brand co-creation as an emblem of a participatory communicative logic of capitalism and its connectedness to social and political structures (Carah, 2010; Dean, 2005; Zwick & Bradshaw, 2016).

The three ramifications above – brand assemblage, brand activism, and brand ecology – may be understood as located on a continuum where they are situated from a "softer" to a "harder" critical approach. With harder and softer critical approaches, we mean that the ramifications to varying degrees enable a critique of the structural conditions of brand co-creation (e.g. social justice issues).

In this regard one can consider brand assemblage as having a critical potential that is not coming to full fruition in its present use in marketing theory (e.g. Parmentier & Fischer, 2015; Rokka & Canniford, 2016). This is unfortunate, since a more explicit critical agenda conceptualizing brands as assemblages would be able to counterbalance the heroic depictions of both managers and consumers as responsible for creating brand value. Furthermore, this perspective has the potential to undermine the fantasy of relative harmony existing within brand assemblages to instead stress the constant tensions at play as assemblages de- and re-territorialize. Because of the presently unleashed potential of the brand assemblage perspective, this ramification thus ends up on the softer end of the spectrum.

The second ramification of brand activism may be placed in the middle of the continuum as it has a stronger emphasis on the political and ethical potential of brand co-creation tied to market activism, protest, and resistance. It proposes that meanings of activist brands emerge in embodied actions in the public sphere and are related to vulnerability as a mode of activism. The concept of vulnerability, as it is used in this chapter, highlights the potential for dependency of actors due to their embodied conditions (i.e. as humans we are equally subjected to suffering and loss). Thus, it challenges the view of co-creation as involving individual autonomous performances of brand managers and consumers. The co-creation of activist brand meanings may be understood as performed in and through public assemblies in which people come together to expose conditions of social injustice in ways that often go beyond speech. This raises questions of the fruitfulness of understanding this type of brand co-creation as taking place within certain consumer communities or crowds and how each and one of us are caught up in the performativity of activist brands. The recognition that we depend on others and that others depend on us, can open up a space to embrace critical stances that question power asymmetries and forms of exploitations in co-creation processes.

Finally the third ramification, the ecological perspective, contains maybe the hardest, or rather radical, critical edge as the entire theoretical apparatus is motivated by understanding brand co-creation as biopolitical ecology of situated and transforming practices devoted to political potency, thus being fully performative in the sense that can set the stage for important revisiting of the relationship between the notion of brand and co-creation and the way they are theorized and practised at the same time. The criticality here resides in the radical political potency of controversies that can be encountered in the experimentation of practices that are done by both researchers and the different stakeholders which might lead to change. Brand co-creation could thereby be conceptualized as always in change, holding "potentiality" for transforming relations, for the good and for the bad.

Although the three different ramifications sketched above thus differ in their level of critique, they nevertheless rest on a common ground that can be summarized in three points that resonate with the overall non-representational ethos:

1. They are dispersed, emergent and epistemic viewpoints on the way in which brand co-creation is materializing and creating relations. They thus illustrate the principle that brand co-creation studies must take into consideration more elements that make up a brand than what is typically done in both traditional brand management research as well as critical branding studies. In order to analyse how, what and why brand co-creation emerges one needs to "examine the often 'unrepresentable' details or minutiae of life through post-human phenomenological accounts of culture; 'precognitive' explanations of networked agency as well as investigating affective and atmospheric intensities that play a part in the assemblage of markets and consumer cultures" (Hill et al., 2014, p. 378). By contrast to focusing on the idealized, heroic stories of how managers and consumers co-create brands, attention should instead be directed to the constitutive role of brand co-creation and the material, embodied, and lived outcomes of its performativity.

2. They rest on a strategic reimagining of social relations in brand co-creation processes, which allows for affirmative action and new possibilities of engagement among different actors, such as consumers, companies, and institutions. In this sense, the critical account proposed here does not seek to understand brand co-creation as it currently stands, but to rethink some of its core premises. Giving attention to instances of performativity and the way that they question and rearticulate material, networked and corporeal boundaries in brand co-creation processes may lead to more meaningful and ethical engagement among actors.

3. They build on an idea of ideology as an important, albeit many times invisible, element of everyday activity that gets reinforced through scholarship. A concept such as brand co-creation thus has to be treated as an ideological apparatus in becoming. Such an acknowledgement, then, potentially leads to research, and ideally also to management practices, that have a more nuanced view of how brands are indeed co-created.

All in all, this means that paying more attention to the minutiae of all the human and non-human actors implicated in brand co-creation would enable us to expose how the value supposedly created by brands does not appear out of thin air. Rather, history seems to repeat itself in the sense that the division of winners and losers in brand value co-creation seems to be following, and reinforcing, the usual patterns of haves and have-nots in society. While there is no reason to regurgitate the Marxist notions of false consciousness that we accounted for above, we still feel it pertinent to paraphrase Marx and Engels as a plea to take a more nuanced and inclusive stance to the field of brand co-creation henceforth: Co-creators of the world, unite!

## REFERENCES

Aaker, D.A. (1991). *Managing Brand Equity: Capitalizing on the Value of a Brand Name*. New York, NY: Free Press.
Arnould, E.J. (2006). Service-dominant logic and consumer culture theory: Natural allies in an emerging paradigm. *Marketing Theory*, *6*(3), 293–297.
Arnould, E.J., & Thompson, C.J. (2005). Consumer culture theory (CCT): Twenty years of research. *Journal of Consumer Culture*, *31*(4), 868–882.
Aronczyk M. (2013). *Branding the nation: The global business of national identity*. New York: Oxford University Press.
Arvidsson, A. (2006). *Brands: Meaning and Value in Media Culture*. London: Routledge.
Arvidsson, A. (2008). The ethical economy of customer coproduction. *Journal of Macromarketing*, *28*(4), 326–338.
Arvidsson, A., & Caliandro, A. (2016). Brand public. *Journal of Consumer Research*, *42*(5), 727–748.
Austin, John L. (1962). *How to do Things with Words*. Oxford: Clarendon Press.
Bajde, D. (2013). Consumer culture theory (re) visits actor–network theory: Flattening consumption studies. *Marketing Theory*, *13*(2), 227–242.
Barad, K. (2007). *Meeting the Universe Halfway: Quantum Physics and the Entanglement of Matter and Meaning*. Durham, NC: Duke University Press.
Bertilsson, J., & Tarnovskaya, V. (2017). *Brand Theories: Perspectives on Brands and Branding*. Lund: Studentlitteratur AB.
Bryar, T. (2018). Preferring Zizek's Bartleby Politics. *International Journal of Žižek Studies*, *12*(1), accessed 2021-02-09 at http://zizekstudies.org/index.php/IJZS/article/view/993/1074.
Butler, J. (1993). *Bodies that Matter: On the Discursive Limits of Sex*. London: Routledge.
Butler, J. (2015). *Notes Toward a Performative Theory of Assembly*. Cambridge, MA: Harvard University Press.
Butler, J. (2016). Rethinking vulnerability and resistance. In Butler, J., Zeynep Gambetti, Z., & Sabsay, L. (eds), *Vulnerability in Resistance* (pp. 12–27). Durham, NC: Duke University Press.
Canniford, R., & Shankar, A. (2013). Purifying practices: How consumers assemble romantic experiences of nature. *Journal of Consumer Research*, *39*(5), 1051–1069.
Carah, N. (2010). *Pop Brands: Branding, Popular Music, and Young People*. New York, NY: Peter Lang.
Carducci, V. (2006). Culture jamming: A sociological perspective. *Journal of Consumer Culture*, *6*(1), 116–138.
Cluley, R., & Brown, S.D. (2015). The dividualised consumer: Sketching the new mask of the consumer. *Journal of Marketing Management*, *31*(1–2), 107–122.
Cova, B. (1997). Community and consumption: Towards a definition of the "linking value" of product or services. *European Journal of Marketing*, *31*(3/4), 297–316.
Cova, B., & Dalli, D. (2009). Working consumers: The next step in marketing theory? *Marketing Theory*, *9*(3), 315–339.
Cova, B., Dalli, D., & Zwick, D. (2011). Critical perspectives on consumers' role as "producers": Broadening the debate on value co-creation in marketing processes. *Marketing Theory*, *11*(3), 231–241.

Cova, B., Pace, S., & Skålén, P. (2015). Brand volunteering: Value co-creation with unpaid consumers. *Marketing Theory*, *15*(4), 465–485.

Dean, J. (2005). Communicative capitalism: Circulation and the foreclosure of politics. *Cultural Politics*, *1*(1), 51–74.

Derrida, J. (1986). Declarations of independence. *New Political Science*, *15* (Summer), 7–15.

Eckhardt, G.M., Varman, R., & Dholakia, N. (2018). Ideology and critical marketing studies. In *Routledge Companion to Critical Marketing Studies* (pp. 306–318). New York, NY: Routledge.

Elliott, R., & Wattanasuwan, K. (1998). Brands as symbolic resources for the construction of identity. *International Journal of Advertising*, *17*(2), 131–144.

Esposito, R. (2011). *Immunitas: The Protection and Negation of Life*. Cambridge: Polity.

Gibson-Graham, J.K. (2008). Diverse economies: Performative practices for other worlds. *Progress in Human Geography*, *32*(5), 613–632.

Giovanardi, M., Lucarelli, A., & Pasquinelli, C. (2013). Towards brand ecology: An analytical semiotic framework for interpreting the emergence of place brands. *Marketing Theory*, *13*(3), 365–383.

Hackley, C. (2003). We are all customers now... Rhetorical strategy and ideological control in marketing management texts. *Journal of Management Studies*, *40*(5), 1325–1352.

Haraway, D. (1988). Situated knowledges: The science question in feminism and the privilege of partial perspective. *Feminist Studies*, *14*(3), 575–599.

Harold, C. (2004). Pranking rhetoric: "Culture jamming" as media activism. *Critical Studies in Media Communication*, *21*(3), 189–211.

Hietanen, J., Andéhn, M., & Bradshaw, A. (2018). Against the implicit politics of service-dominant logic. *Marketing Theory*, *18*(1), 101–119.

Hietanen, J., Rokka, J., & Schouten, J.W. (2014). Commentary on Schembri and Boyle (2013): From representation towards expression in videographic consumer research. *Journal of Business Research*, *67*(9), 2019–2022.

Hill, T., Canniford, R., & Mol, J. (2014). Non-representational marketing theory. *Marketing Theory*, *14*(4), 377–394.

Hoffmann, J., Nyborg, K., Averhoff, C., & Olesen, S. (2020). The contingency of corporate political advocacy: Nike's "dream crazy" campaign with Colin Kaepernick. *Public Relations Inquiry*, *9*(2), 155–175.

Iglesias, O., Ind, N., & Alfaro, M. (2017). The organic view of the brand: A brand value co-creation model. In *Advances in Corporate Branding* (pp. 148–174). London: Palgrave Macmillan.

Klein, N. (2000). *No Logo: Taking Aim at the Brand Bullies*. Toronto: Knopf Canada.

Lazzarato, M. (1996). Immaterial Labour. In Virno, P. & Hardt, M. (eds), *Radical Thought in Italy: A Potential Politics* (pp. 133–147). Minneapolis, MN: University of Minnesota Press.

Lessig, L. (2005). *Free Culture: The Nature and Future of Creativity*. London: Penguin Books.

Lucarelli, A. (2019). Constructing a typology of virtual city brand co-creation practices: An ecological approach. *Journal of Place Management and Development*, *12*(2), 227–247.

Lucarelli, A., & Hallin, A. (2015). Brand transformation: A performative approach to brand regeneration. *Journal of Marketing Management*, *31*(1–2), 84–106.

Lury, C. (2004). *Brands: The Logos of the Global Economy*. London: Routledge.

Lury, C. (2009). Brand as assemblage: Assembling culture. *Journal of Cultural Economy*, *2*(1–2), 67–82.

Marion, G. (2006). Marketing, ideology and criticism: Legitimacy and legitimization. *Marketing Theory*, *6*(2), 245–262.

McCracken, G. (1986), Culture and consumption: A theoretical account of the structure and movement of the cultural meaning of consumer goods. *Journal of Consumer Research*, *13*(1), 71–84.

Medway, D., & Warnaby, G. (2017). Multisensory place branding: A manifesto for research. In Campelo, A. (ed.), *Handbook on Place Branding and Marketing*. Cheltenham, UK and Northampton, MA, USA: Edward Elgar Publishing, 147–159.

Moorman, C. (2020). Commentary: Brand activism in a political world. *Journal of Public Policy & Marketing*, *39*(4), 388–392.

Mouffe, C. (1999). Deliberative democracy or agonistic pluralism? *Social Research*, *66*(3), 745–758.

Mouffe, C. (2005). *The Return of the Political* (Vol. 8). London: Verso.

Murtola, A.-M. (2012). Materialist theology and anti-capitalist resistance, or What would Jesus buy? *Organization*, *19*(3), 325–344.

Nakassis, C.V. (2012). Brand, citationality, performativity. *American Anthropologist, 114*(4), 624–638.

Onyas, W.I., & Ryan, A. (2015). Exploring the brand's world-as-assemblage: The brand as a market shaping device. *Journal of Marketing Management, 31*(1–2), 141–166.

O'Reilly, D. (2006). Commentary: Branding ideology. *Marketing Theory, 6*(2), 263–271.

Parmentier, M.A. (2016). High heels. *Consumption Markets & Culture, 19*(6), 511–519.

Parmentier, M.A., & Fischer, E. (2015). Things fall apart: The dynamics of brand audience dissipation. *Journal of Consumer Research, 41*(5), 1228–1251.

Pongsakornrungsilp, S., & Schroeder, J.E. (2011). Understanding value co-creation in a co-consuming brand community. *Marketing Theory, 11*(3), 303–324.

Rokka, J., & Canniford, R. (2016). Heterotopian selfies: How social media destabilizes brand assemblages. *European Journal of Marketing, 50*(9/10), 1789–1813.

Sandlin, J.A., & Callahan, J.L. (2009). Deviance, dissonance, and détournement: Culture jammers use of emotion in consumer resistance. *Journal of Consumer Culture, 9*(1), 79–115.

Spicer, A., Alvesson, M., & Kärreman, D. (2009). Critical performativity: The unfinished business of critical management studies. *Human Relations, 62*(4), 537–560.

Stanley, V. (2020). Commentary: Patagonia and the business of activism. *Journal of Public Policy & Marketing, 39*(4), 393–395.

Stengers, I. (2005). Ecology of practices and technology of belonging. *Cultural Studies Review, 11*(1), 183–196.

Stevens, L., Cappellini, B., & Smith, G. (2015). Nigellissima: A study of glamour, performativity and embodiment. *Journal of Marketing Management, 31*(5–6), 577–598.

Tadajewski, M. (2010). Critical marketing studies: logical empiricism, 'critical performativity' and marketing practice. *Marketing Theory*, 10(2), 210–222.

Thrift, N. (2008). *Non-Representational Theory: Space, Politics, Affect.* London: Routledge.

Törmälä, M., & Gyrd-Jones, R.I. (2017). Development of new B2B venture corporate brand identity: A narrative performance approach. *Industrial Marketing Management, 65*, 76–85.

Vargo, S.L., & Lusch, R.F. (2004) Evolving to a new dominant logic for marketing. *Journal of Marketing, 68*(1), 1–17.

Vargo, S.L., Akaka, M.A., & Vaughan, C.M. (2017). Conceptualizing value: A service-ecosystem view. *Journal of Creating Value, 3*(2), 117–124.

Von Wallpach, S., Hemetsberger, A., & Espersen, P. (2017a). Performing identities: Processes of brand and stakeholder identity co-construction. *Journal of Business Research, 70*, 443–452.

Von Wallpach, S., Voyer, B., Kastanakis, M., & Mühlbacher, H. (2017b). Co-creating stakeholder and brand identities: Introduction to the special section. *Journal of Business Research, 70*, 395–398.

Vredenburg, J., Kapitan, S., Spry, A., & Kemper, J. A. (2020). Brands taking a stand: Authentic brand activism or woke washing? *Journal of Public Policy & Marketing, 39*(4), 444–460.

Žižek, S. (1989). *The Sublime Object of Ideology.* London: Verso.

Zwick, D. (2013). Utopias of ethical economy: A response to Adam Arvidsson. *Ephemera, 13*(2), 393–405.

Zwick, D., & Bradshaw, A. (2016). Biopolitical marketing and the ideology of social media brand communities. *Theory, Culture & Society, 33*(5), 91–115.

Zwick, D., & Cayla, J. (eds) (2011). *Inside Marketing: Practices, Ideologies, Devices.* Oxford: Oxford University Press.

Zwick, D., Bonsu, S.K., & Darmody, A. (2008). Putting consumers to work: Co-creation and new marketing governmentality. *Journal of Consumer Culture, 8*(2), 163–196.

# PART II

# CO-CREATION OF INTANGIBLE BRAND ASSETS

# 5. Co-creation of intangible brand assets: an integrative S-D logic/organic view of brand-based conceptual framework

*Victor Saha, Venkatesh Mani, Praveen Goyal and Linda D. Hollebeek*

## 1. INTRODUCTION

Service-dominant (S-D) logic has generated a paradigm shift in the way value creation is examined. That is, while brands were previously conceived of as physical entities or mental representations (Stern, 2006), an S-D logic perspective of brands emphasizes their evolving phenomenological or experiential process. Consistent with S-D logic's sixth foundational premise, which reads: "The customer is always a co-creator of value" (Vargo and Lusch, 2016, p. 7), brands are increasingly conceptualized as co-creative, experiential entities by service system stakeholders, including customers and firms.

This conceptualization of brands derived from S-D logic is consistent with the organic view of the brand (OVB), which emphasizes that brands are co-created through the resource contributions made by various stakeholders, including firms, customers and so on (Iglesias et al., 2013). S-D logic classifies these resource contributions as *operand resource* contributions (i.e., those which are acted upon to produce a product/item) and *operant resource* contributions (i.e., those which are used to act upon the operand resources; Hollebeek, 2019). Both firms and their customers draw on operand as well as operant resources to (co-)create intangible brand assets (Wang et al., 2020), which refer to non-physical (vs. physical as in the case of tangible brand assets) brand attributes that enable firms to improve their efficiency and effectiveness in the marketplace (Srivastava et al., 1998).

Thus, drawing on the S-D logic and OVB perspectives, we argue that a firm's intangible brand assets are dynamic (vs. static) entities that emerge from the collaborative involvement of firms and their customers in their co-creation (i.e., the intangible assets; Kucharska et al., 2018). That is, by contributing their respective resources, service system stakeholders – in particular, firms and their customers – jointly co-create intangible brand assets (Hollebeek et al., 2019a). In particular, we focus on the intangible brand assets of *brand heritage*, *brand identity*, and *brand meaning* due to their wide emphasis in the brand co-creation literature (Weidmann et al., 2011; Kennedy and Guzmán, 2016; Berthon et al., 2009). We selected these particular intangible brand assets, as they are the most widely researched intangible brand-related assets in the literature. That is, given the extensive availability of high-quality research for each of these constructs, our resulting conceptual model (developed later in this chapter) reflects a high level of theoretical grounding and rigor.

However, the existing brand co-creation literature has failed to keep up with the role of actors' resource contributions (i.e., engagement) in co-creating these intangible brand assets (Kamasak, 2017). That is, while the brand co-creation literature has addressed the generic idea of actors investing their resources in their brand interactions (Hollebeek et al., 2019a; Kumar et al., 2019), it has largely overlooked the specific resource contributions made by particular actors in co-creating these intangible brand assets. In this chapter, we thus extend Srivastava et al.'s (1998) work on intangible market-based assets, which are those assets that commingle with the firm's external environment (e.g., customers) to create value, and that of Hollebeek et al. (2019a), which addresses the role of customers' resource investments in co-creating brand value. However, despite their contribution, these latter authors' more general analyses do not address the role of these customer and firm contributions in the co-creation of intangible brand assets, as undertaken in this chapter.

Based on this gap, we provide insight into the strategic adoption of value co-creation to develop a brand's intangible heritage, identity, and meaning-related assets (Merchant and Rose, 2013; Vallaster and Von Wallpach, 2013; Kennedy and Guzmán, 2016). Through these analyses, we offer a phenomenological, experience-centric re-conceptualization of these intangible assets, which are viewed to be dynamic (vs. static) in nature. We also detail firms' and customers' specific resource contributions that facilitate the co-creation of these intangible assets. Through these analyses, we then develop a conceptual framework that highlights firm/customer resource contributions in co-creating the intangible brand assets of brand meaning, brand heritage and brand identity.

Our contributions are as follows. First, adopting the S-D logic and OVB, we contribute to the brand co-creation literature by investigating the specific resource investments made by a firm and its customers in co-creating a brand's intangible assets. These insights about resource investments required for co-creating intangible brand assets provide evidence for the dynamic nature of these assets.

Second, we develop a conceptual framework that proposes our key, dynamic intangible brand assets of *brand heritage*, *brand identity* and *brand meaning* to help managers design their brand co-creation strategies. The framework provides specific resource contributions of the firm and their customers in co-creating these dynamic intangible brand assets. As such, the framework helps managers to nurture specific benefits from customers' and the firm's brand-related resource contributions. For instance, managers can develop effective co-creation mechanisms where these resource contributions can be leveraged, thereby creating a strong brand in the process.

The chapter's remainder is structured as follows. We next review a customer co-created brand (CCB) based on the S-D logic and OVB perspective, followed by the development of a conceptual framework that shows how the intangible assets of brand heritage, brand identity and brand meaning are co-created through customer/firm interactions. We conclude by offering important implications that arise from our analyses.

## 2. CUSTOMER CO-CREATED BRAND: AN INTEGRATIVE S-D LOGIC/ORGANIC BRAND PERSPECTIVE

The American Marketing Association defines a brand as "A name, term, design, symbol, or any other feature that identifies one seller's good or service as distinct from those of other sellers" (AMA, 2017). Brands are no longer confined to the traditional boundaries of customer/firm interactions, where the firm typically decides upon the idea of what the "brand" stands for, and consumers would subsequently adopt (or reject) that idea based on their brand-perceived value

proposition (Srivastava et al., 1998; Iglesias et al., 2020). That is, consumers actively participate in the process of creating valuable brand experiences, rather than just acting as passive
purchasers (Brodie et al., 2011; Hollebeek et al., 2014, 2017; Naidoo and Hollebeek, 2016).
Consequently, brand co-creation extends beyond the customer/firm dyad to encompass other
stakeholders, including suppliers, competitors, and so on, in line with the AMA's definition of
marketing (Hatch and Schultz, 2010; Hollebeek et al., 2020a).

In this vein, Iglesias et al.'s (2013) organic brand view-based perspective posits that "brands
are organic entities because they are built together with various stakeholders and many parts of
this process are beyond the control of the organization" (p. 671). At its core, the organic brand
view suggests that brand value is co-created by multiple stakeholders in a fluid space through
ongoing negotiation (Iglesias et al., 2013). However, while this perspective emphasizes the
role of different stakeholders in co-creating brands, it does not explain the fundamental features and characteristics that co-created brands possess.

Based on this gap, we integrate the organic brand perspective with an S-D logic-informed
view to deduce the hallmarks of co-created brands, which we refer to as *customer co-created
brands* (CCBs). CCBs refer to brands that are co-created by virtue of the active investments
made by a firm and its customers, which may also be affected by other brand stakeholders and
their (inter)actions and decision-making (Hollebeek et al., 2019b). Therefore, CCBs comprise
aspects that are beyond the control of the firm, as well as customers.

## 3.    CONCEPTUAL FRAMEWORK

We next develop a conceptual framework of CCBs that shows how a brand's intangible
heritage-, identity-, and meaning-based assets are co-created by virtue of customer/firm interactions (Figure 5.1). We discuss the framework's components below.

### 3.1    Brand Heritage

Brand heritage refers to a brand's history and longevity that stands as proof for its performance
or reliability (Weidmann et al., 2011). A strong-heritage brand is imbued with strong values
that have been carried forward from the past into its present-day brand (Hakala et al., 2011).
For example, owing to its strong brand heritage, consumers of all ages recognize the brand
Coca-Cola through the years, even though it is over 100 years old (Merchant and Rose, 2013).

Brand heritage is not developed by the firm alone; it also requires specific consumer contributions. For instance, while a firm contributes its history, core values and brand symbols to
build a strong brand heritage, consumers, likewise, contribute factors including brand-related
nostalgia, imagery and word-of-mouth to enable the brand heritage to be successfully
co-created.

Firms contribute to brand heritage co-creation through their history that represents a rich,
eventful past developed through effective brand communication and consumer benefits
(Hakala et al., 2011). However, this firm-provided history would not suffice without consumer
reciprocation through their brand-perceived nostalgia (Mencarelli et al., 2020). Consumer
nostalgia sees them trust the brand and thus, boosts their brand loyalty (Wen et al., 2019).

Firms also contribute core values to brand heritage co-creation, which represent the brand's
consistent guiding principles (Hakala et al., 2011). These core values are not modified under

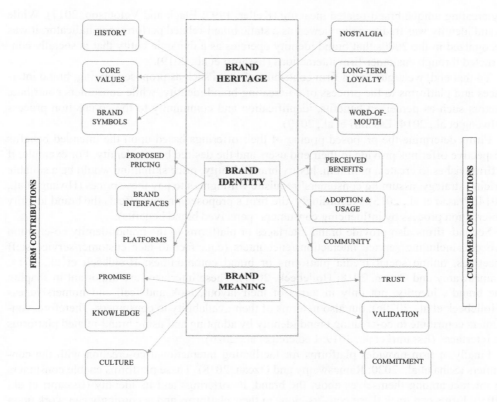

*Figure 5.1      Conceptual framework*

changing trends or market conditions (Stylidis et al., 2020). In response, consumers will tend to contribute their long-term loyalty in building the brand's heritage (Alrawadieh et al., 2019). Consumer loyalty, in turn, motivates the firm to stick to the brand's core values even in challenging times. Consequently, the brand's heritage is strengthened through its enhanced consumer-perceived reliability.

Finally, firms use symbols to display their brand heritage to consumers (Rose et al., 2016). These symbols can be in the form of brand-related logos, taglines, or any other visual identity (e.g., color, trademarks; Urde et al., 2007). That is, a strong-heritage brand contributes to the co-creation process through the provision of strong symbols, essentially reminding consumers about its reliability and performance (Hakala et al., 2011). Correspondingly, consumers contribute to the brand heritage co-creation process by spreading (positive) brand-related word-of-mouth.

### 3.2      Brand Identity

Brand identity refers to the unique set of associations that a brand desires to create for itself, based on which its perceptual image is being developed (Aaker, 1996; Burmann et al., 2009; Kennedy and Guzmán, 2016). A strong identity differentiates a brand from its competitors by creating unique brand-related meaning (Keller, 1993; Black and Veloutsou, 2017). While brand identity was traditionally viewed as a static brand-related performance indicator, it was recognized in the 2000s that brand identity operates as a dynamic entity that is socially constructed through customer/firm interactions (Essamri et al., 2019).

To that end, we argue that a firm contributes factors such as proposed pricing, brand interfaces and platforms to the process of co-creating brand identity, while consumers contribute factors such as perceived benefits, identification and community to the co-creation process (Hwang et al., 2014; Essamri et al., 2019).

Firms determine the proposed pricing of their offerings based upon the intended benefits respective offerings provide to their end users and the desired brand identity. For example, if a firm wishes to create a premium, luxury brand identity, price skimming would be a suitable pricing strategy, assuming consumers' requisite willingness to pay these prices (Hwang et al., 2014; Prasad et al., 2015). Accordingly, the firm's proposed pricing affects the brand identity co-creation process by influencing consumers' perceived brand benefits).

Second, firms also provide brand interfaces or platforms in the brand identity co-creation process, including service interactions/encounters (e.g., face-to-face customer/service staff meetings, online social media platforms or brand communities; Breidbach et al., 2014; Ramaswamy and Ozcan, 2018; Hollebeek, 2019). These interfaces are important in shaping the brand's identity, not only in terms of their layout, look and feel, and immersiveness (Hollebeek et al., 2020b), but also in terms of their availability to consumers. Therefore, consumers contribute to co-creating brand identity by adopting and using brand-related platforms or interfaces (Essamri et al., 2019; Leclercq et al., 2020).

Finally, a firm provides platforms for facilitating interactional co-creation with the consumers (Saha et al., 2020; Ramaswamy and Ozcan, 2018). These platforms enable consumers to interact among themselves about the brand, its offerings and its identity (Essamri et al., 2019). Firms can track these conversations in their platforms and accordingly can work upon strengthening their intended identity for the brand. Correspondingly, consumers contribute to co-creating the brand identity by forming communities that interact across various social platforms (Essamri et al., 2019). The perspective of the communities, as evident from the interactions on the platforms, essentially reveals the nature of identity that a brand has acquired for itself.

### 3.3    Brand Meaning

Given the dynamic nature of brands, brand meaning, rather than being controlled by the firm alone, is co-created through customer–firm and customer-to-customer (or peer) interactions (Berthon et al., 2009; Clark et al., 2020). Co-created brand meaning has been defined as "a discursive social process in which salient stakeholders may directly or indirectly, purposefully or coincidentally, interact via text to shape certain aspects of a brand's social reality" (Vallaster and Von Wallpach, 2013, p. 1506). Through these interactive processes, firms contribute a number of key factors to the co-creation of brand meaning such as promise, knowledge and culture, while consumers contribute factors such as trust, experience and commitment (Bindroo et al., 2016; Rajagopal, 2017; Rosenthal and Brito, 2017).

First, to position their brand in (prospective) customers' consideration set, firms tend to lay out specific promises around the brand's central value proposition (Bindroo et al., 2016). In the process of making, delivering, and keeping promises, consistency is important to foster and maintain customer trust (Hollebeek and Macky, 2019). By contrast, abandoning promises can create significant backlash from consumers, including negative word-of-mouth or boycotting the brand (Berthon et al., 2009; Bowden et al., 2017). Therefore, managing brand-related promises represents an important firm contribution in the brand meaning co-creation process. Consequently, consumers contribute their trust to the co-creation process when they perceive the brand to be authentic and credible (Wang et al., 2020). Without the presence of trust, a brand cannot acquire its desired meaning. Hence, trust forms an essential contribution of the consumers to the process of brand meaning co-creation.

Second, firms provide brand-related knowledge to consumers that is intended to create brand awareness, strong brand perceptions, and preference (Berthon et al., 2009; He et al., 2016), thus facilitating the co-creation of brand meaning. However, consumers would expect this knowledge to be factual and reliable (Brown et al., 2003). Accordingly, they would provide validation of the knowledge provided by the firm, which in turn would place the brand in consumers' consideration set (Rajagopal, 2017). Hence, validation of the knowledge constitutes consumers' contribution to the co-creation of brand meaning.

Third, brand culture is important in shaping brand meaning (Rosenthal and Brito, 2017). Brand culture is first incited by the firm, after which brand meaning is co-constructed and co-created by its audiences, including customers. Strong-culture brands tend to be favorably judged by consumers, particularly when brand culture is rooted in strong core brand values (e.g., the BodyShop's anti-animal testing stance). Consequently, consumers are expected to display elevated levels of commitment to strong-culture brands, in turn stimulating their growth (Terglav et al., 2016).

## 4.    DISCUSSION, IMPLICATIONS, AND FURTHER RESEARCH

In this chapter, we explored customer brand co-creation, which we viewed from a dynamic S-D logic/organic brand perspective. We identified the central intangible assets of a customer co-created brand (CCB): brand meaning, brand heritage, and brand identity, based on which we developed a conceptual framework. The framework highlights the role of firm as well as customer contributions in co-creating these intangible brand assets, as also detailed in the chapter.

The resource contributions that we have highlighted in our study are either firm-initiated or consumer-initiated. These resources require stimulus from both the involved actors. Though some of the resources can be argued to be contributed by both consumers and firms, however, our focus in this study is to present those resources which can be initiated only by either of the actors, and not by the other. For instance, nostalgia is memory-related emotions that can be perceived by individuals (i.e., consumers) only, and not by non-physical entities (i.e., firms). Though firms do provide stimulus for creating nostalgia, nostalgia as a resource contribution to co-create brand heritage can be provided by consumers only. Hence, we have marked nostalgia as customer contributions. Similarly, symbols such as logos, taglines and trademarks can be provided by firms only, and not by consumers. Though consumers can express their judgment about these symbols, the contribution of these symbols in co-creating brand heritage lies in the purview of the firm only. Next, brand interfaces are the platforms that firms create to engage with the customers. These platforms are provided and curated by the firms only (and not customers). Though there are instances where consumers have created platforms on social media to discuss a brand, those platforms are not considered official by the firm and hence firms do not necessarily actively respond to and participate in those platforms. Instead, firms create their own platforms (brand interfaces) which they have control over, and which they use to actively respond to customer queries, concerns and community discussions.

Based on these analyses, we offer the following theoretical and managerial contributions and implications for further research. First, while the brand co-creation literature has burgeoned in recent years, research addressing primary stakeholders' (e.g., customer/firm) contributions to co-creating intangible brand-related assets lags behind to date. Based on this gap, we provide insight into the co-creation of intangible brand assets through resource contributions by primary stakeholders (Hollebeek et al., 2020a), thus making an important contribution to the brand co-creation literature.

Second, by developing a framework that highlights the role of intangible brand assets in co-creating brand value, our analyses provide managers with an enhanced understanding of brand heritage, brand identity, and brand meaning, which can be strategically leveraged. Managers can leverage these intangible assets by facilitating an effective co-creation mechanism through which our suggested resource contributions can be exchanged with customers to elevate brand value. Overall, our analyses reveal that brand-related resource contributions can advance brand-related co-created value development, while also capitalizing on customer resource contributions that may engender firm cost savings (Hollebeek et al., 2019a).

Finally, this study can help managers in moving away from the traditional static conceptualization of intangible brand assets (brand heritage, brand identity, and brand meaning), and instead consider them as dynamic entities that are built through consumer-based co-creation processes (see also Srivastava et al., 1998). This understanding would significantly alter prevailing branding tactics and strategies and, in turn, inspire them to adopt new strategies ensuring consumers' more active engagement.

We also lay out important directions for further research. First, future research may wish to build on our work by conducting empirical study (qualitative or quantitative) that examines those resource types that firms/customers are particularly willing (vs. less willing) to offer in brand co-creation processes and their respective outcomes (Hollebeek et al., 2019a).

Second, while our analyses integrate an S-D logic and organic brand view, we encourage the undertaking of further study that explicitly incorporates key elements from S-D logic's evolving lexicon into its analyses (e.g., resource integration, service systems, institutions; Vargo and Lusch, 2016). Further, alternate theoretical frames may be used to guide further research in this area, including social practice theory or service logic.

Finally, we note that some of the constructs in our conceptual framework may be inter-related. Given that our proposed constructs are related to different brand facets, specific construct inter-relationships may inevitably exist. For example, culture/symbols may be related to brand identity, since culture/symbols play an important role in creating brand identity. To tease out these issues, future research may wish to investigate particular construct inter-relationships, thereby refining our attained insight.

## REFERENCES

Aaker, D. A. (1996). Measuring brand equity across products and markets. *California Management Review, 38*(3), 102–120.

Alrawadieh, Z., Prayag, G., Alrawadieh, Z., & Alsalameen, M. (2019). Self-identification with a heritage tourism site, visitors' engagement and destination loyalty: The mediating effects of overall satisfaction. *Service Industries Journal, 39*(7–8), 541–558.

American Marketing Association (AMA) (2017). Definition of Brand. Approved by the AMA Board of Directors. Retrieved from https://www.ama.org/the-definition-of-marketing-what-is-marketing/ on 20 June, 2020.

Berthon, P., Pitt, L., Parent, M., & Berthon, J. P. (2009). Aesthetics and ephemerality: Observing and preserving the luxury brand. *California Management Review, 52*(1), 45–66.

Bindroo, V., He, X., & Echambadi, R. (2016). Satisfaction–repurchase intentions relationship: Exploring the contingent roles of consideration set size and price consciousness. *Customer Needs and Solutions, 3*(3–4), 115–125.

Black, I., & Veloutsou, C. (2017). Working consumers: Co-creation of brand identity, consumer identity and brand community identity. *Journal of Business Research, 70*, 416–429.

Bowden, J., Conduit, J., Hollebeek, L., Luoma-Aho, V., & Solem, B. (2017). Engagement valence duality and spillover effects in online brand communities. *Journal of Service Theory and Practice, 27*(4), 877–897.

Breidbach, C., Brodie, R., & Hollebeek, L. (2014). Beyond virtuality: From engagement platforms to engagement ecosystems. *Managing Service Quality, 24*(6), 592–611.

Brodie, R., Hollebeek, L. D., Ilic, A., & Juric, B. (2011). Customer engagement: Conceptual domain, fundamental propositions & implications for research in service marketing. *Journal of Service Research, 14*(3), 252–271.

Brown, P., Hesketh, A., & Williams, S. (2003). Employability in a knowledge-driven economy. *Journal of Education and Work, 16*(2), 107–126.

Burmann, C., Hegner, S., & Riley, N. (2009). Towards an identity-based branding. *Marketing Theory, 9*(1), 113–118.

Clark, M., Lages, C., & Hollebeek, L. (2020). Friend or foe? Customer engagement's value-based effects on fellow customers and the firm. *Journal of Business Research*, in press, DOI: https://doi.org/10.1016/j.jbusres.2020.03.011.

Essamri, A., McKechnie, S., & Winklhofer, H. (2019). Co-creating corporate brand identity with online brand communities: A managerial perspective. *Journal of Business Research, 96*, 366–375.

Hakala, U., Lätti, S., & Sandberg, B. (2011). Operationalising brand heritage and cultural heritage. *Journal of Product and Brand Management, 20*(6), 447–456.

Hatch, M. J., & Schultz, M. (2010). Toward a theory of brand co-creation with implications for brand governance. *Journal of Brand Management, 17*(8), 590–604.

He, K., Zhang, X., Ren, S., & Sun, J. (2016, October). Identity mappings in deep residual networks. In *European Conference on Computer Vision* (pp. 630–645). Cham: Springer.

Hollebeek, L. D. (2019). Developing business customer engagement through social media engagement-platforms: An integrative S-D logic/RBV-informed model. *Industrial Marketing Management, 81*(Aug), 89–98.

Hollebeek, L. D., & Macky, K. (2019). Digital content marketing's role in fostering consumer engagement, trust, and value: Framework, fundamental propositions, and implications. *Journal of Interactive Marketing, 45*(1), 27–41.

Hollebeek, L., Clark, M., Andreassen, T., Sigurdsson, V. & Smith, D. (2020a). Virtual reality through the customer journey: Framework and propositions. *Journal of Retailing & Consumer Services*, in press, DOI: https://doi.org/10.1016/j.jretconser.2020.102056.

Hollebeek, L. D., Glynn, M., & Brodie, R. (2014). Consumer brand engagement in social media: Conceptualization, scale development and validation. *Journal of Interactive Marketing, 28*(2), 149–165.

Hollebeek, L. D., Juric, B., & Tang, W. (2017). Virtual brand community engagement practices: A refined typology and model. *Journal of Services Marketing, 31*(3), 204–217.

Hollebeek, L., Kumar, V., & Srivastava, R. K. (2020b). From customer-, to actor-, to stakeholder engagement: Taking stock, conceptualization, and future directions. *Journal of Service Research*, forthcoming, DOI: 10.1177/1094670520977680.

Hollebeek, L., Sprott, D., & Andreassen, T. (2019a). Customer engagement in evolving technological environments. *European Journal of Marketing, 53*(9), 1665–1670.

Hollebeek, L. D., Srivastava, R. K., & Chen, T. (2019b). S-D logic-informed customer engagement: Integrative framework, revised fundamental propositions, and application to CRM. *Journal of the Academy of Marketing Science*, *47*(1), 161–185.

Hwang, Y., Ko, E., & Megehee, C. M. (2014). When higher prices increase sales: How chronic and manipulated desires for conspicuousness and rarity moderate price's impact on choice of luxury brands. *Journal of Business Research*, *67*(9), 1912–1920.

Iglesias, O., Ind, N., & Alfaro, M. (2013). The organic view of the brand: A brand value co-creation model. *Journal of Brand Management*, *20*, 670–688.

Iglesias, O., Landgraf, P., Ind, N., Markovic, S., & Koporcic, N. (2020). Corporate brand identity co-creation in business-to-business contexts. *Industrial Marketing Management*, *85*, 32–43.

Kamasak, R. (2017). The contribution of tangible and intangible resources, and capabilities to a firm's profitability and market performance. *European Journal of Management and Business Economics*, *26*(2), 252–275.

Keller, K. L. (1993). Conceptualizing, measuring, and managing customer-based brand equity. *Journal of Marketing*, *57*(1), 1–22.

Kennedy, E., & Guzmán, F. (2016). Co-creation of brand identities: Consumer and industry influence and motivations. *Journal of Consumer Marketing*, *33*(5), 313–323.

Kucharska, W., Flisikowski, K., & Confente, I. (2018). Do global brands contribute to the economy of their country of origin? A dynamic spatial approach. *Journal of Product & Brand Management*, *27*(7), 768–780.

Kumar, V., Rajan, B., Gupta, S., & Dalla Pozza, I. (2019). Customer engagement in service. *Journal of the Academy of Marketing Science*, *47*(1), 138–160.

Leclercq, T., Hammedi, W., Poncin, I., Kullak, A., & Hollebeek, L. (2020). When gamification backfires: The impact of perceived justice on online community contributions. *Journal of Marketing Management*, *36*(5–6), 550–577.

Mencarelli, R., Chaney, D., & Pulh, M. (2020). Consumers' brand heritage experience: Between acceptance and resistance. *Journal of Marketing Management*, *36*(1–2), 30–50.

Merchant, A., & Rose, G. M. (2013). Effects of advertising-evoked vicarious nostalgia on brand heritage. *Journal of Business Research*, *66*(12), 2619–2625.

Naidoo, V., & Hollebeek, L. D. (2016). Higher education brand alliances: Investigating consumers' dual-degree purchase intentions. *Journal of Business Research*, *69*(8), 3113–3121.

Prasad, A., Venkatesh, R., & Mahajan, V. (2015). Product bundling or reserved product pricing? Price discrimination with myopic and strategic consumers. *International Journal of Research in Marketing*, *32*(1), 1–8.

Rajagopal, A. (2017). Research continuum on consumer education and brand knowledge: A critical analysis. *Journal of Transnational Management*, *22*(4), 235–259.

Ramaswamy, V., & Ozcan, K. (2018). What is co-creation? An interactional creation framework and its implications for value creation. *Journal of Business Research*, *84*, 196–205.

Rose, G. M., Merchant, A., Orth, U. R., & Horstmann, F. (2016). Emphasizing brand heritage: Does it work? And how? *Journal of Business Research*, *69*(2), 936–943.

Rosenthal, B., & Brito, E. P. Z. (2017). The brand meaning co-creation process on Facebook. *Marketing Intelligence & Planning*, *35*(7), 923–936.

Saha, V., Mani, V., & Goyal, P. (2020). Emerging trends in the literature of value co-creation: A bibliometric analysis. *Benchmarking: An International Journal*, *27*(3), 981–1002.

Srivastava, R. K., Shervani, T., & Fahey, L. (1998). Market-based assets and shareholder value: A framework for analysis. *Journal of Marketing*, *62*(1), 2–18.

Stern, B. B. (2006). What does brand mean? Historical-analysis method and construct definition. *Journal of the Academy of Marketing Science*, *34*(2), 216–223.

Stylidis, K., Hoffenson, S., Rossi, M., Wickman, C., Söderman, M., & Söderberg, R. (2020). Transforming brand core values into perceived quality: A Volvo case study. *International Journal of Product Development*, *24*(1), 43–67.

Terglav, K., Ruzzier, M. K., & Kaše, R. (2016). Internal branding process: Exploring the role of mediators in top management's leadership–commitment relationship. *International Journal of Hospitality Management*, *54*, 1–11.

Urde, M., Greyser, S. A., & Balmer, J. M. (2007). Corporate brands with a heritage. *Journal of Brand Management, 15*(1), 4–19.

Vallaster, C., & Von Wallpach, S. (2013). An online discursive inquiry into the social dynamics of multi-stakeholder brand meaning co-creation. *Journal of Business Research, 66*(9), 1505–1515.

Vargo, S. L., & Lusch, R. F. (2016). Institutions and axioms: An extension and update of service-dominant logic. *Journal of the Academy of Marketing Science, 44*(1), 5–23.

Wang, X., Tajvidi, M., Lin, X., & Hajli, N. (2020). Towards an ethical and trustworthy social commerce community for brand value co-creation: A trust-commitment perspective. *Journal of Business Ethics, 167*(1), 137–152.

Wen, T., Qin, T., & Liu, R. R. (2019). The impact of nostalgic emotion on brand trust and brand attachment. *Asia Pacific Journal of Marketing and Logistics, 31*(4), 1118–1137.

Wiedmann, K. P., Hennigs, N., Schmidt, S., & Wuestefeld, T. (2011). The importance of brand heritage as a key performance driver in marketing management. *Journal of Brand Management, 19*(3), 182–194.

# 6. Co-creation or co-destruction? Value-based brand formation

*Andrea Hemetsberger, Maria Kreuzer and Hans Mühlbacher*

## 1. FROM VALUE CO-CREATION TO INTERACTIVE VALUE FORMATION

Since its inception in marketing and branding literature, the idea of value formed in interaction between co-creating actors (Iglesias et al., 2013; Prahalad & Ramaswamy, 2004; Ramirez, 1999; Vargo & Lusch, 2004) has enjoyed ample attention and developed into a full-fledged "dominant" logic of co-creation (Vargo & Lusch, 2016). Standing on the shoulders of important thinkers of the Scandinavian school of services marketing (Grönroos, 1982; Gummesson, 1987, 2006) that introduced the notion of "interactive marketing", or the French school's idea of "servuction" that production and consumption of services are closely interwoven (Eiglier & Langeard, 1987), contemporary management research accords that value-in-use is produced in interaction (Grönroos & Voima, 2013; Vargo & Lusch, 2004, 2016) rather than through transaction. Prahalad and Ramaswamy (2004, p. 16), for example, understand value co-creation as consumer and firm being "intimately involved in jointly creating value that is unique to the individual consumer."

Branding literature enjoyed a parallel development of perspectives regarding meaning co-creation but also co-creation of branded objects as such. The concepts of brand co-creation and customer brand engagement (van Doorn et al., 2010) have radically altered previous perspectives on the creation and development of brands. Literature enjoys abundant empirical evidence of active consumers, who intensively follow the actions of brand managers, comment brand management decisions, negotiate brand meaning (Brodie et al., 2013; Kozinets et al., 2010; Schroll et al., 2018), take initiative in creating new brand manifestations (Berthon et al., 2015; Fisher & Smith, 2011; Füller et al., 2007; O'Sullivan et al., 2011), or even become "brand developers" themselves (Füller et al., 2008; von Wallpach et al., 2017).

Most of the co-creation literature focuses on the positive side of active engagement of consumers in value co-creation processes (Brodie et al., 2013). Much less, however, has been said about consumer engagement that has destructive consequences for brand value. Critical accounts of value co-creation (Bonsu & Darmody, 2008; Cova & Dalli, 2009; Zwick et al., 2008), evidence of negative contributions to interactive value creation (Cova & White, 2010; Hollenbeck & Zinkhan, 2010; Kashif & Zarkada, 2015), and value co-destruction (Andriopoulou et al., 2019; Järvi et al., 2018; Makkonen & Olkkonen, 2017; Prior & Marcos-Cuevas, 2016) provide increasing evidence of the "dark side of co-creation".

Based on the firm belief that different levels of value are nested within each other, Akaka et al. (2015) provide a more differentiated view on value creation and destruction. The authors suggest that what might be valuable to one actor might not be valuable for another actor, or even for the same actor in a different context. In developing the concept of "interactive value formation", Echeverri and Skålén (2011) find that interaction partners in a service delivery both act as value co-creators and value recoverers, as value co-reducers and value destroyers. Value creation presumes a shared understanding of proper procedures, understandings, and engagements. Vice versa, value is destroyed, when interaction partners draw on incongruent elements (Echeverri & Skålén, 2011), or in other words, when they hold different meanings of what is value and what not. Cabiddu et al. (2019), and Dolan et al. (2019) echo the observation that value co-creation and co-destruction happen in parallel. Cabiddu et al. (2019) even suggest to conceptually situate the two concepts in a value variation space rather than viewing them as mutually exclusive. Pera et al. (2021) recently introduced an interesting processual perspective when co-creation turns into co-destruction over time due to rising misbehaviors in a creative community. Echoing Akaka et al. (2015), Echeverri and Skålén (2011) argue that future studies should consider not just two actors involved in value formation but multiple ones. It has become common sense that value co-creation (Vargo & Lusch, 2016) and brand co-creation (Gyrd-Jones & Kornum, 2013) take place in a network or ecosystem of stakeholder relationships. These dynamic stakeholder networks also imply more complex value creation/destruction dynamics first, because not all stakeholders are brand fans and second, because stakeholders hold different positions, goals and understandings of brands' value. The following section carves out different roles of stakeholders in brand value formation in more detail.

## 2. A STAKEHOLDER PERSPECTIVE ON INTERACTIVE BRAND FORMATION

Merz et al. (2009, p. 340) prominently stated that "a brand constitutes a collaborative, value co-creation activity involving all stakeholders and the firm". Similarly, Mühlbacher and Hemetsberger (2008; 2013) acknowledge the prominent role of brand stakeholders in brand meaning co-creation (Iglesias et al., 2020) and co-production of brand manifestations (Asmussen et al., 2012) as well as in the formation of brand-interested stakeholder groups (Christopher & Gaudenzi, 2009; Kornum and Mühlbacher, 2013).

Brand stakeholders, however, have diverse and sometimes even opposing goals (Kornum et al., 2017; Mühlbacher & Hemetsberger, 2013). Ingenbleek and Imminik (2010), for example, find diverse, partly conflicting interests of stakeholders concerning the formulation of corporate social responsibility standards. Additionally, stakeholders take a great variety of roles in interactive value formation processes (von Wallpach et al., 2017) at different times (Vallaster & von Wallpach, 2013). It seems important to carefully account for the multiplicity of diverse stakeholders (Frow & Payne, 2011; Neville & Menguc, 2006) as these roles and the complexity of stakeholder relations with brands often lead to paradoxical constellations (Hillebrand et al., 2015), where value is created for some stakeholders and destroyed for others at the same time. The recent pandemic, when international winter tourism almost vanished, for example, turned out quite harmful for big ski resorts, service providers, gastronomy and their business partners, but considerably increased value for locals, regional tourists, the construction industry that renovated accommodation and tourist sites, and environmental activists.

Stakeholders construct their own roles in brand formation processes (Carlson et al., 2008; Crane & Ruebottom, 2011) depending on the perceived relevance of the brand to them (Johnson et al., 2011) and the roles ascribed to other stakeholders. Stakeholders discursively assign roles to others, for example as gatekeepers, mentors, historian, talent scout, influencer, or celebrity to other stakeholders (Beverland et al., 2010) depending on perceived stakeholder legitimacy (Hollenbeck & Zinkhan, 2010; Santana, 2012) and the perceived relationship of these stakeholders with the brand (Beverland et al., 2010). However, not all stakeholders of a brand actively participate in brand processes. Brand co-creation can happen rather accidentally without stakeholder intent (Hollebeek et al., 2020). Further, not every co-creation activity is collaborative, however, it is always socially mediated (Hemetsberger & Mühlbacher, 2014).

Stakeholders have various goals when they participate in brand formation processes and contribute to brand formation in various ways (Echeverri & Skålén, 2011). Their specific roles strongly influence value formation behavior and communication. Managers, employees, intermediaries, and customers engage in impression management (Schlenker, 1980) and act as gatekeepers of information aiming to actively communicate brand values and recommend branded products, services, or organizations (Brodie et al., 2013; Johnson & Rapp, 2010). Other, less influential stakeholders help others acquire and develop shared attitudes, norms, and language (Dion & Borraz, 2017); share relevant information and expertise with other brand stakeholders (Hemetsberger & Reinhardt, 2009); educate them through knowledge transfer and mentoring or brand adequate behavior (Dion & Borraz, 2017); lend emotional and physical support to other stakeholders (Hartmann et al., 2015; McAlexander et al., 2002); and establish rules and regulations that provide explicit directions for engagement within their brand stakeholder group (Schau et al., 2009). Such practices may compete with others that follow oppositional goals. Brand antagonists pursue similar impression management practices to influence the judgment and actions of others (Bagozzi & Dholakia, 2006) or resist dominant brand meaning (Krishnamurthy & Kucuk, 2009; Lüdicke et al., 2010).

Interestingly, as Echeverri and Skålén (2011) argue, all of these practices can be co-creative or rather co-destructive in nature. Depending on contextual conditions (Aaker et al., 2004), the importance of the brand relationship to the self (Johnson et al., 2011) or to the social group (Lüdicke et al., 2010), active stakeholders may tend to sustain the coherence of brand meaning (Canniford & Shankar, 2013), but may also bring forward diverse or even conflicting ideas, feel betrayed, disengage, or become brand antagonists (Grégoire & Fisher, 2006). Other value-destroying practices, for example acting in an inappropriate or unexpected manner, are less obvious and often unintentional (Plé & Chumpitaz Cáceres, 2010). Engen et al. (2020), for example, recently found that brand destruction might occur in the interaction of several types of actors due to inability (because of technical breakdowns or long waiting lines), mistakes, lack of functional competence, and lack of transparency. Even organizational branding activities can destroy brand value for stakeholders, when employer and consumer expectations to service employees clash (Plé & Chumpitaz Cáceres, 2010) or discursive closure or hypocrisy take over, marginalizing or neglecting essential operations or shortcomings of an organization (Bertilsson & Rennstam, 2018). This literature stream adds an important brand internal perspective to an otherwise quite externally oriented stakeholder perspective and suggests incorporating a multitude of "internal" and "external" stakeholder groups in researching brand formation processes. As these groups all participate in the formation of brands, we actually argue that they all are integral to a brand, thus "internal", and worthy of being considered in brand formation research.

In light of these various practices of stakeholders and companies in a complex social process called "brand" that may be collaborative to controversial, constructive to destructive, individual to interactive, intended to unintended, we look at brands as continually forming at the crossroads of value co-creation and co-destruction. We assume that brand value formation is in the eyes of many beholders and therefore builds a continuum of being more or less "creative" or "destructive" for stakeholders at the same time in a given situation. This chapter aims to disentangle the paradoxical nature of simultaneous brand co-creation and -destruction and uncover the underlying logic of (un-)intentional brand formation practices pursued by multiple stakeholders.

## 3. ORDERS OF WORTH AND THE FORMATION OF BRANDS

As stakeholders commonly do not intentionally seek to co-destruct brands, except for brand contestation, brand hate, boycotting and willful movemental action (Lüdicke et al., 2010; Zarantonello et al., 2016), understanding brand co-destruction necessitates a more differentiated perspective on the underlying logics of "destructive" practices. Stakeholders often act to the best of their knowledge and with the best possible intentions, unaware of the potential detrimental effects of their actions. This is particularly so for professional brand workers. Every day brand co-destruction can arise as an outflow of deliberate, well-justified practice and based on legitimate action that accords with the world views, values, goals and role dependencies of stakeholders that might clash (Bertilsson & Rennstam, 2018). While this view of brand formation and stakeholders' interactive contributions provides a differentiated understanding of individual action, Boltanski and Thévenot's (2006) justification lens suggests a valuable alternative framework to capture differences in stakeholder actions on a broader scale, based on orders of worth that surpass individual value systems. Drawing on Bertilsson and Rennstam (2018), who use a macro, orders of worth perspective to focus on understanding and analyzing branding as a destructive practice, this chapter outlines brand formation as both—a constructive as well as destructive practice—and from a micro- as well as macro-level perspective. In other words, how is value formed by and for brand stakeholders and society at large?

In their work on justification, Boltanski and Thévenot (2006) summarize several general principles of order individuals rely on when justifying their actions. Boltanski and Thévenot describe ideal-type "orders of worth" that determine the worth of people, objects and practices and give direction to distinguish what is right. While the *inspired worth* derives its legitimacy from creativity, passion and spirit, *domestic worth* is based on paternal authority, respect and tradition. Reputation is the main basis of *fame worth*, accompanied by visibility, success and image of the distinguished person. Contrary to fame worth, the *civic worth* puts collectivities center stage, where persons are representatives and gain worth when they strive to unify people and become members of a greater unity. Human desire is the basis of *market worth* measurable in monetized value and related to commercial exchange, competition and profit, while the *industrial worth* derives its value from technology and scientific methods, performance, efficiency, reliability and functionality. These "orders of worth" have been extended later with new kinds of worth that emerged from field reconfigurations and include "projective" worth, based on connectivity and flexibility in the new spirit of capitalism (Boltanski & Chiapello, 2005), and "green" worth based on principles of environmental friendliness (Lafaye & Thévenot, 1993; Lamont & Thévenot, 2000). Reinecke, van Bommel and Spicer (2017) provide a comprehensive overview of these seven orders of worth and their respective implications as shown in Table 6.1.

*Table 6.1*        *Orders of worth*

| | Market | Fame | Industrial | Inspired | Domestic | Civic | Projective | Green |
|---|---|---|---|---|---|---|---|---|
| Common higher principle | Competition | Public Opinion | Efficiency | Inspiration | Tradition | Collectives | Flexible connectivity | Sustainability |
| State of worthiness | Desirable | Fame | Efficient | Inexpressible and etheral | Hierarchical superiority | Rule governed and representative | Flexible | Sustainable |
| Human dignity | Interest | Desire to be recognized | Work | Creation | Habit | Civil rights | Spontaneity | Preservation |
| Subjects | Competitors | Stars and their fans | Professionals | Visionaries | Superiors and Inferiors | Collective persons and their representatives | Partners and brokers | Inhabitants |
| Objects | Wealth | Names in the media | Means | The waking dream | Rules of etiquette | Legal forms | Projects | Nature |
| Investment formula | Opportunism | Giving up secrets, reveal everything to the public (e.g. stars revealing their private lives), make messages simple to appeal to majority opinion | Progress | Escape from habits and routine, calling into question, risk, detour, shed one's rational mental outlook, demonstrate creativity and inventiveness | Rejection of selfishness, consideration, duties (and debt) with respect to those for whom one is responsible, making relations harmonious | The renunciation of the particular, solidarity, transcending divisions, renunciation of immediate interest in favour of collective interests, struggle for a cause | Establish connections | No discount of present utility |
| Model tests | Deal | Presentation of the event, demonstration, press conference, inauguration, open house | Trial | Vagabondage of the mind, adventure, quest, mental vogue, pathfinding, lived experience | Family ceremonies, celebration, social events, nomination, conversation, distinction. | Demonstration of a just cause | Mobilization of network | Greening |
| Judgement | Price | Public opinion | Effective | The stroke of genius | Knowing how to bestow trust | The verdict of the vote | Ease of connectivity | Ecological balance |
| Evidence | Money | Success | Measurement | Intuition | Exemplary anecdote | Legal test | Number of connections | Long-term impact |
| State of Deficiency | Enslavement to money | Indifference and banality | Instrumental action | Temptation to come down to earth | Lack of inhibition | Devision | Bondage | Pollution |

*Source:* Reinecke et al. (2017, p. 45–46).

As Reinecke et al.'s (2017) overview shows, each order of worth has its underlying principles, understandings and norms which may not be compatible with each other. Depending on the order of worth stakeholders prioritize in general, or in a given situation, their actions will differ, or at least justifications for a particular action taken will be based on these different principles. However, stakeholders may face situations which are subject to several, at times conflicting, orders of worth, delegitimizing actions. These instances potentially lead to stake-holder actions based on different orders of worth and brand value co-destruction. Conversely, orders of worth also need adequate "translation" into everyday practice, which is not based on an individual, idiosyncratic understanding of adequate action but rather needs a common understanding congruent with orders of worth applied in specific situations and service deliveries. The following section illustrates such situations using the case study (Yin, 2011) of a private European medical clinic, in which one-on-one interviews with medical staff and patients, and general observations and experiences from the clinic's management allowed a deeper understanding on how value is co-deconstructed. The situation of the medical clinic serves as a representative case, in which many different stakeholder groups add to the medical service process, and create but also destroy value because of diverging expectation and moral attitudes.

# 4. AN ILLUSTRATIVE EXAMPLE: THE CASE OF A MEDICAL CLINIC

Like in other forms of complex service organizations, continuous and complex interactions among a multitude of different stakeholders characterize the medical service ecosystem. Stakeholders included in medical service processes are, for example, physicians, nurses, service workers, managers, patients and their beloved others, suppliers, public and private insurances, public administration and regulatory bodies, and media (Frow et al., 2016). Co-creational practices between these different stakeholders can take place on different levels of the medical ecosystem (i.e., micro, meso, macro or mega level) and can impact the whole system positively or negatively (Frow et al., 2016). Furthermore, the different layers in the medical ecosystem are dynamic and change throughout the medical service process. For example, during the actual intervention stakeholders from the micro level like the focal patient, nursing staff, medical doctors, family members are key, while during the recovery process, stakeholders from the meso and macro level such as insurances, social services, home care visits of physiotherapists become relevant (Frow et al., 2016).

Each individual member of these stakeholders has a specific role in the medical service process and is embedded in a social world that is constituted by co-existing orders of worth or different worlds of valuation (Boltanski & Thévenot, 2006). These orders of worth interact and overlap, and can clash during daily routines, processes, and interactions of different stakeholders. Stakeholders might be caught in divergent orders of worth in specific situations, which causes tensions and difficult trade-offs in decision-making processes, where compromises are difficult to find. Diverging orders of worth that inform everyday work and value-congruent actions can cause trouble in the formation and the "daily living" of the medical brand. Even though central stakeholders such as medical doctors, nurses and clinic management share the goal of participating in an attractive strong brand, their actions might be partly destructive (e.g., Frow et al., 2016). Empirical observations suggest three main situational value constellations that commonly lead to value-destructive tendencies: enacting different orders of worth, conflicting practices based on the same order of worth, and intra-role conflict based on contradictory orders of worth. Based on the case study of the medical clinic, we discuss these value-destructive practices below.

## 4.1 Enacting Different Orders of Worth

A first source of value co-destruction flows from routinized practices of brand stakeholders that apply the logics of different orders of worth. The management of a private medical clinic and its shareholders most likely follow the traditional managerial approach towards brand formation (e.g., Aaker, 1992). Here market, industrial, and reputational forms of valuation are major orders of worth at play. Management's task is to achieve a certain brand equity in the form of price premia, financial profit, and market reputation (Merz et al., 2009). Efficiency and effectiveness in the medical service process is a major priority to stay within predefined budgets and guarantee appropriate financial remuneration to shareholders. Such market and industrial arguments that prioritize price, profit and cost efficiency can clash with a more civic or inspirational order of worth that medical professionals and especially nurses have embodied, live and pass on in their everyday practices and engagements. For example, nurses in their roles as caregiver feel morally obliged to a so-called culture of care, where they want to take as much time as needed for individualized care in the treatment of patients. Via a prosocial orientation towards interpersonal interactions, nurses compensate negative emotions of patients and touch the human and spiritual side of the medical service experience (Kreuzer et al., 2020). Such a civic order of worth stands in sharp contrast with a market and industrial form of brand valuation in which management dictate predefined budgets and time slots per patient for medical interventions and caregiving. Depending on the power relationship between nurses and management, different forms of value destruction will emerge. Sticking to time slots adds a production line flavor to the treatment of healthcare consumers and can not only spoil their experience but also cause severe treatment failure, for example, when efficiency demands determine surgery time and limit life-saving service. Additionally, nurses are unable to deliver and live their values inherent to their role understanding, and the market orientation will add an exploitative nuance in the management–nurse relationship. The outcome is a below-the-expectation and prosaic medical service experience for patients and for nurses as well. Conversely, taking as much time as needed in the medication and caregiving for individual patients, will negatively impact brand performance and eat into profit margins and financial brand equity. When put to the extreme, patients could die, and clinics go bankrupt.

Taking on a macro perspective, policy makers and state health authorities strive for an equal medical service system for all people within their administrative sovereignty. This includes an equal and fair access to medical resources irrespective of the social background, the health insurance (i.e., private or public), and the treatment a person gets. The current situation, however, often differs from the aim of policy makers as public and private medical clinics have different prerequisites for their medical service processes. Private clinics normally have better and faster resources and can provide more attractive conditions to medical staff. Leading doctors are less willing to work in public medical institutions for less money and less attractive working conditions compared to private ones. This increases the bottleneck in public clinics, medical services are more and more reduced, and patients who can afford the treatment in private institutions switch because of very long waiting times. This development thwarts the overall moral and social aim of policy makers to provide fair and equal opportunities for all people irrespective of their social background and creates an imbalance within the whole ecosystem (Frow et al., 2016).

### 4.2    Conflicting Practices Based on the Same Order of Worth

Value creation is not just a matter of applying the same principles or orders of worth. Understanding how to "translate" orders of worth into situation-specific measures and according value-creating practices is key to mutual brand value formation. Our example of the medical clinic demonstrates how the same orders of worth lead to brand co-destruction. In executing their profession, medical doctors and nurses are obliged to not harm their patients, and take pride in being good caretakers, which represents a reputable value and corresponds to the desire to be recognized (Boltanski & Thévenot, 2006). Both doctors and nurses strongly believe in doing good and caring for their patients which can result in an informal (and often official) fight over who is the better caretaker, if they have a different understanding of what caretaking means. For example, doctors often consider the pure characterization of the diagnoses only and prescribe their patients a medical treatment at exactly twelve hour intervals to minimize risks and to maximize the recovery process. Thus, they follow strict treatment standards and processes, monitor, and record the process of recovery, and if needed, adapt the treatment to care in their best and most objective manner for the patient. Such a strict treatment and positivist biomedical approach (Watson, 2002) follows the requirements from an industrial valuation perspective. From a physician's standpoint sticking to this medical regulatory framework can present his/her understanding of care. Thus, the industry structures guide physicians in practicing their medical profession and shape their understanding of care. Conversely, nurses are not only interested in a clear diagnosis of the patient's problem, but tend to take a more holistic, emotional and spiritual perspective on care (Watson, 2002). From their understanding of caregiving, nurses try to establish an authentic relationship by approaching the patient-as-a-person in his/her wholeness. The nurses' understanding of their role as caregiver is very much related to values like humanity and respecting dignity (Watson, 2002). As such, nurses may, for example, respect when people are asleep or when beloved others are visiting and postpone the treatment for a justifiable time.

Another example of the same values resulting in conflicting actions refers to the clinic's management and external insurance companies. Managers at medical clinics as well as insurance companies aim to run their business and underlying processes highly efficiently (industrial valuation) and aim to achieve a certain return on investment (market valuation). Especially, patients with private insurance contracts are most welcomed cash cows for a clinic. For management it is highly profitable to keep patients longer than needed, run expensive examination procedures, or prescribe examinations and treatments that go beyond what is necessary. State insurance that follows a civic order of worth, and particularly private insurance companies which follow a market and industrial form of valuation, oppose this game. Insurances will fight over-examinations and force a more preventive perspective on healthcare in order to reduce the number of treatments to a meaningful level.

Additionally, a market worth orientation of clinics and the resulting differentiation between patients with public or private insurance leads to another form of brand co-destruction. While patients with private insurance are (over)treated under more favorable conditions (i.e., faster, better and more (unnecessary) treatments, no waiting times, etc.), publicly insured patients wait much longer to get a required appointment or treatment. Such a two-class medical system is subject to immanent structural and political problems, as technical methods, laboratory tests and invasive procedures are often far better rewarded than preventive or alternative forms for healthcare. Public authorities and policy makers who are responsible for the definition of the legal, civic and medical framework in which medical clinics and insurance companies operate are increasingly subject to values and evaluative principles of a market order in which the price and cost of providing medical services come to the fore (McLoughlin et al., 2017). As such policy makers define and orchestrate a market-oriented medical system in which stakeholders are embedded and in which different orders of valuation that are incompatible with this market worth orientation result in brand co-destruction.

### 4.3 Intra-Role Conflict Based on Conflicting Orders of Worth

Stakeholders embody different roles and values in their lives as they move between different domains of living. Yet, these value orders are not strictly delineated and may become salient in specific situations that touch upon a different value domain. Medical doctors are a prime example of a profession that often lives and acts according to different orders of worth, depending on their saliency in a given situation. On the one hand and very obviously, it is their civic and moral duty to help and not to harm patients (or any other person) during a medical examination (Hippocratic Oath). This civic obligation does not only relate to interventions regarding the physical body but also extends to the emotional and spiritual well-being of the patient (Watson, 2002). Such a civic value orientation requires a prosocial approach in the interaction between physician and patient. This implies that medical doctors respect the patients and their socioeconomic lifeworld, adapt their language, forms of communication, and interaction fully to the patient's situation (Kreuzer et al., 2020). However, medical doctors are often caught in the fame worth through their expert status which adds reputational value to their profession and to their individual self. They conduct and publish research in their area of expertise, give presentations or press conferences, and are often the stars of a medical institution. The reputation game is further emphasized by clinics, patients, clinic owners and other stakeholders, in order to strengthen their own reputation. Such a reputational valuation may clash with a more civic-oriented value orientation. The expert status can translate into an asymmetrical power relationship between patient and medical doctor (Ishikawa et al., 2013). Medical jargon, closed questions, or leading the dialog express superiority and overemphasizes the "voice of the medicine". Being in the star role, medical doctors may ignore the patient as a person and marginalize the civic worth of his profession, which is the basis for attractive brand meaning to other stakeholders in a clinic in the first place. Being torn between fame, industrial functionality, civic duty and market worth, the profession of medical experts is a prime example of intra-role struggles based on a plethora of demands from different "worlds".

## 5.   CONCLUSION

This chapter introduces a new perspective to brand destructive actions and has important implications for the understanding of interactive brand formation in complex social systems with a multitude of interacting stakeholders. Based on an extended view of stakeholder actions relevant for brand process and meaning formation and a justification lens (Boltanski & Thévenot, 2006), this chapter exemplifies that unintentional brand co-destruction is a quite common phenomenon in everyday practice, rooted in different underlying orders of worth, conflicting practices rooted in the same order of worth, or intra-role conflicts based on conflicting orders of worth. Brand (co-)destruction is not simply a result of the complex interplay of multiple stakeholders, who hold different positions. While individual values, goals and roles allow a differentiated understanding of actions of individual brand stakeholders, the theory of justification (Boltanski & Thévenot, 2006) provides a valuable general framework to capture differences in stakeholder actions on a broader scale, based on orders of worth that surpass individual value systems. The presented example also demonstrates that value formation rests on according value-congruent stakeholder action. While some practices seem value-congruent, their consequences might run counter their initial intention. Lastly, also situation-specific demands and intra-role conflicts in which stakeholders are entangled might undermine concerted co-creative action. Considering the different constellations outlined in our illustrative example allows a more general understanding of simultaneous brand co-creation and co-destruction processes, that means, the ongoing brand formation.

Drawing on Boltanski and Thévenot's approach directs attention to the question of "what is value" in the first place. Whether value is created or destroyed is a matter of the underlying "orders of worth" that are at play in a specific domain and given situation. Different value regimes inform everyday practice, often with the best intentions. While it is well known that individual values and interests of different stakeholders often lead to conflicting thinking and action (e.g., Donaldson & Preston, 1995; Hillebrand et al., 2015), "orders of worth" work at the level of civil understanding and are easy to understand and share, yet they must be negotiated and adapted to organizations, brands, and specific situations. Clear brand positioning and mission statements are a condition sine qua non; concrete and transparent recommendations for everyday practice, based on situation-specific demands, are imperative. As Engen et al. (2020) show, lack of transparency is one of the four "pillars" of service value destruction.

Even if managerial implications seem obvious, an "orders of worth" perspective draws managerial attention to a broader level of value creation, namely that of civil society. It actually draws attention to the definition of "value" in value creation in the first place. Emphasizing value-in-use (Vargo & Lusch, 2004, 2016) as the *ultima ratio* of value co-creation by multiple actors first overlooks value co-destruction processes, and second, comes short of accounting for other value systems that go far beyond "value-in-use" as defined by a market "order of worth". An "orders of worth" perspective teaches us to include other definitions of value worthy of consideration. Corporate social responsibility, business ethics, environmentally conscious conduct of business, and moral standards of humanity are based on political systems and societal orders. But also more mundane values, rooted in the domestic world, fame, the market and industrial world are important pillars of society demand consideration. An explicit consideration of different orders of worth and their implications for continuous interactive brand formation among stakeholders could potentially lead to more fruitful negotiations of how to create brand value and value for all. As the illustrative case example shows, different underlying orders of worth need to be made explicit in order to navigate situation-specific demands.

Boltanksi and Thévenot (2006) suggest compromise as a way to deal with different value systems and moral schemes. Reinecke et al. (2017) suggest two more possible strategies to resolve orders of worth conflicts/situations of value multiplexity: transcendence and antagonism. Doctors, nurses and patients, the clinic, and insurances all might find workable solutions in explicit negotiations of compromises and courses of action between different worlds. Compromising does not lead to a suspension of a clash of worlds but enhances understanding and results in agreements on workable solutions. Reinecke et al. (2017) suggest the construction of moral hybrids which bring together different moral schemes on equal terms. Public policy makers, for example agree on maximum costs of pharmaceutical products per treatment according to their civic and market logic, while clinics decide on the optimal treatment for that flat rate of reimbursement, in accordance with their own market frame, industrial order of worth, and civic duty.

Conflicting practices based on the same order of worth are relatively easier to cope with as soon as the underlying order of worth is being made explicit. Negotiations then, revolve around appropriate means and actions to the achievement of a common goal, rather than conflicting orders of worth. As a matter of fact, public policy and health insurances in Austria, for example, in accordance with many clinics, personnel in the health sector, and most obviously patients, more and more adopt a civic perspective of the common good of health, and invest in preventive healthcare, rather than sticking to a short-sighted market order of worth. In the long run, these negotiations also contribute to the industrial and market value. Reinecke et al. (2017) describe such effects, for example as outcomes of negotiations of transcendence. Transcendence involves the creation of a new moral reference that helps align conflicting values and actions. Preventive healthcare, for example, is such a reference point that transcends the mainly restorative focus of the health industry beyond systemic constellations of orders of worth.

Third, brands often suffer from intra-role conflicts of important stakeholders, which potentially destroys value on several sides. In the discussed example, conflicting interests among market and industrial orders in the management of a clinic or public health insurance could be detrimental. If public health institutions are not willing to invest into health technology and effectiveness, people might not get the best possible treatment. On an individual level, when medical doctors need to decide between financial aspects, medical technology, fame, and civic orders of worth like care, intra-role conflict becomes almost impossible to solve. Here, antagonistic negotiations, which entails strong siding with one particular moral order and counter-posing it against another, are often necessary in order to settle these conflicts. Often, the concrete situation and vulnerabilities of entangled stakeholders is the only reference point at hand to decide which order to follow. Table 6.2 summarizes the three problematic value constellations that can lead to value co-(deconstruction) and provides possible solutions to overcome these conflicting situations.

*Table 6.2    Co-deconstructive situations and possible solutions*

| Problematic co-deconstructive constellations | Illustrative example | Possible solutions to solve the conflicting constellation |
| --- | --- | --- |
| Enacting different orders of worth | Value clash between different stakeholder groups. For example, different cost models and billing schemes of public policy makers and medical clinics. | – Constant antagonistic negotiations<br>– Feedback rounds to build "moral hybrids"<br>– Empathizing with others, understanding different value perspectives<br>– Constant training of value proposition and its implication for daily work |
| Conflicting practices based on the same order of worth | Value clash due to a different understanding of the same value between different stakeholders. For example, medical doctors and nurses have a different understanding of caretaking. | – Sensemaking of values<br>– Pursue common goals in brand formation<br>– Feedback rounds and empathizing with others<br>– Constant training of value proposition and its implication for daily work |
| Intra-role conflict based on conflicting orders of worth | Value clash within a single stakeholder. For example, the focus of a medical doctor on process efficiency versus humanity in medical service processes. | – Individual coaching and supervision<br>– Clarification of expectations towards one's role<br>– Constant training of value proposition and its implication for daily work |

In generalizing these important insights, we may conclude that (service) brand co-creation and co-destruction are just two sides of the same coin of interactive brand formation. When stakeholders act in the best of their interests, they might harm other stakeholders' interests. This chapter suggests a more encompassing view on brand co-creation that trespasses the meso-level market domain. This seems important for at least two reasons. First, brand co-creation by consumers and other stakeholders most often does not follow a market logic but occurs in private, inspired or civic domains; or from an industrial order of worth, for example in the case of producers. Second, being a sustainable and responsible (corporate) brand necessarily means to take responsibility, not only at a market level but beyond, including civic and green orders of worth. Brand value co-creation, therefore, will strongly benefit from a redefinition and enlargement of brand value as "value-in-use", or "value-in-cultural-context" (Akaka et al., 2015; Edvardsson et al., 2011) to a "value-in-society" perspective, to avoid value co-destruction in different domains. The clear and concise definition of a brand's "value-in-society", its transparent communication and translation into concrete action, therefore, constitutes a core responsibility of branding.

# REFERENCES

Aaker, D.A. (1992). The value of brand equity. *Journal of Business Strategy, 13*(4), 27–32.

Aaker, J., Fournier, S., & Brasel, A.S. (2004). When good brands do bad. *Journal of Consumer Research, 31*(June), 1–16.

Akaka, M.A., Vargo, S.L. & Schau, H.J. (2015). The context of experience. *Journal of Service Management, 26*(2), 206–223.

Andriopoulou, A., Skourtis, G., Giannopoulos, A., Strapchuk, S., & Koniordos, M. (2019). *Understanding Value Co-destruction in Tourism Service Ecosystem.* 11th International Scientific Conference, Mecavnik-Drvengrad, Uzice, Serbia.

Asmussen, B., Harridge-March, S., Occhiocupo, N., & Dawes-Farquhar, J. (2012). The multi-layered nature of the internet-based democratization of brand management. *Journal of Business Research, 66*(9), 1473–1483.

Bagozzi, R.P., & Dholakia, U.M. (2006). Antecedents and purchase consequences of customer participation in small group brand communities. *International Journal of Research in Marketing, 23*(1), 45–61.

Berthon, P., Pitt, L., Kietzmann, J., & McCarthy, I.P. (2015). CGIP: Managing consumer-generated intellectual property. *California Management Review, 57*(4), 43–62.

Bertilsson, J., & Rennstam, J. (2018). The destructive side of branding: A heuristic model for analyzing the value of branding practice. *Organization, 25*(2), 260–281.

Beverland, M.B., Farrelly, F., & Quester, P.G. (2010). Authentic subcultural membership: Antecedents and consequences of authenticating acts and authoritative performances. *Psychology & Marketing, 27*(7), 698–716.

Boltanski, L., & Chiapello, E. (2005). *The New Spirit of Capitalism.* Verso: London & New York.

Boltanski, L. & Thévenot, L. (2006). *On Justification: Economies of Worth.* Princeton Studies in Cultural Sociology, Princeton University Press: Princeton.

Bonsu, S.K., & Darmody, A. (2008). Co-creating second life: Market–consumer cooperation in contemporary economy. *Journal of Macromarketing, 28*(4), 355–368.

Brodie, J., Ilic, A., Juric, B., & Hollebeek, L. (2013). Consumer engagement in a virtual brand community: An exploratory analysis. *Journal of Business Research, 66*(1), 105–114.

Cabiddu, F., Frau, M., & Lombardo, S. (2019). Toxic collaborations: Co-destroying value in the B2B context. *Journal of Service Research, 22*(3), 241–255.

Canniford, R., & Shankar, A. (2013). Purifying practices: How consumers assemble romantic experiences of nature. *Journal of Consumer Research, 39*(February), 1051–1069.

Carlson, B.D., Suter, T.A., & Brown, T.J. (2008). Social versus psychological brand community: The role of psychological sense of brand community. *Journal of Business Research, 61*(4), 284–291.

Christopher, M., & Gaudenzi, B. (2009). Exploiting knowledge across networks through reputation management. *Industrial Marketing Management, 38*(2), 191–197.

Cova, B., & Dalli, D. (2009). Working consumers: The next step in marketing theory? *Marketing Theory, 9*(3), 315–339.

Cova, B., & White, T. (2010). Counter-brand and alter-brand communities: The impact of Web 2.0 on tribal marketing approaches. *Journal of Marketing Management, 26*(3–4), 256–270.

Crane, A., & Ruebottom, T. (2011). Stakeholder theory and social identity: Rethinking stakeholder identification. *Journal of Business Ethics, 102*(1), 77–87.

Dion, D., & Borraz, S. (2017). Managing status: How luxury brands shape class subjectivities in the service encounter. *Journal of Marketing, 81*(5), 67–85.

Dolan, R., Seo, Y., & Kemper, J. (2019). Complaining practices on social media in tourism: A value co-creation and co-destruction perspective. *Tourism Management, 73*, 35–45.

Donaldson, T., & Preston, L. (1995). The stakeholder theory of the corporation concepts, evidence, and implications. *Academy of Management Review*, *20*, 65–91.

Echeverri, P., & Skålén, P. (2011). Co-creation and co-destruction: A practice theory based study of interactive value formation. *Marketing Theory*, *11*, 351–373.

Edvardsson, K., Tronvoll, B., & Gruber, Th. (2011). Expanding understanding of service exchange and value co-creation: A social construction approach. *Journal of the Academy of Marketing Science*, *39*(2), 327–339.

Eiglier, P., & Langeard, E. (1987). *Servuction – Le Marketing des Service*. McGraw-Hill: Paris.

Engen, M., Fransson, M., Quist, J., & Skålén, P. (2020). Continuing the development of the public service logic: A study of value co-destruction in public services. *Public Management Review*, *23*(6), 886–905.

Fisher, D., & Smith, S. (2011). Cocreation is chaotic: What it means for marketing when no one has control. *Marketing Theory*, *11*(3), 325–350.

Frow, P., & Payne, A. (2011). A stakeholder perspective of the value proposition concept. *European Journal of Marketing*, *45*(1/2), 223–240.

Frow, P., McColl-Kennedy, J.R., & Payne, A. (2016). Co-creation practices: Their role in shaping a health care ecosystem. *Industrial Marketing Management*, *56*, 24–39.

Füller, J., Jawecki, G., & Mühlbacher, H. (2007). Innovation creation by online basketball communities. *Journal of Business Research*, *60*(1), 60–71.

Füller, J., Lüdicke, M.K., & Jawecki, G. (2008). How brands enchant: Insights from observing community driven brand creation. *Advances in Consumer Research*, *35*, 359–366.

Grégoire, Y., & Fisher, R.J. (2006). The effects of relationship quality on customer retaliation. *Marketing Letters*, *17*(1), 31–46.

Grönroos, C. (1982). An applied service marketing theory. *European Journal of Marketing*, *16*(7), 30–41.

Grönroos, C., & Voima, P. (2013). Critical service logic: Making sense of value creation and co-creation. *Journal of the Academy of Marketing Science*, *41*(2), 133–150.

Gummesson, E. (1987). The new marketing—Developing long-term interactive relationships. *Long Range Planning*, *20*(4), 10–20.

Gummesson, E. (2006). *Many-to-Many Marketing as Grand Theory: A Nordic School Contribution*. Sharpe: New York.

Gyrd-Jones, R., & Kornum, N. (2013). Managing the co-created brand: Value and cultural complementarity in online and offline multi-stakeholder ecosystems. *Journal of Business Research*, *66*(9), 1484–1493.

Hartmann, P.J., Wiertz, C., & Arnould, E.J. (2015). Exploring consumptive moments of value-creating practice in online community. *Psychology & Marketing*, *32*(3), 319–340.

Hemetsberger, A. & Mühlbacher, H. (2014). *Brands as Socially-mediated Processes*. Proceedings of the BBR (Brands and Brand Relationships) Conference, Boston.

Hemetsberger, A., & Reinhardt, C. (2009). Collective development in open-source communities: An activity theoretical perspective on successful online collaboration. *Organization Studies*, *30*(9), 987–1008.

Hillebrand, B., Driessen, P.H., & Koll, O. (2015). Stakeholder marketing: Theoretical foundations and required capabilities. *Journal of the Academy of Marketing Science*, *43*(4), 411–428.

Hollebeek, L.D., Kumar, V., & Srivastava, R.K. (2020). From customer-, to actor-, to stakeholder engagement: Taking stock, conceptualization,and future directions. *Journal of Service Research*, https://doi.org/10.1177/1094670520977680.

Hollenbeck, C.R., & Zinkhan, G.M. (2010). Anti-brand communities, negotiation of brand meaning, and the learning process: The case of Wal-Mart. *Consumption Markets & Culture*, *13*(3), 325–345.

Iglesias, O., Ind, N., & Alfaro, M. (2013). The organic view of the brand: A brand value co-creation model. *Journal of Brand Management*, *20*(8), 670–688.

Iglesias, O., Landgraf, P., Ind, N., Markovic, St., & Koporcic, N. (2020). Corporate brand identity co-creation in business-to-business contexts. *Industrial Marketing Management*, *85*, 32–43.

Ingenbleek, P.T.M., & Imminik, V.M. (2010). Managing conflicting stakeholder interests: An exploratory case analysis of the formulation of corporate social responsibility standards in the Netherlands. *Journal of Public Policy & Marketing*, *29*(1), 52–65.

Ishikawa, H., Hashimoto, H., & Kiuchi, T. (2013). The evolving concept of "patient-centeredness" in patient–physician communication research. *Social Science & Medicine, 96*, 147–153.

Järvi, H., Kähkönen, A.-K., & Torvinen, H. (2018). When value co-creation fails: Reasons that lead to value co-destruction. *Scandinavian Journal of Management, 34*(1), 63–77.

Johnson, A.R., Matear, M., & Thomson, M. (2011). A coal in the heart: Self-relevance as a post-exit predictor of consumer anti-brand actions. *Journal of Consumer Research, 38*(June), 108–125.

Johnson, J.W., & Rapp, A. (2010). A more comprehensive understanding and measure of customer helping behavior. *Journal of Business Research, 63*(8), 787–792.

Kashif, M., & Zarkada, A. (2015). Value co-destruction between customers and frontline employees: A social system perspective. *International Journal of Bank Marketing, 33*(6), 672–691.

Kornum, N., & Mühlbacher, H. (2013). Multi-stakeholder virtual dialogue: Introduction to the special section. *Journal of Business Research, 66*(9), 1460–1464.

Kornum, N., Gyrd-Jones, R., Al Zagir, N., & Brandis, A. (2017). Interplay between intended brand identity and identities in a Nike related brand community: Co-existing synergies and tensions in a nested system. *Journal of Business Research, 70*(1), 432–440.

Kozinets, R.V., de Valck, K., Wojnicki, A.C., & Wilner, S.J.S. (2010). Networked narratives: Understanding word-of-mouth marketing in online communities. *Journal of Marketing, 74*(2), 71–89.

Kreuzer, M., Cado, V., & Raïes, K. (2020). Moments of care: How interpersonal interactions contribute to luxury experiences of healthcare consumers. *Journal of Business Research, 116*, 482–490.

Krishnamurthy, S., & Kucuk, U.S. (2009). Anti-branding on the internet. *Journal of Business Research, 62*(11), 1119–1126.

Lafaye, C., & Thévenot, L. (1993). Une justification écologique ? Conflits dans l'aménagement de la nature. *Revue Française de Sociologie, 34*(4), 495–524.

Lamont, M., & Thévenot, L. (2000). *Rethinking Comparative Cultural Sociology*. Cambridge University Press: Cambridge.

Lüdicke, M.K., Thompson, C.J., & Giesler, M. (2010). Consumer identity work as moral protagonism: How myth and ideology animate a brand-mediated moral conflict. *Journal of Consumer Research, 36*(6), 1016–1032.

Makkonen, H., & Olkkonen, R. (2017). Interactive value formation in interorganizational relationships: Dynamic interchange between value co-creation, no-creation, and co-destruction. *Marketing Theory, 17*(4), 517–535.

McAlexander, J.H., Schouten, J.W., & Koenig, H.F. (2002). Building brand community, *Journal of Marketing, 66*(1), 38–54.

McLoughlin, I.P., Garrety, K., & Wilson, R. (2017). *The Digitalization of Healthcare: Electronic Records and the Disruption of Moral Orders*. Oxford University Press: New York.

Merz, M., He, Y., & Vargo, S. L. (2009). The evolving brand logic: A service-dominant logic perspective. *Journal of the Academy of Marketing Science, 37*(3), 328–344.

Mühlbacher, H., & Hemetsberger, A. (2008). Cosa diamine è un brand? Un tentativo di integrazione e le sue conseguenze per la ricerca e il management. *Micro & Macro Marketing, 2*, 271–292.

Mühlbacher, H., & Hemetsberger, A. (2013). Brands as processes: A social representations perspective. In J. Scholderer, & K. Brunso (eds.), *Marketing, Food and the Consumer*, Festschrift in Honour of Klaus G. Grunert, Pearson, pp. 31–46.

Neville, B.A., & Menguc, B. (2006). Stakeholder multiplicity: Toward an understanding of the interactions between stakeholders. *Journal of Business Ethics, 66*(4), 377–391.

O'Sullivan, S.R., Richardson, B., & Collins, A. (2011). How brand communities emerge: The Beamish conversion experience. *Journal of Marketing Management, 27*(9–10), 891–912.

Pera, R., Menozzi, A., Abrate, G., & Baima, G. (2021). When cocreation turns into codestruction. *Journal of Business Research, 128*(C), 222–232.

Plé, L., & Chumpitaz Cáceres, R. (2010). Not always co-creation: Introducing interactional co-destruction of value in service-dominant logic. *Journal of Services Marketing, 24*(6), 430–437.

Prahalad, C.K. and Ramaswamy, V. (2004) *The Future of Competition: Co-Creating Unique Value With Customers*. Boston, MA: Harvard Business School Press.

Prior, D., & Marcos-Cuevas, J. (2016). Value co-destruction in interfirm relationships: The impact of actor engagement styles. *Marketing Theory, 16*(4), 533–552.

Ramirez, R. (1999). Value co-production: Intellectual origins and implications for practice and research. *Strategic Management Journal, 20*(1), 49–65.

Reinecke, J., van Bommel, K., & Spicer, A. (2017). When orders of worth clash: Negotiating legitimacy in situations of moral multiplexity: Contributions from French pragmatist sociology. *Research in the Sociology of Organizations, 52*, 33–72.

Santana, A. (2012). Three elements of stakeholder legitimacy. *Journal of Business Ethics, 105*(2), 257–265.

Schau, H.J., Muñiz, A.M., & Arnould, E.J. (2009). How brand community practices create value. *Journal of Marketing, 73*(September), 30–51.

Schlenker, B. (1980). *Impression Management: The Self Concept, Social Identity and Interpersonal Relations.* Brooks-Cole: Monterey, CA.

Schroll, R., Schnurr, B., & Grewal, D. (2018). Humanizing products with handwritten typefaces. *Journal of Consumer Research, 45*(3), 648–672.

Vallaster, C., & von Wallpach, S. (2013). An online discursive inquiry into the social dynamics of multi-stakeholder brand meaning co-creation. *Journal of Business Research, 66*(9), 1505–1515.

van Doorn, J., Lemon, K.N., Mittal, V., Nass, S., Pick, D., Pirner, P., & Verhoef, P.C. (2010). Customer engagement behavior: Theoretical foundations and research directions. *Journal of Service Research, 13*(3), 253–266.

Vargo, S.L., & Lusch, R.F. (2004). Evolving to a new dominant logic for marketing. *Journal of Marketing, 68*(1), 1–17.

Vargo, S.L., & Lusch, R.F. (2016). Institutions and axioms: An extension and update of service-dominant logic. *Journal of the Academy of Marketing Science, 44*(1), 5–23.

von Wallpach, S., Hemetsberger, A., & Espersen, P. (2017). Performing identities: Processes of brand and stakeholder identity co-construction. *Journal of Business Research, 70*(1), 443–452.

Watson, J. (2002). Intentionality and caring-healing consciousness: A practice of transpersonal nursing. *Holistic Nursing Practice, 16*(4), 12–19.

Yin, R.K. (2011). *Applications of Case Study Research.* Sage: Thousand Oaks, CA.

Zarantonello, L., Romani, S., Grappi, S., & Bagozzi, R. (2016). Brand hate. *Journal of Product & Brand Management, 25*(1), 11–25.

Zwick, D., Bonsu, S.K., & Darmody, A. (2008). Putting consumers to work: "Co-creation" and new marketing govern-mentality. *Journal of Consumer Culture, 8*(2), 163–196.

# 7. Dealing with discrepancies of a brand in change: recomposition of value and meanings in the network

*Anu Norrgrann and Saila Saraniemi*

## 1. INTRODUCTION

Research literature demonstrates that multiple actors participate in the co-creation of brands and therefore of brand meanings. Further, it is suggested that brands are created in networks (e.g. Mäläskä et al., 2011). The opposing process of co-destruction of brands from a multi-stakeholder perspective has also been addressed, but to a lesser degree, and in a more fragmented way. These prior studies mostly have the research streams of consumer activism or anti-branding as their departure point (Hollenbeck & Zinkhan, 2010), and look less at brands at the B2B interaction level. This raises the question of how brands become shaped – co-created, co-destroyed, or altered in other ways – by interaction processes in the multi-stakeholder network, in which they are embedded. There is a need to broaden the perspective on the implications of interaction that go beyond co-creation and examine the discrepancies in how brands are approached by diverse stakeholders, and what might be the consequences of such discrepancies. The purpose of this chapter is to elaborate on the co-destruction of brands in multi-stakeholder networks to acquire an understanding of the dynamic nature of brands and the changes in the value they provide.

This chapter examines co-destruction in a brand network from the food industry and shows how changes to end-customer needs trigger a re-evaluation of a supplier brand's role, including its meanings and value, in the entire network. What may look like the destruction of the existing way of creating value in the network may later lead to successful co-creation of the offering through changing interactions. We examine a case study featuring a vegetable wholesale intermediary and its process of turning the bulk produce it sells into a consumer brand. This strategically chosen case illuminates brand-related discrepancies and brand meaning co-destruction exposed in the process of branding, which constitutes a re-evaluation of the brand in the network by the stakeholders. We draw on in-depth personal interviews, observational data, and company documents, generated on several occasions between 2014 and 2020; an approach that enables a processual examination of the case brand and the development of the network relationships surrounding it.

The chapter contributes particularly to socioculturally informed literature (e.g. Vallaster & von Wallpach, 2013) and also to process-oriented brand literature (e.g. Wider et al., 2018) that each address interactive processes related to brands, while also in part touching upon other relevant marketing literature such as industrial marketing and purchasing (IMP), market studies, and practice theory. Within each of these streams of research, the concept of co-destruction has been considered in parallel with the notion of co-creation, as a dark side of it (see Michel, 2017). Echeverri and Skålen (2011) suggested duality in terms of value outcomes: meaning co-creation and co-destruction. Lessons from IMP literature (e.g. Norrgrann & Luokkanen-Rabetino, 2011) point to examining the relationship and network dynamics and the broader network effects of brands; if value becomes co-destructed in interaction, what can we learn of its implications for multi-stakeholder networks? We highlight that contradictions in business relationships need not necessarily have only negative implications but can later be reconfigured into more positive outcomes too. Further, this study addresses changes over time in the brand's internal and external environment that create tensions in managing the brand, while also addressing the research gap highlighted by Melewar et al. (2012) regarding the need for a dynamic approach to managing corporate brands.

## 2.  THEORETICAL BACKGROUND

Recent branding research has recognised brands as dynamic social processes that are not only identities embedded in products or firms but are also ongoing, social value co-creation processes (Merz et al., 2009; Evans et al., 2019). This understanding of brands and their value generated in complex stakeholder interactions (e.g. Brodie et al., 2017) has inspired many important developments in research. Wider et al. (2018), for example, refer to these brand-related interactions as a multiplicity of brands (or *rhizomic brands*) that occurs when stakeholders in a brand's network are continuously and reciprocally interrelated, thus influencing one another. What is more, "changes to or additions or omission of any one element have an impact on all the other elements" in the brand's network (Wider et al., 2018, p. 302).

Accordingly, we suggest that such a multiplicity results in possible discrepancies in the brand's network, change being central not only to interactions but also with regard to revealing those discrepancies. Even if a focal firm pursues a shared understanding of its brand identity and image (e.g. Mäläskä et al., 2011), it is not possible to control all brand meanings in the network. In B2B settings, these interactions have been described as the brand's activities as influenced by prevailing contextual factors such as responsiveness to markets (Törmälä & Gyrd-Jones, 2017) and stakeholder performance (Iglesias et al., 2020) both of which co-create corporate brand identity. The above-referenced studies illustrate the ongoing negotiation between a company and its stakeholders around corporate brand identity. They also show the processuality of the brand identity incorporating certain developmental phases (Törmälä & Gyrd-Jones, 2017) and recurring stakeholder performances (Iglesias et al., 2020). The particular focus in this chapter lies in the tensions between a company and its stakeholders as well as the disruptive changes that occur as stakeholders contest the corporate brand identity (see, e.g. Iglesias et al., 2020). The last referenced study demonstrates how tensions can arise when stakeholders see a contrast between the brand identity and their perceptions of the brand while management wishes to protect current brand meanings. That recurring process of adjusting and clarifying the brand identity (see Törmälä & Gyrd-Jones, 2017) is our focus because it reveals ongoing changes to brand meanings and value. The focus is valuable because existing literature does not expressly consider such changes from the perspective of discrepancies, that is, disruptive changes in a brand's network.

Brand creation is a collaborative process with empowered stakeholders marked by the potential for brand co-creation to push brand meaning in an undesirable direction (see Ind, 2014). In the context of higher-education branding, Aspara et al. (2014) suggested that mutual value co-creation and interaction between stakeholders do not necessarily construct strong brands. Further, Onyas and Ryan (2015) highlighted that brand processes are likely to be characterised by disagreements between market actors.

Echeverri and Skålen (2011) define co-destruction of value as the collaborative destruction or diminution of value by providers and customers. Thus, co-destruction of value is part of that interaction by those parties, just as the co-creation of value is (see also Plé & Chumpitaz Cáceres, 2010). In line with that concept, Mäläskä et al. (2011) found that business partners can damage the brand, even if unintentionally, particularly if a business has not assigned the necessary resources and expertise for co-creation of the brand. Research has identified multiple reasons for value co-destruction. In a B2B setting, Vafeas et al. (2016) suggest reasons including the absence of trust, inadequate communication and coordination, inadequate human capital, and a power or dependence imbalance. Järvi et al. (2018) conducted research spanning multiple sectors and found that a provider's or customer's inability to change, the absence of clear expectations on the part of the customer, misbehaviour, or assigning blame could cause value co-destruction in relationships. The reasons are often behavioural or caused by a failure to integrate resources between business partners.

Issues such as tensions and conflicts have been addressed in B2B marketing literature for instance in relation to technological embeddedness and co-opetition (see, e.g. Håkansson & Waluszewski, 2001, 2002; Mele, 2011; Tidström, 2014). That body of research reports that inconsistencies among actors do not necessarily only have negative consequences, but can be a source of dynamic progress and development. Different market actors' disharmonious and contradicting interests related to a brand may lead to new, creative reinterpretations of the brand meanings (Fyrberg Yngfalk, 2013). Similarly, while the resource structure around a brand can be seen as inert and limiting for some relationships, it can provide new value when coupled to new relationships and resources (Norrgrann & Luokkanen-Rabetino, 2011; Gidhagen & Havila, 2016). Surprisingly, such discrepancies in networks and business relationships that relate to brands have remained rather unstudied.

Furthermore, Wider et al. (2018) suggest brands are "processes in constant flux [that] escape the control of managers". Evidently, branding, even if referred to as a deliberate activity among multiple stakeholders, is not straightforward. Brands, in a traditional sense, may not be manageable, but branding entities do need goals, visions, or actions to ensure their stakeholders' actions towards the brand are harmonised (see Wider et al., 2018). We see this orchestration as a source of enduring corporate brand identity (see also Iglesias et al., 2020). It is suggested that firms should identify their key stakeholders and particularly those business partners with whom they co-create their brand meanings; something even more important for SMEs with limited resources (see Mäläskä et al., 2011; Törmälä & Saraniemi, 2018). Wider et al. (2018) among others suggest the term *orchestration* rather than *management* to capture the essence of this novel mindset of brand management. This argument is supported by Michel (2017) who uses the term *brand conductor* for a similar purpose. As tensions and discrepancies rise in parallel with brand co-creation, it is also important to find mechanisms to orchestrate the efforts of the brand's network to address those challenges.

Combining the views discussed above prompted an exploration of the implications for brand-related discrepancies in networks. To reveal these discrepancies, we next scrutinise stakeholder relationships relating to a food industry brand and also discuss the mechanisms applied to turn the co-destruction of brand value and brand meanings into positive outcomes; in other words, to recompose the brand meanings. Although we focus on the implications for certain relationships, the sources of discrepancies may lie in multiple stakeholder relationships and their effects can produce broad impacts throughout the brand's network.

## 3.    DISCREPANCIES IN BRAND CO-CREATION: FROM GENERIC PRODUCE TO A CONSUMER BRAND

The following empirical case illustrates how brand discrepancies can manifest and how they can be overcome. In the case, the brand governor has the express aim of changing the brand significantly by making it recognisable as a consumer brand, rather than just a corporate brand known primarily by trade customers. The examined change process thus explicates how an existing brand identity is contested, and how various stakeholders adjust to the change, (cf. Törmälä & Gyrd-Jones, 2017; Iglesias et al., 2020) involving the co-destruction of the old brand meanings and value and their recomposition into new forms.

The case study draws on multiple types of data, gathered between 2014 and 2020. In addition, one of the authors has background knowledge that helps contextualise the data, from having grown up in the area where the case company and its producer network operate, which gives rise to multiple personal touchpoints with both the case company itself and with other industry actors in the network. The data include extensive personal interviews with the case company's sales and marketing director in 2014, 2015, and 2020, supplemented with company-generated documents such as company presentations and social media content. The final case description was also checked by the key informant to ensure the credibility and salience of the empirical accounts. Observational data from visits to the focal company's packaging facilities, as well as following the brand's visibility in retail environments from a consumer-observer's viewpoint also helped corroborate the case. The timing of the interviews has provided a perspective on the brand at different points in time; from the early stages of the consumer branding efforts to six years later, thereby enabling a longitudinal view of brand-related changes and their network-level implications. While the first stages of data elicitation depicted the brand at the beginning of a change process and revealed discrepancies at the outset, the later interview, along with tracking the brand's media presence, provided insight into how the focal company's brand orchestration efforts turned out; the means through which new brand meanings and value were created, and how the initial discrepancies were addressed. The latter stage of data elicitation also enabled broadening the brand's stakeholder network to include new actors and their contributions to the brand, especially in terms of the communication of brand meanings.

The case description relies most significantly on interviews with the sales and marketing director of the focal firm – the person employed to implement the branding process – and hence the brand's network is largely depicted from the perspective of that specific actor.

## 4.    BACKGROUND: THE NEED FOR A NEW BRAND STRATEGY

The focal actor in the case, Närpes Grönsaker is a Finnish farmer-owned vegetable wholesale cooperative that specialises in producing greenhouse-grown vegetables such as tomatoes and cucumbers. It packages and sells vegetables to the big national food wholesale chains, and through them to supermarkets and other grocery stores, as well as food service suppliers throughout the country. It has a dominant market position, being the biggest supplier of tomatoes and the second-biggest supplier of cucumbers to the Finnish market. The name of the company (which translates as Närpes vegetables) reflects that the products are grown around the municipality of Närpes in Western Finland, which is the geographical area where about 70 per cent of Finnish tomatoes are grown (Finnish Glasshouse Farmers' Association, 2020).

The customer market in Finland is highly concentrated and dominated by big chains like Kesko (a chain of entrepreneur-owned outlets ranging from hypermarkets to corner shops), SOK (a similar chain of regional cooperatives), and the German retailer, Lidl. The market is then completed with other smaller wholesale and retail actors and food service customers. The traditional role of the case company has been to distribute the crop of the owner-farmers to various customers. The role has therefore been a logistical one, characterised by transaction type of customer interactions where the contact points have concerned routine processes of handling orders and price negotiations, or evening out temporary excess supply though pricing campaigns. The exchange has concerned generic, bulk produce, where at best, only the domestic origin has functioned as a differentiating characteristic. Exposure to competition in such a market has been high.

The market situation had been changing owing to increasing competition from foreign and private-label products (creating co-opetition between buyer and seller) and the threat of the larger-scale farmers to develop their own packaging and direct sales routes – a new form of competition. Against this setting, the case company began a strategy process in 2012, involving, among other things, employing a sales and marketing director, and devoting resources to redirecting the offering of the company from a generic bulk to a more branded outward face in the hope that doing so would add value to the offering and shield the firm from price competition, thereby also helping to sustain profitability upstream among the farmers. Moreover, such a change from selling bulk products to becoming a recognised and appreciated brand among end-users was also expected to change the nature of the business customer relationships and move them in a more co-creative direction.

## 5.    RECOMPOSING THE BRAND

In their pursuit of developing a branded offering instead of being seen as only a provider of anonymous, bulk produce, Närpes Grönsaker focused on three main areas of development: changing the offering, developing its brand communications and relationships with consumers, and revising its sales strategy. These changes necessitated such major shifts in the resources it developed and acquired upstream and offered downstream to customers, that we choose to label the process *recomposing* the brand. Through this analogy with a musical term, we draw attention to a brand not only being adjusted or repositioned but rather being recreated as something significantly different from what went before. Moreover, just as a musical composition brings together various instruments and their melodies, brand recomposition, although being set in motion by one actor, similarly requires consideration of the stakeholders involved and the way their collective performance is coordinated, or *reorchestrated*.

The first type of tangible brand adjustment action in the case addressed product development. The aim was to move supply in a direction that had the consumer sphere and situations of use as its point of departure, rather than, for example, what was productive for the farmers to cultivate. This, in other words, implied a major perspective shift from a production orientation to a customer (use) orientation, as the following extract from an interview with the sales and marketing director exemplifies:

> We try to teach consumers to use the products in a different way. It supports the idea of a broader product assortment and different varieties for different use purposes, like some specifically for warm dishes and others to be eaten as snacks as such, because they are so tasty.

While generic bulk tomatoes had previously been offered as a single solution, the focus on differentiated product usage (e.g. tomatoes to be eaten fresh, on the go, barbecued, or in slow-cooked dishes), meant more diversified product categories for the company, which in turn relied on changing the requirements of which varieties to cultivate to best suit each type of use set for the farmers. The sales and marketing director explains this as a supplier relationship issue between the cooperative and its farmer-owners:

> The producers are still individual entrepreneurs. Of course, they listen to us, and what we advise, but their investment decisions are always their own.

In other words, the brand recomposition in terms of new product development was reliant on and affected other stakeholders, as the existing brand identity became contested and recomposed. In this process, the new market-driven development directions identified by the case firm need to be sold to the farmer-owners, for instance through arguments related to the prices farmers could expect from switching to new varieties.

This branding aim has also created a need to make consumers more aware of and knowledgeable on, for example, which varieties of tomatoes to use for which purpose. Creating new use-based segments brought about changes to central brand meanings and the value that they provided. Encouraging consumers to pay attention to new, qualitative characteristics as product choice criteria, also had implications for producers. Taste, for example, was emphasised as a central appeal, as the sales and marketing director illustrates:

> We go taste first into all the product development processes. You can cultivate and aim for high crop levels and be interested in kg/m$^2$, but we think, in the long run, no one buys all those kilos if they don't taste good.

*Taste* is also the title of one of the firm's first promotional videos, depicting a farming family and their pursuit of good products, which also exemplifies the focal firm's desire to shift brand meanings away from economic sales arguments, something that requires adjustment for other brand stakeholders, such as trade customers, and how they market and display tomatoes.

In addition to product development, the second area of development was to increase the share of products that are consumer packaged, rather than sold as generic *pick and weigh* commodities. Through increased use of product packaging, the corporate brand could be made visible and recognisable to consumers, and more marketing messages and information conveyed in the retail environments, as illustrated by Figures 7.1 and 7.3. Moreover, packages enabled the more efficient display of more specialised, new products such as pearl tomatoes or cherry tomatoes on the vine. For the retail level stakeholders, the move meant exploring their ways of using shelf and floor space and thus required adjustment and negotiation.

*Photo:* Närpes Grönsaker.

*Figure 7.1    Supermarket display of consumer packaged tomatoes*

The sales and marketing director further describes the path to a more nuanced, packaged, and branded offering, and the implications of that offering for value across the network:

> The goblet products [small tomatoes in plastic cups or "goblets"] are typical examples of successful product development and commercialisation. … With that product, we have maintained a pull on the market, demand has exceeded supply. And this has enabled an acceptable price level, also for our producers. So, developing the market without ruining market prices.

Moreover, the brand strategy necessitated investments in marketing communication, from redesigning the logo and other visual materials, sales promotion activities, and establishing a presence in communication channels that enabled direct dialogue between the company and consumers. The communication strategy involved providing information and ideas related to product use but also promoting the transparency of the company's operations, which is a significant factor in the food industry. Such transparency required the firm to show its brand audiences where the products come from and who grows them. Doing so lends familiarity and trustworthiness to the brand's character and helps convey sustainability arguments. As the sales and marketing director expressed it:

> One of our main aims is to increase the transparency of what we do. The farmers, what they do, how they do it. Nowadays the consumer is super interested in that in the food sector.

Communicating transparently about product origins also plays a role in meaning-making and building consumer–brand relationships, which constituted a broadening of the brand's network compared to the earlier corporate brand that had little recognition beyond B2B relationships:

> You get a different relationship with the end-user when production phases are shown transparently. It increases trust. Because there are still issues with consumer scepticism of the sustainability of Finnish greenhouse production. But there are still a lot of adjectives left to use, and claims we can make, that we can and want to use in marketing.

In its more tactical marketing communication efforts, Närpes Grönsaker has utilised input from several external advertising and media agencies and their sub-suppliers, thus orchestrating a set of meaning-creating resources related to commercialisation, creative and visual content production, and cooperation initiatives with social media influencers. Furthermore, within the organisation, marketing has gradually grown in terms of allocated budget, staffing, and use of market research. The different actors involved with the brand's ecosystem are illustrated in Figure 7.2.

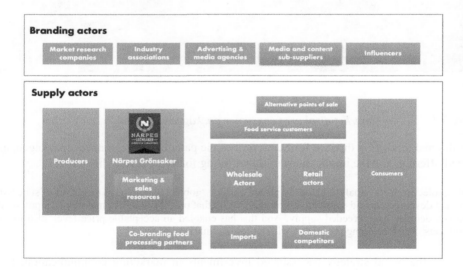

*Figure 7.2    The brand's ecosystem*

In addition to the visible aspects of recomposing the brand through product development, packaging, and communication efforts described above, a fourth, more strategic level change was a major shift in the sales strategy of the firm. That shift required the firm to move on from a customer-order handling stance to become more proactive in its attempts to maintain and develop true business customer relationships at different levels. The sales function was reconstructed to reflect the importance of key account management instead of order handling.

An illustrative detail is also the job title of the informant, sales and marketing director, which highlights the integration of the sales and marketing functions in the case firm.

Gathering information on customer preferences through direct consumer communication channels in social media and conducting market research led to a change in the content of the case firm's sales relationships, and enabled the sales negotiations to revolve around meanings and value, rather than generic products and prices. The sales and marketing director describes the current situation:

> Today, we can offer value through the brand, whose recognition has gone up from 6% to over 73% in six years. That's a direct result of our marketing work. We have managed to create product-related values so that consumers tend to prefer our products to competitors if the alternatives are similar. That's added value that those in the trade can't ignore anymore.

The informant perceived the firm's marketing intelligence and branding efforts to have altered the division of work in the sales relationships, but states that "we gladly do part of the intermediary's job if it generates business for us". By possessing better knowledge of consumer behaviour and the sales potential of its products, the firm has also equipped itself to address customer relationships on the category management level, rather than only with the customer's purchasing function.

## 6.    BRAND DISCREPANCIES IN THE NETWORK

When the company first launched its new branding strategy, the initiative was applauded by representatives of the major customer chains: One key customer told the sales and marketing director, "Finally someone is doing something within the greenhouse segment". The retail chains also appreciated having an active counterpart in the business relationship, in contrast to the previous routinised transactions. Nevertheless, the transition from the old role and position to the new was not entirely smooth and did involve tensions and inconsistencies, which are typical in change processes and dynamics that span organisational boundaries. Here we use the term *brand discrepancies* to describe issues experienced by the parties to the brand's network during the process of reconfiguring the brand and its meanings, and the value it provided. In a sense, all parties were involved in co-destroying the old positions and reconfiguring them anew, even if the business relationships in which the changes took place remained the same. This reconfiguration meant a new role for the case firm in relation to its customers now being able to contribute with new types of resources (products, brand recognition, consumer insight) and the meanings and value they could provide.

When one relationship counterpart levels up in terms of its position and bargaining power – as Närpes Grönsaker did through the branding efforts described – the relationship dynamics change as well. Even if the related actors in principle agree on the new development direction, the pace at which they adapt can vary, and thus create tension that reveals brand discrepancies. This outcome is in line with the findings of prior research into value co-destruction in relation to the ability to integrate resources and adapt to change, for example (see also Järvi et al., 2018).

In the supply network, such a temporal discrepancy is identifiable in the interface between producers (farmers) and the focal firm. Product development cycles are long – when new product varieties are developed, it may take several growing seasons until supply and demand are correctly aligned. The asynchrony and uncertainty related to how demand develops in relation to allocated cultivation capacity pose challenges for the supply network, not least upstream. While producers supplying Närpes Grönsaker generally supported the redirection, the time horizon in which they anticipated it would yield benefits has been a cause of some tension and misaligned expectations.

On the customer relationship side, the major retail chains are characterised by a strong focus on logistical efficiency and cost considerations, which constitutes a kind of a counter-force to the aim to provide a more nuanced, branded offering; the same actor, who has an interest in providing value for its end-user can also hinder developments that will ultimately deliver such customer value. From the logistics-driven perspective, a simple bulk product is an easier resource to handle (compare and purchase) than a more complex, branded offering that involves the purchasing department in more work. When Närpes Grönsaker's position changed to being a firm possessing a consumer brand and new and enhanced knowledge of consumers and product use, it became a new type of negotiating partner, having previously been one where negotiations most revolved around price and delivery schedules. The new situation reflected changed power and dependence relations as sources of co-destruction (see Vafeas et al., 2016), at the same time revealing a need for reorchestration.

When Närpes Grönsaker became a consumer brand, the firm had to pay attention to making the brand visible to consumers through its choice of packaging and display materials, such as the ones seen in Figure 7.3. This consideration meant issues such as shelf and floor space display choices became critical points of negotiation between seller and retailer. The retail chain customers initially mostly declined to use supplier-provided point of purchase displays "Not aligning with the store concept" being the response of the sales and marketing director received from the chain customers. Similarly, as Närpes Grönsaker positioned some of the new products based on their use as snacks, rather than generally as vegetables, the sales and marketing director would have liked to have seen them placed near the checkouts to encourage impulse buys; the supermarket chains, however, were not very keen to adopt this idea, despite the strategy of replacing confectionary with healthier products at the checkout being adopted in other countries.

While the main supermarket chains contested some ways of jointly conveying brand identity, the type and extent of discrepancies in transitioning to dealings with a branded supplier differ from one customer relationship to another. The change was more easily handled with customers with smaller and flatter organisations and where personal bonds between interacting parties extended over a longer period. In this case, Lidl is such an example.

> There is a significant difference in the step from business opportunity to decision; there are fewer people to be in contact with and have relationships with. Others are bigger and heavier in their administration.

Thus, the speed of renewal was faster and the decision processes simpler in some smaller organisations than in the bigger ones, where multiple levels of decision-makers had to be identified and convinced, a situation that reverberates with Järvi et al.'s (2018) observation of the inability to change being a source of co-destruction. The different wholesale customers also vary in the volume of competing products they buy, and how well they can forecast the product volume demanded by individual stores.

*Photo:* Närpes Grönsaker.

*Figure 7.3    In-store display of snack tomatoes*

The sales and marketing director notes:

> Lidl's flow of goods is 100% centralised so they have a better grasp of what is sold where. But Kesko, for example, consists of independent shop owners so the local shops can buy in whatever they want, it's the same in SOK's regional cooperatives. So, the chains can estimate but don't know for sure the flow of goods from one week to the next. This is much more straightforward with Lidl.

In this sense, the Lidl network offered a lower degree of complexity and thus fewer potential sources of discrepancy compared to the bigger chain customers.

A different type of discrepancy from those in the supply network can be seen among the stakeholders that are brand specialists (see Törmälä & Saraniemi, 2018), and directly connected to the branding process. As brand meanings had been articulated and visualised almost from scratch, the process also revealed the difficulty faced by external actors in understanding the essence of their client's identity and the most appropriate means through which to express it. This learning process led to re-evaluating communication media and reassessing advertising agency cooperation during the brand development process. The sales and marketing director illuminates these challenges in the following way:

> A problem has been that it's too project-based, one campaign and activity at a time. The red thread has been missing and the messages have been unlinked. There is a focus on the artsy and visual but a business understanding of the customer is often poorer. We have ditched many agencies because of this.

Although the case firm's idea to transform a relatively unbranded commodity into a consumer brand has been portrayed as a win–win situation at the idea level for the different stakeholders involved, the practical activities undertaken to this end exposed discrepancies among the stakeholders, as the prior substance of exchange, and negotiating positions were co-destructed to pave way for the new. The change created tensions; and required negotiation, clarification, and adjustment in orchestrating the brand across the different organisations involved. Below, we discuss how these discrepancies were dealt with.

## 7.    OVERCOMING DISCREPANCIES AND RECONFIGURING MEANINGS AND VALUE

Six years after the launch of the brand strategy, Närpes Grönsaker had managed to raise its brand recognition from 6 per cent to 73 per cent, indicating the effectiveness of the changed brand identity from a B2B commodity supplier to become a consumer brand. The share of the bulk of the sold output has decreased markedly; measured in product units, the sale of packaged and branded products has gone up from 200 000 per year to almost 14 million, that is, a 70-fold increase. What has Närpes Grönsaker done to overcome the discrepancies among its stakeholders and achieve its new position as a modern, consumer-oriented food industry brand that is also valuable in a new way for its network?

The investments made, starting with market research and gaining an understanding of end-user needs, using that knowledge to drive product development processes, meaning-making, and devoting resources to brand development and recognition building among consumers, has over time accumulated a brand value that, in the words of the sales and marketing director "the trade actors can't ignore anymore". Compared to the beginning of the branding process, it has taken time for the brand-related competence of the focal firm to become sufficiently convincing to affect consumer preferences for and recognition of the brand so that the firm could utilise its position as a resource in its interactions with business customers. In a successful product development project, the sales and marketing director says "we have done our homework and know what the consumer wants, what product characteristic this requires, what it can cost, and where they want to buy it. This is information that we can give to the customer". Thus, the reconfiguration means that one party has new and useful resources to bring to the relationship. Even if those resources might initially be challenging to adjust to for the stakeholders, once aligned and reorchestrated, they can provide new kinds of meanings and value across the network.

Närpes Grönsaker has gradually also increased its understanding of the dynamics that drive the business customers as a whole, which aligns with Vafeas et al.'s (2016) considerations of human capital and adequacy of communication considerations and generally reflects the way in which actors' resources become better aligned and integrated. While the discrepancy related to a focus on price and logistics versus qualitative brand characteristics and meanings can still be identified within interactions with the purchasing functions of the buyer organisations, Närpes Grönsaker has increasingly strengthened its ties with the customer through interactions with other functions within the wholesale and retail chains. "What we've changed, is that we work on several different levels today", the sales and marketing director states. Discussing the brand's retail presence increasingly with the category management and sales functions within the customer organisation has provided arenas to focus not only on price but on developing and utilising the sales potential of products. The focus in these interactions is directed more to generating revenue. In other words, understanding the customer's decision-making structures, identifying and investing in relationships with the right internal stakeholders and gatekeepers to jointly be able to maximise the brand's value potential, has been an important step in brand reconfiguration and a means of reducing brand discrepancies.

The issue of discrepancies related to retail space and brand visibility is partly a continuous negotiation, as Närpes Grönsaker remains keen to expand its presence from the fruit and vegetable sections to other spaces that would encourage first-time trial purchases of new products or impulse buys of snacks, for instance. One avenue for enabling such a use purpose-centric path to a specific product is to consider new types of sales points that would provide a brand presence in a specific consumption context, such as gyms or cinemas. Another alternative pathway to product use is Närpes Grönsaker investigating brand cooperation with a company that makes tomato sauce from tomatoes that do not meet the EU directive appearance criteria to be sold in shops. While this customer relationship is still economically less significant than other sales channels, there is a goodwill value to being part of such a sustainability promotion and food waste utilisation venture. Moreover, other potential brand cooperation initiatives involving brand meanings relevant to Närpes Grönsaker that could be reinforced through association with other parties are planned. Such efforts can be seen as examples of reconfiguration; challenging the idea of what type of distribution actors that are needed in the network in order for the brand to provide value and meanings for consumers.

In line with the suggestions in prior literature, relationship mechanisms in the form of increased openness and communication have also reduced the discrepancies between the company and its farmer-owners, as the following statement from the sales and marketing director illustrates:

> They are better at telling us things about the conditions of cultivation, and we provide continuous information about the market … We know much more than 5 or 6 years ago. And what we know, we also communicate to the producers. So they are aware of the market expectations.

Better communication and thorough customer understanding are also central to the process of handling discrepancies in brand meaning-making that involve advertising content and media stakeholders. Currently, Närpes Grönsaker uses three different agencies as a kind of networked pool of external brand specialists. While the agencies have previously mainly viewed each other as competitors for the account, Närpes Grönsaker has instead sought to orchestrate (see Wider et al., 2018) the brand meaning-making inputs of the agencies and their sub-suppliers into a whole, where each actor contributes its particular strengths and competence. As the agencies have become used to working together rather than competing their creative suggestions have also become aligned. The sales and marketing director explains:

> They all have their strengths, and we try to make a good team out of them. Previously they had very divergent ideas, but now the red thread and the key message is clearer … I take it as a sign of [the agencies] understanding the brand's needs better.

In sum, while the customer chains have welcomed the idea of branded tomatoes, which retailers can use to provide more value for their customers, the change process also revealed tensions and required adjustment. A firm that has a consumer brand and new and enhanced knowledge of its target consumers and their product use, becomes a new type of negotiating partner, compared to one primarily concerned with negotiating price and delivery schedules. In this new situation, for instance, shelf and floor space and display choices – through which the brand is made visible to consumers through packaging and point of purchase display materials – became new critical points of negotiation between buyer and seller.

This case highlights the typical challenges of FMCG suppliers in their fight for a place on the shelves of a powerful distributor. What is particular, however, is that this food brand did not enter the network as a completely new one, but that the brand-related interactions lay on a foundation of existing business relationships together with an established familiarity with and trust in the focal actor. The introduction of new resources (products, brands, knowledge, meanings, etc.) and new management issues related to them temporarily changed the dynamics and roles of the parties, revealing brand discrepancies. Orchestrating the brand as a co-created effort has, however, helped overcome such discrepancies and recompose value and meanings. However, as market expectations and developments are ever-changing and business networks never stand still, the co-creation process related to brand meanings and value is also an ongoing negotiation, albeit one that is sometimes more disruptive and requiring of extensive reconfiguration and reorchestration.

## 8.    CONCLUSIONS

The case depicted in this chapter illuminates the networked character of brands. The process involved defining brand discrepancies, that is, the inconsistencies and other triggering infractions in business relationships that can prompt a co-destruction of the brand and ultimately a reconfiguration of meanings and value in the brand's ecosystem. Our findings show that the management of brands should be approached as a continuous process of orchestration in a multi-stakeholder setting, rather than as something conducted unilaterally by a brand governor. Our study contributes to the brand co-creation literature by explicating the concept of brand co-destruction and illustrating that it is not always the dark side of co-creation (see Michel, 2017). Brand co-destruction can have positive outcomes by spurring the reconfiguration, recomposition, and reorchestration of brand meanings and value in the ecosystem. While these terms may seem interchangeable, we make a small but significant semantic distinction between them to highlight the nuances of this phenomenon. *Recomposition* refers to creating meanings and value, possibly even with new actors, in a distinctly different way than before. *Reconfiguration* again refers to novel brand elements, resources, and actors that become integrated into the co-creation of brand meanings and value. Both recomposition and reconfiguration need *reorchestration* in the network. This term, in turn, has a more managerial angle, illustrating the process of for instance a brand governor in coordinating the different brand-related resources of interlinked stakeholders to the desired end, which is analogous to orchestrating a musical performance.

The longitudinal character of this case study exposed the process nature of brands, even in instances when the brand resides in a seemingly stable, long-term business relationship. We show that changes in a brand's external and internal context (see Törmälä & Gyrd-Jones, 2017; Iglesias et al., 2020), for example, downstream in the network in consumer trends or valued product characteristics (such as the sustainability of production or the traceability of foods), may trigger a re-evaluation of the kind of value the brand can offer, thus causing the destruction of the existing value in some business relationships and reconfiguring the value proposition and meanings in the whole ecosystem. Accordingly, the company's responsiveness to changes and co-creation of offerings with stakeholders serves as an example of a triggering discrepancy prompting further discrepancies and dynamics in other stakeholder relationships. Time and the asynchrony of the parties' adaptation to change is a central factor to consider in such dynamics. Even if stakeholders share similar ideas of the brand and its future development direction in principle, they move at different speeds. Some are more motivated than others, some limited by intra-organisational complexity and rigidity, some have different expectations of shorter-term activity or results than others. Asynchronous adjustments to a recomposed brand are something that needs to be acknowledged when the brand is orchestrated.

The Närpes Grönsaker case illustrates how the brand discrepancies and a following successful brand reconfiguration necessitates the activation of existing resources and capitalising on those relating to market intelligence, corporate reputation, and existing actor bonds, for example; in other words, the orchestration of the ecosystem. In addition to such positive network effects, the embeddedness of the brand in multi-stakeholder networks also exposed their downside, in that change was hindered by the differing aims of the various stakeholders, as illustrated by the negotiation between value, cost, and logistics considerations in the food distribution network.

In light of the findings, brand discrepancies can be viewed as forces for change of various character leading to the instability and inconsistency of the brand in a network. They challenge and even co-destruct the value and meanings of the brand on a given occasion, but their outcomes – particularly when considered in a more extended temporal horizon – may be positive for the brand, such as when the network effects offer a foundation for new forms of brand value. Accordingly, compared to, for example, repositioning or rebranding (see Koch & Gyrd-Jones, 2019), the brand discrepancies revealed in our case study cover a broader range of processuality and multiplicity (see also Wider et al., 2018) of brands' reality. Ultimately, repositioning as such is a management process, but coupled with the discrepancies surrounding it externally and internally (see, e.g. Schmeltz & Kjeldsen, 2019), reveals the ever-changing nature of the reality surrounding brands. In line with Wider et al. (2018), we suggest that for managers, adopting a dynamic and networked perspective to brands requires a different mindset; one of orchestration rather than control in the context of a brand network, but also offers the promising possibility of creating an authentic brand that welcomes different voices in the network and draws upon diversities in the brand's time and space.

In further studies, an interesting avenue would be to adopt a processual and interactional approach to brands as agentic assemblages with multiplicity (see Onyas & Ryan, 2015; Ramaswamy & Ozcan, 2018; Wider et al., 2018), which could provide an even more detailed network-level understanding of how brand meanings and value emerge and develop, and also of how they can come to be contested or even fail to provide the value intended for them.

# REFERENCES

Aspara, J., Aula, H.-M., Tienari, J. & Tikkanen, H. (2014), "Struggles in organizational attempts to adopt new branding logics: The case of a marketizing university," *Consumption Markets and Culture*, 17(6), 522–552.
Brodie, R.J., Benson-Rea, M. & Medlin, C.J. (2017), "Branding as a dynamic capability: Strategic advantage from integrating meanings with identification," *Marketing Theory*, 17(2), 183–199.
Echeverri, P. & Skålen, P. (2011), "Co-creation and co-destruction: A practice-theory based study of interactive value formation," *Marketing Theory*, 11(3), 351–373.

Evans, B.P., Starr, R.G. & Brodie, R.J. (2019), "Counterfeiting: Conceptual issues and implications for branding," *Journal of Product & Brand Management*, 28(6), 707–719.

Finnish Glasshouse Farmers' Association (2020), Tietoa kasvihuonealasta [Information about the glasshouse industry]. Website. Quoted 30.6.2020. Available at https://kauppapuutarhaliitto.fi/tietoa-kasvihuonealasta/vihannesten-viljely-kasvihuoneissa/tomaatti/.

Fyrberg Yngfalk, A. (2013), "'It's not us, it's them!' – Rethinking value co-creation among multiple actors," *Journal of Marketing Management*, 29(9–10), 1163–1181.

Gidhagen, M. & Havila, V. (2016), "From Business Remains to Reactivated Business Relationships", in Thilenius, P., Pahlberg, C. & Havila, V. (eds.), *Extending Business Network Approach – New Territories, New Technologies, New Terms*. Basingstoke: Palgrave Macmillan.

Håkansson, H. & Waluszewski, A. (2001), "Co-evolution in technological development – the role of friction", Proceedings of the 17th IMP conference, Oslo, Norway.

Håkansson, H. & Waluszewski, A. (2002), *Managing Technological Development. IKEA, the Environment and Technology*. London: Routledge.

Hollenbeck, C.R. & Zinkhan, G.M. (2010), "Anti-brand communities, negotiation of brand meaning, and the learning process: The case of Wal-Mart," *Consumption Markets & Culture*, 13(3), 325–345.

Iglesias, O., Landgraf, P., Ind, N., Markovic, S. & Koporcic, N. (2020), "Corporate brand identity co-creation in business-to-business context," *Industrial Marketing Management*, 85, 32–43.

Ind, N. (2014), "How participation is changing the practice of managing brands," *Journal of Brand Management*, 21(9), 734–742.

Järvi, H., Kähkönen, A.-K. & Torvinen, H. (2018), "When value co-creation fails: Reasons that lead to value co-destruction," *Scandinavian Journal of Management*, 34, 63–77.

Koch, C.H. & Gyrd-Jones, R.I. (2019), "Corporate brand positioning in complex industrial firms: Introducing a dynamic, process approach to positioning," *Industrial Marketing Management*, 81, 40–53.

Mäläskä, M., Saraniemi, S. & Tähtinen, J. (2011), "Network actor's participation in B2B SME branding," *Industrial Marketing Management*, 40, 1144–1152.

Mele, C. (2011), "Conflicts and value co-creation in project networks," *Industrial Marketing Management*, 40(8), 1377–1385.

Melewar, T.C., Gotsi, M. & Andriopoulis, C. (2012), "Shaping research agenda for corporate branding: Avenues for future research," *European Journal of Marketing*, 46(5), 600–608.

Merz, M., He, Y. & Vargo, S. (2009), "The evolving brand logic: A service-dominant logic perspective," *Journal of the Academy of Marketing Science*, 37(3), 328–344.

Michel, G. (2017), "From brand identity to polysemous brands: Commentary on 'Performing identities: Processes of brand and stakeholder identity co-construction'," *Journal of Business Research*, 70, 453–455.

Norrgrann, A. & Luokkanen-Rabetino, K. (2011), "Inertia in business relationships: The case of a designer furniture manufacturer," *International Journal of Entrepreneurial Venturing*, 3(1), 44–62.

Onyas, W.I. & Ryan, A. (2015), "Exploring the brand's world-as-assemblage: The brand as a market shaping device," *Journal of Marketing Management*, 31(1–2), 141–166.

Plé, L. & Chumpitaz Cáceres, R.A. (2010), "Not always co-creation: Introducing interactional co-destruction of value in service-dominant logic," *Journal of Services Marketing*, 24(6), 430–437.

Ramaswamy, V. & Ozcan, K. (2018), "What is co-creation? An interactional creation framework and its implications for value creation," *Journal of Business Research*, 84, 196–205.

Schmeltz, L. & Kjeldsen, A.K. (2019), "Co-creating polyphony or cacophony? A case study of a public organization's brand co-creation process and the challenge of orchestrating multiple internal voices," *Journal of Brand Management*, 26, 304–316.

Tidström, A. (2014), "Managing tensions in coopetition," *Industrial Marketing Management*, 43(2), 261–271.

Törmälä, M. & Gyrd-Jones, R. (2017), "Development of new B2B venture corporate brand identity: A narrative performance approach," *Industrial Marketing Management*, 65, 76–85.

Törmälä, M. & Saraniemi, S. (2018), "The roles of business partners in corporate brand image co-creation," *Journal of Product and Brand Management*, 27(1), 29–40.

Vafeas, M., Hughes, T. & Hilton, T. (2016), "Antecedents to value diminution: A dyadic perspective," *Marketing Theory*, 16(4), 469–491.

Vallaster, C. & von Wallpach, S. (2013), "An online discursive inquiry into the social dynamics of multi-stakeholder brand meaning co-creation," *Journal of Business Research*, 66(9), 1505–1515.
Wider, S., von Wallpach, S. & Mühlbacher, H. (2018), "Brand management: Unveiling the delusion of control," *European Journal of Management*, 36, 301–305.

# 8. The role of brand-facing actors in shaping institutions through brand meaning co-creation

*Kieran D. Tierney, Ingo O. Karpen and Kate Westberg*

## 1. INTRODUCTION

Institutional theory provides a means to understand social structures and is emerging as an influential perspective in marketing (e.g., Koskela-Huotari et al., 2020; Slimane et al., 2019; Vargo & Lusch, 2016). Institutions are the socially constructed rules, norms and guidelines that provide structure and govern behavior (Giddens, 1984; Scott, 2013). Yet the role of an institutional perspective in accounting for the influence of social structures in brand research is still limited. This is surprising given that brand-facing actors, such as consumers, politicians, advocacy groups and the broader community, determine the legitimacy of brands, as they are the ultimate judges about what is appropriate and acceptable brand behavior. While institutional theory recognizes the mutually influential relationship between people and social structures in general (Lawrence et al., 2009), brand-facing actors have been largely overlooked in institutional theorizing and change, which researchers are increasingly criticizing (e.g., Delmestri, 2006; Lawrence et al., 2009; Slimane et al., 2019). Furthermore, the limited role of institutional theory in branding is also surprising given the relevance of brands in both aligning with and shaping meaning-making, and in doing so, influencing institutional arrangements – that is, the combined rules and conventions that guide actors' behavior – in their favor (Scott, 2013).

The limited brand research that does leverage institutional theory focuses primarily on an organizational/strategic perspective; for example, how firms and their brands can navigate and shape the institutional arrangements and expectations within and/or across markets (e.g., Ertimur & Coskuner-Balli, 2015; Stuart, 2018), or how institution-congruent employee behavior contributes to reinforcing brand positioning (e.g., Dion & Borraz, 2017). Similarly, research also demonstrates that the actions of the firm can diverge from expectations in the meaning-making processes of consumers (Gambetti & Graffigna, 2015) and that brand-related interactions can result in institutional misalignment with consumer expectations and identities (Zanette & Scaraboto, 2019). Yet the use of an institutional theory lens to explore the role and contribution of individual and collective brand-facing actors through the co-creation of brand meaning is limited. Brand meaning is an idiosyncratic and evolving emotional and cognitive understanding attributed to a brand as a result of a socially negotiated process (Tierney et al., 2016). The lack of institutional theorizing in a brand co-creation context is problematic because current understanding does not sufficiently account for the influence of actors in the brand co-creation process and the institutions that both shape, and are shaped, in this process. As demonstrated through the vignettes presented in this chapter, this is important for brand managers given the role of brand-facing actors in view of shaping institutions through brand meaning co-creation, potentially challenging the effectiveness of brand strategy.

While it is accepted that brand meaning is a mechanism through which organizations can connect with brand-facing actors and stimulate emotions, these actors are not passive receivers of communications or organizational actions that influence meaning-making processes (Tierney et al., 2016). Indeed brand-facing actors are influential in responding to perceived institutional misalignment in brand-related interactions (Zanette & Scaraboto, 2019). Further, while institutions frame meaning-making processes (Scott, 2013), meaning is an instrument that recursively shapes institutions particularly when institutions are perceived to be misaligned with the experiences and expectations of market actors (Karpen & Kleinaltenkamp, 2018).

This chapter seeks to advance knowledge in relation to the nexus between institutional theory and branding. In doing so, we give primacy to brand-facing actors rather than the organizational perspective. Specifically, we examine the nature of brand meaning co-creation, a process that encompasses brand-related, resource-integrating activities and interactions among multiple market actors within service ecosystems, leading to a socially negotiated and idiosyncratically determined brand meaning (Tierney et al., 2016), and the agency of brand-facing actors in this process. In particular, we demonstrate through three illustrative vignettes how divergence between community and organizational institutions influences brand meaning co-creation and can result in brand-facing actors putting pressure on these institutions to converge again and (re)align with expectations. We then argue that brand meaning co-creation represents a meaningful mechanism for institutional (re)shaping, which can be initiated by brand-facing actors. This leads us to present a conceptual framework theorizing and visualizing this process. Finally, we propose a set of theoretical propositions to prompt further explanation and exploration of this perspective to empirically demonstrate the reciprocal influence of institutions and meaning-making within the context of brand meaning co-creation. By adopting an institutional lens through which to examine brand meaning co-creation, our chapter contributes to the limited research exploring the role of brand-facing actors in shifting, and even transforming, institutions both internal and external to the firm and the reciprocal nature of this process. Our illustrations are applicable to and consider multiple brand-facing actors such as consumers, politicians, advocacy groups and other stakeholders. However, for illustrative purposes many examples here relate to the consumer perspective as the key brand interactant and determinant.

## 2.    THEORETICAL BACKGROUND

Institutional theory traditionally has engaged with social structures, their maintenance and developments, primarily at the macro (often field) level (e.g., Lawrence et al., 2011). Scholars endeavor, for example, to understand the evolving legitimacy and shared understandings and rules in an organizational field (Lawrence & Phillips, 2004). Therefore, researchers might study a focal firm (and/or its internal actor(s)) that seeks to navigate and potentially shape institutional environments and specific institutional arrangements for their competitive benefit; and in doing so, consumers are often not fully recognized as active participants in institutional change (Furnari, 2014; Slimane et al., 2019). However, this view, particularly the impetus for institutional change, is increasingly being challenged by researchers, building on an understanding that social structures guide human behavior and are influenced by humans and their behavior (e.g., Lawrence & Suddaby, 2006). For instance, practice-driven institutionalism, improvised behaviors of individuals in responding to institutional complexity, acknowledges the role of more micro-level contributions (e.g., individual yet relational actions) to institutional maintenance and developments (e.g., Smets et al., 2017). Further, researchers call for theorizing that more actively considers the role of consumers in not only being exposed to institutional arrangements but also in shaping them and in doing so, engage in institutional work (e.g., Delmestri, 2006; Lawrence & Suddaby, 2006; Lawrence et al., 2009). In combination, these movements allow for more bottom-up (from the individual up rather than the organization down) as well as external (rather than internal) institutional influence.

While there is a rapidly emerging corpus of research connecting institutional theory and marketing, an institutional theory perspective (e.g., Koskela-Huotari et al., 2020) in branding research is rather scant. Marketing research to date, for example, highlights by way of service-dominant logic the role of institutional arrangements in shaping value co-creation contexts and processes (Vargo & Lusch, 2016). This line of thought has been further advanced in the context of innovation processes and systems (Ansari & Phillips, 2011; Koskela-Huotari et al., 2016), whereby consumers play an important role in contributing to co-creation and co-innovation efforts. Marketing researchers also highlight the challenges of individual consumers in navigating institutional complexity in these contexts, particularly in dealing with various institutional expectations across service systems (e.g., Chandler et al., 2019; Karpen & Kleinaltenkamp, 2018).

Research that focuses on the nexus of institutional theory and branding, however, is in its infancy (Vargo et al., 2015), despite the fact that brand meaning is an essential ingredient for firm success. Branding scholars have started to embrace an institutional perspective to better understand strategic challenges and opportunities for brand managers and organizations. For instance, one stream of research takes an organizational perspective to examine how brands face the complexity of navigating multiple, often competing or conflicting, institutional logics (e.g., Ertimur & Coskuner-Balli, 2015; Stuart, 2018). On the other hand, researchers are beginning to consider a more active role of consumers in maintaining or shaping institutional order. For example, research has studied collective consumer action and identity in disrupting institutions through social movements and boycotts, in view of shaping markets in their favor (e.g., increasing market choice, see Scaraboto & Fischer, 2013). Consumers as "institutional entrepreneurs" might be both individuals (e.g., influential bloggers) and collectives (e.g., the blogger's follower community), working to instigate direct changes in field logics or at market level either intentionally (e.g., Kjeldgaard et al., 2017; Scaraboto & Fischer, 2013) or unintentionally (Dolbec & Fischer, 2015).

Additionally, research has acknowledged the co-creative nature of brand meaning construction through multiple market actors (Berthon et al., 2009; Rosenthal & Brito, 2017; Tierney et al., 2016; Wilson et al., 2014). Indeed, combinations of these institutions frame actors' meaning-making processes and influence brand perceptions and reactions. Yet, the role of the brand-facing actor actions that influence institutional change through brand meaning co-creation remains undertheorized and understudied (Slimane et al., 2019). Researchers call for theorizing that actively considers the role of brand-facing actors in not only being exposed to institutional arrangements but also in shaping them.

While institutional theory recognizes the mutual influence of institutions and actors (Lawrence et al., 2011), the role of brand meaning co-creation in this context remains poorly understood. To date, research acknowledges the role of institutions in terms of framing brand meaning-making (Tierney et al., 2016). For example, it is acknowledged that brand meaning co-creation takes place in contexts that are guided by an organization's internal rules, norms and guidelines as well as external market and societal expectations (Chandler & Vargo, 2011). Yet, the role of brand meaning co-creation in shaping these internal and external institutions is unclear. Given the marginal extant theorizing and empirical investigations, managerial insight into the relationship between brand meaning co-creation and institutions is limited. Investigating how brand meaning recursively influences institutions could shed light on how brand-facing actors co-create brand meaning and influence institutional change in brands and the broader socio-cultural environment. Without this understanding it is difficult for brand managers to develop strategies to instigate change in regulative and normative institutions that support brand legitimacy and contribute to positive brand meaning co-creation.

## 3. INSTITUTIONS AND BRAND MEANING CO-CREATION: BRAND VIGNETTES

Following the synthesis of institutional, branding and brand co-creation literatures, we now examine the relationship between institutional arrangements in brand interactions; in doing so, we draw on the regulative, normative, and cultural-cognitive elements of institutions, and their influence on brand meaning co-creation. Regulative institutions are the formal rules that enable and constrain behavior; normative institutions are the behavioral expectations and standards; cultural-cognitive institutions are taken-for-granted assumptions that frame the perception and interpretation of social reality through which meaning is made (Scott, 2013). To aid this discussion, we use three illustrative vignettes in which brand actions are perceived to be incongruent with evolving socially constructed rules, norms and values operating in the firm's external environment. This divergence contributes to the co-creation of negative brand meaning and triggers subsequent purposive grassroots brand-facing actor responses that create the impetus for change in institutions internal to the firm, and in doing so, reinforce changing external institutions.

The first vignette focuses on Aunt Jemima, an iconic American pancake and syrup brand with a long legacy. However, increasing intolerance of brands that perpetuate racist stereotypes, propelled by the Black Lives Matter social movement, as well as media and academic commentary and a vocal public, has resulted in the co-creation of negative brand meaning for Aunt Jemima, prompting the company to re-shape the brand. The second vignette features Adidas, a leading German sportswear brand that became mired in controversy in response to what was perceived as an attempt to take unfair advantage of the German government's COVID-19 business support package. The company's actions elicited brand-damaging condemnation from political and community leaders and public outcry on social media, necessitating a swift turnaround on their decision. The final vignette highlights the actions of Liverpool Football Club, one of the most successful football clubs not only in the English Premier League but worldwide. Similar to Adidas, due to COVID-19 business-related pressures, Liverpool FC sought to take advantage of government initiatives to support furloughed staff. Given the wealth of the club, as well as the brand's socialist values and community positioning, their actions were incongruent with the expectations of their constituents, resulting in significant backlash for the brand causing management to change their position.

These illustrative brand vignettes are discussed in the following sections and each concludes with a theoretical reflection on the nexus between institutions and brand meaning co-creation.

The experience of these three brands demonstrates the influence of regulative, normative and cultural-cognitive institutions (Scott, 2013) external to organizations in shaping brand meaning co-creation and the brand repercussions of a misalignment between internal and external institutions. Further, these vignettes demonstrate how, individually and collectively, brand-facing actors can play a powerful role in shifting not only institutions but also brand meaning. While it has been acknowledged that consumer movements and pressure can influence the norms and standards in both companies and governments, more knowledge is needed on how these activities achieve institutional change (Slimane et al., 2019). Following the presentation of these vignettes, we theorize the relationship between institutions and brand meaning co-creation, and present five propositions to stimulate future empirical investigation.

## VIGNETTE 1: AUNT JEMIMA – FROM EVOLUTION TO REVOLUTION IN ORGANIZATIONAL INSTITUTIONS THROUGH BRAND MEANING CO-CREATION

Aunt Jemima is one of several brands that have come under scrutiny in the wake of the Black Lives Matter (BLM) movement and the death of George Floyd in Minneapolis police custody in May 2020. The popular pancake mix and syrup brand has been around for over 130 years and was nominated seventh in Advertising Age's list of the top ten ad icons of the 20th century. This list celebrates those "images that have had the most powerful resonance in the marketplace" (Ad Age, 1999). The criteria include effectiveness, longevity, recognizability and cultural impact. However, in 2021, the familiar brand image will disappear, and a new brand name will be introduced.

The name "Aunt Jemima" came from a minstrel song written in 1875 and the original accompanying image of a Black woman in a headscarf reflected the "mammy" stereotype. In an opinion piece for the *New York Times*, Riché Richardson, an associate professor in the Africana Studies and Research Center at Cornell University, commented that the Aunt Jemima logo represented

> an outgrowth of Old South plantation nostalgia and romance grounded in an idea about the "mammy", a devoted and submissive servant who eagerly nurtured the children of her white master and mistress while neglecting her own. Visually, the plantation myth portrayed her as an asexual, plump black woman wearing a headscarf.[1]

Despite the brand's owner, Quaker Oats, stating that the brand "has evolved over time with the goal of representing loving moms from diverse backgrounds who want the best for their families" (Quaker Oats, 2020) the brand's meaning has been interpreted very differently by many consumers, as well as members of the general public and Black community leaders. A TikTok video from singer-songwriter Kirby (n.d.), "How to Make a Non-racist Breakfast" received hundreds of thousands of views as she educated viewers on the racist history of Aunt Jemima, concluding by pouring the pancake mix down the sink, stating, "black lives matter, people, even over breakfast" (Kesslen, 2020). While the brand's imagery has evolved over the years, in the face of rising public pressure, on June 17, 2020, the company issued a statement which acknowledged the incongruence between the organization's view of the brand and that of the wider community.

Acknowledging that the brand needed to reflect the values of the organization as well as meeting customer expectations, Kristin Kroepfl, Vice President and Chief Marketing Officer, Quaker Foods North America stated,

> We recognize Aunt Jemima's origins are based on a racial stereotype. While work has been done over the years to update the brand in a manner intended to be appropriate and respectful, we realize those changes are not enough. [...] We acknowledge the brand has not progressed enough to appropriately reflect the confidence, warmth and dignity that we would like it to stand for today. We are starting by removing the image and changing the name. We will continue the conversation by gathering diverse perspectives from both our organization and the Black community to further evolve the brand and make it one everyone can be proud to have in their pantry. (Quaker Oats, 2020)

Daina Ramey Berry, a professor of history at the University of Texas, commented on the significance of the impending change by Quaker Oats as Aunt Jemima normalized a racist depiction of Black women (Kesslen, 2020). In addition to the move by Quaker Oats, public support of the BLM movement has prompted several companies to re-consider the meaning of their brands resulting in significant proposed changes to familiar brands like Uncle Ben's rice, Mrs. Butterworth's syrup and Cream of Wheat cereal (Maguire, 2020). Mars, the owner of the Uncle Ben's brand, issued a media release in June 2020 stating, "As we listen to the voices of consumers, especially in the Black community, and to the voices of our Associates worldwide, we recognize that now is the right time to evolve the Uncle Ben's brand, including its visual brand identity, which we will do" (Mars, 2020).

The Aunt Jemima example illustrates the influence of regulative, normative and cognitive cultural institutions external to organizations in shaping the co-creation of brand meaning by the consumer (cf. Scott, 2013). These community-level institutions prompted market actors such as consumers to challenge the organization's regulative (e.g., internal brand guidelines and policies), normative (e.g., internal acceptability of the brand's racist origins) and cultural-cognitive (e.g., normalization of racist stereotypes and racial equality) institutions. For the Aunt Jemima brand, this shift was prompted not only by consumers, but also other individual actors such as social media influencers, celebrities, academics and media commentators, condemning the misalignment between the emerging external and internal institutional environment.

The revolutionary change at the internal brand level, as illustrated by the Aunt Jemima example, has a reciprocal effect on external community institutions; in this case, further strengthening the BLM movement, and amplifying the unacceptability of racism in business as well as the community more generally. In addition to the brand changes, Quaker Oats has also pledged a minimum of US$5 million to engage with the Black community and its parent company, PepsiCo, has pledged US$400 million over five years to support a range of programs to address racial inequity and to increase Black representation at the company.[2] While challenging and modifying firm institutions as a consequence of the brand meaning co-creation taking place in the market, this institutional change within the organization further reinforces the emerging external institutional environment, for example through the launch of diversity programs.

## VIGNETTE 2: ADIDAS – A CALL FOR MORAL ACTION SHAPES ORGANIZATIONAL INSTITUTIONS

In response to COVID-19, the German government passed a package of laws and measures to support businesses and the community. This included granting temporary relief to tenants by allowing for rent deferrals (not cancellations), manifesting in a "change to tenancy laws that bans landlords from evicting tenants if they fail to pay their rents between April 1 and June 30 2020" (Buck & Storbeck, 2020). While this emergency legal framework did not explicitly exclude large or stock listed companies, government officials made clear that it was intended for those business and private tenants with financial difficulties due to the crisis (ibid.).

Yet, Adidas, the second largest sportswear manufacturer and one of the most valuable sports brands in the world, decided during the early stages of the COVID crisis to freeze its rent payments, with a spokesperson saying: "Adidas, like many other companies, has temporarily suspended rental payments where our shops are closed", and "this is not about not paying the rent for April. This is only about a deferral." This action was a rather surprising response to the government's intended emergency relief for financially troubled tenants, given that the Adidas group reported a 2.56 billion Euro profit for 2019.

As a consequence of this decision, Adidas attracted a huge number of public reactions. This included, for example, statements from all major ministers of the German government. Among them, the German Justice Minister, Christine Lambrecht, argued that "it is indecent and unacceptable for financially strong companies to stop paying their rents" (Buck & Storbeck, 2020). Similarly, the German Finance Minister, Olaf Scholz, found it "irritating when big companies simply announce a halt to rental payments [...] Now is the time for co-operation [...] We will only get through this crisis together if we show consideration and cohesion. Corona teaches us that we will fail if we show egoism." Similarly, the German Labor Minister, Hubertus Heil, "called the behavior irresponsible and noted that the company had made hefty profits in recent years" (Thomasson, 2020).

There was general disbelief, disappointment and moral questioning of Adidas's behavior among German politicians, up to Chancellor Angela Merkel's office calling it "wrong", suggesting that Adidas is "taking unfair advantage of the measure" (Chochrek, 2020). Similarly, the Vice-president of the European Parliament, Katarina Barley, posted a tweet showing her Adidas sneakers, with the comment: "Those are the last Adidas that we bought. For a global group [...] to exploit protection clauses for tenants with existential problems is shabby." The example of Katarina Barley is interesting as she moves away from her political role to comment on the Adidas events as a private consumer, which attracted considerable attention. Importantly, her post is symbolic for Adidas being "blasted on social media for its decision last week to defer rental payments" (Thomasson, 2020). Adidas recognized an exploding social media mention, albeit largely and often strongly negative.

A study of social media reactions to the Adidas brand, analyzing more than 10,000 comments, identified a threefold negative effect: (1) a strong and negative sentiment in the public outcry; (2) the Adidas brand was damaged by a call to action from many market participants to boycott Adidas; and (3) market participants recommended buying competitor products with higher moral and responsibility standards (Kübler, 2020). In addition to the broader community, industry experts further stimulated the debate arguing that "While sports facilities and fast-fashion brands are proving by these decisions that ethics is not a key pillar of their industrial policy, the major French and Italian luxury groups are taking the diametrically opposite path by putting in place measures that exalt their responsible commitment" (Devintre, 2020).

The brand saga was diffused to some extent when Adidas released an extended statement with the following acknowledgment: "We would therefore like to apologize to you formally. We have paid our landlords the rent for April" (Thomasson, 2020).

Based on the significant public backlash, the damage done for Adidas is likely to be significant in Germany and goes beyond short-term consumer memory. Specifically, while extant research argues that institutions frame brand meaning co-creation (Tierney et al., 2016), the Adidas events also demonstrate how public brand engagement recursively shapes institutions. For example, the call to action such as boycotting Adidas and recommending more responsible competitor brands, is indicative of and in fact reinforcing changing normative and cultural-cognitive standards and institutions in the German community. Increasingly the community is holding organizations accountable for their actions, expecting businesses to take leadership and responsibility seriously in moving toward more sustainable and responsible living.

Particularly, COVID-19 has challenged brands to engage differently with consumers, being more attuned to existential questions and supporting standards of living and being (Karpen & Conduit, 2020). Brand meaning co-creation, specifically through social media interactions, has contributed and still is contributing to changes in internal and external institutions across various societal/market participants, including consumers, industry experts and politicians. In particular, politicians, through their contributions to brand meaning, have acted as guardians or stewards of regulative institutions, reinterpreting and clarifying legal frameworks and their intentions, to ensure that wealthy brands, such as Adidas, comply with said frameworks, further shaping market expectations through brand meaning co-creation. At the same time, consumers with their call for action and voicing of brand frustrations, for instance, further shape normative and cultural-cognitive institutions in the community. Ultimately, the institutional bar across all three pillars is raised through brand meaning co-creation.

## VIGNETTE 3: LIVERPOOL FC – MAINTAINING SOCIAL(IST) INSTITUTIONS THROUGH BRAND MEANING CO-CREATION

In April 2020, as COVID-19 ravaged the UK and caused the suspension of the English Premier League, Liverpool FC announced that it would furlough around 200 non-playing staff. Under the Coronavirus Job Retention scheme, the UK Government would pay 80 percent of the wages of furloughed staff and the club would make up the difference. Liverpool stood to make a saving of £1.5m through the scheme (BBC Sport, 2020). However, Liverpool are currently the world's seventh richest football club, and their announcement to seek government support came six weeks after revealing a £32m profit and increased turnover of £533m (Hunter, 2020). Understandably, the public questioned the morality of this decision when many small companies, for whom the scheme was designed to help, were struggling to stay in business (Meehall Wood, 2020a).

Yet Liverpool is a globally renowned football club, and proud of its strong socialist values and local community connections (Reddy, 2020). Indeed, the CEO had only recently reinforced these values in an interview with Spanish daily newspaper *El Pais*, stating that what differentiated the club from other teams in the world of football is,

> we had this amazing historical figure Bill Shankly, a Scottish socialist, who built the foundation. Even today, when we talk about business, we ask ourselves: "What would Shankly do? What would Bill say in this situation?" In the marketing department we got together and said: "Let's put this into words". (Reddy, 2020)

There was, therefore, a sense of betrayal and disbelief among fans and the broader sporting community at the actions of the club whose brand meaning was encapsulated in their slogan "We are Liverpool, this means more", and in the sentiment of the club anthem "You'll never walk alone" (Reddy, 2020).

The response to the club's actions exposed the depth of feeling about how this was perceived as incongruous with their brand meaning. The supporters' union demanded an explanation from the CEO amid concern "about the damage this is causing to our club's reputation and values" (Meehall Wood, 2020a). The city's mayor held talks with the club to re-consider its actions, while a past player commented that "it is contrary to the morals and values of the club I got to know", and a member of the non-playing staff commented, "the club call their staff their family – I'm not feeling like a family member" (BBC Sport, 2020).

Under the weight of this public opprobrium, the club reversed their decision a week later. In an open letter to supporters, the CEO wrote "a range of possible scenarios were considered, including but not restricted to applying to the coronavirus job retention scheme […] we believe we came to the wrong conclusion last week and we are truly sorry for that" (Meehall Wood, 2020b). Fans, public figures, ex-players and professional commentators forcibly challenged the brand over behavior they perceived as incongruent with social norms as well as the values associated with the brand. Indeed, this brand meaning co-creation process served to de-legitimize the club's actual decisions and behavior, while seeking to preserve the social side of the legacy brand. In so doing, the reactions of consumers and the public on one hand aimed at maintaining the values associated with the brand, while on the other hand seeking congruence with the social responsibility expected or taken for granted in line with broader community institutions. As a consequence of this, the resulting climb-down by the club demonstrates the influence of individual "consumers" in these situated interactions, and how brand meaning co-creation is at once shaped by and in turn shapes institutions.

Taking this a step further, the continued fall-out and negative impact on the Liverpool FC brand meaning pointed toward the foundation for proto-institutions; that is, "institutions in the making" (Lawrence et al., 2002, p. 282) that have not yet reached a tipping point of wider social diffusion and adoption (see also Kleinaltenkamp et al., 2018). While these "consumer" reactions were focused on the Liverpool FC brand, supporters of a rival team were aware that their club was also planning to furlough staff. The rival Supporters' Trust urged their club to learn from Liverpool's experience. It tweeted: "We are now saying it clearly and in public – do not further damage the Club's reputation, listen to your fans" (Hunter, 2020), again showing the recursive relationship between internal and external institutions and brand meaning co-creation.

## 4.    DISCUSSION

Institutional theory is emerging as a useful perspective in marketing to understand social structures and social dynamics (e.g., Koskela-Huotari et al., 2020; Slimane et al., 2019). Yet, the link between institutional theory and brand co-creation research to date has been limited. Consequently, existing theorizing does not meaningfully account for the reciprocal influence between regulative, normative and cultural-cognitive institutions in the context of brand meaning co-creation. While current research highlights that institutions frame meaning-making (Scott, 2013), the role of brand meaning co-creation in institutional change remains undertheorized and understudied. While giving primacy to consumers, this chapter considers the role of other brand-facing actors, such as politicians and influencers, in brand meaning co-creation and institutional shaping.

By way of three illustrative vignettes featuring Aunt Jemima, Adidas and Liverpool FC, and in the context of very recent socio-political developments, this chapter proposes the reciprocal influence of brand meaning co-creation and institutions. This mutually constitutive relationship is visualized in Figure 8.1. Specifically, internal organizational and external institutions constantly evolve and consequently may diverge over time. To retain or regain legitimacy (e.g., acceptance in the market), organizations might seek to realign with, for example, the external institutions in which they are embedded or even seek to shape such community institutions. This divergence and convergence of institutions can be significantly influenced by the brand meaning co-creation process. In the following discussion we will further examine the interplay between these phenomena from a theoretical perspective.

As we have seen across the three vignettes, organizations and their brands can be profoundly influenced by emerging external institutions. Whether it is the influence of the BLM movement, COVID-19 or rebelling influencers and consumers, the emerging social and cultural change puts pressure on organizations and brands to live up to the new standards and conventions (Ertimur & Coskuner-Balli, 2015). This is in line with previous research that argues that institutions frame meaning-making (e.g., Zilber, 2017). While organizations sought for a long time to control and/or dominate the brand meaning-making process (Wider et al., 2018) in parallel to the framing of institutions, the current dynamics in the market highlight that brand meaning co-creation shapes both brand perceptions far beyond the control of market actors and even further shape institutions relevant to the focal organization.

We advance theorizing of the interface between brand co-creation and institutional theory by way of five propositions that capture the emerging perspective and build a foundation for future empirical research. In the three preceding vignettes though, brand meaning co-creation takes a special role in enforcing or stabilizing emerging institutions. Indeed, as part of the brand meaning co-creation process, community members such as consumers, industry experts, and politicians voice their emerging institutionally influenced perspectives, which in turn shape organizational institutions over time. Aunt Jemima, Adidas and Liverpool FC all recognized that their policies and behavior are incongruent with the wider community-based expectations, and accordingly challenged or sought to realign their internal institutions. Previous research has found that successful co-creation requires an alignment across cultural environments (Gyrd-Jones & Kornum, 2013). As a result, consumers and other brand-facing actors influence the institutional environment through their brand co-creation activities, while being influenced by these institutions at the same time. This leads to our first two propositions:

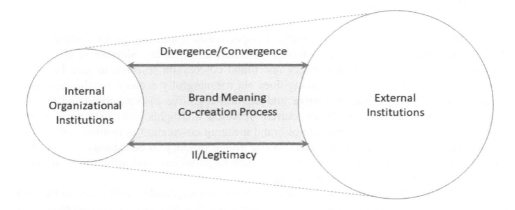

*Figure 8.1    Institutional shaping through brand meaning co-creation*

*P1: Brand meaning co-creation functions as a key mechanism for institutional shaping across normative, regulative and cultural-cognitive pillars.*

*P2: Brand meaning co-creation influences institutions in both ways, from external to internal institutions and vice versa.*

While institutional theory acknowledges the reciprocal influence between social structures and market actors (e.g., Lawrence et al., 2011), the specific role of consumers in shaping institutions through brand co-creation is only just emerging (cf. Slimane et al., 2019). Indeed, theorizing that considers the agency of consumers in shaping the brand dialogue and the institutional environment through engaging in institutional work in turn is limited. While there is emerging research that acknowledges the role of key social media influencers in promoting or boycotting a focal brand (e.g., Scaraboto & Fischer, 2013), the implications for institutional maintenance, disruption or creation, lack in-depth theorizing.

Beyond the individual agency, there are community-level institutions, such as commonly taken-for-granted beliefs or shared schemas that influence brand meaning co-creation (Ertimur & Coskuner-Balli 2015). These community-level institutions frame or influence consumers' meaning-making processes through the interpretive filters (e.g., expectations) these institutions create. Yet, across the Aunt Jemima case, for example, it becomes clear brand meaning co-creation also shapes these community-level institutions. Indeed, social media influencers such as artists may enhance the emergence of new or disrupt existing institutions by publicly questioning brand behavior and brand associations. This leads us to our third and fourth propositions:

*P3: Internal and external institutions frame the brand meaning co-creation process.*

*P4: Individual and collective consumer brand actions influence the disruption, maintenance or creation of new institutions.*

On the other hand, the Liverpool FC vignette further highlights that brand meaning co-creation can also serve to stabilize or re-instate existing institutions across community and organizational levels that are part of a focal ecosystem. For example, while Liverpool FC rose from a socially oriented brand heritage at the organizational level, the public uproar and resulting brand meaning co-creation driven by community-level external institutions (e.g., taken-for-granted beliefs that wealthy football clubs do not need to or should not draw on government support), also helped revive and ensure organization-level, internal institutions (e.g., the socially oriented brand heritage).

In addition to this preserving nature, brand meaning co-creation can also have the opposite effect of creating proto-institutions at alternate levels across the organization and the community in which it is embedded. For instance, through legitimacy pressures of the community, Adidas had to iterate and test proto-institutions (cf. Kleinaltenkamp et al., 2018) to realign itself with the moral standards and expectations of the community. This constant and increasingly dynamic emergence puts pressure on brand managers to anticipate institutional changes in the community environment, whether they are desirable or undesirable. This leads to our final proposition:

*P5: Brand meaning co-creation processes can (re)create proto-institutions across ecosystem levels as a foundation for institutional diffusion and stabilization.*

## 5.    CONCLUSION AND FUTURE RESEARCH

With this chapter we demonstrate the important role of brand meaning co-creation as a mechanism for institutional change. Through brand meaning co-creation, organizations may be seen to diverge from, or converge with, regulative, normative and cultural-cognitive institutions embedded in the community environment. We thus argue that brand managers might proactively question or challenge what is currently perceived as legitimate behavior or might seek to realign their brand(s) with emerging institutions and resulting legitimacy criteria in the external environment. In combination, we further develop our understanding of how institutions frame brand meaning co-creation, while brand meaning co-creation shapes institutions, visualized in our conceptual framework in Figure 8.1 and further theorized by way of five propositions.

We also highlight the role of consumer agency, showing their influence in shaping institutions through their contributions to brand meaning co-creation, which may also be complemented by other brand-facing actors. In extant branding research, the role of consumers in the context of institutional change through brand contributions is rather limited, in contrast to the relative extensive research on consumer contributions to value co-creation (cf. Pongsakornrungsilp & Schroeder, 2011). Individual consumers, or their scaled version as influencers with significant followers (e.g., the artist Kirby in the Aunt Jemima vignette, the Vice-President of the European Parliament in the Adidas vignette, or the fans in the Liverpool FC vignette), can significantly shape the brand meaning co-creation process, and hence also significantly influence institutional divergence or convergence.

However, consumers are just one type of constituent or brand-meaning contributor, acknowledging the role of the organization itself and other brand-facing actors. Ultimately though, institutional shaping through brand meaning co-creation can be facilitated by various brand-facing actors. This influence can unfold across levels (e.g., organizational, community) and can be initiated internally or externally. Indeed, in some cases stimulus for changing organizational institutions might emerge from the external environment, while in other cases changes in the external environment might emerge from organizational efforts (while acknowledging internal dynamics too).

Given the influence of mass and social media, which might trigger a powerful public outcry in a very short amount of time, brand managers thus need to sharpen their abilities in sensing and shaping institutions and their developments. It could be argued, for instance, that the brand managers of Aunt Jemima waited for too long until any meaningful response emerged to changing community-based institutions. At the same time, brand managers need to find the right balance between having access to meaningful data *and* meaningful insight. "Big data" does not automatically mean "big insights". Rather, brand managers need to understand, for instance, brand sentiment developments and respective institutional relationships.

To guide managers in such endeavors, future research needs to zoom into the practices that constitute the organizational brand meaning co-creation process to deal with and account for institutional influences, in particular as these practices relate to the reciprocal influence of internal and external institutions. For example, frontline employees may struggle with the demands of multiple institutions in service interactions, and hence more research is needed that seeks to understand how employees navigate complex institutional environments. Moreover, further research is required to better understand individual and collective consumer brand co-creation practices and their role as institutional work, seeking to maintain, disrupt or create institutions. A multi-actor or ecosystem perspective could shed meaningful light on how various brand-facing actors shape the divergence or convergence of institutions. Finally, future research might also investigate how proto-institutions diffuse and ultimately become institutionalized through the brand meaning co-creation process.

## NOTES

1. See https://www.nytimes.com/roomfordebate/2015/06/24/besides-the-confederate-flag-what-other -symbols-should-go/can-we-please-finally-get-rid-of-aunt-jemima.
2. See https://www.pepsico.com/about/diversity-and-engagement/racial-equality-journey-black-ini tiative.

## REFERENCES

Ad Age (1999). Ad Age advertising century: Top 10 icons. Accessed online (August 12, 2020): https:// adage.com/article/special-report-the-advertising-century/ad-age-advertising-century-top-10-icons/ 140157.

Ansari, S., & Phillips, N. (2011). Text me! New consumer practices and change in organizational fields. *Organization Science, 22*(6), 1579–1599.

BBC Sport (April 4, 2020). Liverpool place some non-playing staff on furlough. Accessed online (August 4, 2020): https://www.bbc.com/sport/football/52165826.

Berthon, P., Pitt, L.F., & Campbell, C. (2009). Does brand meaning exist in similarity or singularity? *Journal of Business Research, 62*(3), 356–361.

Buck, T., & Storbeck, O. (2020). Adidas under fire for holding back rent payments because of coronavirus. Accessed online (August 15, 2020): https://www.ft.com/content/8bfe8e86-39b2-48c1-9a7c -5a527e60d120.

Chandler, J.D., & Vargo, S.L. (2011). Contextualization and value-in-context: How context frames exchange. *Marketing Theory, 11*(1), 35–49.

Chandler, J.D., Danatzis, I., Wernicke, C., Akaka, M.A., & Reynolds, D. (2019). How does innovation emerge in a service ecosystem? *Journal of Service Research*, *22*(1), 75–89.

Chochrek, E. (2020). Adidas accused of "exploiting" German rent deferral law as coronavirus bruises business. Accessed online (August 15, 2020): https://news.yahoo.com/adidas-accused-exploiting -german-rent-200351586.html.

Delmestri, G. (2006). Streams of inconsistent institutional influences: Middle managers as carriers of multiple identities. *Human Relations*, *59*(11), 1515–1541.

Devintre, H. (2020). Fashion companies' reputations helped or hurt by reaction to crisis. Accessed online (August 15, 2020): https://fashionunited.com/news/business/hermes-exemplary-h-m-indecent -companies-reputations-helped-or-hurt-by-reaction-to-crisis/2020040632963.

Dion, D., & Borraz, S. (2017). Managing status: How luxury brands shape class subjectivities in the service encounter. *Journal of Marketing*, *81*(5), 67–85.

Dolbec, P.Y., & Fischer, E. (2015). Refashioning a field? Connected consumers and institutional dynamics in markets. *Journal of Consumer Research*, *41*(6), 1447–1468.

Ertimur, B., & Coskuner-Balli, G. (2015). Navigating the institutional logics of markets: Implications for strategic brand management. *Journal of Marketing*, *79*(2), 40–61.

Furnari, S. (2014). Interstitial spaces: Microinteraction settings and the genesis of new practices between institutional fields. *Academy of Management Review*, *39*(4), 439–462.

Gambetti, R.C., & Graffigna, G. (2015). Value co-creation between the "inside" and the "outside" of a company: Insights from a brand community failure. *Marketing Theory*, *15*(2), 155–178.

Giddens, A. (1984). *The Constitution of Society: Outline of the Theory of Structuration*. Los Angeles: University of California Press.

Gyrd-Jones, R.I., & Kornum, N. (2013). Managing the co-created brand: Value and cultural complementarity in online and offline multi-stakeholder ecosystems. *Journal of Business Research*, *66*(9), 1484–1493.

Hunter, A. (2020). Liverpool reverse decision to furlough staff after fierce criticism. Accessed online (July 28, 2020): https://www.theguardian.com/football/2020/apr/06/liverpool-reverse-decision-to -furlough-staff-after-fierce-criticism-coronavirus.

Karpen, I.O., & Conduit, J. (2020). Engaging in times of COVID-19 and beyond: Theorizing customer engagement through different paradigmatic lenses. *Journal of Service Management*, ahead-of-print. https://doi.org/10.1108/JOSM-05-2020-0156.

Karpen, I.O., & Kleinaltenkamp, M. (2018). Coordinating resource integration and value cocreation through institutional arrangements: A phenomenological perspective. In S.L. Vargo, & R.F. Lusch (eds.), *The SAGE Handbook of Service-Dominant Logic*. London: Sage, pp. 284–298.

Kesslen, B. (2020). Aunt Jemima to change brand name, remove image that Quaker says is "based on a racial stereotype". NBC News. Accessed online (August 11, 2020): https://www.nbcnews.com/ news/us-news/aunt-jemima-brand-will-change-name-remove-image-quaker-says-n1231260.

Kirby (n.d.). https://twitter.com/singkirbysing/status/1273053553876074496.

Kjeldgaard, D., Askegaard, S., Rasmussen, J.Ø., & Østergaard, P. (2017). Consumers' collective action in market system dynamics: A case of beer. *Marketing Theory*, *17*(1), 51–70.

Kleinaltenkamp, M., Corsaro, D., & Sebastiani, R. (2018). The role of proto-institutions within the change of service ecosystems. *Journal of Service Theory and Practice*, *28*(5), 609–635.

Koskela-Huotari, K., Edvardsson, B., Jonas, J.M., Sörhammar, D., & Witell, L. (2016). Innovation in service ecosystems – Breaking, making, and maintaining institutionalized rules of resource integration. *Journal of Business Research*, *69*(8), 2964–2971.

Koskela-Huotari, K., Vink, J., & Edvardsson, B. (2020). The institutional turn in service research: Taking stock and moving ahead. *Journal of Services Marketing*, *34*(3), 373–387.

Kübler, R. (2020). Dreifachschaden für Adidas – Warum sich das Aussetzen von Mietzahlungen nicht lohnt. Münster Practice and Policy Series. Accessed online (August 15, 2020): https://www.wiwi.uni -muenster.de/fakultaet/sites/fakultaet/files/mpp_16_01042020_1.pdf.

Lawrence, T.B., and Phillips, N. (2004). From Moby Dick to Free Willy: Macro-cultural discourse and institutional entrepreneurship in emerging institutional fields. *Organization*, *11*(5), 689–711.

Lawrence, T.B., & Suddaby, R. (2006). Institutions and institutional work. In S.R. Clegg, C. Hardy, T.B. Lawrence, & W.R. Nord (eds.), *Handbook of Organization Studies*. London: Sage, pp. 215–254.

Lawrence, T.B., Hardy, C., & Phillips, N.W. (2002). Institutional effects of organizational collaboration: The emergence of proto-institutions. *Academy of Management Journal*, *45*(1), 281–290.

Lawrence, T.B., Suddaby, R., & Leca, B. (2009). Introduction: Theorizing and studying institutional work. In T.B. Lawrence, R. Suddaby, & B. Leca (eds.), *Institutional Work: Actors and Agency in Institutional Studies of Organizations*. Cambridge: Cambridge University Press, pp. 1–27.

Lawrence, T.B., Suddaby, R., & Leca, B. (2011). Institutional work: Refocusing institutional studies of organization. *Journal of Management Inquiry*, *20*(1), 52–58.

Maguire, D. (2020). Uncle Ben's, Aunt Jemima and Mrs Butterworth products to get new look to remove racial stereotypes. ABC News, June 23. Accessed online (August 15, 2020): https://www.abc.net.au/news/2020-06-19/uncle-bens-aunt-jemima-mrs-butterworths-racial-stereotype/12373834.

Mars (2020). Uncle Ben's brand evolution. Press release. Accessed online (August 20, 2020): https://www.mars.com/news-and-stories/press-releases/uncle-bens-brand-evolution.

Meehall Wood, M. (2020a). Liverpool cop criticism for furloughing staff while Man United, City promise to pay staff in full. Accessed online (July 28, 2020): https://www.forbes.com/sites/mikemeehallwood/2020/04/06/liverpool-cop-criticism-for-furloughing-staff-at-uk-government-expensebut-united--city-promise-to-pay-staff-in-full/#5c8ef2d28bcd.

Meehall Wood, M. (2020b). Liverpool FC u-turns on furlough decision as public pressure takes toll. Accessed online (July 28, 2020): https://www.forbes.com/sites/mikemeehallwood/2020/04/07/liverpool-in-covid-19-furlough-u-turn-as-public-pressure-takes-toll/#37c89f1bad56.

Pongsakornrungsilp, S., & Schroeder, J.E., (2011). Understanding value co-creation in a co-consuming brand community. *Marketing Theory*, *11*(3), 303–324.

Quaker Oats (2020). Media release. Accessed online (August 12, 2020): https://www.prnewswire.com/news-releases/aunt-jemima-brand-to-remove-image-from-packaging-and-change-brand-name-301078593.html.

Reddy, M. (2020). This means more is exactly why Liverpool can't escape criticism for furloughing staff in coronavirus lockdown. Accessed online (July 30, 2020): https://www.independent.co.uk/sport/football/premier-league/liverpool-furlough-coronavirus-premier-league-criticism-this-means-more-a9448826.html.

Rosenthal, B., & Brito, E.P.Z. (2017). The brand meaning co-creation process on Facebook. *Marketing Intelligence & Planning*, *35*(7), 923–936.

Scaraboto, D., & Fischer, E. (2013). Frustrated fatshionistas: An institutional theory perspective on consumer quests for greater choice in mainstream markets. *Journal of Consumer Research*, *39*(6), 1234–1257.

Scott, W.R. (2013). *Institutions and Organizations: Ideas, Interests, and Identities*, 4th ed. Thousand Oaks, CA: Sage.

Slimane, K.B., Chaney, D., Humphreys, A., & Leca, B. (2019). Bringing institutional theory to marketing: Taking stock and future research directions. *Journal of Business Research*, *105*, 389–394.

Smets, M., Aristidou, A., & Whittington, R. (2017). Towards a practice-driven institutionalism. In R. Greenwood, C. Oliver, T.B. Lawrence, & R. Meyer (eds.), *The Sage Handbook of Organizational Institutionalism*, 2nd ed. London: Sage, pp. 384–411.

Stuart, H. (2018). Corporate branding and rebranding: An institutional logics perspective. *Journal of Product & Brand Management*, *7*(1), 96–100.

Thomasson, E. (2020). Adidas apologizes for deferring store rent, will pay up. Accessed online (August 15, 2020): https://www.reuters.com/article/us-adidas-stores/adidas-apologizes-for-deferring-store-rent-will-pay-up-idUSKBN21J5J7.

Tierney, K.D., Karpen, I.O., & Westberg, K. (2016). Brand meaning cocreation: Toward a conceptualization and research implications. *Journal of Service Theory and Practice*, *26*(6), 911–932.

Vargo, S.L., & Lusch, R.F. (2016). Institutions and axioms: An extension and update of service-dominant logic. *Journal of the Academy of Marketing Science*, *44*(1), 5–23.

Vargo, S.L., Wieland, H., & Akaka, M.A. (2015). Innovation through institutionalization: A service ecosystems perspective. *Industrial Marketing Management*, *44*, 63–72.

Wider, S., von Wallpach, S., & Mühlbacher, H. (2018). Brand management: Unveiling the delusion of control. *European Management Journal*, *36*(3), 301–305.

Wilson, E.J., Bengtsson, A., & Curran, C. (2014). Brand meaning gaps and dynamics: Theory, research, and practice. *Qualitative Market Research: An International Journal*, *17*(2), 128–150.

Zanette, M.C., & Scaraboto, D. (2019). From the corset to Spanx: Shapewear as a marketplace icon. *Consumption Markets & Culture*, *22*(2), 183–199.

Zilber, T.B. (2017). The evolving role of meaning in theorizing institutions. *The Sage Handbook of Organizational Institutionalism*, 2nd ed. London: Sage, pp. 651–678.

# 9. Co-creation of multi-sensory brand experiences: a manufacturer perspective

*Clarinda Rodrigues, Andreas Aldogan Eklund, Adele Berndt and Susanne Sandberg*

## 1. INTRODUCTION

Brands are among the most valuable assets for companies and the basis for strong competitive advantages (Madden et al., 2006). The recognition of its relevance in an increasingly competitive arena has led companies to intensify the level of resources they devote to brand-building strategies focused on value creation (Eklund, 2019). Indeed, the concept of the experience economy sheds light on shifting the value from transactions to creating memorable experiences (Pine & Gilmore, 1998). Over the last two decades, sensory marketing research has demonstrated that brands can offer value by embedding sensory cues in their products and services (Brakus et al., 2009; Chang & Chieng, 2006; Hepola et al., 2017; Khan & Fatma, 2017; Rodrigues & Rodrigues, 2019). More specifically, it is evident that brands and consumers are operant resources in the value-generating process of multi-sensory brand experiences (Eklund, 2019). This assumption is based on service-dominant (S-D) logic which posits that the value proposition is designed by manufacturers (Vargo & Lusch, 2004, 2008; Vargo et al., 2016), and value-in-use is represented by the value derived by consumers when co-creating the brand with manufacturers (Grönroos & Gummerus, 2014; Sandström et al., 2008; Vargo & Lusch, 2004, 2008).

Consumer research has begun to focus on the networked nature of brands and their meanings (e.g., Hatch & Schultz, 2010). Brand co-creation theories also suggest that the co-creation process occurs within a multi-stakeholder ecosystem (Pera et al., 2016; Ramaswamy & Ozcan, 2016; Sarkar & Banerjee, 2019) which includes consumers, organizations, and suppliers. This view is aligned with the notion of a "brand as a collaborative, value co-creation activity of firms and all of their stakeholders" (Merz et al., 2009, pp. 328–329). The brand value co-creation process is described as a social, continuous, highly interactive, and dynamic process between the company, the brand, and all its stakeholders (Merz et al., 2009). This process is extremely relevant in the context of luxury car brands where manufacturers are expected to deliver high levels of symbolic, experiential, and functional value (Berthon et al., 2009). In order to convey the value proposition of luxury cars, manufacturers may have to rely on a dynamic brand co-creation process that encompasses brand-related and resource-integrating activities and relies on interactions between individuals (micro-level), groups (meso-level), or complex networks of actors such as at the societal level (macro-level) (Tierney et al., 2016).

Despite the extensive research on brand co-creation and sensory marketing, there is a lack of studies on how manufacturers, suppliers, and consumers engage in the value co-creation process from a multi-sensory brand perspective, especially in the luxury segment. Most studies focus on the sensory aspects of brand image (Cho & Fiore, 2015; Rodrigues & Rodrigues, 2019) and experiential brand value (Chang & Chieng, 2006; Delgado-Ballester & Sabiote,

2015). With their focus on the customer perspective, these studies neglect the active role of several stakeholders in the value-generating process (Prahalad & Ramaswamy, 2004), which relies on the interaction of the brand, user, and context (Starr & Brodie, 2016). Responding to this research gap, the authors aim at answering the following research questions: (a) what is the role of the different stakeholders in the brand co-creation process? and (b) how do manufacturers design multi-sensory brand experiences as the result of a co-creation process? Thus, the chapter offers a threefold contribution: first, a review of the main theories on brand co-creation, value creation, and sensory marketing. Second, it explores the process of co-creation of multi-sensory brand experiences through a case study of a global car manufacturer in the premium segment. Third, it proposes a framework of co-creation of multi-sensory brand experiences from the manufacturer's perspective. Following our introduction, the theoretical framework is presented. In the methodology section thereafter, the case study design and method are described and motivated. The findings of the study are then presented and discussed, also proposing a "framework of co-creation of multi-sensory brand experiences". The chapter concludes with implications for theory and practice.

## 2.    THEORETICAL FRAMEWORK

### 2.1    Brands as a Value Proposition

Brands are intangible assets that are indistinguishably associated with the value they offer to their stakeholders (Starr & Brodie, 2016). This value is often subsumed as a value proposition, that is, a concise statement of the total sum of benefits a customer may derive from using a specific brand (ibid.). The value proposition concept is derived from the brand management work conducted at Procter & Gamble and was later expanded by McKinsey (ibid.). From an academic perspective, the value proposition is conceptualized as "a statement of the functional benefits, emotional benefits, and self-expressive benefits that provide value to the customer" (Aaker, 1996, p. 95). This assumption is highly relevant in the context of luxury brands, since they are expected to deliver high levels of symbolic, experiential, and functional value at the extreme luxury end of the utilitarian–luxury continuum (Berthon et al., 2009) through customer experiences (Tynan et al., 2010). In other words, the value proposition of luxury goods and services is deeply grounded on the luxury core values of excellent quality, high prices, aesthetic beauty, authenticity, and scarcity or uniqueness (Atwal & Williams, 2009; Jung et al., 2014; Kapferer, 1997). In order to convey the value proposition, luxury brands design and deliver experiences that aim at appealing to and delighting consumers through functional and experiential values (Rodrigues, 2018). In this regard, value resides both in the object of consumption (e.g., utilitarian brand attributes) and in the experience of searching, shopping, and consuming brands (e.g., experiential brand attributes) (ibid.).

The traditional view of branding posits that consumers store brand knowledge in their memory as abstract and stable brand associations (e.g., Aaker, 1991; Keller, 1993). Nevertheless, the assumption that brand knowledge consists mainly of rational and verbal representations has been challenged by embodied cognition theory (Von Wallpach & Kreuzer, 2013). This new stream of research proposes that embodied brand knowledge results from multi-sensory brand experiences, predominantly stored at a non-conscious and modality-specific level (ibid.). Research shows that consumers can transform multi-sensory and introspective (i.e., internal cognitive) brand experiences into multi-sensory images (ibid.). In this regard, consciously and non-consciously experiencing the brand through the five human senses leads to the development of embodied brand knowledge (ibid.). For example, a consumer can mentally simulate the experience of driving a car without having such a brand experience. Consequently, the driver can fantasize about how the engine would sound, how the leather seats would smell, how it would feel to touch the metal of the engine hood, and ultimately how other drivers would react to the car (ibid.). More specifically, consumers cognitively transform multi-sensory images into verbal metaphors that enable them to mentally re-experience a brand, even in its total absence (ibid.).

A large body of research identifies experiential value as a key driver of competitiveness since it is more difficult for competitors to copy and is less vulnerable to product-related changes (e.g., Delgado-Ballester & Sabiote, 2015). According to Brakus et al. (2009), brand experience consists of sensory, affective, cognitive, behavioral, and relational stimuli, which all provide consumers with pleasurable and memorable experiences in the pre-consumption and consumption process. This conceptualization reflects the experiential dimensions of consumption (fantasies, feelings, and fun) proposed by Hirschman and Holbrook (1982) and stresses the importance of the brand experiential value in strengthening positive consumer–brand relationships such as brand love (Rodrigues & Rodrigues, 2019).

Interestingly, this multi-sensory brand approach has been gaining attention among scholars, especially in the fields of fashion (Cho & Fiore, 2015; Rodrigues & Rodrigues, 2019) and tourism (Huang & Gross, 2010; Son & Pearce, 2005; Xiong et al., 2015). In this domain, sensuality has been identified as a relevant sensory-focused dimension of brand image (Cho & Fiore, 2015), shaped mainly by direct experiences with products and retail-environment-related attributes (Hultén, 2011; Krishna, 2011). Moreover, sensuality is deeply grounded on hedonic consumption and derives a set of visual, auditory, gustatory, tactile, and olfactory sensations that elicit sensory pleasure (Cho & Fiore, 2015; Rodrigues & Rodrigues, 2019). Hultén (2011) stressed the significance of the human mind and senses in the value-generating process by identifying the central role of multi-sensory experiences in engaging consumers emotionally. In this regard, "a multi-sensory brand-experience supports individual value creation and refers to how individuals react when a firm interacts, and supports their purchase and consumption processes through the involvement of the five human senses in generating customer value, experiences, and brand as image" (Hultén, 2011, p. 259).

## 2.2    Co-Creation of Multi-Sensory Brand Experiences

It is worth noting that whereas the branding perspective highlights the customer experience of a brand after being primed to expect a set of benefits, the network perspective offers a more integrative approach that focuses on the co-creation of value and recognizes the need for customer engagement in the value-perception process (Starr & Brodie, 2016). Vargo and Lusch (2004) conceptualized co-creation as the dynamic interaction and involvement of customers with their suppliers in each phase of the value-creation process. Consequently, the notion of co-creation implies an active role of the customer in the value-generating process (Prahalad & Ramaswamy, 2004) and emphasizes the interaction of the brand, user, and context (Starr & Brodie, 2016). In this regard, value is delivered only when engagement and resource integration takes place among two or more parties (Starr & Brodie, 2016) and across one or more stages of production and consumption (Hoyer et al., 2010; Payne et al., 2008; Roggeveen et al., 2012;

Tynan et al., 2010). This new brand logic implies that brands have evolved from being markers of identification and product differentiation to being a dialogue between multiple stakeholders which facilitates their co-creation of value and brand meaning (Gyrd-Jones & Kornum, 2013; Ind et al., 2013; Von Wallpach et al., 2017). Moreover, as value has shifted progressively to experiences, the market has become a forum for interactions and conversations between companies, consumers, and consumer communities (Prahalad & Ramaswamy, 2004). Strong relationships and high-quality interactions and dialogue are considered as successful value co-creation factors (Jaakkola & Alexander, 2014) in the era of stakeholder-focused branding (Merz et al., 2009).

It is commonly acknowledged that there are two types of co-creation: one is co-creation initiated by consumers (e.g., co-creation in blogs), and the other is firm-sponsored co-creation conducted on behalf of a company (Hsieh & Chang, 2016). The literature on value co-creation also distinguishes between two components of value co-creation (Lusch & Vargo, 2006; Ranjan & Read, 2016). The first component is co-production, which involves the participation of customers in the creation of the core offering itself. It can occur with customers and any other stakeholder in the value network through co-design, shared inventiveness, or shared production of related goods. In other words, co-production consists of a set of activities carried out by social and economic actors together with networks, which implies interactivity, deep engagement, and the ability and willingness on both sides to act (Prahalad & Ramaswamy, 2004; Ranjan & Read, 2016). On the other hand, the second component of value co-creation occurs at the intersection of the offer and the customer over time and is referred to as value-in-use (Lusch & Vargo, 2006). Consequently, both suppliers and customers have the opportunity to create value through interactive, customized, co-produced offerings and thus improve the front-end process of identifying customers' needs and wants (Lusch & Vargo, 2006; Payne et al., 2008) when designing and creating multi-sensory brand experiences.

Research on new product development has proposed co-creation as a process that integrates brand information from the manufacturer with idiosyncratic customer knowledge (Starr & Brodie, 2016). The brand-embedded interaction (Kim & Slotegraaf, 2016) results from a growing involvement of informed, active, empowered, and networked consumers in the process of co-creating value with companies (Prahalad & Ramaswamy, 2004). The co-creation process allows consumers to play an active and central role as participants in the New Product Development process, including ideation, product development, commercialization, and post-launch activities (Hoyer et al., 2010). Companies that are highest in their scope of co-creation will collaborate with consumers in the entire product development process, whereas companies that are highest in their intensity of co-creation at a specific stage of product development would rely exclusively on consumers for their development activities (ibid.). Involving customers in helping to shape services, spaces, and products is grounded in the notion of participatory design, a Scandinavian design approach that began in the 1970s (Ind et al., 2013) and rapidly accepted worldwide.

Research on value co-creation also stresses that the co-creation process extends beyond the production chain to the consumption and value delivery chain (Ranjan & Read, 2016). It is demonstrated that co-creation of value could also occur at the consumption stage when consumers use or consume the product following the production and the launch stages (Roberts & Darler, 2017). Prahalad and Ramaswamy (2004) view the experience as the brand and identify co-creation as a process that evolves through personalized experiences. Customers are active partners in this value-generating process (Tynan et al., 2010). Experience has an intrinsic value that results from empathetic, emotional, and memorable interactions (Ballantyne & Varey, 2008; Lusch & Vargo, 2006). According to Pine and Gilmore (1998), experiences are the most evolved form of value creation. In other words, whereas economic offerings are external to customers, experiences are personal and only exist in the mind of individuals (ibid.). This experience-centric view posits that value can be delivered by sensory, emotional, cognitive, behavioral, and relational components of brands (Brakus et al., 2009) through the co-creation process. Value is then, according to Etgar (2008), achieved through co-creative experiences independently of the nature of the services and products created. Consequently, by highlighting some sensory aspects of the brand, the value proposition primes customers to frame their perceptions by concentrating their attention on the most salient sensory attributes and benefits (Starr & Brodie, 2016). This approach to co-creation of multi-sensory brand experiences may facilitate brand co-creation as a process that encompasses brand-related, resource-integrating activities and relies on interactions between individuals (micro-level), groups (meso-level), or complex networks of actors such as at the societal level (macro-level) (Tierney et al., 2016).

In sum, the branding literature highlights the involvement of different stakeholders in the brand co-creation process and stresses the relevance of multi-sensory brand experiences as drivers of value creation (e.g., Eklund, 2019; Starr & Brodie, 2016). In the luxury segment, multi-sensory brand experiences are suggested as key elements for creating value propositions based on high levels of experiential value (Berthon et al., 2009; Rodrigues & Rodrigues, 2019). This multi-sensory brand approach, which has been gaining attention among scholars and practitioners over the last decade, calls for an active and interactive role of manufacturers, suppliers, and consumers during several phases of the value-creation process (e.g., Von Wallpach & Kreuzer, 2013). As such, the luxury brand logic has evolved from being markers of high-quality levels and aesthetic beauty to a dialogue between multiple stakeholders grounded on strong relationships and high-quality interactions. In this context, the brand co-creation process occurs in two different interlinked stages (Prahalad & Ramaswamy, 2004; Starr & Brodie, 2016). The first component is co-production led by the manufacturers in close collaboration with their network of suppliers and panels of consumers (Prahalad & Ramaswamy, 2004; Ranjan & Read, 2016). Moreover, the second component of value co-creation occurs over time and is led by consumers when consuming the luxury products or services (Lusch & Vargo, 2006; Payne et al., 2008). Here, the focus lies on the first component of the brand co-creation process of premium cars, in which the manufacturers play a key role.

## 3.    METHODOLOGY

Following the threefold aims of the chapter, a case study with a global car manufacturer in the premium segment was employed to gain insight into and knowledge of value co-creation regarding a multi-sensory brand experience. A case study was chosen to move beyond the observed phenomenon, which is required for theory building (Eisenhardt, 1989; Yin, 2014). The selected case carried sufficient experience to learn from (Stake, 1994), to gain in-depth knowledge. Few industries besides the automotive business face such fierce competition from other brands. Since cars are complex, highly engineered products, manufacturers are encouraged to be creative in positioning the brand (Kirca et al., 2020). The car's interior is one such opportunity, since the inside of the vehicle is a setting to which consumers are continuously exposed when driving. Thus, we adopted a qualitative approach involving the acquisition of detailed and rich data (Kauppinen-Räisänen & Grönroos, 2015) through the use of personal interviews with employees of a global manufacturer in the premium segment. This research method is most appropriate for exploring phenomena in-depth and obtaining truthful insights (Rowley, 2012), and responding to "how", "what", and "why" questioning (Yin, 2014). It should be noted that the qualitative approach was part of a larger data collection; for a detailed review, see Eklund (2019).

To successfully capture a rich empirical understanding of the phenomenon, purposeful sampling was used in accordance with Kumar et al. (1993). The advantage of selecting purposeful sampling was to identify key informants who possessed the right competence and knowledge about the studied phenomenon (Patton, 2014), namely how brand experience is created via the car's interior and different stakeholder roles in that process. Between 2014 and 2015, a total of 14 personal in-depth interviews were conducted at the manufacturer's headquarters. A manager was assigned to assist with the study and to ensure that key informants with relevant knowledge could be interviewed. As a result, all informants had been involved in the product development and design process of the car's interior and had titles in the areas of customer experience, engineering, or design. The interviews were conducted until the informants' narratives became similar to one another, indicating empirical saturation. The "voice" of the manufacturer is represented in the response from all informants. Due to a non-disclosure agreement, the participants and the manufacturer remain anonymous.

As a basis for the interviews, a semi-structured interview guide based on the theoretical themes "sensory cues" and "brand experience" was developed, following the guidelines of Brinkmann and Kvale (2015). The interviews ranged from ten to 62 minutes – with an average of 45. It should be noted that the one ten-minute interview was not scheduled in advance. An opportunity for that particular interview occurred when another informant suggested that a certain colleague had better insight into and knowledge on a specific question; thus, it became an additional, but short, interview. Moreover, all interviews were audio-recorded and transcribed with the informants' consent. In accordance with Brinkmann and Kvale (2015), the transcribed interviews were sent to each interviewee, respectively, to avoid reflections and misunderstandings when retelling the interviewee's narrative. All interviews were conducted in Swedish, given that the informants and interviewer are native Swedes. Narratives and quotations presented in the findings were translated by the researchers and approved by the informants.

The analysis of the empirical findings focused on how and why (Yin, 2014) to understand the brand value-creation process. As we closely monitored the informants' narratives, i.e., how sensory cues and brand experience were employed emerged. The "why" allowed for reflection of sensory cues and brand experience in the study. This allowed the researchers to move beyond the obvious in the narratives to enable the informants to guide the development of a theoretical framework (Eisenhardt, 1989). To ensure the trustworthiness of the findings and analysis, Lincoln and Guba's (1985) four techniques, recently also elaborated upon in Zeithaml et al. (2020), were followed. These are "credibility" through interviewing relevant and knowledgeable informants, "transferability" through aiming for empirical saturation, "dependability" via theme-led, recorded, and transcribed interviews, and "conformability" through the narratives being the informant's own. The trustworthiness was secured by allowing informants to review and comment upon the transcripts and the translations.

## 4.     FINDINGS

### 4.1     Involving Various Stakeholders in the Brand Co-Creation Process

In terms of consumers, the manufacturer first visited their private homes to talk to them and take pictures to understand the consumers' daily life. For example, what interior do they have, what colors, and how they live, all to gain an understanding of how to design the car's interior. Second, the manufacturer conducted focus groups with consumers. Participants were selected with regard to their personal experience and knowledge of premium brands. The focus groups revealed that premium consumers value the right brands, material, shoes and see the importance of having an elegant and exclusive watch. One conclusion drawn from this by the manufacturer was:

> The consumer spends time inside the car. That's where he wants to spend time. We are valuing the car's interior more than the exterior. It relates to our brand, where we care about the consumer the most. It means luxury is the experience we provide.

Third, the manufacturer conducted customer clinics to test the car's interior. The clinics were intended to examine consumer preferences for functional and emotional dimensions in the car's interior. Individuals of various heights and weights test drove the car to ensure, for example, that the seating and steering wheel would fit the majority of drivers. Subsequentially, the manufacturer received feedback on the comfort and ergonomics of the seating and steering wheel. In addition, individuals provided input on how the seating felt and to hold the steering wheel, as well as the perception of the leather itself. If it looks like leather, the material needs to be leather to convey the right impression. Subsequently, the manufacturer wanted to gain consumer perceptions of the car's interior, in reality, to be able to make final adjustments if needed. Fourth, the manufacturer used customer complaints from owners on previous car interiors. Thus, complaints, demands, and feedback from consumers who owned previous car models were sought to identify strengths and weaknesses, to be able to improve the current car's interior. The complaints served as input for improving the car's interior based on quality and warranty issues. For example, complaints stated that the seating became sagged after a while, there was little leg space, and leather abrasion which led to an old-fashioned-looking interior not associated with premium over time.

According to the manufacturer, suppliers played an essential role in creating the brand experience in the car's interior. The suppliers were involved earlier in the product development and design process for the car's interior. Before becoming an official partner, suppliers participated in a design competition arranged by the manufacturer. The idea was to let several suppliers present a prototype interior, respectively, based on the design theme provided by the manufacturer. The approach aimed at involving several suppliers for each interior component early on to be able to obtain input to the predefined interior design and its attributes. During this process, suppliers provided insight and knowledge on whether the manufacturer's design was feasible or not, before selecting the official suppliers. Up to this point, the suppliers could influence the interior design if underlying components related to, for example, ergonomics and heating did not fit inside the predefined interior design. However, once a contract was signed, the suppliers were limited in influencing the interior design. The manufacturer summarized the situation as follows:

The suppliers were crucial for manufacturing and delivering the interior design. However, the suppliers were limited in modifying the interior design when an official partner. Rather the suppliers' role was to provide insight and knowledge early on the underlying structure, such as if and how the technical attributes of heating could become feasible in the car's interior design.

## 4.2    Designing a Value Proposition with Brand-Related Stimuli

From the manufacturer's perspective, the brand heritage was an imperative inspiration when planning and designing the brand experience for the car's interior. Since the car manufacturer's origin is Scandinavia, brand-related stimuli associated with the Nordic countries were embedded. It was a strategic decision to offer consumers a brand experience that builds upon the characteristics of Scandinavia to ensure a holistic appearance of a high-quality car interior that translates into a premium brand experience:

> The car's interior has approximately 284 components. We are responsible for stringing it all together. We needed to ensure that all of these fitted with another. An attractive interior that fulfills consumer expectations was developed with a modern and appealing design. We are responsible for making sure that everything the consumers see, smell, hear, and feel provide harmony.

For example, exclusive materials such as crystal, birchwood, and leather were embedded in the car's interior. A gear-lever knob in crystal was positioned in the car since this is considered one of the most exclusive Scandinavian materials, which was confirmed from results from the conducted consumer clinics undertaken when visiting their homes. Birchwood was used in the door panels and dashboard since it is a common tree in the Scandinavian forest. Leather was used in the seating and steering wheel, as well as an optional add-on for the dashboard. Although leather is not needed for utility, it was added to provide consumers with sentiments and feelings of exclusivity regarding the car's interior. Calm and cool colors inspired by the Scandinavian coastline were used to remind consumers, from a sensory perspective, of the landscape in the Nordic countries.

Moreover, the manufacturer wanted to convey other characteristics of Scandinavia to the consumers. For example, silence and simplicity are characteristics the manufacturer embedded in the car's interior. Silence is provided by a soundless cabin that shelters noise from the outside, so consumers can hear and talk with one another. However, if the driver accelerates fast, the sound of the engine can be heard. Simplicity imbues the car's interior design. All the interior components were designed with regard to the purity of Scandinavia. However, this can also be seen in some of the interior features. For example, only a few buttons are located in the cabin since most functions are controlled by the tablet. The tablet employs a user-friendly menu so that consumers do not need to engage in mental activities when looking for a particular setting.

In addition, the car's interior, such as seating and steering wheel, has been designed to be comfortable and ergonomic. Attributes like these became feasible due to suppliers' competence, knowledge, and skills to develop a quality interior. Subsequentially, suppliers' involvement enables consumers to experience a comfortable long-distance ride and enjoy the car's interior. Thus, consumers are supposed to want to feel comfortable and enjoy the car's interior since they not only enter the car but transport themselves experientially. In other words, the car's interior has been planned and designed with consumers' expectations in mind to ensure that consumers feel welcome when they enter and drive the car. They are also intended to stand outside and gaze at the car's interior and feel that this is the one they want to have:

> Investigating and listening on consumer expectations and involving end-consumers was imperative. At the end of the day, they are the ones the car is manufactured for and determine meaning and value. They are the ones who will drive it. It was crucial we provide them with the premium interior they expect and want.

## 4.3　Co-Creating Multi-Sensory Brand Experiences

As stated previously, the definition of the experiential value proposal leads to the creation of an internal brand strategy that relies on multi-sensory brand experiences to engage consumers emotionally. As such, the car manufacturer defined clear guidelines based on Scandinavia as the major theme for creating the multi-sensory brand experience. Vision, touch, and sound were strategically selected to create brand-related stimuli in connection with the chosen interior design theme. These guidelines allowed the manufacturer to strategically define a completely new car model personality that moved beyond the safety and utilitarian benefits. The multi-sensory brand experience resulted from an interactive and continuous brand co-creation process that involved the car manufacturer, consumers, and a network of suppliers. Each one of these actors played a part in the car's interior. The manufacturer was the one responsible for stringing it all together. Consumers contributed with the thoughts and expectations of what makes a luxury interior from an experiential perspective. Suppliers aided the manufacturer with the know-how to develop and manufacture a luxury interior.

> The suppliers played an extremely important role. It does not matter how much work we do ourselves if the suppliers cannot produce and deliver the interior to the right quality and dimensions on time. We can't create a product without seats, infotainment, or steering wheel in it. It's all got to come together and be of the right quality. So that puts real importance on the suppliers.

Moreover, the car manufacturer was the driving actor of the production process to ensure the implementation of the multi-sensory experience in a harmonious manner. In that regard, suppliers had to become official partners and played different roles in the network. The color tonality of calm and cool was coded into numbers, so that they have the identical hue for all the car's interior. Material such as leather was a bit more complex since it may vary in tonality, shininess, and quality. Therefore, all suppliers used leather from a particular sub-supplier. This strategy ensured a coherent and unified visual impression in the car's interior. An interior such as seating and the steering wheel was developed over time in terms of comfort and ergonomics. It was achieved by a continuous evaluation and input for the interior to ensure tactile response such as solid, robust, and premium. Moreover, buttons and panels were developed to have the right pressure encumberment. Similar to color tonality, the hardness and softness were coded into numbers to ensure the right touch-pressure sensation when pressed and touched.

> A visual appealing design is the starting point. But it goes beyond that. Other senses should relate and maintain that impression. For example, if the steering wheel looks to have high quality, the consumer needs to feel that it's comfortable, natural, and pleasant when holding. Identifying and providing that feeling when touching the material is crucial. At the end of the day, these feelings influence the premium impression.

Sounds in the car's interior have a twofold purpose. On the one hand, the car's cabin was designed to resemble the silence of Scandinavia. For example, when pressing buttons and panels, no sound should occur since a noise or squeak is associated with poor quality. Also, being a family car, consumers should be able to have a conversation with each other without disturbing background noises such as clattering, squeaks, and road noise. On the other hand, despite the silence in Scandinavia, the car manufacturer wanted some sounds present. For instance, the engine was developed to have a nice tone without just being loud. The pleasant sound responds and soars when accelerating, so the consumer can hear the engine noise if required without overwhelming the quietness inside the cabin. Furthermore, technology such as mobile phones and tablets are part of consumers' daily lives. Therefore, the manufacturer developed a particular response sound in the car's tablet. The sound was designed to resemble the chimes of mobile phones and tablets, to foster a quality impression. A similar logic was developed for the car's indicators. Although the sound is still the same as before, the indicator sound is now amplified via the speaker system for quality purposes.

It is worth noting that the car manufacturer did not consider a particular scent in the car's interior, in keeping with following the Scandinavian theme. Instead, it focused on eliminating odors in the car's interior. However, as consumers expected leather to have a particular scent, this sensory cue was added to elicit the feeling of a new car.

## 5. PROPOSING A FRAMEWORK OF CO-CREATION OF MULTI-SENSORY BRAND EXPERIENCES

The informants' narrative reveals how the co-creation of multi-sensory brand experiences occurs from a manufacturer's perspective. As the case study shows, this is achieved by employing the brand heritage theme in designing a value proposition for a luxury car. However, following the logic of a multi-stakeholder ecosystem (Pera et al., 2016; Ramaswamy & Ozcan, 2016; Sarkar & Banerjee, 2019), the manufacturer cannot co-create value in isolation (Vargo & Lusch, 2004). Consequently, the manufacturer involved stakeholders such as consumers and suppliers in the process of designing a brand value proposition that combines: (a) the strategic definition of brand-related stimuli by the manufacturer to incorporate in the car design to assure a consistent brand image; (b) the competence, knowledge, and skills of suppliers to upgrade the overall experience, and (c) sensations experienced by all the stakeholders involved in the process of designing a luxury car.

The findings show that the three actors played a different role in the process of co-creating the luxury car multi-sensory experience. The manufacturer was the stakeholder who initiated the co-creation of a multi-sensory brand experience by defining an overarching theme (brand heritage) that could guide the process of designing and manufacturing a luxury car. The definition of an overarching theme is crucial to incorporate brand-related stimuli into the brand value proposition from a multi-sensory brand perspective. Moreover, the manufacturer also played a key role in collecting insights from consumers and promoting discussions with suppliers. In other orders, the manufacturer acted as a moderator in the co-creation process with the consumers and the suppliers. On the other hand, suppliers also had a key role through their competence, knowledge, and skills in ideating the car's interior based on the chosen Scandinavian theme. This interactive and open-minded dialogue between the supplier and the manufacturer was crucial to develop the intended value proposition. Finally, the consumers also participated actively in the co-creation process by helping the manufacturer to identify which factors contribute to an outstanding multi-sensory experience in what concerns a luxury car interior.

In this regard, the proposed framework (Figure 9.1) shows that the different stakeholders contribute with various facets in the co-creation of a luxurious multi-sensory brand experience. It should be noted that the present study only explored the manufacturer's perspective, that is, how value is co-created from the ideation to product development phases to offer a unique value proposition. It is important to stress that the co-creation process of a luxurious product suggests a value system where all the stakeholders generate value through the integration of their resources, skills, and knowledge. More specially, it implies that all the stakeholders collaborate actively in designing and co-producing the offer by strategically engaging the human senses. Nevertheless, the creation of value is not limited to the co-creation process between manufacturers, suppliers, and consumers (co-creation component). After the luxurious product is launched in the market, customers are the ones who will make sense of the manufacturer's brand value proposition by actively using the product (value-in-use). It points to the need to regularly analyze the customers' emotional responses to the multi-sensory brand experience (Hultén, 2011; Rodrigues & Rodrigues, 2019) since the value co-creation of a value proposition is determined by the end-user. In conclusion, the dynamic and interactive value-generation process results from the combination of the value co-creation (creation and offer of the luxury value proposition) and the value-in-use (value is recognized and accepted by the customers when using the product).

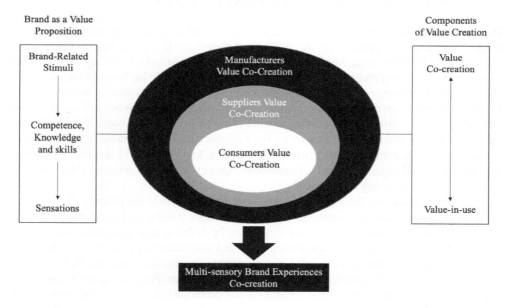

*Source:* Author.

Figure 9.1    *Framework of co-creation of multi-sensory brand experiences:*
*a manufacturer perspective*

## 6.   IMPLICATIONS FOR RESEARCH AND PRACTICE

Our study contributes to a better understanding of the process of co-creating multi-sensory brand experiences from a manufacturer perspective and sets the scene for further studies in this regard. Building on a co-creative approach to brand building, we underpin the importance of involving several stakeholders in the process of co-creating multi-sensory brand experiences. As such, we expand on previous studies on sensory marketing, which recognize the importance of sensory dimensions of brand image (e.g., Cho & Fiore, 2015; Rodrigues & Rodrigues, 2019) and the experiential brand value (Chang & Chieng, 2006; Delgado-Ballester & Sabiote, 2015), but neglect the concept of the multi-sensory brand experience as a co-creation process that involves consumers, manufacturers, and suppliers. Our qualitative study also accounts for the need to rethink the role of all stakeholders in the value-generating process from a micro to a macro-level (Tierney et al., 2016). Moreover, we also acknowledge the relevance of a consistent and unique value proposition in the value-generating process of luxury brands by acknowledging that value is generated in the new product development process (value co-creation) and when experiencing the product using the five senses (value-in-use). This assumption is relevant in the context of brand co-creation since it highlights the primary role of the manufacturer in the co-creation network, which has not been investigated in previous studies (Pera et al., 2016; Ramaswamy & Ozcan, 2016; Sarkar & Banerjee, 2019). The derived theoretical framework (Figure 9.1) summarizes our findings by proposing a conceptual model that we suggest may be useful for future research activities. For example, based on our findings, researchers may want to explore whether the proposed model applies to other types of brands or services.

The results presented in this chapter are not only relevant for research. The contribution of our qualitative study to companies is manifold, and our insights should enable manufacturers to understand how the multi-sensory brand experience can be created at different levels and thus generate value. First, car manufacturers need to acknowledge that the creation of multi-sensory brand experiences should rely on regular interaction between the company, the suppliers, and the consumers. Our study supports the notion that the network-perspective approach offers a more integrative approach that focuses on the co-creation of value (Starr & Brodie, 2016; Vargo & Lusch, 2004). Moreover, it highlights the importance of relationships, high-quality interaction, and dialogue as successful value co-creation factors (Jaakkola & Alexander, 2014). Second, car manufacturers should adopt a stepwise approach to creating a strong value proposition. The first stage corresponds to the definition of all brand-related stimuli that should be incorporated into the product development. The selection of a theme that conveys the brand identity is relevant to creating a consistent and unique value proposition (e.g., Scandinavian heritage). The second stage involves choosing the suppliers, so as to use the right competences, knowledge, and skills in product development. Detailed and clear guidelines are crucial to fulfilling the desired value proposition. In the final stage, a constant dialogue with consumers is essential for ensuring that sensations provided by the car generate the expected results and sensory gratification as planned. Another relevant implication for management is that value extends beyond the multi-sensory characteristics of a car in new product development (value co-creation). Being an interactive process, the value-generating process also includes value-in-use through the multi-sensory brand experience, which entails the need for a regular audit of how consumers feel about a car, following the production and the launch stages (Roberts & Darler, 2017).

# REFERENCES

Aaker, D. A. (1991). *Managing brand equity: Capitalizing on the value of a brand name*. New York: Free Press.

Aaker, D. A. (1996). *Building strong brands: Building, measuring, and managing brand equity*. New York: The Free Press.

Atwal, G., & Williams, A. (2009). Luxury brand marketing – The experience is everything. *Journal of Brand Management, 16*(5–6), 338–346. doi:10.1057/bm.2008.48

Ballantyne, D., & Varey, R. J. (2008). The service-dominant logic and the future of marketing. *Journal of the Academy of Marketing Science, 36*(1), 11–14.

Berthon, P., Pitt, L., Parent, M., & Berthon, J.-P. (2009). Aesthetics and ephemerality: Observing and preserving the luxury brand. *California Management Review, 52*(1), 45–66.

Brakus, J. J., Schmitt, B. H., & Zarantonello, L. (2009). Brand experience: What is it? How is it measured? Does it affect loyalty? *Journal of Marketing, 73*(3), 52–68.

Brinkmann, S., & Kvale, S. (2015). *Interviews: Learning the craft of qualitative research interviewing* (Vol. 3). Thousand Oaks, CA: Sage Publications.

Chang, P. L., & Chieng, M. H. (2006). Building consumer–brand relationship: A cross-cultural experiential view. *Psychology & Marketing, 23*(11), 927–959.

Cho, E., & Fiore, A. M. (2015). Conceptualization of a holistic brand image measure for fashion-related brands. *Journal of Consumer Marketing, 32*(4), 255–265. doi:10.1108/JCM-07-2014-1063

Delgado-Ballester, E., & Sabiote, E. F. (2015). Brand experimental value versus brand functional value: Which matters more for the brand? *European Journal of Marketing, 49*(11/12), 1857–1879.

Eisenhardt, K. M. (1989). Building theories from case study research. *Academy of Management Review, 14*(4), 532–550. doi:10.5465/AMR.1989.4308385

Eklund, A. (2019). *Harmonising value in a car's interior using sensory marketing as a lens*. (Doctorate). Kalmar: Linnaeus University Press.

Etgar, M. (2008). A descriptive model of the consumer co-production process. *Journal of the Academy of Marketing Science, 36*(1), 97–108.

Grönroos, C., & Gummerus, J. (2014). The service revolution and its marketing implications: Service logic vs. service-dominant logic. *Managing Service Quality: An International Journal, 24*(3), 206–229. doi:10.1108/msq-03-2014-0042

Gyrd-Jones, R. I., & Kornum, N. (2013). Managing the co-created brand: Value and cultural complementarity in online and offline multi-stakeholder ecosystems. *Journal of Business Research, 66*(9), 1484–1493.

Hatch, M. J., & Schultz, M. (2010). Toward a theory of brand co-creation with implications for brand governance. *Journal of Brand Management, 17*(8), 590–604.

Hepola, J., Karjaluoto, H., & Hintikka, A. (2017). The effect of sensory brand experience and involvement on brand equity directly and indirectly through consumer brand engagement. *Journal of Product & Brand Management, 26*(3), 282–293. DOI:10.1108/JPBM-10-2016-1348

Hirschman, E. C., & Holbrook, M. B. (1982). Hedonic consumption: Emerging concepts, methods, and propositions. *Journal of Marketing, 46*(3), 92–101.

Hoyer, W. D., Chandy, R., Dorotic, M., Krafft, M., & Singh, S. S. (2010). Consumer co-creation in new product development. *Journal of Service Research, 13*(3), 283–296.

Hsieh, S. H., & Chang, A. (2016). The psychological mechanism of brand co-creation engagement. *Journal of Interactive Marketing, 33*, 13–26.

Huang, S., & Gross, M. J. (2010). Australia's destination image among mainland Chinese travelers: An exploratory study. *Journal of Travel & Tourism Marketing, 27*(1), 63–81.

Hultén, B. (2011). Sensory marketing: The multi-sensory brand-experience concept. *European Business Review, 23*(3), 256–273.

Ind, N., Iglesias, O., & Schultz, M. (2013). Building brands together: Emergence and outcomes of co-creation. *California Management Review, 55*(3), 5–26.

Jaakkola, E., & Alexander, M. (2014). The role of customer engagement behavior in value co-creation: A service system perspective. *Journal of Service Research, 17*(3), 247–261.

Jung, H. J., Lee, Y., Kim, H., & Yang, H. (2014). Impacts of country images on luxury fashion brand: Facilitating with the brand resonance model. *Journal of Fashion Marketing and Management, 181*(2), 187–205.

Kapferer, J.-N. (1997). Managing luxury brands. *Journal of Brand Management, 4*(4), 251–259.

Kauppinen-Räisänen, H., & Grönroos, C. (2015). Are service marketing models really used in modern practice? *Journal of Service Management, 26*(3), 346–371.

Keller, K. L. (1993). Conceptualizing, measuring, and managing customer-based brand equity. *Journal of Marketing, 57*(1), 1–22. doi:10.2307/1252054

Khan, I., & Fatma, M. (2017). Antecedents and outcomes of brand experience: An empirical study. *Journal of Brand Management, 24*(5), 439–452.

Kim, Y., & Slotegraaf, R. J. (2016). Brand-embedded interaction: A dynamic and personalized interaction for co-creation. *Marketing Letters, 27*(1), 183–193.

Kirca, A. H., Randhawa, P., Talay, M. B., & Akdeniz, M. B. (2020). The interactive effects of product and brand portfolio strategies on brand performance: Longitudinal evidence from the US automotive industry. *International Journal of Research in Marketing, 37*(2), 421–439.

Krishna, A. (2011). *Sensory marketing: Research on the sensuality of products*. London: Routledge.

Kumar, N., Stern, L. W., & Anderson, J. C. (1993). Conducting interorganizational research using key informants. *Academy of Management Journal, 36*(6), 1633–1651.

Lincoln, Y. S., & Guba, E. G. (1985). *Naturalistic inquiry* (Vol. 75). Newbury Park, London: Sage Publications.

Lusch, R. F., & Vargo, S. L. (2006). *The service-dominant logic of marketing: Dialog, debate, and directions*. Armonk, New York: M.E. Sharpe.

Madden, T. J., Fehle, F., & Fournier, S. (2006). Brands matter: An empirical demonstration of the creation of shareholder value through branding. *Journal of the Academy of Marketing Science, 34*(2), 224–235.

Merz, M. A., He, Y., & Vargo, S. L. (2009). The evolving brand logic: A service-dominant logic perspective. *Journal of the Academy of Marketing Science, 37*(3), 328–344.

Patton, M. Q. (2014). *Qualitative research & evaluation methods: Integrating theory and practice*. London: Sage Publications.

Payne, A. F., Storbacka, K., & Frow, P. (2008). Managing the co-creation of value. *Journal of the Academy of Marketing Science, 36*(1), 83–96.

Pera, R., Occhiocupo, N., & Clarke, J. (2016). Motives and resources for value co-creation in a multi-stakeholder ecosystem: A managerial perspective. *Journal of Business Research, 69*(10), 4033–4041.

Pine, B. J., & Gilmore, J. H. (1998). Welcome to the experience economy. *Harvard Business Review, 76*(4), 97–105.

Prahalad, C. K., & Ramaswamy, V. (2004). Co-creation experiences: The next practice in value creation. *Journal of Interactive Marketing, 18*(3), 5–14.

Ramaswamy, V., & Ozcan, K. (2016). Brand value co-creation in a digitalized world: An integrative framework and research implications. *International Journal of Research in Marketing, 33*(1), 93–106.

Ranjan, K. R., & Read, S. (2016). Value co-creation: Concept and measurement. *Journal of the Academy of Marketing Science, 44*(3), 290–315.

Roberts, D. L., & Darler, W. (2017). Consumer co-creation: An opportunity to humanise the new product development process. *International Journal of Market Research, 59*(1), 13–33.

Rodrigues, C. (2018). Multi-sensory brand experiences and brand love: Myth or reality? In *Driving customer appeal through the use of emotional branding* (pp. 1–21). Pennsylvania: IGI Global.

Rodrigues, C., & Rodrigues, P. (2019). Brand love matters to Millennials: The relevance of mystery, sensuality and intimacy to neo-luxury brands. *Journal of Product & Brand Management, 28*(7), 830–838.

Roggeveen, A. L., Tsiros, M., & Grewal, D. (2012). Understanding the co-creation effect: When does collaborating with customers provide a lift to service recovery? *Journal of the Academy of Marketing Science, 40*(6), 771–790.

Rowley, J. (2012). Conducting research interviews. *Management Research Review, 35*(3/4), 260–271.

Sandström, S., Edvardsson, B., Kristensson, P., & Magnusson, P. (2008). Value in use through service experience. *Managing Service Quality: An International Journal, 18*(2), 112–126.

Sarkar, S., & Banerjee, S. (2019). Brand co-creation through triadic stakeholder participation. *European Business Review, 31*(5), 585–609.

Son, A., & Pearce, P. (2005). Multi-faceted image assessment: International students' views of Australia as a tourist destination. *Journal of Travel & Tourism Marketing, 18*(4), 21–35.

Stake, R. (1994). Case studies. In N. K. Denzin & Y. S. Lincoln (Eds.), *Handbook of qualitative research* (pp. 236–247). Thousand Oaks, CA: Sage Publications.

Starr, R. G., & Brodie, R. J. (2016). Certification and authentication of brand value propositions. *Journal of Brand Management, 23*(6), 716–731.

Tierney, K. D., Karpen, I. O., & Westberg, K. (2016). Brand meaning co-creation: Toward a conceptualization and research implications. *Journal of Service Theory and Practice, 26*(6), 911–932.

Tynan, C., McKechnie, S., & Chhuon, C. (2010). Co-creating value for luxury brands. *Journal of Business Research, 63*(11), 1156–1163.

Vargo, S. L., & Lusch, R. F. (2004). Evolving to a new dominant logic for marketing. *Journal of Marketing, 68*(1), 1–17. doi:https://doi.org/10.1509%2Fjmkg.68.1.1.24036

Vargo, S. L., & Lusch, R. F. (2008). Service-dominant logic: Continuing the evolution. *Journal of the Academy of Marketing Science, 36*(1), 1–10. https://doi.org/10.1007/s11747-007-0069-6

Vargo, S. L., Wieland, H., & Akaka, M. A. (2016). Innovation in service ecosystems. *Invited Paper Journal of Serviceology, 1*(1), 1–5.

Von Wallpach, S., Hemetsberger, A., & Espersen, P. (2017). Performing identities: Processes of brand and stakeholder identity co-construction. *Journal of Business Research, 70*, 443–452.

Von Wallpach, S., & Kreuzer, M. (2013). Multi-sensory sculpting (MSS): Eliciting embodied brand knowledge via multi-sensory metaphors. *Journal of Business Research, 66*(9), 1325–1331.

Xiong, J., Hashim, N. H., & Murphy, J. (2015). Multisensory image as a component of destination image. *Tourism Management Perspectives, 14*, 34–41.

Yin, R. K. (2014). *Case study research and applications: Design and methods* (5th ed.). Thousand Oaks: Sage Publications.

Zeithaml, V. A., Jaworski, B. J., Kohli, A. K., Tuli, K. R., Ulaga, W., & Zaltman, G. (2020). A theories-in-use approach to building marketing theory. *Journal of Marketing, 84*(1), 32–51.

# 10. B2B branding in global commodity networks: a cultural branding analysis of a Danish company going global

*Christian Dam and Dannie Kjeldgaard*

## 1. INTRODUCTION

An enduring thought in the branding literature is that business-to-consumer (B2C) brands are oriented toward creating symbolic benefits, while business-to-business (B2B) brands are oriented toward creating functional benefits. However, the symbolic side of B2B branding is gaining prominence in the literature, exemplified through claims that B2B branding is more than just rational persuasion (Mudambi et al., 1997), and that branding has a positive impact on B2B companies (Cretu & Brodie, 2007; Michell et al., 2001). On the basis of this idea, researchers have advocated for emotional aspects to be assimilated into B2B brands (Leek & Christodoulides, 2012; Lynch & Chernatony, 2004, 2007). Researchers have further found that global B2B brands should emphasize their symbolic attributes (Beverland et al., 2007), as they are affected by their involvement in cultural collectives (Bruhn et al., 2014; Cayla et al., 2013). In other words, B2B brands are global actors shaped by symbolism and their cultural context. Along the lines of the purpose of this book, we ask how is global brand symbolism co-created for B2B brands? We answer this question by showing how mythologies that circulate in global commodity networks affect brand meanings by being co-created by different actors.

To explicate how mythologies interact with brand meanings, we take the case of a Danish company in the creative industry whose production activities take place mainly in Southeast Asia. In the wake of the brand becoming globalized, the company found its brand meanings becoming distorted. The distortion stemmed from the way that outsourced production and associated working conditions in Southeast Asia were mythologized. These new meanings were not related to a specific country; hence, it was not country-of-origin that was at play but rather ideas about globalization in general—customers were confused about whether the company was Danish or Southeast Asian and they therefore expressed doubt about the global nature of the company.

The main issue in this case is how the brand was challenged in navigating a new global terrain of symbolism. To gain a deeper understanding of this issue, we propose three analytical tools. The first tool is examining the mythologies that the brand is associated with. The brand's new cultural context led to new ideas about it, thus showing that mythologies (Holt, 2004; Thompson, 2004) were interfering with the brand's intended meanings. These mythologies were embedded in the brand, thus we need to understand how mythologies serve as a subtext in B2B branding to better grasp the symbolic side of B2B branding.

The second tool revolves around the co-creation process and how mythologies serve as resources to mobilize in co-creation processes, that is, how the brand and its customers contribute to the brand meanings. Previous research has shown that multiple stakeholders co-create brand meanings (Iglesias et al., 2019; Mäläskä et al., 2011), making it crucial to examine the role that external cultural actors play in endowing the brand with new meaning.

The third analytical tool in examining the cultural shifts the brand experienced is the commodity network. As the mythologies arose after the company moved its production to Southeast Asia, it is important to focus on how changes to the commodity network generated new meanings for the brand. Foster (2005) showed that when the symbolic links of the network were in discord, new brand meanings were created. We explore the links of the commodity network in depth, which leads us to identify that bringing producers and consumers closer together can generate a deeper understanding of each other's working conditions (Foster, 2005).

This chapter shows how concepts like mythology, co-creation, and commodity networks are interconnected and how they are related to B2B branding. Moreover, it advances existing knowledge on the symbolic side of B2B branding by explicating how mythology functions as an element of B2B branding. The topic will be approached through a qualitative lens, responding to researchers' calls for more qualitative work on B2B branding (Keränen et al., 2012).

## 2.   MARKETPLACE MYTHOLOGIES IN B2B CONTEXTS

Mythologies in markets are powerful as they provide the marketplace with meanings and metaphors, which invoke specific ideologies that can be connected to brands (Thompson, 2004). A mythology can become part of a brand, meaning that a brand becomes a carrier of these ideological meanings (Askegaard, 2006). According to Holt (2004), a compelling myth is pivotal in establishing what he terms an iconic brand. Myths function as a story that has the potential to answer an ideological tension etched into society. Holt defines myth as "a simple story that resolves cultural contradictions" (2004, p. 11). Myths bring the brand ideology to life and enable the embedded meanings of the brand to bridge cultural contradictions. Furthermore, myths have been characterized as foundational and relatable stories that transcend time and place. These compelling stories help people to understand social life and their own position in society, which is dramatized around binary oppositions (Arnould, 2008) such as past/future, local/global or tradition/modernity. It is important to note that we in this case are not following Holt's (2004) thinking on cultural branding completely, as the aim is not to show how the case company can rise to iconic status. Rather, we see the concept of mythology (Holt, 2004) to show that mythology exists in the symbolic layers of a brand, regardless of whether the brand deliberately engages with its mythology. Furthermore, mythologies are not only leveraged by the brand but also by the brand's stakeholders. Hence, we understand mythology as culturally entrenched meanings and metaphors that carry ideological agendas (Thompson, 2004) and that can be mobilized by multiple stakeholders to ultimately co-create brand meaning.

Using the mythology concept will help us understand how B2B brands are affected by mythological stories. Hence, our focus is not on mythologies as something that consumers engage with through identity work. In B2B branding, mythology is an element that customers intentionally or unintentionally evaluate the brand by. For the Danish brand, mythologies are not related to country-of-origin effects; instead, mythologies emerge from the global nature of their production. Although cultural meanings in B2B contexts are relatively unexplored, researchers have shown how specific industries can be embedded with cultural meaning (Bajde, 2019) and that sociocultural processes affect B2B industries, articulated through mythologies.

Integrating the co-creation perspective with the commodity network perspective advances knowledge on how B2B brands are affected by myths. This is because brand meaning is not merely an outcome of the work done by brand managers but is also shaped by a variety of links within the commodity network and how those links are mythologized. This indicates that the symbolic aspects of B2B brands should not be neglected, as it becomes a crucial factor in customers' evaluation of a supplier. Our study joins the emergent conversation on symbolism in B2B marketing (Bengtsson & Servais, 2005; Cretu & Brodie, 2007; Gomes et al., 2016; Leek & Christodoulides, 2012). We aim to add to the conversation by showing how mythology exists among B2B brands and how neglecting it can damage a brand. For the Danish brand, the mythologies are tied to the global nature of the company and its operations in Denmark and Southeast Asia. It is important to note that it is not country-of-origin effects that are at play here, as country-of-origin is always affected by several mythologies (Ostberg, 2011), but rather mythologies around globalized systems of production which not only generate economic value but also generate symbolic meanings (Karababa & Kjeldgaard, 2014).

## 3. COMMODITY NETWORKS AND VALUE CREATION

In order to understand how these mythologies are shaped, we need to understand how value is created in the company's production. Our conception of production is not as a linear "chain"; rather, we draw on Foster's (2005) idea of production as part of a commodity network with multiple actors. Furthermore, the term "commodity" should be understood as a term covering both tangible and intangible products. Foster (2005) argues that consumers and producers should be located close to each other in the network, as large spatial separation between the two could lead to a dissociated understanding between them. Foster's finding corresponds with studies showing how it has been beneficial to connect the producer with the end-user as, for example, when Tanzanian tulip producers went to the Netherlands to learn about the end-stage of their products (Arce, 1997). Similarly, it has been shown how British consumers of Jamaican papaya have little understanding of the working conditions of the producers (Cook, 2004). These examples thereby support that spatial distance results in a constructed ignorance (Cook & Crang, 1996), which ultimately inhibits the consumer from forming a strong relationship with the brand (Foster, 2005).

The commodity network is characterized as a process of linking a commodity with households, companies, and states in a global network (Gereffi et al., 1994). The conceptualization of the commodity network identifies the set of actors at play, which in turn enables the identification of where in the process value is created (Bair, 2005). Foster (2005) advocates focusing on different types of value creation rather than simply on economic value creation, in keeping with Graeber's (2001) three notions of value: economic, social, and symbolic. It is important to note that these different types of value are interrelated, and although value can seem social or symbolic, it could transform into economic value in the long run.

The commodity network approach offers a cultural perspective on value chains, which can shed light on the circulating mythologies about global production systems. A brand as a cultural entity (Cayla & Arnould, 2008) accumulates meanings from a variety of actors. The commodity network approach is therefore especially helpful to explain the co-generative value creation that occurs in the networks of these actors (Karababa & Kjeldgaard, 2015).

## 4.    BRAND CO-CREATION—MEANINGS AND MYTHOLOGIES

There is wide agreement that B2B branding is a result of multiple stakeholders intervening in the process of meaning-creation for the brand, that is, brand meaning is a process of co-creation (Iglesias et al., 2019; Vallaster & von Wallpach, 2013; von Wallpach et al., 2017). These co-created meanings are crucial in value being created for the brand. The co-creation of value entails the involvement of several parties in mutually beneficial synergistic relationships (Gyrd-Jones & Kornum, 2013). To avoid a multiplicity of brand meanings, brands should actively engage with these other actors. By nurturing the co-created meanings (Berthon et al., 2009), brand managers could offer different mythologies or work with different types of valorization.

The key elements that should lead to co-creation are dialog, access, transparency, and understanding of risk–benefit (Prahalad & Ramaswamy, 2004). These characteristics align with Foster's (2005) argument to keep the links in the commodity network close to each other to ensure joint understanding. These elements also coincide with Hatch and Schultz's (2010) framework for co-creation, which stresses that transparency and dialog are key to successfully implementing co-creation.

As co-created value is a result of the co-created meanings of the brand, it is necessary to recognize how these meanings emerge. Co-created meanings can be created intentionally through the careful development of branding strategies or they can emerge unintentionally, as other actors intervene in the meaning-making processes (Mäläskä et al., 2011). The brand will thereby be in a state of constant flux, as all actors are constantly re-negotiating its meanings (Iglesias et al., 2019). Hence, it is no longer solely the company that manages its brand meanings but external factors as well (Vallaster & von Wallpach, 2013).

One external factor that intervenes with the meaning-making process is developments in the cultural landscape, which occurs in parallel with managers' strategic efforts. Brands are not merely recognizable signs for customers; they are also carriers of cultural codes shaped by the sociocultural milieu to which they belong (Holt & Cameron, 2010), that is, the value networks. Culture is not an ingredient that brand managers can choose to add to or leave out. Instead, the brand in itself acts as a culturally informed and culturally shaping entity, meaning that the brand will engage with the cultural landscape regardless of management decisions (Cayla & Arnould, 2008).

In this hodgepodge of cultural patterns reside not only B2C brands but also entire industry brands (Bajde, 2019), which means B2B brands are likewise affected by these cultural codes. Mythologies, as carriers of cultural codes, are an outcome of cultural shifts in society (Holt, 2004). These shifts occur as a result of a multitude of cultural actors shaping the cultural discourse in a co-creational process. These cultural actors involve managers, customers, end-consumers, producers as well as actors within popular culture. If brands could identify co-creational shifts in the cultural landscape through mythologies, they could develop a competitive advantage (Holt & Cameron, 2010). Identifying these shifts would entail the brand understanding its own role in engaging with the co-creational cultural process. If a brand fails to read the broader cultural context in which it resides, it could prove damaging for the brand, as will be shown in the upcoming analysis.

Overall, this chapter will be based on three analytical tools (Mythology, commodity network, brand co-creation), which, when synthesized, will provide a cultural explanation for how B2B brands are shaped by mythologies in the broader cultural context. The production in the commodity network will have an effect on which mythologies will revolve around the brand. As these mythologies will be interpreted and shaped in co-creational processes by several cultural actors, they will ultimately lead to specific brand meanings.

## 5.    CASE BACKGROUND

This case is about a Danish company with a subsidiary in Southeast Asia. The company is a creative studio, providing services such as graphic design, image-editing, computer-generated imaging, and motion graphics for multiple larger international clients in various industries. It has always been considered a high-end brand in terms of the quality of work it provides. In order to continue providing high-quality work without increasing its fees, it felt compelled to move parts of its production to a low-wage country. Initially, only the basic services were moved to the office in Southeast Asia. Over the years, more complex tasks were also moved there, substantially expanding the operation.

The company faced skepticism about the quality of its work from customers and potential customers because of its Asian location, as customers were influenced by a negative mythology about production in Asia. This negative image was formed despite the company always focusing on securing good working conditions for all its employees. Moreover, the company made notable efforts in terms of corporate social responsibility actions—for example, it educated disabled people to do graphic work. Although the company did not produce any physical products and only provided graphic tasks performed on computers, the data revealed that it unwittingly acquired mythological meanings related to poor working conditions in Asia.

## 6.    METHODS

To understand the links in the commodity network, we conducted interviews with several key players in the network (see Table 10.1) to arrive at a multifaceted understanding of the empirical context and to uncover disparate brand meaning articulations. Among the interviewees were the CEO of the Danish company and that of the Southeast Asian subsidiary. Furthermore, we conducted qualitative interviews with six major customers of the company to attain customers' perspectives on the brand and its meanings. Interviewing both managers and customers offered us a peek into how the cultural meanings of the brand were co-created. We were welcomed behind the curtain of how these dialectical constructed meanings emerged (Bengtsson & Ostberg, 2006). These interviews were later transcribed and coded according to the themes that emerged in the data collection.

In addition to the interviews, one of the authors followed the day-to-day activities of the company for four months, where observations were recorded in an ethnographic diary. It included observations of daily practices and the deeper meanings of the company and its meaning-making activities. This type of ethnographic inquiry is rare in B2B research but can offer unique data as it provides direct access to the site of action (Gummeson, 2003). Furthermore, ethnography has proven helpful in uncovering symbolic meanings on the B2B side of marketing (Rinallo et al., 2010). Since global brands exist as cultural actors in a dialectical relationship with the cultural world, brands need to be contextualized in relation to the global cultural system (Cayla & Arnould, 2008). This contextualization was ensured by gathering a collection of press releases and blog posts, which functioned as archival accounts of how the brand developed (Bengtsson & Ostberg, 2006). This background material provided the data with richness, as several types of data were collected.

*Table 10.1    List of informants*

| Title of Informant | Industry of Customer | Number of Employees |
| --- | --- | --- |
| CEO, Southeast Asian branch of case company | Creative industry | 80–100 |
| CEO, Danish branch of case company | Creative industry | 80–100 |
| Communication Manager | Public sector | 10,000+ |
| Project Manager | Distributor of technology products, services, and solutions | 70 |
| Contact Manager | Advertising agency | 50–200 |
| Marketing Manager | DIY retailer | 500–1000 |
| Creative Director | Magazine publisher | 500–1000 |
| Visual Merchandise Coordinator | Luxury accessories | 10,000+ |

## 7.    MOBILIZING A MYTHOLOGY OF ANTI-GLOBALIZATION

When taking a cultural approach to branding, it is imperative to identify the cultural tensions that cause problems for the brand (Holt & Cameron, 2010). The CEO of the Danish company expressed how the company occasionally encountered customers that were skeptical about its globalization. According to him, this skepticism became a particularly delicate issue in light of the political push globally toward protectionism in recent years:

> They think that we should build a big wall and keep everything within the borders. And they are definitely supporters of Trump's core value of no globalization and that globalization is bad for me and my everyday life and my family. (CEO, Danish branch)

As he explains the views of the brand's customers, it becomes clear that the company's image is related to broader sociocultural and political developments, a finding that corresponds with Mäläskä et al. (2011) who argue that externalities play a role in shaping the brand. In this case, developments in the cultural milieu intervene with the intended brand meaning, illustrating how challenging it can be to manage brand meaning when numerous stakeholders are involved. The capricious domain of culture further complicates branding, but can be managed by employing suitable strategies that specifically engage with culture (Holt & Cameron, 2010). As these cultural influences could be factors influencing a co-creational relationship, brand managers could benefit from engaging with the co-created meanings (Berthon et al., 2009), which is what the Danish company neglected to do in its branding activities when its production moved abroad. The company continued in the same vein, with a marketing strategy based on empty slogans, which is what Holt and Cameron call mindshare marketing. Therefore, their strategy aimed at winning space in its customers' minds, while leaving out the cultural context. This implies that their move to Southeast Asia was significant only for production optimization and carried no symbolic meaning. As the brand ignored its cultural context, the meanings attached to the brand changed (Holt & Cameron, 2010). In order to better understand how these meanings changed, we need to dig deeper into what it meant to make changes in the commodity network.

What were the consequences to the brand image when the company moved its production abroad? One clear outcome was that all communication was routed through online technology. The online system they used for communication enabled the easy transfer of graphic work between the company and its clients, but it also created an extra link between producer and customer, as they now had to communicate through the online system without seeing each other. One customer had for years been in the belief that she had been communicating with an Indian man, when she in fact had been communicating with a woman at the Southeast Asian office. This had caused frustration, as she thought that an Indian man would never understand their issues and therefore she expressed dissatisfaction with the company. This example show how a lack of understanding for the producer can be damaging, as it can be projected onto the brand.

Closely examining the commodity network reveals the consequences of moving abroad. Customers' limited knowledge of Southeast Asia and the working conditions there arises as one factor hampering the brand image. One customer expresses:

> I think it is a budget solution. I don't know what kind of people they are but I believe that they do what they are told. And if they are told to do it quickly and they get 10 minutes for this task, then they are not going to sit and play with the expression. Then they do it in the easiest and fastest way. (Customer)

This quote suggests that the customer had preconceived ideas about workers in Southeast Asia and their working conditions. They believed that the pressure of working at the company would lead to a decrease in creativity. This belief persisted despite the high quality of work the company continued to produce, highlighting how customers create certain ideas about collaborations in Southeast Asia. This bias could ultimately overshadow perceptions of product quality and brand meanings, and indicates how the links in the commodity network were stretched to where producer and customer had lost their understanding of each other. This time–space distanciation required alternative sense-making schemes to overcome the mythology of low-skilled, sweatshop production, demonstrated in the following quote from another customer:

> There is what is needed. A chair, a computer, and a desk. And I don't think you have your own computer or your own desk or your own […] maybe you just have your work schedule and then you are placed somewhere depending on the time […] I think it is very simple. I could not imagine that they spend time on putting the right designer chair in the office or putting a cozy light or anything. So, I think it's a very basic office, a plain office. (Customer)

Similar to the previous quote, this customer also expresses negative preconceived ideas about working conditions at the office in Southeast Asia. This bleak view of the working conditions are in stark contrast to the actual work facilities, showing how these views tap into existing mythologies of production in Asia. Concurrently, several customers expressed that the services from the Southeast Asian office were too expensive. This seems contradictory, as they simultaneously feared that the workers had poor working conditions. This ambiguity in the relationship with the producer suggests that the customers tend to forget that it is real human beings that they were communicating with through the online system. This is because the online system allows the customers to dehumanize the producer. When a customer perceives the producer as solely a production unit, the deeper personal brand relationship becomes complicated (Foster, 2005). To fill this void of meaning that emerged from distanciated relations and lack of interaction, members of the commodity network tend to draw upon the mythologi-zation of different parts of the value chain, for example through the cultural binary opposition of perceived low-skilled labor in foreign production contexts and highly skilled labor in local/Western contexts.

Making changes in the commodity network by moving the production to Southeast Asia affected the company on a symbolic level (Karababa & Kjeldgaard, 2014). As a container of meanings (Askegaard, 2006), the brand absorbed the meanings attached to a global company, which were co-created by several actors. Customers play a major role in creating these new meanings as they interpret the brand, as do developments in the cultural landscape. These findings show that the brand is related to existing mythologies of production in Asia and about poor working conditions, even if the digital graphics work is a far cry from the image of the manual labor conducted in goods-manufacturing sweatshops. The CEO of the Danish branch articulates how these mythologies affected the brand:

> There are certain myths and they paint a picture. Through the years, when I have met customers for the first time, I have shown them pictures of our office in Southeast Asia. I have done so because the first comment I get from most customers is: "Jeez, it looks like a Danish company." And then I look at them and say, "Actually, it is that too." (CEO, Danish branch)

This quote indicates the confusion customers experienced in telling whether the brand was Danish or Southeast Asian. This confusion was not only due to an external cultural impact; the brand also contributed to negative meanings of producing in Asia. In failing to commu-nicate its Southeast Asian connection, the brand invited stakeholders to interpret its actions as being furtive, its absence particularly noticeable on its main communication channel, its website. The company opted for a minimalistic design to mobilize a Danish mythology related to Scandinavian design traditions. In lieu of expressing its Southeast Asian affiliation, it repeatedly shared pictures and information about its Danish operations. This silence about the Southeast Asian operations would likely confuse customers, as they would fail to comprehend how those operations formed a part of the company, which would in turn invite them to inter-pret the Southeast Asian operations in any way they chose.

Overall, different actors shape the brand by co-creating a meaning of anti-globalization. These meanings tap into an existing mythology of the Asian sweatshop. The mythology is partly a result of decades of narratives about Western companies exploiting low-paid workers in the East under poor working conditions. This idea about the exploited workers serves as the first component of the mythology, which is accompanied by a general discontent for globalization. The informants express skepticism toward globalization, as they seem to favor protectionism.

The interviews make clear that customers have limited knowledge about the producers and the region in which they are located. Thus, lack of knowledge could be a second component of the mythology. The mythology is shaped by how the company failed to communicate its ties to Southeast Asia, which could be interpreted as hiding something. Likewise, custom-ers' interpretations are crucial as their disconnection in the commodity network led them to create negative imaginings of the working conditions. Finally, the cultural developments that occurred in parallel also intervened with the brand meanings. We can therefore clearly say that the brand attracted a co-created mythology of anti-globalization which illuminates the cultural tension of globalization vs. localization.

# 8.    LACK OF CO-CREATION AS AN ENFORCER OF MYTHOLOGY

The Danish company experienced a cultural challenge, which is problematic for the managers, as it could be argued to be one of those external stakeholders that intervene with the brand meaning (Vallaster & von Wallpach, 2013). When dealing with a challenge, cultural competences are needed to navigate the cultural landscape. Cultural tension can be an opportunity for brand innovation but it requires the brand to engage with relevant cultural movements in a compelling manner (Holt & Cameron, 2010). The company did find itself in such a situation but chose to continue branding itself through mindshare marketing (Holt & Cameron, 2010)— conquering cognitive space through catchy but empty slogans. As the company was caught in issues related to cultural changes, it should have created a strategy that was grounded in historical developments, which would have enabled it to respond and adapt to cultural changes. Therefore, to approach the branding only as a psychological phenomenon in the mind while neglecting any focus on society and culture is inadequate (Holt & Cameron, 2010).

The anti-globalization mythology was activated as a result of changes in the commodity network. Moving the production abroad gave rise to a welter of brand meanings connected to globalization. Specifically, customers reported a lack of knowledge about their collaborators in Southeast Asia. The lack of knowledge is problematic, as it ultimately hinders the co-creation of value in the company. Berthon et al. (2009) have argued that brands must actively engage with situations when multiple meanings are being generated; the company's non-compliance left the situation open for interpretation by others (Hatch & Schultz, 2010; Prahalad & Ramaswamy, 2004). The lack of transparency and access in particular inhibited its potential to co-create meaning. The issue in terms of access related to how the company did not allow its customers access to see the production facilities. Subsequently, this caused a low degree of transparency, which ultimately resulted in a general lack of knowledge. During the interview, one customer reflected upon their lack of knowledge:

> I just think that we don't know anything about them. You were asking all these questions and it seems very easy to just deliver our briefs and get the material back and everything looks fine, but we have no idea about what they do there and how they work. It would be interesting to know more. (Customer)

A recurrent theme across interviews was that customers had inadequate information about the Southeast Asian branch of the company. This situation is a major obstacle for managing co-creation in the brand. Prahalad and Ramaswamy (2004) highlight four elements of co-creation: dialog, access, transparency, and understanding of risk. As shown in the last section, the customers had a low degree of *dialog* and *access* since the company failed to communicate its ties to Southeast Asia. By actively communicating its new production facilities in its marketing, it could have provided customers with information to make up for their lack of access. There is a similar issue in terms of *transparency*—given no information, customers imagined poor working conditions in the new offices and cultivated a negative perception of *risk* in collaborating with the Danish company. Similarly, the company could have enhanced its transparency had it prioritized communications about its new ties to Southeast Asia in its marketing activities. Doing so would have eased the integration of other actors into the co-creation process, and they would have been less likely to create negative values regarding work conditions and similar issues. This approach would be in line with Foster's (2005) recommendations on how connecting producer and customer create a better understanding of each other.

The Danish company's problem was that mythologies which negatively valorize globalized commodity networks were intervening with its brand. This section has explained why these mythologies were a threat to the brand and why the company was challenged in managing the anti-globalization mythology. Its infrastructure for co-creation was undeveloped, which means that it was not able to engage with the mythology that was co-created as well. By not managing the co-creation elements, the company invited multiple interpretations of its brand (Berthon et al., 2009).

## 9.    STRATEGY TO COUNTER A CO-CREATED MYTHOLOGY

The Danish company was challenged by a mythology relating to negative discourses on production in Asia, and which have inadvertently been applied to it. It was not possible to overcome this issue due to an insufficient co-creation infrastructure. In order to counter the mythology with alternative mythologization, the company would have to improve its effort to co-create with other actors. One way of achieving this could be through social media efforts that could invite customers behind the company's curtains (Potts et al., 2008). This solution would help overcome its prior failure to communicate its ties to Southeast Asia, and would help in creating a higher degree of transparency for the brand.

When communicating about its subsidiary, the company should simultaneously incorporate the cultural codes of the location in its marketing. Several customers wished to learn more about the cultural roots of the subsidiary. However, at the same time, they expressed confusion about whether the company was Danish or Southeast Asian. Hence, it is important not to localize the brand but rather to glocalize it (Kjeldgaard et al., 2015), best achieved by actively promoting both the Danish origin and the Southeast Asian subsidiary. Following Thompson (2004) who argues that myths contain ideologies, we suggest that the company formulate a counter-myth of mixing cultures to oppose the ideology of anti-globalization. This new myth could help resolve the cultural tensions of globalization vs. localization because it would deliver counter-narratives that mythologize globalized commodity networks positively and would enroll customers to co-create such a mythologization. Indeed, a company manager voiced a similar idea during an interview. Glocalizing its brand would be one strategy to engage in the multiple co-created meanings that circulate among its affiliated actors.

## 10.    IMPLICATIONS AND LIMITATIONS

In this chapter, we have shown how mythologies can interfere with a B2B brand. Research on B2B brands should pay attention to the sociocultural side of the co-creation process, as these brands too are shaped by cultural movements. We have shown this to be the case by analyzing the challenges faced by a Danish company that moved parts of its production to Southeast Asia. Our analysis shows how mythologies are part of the co-creation process and emerge as an outcome of changes in the commodity network. Furthermore, the case shows how difficult it is to manage these mythologies when the company does not accommodate the key elements of co-creation. Finally, it leads us to propose a glocal branding strategy.

We do not argue that there is anything new in proposing a glocal branding strategy nor are we arguing that all issues relating to mythologies can be treated by developing a glocal branding strategy. Hence, this is not where we see the contribution of this chapter. Our contribution lies in demonstrating how mythologies are part of the co-creation branding process in B2B markets. We are also able to open up the research frontier of cultural branding further to include glocalized B2B contexts.

We would like to call for more research on the sociocultural side of B2B branding. As we have focused on how global production systems shape brand mythologies, we would also like to see research focusing on how local production systems might affect B2B brands through mythologies of specific forms of localness and globalness.

The implication of this research for brand stakeholders is that they should consider the sociocultural side of B2B branding. This case showed how managerial decisions could lead to changes in the cultural meanings of a brand, which could ultimately create negative brand meanings. Taking into consideration how multiple actors co-create brand mythologies is paramount, ultimately making it easier to manage them.

Since this is the first study to focus on mythologies in B2B branding, we refrain from making grand generalizations. Instead, we see our study as an extension to the current debate on B2B branding and as an initiation of research into B2B mythologies. We hope our study sparks an interest in how mythologies intervene with the B2B world, and ultimately how the theoretical fields of cultural branding, B2B branding, and brand co-creation can cross-pollinate.

## REFERENCES

Arce, A. (1997). Globalization and food objects. In H. d. Haan & N. Long (Eds.), *Images and Realities of Rural Life*. Assen: Van Gorcum.

Arnould, E. J. (2008). Commercial mythology and the global organization of consumption. In A. Y. Lee & D. Soman (Eds.), *Advances in Consumer Research* (Vol. 35). Duluth, MN: Association for Consumer Research.

Askegaard, S. (2006). Brands as a global ideoscape. In J. E. Schroeder & M. Salzer-Mörling (Eds.), *Brand Culture*. New York: Routledge.

Bair, J. (2005). Global capitalism and commodity chains: Looking back, going forward. *Competition & Change, 9*(2), 153–180.

Bajde, D. (2019). Branding an industry? Conceptual development and relevance. *Journal of Brand Management, 26*(5), 497–504.

Bengtsson, A., & Ostberg, J. (2006). Researching the cultures of brands. In R. W. Belk (Ed.), *Handbook of Qualitative Research Methods in Marketing*. Cheltenham, UK and Northampton, MA, USA: Edward Elgar Publishing.

Bengtsson, A., & Servais, P. (2005). Co-branding on industrial markets. *Industrial Marketing Management, 34*, 706–713.

Berthon, P., Pitt, L. F., & Campbell, C. (2009). Does brand meaning exist in similarity or singularity? *Journal of Business Research, 62*, 356–361.

Beverland, M., Napoli, J., & Lindgreen, A. (2007). Industrial global brand leadership: A capabilities view. *Industrial Marketing Management, 36*, 1082–1093.

Bruhn, M., Schnebelen, S., & Schäfer, D. (2014). Antecedents and consequences of the quality of e-customer-to-customer interactions in B2B brand communities. *Industrial Marketing Management, 43*, 164–176.

Cayla, J., & Arnould, E. J. (2008). A cultural approach to branding in the global marketplace. *Journal of International Marketing, 16*(4), 86–112.

Cayla, J., Cova, B., & Maltese, L. (2013). Party time: Recreation rituals in the world of B2B. *Journal of Marketing Management, 29*(11–12), 1394–1421.

Cook, I. (2004). Follow the Thing: Papaya. *Antipode, 36*(4), 642–664.

Cook, I., & Crang, P. (1996). The world on a plate: Culinary culture, displacement and geographical knowledges. *Journal of Material Culture, 1*(2), 131–153.

Cretu, A. E., & Brodie, R. (2007). The influence of brand image and company reputation where manufacturers market to small firms: A customer value perspective. *Industrial Marketing Management, 36*, 230–240.

Foster, R. J. (2005). Commodity futures: Labour, love and value. *Anthropology Today, 21*(4), 8–12.

Gereffi, G., Korzeniewicz, M., & Korzeniewicz, R. P. (1994). Introduction: Global commodity chains. In G. Gereffi & M. Korzeniewicz (Eds.), *Commodity Chains and Global Capitalism*. Westport, CT: Praeger.

Gomes, M., Fernandes, T., & Brandão, A. (2016). Determinants of brand relevance in a B2B service purchasing context. *Journal of Business & Industrial Marketing, 31*(2), 193–204.

Graeber, D. (2001). *Toward an Anthropological Theory of Value: The False Coin of Our Own Dreams*. New York: Palgrave.

Gummeson, E. (2003). All research is interpretive! *Journal of Business & Industrial Marketing, 18*(6/7), 482–492.

Gyrd-Jones, R. I., & Kornum, N. (2013). Managing the co-created brand: Value and cultural complementarity in online and offline multi-stakeholder ecosystems. *Journal of Business Research, 66*, 1484–1493.

Hatch, M. J., & Schultz, M. (2010). Toward a theory of brand co-creation with implications for brand governance. *Journal of Brand Management, 17*(8), 590–604.

Holt, D. (2004). *How Brands Become Icons: The Principles of Cultural Branding*. Boston, MA: Harvard Business Press.

Holt, D., & Cameron, D. (2010). *Cultural Strategy: Using Innovative Ideologies to Build Breakthrough Brands*. Oxford: Oxford University Press.

Iglesias, O., Landgraf, P., Ind, N., Markovic, S., & Koporcic, N. (2019). Corporate brand identity co-creation in business-to-business contexts. *Industrial Marketing Management, 85*, 32–43.

Karababa, E., & Kjeldgaard, D. (2014). Value in marketing: Toward sociocultural perspectives. *Marketing Theory, 14*, 119–127.

Karababa, E., & Kjeldgaard, D. (2015). Understanding the complexity of value and its co-constitution in a global network: Insights from a global fashion brand value constitution context. *Journal of Consumer And Consumption Research, 7*, 1–21.

Keränen, J., Piirainen, K. A., & Salminen, R. T. (2012). Systematic review on B2B branding: Research issues and avenues for future research. *Journal of Product & Brand Management, 21*(6), 404–417.

Kjeldgaard, D., Askegaard, S., & Eckhardt, G. M. (2015). The role of cultural capital in creating "glocal" brand relationships. In S. Fournier, M. Breazeale, & J. Avery (Eds.), *Strong Brands, Strong Relationships*. New York: Routledge.

Leek, S., & Christodoulides, G. (2012). A framework of brand value in B2B markets: The contributing role of functional and emotional components. *Industrial Marketing Management, 41*, 106–114.

Lynch, J., & Chernatony, L. d. (2004). The power of emotion: Brand communication in business-to-business markets. *Journal of Brand Management, 11*(5), 403–419.

Lynch, J., & Chernatony, L. d. (2007). Winning hearts and minds: Business-to-business branding and the role of the salesperson. *Journal of Marketing Management, 23*(1–2), 123–135.

Mäläskä, M., Saraniemi, S., & Tähtinen, J. (2011). Network actors' participation in B2B SME branding. *Industrial Marketing Management, 40*, 1144–1152.

Michell, P., King, J., & Reast, J. (2001). Brand values related to industrial products. *Industrial Marketing Management, 30*, 415–425.

Mudambi, S. M., Doyle, P., & Wong, V. (1997). An exploration of branding in industrial markets. *Industrial Marketing Management, 26*, 433–446.

Ostberg, J. (2011). The mythological aspects of country-of-origin: The case of the Swedishness of Swedish fashion. *Journal of Global Fashion Marketing, 2*(4), 223–234.

Potts, J., Hartley, J., Banks, J., Burgess, J., Cobcroft, R., Cunningham, S., & Montgomery, L. (2008). Consumer co-creation and situated creativity. *Industry and Innovation, 15*(5), 459–474.

Prahalad, C. K., & Ramaswamy, V. (2004). Co-creation experiences: The next practice in value creation. *Journal of Interactive Marketing, 18*(3), 5–14.

Rinallo, D., Borghini, S., & Golfetto, F. (2010). Exploring visitor experiences at trade shows. *Journal of Business & Industrial Marketing, 25*(4), 249–258.

Thompson, C. J. (2004). Marketplace mythology and discourses of power. *Journal of Consumer Research, 31*(1), 162–180.

Vallaster, C., & von Wallpach, S. (2013). An online discursive inquiry into the social dynamics of multi-stakeholder brand meaning co-creation. *Journal of Business Research, 66,* 1505–1515.

von Wallpach, S., Hemetsberger, A., & Espersen, P. (2017). Performing identities: Processes of brand and stakeholder identity co-construction. *Journal of Business Research, 70,* 443–452.

# PART III

# CO-CREATION OF BRAND OFFERINGS

# 11. Freedom and control in brand co-creation communities
*Nicholas Ind and Oriol Iglesias*

## 1. INTRODUCTION

In the last decade, co-creation has moved out of the shadows into the light and has become the go-to method for organizations to get close to stakeholders and to build brands. However, in spite of its ubiquity, has co-creation optimized its potential as a source of innovation in the development of products and services? In one sense it has, in that organizations have understood the value of becoming closer to stakeholders and reaping such benefits as sharing knowledge, building insights and reducing risk (Prahalad and Ramaswamy, 2004, Hatch and Schultz, 2010). In another sense, much co-creation has emphasized the 'co' rather than 'creation' (Ramaswamy and Ozcan, 2018). Organizations have involved consumers and other stakeholders through online platforms, but they have not been so willing to adopt a participative approach to the collaborative and creative acts involved in defining new experiences. Managers have often had a tendency to use co-creation as a tool to stay closer to customers and to test out internally generated concepts, rather than focus on the 'creation' dimension of working with community members to build knowledge, ideas and innovations (Ind et al., 2017). The 'creation' approach implies a more transformative effect in terms of processes and experiences, a culture that appreciates the creativity of others (Leadbeater, 2008) and a willingness to give freedom to stakeholders as a way to create innovations together.

In this chapter, we build on the work of the philosopher Isaiah Berlin, who makes explicit two types of freedom (negative and positive). Berlin's distinction provides a lens that enables us to see the sometimes subtle variations that define the different typologies of brand co-creation communities and the implications this has for the way they are managed. Our purpose in using Berlin's idea is to give emphasis to the way freedom affects how such communities are constructed and facilitated and the roles of organizations and participants. Through the example of Lego in particular, we show that organizations can use different forms of community at the same time. We conclude with some specific recommendation as to how freedom can be managed in brand co-creation. Before turning to Berlin's ideas about freedom, we first look at the role freedom plays in motivating consumers to participate in brand co-creation communities.

## 2. WHY FREEDOM MATTERS TO CONSUMERS IN BRAND CO-CREATION

Brand co-creation provides the opportunity for people to participate with others in sharing their lives, interacting with an organization and developing new ideas. As Nambisan and Baron (2007) note, this can be a stimulating experience and participants can be surprisingly passionate and intense (Ind et al., 2013). Communities also create opportunities for sociality, fun, self-expression, creativity and the development of operant resources (Vargo and Lusch, 2004; Arnould, 2007; Ind et al., 2013; Arnould et al., 2014). However, these intrinsic benefits require sufficient freedom to be realized (Ind et al., 2020). In a series of studies, the psychologists, Deci and Ryan showed that people have innate psychological needs in the form of competence, autonomy and relatedness, that lead to emotional engagement (Deci, 1972; Deci and Ryan, 1985; Deci et al., 1999; Ryan and Deci, 2000). In their Self-Determination Theory, they argue that if you try to limit people's freedom you negate their desire for autonomy and diminish intrinsic motivation, while if you give them greater freedom, you enhance it. They also found that you can improve intrinsic motivation through positive and genuine feedback. By way of contrast, extrinsic rewards tend to make a relationship transactional, which undermines engagement and motivation (Frey and Goette, 1999; Gneezy and Rustichini, 2000; Shirky, 2010).

The implication is that creativity is best nurtured in environments that provide sufficient freedom to enable the intrinsic benefits of participation connected to social, self-development and hedonic factors to be realized (Schau et al., 2009; Carù and Cova, 2015; Hsieh and Chang, 2016; Ind et al., 2020). As Amabile notes, 'Autonomy around process fosters creativity because giving people freedom in how they approach their work heightens their intrinsic motivation and sense of ownership. Freedom about process also allows people to approach problems in ways that make the most of their expertise and their creative-thinking skills' (Amabile, 1998, 82). Amabile further points out that this emphasis on ensuring there is freedom as to how to do something, does not preclude participants from also taking part in defining the purpose of the process. However, this is not seen as essential in motivational terms. Rather the important point is the clarity of what is required, so that people understand the value and relevance of the activity. In this perspective, killing creativity is a result of poor elucidation and/or an inauthentic approach to freedom.

## 3.    NEGATIVE AND POSITIVE FREEDOM

What Amabile and Deci and Ryan argue, and what Berlin makes explicit, is that freedom is an instrumental freedom in that it enables discovery and creativity by allowing for spontaneity and individual variation (Berlin, 2005). However, Berlin also notes that there has been an ongoing struggle between the desire for order and control and the quest for freedom (Berlin, 2003). In co-creation this tension is played out in communities and networks. The order that derives from a brand co-creation community's guiding purpose plus its guidelines, rules and protocols is counterpointed by participants' desire to be free to express themselves. We can connect this idea of freedom and control to Berlin's concept of two types of freedom – negative (freedom *from*) and positive (freedom *to*). While the former is concerned with the space of freedom, 'liberty in this sense is principally concerned with the area of control, not with its source' (Berlin, 2005, 176), the latter is concerned with people making their own choices and having the freedom to achieve self-realization. Berlin encapsulates negative and positive freedom in terms of answers to the following questions: 'What is the area within which the subject – a person or group of persons – is or should be left to do or be what he is able to do or be, without interference by other persons?' and 'What, or who, is the source of control or interference that can determine someone to do, or be, this rather than that?' (Berlin, 2005, 169).

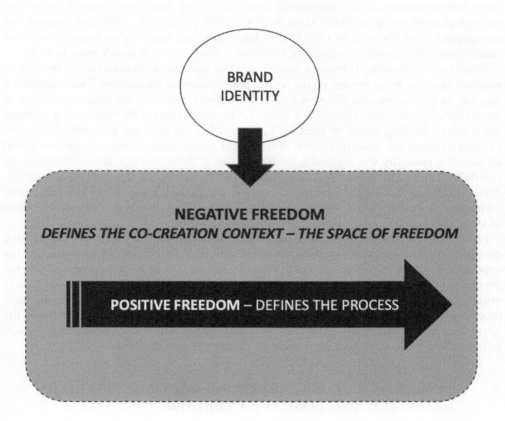

*Figure 11.1    Negative and positive freedom*

In essence, as illustrated in Figure 11.1, negative freedom tries to define the boundaries of a brand co-creation community by setting out its scope, purpose and objectives. Additionally, knowledge of the brand identity influences participants in the way they think and behave (Arvidsson, 2005). When a community is initiated and run by fans it allows for more negative freedom by enabling people to explore possibilities. When a company owns a community, the space of negative freedom is reduced, as boundaries and objectives are defined by the interests of the organization. In contrast, positive freedom defines the degree of freedom that the community members will have in terms of how they do things in the co-creation process, within the space of negative freedom. Organizations can limit positive freedom by focusing on the 'co' and directing community participants to undertake tasks in a specific way. This limiting of positive freedom often seems to be based on the assumption that while participants can sometimes inspire insiders, and 'work up', 'test' and 'refine' concepts they lack the knowledge and skills to be creative and to contribute new and relevant ideas, which can only come from experts inside the organization (Ind et al., 2017). This view can be challenged by research (Kristensson et al., 2004; Matthing et al., 2004; Füller et al., 2009) that suggests that consumers can be liberated by their lack of knowledge and can develop more original and creative ideas than insiders – especially if they are given the tools to enable them to do so.

When positive freedom is broader, participants can be more creative and act as innovation partners. Here the focus is more on the 'creative' dimension of co-creation. This is important because, as the linguist and philosopher, Noam Chomsky, notes, 'A fundamental element of human nature is the need for creative work, for creative enquiry, for free creation without the arbitrary limiting effect of coercive institutions' (Chomsky and Foucault, 2006, 37). Chomsky's argument in this discussion with Michel Foucault about justice and power was that all too often creativity was repressed, yet he suggests a 'decent society should maximise the possibilities for this fundamental human characteristic to be realized' (Chomsky and Foucault, 2006, 38). When a company initiates co-creation, maximizing positive freedom can enable participants to realize their desire for creative expression and contribute to the development of ideas.

From Berlin's perspective of political philosophy, negative and positive freedom have developed different trajectories and are in conflict with each other, but rather than treat them as oppositional, we use them here as a lens to view co-creation. The value of the perspective is that the practice of brand co-creation involves the management of freedom. Whether co-creation is organic (as typified by fan-based communities) or directed (as in the case of company-initiated processes) there is always a confluence of interests, whereby organizers must determine the appropriate degree of freedom *from* man-made barriers that will enable participants to attain fulfilment while allowing them the freedom *to* choose how they do things.

## 4.    TOWARDS A CO-CREATION TYPOLOGY INSPIRED BY NEGATIVE AND POSITIVE FREEDOM

Berlin's distinction between negative and positive freedom can serve as the basis to build a typology of co-creation (see Figure 11.2). The four typologies are explained below, but it should be noted that while each typology has distinct attributes, there are varying degrees of freedom within them. For example, within 'company-based co-creation community' there are communities that limit the process by creating precise rules and toolkits, and in contrast, there are communities that place very little limit on process and encourage participants to see the community as their own and in which they have greater freedom to create on their own terms. The first typology is company-based insights communities, where both negative and positive freedom are limited. These are communities owned and steered by the organization, where the key objective is to get insights from the participants or to test internally generated ideas. This is a view of co-creation (Ind et al., 2017), which is quite similar to some traditional market research, that seeks to evaluate rather than create. Think for instance about the online communities, such as the ones powered by Qualtrics, that are used to conduct A/B testing of commercials and social media strategies.

When negative freedom is broad, but positive freedom is limited, we find fan-based communities based on interest. These are specialist communities 'based on a structured set of social relations among admirers of a brand' (Muniz and O'Guinn, 2001, 412). These communities mostly develop organically based on self-imposed guidelines and are run by brand fans as a way to socialize, learn about, and discuss the brands that interest them (Pongsakornrungsilp and Schroeder, 2011; Carù and Cova, 2015; Skålén et al., 2015). These communities do not try to influence brands directly, but they are influenced by the brand identity. For example, take the NBRO Nike community (Kornum et al., 2017), which is an initiative led by a group of Nike fans to organize running activities in Copenhagen. Within the NBRO community, the emphasis is on the 'co' dimension of co-creation as a way to support the gathering of a certain collective of people who share a passion for running and for Nike.

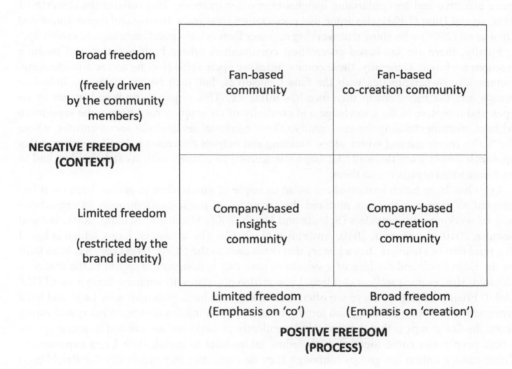

*Figure 11.2    Typologies of brand co-creation*

The third typology is company-based co-creation communities, where there is a stronger emphasis on creation. Typically, these communities are initiated by organizations to meet specific goals and to develop innovations within the framework defined by the brand identity. Here negative freedom is limited through the influence of the organization that sponsors the community, but positive freedom is broad in that community members have the opportunity to determine how they work with the challenges defined by the organization. There will be active moderation provided by company appointed facilitators, whose role is to steer the direction and support conversations. Membership of such co-creation communities is often determined by the organization – it sets the specification for participation and recruits and rewards people accordingly – and is not open to non-members. These communities can be time limited or ongoing. In a study of six such online brand co-creation communities (Ind et al., 2013), sponsored by such organizations as Tata Beverages, Danone and Sony Music, the emphasis was more on creation, but it was also evident that creation only emerged as participants began to socialize and to feel connected. Participants need to become confident and trusting of each other and the sponsoring brand. For example, in the case of Danone, a strong sense of community emerged amongst the 400 members, based on a shared interest in the brand being co-created. This made participation meaningful for the members and productive for Danone, as demonstrated by independent research into the process that showed co-creation generated more effective and less polarizing insights than other methods. This reflects the research of Morgan and Hunt (1994) who argue that cooperation emerges with trust and commitment and Hirst et al. (2009) who show that working together fosters individual learning and creativity.

Finally, there are fan-based co-creation communities where both negative and positive freedom are broad. Generally, these communities are open, self-selecting and self-moderating. Community ownership lies with the fans themselves, but such communities are linked to brands and the membership therefore has influence. This requires the brand owner to be open and receptive to the knowledge and creativity of community members; to be supportive without instrumentalizing the community. These communities are both social entities, where the 'co' is important and where ideas, meaning and outputs are created. An illustration of this approach comes from the way that Lego has learned to connect with its stakeholders and to co-create ideas together with them.

Lego has been much written about as an example of co-creation in action, because it has adopted an approach that has nurtured the creativity of participants through an empathetic way of working with outsiders (Schultz and Hatch, 2006; Hatch and Schultz, 2008; Ind and Schultz, 2010; Kornberger, 2010; Antorini et al., 2012). The toymaker, Lego, which is based in a rural part of Denmark, has a history that dates back to the 1930s. Its success has been built on the Lego brick and the idea of a system of play that is designed to appeal to the maker in children. However, as well as children, Lego is also popular with what are known as AFOLs (Adult Friends of Lego). These are often individuals who have grown up with Lego and have remained enthusiasts, forming, and joining in later life, online fan groups. What is interesting about the fan groups is that they exist independently of Lego and are created as social spaces where people can come together with fellow enthusiasts to enrich their Lego experiences. These mostly online fan groups (although they do come together physically for BrickFests) have developed new games, new building standards and specialized software. As Antorini et al. (2012, 74) note, 'The innovations have created value for the innovator and encouraged deeper community engagement and community vitality.' Adult fans have also uploaded their own Lego creations (300,000 of them) and posted more than 4.5 million photos, drawing and instructions (Antorini et al., 2012).

It is important to note that these fan-based co-creation communities do not belong to Lego. Lego can support, listen to and ask for input, but they cannot direct them: 'they are not just extensions of the company – they are independent entities' (Antorini et al., 2012, 78). That these communities provide valuable inspiration and help focus ideas for the company is because of the way participants are intrinsically motivated to contribute. This is partly about socialization, but also about the way people construct their identities through participation. Von Wallpach et al. (2017) found in a study of Lego that individual identities are constructed through the performativity of language and practices as interviewees socially interact both online and offline. One of the conclusions they come to is that managers should support the playful, creative and social qualities of interactions by engaging stakeholders and meeting their identity needs and providing the technology and places to enable fruitful interactions. We might note that in this context the space of freedom within such communities is determined not by Lego, but by the norms established by community participants. From this perspective, the participants in these fan-based co-creation communities enjoy a large space of negative freedom and broad levels of positive freedom in which they create meaning and tangible outputs.

In addition to fan-based co-creation communities, Lego has also established its own co-creation projects (company-based co-creation communities) through such initiatives as the Lego Ambassador Network (which provides a way for Lego to build relationships with adult fans and to generate ideas and feedback) and Lego Ideas (which is a toolkit to enable fans to contribute product ideas). The basic format of Lego Ideas is that a fan has to submit a product concept using a pre-designed structure. This is then discussed and voted on by the community and if it receives more than 10,000 votes, is considered for production – for which the idea developer receives a fixed royalty, if the product makes it to market. Lego Ideas is a company initiative and its purpose and rules are defined by Lego. Here the space of freedom is more constrained, as Lego is restricting negative freedom, because the generated ideas have to follow the specific and detailed rules laid down by Lego that cover production requirements, intellectual property and development processes. Lego Ideas extends the Lego brand within clear and specific limits that do not challenge internally accepted rules and procedures.

Integral to Lego's ability to engage stakeholders, whether through fan-based communities or more directed ones, is a subtle yet influential barrier, which is the influence of the brand itself. Alongside the company's willingness to let go of its brand and to encourage outsiders to help co-create it though communities, by giving them the 'right to hack' existing products and by inviting passionate AFOLs to work at the headquarters with designers on new ideas, was a re-thinking of the purpose and values of the brand (Ind and Schultz, 2010). This was a contrast to the dark days of the late 1990s and early 2000s, where Lego had over-expanded into diverse areas and got itself into financial difficulties. Its resurrection was due to a recognition of the importance of re-establishing the pre-eminence of the brick and the concept of a system of play. By developing a pellucid statement that through workshops, brand schools and everyday usage became well-understood by employees, Lego had the confidence to make the transition from being a manufacturing company to being a platform company that is networked to a wide array of companies and individuals (Hatch and Schultz, 2008). This change was not without its tensions in that the company had to find the right balance between freedom and control by shifting between centralizing and decentralizing modes (Schultz and Hatch, 2006). However, as Lego has come to understand its brand better, so it has enabled insiders and outsiders to shape the brand within a space defined by a shared understanding of the purpose and values and with a broad degree of positive freedom, 'The brand offers the only recognizable interface that frames the conversation between producers and consumers … external communities that crystallize around it are quasi-extensions of internal culture. In fact, culture cannot be confined within the bounds of the organization' (Kornberger, 2010, 40).

## 5.    MANAGING FREEDOM

Understanding and managing freedom is an essential requirement, especially when co-creation communities ask people for their creativity in helping to create and hone new products and services (Füller, 2010). This requires a nuanced view of freedom, whereby managers think about the space of freedom that they initiate and how they can best enable participants to achieve self-realization through an empathetic and nurturing approach to community moderation and feedback. It should be noted here that the management of the two types of freedom is inter-dependent and dynamic. It needs to be adapted to changing circumstances depending on the purpose of the community and who owns and initiates it. When a task is broad, such as in an initial ideation or brainstorming phase, the space of freedom can be broader. We want people to imagine new possibilities and indeed to challenge the boundaries. However, as a process develops, we may also want to bring more focus into the process and to look at specific issues or tasks. Even within these phases, moderators need to be aware of the needs of participants and their desire for self-realization and to adapt the space accordingly.

While co-creation should be rooted in openness and freedom, there is a recurring deterministic approach that emphasizes unity and control (Ind et al., 2017). Managers sometimes believe that by opening up the brand to the influence of online community members, there is a danger that the brand's meaning will evolve in unintended ways and perhaps lose coherence (Fisher and Smith, 2011; Iglesias et al., 2013; Schmeltz and Kjeldsen, 2019). This leads managers to emphasize the 'co' of co-creation, whereby they see value in generating insights and opinions, but no more. This orientation may be self-fulfilling in that the tactical approach leads to a reduction in negative freedom and a lack of attention to positive freedom – after all if the use of co-creation is narrow and instrumental there is no need to pay attention to people's self-realization needs. Co-creation here is a transaction.

In the case of company-initiated co-creation communities, where managers want to emphasize 'creation' and tap into the knowledge and creativity of people there are three simple steps. First, managers should set clear (but adaptable) boundaries based around a sense of community purpose. As John Stuart Mill argues, we should try to maximize freedom, not because of a belief in its ethicality, but because it is more effective: 'leaving people to themselves is always better, *ceteris paribus*, than controlling them' (Mill, 2002, 99). Creating this space of freedom is valuable because as Amabile and Deci and Ryan suggest it feeds into people's intrinsic desires to develop and express themselves. Thus, instead of managers erring on the side of control and thinking what can we let go, they should start from a position of freedom and think, what do we need to constrain. This perspective aligns with that of Carù and Cova who recommend companies should not aim to control experience, but rather to reduce unmanageability: 'managers should position themselves as community enhancers who support the creation and development of creative practices' (2015, 289).

Second, managers ought to recognize people's desire for self-realization and to create processes and moderation that enable it. This suggests a focus on the intrinsic motivations of those that participate in brand co-creation and a willingness to listen to people's differing needs and to adapt accordingly. As a general principle, managers should not interfere with the how – if community participants are set a clear task, then it should be the choice of the participants as to the inspirations and tools they draw on to address it. Mill (who was an important influence on Berlin), argues that we should recognize and cherish diversity. As long as people's diverse opinions do not do harm to others, we should encourage it. Indeed, it is by enabling people to communicate their own ideas with spontaneity and originality that new ways of thinking and doing are challenged and improved upon (Mill, 2002).

Third, too often organizations put the focus on the tools that are required to enable brand co-creation to be realized. Often there is a focus here on online communities, but it is also the case that much co-creation is face-to-face, especially in business-to-business contexts, where professional participants within networks of innovation come together to create new products and services. However, much more important than the tools is the belief that outsiders can make valid contributions to organizations and can help to create new ways of thinking and acting. The key concern for organizations should be fostering a supportive corporate culture where co-creation can flourish. This is about promoting openness, managing negative and positive freedom, and embracing a more empathetic and participative leadership style.

# REFERENCES

Amabile, T. M. (1998). How to kill creativity. *Harvard Business Review*, *87*(September–October), 77–87.

Antorini, Y. M., Muñiz Jr, A. M., & Askildsen, T. (2012). Collaborating with customer communities: Lessons from the LEGO Group. *MIT Sloan Management Review*, *53*(3), 73–79.

Arnould, E. J. (2007). Service-dominant logic and consumer culture theory: Natural allies in an emerging paradigm. In R., Belk & J. Sherry (Eds.), *Consumer Culture Theory* (pp. 57–76). Bingley: Emerald Group Publishing.

Arnould, E. J., Price, L. L., & Malshe, A. (2014). Toward a cultural resource-based theory of the customer. In *The Service-Dominant Logic of Marketing* (pp. 109–122). Abingdon, UK: Routledge.

Arvidsson, A. (2005). Brands: A critical perspective. *Journal of Consumer Culture*, *5*(2), 235–258.

Berlin, I. (2003). *The Crooked Timber of Humanity: Chapters in the History of Ideas* (Edited by H. Hardy). London: Pimlico.

Berlin, I. (2005). *Liberty* (Edited by H. Hardy). Oxford: Oxford University Press.

Carù, A., & Cova, B. (2015). Co-creating the collective service experience. *Journal of Service Management*, *26*(2), 276–294.

Chomsky, N., & Foucault, M. (2006). *The Chomsky–Foucault Debate on Human Nature*. New York: The New Press.

Deci, E. L. (1972). The effects of contingent and noncontingent rewards and controls on intrinsic motivation. *Organizational Behavior and Human Performance*, *8*(2), 217–229.

Deci, E. L., & Ryan, R. M. (1985). Cognitive evaluation theory. In *Intrinsic Motivation and Self-Determination in Human Behavior* (pp. 43–85). Boston, MA: Springer.

Deci, E. L., Koestner, R., & Ryan, R. M. (1999). A meta-analytic review of experiments examining the effects of extrinsic rewards on intrinsic motivation. *Psychological Bulletin*, *125*(6), 627–668.

Fisher, D. & Smith, S. (2011). Cocreation is chaotic: What it means for marketing when no one has control. *Marketing Theory*, *11*(3), 325–350.

Frey, B. S., & Goette, L. (1999). Does pay motivate volunteers? Working paper/Institute for Empirical Research in Economics, *7*.

Füller, J. (2010). Refining virtual co-creation from a consumer perspective. *California Management Review*, *52*(2), 98–122.

Füller, J., Mühlbacher, H., Matzler, K., & Jawecki, G. (2009). Consumer empowerment through internet-based co-creation. *Journal of Management Information Systems*, *26*(3), 71–102.

Gneezy, U., & Rustichini, A. (2000). A fine is a price. *Journal of Legal Studies*, *29*(1), 1–17.

Hatch, M. J., & Schultz, M. (2008). *Taking Brand Initiative: How Companies can Align Strategy, Culture, and Identity through Corporate Branding*. New York: John Wiley & Sons.

Hatch, M. J., & Schultz, M. (2010). Toward a theory of brand co-creation with implications for brand governance. *Journal of Brand Management*, *17*(8), 590–604.

Hirst, G., Van Knippenberg, D., & Zhou, J. (2009). A cross-level perspective on employee creativity: Goal orientation, team learning behavior, and individual creativity. *Academy of Management Journal, 52*(2), 280–293.

Hsieh, S. H., & Chang, A. (2016). The psychological mechanism of brand co-creation engagement. *Journal of Interactive Marketing, 33*, 13–26.

Iglesias, O., Ind, N., & Alfaro, M. (2013). The organic view of the brand: A brand value co-creation model. *Journal of Brand Management, 20*(8), 670–688.

Ind, N., & Schultz, M. (2010). Brand building, beyond marketing. *Strategy + Business*, 1–4.

Ind, N., Coates, N., & Lerman, K. (2020). The gift of co-creation: What motivates customers to participate. *Journal of Brand Management, 27*(2), 181–194.

Ind, N., Iglesias, O., & Markovic, S. (2017). The co-creation continuum: From tactical market research tool to strategic collaborative innovation method. *Journal of Brand Management, 24*(4), 310–321.

Ind, N., Iglesias, O., & Schultz, M. (2013). Building brands together: Emergence and outcomes of co-creation. *California Management Review, 55*(3), 5–26.

Kornberger, M., (2010). How brand communities influence innovation and culture. *Market Leader, Q3*, 39–41.

Kornum, N., Gyrd-Jones, R., Al Zagir, N., & Brandis, K. A. (2017). Interplay between intended brand identity and identities in a Nike related brand community: Co-existing synergies and tensions in a nested system. *Journal of Business Research, 70*, 432–440.

Kristensson, P., Gustafsson, A., & Archer, T. (2004). Harnessing the creative potential among users. *Journal of Product Innovation Management, 21*(1), 4–14.

Leadbeater, C. (2008). *We-Think.* London: Profile Books.

Matthing, J., Sandén, B., & Edvardsson, B. (2004). New service development: Learning from and with customers. *International Journal of Service Industry Management, 15*(5), 479–498.

Mill, J. S. (2002). *The Basic Writings of John Stuart Mill.* On Liberty (1863), The Subjection of Women (1870), Utilitarianism (1871). New York: The Modern Library.

Morgan, R. M., & Hunt, S. D. (1994). The commitment–trust theory of relationship marketing. *Journal of Marketing, 58*(3), 20–38.

Muniz, A. M., & O'Guinn, T. C. (2001). Brand community. *Journal of Consumer Research, 27*(4), 412–432.

Nambisan, S., & Baron, R. A. (2007). Interactions in virtual customer environments: Implications for product support and customer relationship management. *Journal of Interactive Marketing, 21*(2), 42–62.

Pongsakornrungsilp, S., & Schroeder, J. E. (2011). Understanding value co-creation in a co-consuming brand community. *Marketing Theory, 11*(3), 303–324.

Prahalad, C. K., & Ramaswamy, V. (2004). *The Future of Competition: Co-Creating Unique Value with Customers.* Boston, MA: Harvard Business Press.

Ramaswamy, V., & Ozcan, K. (2018). What is co-creation? An interactional creation framework and its implications for value creation. *Journal of Business Research, 84*, 196–205.

Ryan, R. M., & Deci, E. L. (2000). Self-determination theory and the facilitation of intrinsic motivation, social development, and well-being. *American Psychologist, 55*(1), 68–78.

Schau, H. J., Muñiz Jr, A. M., & Arnould, E. J. (2009). How brand community practices create value. *Journal of Marketing, 73*(5), 30–51.

Schmeltz, L., & Kjeldsen, A. K. (2019). Co-creating polyphony or cacophony? A case study of a public organization's brand co-creation process and the challenge of orchestrating multiple internal voices. *Journal of Brand Management, 26*(3), 304–316.

Schultz, M., & Hatch, M. J. (2006). A cultural perspective on corporate branding. In Schroeder, J. E., & Salzer-Mörling, M. (Eds.), *Brand Culture* (pp. 15–31). London: Routledge.

Shirky, C. (2010). *Cognitive Surplus: Creativity and Generosity in a Connected Age.* London: Penguin UK.

Skålén, P., Pace, S., & Cova, B. (2015). Firm-brand community value co-creation as alignment of practices. *European Journal of Marketing, 49*(3/4), 596–620.

Vargo, S. L., & Lusch, R. F. (2004). Evolving to a new dominant logic for marketing. *Journal of Marketing, 68*(1), 1–17.

Von Wallpach, S., Hemetsberger, A., & Espersen, P. (2017). Performing identities: Processes of brand and stakeholder identity co-construction. *Journal of Business Research, 70*, 443–452.

# 12. Exploring the brand co-creation–brand performance linkage and the roles of innovation and firm age: resource-based and dynamic capabilities views

*Ahmed Rageh Ismail*

## 1. INTRODUCTION

> According to the Huffington Post, 70 percent of companies that deliver outstanding customer experience rely on customer feedback. Smart brands have long since realized that its customers control whether a product or service goes to market successfully. Co-creation is the process where brands and consumers work together to create better ideas, products and services, is a happy medium. Brands still steer product innovation, but customers have a seat at the (head of the) table. (Alida, 2016)

In co-creation, customers are involved throughout the process. Real-time feedback during co-creation reduces misunderstandings and ensures a richer value proposition for every development (Hurni & Grösser, 2017). Co-creating with customers benefits the product, the consumer, the organization and, ultimately, the bottom line (Sheth, 2019). It boosts brand loyalty because it creates perceived ownership and products and services are often more integral to customer lives when organizations get involved in co-creating with customers (Yazdanparast et al., 2010). Obviously, co-creation helps brands to achieve their goals and increase their value. However, little is known about how brand co-creation improves brand performance in the context of Egypt and also little attention is paid to the moderating roles of firm age as well as the innovation role in co-creation–brand performance linkage.

The key purpose of this chapter is to offer original and useful insights into the brand co-creation body of knowledge and provide better understanding of the relationship between brand co-creation and brand performance. In this study, the resource-based view and dynamic capabilities will be the lens through which research problems and research questions will be evaluated. The resource-based view (RBV) suggests that if a firm is to achieve a competitive advantage, it must acquire and control valuable, rare, inimitable, and non-substitutable (VRIN) resources and capabilities (Barney, 1986, 1991, 1994, 2002; Dierickx & Cool, 1989; Peteraf, 1993; Newbert, 2007a). These resources and capabilities can be viewed as bundles of tangible and intangible assets. Amit and Schoemaker define resources as "stocks of available factors that are owned or controlled by the firm" (1993, p. 35). Resources consist of tangible components like financial and physical assets like property, plant and equipment, and intangible components include human capital, firm's management skills, its innovation culture, its organizational processes and routines, and the information and knowledge it controls, patent, technology know-how (Grant, 1991; Amit & Schoemaker, 1993; Nath et al., 2010). Capabilities are "information-based, tangible or intangible processes that are firm-specific and are developed over time through complex interactions among the firm's resources" (Amit & Schoemaker, 1993, p. 35). It is like "intermediate goods" generated by the firm using organizational processes to provide "enhanced productivity to its resources" (Amit & Schoemaker, 1993). Capabilities are "invisible assets", tangible or intangible organizational processes developed by a firm over a period of time that "cannot be easily bought; they must be built" (Teece et al., 1997, cited in Nath et al., 2010).

Marketing scholars have extensively used the RBV theory to understand firm performance and concluded that there is a significant relationship between capabilities and performance (Barney, 1986; Peteraf, 1993; Dutta et al., 1999; Makadok, 2001; Liebermann & Dhawan, 2005; Song et al., 2005, 2007, 2008). Following the same line of thinking, the current study argues that competitive advantage can be derived from a firm's resources and capabilities.

Dynamic capabilities, on the other hand, are "the firm's ability to integrate, build, and reconfigure internal and external competences to address rapidly changing environments in which there is deep uncertainty" (Teece et al., 1997, p. 516; 2016). In the dynamic capabilities perspective, recombining and reconfiguring organizations' assets is a key to sustain performance (Teece et al., 2016). This "orchestration" process involves the modification, addition, divestment, and alignment of tangible and intangible assets. This requires shifting resources such as talent and money to where they will deliver the most value (Helfat et al., 2007).

There are three clusters of dynamic capabilities that can help brands effectively reap the full benefits of co-creation. First, co-creation requires *sensing*. The sensing capability can assist companies in identifying and evaluating valuable knowledge; it is critical to be able to attract lots of ideas, and then evaluate, select, and remove the bad ones (Bogers et al., 2019). Second, is *seizing* – companies also need to realign their organizations to integrate external knowledge sources, which often requires transforming capability. Integrating external knowledge may cause disruption and require a cultural change. Third, is *transforming capability* – co-creation helps to realign the organization to integrate knowledge and develop a culture that promotes collaboration (Bogers et al., 2019).

Furthermore, on the basis of RBV theory and the dynamic capability view of the firm (Teece et al., 1997), this study argues that firms that have brand co-creation as an intangible resource and a certain level of innovation as capabilities will achieve a competitive advantage and consequently improve brand performance (see Figure 12.1). The reason behind this argument is that the mere availability of brand co-creation strategies cannot achieve a competitive advantage and brand performance will not depend only on brand co-creation but will depend also on the inimitable capability of innovation (Rumelt, 1984, 1987; Day & Wensley, 1988; Barney, 1991; Peteraf, 1993; Song et al., 2007).

The present research is motivated by three factors. First, it provides insight into the role of brand co-creation in brand performance. Despite the considerable amount of research focus brand co-creation, relatively little attention has been paid to the relationship between brand co-creation and brand performance, for instance, the study of brand value co-creation and its impacts upon customer perception and brand performance in the B2B context (Zhang & He, 2014). This study, therefore, explores this relationship both theoretically and empirically to address this research gap. Second, the study reviews recent research on brand co-creation and its relationship to brand performance. Over the past decades a few studies have investigated several antecedents and consequences of brand co-creation, however little is known about the roles of firm age and innovation in this relationship, therefore this study is attempting to summarize what we now know about brand co-creation and explore what we don't know about firm age and innovation. Third, existing empirical studies on brand co-creation are limited in the generalizability of the knowledge they produce about the concept and illuminate only one part of the puzzle. Taken together, the existing literature left researchers with a big task of exploring and researching brand co-creation.

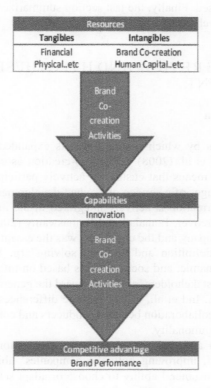

*Figure 12.1    Resource-based view as a theoretical foundation of the study*

Thus, data was collected from a sample of marketing and branding managers via an online survey to test the proposed conceptual framework. Consequently, the research questions are formulated as follows: RQ1: What impact does brand co-creation have on brand performance? RQ2: what roles, if any, do firm age and innovations play in the relationship between brand co-creation and brand performance? This study is expected to contribute to the current body of literature on brand co-creation as follows.

First, there is a paucity of theoretically grounded research that examines the link between brand co-creation and brand performance in countries other than US and European countries. Second, existing studies overlooked the role of firm age and innovations. This study aims to include those two constructs in the research model to better understand their impact on brand performance along with brand co-creation. Therefore, we can have a better understanding of brand co-creation. Third, this study investigates how brand co-creation influences brand performance through the lenses of resource-based view theory and dynamic capabilities theory. The findings from this study may provide brand managers with insights about how to better manage the brand co-creation process.

The remainder of this chapter is organized as follows. First, the literature review and hypotheses development are presented. Second, the methodology is outlined, and third, the empirical results are discussed. Finally, the last section summarizes conclusions, discussions, limitations and future research directions.

## 2.   LITERATURE REVIEW AND HYPOTHESES DEVELOPMENT

### 2.1   Brand Co-creation

Co-creation is "the process by which mutual value is expanded together" (Ramaswamy, 2011, p. 195). Also, Füller et al. (2008) defined co-creation as customers' participation in product development. This means that customers actively participate in the generation and evaluation of ideas at all stages of a service or product development process. With this form of co-creation, market information is actively integrated in the innovation process through customer participation. Moreover, Prahalad and Ramaswamy (2004, p. 8) stated that "joint creation of value by the company and the customer" was the essential element of co-creation, including "joint problem definition and problem solving" (p. 8). Another definition of co-creation is an active, dynamic, and social process based on interactions and relationships between firms and external stakeholders, oriented toward the generation of new products (i.e., goods and/or services) (e.g., Ind et al., 2013). Despite differences in the articulation of the concept of co-creation, the collaboration between producers and consumers for the purpose of creating value is a major commonality.

"Through the interaction and dialogue elements of co-creation, mutual knowledge and understanding is developed, improving both the companies' ability to provide what the consumers want and the consumers' ability to choose or adapt services that fit their needs" (Nysveen & Pedersen, 2014, p. 811). Therefore, the importance of including consumers in innovation processes is emphasized (Roberts et al., 2005). Practically, firms increasingly embrace co-creation initiatives to build a competitive edge (Kazadi et al., 2016). Co-creation is argued to help firms generate new products/services ideas, reduce risk, lower costs and improve innovation performance (e.g., Faems et al., 2005; Hatch & Schultz, 2010; Ind et al., 2017).

### 2.2   Brand Co-creation and Brand Performance

Brand performance refers to the success of the brand in the markets (Wong & Merrilees, 2005). Brand image, brand awareness, customer brand loyalty, and brand reputation are identified as factors pertaining to the concept (Wong & Merrilees, 2008). Brand co-creation is argued to increase the strength of the brand (Markovic & Bagherzadeh, 2018). Strong brands are built by means of co-creation processes involving different stakeholders (Sherry, 1998; Brown et al., 2003; Coupland et al., 2005 in Boyle, 2007; Brakus et al., 2009; Ismail, 2011; Ismail et al., 2011; Ind et al., 2013). Stakeholders' engagement is crucial in achieving high brand performance (i.e., involvement and loyalty) (Casaló et al., 2008; Hatch & Schultz, 2010). Furthermore, companies engage in co-creation projects to discover customer interest and value, which they can turn into innovation (as will be discussed in the next hypothesis development) and competitive advantage. In brand co-creation, companies solicit new ideas, suggestions or designs from customers and other stakeholders, through contests or open-ended appeals, for subsequent use in the design and development of products and services (Bhalla, 2016). They also refine one or more features of a target product or service, to help improve its physical performance, leading to a better customer experience and enhanced brand performance (ibid.). Thus, the present study puts forward the following hypothesis:

*H1: Brand co-creation will positively influence brand performance.*

### 2.3    Innovation

Innovation is suggested to be one of the most critical factors determining business success (Day, 1996; Wind & Mahajan, 1997; Golder, 2000). Innovation can be defined as the market effectiveness of new or significantly improved products (Faems et al., 2005). Innovation also is viewed as the process of transformation of creative ideas into practical applications by using the firm's capabilities in an effective way; therefore, it includes not only the products or service level but also the process and systemic change (Cram, 1996). Thus, in this study the items of innovation construct include both product/service level and the process aspect as well.

**Brand co-creation and innovation**
Fifty-eight per cent of businesses are now piloting co-creation projects to help drive innovation (*Telegraph*, 2018). The rapid evolution of information technologies has impacted the way brands interact with their stakeholders (Zolkiewski et al., 2006). Brands have, now, more opportunities to involve their key stakeholders in co-creation projects (Ind et al., 2017). Customers and other stakeholders are not passive receivers of brand innovations anymore, but they share their knowledge and skills to actively co-create the brand (Cova & Dalli, 2009). Accordingly, informed, networked, empowered, and active stakeholders participate ideally in every stage of the co-creation process, from idea generation to implementation (Payne et al., 2008). This co-creation process has nurtured innovation (Gyrd-Jones & Kornum, 2013; von Wallpach et al., 2017; Markovic & Bagherzadeh, 2018). Co-creation provides firms with a wide range of insights and ideas that contribute to the creation of products that are more relevant to customers (Iglesias et al., 2013; Ind et al., 2017). Therefore, the risk of non-acceptance of new products in the marketplace is likely to decrease (Ind et al., 2013; Markovic & Bagherzadeh, 2018). As a result, co-creation is likely to improve innovation performance (Tsai, 2009; Ferreras-Méndez et al., 2015; Markovic & Bagherzadeh, 2018). Therefore, it is hypothesized that:

*H2: Brand co-creation will positively influence innovation.*

**Innovation and brand performance**
Innovation cultures in SMEs are characterized by relatively low resistance to change, low risk aversion, and tolerance of ambiguity (Saleh and Wang, 1993; Acs et al., 1997; O'Regan et al., 2005), whereas innovation cultures in large organizations tend to be more formalized and based on research capabilities and operating procedures (Damanpour, 1992). Previous studies have demonstrated that innovation can improve firm performance (Merrilees & Miller, 2001a, b; Noble et al., 2002; Faems et al., 2005; Knudsen, 2007). It is also argued to boost brand per-

formance in SMEs (Weerawardena et al., 2006). However, other studies have shown a negative effect (e.g., Knudsen, 2007; Knudsen & Mortensen, 2011). Following the dynamic capabilities approach, which originates from activities undertaken by firms (Amit & Schoemaker, 1993; Verona, 1999) and represent a firm's ability to persistently modify or create organizational configurations for competitive advantage (Helfat, 1997), the study is focusing on innovation as a specific dynamic capability of the firm. It is argued, therefore, that when brands are more innovative, their performance increases (O'Sullivan & Abela, 2007) because the innovative products/services attract more customers; that is brand awareness. Additionally, when firms adopt innovation, they will outperform competitors, have a good reputation and consequently will cultivate brand loyalty and gain a formidable competitive edge (Gunday et al., 2011; Dibrell et al., 2014; Zaefarian et al., 2017). Thus:

*H3: Innovation will positively influence brand performance.*

The resource-based view (RBV) addresses that when firms possess valuable, rare, inimitable and non-substitutable VRIN resources, they can achieve sustainable competitive advantage and that competitive advantage is likely to improve firm's performance through innovative strategies that competing firms will have difficulty in duplicating (Wernerfelt, 1984; Barney, 1986; Dierickx & Cool, 1989; Grant, 1991; Ray et al., 2004; Acedo et al., 2006; Armstrong & Shimizu, 2007; Newbert, 2007b; Lockett et al., 2009). Innovation here is considered a VRIN resource through which firms are provided with opportunities to acquire new skills and knowledge that will improve brand performance. Therefore,

*H4: Innovation will positively mediate the relationship between brand co-creation and brand performance.*

## 2.4     Firm Age

The interest in firm age as a control variable has grown in studies investigating the determinants of firm performance (Autio et al., 2000; Gilbert et al., 2008). However, there is a scarcity of empirical research examining this variable in brand co-creation studies. The rationale for selecting firm age as a moderating variable lies in the possibility that old firms might have improved their brand co-creation process over time and in turn their brand performance compared to younger firms. Past studies suggest new firms are more prone to failure than are older, more established firms (Stinchcombe, 1965). Compared to older firms that are characterized by established processes, routines and organizational norms, younger firms lack stable ties with the customers they wish to serve, lack knowledge about what they can do or should do (Jovanovic, 1982; Lippman & Rumelt, 1982) and may lack sufficient resources to implement their strategies (Venkataraman et al., 1990; Lussier, 1995). Moreover, younger firms "lack established routines and processes that may provide guidance and discipline in strategic decision-making" (Anderson & Eshima, 2013, p. 413).

Hirvonen et al. (2013) note that as "young firms may also lack an explicit business strategy", it is "difficult for them to coordinate their brands as strategic resources as the overall direction of the business is still developing" (p. 628). Brand co-creation requires knowledge and skills that may not be available during the early stages of the business (Calantone et al., 2002). Thus, brand managers of younger firms are often engaged in excessive trial and error behaviour without a clear strategic purpose, resulting in a weak link between brand co-creation and performance outcomes (Slevin & Covin, 1997). Additionally, Sørensen and Stuart (2000) stated that older firms tend to engage in more frequent innovation than younger firms, because of the firm's existing knowledge stock. Therefore, firm age is theoretically meaningful in explaining the innovation–performance linkage (Luo et al., 2005; Rauch et al., 2009; Rosenbusch et al., 2011), and this study posits firm age as a control variable that moderates all the relationships among the study constructs (see Figure 12.2).

*H5: The relationship between brand co-creation and brand performance will be positively moderated by firm age.*

*H6: The relationship between brand co-creation and innovation will be positively moderated by firm age.*

*H7: The relationship between innovation and brand performance will be positively moderated by firm age.*

## 3.    METHODOLOGY

### 3.1    Questionnaire and Measures

All measurement items are borrowed from the relevant literature. To measure brand co-creation, six items were adapted from Nysveen and Pedersen (2014). The four-item brand performance scale is adapted from Wong and Merrilees (2005). Finally, innovation is operationalized with the four items used in Wong and Merrilees's (2008) work. A seven-point Likert scale, 1 = decreased enormously, to 7 = increased enormously, is used for the brand performance construct. For all the other constructs, responses are recorded by means of a seven-point Likert scale, that ranged from 1 = "strongly disagree" to 7 = "strongly agree".

### 3.2    Data Collection

This study is based on SMEs operating in Egypt from a cross-section of industries. The sample is drawn from a professional database company in Egypt. In January 2019, emails were sent to the firms with a covering letter explaining the purpose of the study and a hyperlink for an online questionnaire in Google form. After two weeks a reminder email was sent for those firms that didn't respond. In this study marketing managers or brand managers or owners/CEOs were selected as the key informant not only because they are policymakers but also responses provided by them are argued to be more reliable and less biased (Zahra & Covin, 1993; Heide & Weiss, 1995).

In total, 131 out of 1023 completed questionnaires were returned after two reminders, accounting for approximately a 13 per cent response rate. Non-response bias was examined by comparing responses before the first reminder and after a second reminder (Armstrong & Overton, 1977). The results showed no significance difference between scale items (at $p < 0.05$), which confirms that non-response bias is not a major concern. The surveyed firms covered the following industries: advertising (19.8 per cent), manufacturing (16.8 per cent), retailing (16 per cent), telecommunications (9.2 per cent), real estate (6.1 per cent), service industry including medical services, restaurants, educational and training services, publishing and consultancy (22.1 per cent) and others (9.9 per cent). Eighty-three respondents were marketing managers (63.4 per cent), 29 were owner/CEOs (22.1 per cent), 19 were brand managers (14.5 per cent). The sample included both younger and older firms – 64.9 per cent of the firms were less than 20 years old, and 35.1 per cent were more than 20 years old. With respect to firm size, 13.7 per cent of the firms had less than 10 employees, 37.4 per cent of the firms had from 10 to 49 employees and 48.9 per cent of the firms had more than 50 employees to less than 250 employees, following the cut-off for small and medium-sized enterprises by Wiklund and Shepherd (2003).

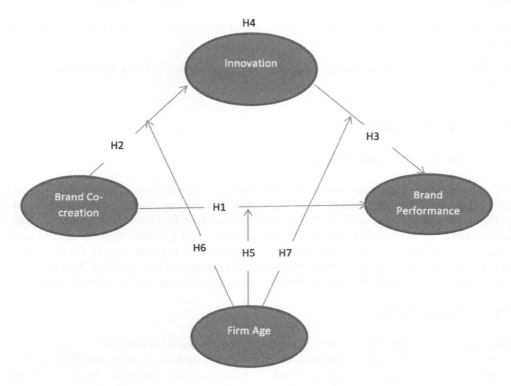

*Figure 12.2    Conceptual framework*

## 4.    DATA ANALYSIS AND RESULTS

Partial least squares structural equation modelling (PLS-SEM) is applied using SmartPLS 3.0, considering the small sample size. PLS is also used when the analysis is concerned with testing a theoretical framework from a prediction perspective (Hair et al., 2019, p. 5). In this study exploring the roles of innovation and firm age in addition to brand co-creation in the prediction of brand performance is the main aim of the research, it is, therefore, predictive and explora-tory in nature and the use of PLS-SEM is recommended (Hair et al., 2016) to use PLS-SEM.

## 4.1   Outer Model Results

Prior to testing the hypotheses, it is essential to establish the reliability and validity of the measurement model (i.e., outer model) first. The hypothesized model was comprised of three reflective constructs: brand co-creation, innovation and brand performance. With the exception of one item (CO_4), the results indicate that no measurement item loading is less than 0.65, showing an acceptable loading that ranged from 0.65 to 0.93, and were significant (t > 1.96) (Hair et al., 2016) as shown in Table 12.1 and Figure 12.3. The Cronbach's α value is 0.89, 0.86 and 0.84 for brand co-creation, innovation and brand performance respectively. Cronbach's α value above 0.60 is considered acceptable (Nunnally, 1978).

Table 12.1 shows the average variance extracted (AVE) values and composite reliability (CR) value. Convergent validity was confirmed by the Cronbach's α value which is above the threshold (0.7) suggested by Hair et al. (1998). Also, all loadings were statistically significant (p < 0.01), and accounted for more than 50 per cent of their respective constructs, supporting convergent validity. CR values were above the accepted limit (0.70) suggested by Bagozzi and Yi (1988); and AVE values were also above the cut-off value (0.50) suggested by Fornell and Larcker (1981).

Table 12.2 shows correlations between constructs did not exceed 0.77 and were significantly less than one (Bagozzi & Yi, 1988); the square root of AVE is greater for all variables than the corresponding correlation between those variables, showing the discriminant validity achieved (Fornell & Larcker, 1981; Anderson & Gerbing, 1988). Another method to test the discriminant validity is the heterotrait–monotrait (HTMT) method, which is a stringent method of testing discriminant validity (Voorhees et al., 2016). It involves the examination of the HTMT and if the ratio is significantly different from one, then the discriminant validity is established. The results of the HTMT method showed that HTMT ratios ranged from 0.11 to 0.88, thus confirming discriminant validity (see Table 12.2). Finally, to check for multicollinearity issues, VIF is examined. All VIFs were well below the recommended level of 5 (i.e., ranged from 1.64 to 2.72), with the exception of one item (Innov_4) which is later dropped. Also, all factor-level VIFs resulting from the full collinearity test are less than 3.3. Therefore, the model can be considered free of common method bias (Kock, 2015, p. 7). Additionally, the correlation matrix (Table 12.2) does not indicate any highly correlated factors (r > 0.90) (Pavlou et al., 2007). Therefore, CMB is not to a serious threat in analysis.

## 4.2   Inner Model Results

The hypothesized relationships are tested through the structural (inner) model (Diamantopoulos & Winklhofer, 2001). The structural model assessment includes the examination of the $R^2$ estimates, standardized path coefficients (b) and p-values. The results showed that brand co-creation and innovation predict a 61 per cent $R^2$ variance in the brand performance, larger than the cut-off value of 0.10 (Falk & Miller, 1992), which indicates a moderate prediction (Hair et al., 2012). Regarding the path significance, results showed that the direct relationship between brand co-creation and brand performance is insignificant (b = 0.10; t-value = 1.62) as shown in Figure 12.4. Therefore, H1 is not supported. The finding seems to be unanticipated; however, the indirect effect of brand co-creation on brand performance through innovation is significant as shown in the mediation analysis in Table 12.3. Therefore, H4 is supported.

*Table 12.1*   *Measures, factor loadings, Cronbach's α, composite reliability and AVE values*

| Construct | Items | Mean | SD | Outer loadings | Cronbach's α | CR | AVE |
|---|---|---|---|---|---|---|---|
| Brand co-creation | Our customers often express their personal needs to the brand | 0.72 | 0.18 | 0.78 | 0.89 | 0.91 | 0.67 |
| | Our customers often suggest how this brand can improve its products and/or services | 0.83 | 0.25 | 0.93 | | | |
| | Our customers participate in decisions about how the brand offers its products and/or services | 0.80 | 0.21 | 0.88 | | | |
| | Our customers often find solutions to their problems together with the brand | 0.60 | 0.19 | 0.64 | | | |
| | Our customers are actively involved when the brand develops new products and/or services | 0.73 | 0.17 | 0.79 | | | |
| | The brand encourages customers to create solutions together | 0.67 | 0.19 | 0.70 | | | |
| Innovation | We actively engage in wide search for new ideas | 0.65 | 0.08 | 0.65 | 0.86 | 0.9 | 0.64 |
| | We carefully think through how new ideas need to be adapted for our business | 0.81 | 0.03 | 0.82 | | | |
| | We have good system of identifying, selecting and implementing innovation on a regular basis | 0.81 | 0.05 | 0.81 | | | |
| | Compared with competitors, we have a high rate of product/service innovation | 0.87 | 0.03 | 0.88 | | | |
| | Compared with competitors, we have a high rate of process/organization improvement | 0.86 | 0.03 | 0.87 | | | |
| | Over time, we have been very successful with overall innovation in recent years | 0.81 | 0.03 | 0.82 | | | |
| Brand performance | We have reached the desired image in the market | 0.78 | 0.06 | 0.79 | 0.84 | 0.89 | 0.68 |
| | Our firm has a good reputation | 0.89 | 0.03 | 0.89 | | | |
| | Our firm has built a strong customer brand loyalty | 0.88 | 0.02 | 0.88 | | | |
| | Our brand has strong brand awareness in the market | 0.72 | 0.07 | 0.72 | | | |

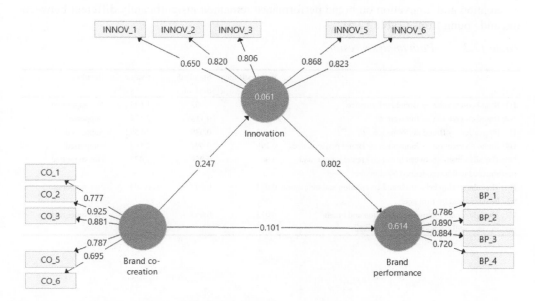

*Figure 12.3*    *The measurement model*

*Table 12.2*    *Construct correlations, Fornell–Larcker criterion analysis and HTMT ratios*

| Constructs | Brand co-creation | Innovation | Brand performance |
|---|---|---|---|
| Brand co-creation | **0.82** | | |
| Innovation | 0.24 (0.21) | **0.80** | |
| Brand performance | 0.10 (0.12) | 0.77 (0.89) | **0.82** |

*Notes:* Figures in bold are the square root of AVE of each factor; the remaining figures represent the correlations (p < 0.01). HTMT ratios are in parentheses.

The study also found that brand co-creation has a positive and significant impact on innovation (b = 0.25; t-value = 2.17). Similarly, there is a positive relationship between innovation and brand performance (b = 0.80; t-value = 20.59). Therefore, the second and the third hypotheses H2 and H3 are supported. Additionally, the Stone–Geisser's $Q^2$ is larger than zero (0.40) and that confirms the model's predictive validity (Hair et al., 2012). However, the moderation effect of firm age was found to be insignificant. As a result, H5, H6 and H7 are rejected.

To understand how the proposed relationships differ across young and old firms, a multi-group analysis (MGA) is performed. First, measurement invariance is an essential pre-requisite for conducting comparison across the two groups. Therefore, the MICOM (measurement invariance of composite models) is assessed prior to the multi-group analysis (Sarstedt et al., 2011; Henseler et al., 2016; Hair et al., 2017). The results showed no significant difference exists between the two groups (Table 12.4). After confirming the existence of invariance, standardized path coefficients across the two groups are compared by conducting a multi-group analysis (Table 12.5) (Sarstedt et al., 2011; Henseler et al., 2016; Hair et al., 2017). The PLS-SEM multi-group analysis failed to show a significant difference as shown in Table 12.5. Thus, the study showed the firm age to be less relevant, as the effects of brand co-creation and innovation on brand performance remained insignificantly different between old and young firms (Table 12.5).

*Table 12.3      Path analysis results*

|  | Path coefficient | Standard deviation | t-value | Results |
|---|---|---|---|---|
| H1: Brand co-creation → Brand performance | 0.101 | 0.062 | 1.623 | Not supported |
| H2: Brand co-creation → Innovation | 0.247 | 0.113 | 2.174 | Supported |
| H3: Innovation → Brand performance | 0.802 | 0.039 | 20.592 | Supported |
| H4: Brand co-creation → Innovation → Brand performance | 0.198 | 0.091 | 2.164 | Supported |
| H5: The relationship between brand co-creation and brand performance will be moderated by firm age | 0.087 | 0.059 | 1.477 | Not supported |
| H6: The relationship between brand co-creation and innovation will be moderated by firm age | 0.077 | 0.097 | 0.794 | Not supported |
| H7: The relationship between innovation and brand performance will be moderated by firm age | 0.073 | 0.053 | 1.397 | Not supported |

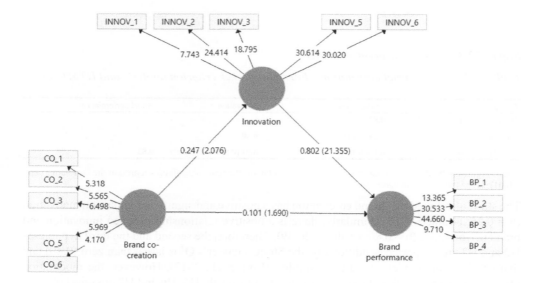

*Figure 12.4      The structural model*

## 5.      DISCUSSION

Findings of this study offer support for the argument of brand performance is derived by brand co-creation and innovation. In light of RBV theory and dynamic capabilities theory, the study showed that when firms embrace brand co-creation as a valuable resource, they can achieve an improved brand performance through innovative strategies that competing firms will have difficulty in duplicating. These results support the consensus that brand co-creation increases the strength of the brand (Sherry, 1998; Brown et al., 2003; Coupland et al., 2005; Boyle, 2007; Casaló et al., 2008; Fang et al., 2008; Brakus et al., 2009; Ismail, 2011; Ismail et al., 2011; Ind et al., 2013; Hatch & Schultz, 2010; Markovic & Bagherzadeh, 2018).

*Table 12.4        Measurement invariance results*

| ° | Outer loadings-difference | p-value |
|---|---|---|
| BP_1 ← Brand performance | −0.251 | 0.065 |
| BP_2 ← Brand performance | 0.035 | 0.543 |
| BP_3 ← Brand performance | 0.005 | 0.771 |
| BP_4 ← Brand performance | 0.037 | 0.722 |
| CO_1 ← Brand co-creation | 0.057 | 0.563 |
| CO_2 ← Brand co-creation | −0.197 | 0.352 |
| CO_3 ← Brand co-creation | −0.13 | 0.604 |
| CO_5 ← Brand co-creation | 0.003 | 0.675 |
| CO_6 ← Brand co-creation | −0.074 | 0.898 |
| INNOV_1 ← Innovation | 0.225 | 0.104 |
| INNOV_2 ← Innovation | 0.014 | 0.787 |
| INNOV_3 ← Innovation | 0.032 | 0.671 |
| INNOV_5 ← Innovation | 0.003 | 0.849 |
| INNOV_6 ← Innovation | 0.015 | 0.738 |

*Table 12.5        MGA results*

| ° | Path coefficient difference | p-value |
|---|---|---|
| Brand co-creation → Innovation | 0.315 | 0.410 |
| Brand co-creation → Performance | 0.168 | 0.298 |
| Innovation → Brand performance | −0.036 | 0.676 |

## 5.1        The Mediation Effect of Innovation

Further, aligned with RBV theory and dynamic capabilities theory, the current study viewed innovation as a capability through which firms are provided with opportunities to acquire new skills and knowledge that will improve brand performance (Wernerfelt, 1984; Barney, 1986; Dierickx & Cool, 1989; Grant, 1991; Ray et al., 2004; Acedo et al., 2006; Armstrong & Shimizu, 2007; Newbert, 2007b; Lockett et al., 2009). Empirically, the importance of innovation is highlighted in this study, as the results showed that influence of brand co-creation on brand performance is mediated by innovation. Therefore, without the innovation the brand co-creation–brand performance may not be realized. Results also suggested that brand co-creation drives innovation; this finding concurs with previous studies which showed that by engaging customers and stakeholders in the co-creation process of the brand, innovation will be fostered (Payne et al., 2008 in von Wallpach et al., 2018; Cova & Dalli, 2009; Gyrd-Jones & Kornum, 2013; von Wallpach et al., 2017; Markovic & Bagherzadeh, 2018). Another interesting finding is the effect of innovation on brand performance. The study found that innovation positively influences brand performance. The finding is consistent with literature that has shown that innovation can enhance brand performance (Weerawardena et al., 2006).

### 5.2    The Moderating Effect of Firm Age

In this study, it is thought that the proposed relationships may be influenced by the firm age. However, the findings relating to the moderating effect of firm age were unanticipated, indicating firm age is not influential. A possible explanation for this finding is that, regardless of firm age, both older and younger firms can benefit from innovation and its role in fostering the impact of brand co-creation on brand performance. For older firms, the established routines and processes facilitate competitive advantage and better brand performance (Freeman et al., 1983; Leonard-Barton, 1992). For the younger firms, the lack of established routine may also encourage firms to be more innovative and improve brand performance. However, the results showed that firm age is not influential. These results may not align with previous studies that showed firm age is important in explaining and understanding brand performance (Slevin & Covin, 1997; Sørensen & Stuart, 2000; Calantone et al., 2002; Luo et al., 2005; Rauch et al., 2009; Rosenbusch et al., 2011). Therefore, further replication of this study is required.

## 6.    THEORETICAL CONTRIBUTION

Overall, this study offers theoretical perspectives on brand co-creation and innovation as major determinants of brand performance. The study theoretically contributes in many ways to the brand co-creation literature that acknowledges the significant role co-creating plays in enhancing brand performance. First, this research, to the best of the author's knowledge, is the first empirical exploration of brand co-creation among Egyptian firms and, in this way, it remedies the research gap of brand co-creation in non-western countries. Second, this chapter not only figures out the relationship between brand co-creation and brand performance, it integrates two important variables into the study conceptual framework (i.e., firm age and innovation) to further develop the existing knowledge on brand co-creation. The two constructs are included in the research model to better understand their impact on brand performance along with brand co-creation. Therefore, we can have a better understanding of brand co-creation, since existing studies overlooked the role of firm age and innovations. Third, this study investigates how brand co-creation influences brand performance through the lenses of the resource-based view (RBV) theory and dynamic capabilities theory. Therefore, the study makes a significant contribution to overcome the existing shortcomings and paucity of theoretically grounded research that examines the link between brand co-creation and brand performance. As a result, the robust findings from this study may provide brand managers with insights about how to better manage the brand co-creation process. Finally, another theoretical contribution lies in extending the RBV theory and dynamic capabilities theory – it is that current literature shows that it is important for organizations to remember that brands are not created by management teams alone; customers and different stakeholders should be closely involved in developing and designing new products (Iglesias et al., 2013; Vallaster & von Wallpach, 2013). The study extended this perspective and suggested that co-creation will enable consumers to contribute key inputs in response to queries, to offer their innovative ideas, to get involved in discussions, and to generate new concepts and ideas, and as a result brand performance will be improved (Ind et al., 2013).

## 7.     MANAGERIAL IMPLICATIONS

Empirically, the findings of this study are of utmost importance for brand managers seeking to improve their brand performance. Therefore, brand managers should embrace brand co-creation as an essential component that drives brand performance, without overlooking the importance of innovation. The old school of thought that managers are passive recipients of brand offerings is no longer true. Therefore, managers should pay attention to the role of customers in brand co-creation and treat them as active creators of brand value. Firms need to cooperate not only with customers, but also should encourage employees and other stakeholders to participate in the co-creation of the brand. There are many paths organizations can follow to improve brand co-creation, for example increase stakeholders' knowledge about the brand and improve brand image and reputation. Also managers should evaluate the co-creation process on a regular basis and identify those problems that may hinder the progress of the co-creation activities. Finally, brand managers of firms need to be receptive to all of the brand co-creation activities that engage consumers and other stakeholders in the co-creation process. They are encouraged to establish online brand communities to foster interactions among consumers and organizations which in turn will help in building trust and commitment and, eventually, facilitate brand loyalty, brand co-creation activities and improve brand performance (Hajli et al., 2017).

## 8.     LIMITATIONS AND FURTHER RESEARCH

The research is exploratory in nature, and as such, findings are indicative rather than conclusive. The fact that the study was conducted on a small sample size from a single country limits the generalization of the study. Therefore, future research should consider larger sample sizes from different countries to explore cultural variation. While the study findings require further exploration, this research increases our knowledge and provides directions for future avenues to pursue. For instance, future research may examine the mediation role of brand trust, commitment and emotional attachment in the brand co-creation and brand performance link. The role of firm size is also worth investigating. Future studies, may compare between different samples of stakeholders, not only customers, but also suppliers, dealers, and so on in different sectors.

## REFERENCES

Acedo, F.J., Barroso, C., & Galan, J.L. (2006). The resource-based theory: Dissemination and main trends. *Strategic Management Journal*, 27(7), 621–636.
Acs, Z.J., Morck, R., Shaver, J.M., & Yeung, B. (1997). The internationalization of small and medium-sized enterprises: A policy perspective. *Small Business Economics*, 9(1), 7–20.

Alida (2016). 5 Examples of Brands Driving Customer-Centric Innovation. Available at: https://www.alida.com/the-alida-journal/5-examples-how-brands-are-using-co-creation retrieved on 9 November 2020.

Amit, R., & Schoemaker, P.J. (1993). Strategic assets and organizational rent. *Strategic Management Journal*, 14(1), 33–46.

Anderson, B.S., & Eshima, Y. (2013). The influence of firm age and intangible resources on the relationship between entrepreneurial orientation and firm growth among Japanese SMEs. *Journal of Business Venturing*, 28(3), 413–429.

Anderson, J., & Gerbing, D. (1988). Structural equation modeling in practice: A review and recommended two-step approach. *Psychological Bulletin*, 103(3), 411–423.

Armstrong, C.E., & Shimizu, K. (2007). A review of approaches to empirical research on the resource-based view of the firm. *Journal of Management*, 33(6), 959–986.

Armstrong, J.S., & Overton, T.S. (1977). Estimating nonresponse bias in mail surveys. *Journal of Marketing Research*, 14(3), 396–402.

Autio, E., Sapienza, H.J., & Almeida, J.G. (2000). Effects of age at entry, knowledge intensity, and imitability on international growth. *Academy of Management Journal*, 43(5), 909–924.

Bagozzi, R.P., & Yi, Y. (1988). On the evaluation of structural equation models. *Journal of the Academy of Marketing Science*, 16(1), 74–94.

Barney, J.B. (1986). Strategic factor markets: Expectations, luck, and business strategy. *Management Science*, 32(10), 1231–1241.

Barney, J.B. (1991). Firm resources and sustained competitive advantage. *Journal of Management*, 17, 99–120.

Barney, J.B. (1994). Bringing managers back in: A resource-based analysis of the role of managers in creating and sustaining competitive advantages for firms. In *Does Management Matter? On Competencies and Competitive Advantage. The 1994 Crafoord Lectures* (pp. 1–36). Lund, Sweden: Lund University, Institute of Economic Research.

Barney, J.B. (2002). *Gaining and Sustaining Competitive Advantage*. Upper Saddle River, NJ: Prentice Hall.

Bhalla, G. (2016). Collaboration and co-creation: The road to creating value. Available at: https://www.marketingjournal.org/collaboration-and-co-creation-the-road-to-creating-value/, retrieved February 2021.

Bogers, M., Chesbrough, H., Heaton, S., & Teece, D.J. (2019). Strategic management of open innovation: A dynamic capabilities perspective. *California Management Review*, 62(1), 77–94.

Boyle, E. (2007). A process model of brand cocreation: Brand management and research implications. *Journal of Product & Brand Management*, 16(2), 122–131.

Brakus, J.J., Schmitt, B.H., & Zarantonello, L. (2009). Brand experience: What is it? How is it measured? Does it affect loyalty? *Journal of Marketing*, 73(3), 52–68.

Brown, S., Kozinets, R.V., & Sherry, J.F. (2003). Teaching old brands new tricks: Retro branding and the revival of brand meaning. *Journal of Marketing*, 67(3), 19–33.

Calantone, R.J., Cavusgil, S.T., & Zhao, Y. (2002). Learning orientation, firm innovation capability, and firm performance. *Industrial Marketing Management*, 31(6), 515–524.

Casaló, L.V., Flavián, C., & Guinalíu, M. (2008). Promoting consumers' participation in virtual brand communities: A new paradigm in branding strategy. *Journal of Marketing Communications*, 14(1), 19–36.

Coupland, J.C., Iacobucci, D., & Arnould, E. (2005). Invisible brands: An ethnography of households and the brands in their kitchen pantries. *Journal of Consumer Research*, 32(1), 106–113.

Cova, B., & Dalli, D. (2009). Working consumers: The next step in marketing theory? *Marketing Theory*, 9(3), 315–339.

Cram, T. (1996). A manager's guide to innovation. *Journal of Product & Brand Management*, 5(5), 15–17.

Damanpour, F. (1992). Organizational size and innovation. *Organization Studies*, 13(3), 375–402.

Day, G.S. (1996). Using the past as a guide to the future: Reflections on the history of the *Journal of Marketing. Journal of Marketing*, 60(1), 14–16.

Day, G.S., & Wensley, R. (1988). Assessing advantage: A framework for diagnosing competitive superiority. *Journal of Marketing*, 52(2), 1–20.

Diamantopoulos, A., & Winklhofer, H. (2001). Index construction with formative indicators: An alternative to scale development. *Journal of Marketing Research*, 38(2), 269–277.

Dibrell, C., Craig, J.B., & Neubaum, D.O. (2014). Linking the formal strategic planning process, planning flexibility, and innovativeness to firm performance. *Journal of Business Research*, 67(9), 2000–2007.

Dierickx, I., & Cool, K. (1989). Asset stock accumulation and sustainability of competitive advantage. *Management Science*, 35, 1504–1513.

Dutta, S., Narasimhan, O., & Rajiv, S. (1999). Success in high-technology markets: Is marketing capability critical? *Marketing Science*, 18(4), 547–568.

Faems, D., Van Looy, B., & Debackere, K. (2005). Interorganizational collaboration and innovation: Toward a portfolio approach. *Journal of Product Innovation Management*, 22(3), 238–250.

Falk, R.F., & Miller, N.B. (1992). *A Primer for Soft Modeling*. Akron, OH: University of Akron Press.

Fang, E., Palmatier, R.W., & Evans, K.R. (2008). Influence of customer participation on creating and sharing of new product value. *Journal of the Academy of Marketing Science*, 36(3), 322–336.

Ferreras-Méndez, J.L., Newell, S., Fernández-Mesa, A., & Alegre, J. (2015). Depth and breadth of external knowledge search and performance: The mediating role of absorptive capacity. *Industrial Marketing Management*, 47, 86–97.

Fornell, C., & Larcker, D. (1981). Evaluating structural equation models with unobservable variables and measurement error. *Journal of Marketing Research*, 18(1), 39–50.

Freeman, J., Carroll, G.R., & Hannan, M.T. (1983). The liability of newness: Age dependence in organizational death rates. *American Sociological Review*, 48, 692–710.

Füller, J., Matzler, K., & Hoppe, M. (2008). Brand community members as a source of innovation. *Journal of Product Innovation Management*, 25(6), 608–619.

Gilbert, B., McDougall, P., & Audretsch, D. (2008). Clusters, knowledge spillovers and new venture performance: An empirical examination. *Journal of Business Venturing*, 23, 405–422.

Golder, P.N. (2000). Insights from senior executives about innovation in international markets. *Journal of Innovation Management*, 17(5), 326–340.

Grant, R.M. (1991). The resource-based theory of competitive advantage: Implications for strategy formulation. *California Management Review*, 33, 114–135.

Gunday, G., Ulusoy, G., Kilic, K., & Alpkan, L. (2011). Effects of innovation types on firm performances. *International Journal of Production Economics*, 133(2), 662–676.

Gyrd-Jones, R.I., & Kornum, N. (2013). Managing the co-created brand: Value and cultural complementarity in online and offline multi-stakeholder ecosystems. *Journal of Business Research*, 66(9), 1484–1493.

Hair Jr, J.F., Anderson, R.E., Tatham, R.L., & Black, W.C. (1998). *Multivariate Data Analysis*. Englewood, NJ: Prentice Hall.

Hair, J.F., Sarstedt, M., Ringle, C.M., & Mena, J.A. (2012). An assessment of the use of partial least squares structural equation modeling in marketing research. *Journal of the Academy of Marketing Science*, 40(3), 414–433.

Hair Jr, J.F., Hult, G.T.M., Ringle, C., & Sarstedt, M. (2016). *A Primer on Partial Least Squares Structural Equation Modeling (PLS-SEM)*. Thousand Oaks, CA: Sage Publications.

Hair, J.F., Jr, Sarstedt, M., Ringle, C.M., & Gudergan, S.P. (2017), *Advanced Issues in Partial Least Squares Structural Equation Modeling*. Thousand Oaks, CA: Sage Publications.

Hair, J.F., Risher, J.J., Sarstedt, M., & Ringle, C.M. (2019). When to use and how to report the results of PLS-SEM. *European Business Review*, 31(1), 2–24.

Hajli, N., Shanmugam, M., Papagiannidis, S., Zahay, D., & Richard, M.O. (2017). Branding cocreation with members of online brand communities. *Journal of Business Research*, 70, 136–144.

Hatch, M.J., & Schultz, M. (2010). Toward a theory of brand co-creation with implications for brand governance. *Journal of Brand Management*, 17(8), 590–604.

Heide, J.B., & Weiss, A.M. (1995). Vendor consideration and switching behavior for buyers in high-technology markets. *Journal of Marketing*, 59(3), 30–43.

Helfat, C.E. (1997). Know-how and asset complementarity and dynamic capability accumulation: The case of R&D. *Strategic Management Journal*, 18(5), 339–360.

Helfat, C.E., Finkelstein, S., Mitchell, W., Peteraf, M., Singh, H., Teece, D., & Winter, S.G. (2007), *Dynamic Capabilities: Understanding Strategic Change in Organizations*. Malden, MA: Blackwell.

Henseler, J., Ringle, C.M., & Sarstedt, M. (2016). Testing measurement invariance of composites using partial least squares. *International Marketing Review*, 33(3), 405–431.

Hirvonen, S., Laukkanen, T., & Reijonen, H. (2013). The brand orientation–performance relationship: An examination of moderation effects. *Journal of Brand Management*, 20(8), 623–641.

Hurni, D., & Grösser, S.N. (2017). Innovation management with an emphasis on co-creation. In: S. Grösser, A. Reyes-Lecuona, & G. Granholm (eds), *Dynamics of Long-Life Assets*. Cham: Springer. https://doi.org/10.1007/978-3-319-45438-2_4

Iglesias, O., Ind, N., & Alfaro, M. (2013). The organic view of the brand: A brand value co-creation model. *Journal of Brand Management*, 20, 670–688.

Ind, N., Iglesias, O., & Markovic, S. (2017). The co-creation continuum: From tactical market research tool to strategic collaborative innovation method. *Journal of Brand Management*, 24(4), 310–321.

Ind, N., Iglesias, O., & Schultz, M. (2013). Building brands together. *California Management Review*, 55(3), 5–26.

Ismail, A.R. (2011). Experience marketing: An empirical investigation. *Journal of Relationship Marketing*, 10(3), 167–201.

Ismail, A.R., Melewar, T.C., Lim, L., & Woodside, A. (2011). Customer experiences with brands: Literature review and research directions. *Marketing Review*, 11(3), 205–225.

Jovanovic, B. (1982). Selection and the evolution of industry. *Econometrica*, 50, 649–670.

Kazadi, K., Lievens, A., & Mahr, D. (2016). Stakeholder co-creation during the innovation process: Identifying capabilities for knowledge creation among multiple stakeholders. *Journal of Business Research*, 69(2), 525–540.

Knudsen, M.P. (2007). The relative importance of inter firm relationships and knowledge transfer for new product development success. *Journal of Product Innovation Management*, 24(2), 117–138.

Knudsen, M.P., & Mortensen, T.B. (2011). Some immediate – but negative – effects of openness on product development performance. *Technovation*, 31(1), 54–64.

Kock, N. (2015). Common method bias in PLS-SEM: A full collinearity assessment approach. *International Journal of e-Collaboration*, 11(4), 1–10.

Leonard-Barton, D. (1992). Core capabilities and core rigidities: A paradox in managing new product development. *Strategic Management Journal*, 13(S1), 111–125.

Liebermann, M.B., & Dhawan, R. (2005). Assessing the resource base of Japanese and US auto producers: A stochastic frontier function production approach. *Management Science*, 51(7), 1060–1075.

Lippman, S.S., & Rumelt, R.P. (1982). Uncertain imitability: An analysis of interfirm differences in efficiency under competition. *Bell Journal of Economics*, 13, 418–438.

Lockett, A., Thompson, S., & Morgenstern, U. (2009). The development of the resource-based view of the firm: A critical appraisal. *International Journal of Management Reviews*, 11(1), 9–28.

Luo, X., Zhou, L., & Liu, S.S. (2005). Entrepreneurial firms in the context of China's transition economy: An integrative framework and empirical examination. *Journal of Business Research*, 58(3), 277–284.

Lussier, R.N. (1995). A nonfinancial business success versus failure prediction model for young firms. *Journal of Small Business Management*, 33(1), 8–20. http://doi.org/papers://BA75DBD3-74D3-4A2D-AAAC-910414082C6C/Paper/p12331

Makadok, R. (2001). Toward a synthesis of the resource-based and dynamic-capability views of rent creation. *Strategic Management Journal*, 22(5), 387–401.

Markovic, S., & Bagherzadeh, M. (2018). How does breadth of external stakeholder co-creation influence innovation performance? Analyzing the mediating roles of knowledge sharing and product innovation. *Journal of Business Research*, 88, 173–186.

Merrilees, B., & Miller, D. (2001a). Innovation and strategy in the Australian supermarket industry. *Journal of Food Products Marketing*, 7(4), 3–18.

Merrilees, B., & Miller, D. (2001b). Radical service innovations. *International Journal of New Product Development and Innovation Management*, 3(1), 45–58.

Nath, P., Nachiappan, S., & Ramanathan, R. (2010). The impact of marketing capability, operations capability and diversification strategy on performance: A resource-based view. *Industrial Marketing Management*, 39(2), 317–329.

Newbert, S.L. (2007a). Value, rareness, competitive advantage, and performance: A conceptual-level empirical investigation of the resource-based view of the firm. *Strategic Management Journal*, 29(7), 745–768.

Newbert, S.L. (2007b). Empirical research on the resource-based view of the firm: An assessment and suggestions for future research. *Strategic Management Journal*, 28(2), 121–146.

Noble, C.H., Sinha, R.K., & Kumar, A. (2002). Market orientation and alternative strategic orientations: A longitudinal assessment of performance implications. *Journal of Marketing*, 66(4), 25–39.

Nunnally, J.C. (1978). *Psychometric Theory*. New York, NY: McGraw-Hill.

Nysveen, H., & Pedersen, P.E. (2014). Influences of cocreation on brand experience. *International Journal of Market Research*, 56(6), 807–832.

O'Regan, N., Ghobadian, A., & Gallear, G. (2005). In search of the drivers of high growth in manufacturing SMEs. *Technovation*, 26(1), 30–41.

O'Sullivan, D., & Abela, A.V. (2007). Marketing performance measurement ability and firm performance. *Journal of Marketing*, 71(2), 79–93.

Pavlou, P., Liang, H., & Xue, Y. (2007). Understanding and mitigating uncertainty in online exchange relationships: A principal–agent perspective. *MIS Quarterly*, 31, 105–136.

Payne, A.F., Storbacka, K., & Frow, P. (2008). Managing the co-creation of value. *Journal of the Academy of Marketing Science*, 36(1), 83–96.

Peteraf, M.A. (1993). The cornerstones of competitive advantage. *Strategic Management Journal*, 14(3), 179–191.

Prahalad, C.K., & Ramaswamy, V. (2004). Co-creation experiences: The next practice in value creation. *Journal of Interactive Marketing*, 18(3), 5–14.

Ramaswamy, V. (2011). It's about human experiences … and beyond, to co-creation. *Industrial Marketing Management*, 40, 195–196.

Rauch, A., Wiklund, J., Lumpkin, G.T., & Frese, M. (2009). Entrepreneurial orientation and business performance: An assessment of past research and suggestions for the future. *Entrepreneurship Theory and Practice*, 33(3), 761–787.

Ray, G., Barney, J.B., & Muhanna, W.A. (2004). Capabilities, business processes, and competitive advantage: Choosing the dependent variable in empirical tests of the resource-based view. *Strategic Management Journal*, 25, 23–37.

Roberts, D., Baker, S., & Walker, D. (2005). Can we learn together? Co-creating with consumers. *International Journal of Market Research*, 47(4), 407–427.

Rosenbusch, N., Brinckmann, J., & Bausch, A. (2011). Is innovation always beneficial? A meta-analysis of the relationship between innovation and performance in SMEs. *Journal of Business Venturing*, 26(4), 441–457.

Rumelt, R.P. (1984). Towards a strategic theory of the firm. In R.B. Lamb (ed.), *Competitive Strategic Management*. Englewood Cliffs, NJ: Prentice-Hall, pp. 556–570.

Rumelt, R.P. (1987). Theory, strategy, and entrepreneurship. In D. Teece (ed.), *The Competitive Challenge*. Cambridge, MA: Ballinger, pp. 556–570.

Saleh, S.D., & Wang, C.K. (1993). The management of innovation: Strategy, structure, and organizational climate. *Engineering Management*, 40(1), 14–21.

Sarstedt, M., Henseler, J., and Ringle, C.M. (2011). Multigroup analysis in partial least squares (PLS) path modeling: Alternative methods and empirical results. In M. Sarstedt, M. Schwaiger & C.R. Taylor (eds), *Measurement and Research Methods in International Marketing*. Bingley, UK: Emerald Group Publishing Limited, pp. 195–218.

Sherry, J. (1998). The soul of the company store: Nike town Chicago and the emplaced brandscape. In J. Sherry (ed.), *The Concept of Place in Contemporary Markets*. Lincolnwood, IL: NTC Business Books, pp. 109–146.

Sheth, J.N. (2019). Customer value propositions: Value co-creation. *Industrial Marketing Management*, 87, 312–315.

Slevin, D.P., & Covin, J.G. (1997). Strategy formation patterns, performance, and the significance of context. *Journal of Management*, 23(2), 189–209.

Song, M., Droge, C., Hanvanich, S., & Calantone, R. (2005). Marketing and technology resource complementarity: An analysis of their interaction effect in two environmental contexts. *Strategic Management Journal*, 26(3), 259–276.

Song, M., DiBenedetto, A., & Nason, R.W. (2007). Capabilities and financial performance: The moderating effect of strategic type. *Journal of the Academy of Marketing Science*, 35(1), 18–34.

Song, M., Nason, R.W., & Di Benedetto, C.A. (2008). Distinctive marketing and information technology capabilities and strategic types: A cross-national investigation. *Journal of International Marketing*, 16(1), 4–38.

Sørensen, J.B., & Stuart, T.E. (2000). Aging, obsolescence, and organizational innovation. *Administrative Science Quarterly*, 45(1), 81–112.

Stinchcombe, A.L. (1965). Social structure and organizations. *Handbook of Organizations*, 7, 142–193.

Teece, D.J., Peteraf, M.A., & Leih, S. (2016). Dynamic capabilities and organizational agility: Risk, uncertainty, and entrepreneurial management in the innovation economy. *California Management Review*, 58(4) (Summer), 13–35.

Teece, D.J., Pisano, G.P., & Shuen, A. (1997). Dynamic capabilities and strategic management. *Strategic Management Journal*, 18, 509–533.

*Telegraph* (2018). What is "co-creation" and what are the benefits for companies? Available at: https://www.telegraph.co.uk/business/social-innovation/benefits-of-co-creation/, accessed on 2 June 2020.

Tsai, K.H. (2009). Collaborative networks and product innovation performance: Toward a contingency perspective. *Research Policy*, 38(5), 765–778.

Vallaster, C., & von Wallpach, S. (2013). An online discursive inquiry into the social dynamics of multi-stakeholder brand meaning co-creation. *Journal of Business Research*, 66(9), 1505–1515.

Venkataraman, S., Van De Ven, A.H., Buckeye, J., & Hudson, R. (1990). Starting up in a turbulent environment: A process model of failure among firms with high customer dependence. *Journal of Business Venturing*, 5(5), 277–295. http://doi.org/10.1016/0883-9026(90)90006-F

Verona, G. (1999). A resource-based view of product development. *Academy of Management Review*, 24(1), 132–142.

von Wallpach, S., Gyrd-Jones, R., & Markovic, S. (2018). Brand co-creation: Innovation opportunities and ethical challenges. special interest group proposal. In K. Hamilton, M. Alexander, S. Gounaris, M. Karampela, & E. Lacka (eds), *Proceedings of the European Marketing Academy (EMAC) Conference 2018: People Make Marketing*. Glasgow: European Marketing Academy (EMAC).

von Wallpach, S., Hemetsberger, A., & Espersen, P. (2017). Performing identities: Processes of brand and stakeholder identity co-construction. *Journal of Business Research*, 70, 443–452.

Voorhees, C.M., Brady, M.K., Calantone, R., & Ramirez, E. (2016). Discriminant validity testing in marketing: An analysis, causes for concern, and proposed remedies. *Journal of the Academy of Marketing Science*, 44(1), 119–134.

Weerawardena, J., O'Cass, A., & Julian, C. (2006). Does industry matter? Examining the role of industry structure and organizational learning in innovation and brand performance. *Journal of Business Research*, 59(1), 37–45.

Wernerfelt, B. (1984). A resource-based view of the firm. *Strategic Management Journal*, 5, 171–180.

Wiklund, J., & Shepherd, D. (2003). Knowledge-based resources, entrepreneurial orientation, and the performance of small and medium-sized businesses. *Strategic Management Journal*, 24(13), 1307–1314.

Wind, J., & Mahajan, V. (1997). Issues and opportunities in new product development: An introduction to the special issue. *Journal of Marketing Research*, 34(1), 1–12.

Wong, H.Y., & Merrilees, B. (2005). A brand orientation typology for SMEs: A case research approach. *Journal of Product & Brand Management*, 14(3), 155–162.

Wong, H.Y., & Merrilees, B. (2008). The performance benefits of being brand-orientated. *Journal of Product & Brand Management*, 17(6), 372–383.

Yazdanparast, A., Manuj, I., & Swartz, S.M. (2010). Co-creating logistics value: A service-dominant logic perspective. *International Journal of Logistics Management*, 21(3), 375–403.

Zaefarian, G., Forkmann, S., Mitręga, M., & Henneberg, S.C. (2017). A capability perspective on relationship ending and its impact on product innovation success and firm performance. *Long Range Planning*, 50(2), 184–199.

Zahra, S.A., and Covin, J.G. (1993). Business strategy, technology policy and firm performance. *Strategic Management Journal*, 14(6), 451–478.

Zhang, J., & He, Y. (2014). Key dimensions of brand value co-creation and its impacts upon customer perception and brand performance. *Nankai Business Review International*, 5(1), 43–69.

Zolkiewski, J., Turnbull, P., Lindfelt, L.L., & Törnroos, J.Å. (2006). Ethics and value creation in business research: Comparing two approaches. *European Journal of Marketing*, 40(3–4), 328–351.

# 13. Toward a co-creation approach to nation branding: an integrative framework

*Mai T. Pham and Roderick J. Brodie*

## 1. INTRODUCTION

Nation branding, commonly understood as the application of branding techniques to nations, is a topic that has drawn attention and prompted considerable discussion for the last two decades (Dinnie, 2010; Fan, 2010; Hao et al., 2021). Globalization, together with the pervasiveness of the internet and other communication technologies, has enabled unprecedented mobility of human and other resources, which has increased competition in nation branding efforts. Countries strive to attain a favourable nation brand image by tourists, investors, and potential migrants (Caldwell & Freire, 2004; Dinnie, 2010; Jaffe & Nebenzahl, 2006). The increasing importance of nation branding can be seen in the development of several industry-led nation brand indexes, including the Anholt Nation Brand Index, the Nation Brands Annual Report by Brand Finance, the Future Brand's Country Index, and the Digital Country Index. Nevertheless, nation branding remains an underdeveloped and fragmented field, with 'a lack of a coherent and explicit theoretical base' (Hao et al., 2021, p. 56).

Since the field of nation branding first emerged in the late 1990s, different established theories in branding literature, including social identity theory, self-congruity theory, resource advantage theory, and attribution theory, were adapted and tested for the context of nation branding (Hao et al., 2021). Several major research themes eventuated as a result, namely nation brand image, nation brand equity, and nation brand personality. Though diverse in approach, the authors agreed that the nation brand is a multi-ownership, multi-stakeholders, and multi-dimensional concept. These themes of literature, however, mostly retain the dominant dyadic perspective in branding research. The perspective assumes the nation brand as a relationship between sellers (the nation) and buyers (customers) and functions as an identity which has an associated image. Depending on the dimensions, the customers in the context of nation branding could be tourists, investors, international students, or potential migrants. This approach has limited managerial implications as it fails to accommodate broader branding issues within the complex marketing network of a nation.

In response to the changing business environment of the digitalized economy, branding theories have evolved to a more relational, integrative, and network perspective (Brodie, 2009; Merz et al., 2009), conceptualized as the brand co-creation approach. The approach recognizes the active role of customers and other stakeholders in collectively creating the brand meanings and value (Caru & Cova, 2003; Merz et al., 2009; Prahalad & Ramaswamy, 2000, 2003, 2004). Literature adopting the brand co-creation approach provides a better understanding of the role that brands play in the value-adding process (Brodie, 2009), and explains the benefits that brand co-creation activities offer both customers and enterprises.

In nation branding research, the co-creation approach is perceived as a tool to generate knowledge and expertise from various actors to develop new value propositions (Hakala &

Lemmetyinen, 2011; Konecnik Ruzzier & de Chernatony, 2013). However, we suggest it is more important to develop a co-creation mindset in viewing the nation brand. This chapter addresses this issue by providing a framework to conceptualize brand co-creation in the context of nation branding. Furthermore, the chapter suggests how the lens of brand co-creation should be applied for research and management in nation branding.

The chapter proceeds as follows: first, we review and examine the existing literature on nation branding, highlighting the use of traditional or contemporary theories that incorporate identification and meanings; hence, justify the need to refresh the nation branding research with a novel, yet more comprehensive approach. We then develop a conceptual framework for the co-creation of the nation brand. To illustrate the framework, we use a case study of Viet Nam's offering as an emerging Southeast Asia tourist destination. The theoretical and managerial implications are then offered. To conclude, limitations and suggestions for future research are provided.

## 2.     THE NATION BRAND AND NATION BRANDING RESEARCH

There is no consensus on the definition of 'nation brand' (Hao et al., 2021; Rojas-Méndez, 2013). Leading scholars mainly agree that 'nation brand' is 'the sum' of 'beliefs and impressions' (Anholt, 2005; Fan, 2010; Kotler & Gertner, 2002) of 'the many stakeholders' (Fan, 2010; Fetscherin, 2010) concerning a 'country's image' over its multiple dimensions or aspects, including culture (Anholt, 2005; Fan, 2010; Fetscherin, 2010), people (Anholt, 2005; Fan, 2010), political, social and economic environment (Anholt, 2005; Fetscherin, 2010), history (Fan, 2010; Fetscherin, 2010), tourist appeal (Anholt, 2005), and global brands (Fan, 2010). In general, the authors acknowledged the multi-stakeholder and multi-faceted nature of the concept, and that a nation brand exists in people's minds rather than being created or controlled by marketing agents. In other words, the nation brand is, by definition, a complex, multi-ownership, and multi-dimensional concept.

First coined as a marketing term, nation branding is now widely considered as an intersection of different academic disciplines, including public policy, public diplomacy, international relations, tourism, and marketing (Dinnie, 2010; Fetscherin, 2010; Rojas-Méndez, 2013). This interdisciplinary nature of nation branding makes it more complex than corporate branding (Fetscherin, 2010), with which it is believed to share some similarities (Rojas-Méndez, 2013). Nation branding is regarded as a tool to augment a country's competitive advantage, or 'the strategy of using the name, logo and other branding elements to create a distinct identity for the country involved, to differentiate the country and its offerings in international markets' (Pappu & Quester, 2010, p. 277). Hence, the theoretical foundations of the field of nation branding draw on contemporary marketing theory and other interrelated disciplines.

In Table 13.1, we provide a selection of studies on nation branding to examine different foundations and theoretical perspectives. A significant body of work in the field to date aims at extending different branding theories to the context of nation branding (D'Astous & Boujbel, 2007; Hakala et al., 2013; Kotler & Gertner, 2002; Papadopoulos & Heslop, 2002; Pappu & Quester, 2010; Pike et al., 2010; Rojaz-Méndez et al., 2015). The major theories adapted were brand identity, brand image (Aaker, 1991, 1996), brand personality (Aaker, 1997), consumer-based brand knowledge, and brand equity (Keller, 1993). Besides these theories, nation branding is also informed by the related fields of marketing, including country-of-origin (or product-country image) branding (Papadopoulos & Heslop, 2002), place branding (Caldwell & Freire, 2004; Konecnik Ruzzier & de Chernatony, 2013; Kotler & Gertner, 2002), and destination branding (Caldwell & Freire, 2004; Pike et al., 2010).

As presented in Table 13.1, authors in the nation brand image research theme described the concept as comprised of stereotypes (Hakala et al., 2013; Papadopoulos & Heslop, 2002) and 'extreme simplifications of the reality' (Kotler & Gertner, 2002, p. 251). On the one hand, country images are stated to be important cues in the customer decision-making process (Diamantopoulos et al., 2011; Kotler & Gertner, 2002; Lee et al., 2010; Sun & Paswan, 2011). On the other hand, product-country image research has confirmed that product brands also influence its nation brand image (Hakala et al., 2013; Sun & Paswan, 2011). The country-of-origin associated image, or the product-country image, is termed as a 'micro image' of the nation, while the country-level associated image is known as the 'macro image' of the country (Pappu & Quester, 2010). At the 'macro' image level, nations are portrayed as brands themselves, competing for tourists, factories, businesses, and talented people (Kotler & Gertner, 2002; Pappu & Quester, 2010). Furthermore, country image is regarded as having cross-cultural differences and a multi-dimensional character (Hakala et al., 2013).

As shown in Table 13.1, scholars investigating the nation brand equity theme used brand equity theory to develop measurements to assess a country's brand equity (Fetscherin, 2010; Pappu & Quester, 2010; Pike et al., 2010). These studies assume that brands possess embedded equity related to their built images (Aaker, 1991; Keller, 1993, 2003; Yoo & Donthu, 2001). Pappu and Quester (2010) and Pike et al. (2010) confirmed the nation brand image has a positive effect on the nation brand equity. The image dimensions include country awareness, macro country image, micro country image, perceived quality, and country loyalty.

The idea that nations have personalities similar to individual personality traits attracted the interest of several scholars in the field (D'Astous & Boujbel, 2007; Rojaz-Méndez et al., 2015). This line of study is inspired by the brand personality research theme, of which Jennifer Aaker (1997) is the pioneer. The empirical results suggested that different countries may possess a different set of personality dimensions. A match of the nation's personality with the audience's personal traits results in a more positive reaction toward that nation's offerings (Rojaz-Méndez et al., 2015).

Our review reveals the majority of nation branding research adopts the dyadic view of brand building, where the nation brand is an identity to be communicated to its target audience. Underpinning this perspective to brand building is the assumption of the predominant role of the seller in promising and delivering value. The customer remains passive in experiencing the brand with the expectation of promised benefits. These studies, therefore, failed to embrace the multi-ownership aspect and the complex stakeholder's network of the nation brand. This leads to a simplified brand management approach to branding nations, such as designing appealing and appropriate logos and slogans (Supphellen & Nyaarsdvick, 2002). While such an approach is still valuable, we suggest it is not adequate in the contemporary branding context. More importantly, it could not accommodate the unique characteristics of a nation brand.

In response to the changing business environment of the 'new economy' (Day & Montgomery, 1999), together with the digitally empowered customers (Schau et al., 2009), marketing theory has been evolved during the last two decades. Thus, recent branding literature assumes the brand meanings and values are co-created by the customers and other stakeholders.

*Table 13.1    Selected studies on nation branding*

| Authors, date | Type of paper | Foundational branding theories | Theoretical perspectives of branding | Major research findings/contributions |
|---|---|---|---|---|
| Kotler & Gertner (2002) | Conceptual | Brand image, brand management | As an identity with an associated image | Country images are important cues with regard to customer decision making; countries may be viewed as 'products' in their own right whilst competing for tourists, factories, businesses, and talented people. |
| Papadopoulos & Heslop (2002) | Conceptual | Product-country image, brand equity | As an identity with an associated image | Country images are powerful stereotypes that influence customer behaviour, but such effects vary depending on circumstances; country brands have built-in equity that individuals in various target markets develop over their lifetime. |
| Gilmore (2002) | Conceptual | Brand positioning | As co-created meanings | Four elements should be considered when developing the brand positioning of a country: macrotrends, target groups, competitors, and core competencies. |
| Supphellen & Nyaarsdvick (2002) | Empirical | Brand awareness, brand image | As an identity with an associated image | Developed a three-step model to empirically test the effects of a country brand slogan before the official launch. |
| Caldwell & Freire (2004) | Empirical | Place branding, destination branding | As an identity with an associated image | Nation brands are more representational and less functional than region and city brands. The functional dimension encompasses the utilitarian aspects of the places, and the representational dimension refers to attributes linked to the individual's self-expression. |

| Authors, date | Type of paper | Foundational branding theories | Theoretical perspectives of branding | Major research findings/ contributions |
|---|---|---|---|---|
| D'Astous & Boujbel (2007) | Empirical | Brand personality | As an identity with an associated image | Identification of six country personality dimensions: agreeableness, wickedness, snobbism, assiduousness, conformity, and unobtrusiveness. |
| Pappu & Quester (2010) | Empirical | Brand awareness, brand image, brand equity | As an identity with an associated image | Country equity is a five-dimensional construct comprising of country awareness, macro country image, micro country image, perceived quality, and country loyalty. |
| Pike et al. (2010) | Empirical | Brand equity, destination branding | As an identity with an associated image | Nation brand salience, perceived quality, and nation brand image have a positive effect on nation brand loyalty. |
| Fetscherin (2010) | Empirical | Brand equity | As an identity with an associated image | An alternative to the existing indexes to measure the strength of nations. |
| Sun & Paswan (2011) | Empirical | Country-of-origin image | As an identity with an associated image | Perceived product quality is a critical variable in shaping a country's image. |
| Hakala et al. (2013) | Empirical | Brand awareness, brand image | As an identity with an associated image | Awareness is a crucial indicator of people's knowledge about a country; country images are based on stereotypes, have cross-cultural differences, are multi-dimensional characters, are influenced by the product brands of the country, and are related to the awareness of celebrities from the nations. |

| Authors, date | Type of paper | Foundational branding theories | Theoretical perspectives of branding | Major research findings/contributions |
|---|---|---|---|---|
| Rojas-Méndez (2013) | Empirical | Brand identify, brand image | As co-created meanings | Determined by a set of dimensions and facets that exist in people's minds with regard to a country brand. The seven dimensions identified were: economy, tourism, geography and nature, culture and heritage, society, science and technology, and government. |
| Konecnik Ruzzier & de Chernatony (2013) | Empirical | Place brand identity | As co-created meanings | Using a stakeholder-based approach to develop a new model for place brand identity, consisting of several elements: vision, mission, values, personality, benefits, and distinguishing preferences. |
| Rojaz-Méndez et al. (2015) | Empirical | Brand personality | As an identity with an associated image | International audiences holding similar personality traits with the nation brand personality traits will be more likely to respond positively toward the country's offerings. |

The approach is based on the argument that customers and other stakeholders, with their expertise, skills, and background, are capable of taking an active role in the value creation process (Caru & Cova, 2003; Prahalad & Ramaswamy, 2003, 2004; Vargo & Lusch, 2004, 2008, 2016). In this co-creation process, the brand meanings are the outcome of simultaneous interactions (Vallaster & von Wallpach, 2013) and dynamically constructed over time (Da Silveira et al., 2013) via joint input from managers and other actors in the service ecosystem.

The co-creation approach implies brands are associated with the value they offer, which can be expressed as value propositions (Merz et al., 2009; Vargo & Lusch, 2004, 2008, 2016). Traditionally, in parallel with the view of the brand as an identity, the brand value proposition is conceptualized as 'a statement of the functional benefits, emotional benefits, and self-expressive benefits that provide value to the customers' (Aaker, 1996, p. 95). Here in the co-creation perspective, a value proposition becomes a statement of the benefits that a customer and stakeholders may derive from using the brand (Starr & Brodie, 2016, pp. 716–717). Hence, the value proposition can be seen as a flexible market offer rather than a firm statement to be transmitted. As Chandler and Lusch (2015) established, the value propositions are the 'invitations from actors to one another to engage in service' (p. 8). In short, this perspective emphasizes the inevitability of engaging customers and other stakeholders in the development of value propositions (Starr & Brodie, 2016). Brand co-creation has become one of the key vectors for diffusing the SD logic in marketing research (Vargo & Lusch, 2017).

Research indicates that engaging in brand co-creation activities is beneficial for both customers and firms. Brand-related collectives such as brand communities are platforms for sharing explicit, discursive knowledge about the brand, and can collectively create value beyond that initiated and anticipated by the firms (Prahalad & Ramaswamy, 2000; Schau et al., 2009, 2019). Customers benefit by engaging in platform activity for self-developmental, social, and hedonic reasons (Caru & Cova, 2003; Schau et al., 2009). On the other hand, firms find these platforms as opportunities to connect to their customers for the distribution of brand-related content, the development of user innovation (Schau et al., 2019), and revitalize the enterprises' offerings (Ind et al., 2017). Therefore, engaging in co-creation helps brands to increase cost efficiencies, speed to market, and competitive advantage (Ind et al., 2017).

A few studies in the field of nation branding have begun to view the nation brand as co-created meanings (Gilmore, 2002; Hakala & Lemmetyinen, 2011; Konecnik Ruzzier & de Chernatony, 2013; Rojas-Méndez, 2013). Rojas-Méndez (2013) employed what is called 'a stakeholder-based approach' to identify the dimensions of the nation brand, using the metaphor of 'molecule'. In other studies, Hakala and Lemmetyinen (2011) and Konecnik Ruzzier and de Chernatony (2013) involved vital influencers and stakeholders in the process of nation brand identity development. The research stressed the advantages of generating knowledge from a range of stakeholders in the network to develop new value propositions within nation branding. However, a solid theoretical foundation for understanding the process of co-creation of the nation brand, especially the marketing relations and interactions that the actors encounter in such a process, is still absent.

## 3. THE CONCEPTUAL FRAMEWORK FOR BRAND CO-CREATION IN THE NATION BRANDING CONTEXT

To develop the conceptual framework, we draw on previous works of Brodie et al. (2006) and Warnaby (2009). The approach, introduced by Calonius (1986), Bitner (1995) and Grönroos (1996, 2006), recognizes three processes: external marketing, interactive marketing, and internal marketing. Brodie et al. (2006) advanced the frameworks of Grönroos (1996, 2006) by linking together brands, value creation, and relationships to introduce the concept of the service brand–relationship–value (SBRV) triangle, with the company, employees, customers, and other stakeholders at each corner of the triangle. It portrays an integrative approach to branding that reflects the marketing relationship among stakeholders in the branding network. Furthermore, it suggests the important role of the brand in integrating resources to co-create value (Brodie, 2009). Recognized the complexity of the organizational mechanism for place branding, Warnaby (2009) suggested viewing the place brand as an umbrella that could accommodate and facilitate the articulation of consistent value propositions of related actors (p. 413). The author, hence, modified the SBRV triangle of Brodie et al. (2006) for the context of city branding. In this chapter, we extend the context to nation branding with further modification to the framework.

Thus, as shown in Figure 13.1, we adapt the previously developed frameworks to provide an integrated understanding of the co-creation of a nation brand. The theoretical framework has three layers. First, it defines the nation brand as collectively perceived and constructed within the nation brand's complex stakeholders' network. This stakeholder network comprises three main groups of actors: the nation branding agency, the local service providers, and finally, customers and other external stakeholders. The nation brand offerings, in this case, are collective meanings for the nation brand's value propositions. Second, the framework emphasizes the role of the nation brand in facilitating and mediating the relationships and interactions of different actors in their marketing activity. It serves as an interface for interactions of related actors, where perceptions and value of the holistic nation brand and the local service brands are determined (Warnaby, 2009). Third, the framework indicates that two continuous and interconnected processes are essential for the co-creation of the nation brand to happen: the knowledge exchange and negotiation of value propositions, and the integration of resources.

The first group of actors, the nation branding agency, is responsible for branding the nation as a holistic place and communicate with other stakeholders about the nation brand value propositions. The nation branding agency could be a specific government body that coordinates a nation branding campaign or initiative, a government agency, or place brand identity organizations (Ahn & Wu, 2015; Casidy et al., 2019; Helmi et al., 2019). The role of this focal actor is similar to that of leaders and management boards in the context of business enterprise. Besides the external interaction to communicate with the external stakeholders, the nation branding agency also has the internal interaction with the local service providers to ensure the development of appropriate value propositions that are consistent with the value propositions of the nation brand. The internal interactions enable and facilitate the meaning and experience associated with the value propositions of the nation.

The second group of actors, the local service providers, are local governments, local businesses, educational institutions, and civil society organizations, among others (Chigora & Hoque, 2018; Dinnie, 2010; Gilmore, 2002; Konecnik Ruzzier & de Chernatony, 2013; Skoko et al., 2018). The term 'service' in this case should be understood as it is used in service-dominant (S-D) logic (Vargo & Lusch, 2004, 2008, 2016), superordinating both 'products' and 'services'. Actors in this group also form the external interactions with the customers and other stakeholders, communicating the value propositions of their service and that of the holistic nation brand. Their direct interactions with the customers and other stakeholders are where meanings and experiences about the nation brand and each service brand are created. This group of actors also engages in internal interactions to benefit from being consistent with the nation brand's value propositions. Their role, therefore, is broader than that of employees in the case of commercial brands.

The third group, customers and other stakeholders, varies according to the distinct dimensions of the nation brand: tourism, education, export, or migration. Hence, this group could be tourists, investors, international students, potential migrants, buyers of services and products from the nation, and the media (Dinnie, 2010; Herrero-Crespo et al., 2016; Kotsi et al., 2018; Schühly & Tenzer, 2017). They interact with both the nation branding agency and the local service providers, thus creating meanings and experiences associated with both the holistic nation brand and each of the service brands.

Communication to exchange knowledge facilitates the learning process among stakeholders allowing the generation of collective meanings and perceptions, while the negotiation defines the value propositions elements. During this continuous process, the perceptions of actors on the value propositions are communicated to other actors in the networks via internal and external interactions. Hence, any group of actors, including customers or internal stakeholders, could initiate the development of new value propositions. Enabled by the knowledge exchange, the value propositions are negotiated until a change in the perceptions and actions of other actors is reached. Therefore, all actors in the network could become operant resources, contributing to the development of coherent and consistent meanings and experiences of the value propositions of a nation brand. In other words, the resource integration process happens in parallel with the exchange of knowledge. The resource, however, is not limited to knowledge, but any other type of human or financial resources. According to Vargo and Lusch (2008, 2017), operant resources are the source of competitive advantage.

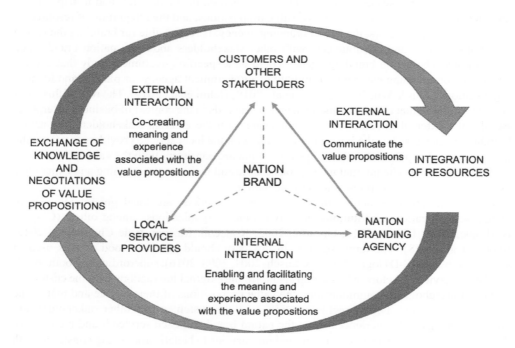

*Figure 13.1    The conceptual model for co-creation of the nation brand*

## 4.    ILLUSTRATIVE CASE STUDY

We provide an illustrative case (Siggelkow, 2007) to give a concrete example of the framework for researchers to visualize how the conceptual framework can be applied. This allows us to elaborate on the marketing relationships among stakeholders in the network of nation branding. The case highlights the role of the nation brand as an umbrella to mediate and facilitate relationships and interactions among stakeholders and the importance of sharing knowledge and integrating resources in the stakeholder network to co-create the value propositions for the nation brand. The marketing relationships among stakeholders to formulate the value propositions of Viet Nam as an exciting tourist destination provides an illustrative case to support the proposed frameworks and imparts further theoretical and practical insights. Thus the case demonstrates how the conceptual framework can be applied in an empirical setting (Siggelkow, 2017).

## 4.1    Overview

Viet Nam, a country in Southeast Asia, bordering with Lao, Cambodia, and China, has a population of over 95 million inhabitants and a GDP per capita (PPP) of US$7,513 (US News, 2020). The economic reforms in 1986 helped the nation transform into a more modern and competitive society (US News, 2020). At present, Viet Nam is gaining a positive reputation internationally, which is reflected in nation branding indexes. It is seen as an attractive destination for tourists, investors, and expatriates (Bloom Consulting, 2019; Brand Finance, 2019; Future Brand, 2019). Particularly about tourism, the country is rising as 'Southeast Asia's most exciting tourist destination' (CNN Travel, 2020). Viet Nam was named 'Asia's Leading Destination' for the first time at the 2018 World Travel Awards (Das, 2019). The country is appreciated for its numerous tourism-related attributes, including beautiful scenery, cultural attractions, rich history, good foods, and an affordable lifestyle (US News, 2020). Lonely Planet (2020) describes the country as 'A land of staggering natural beauty and cultural complexities, of dynamic megacities and hill-tribe villages' and 'both exotic and compelling'. Over the last ten years before COVID-19 (from 2009 to 2018), the number of international arrivals to the country grew by almost 400 per cent. Given the global growth of 150 per cent and 190 per cent of the Asia-Pacific regions (World Bank, 2020), the country is one of the emerging destinations of the world tourism industry.

The country's first tourism identity, 'Viet Nam – the Hidden Charm', was introduced in 2005 (*Vietnam Investment Review* [VIR], 2014), showcasing the country's value as a charming yet unknown tourist destination to be explored. The value propositions were appropriate when the country began to open its doors to the world and attracted the first generation of tourists, the adventurous Westerners (Gwyther, 2020). The identity ended its mission in 2011 (VIR, 2014) when the Viet Nam National Administration of Tourism (VNAT) introduced an evolved slogan, 'Viet Nam – Timeless Charm', in 2012. This new identity encompassed more comprehensive value propositions and was aimed at broader targets: traditional tourism, adventurous tourism, mass tourism, and sustainable tourism (Gwyther, 2020).

## 4.2    Illustrating the Framework

Applying the conceptual framework presented in Figure 13.1, we first examine the interactions of different actors in the network to co-create the nation brand of Viet Nam's tourism. Second, we investigate the knowledge exchange and negotiation of value propositions and the integration of resources.

### The marketing relationships within the stakeholder network for the branding of Viet Nam tourism

The actors in the stakeholders' network of Viet Nam's tourism brand comprise VNAT, local service providers in the tourism and hospitality industry, past and future customers (visitors, tourists/travellers/travel bloggers), and other stakeholders. Among other stakeholders, the key actors are the media in the tourism and hospitality industry and online travel guide services such as Lonely Planet (Lonely Planet, 2020) or Trip Advisor (Trip Advisor, 2020). Analysis of marketing interactions among VNAT, local service providers, and external stakeholders are summarized in Table 13.2. All of the interactions contribute to creating the collective perceptions and meanings of Viet Nam's tourism. The tagline of 'Timeless Charm' serves as the umbrella brand to facilitate and mediate the marketing activities of the stakeholders and, hence, develop more focused value propositions.

*The nation branding agency: the Viet Nam National Administration of Tourism (VNAT)*
The branding activities conducted by VNAT with external stakeholders mostly focused on communicating the value propositions of Viet Nam's tourism. The communication promoted the country as an exciting destination with a dynamic and fast-growing hospitality sector and a diversity of tourism products to cater to different needs and interests (Vietnam Travel, 2020). The communication includes both traditional trade promotion activities and online marketing. In recent years, VNAT has participated in around 14 international tourism fairs each year, including Travex, ITB in Germany, Jata in Japan, MITT in Russia, among others (VIR, 2017). Hosting international events in-country to promote the most appealing tourist destinations for domestic and international tourists is another crucial activity that VNAT facilitates. Notable events in this category include the Da Nang Fireworks Festival, Dalat Flower Festival, Thai Nguyen Tea Festival, Hue Festival, and several international marathons (Vietnamtourism, 2020). The traditional communication channels via international tourism fairs and hosting international events are complemented by online marketing activities. In 2016, VNAT launched its official tourism promotion website, Vietnam Travel (Vietnam Travel, 2020), with highly interactive social media extensions. During the COVID-19 pandemic, in addition to providing information on COVID-related restrictions, the official web portal Vietnam Travel also featured 'Visit Viet Nam from home', which included virtual tours of breathtaking natural and historical sites for visitors to stay engaged with the country (Vietnam Travel, 2020).

Besides the external interactions with customers and other stakeholders, VNAT also has a critical role in the internal interactions with local service providers to enable and facilitate the co-creation of meaning and experience associated with the promised value propositions of the country. These internal interactions centred on two major purposes: consolidating the collective perceptions of local service providers about the value that Viet Nam's tourism promises, or enabling the value propositions, and facilitating the delivery of that promise. Regarding the enabling work, VNAT has orchestrated various activities directly aiming at internal stakeholders, including local authorities, local businesses in the hospitality sector, tour guides, and others. The organization provided a dedicated web database to provide information and guidance for tour guides regarding the certificates and training required to possess (Huongdanvien, 2020). By doing so, VNAT can promote the quality and professionalism of the service and ensure pleasant experiences for visitors, especially at cultural and historical sites. In 2012, after releasing the new tagline of the tourism industry, 'Viet Nam – the Timeless Charm', VNAT also introduced guidelines for tourism agencies and businesses in the hospitality sector for the proper use of the tagline to ensure consistency in communicating the meanings of the brand (Vietnamtourism, 2020). In 2014, VNAT organized a press conference to officially share the fundamental values and meanings underpinning the tagline to a broader audience.

To facilitate the delivery of the value propositions, VNAT facilitates the interactions between internal and external stakeholders, most importantly, between the local hospitality businesses and their potential customers via various channels. All the communications centre

*Table 13.2   Marketing interactions among actors in the stakeholders network of Viet Nam's tourism brand*

| Actor | External interactions | Internal interactions |
| --- | --- | --- |
| Viet Nam National Administration of Tourism (VNAT) | Communicate the value propositions of 'Viet Nam's tourism; Learning from stakeholders' feedbacks to ameliorate the value propositions of Viet Nam's tourism | Coordinate and orchestrate the marketing activities of the local businesses in the tourism and hospitality industry; Coordinate the work of related government agencies and local governments for the amelioration of value propositions; Facilitate the co-creation of meanings and experiences of local service providers and external stakeholders; Orchestrate the organization of training for local businesses to ensure consistency with the value propositions of 'Viet Nam – Timeless Charm'; Learn about the value propositions of Viet Nam's tourism in compliance with the tagline 'Viet Nam – Timeless Charm' |
| Local service providers in the tourism and hospitality industry | Communicate their offerings under the tagline of 'Viet Nam – Timeless Charm'; Interact with the customers and other stakeholders to co-create the meanings and experiences regarding their service brand and the tourism brand of Viet Nam | |
| Visitors/tourists/travellers/travel bloggers | Interact with local service providers and other visitors/tourists/travellers to create meanings and experiences; Exchange information on meanings and experiences regarding the umbrella brand and each service brand | |
| Potential or future visitors/tourists | Learn about the value propositions of the tourism brand of Viet Nam and the promises and offerings of different service providers | |

| Actor | External interactions | Internal interactions |
|---|---|---|
| The media in the tourism and hospitality industry | Learn and communicate the value propositions of different stakeholders<br>Learn and communicate the meanings of umbrella brands and each service brand<br>Learn and communicate the experiences of different stakeholders | |
| Online travel guide services (Lonely Planet, Trip Advisor) | Provide platforms for interactions to co-create meanings and experiences with the umbrella brand and each service brand | |

on creating the common and shared perceptions of the 'Viet Nam – Timeless Charm' offerings: wonderfully diverse, yet fascinating. First, the organization facilitates the interactions by listing on what is considered the 'Official Tourism Website of Viet Nam' (Vietnam Travel, 2020), detailed guidance on the country's offering to tourists, from places to go, what to do to and how to get to destinations, with links to local service providers: hotels and resorts, railways, airlines, tour operators, among others. Participation in international tourism fairs and the organization of festivals in-country has a similar effect: helping to connect potential customers with local businesses. VNAT also fosters co-creation by facilitating communication and the sharing of perceptions between local people and loyal customers with future tourists by organizing various platforms for the exchange of experiences. In 2018, VNAT organized a writing contest titled 'Viet Nam – Timeless Charm', allowing writers, filmmakers, and travellers to share their stories about the country (Vietnam Travel, 2018). 'My Vietnam', a newly launched communication project featured on the official website, Vietnam Travel, in 2019–2020, presents the views of local people regarding popular tourist destinations of Viet Nam, highlighting the attributes each destination has to offer for travellers (Vietnam Travel, 2020). The communication project not only shares the perceptions of local people with potential visitors but also acts as a promise of value offer, simultaneously strengthening the commitment of local people to deliver on that promise.

*The local service providers*
The local service providers in the tourism and hospitality industry are very diverse, ranging from hotels, resorts, and other accommodation providers, airlines, trains, and other vehicle rental services, to tour operators and travel agents, among others. This group of actors directly forms the external interactions with customers and other stakeholders, where they communicate their offerings and interact with the customers and other stakeholders to co-create the meanings and experiences regarding their service brand. These interactions are similar to that of any firm in a regular business context. In addition, the local service providers participate in interactions that are facilitated by VNAT, such as internal tourism fairs, international festivals, or sports events that VNAT and other institutions organized throughout Viet Nam aiming at promoting tourism for the country.

To benefit from the umbrella brand of Viet Nam's tourism, they also engage in internal interactions with the nation branding agency, VNAT, to learn about the value propositions of Viet Nam's tourism and have their offerings promoted under the tagline of 'Viet Nam – Timeless Charm'.

*Customers and other stakeholders*
The customers of Viet Nam's tourism brand include past and future tourists, visitors, and travellers, both local and international. The potential customers interact with both the nation branding agency and the local business providers, where they learn about the value propositions of the tourism brand of Viet Nam and the promises and offerings of different service providers. Once they become the customers, their interactions with local service providers and other customers are to create meanings and experiences with the service brands and the umbrella nation brand. They might then share their information or knowledge on the meanings and experiences with other stakeholders, including other customers, potential customers, the service providers, the nation branding agency, or the media. There are multiple channels for sharing such information with the help of today's information technology, from their own

social media to the website or social media of the service providers, to different online platforms for customer review and feedback.

The online travel guide services such as the Lonely Planet (2020), Trip Advisor (2020), and numerous other travel guide web portals or blogs provide the platforms for knowledge and information sharing among stakeholders, especially past and future customers. These platforms facilitate the interactions to co-create the meanings and value of the umbrella as well as the service brands that it covers. The media also plays a vital role in this co-creation process, where they learn and communicate the value propositions of different stakeholders and learn about the meaning and experience associated with the umbrella brand or each service and communicate these to other actors in the network.

**The knowledge exchange, the negotiation of value propositions, and the integration of resources**
A continuous process of knowledge exchange enables the marketing interactions and the co-creation of the value propositions of Viet Nam tourism. The knowledge, including information and experience, is transmitted from the marketing organizations, VNAT, to other actors in the network via their external and internal interactions. VNAT also learns from stakeholder feedback via events and social media interactions. Hence, knowledge exchange facilitates the learning process within the stakeholder network. Likewise, knowledge is transferred within groups of actors, most significantly among customers and other stakeholders. It helps confirm the promises made by the marketing organization and to share the experience of how the promises may be delivered. Similar to the activities of brand communities in commercial brands, platforms featuring tourism and travel blogs are significant in shaping customer collective perceptions regarding the value propositions of a nation brand. From renowned platforms such as Trip Advisor or Lonely Planet to hundreds of travel blogs, knowledge sharing among customers in the form of reviews and travel notes contributes significantly to the shaping of customers' collective perceptions regarding the value propositions of the country.

Together with the exchange of knowledge, the value propositions are constantly adjusted in accordance with the negotiation process among actors. Value propositions are a flexible offer or a call for engagement from stakeholders (Chandler & Lusch, 2015). By engaging and exchanging knowledge, the actors also negotiate for innovation of the offerings. In the case of Viet Nam, as an emerging country with a fast-growing tourism industry, the country is engaged in a continuous process of improving visitor offerings. The country has adopted a visa exemption system for 24 countries and visas upon arrival for all the others (*Financial Times*, 2020). VNAT, in coordination with other government agencies, is addressing the multiple issues raised by visitors, including overcharging or double pricing encountered by international visitors, the cleanliness of tourism spots, the availability of nightlife, the need to upgrade tourism infrastructures (Nguyen, 2020), among others. During the continuous innovation process, the perceptions of customers and other key actors also undergo change.

In the course of exchanging knowledge and negotiation of value propositions, the actors are contributing resources to co-create the meanings associated with the brand. By facilitating that knowledge exchange, VNAT, or other marketing organizations, are integrating resources for branding the nation. Resource integration also encompasses the financial contribution of members. In this case, the promotional activities organized and facilitated by VNAT were jointly funded from the state budget and contributions from local tourism businesses (VIR, 2017).

# 5.    CONCLUSIONS, IMPLICATIONS, AND FUTURE RESEARCH

This chapter's primary objective was to develop an integrative framework to conceptualize brand co-creation in the context of nation branding, hence, discuss how that brand co-creation lens could pave the way for research and management in nation branding. The conceptual framework illuminates the marketing relationships and interactions among actors to co-create the value propositions for a nation brand. The framework defined the nation brand as the collective perceptions and constructions of value propositions formulated by the marketing interactions of three main groups of actors: the nation branding agency, local service providers, customers, and other stakeholders. Customers of a nation brand could directly interact and learn about the value propositions from both the nation branding agency and each service provider of the nation. Besides the external interactions with the customers and other stakeholders, internal interactions are indeed crucial in the case of nation branding, where the nation brand serves as an umbrella for other service brands. Thus, the consistency in understanding and the communication of the value propositions of the nation, often under one tagline, is crucial for building a holistic brand for the nation that its local service brands could benefit from. The framework also highlights the processes that enable such marketing interactions to take place: (i) the knowledge exchange and negotiation of value propositions, and (ii) the integration of resources. Hence, the chapter provides a perspective and theoretical framework with which to understand the co-creation of a nation brand. It expanded upon previous works on brand co-creation to the context of nation branding.

The case study illustrates the conceptual framework in the real-life context. It demonstrates that the success of the Viet Nam tourism industry is due to its ability to strategically develop a nation brand that acts as an umbrella brand for tourism. It highlights the role of the nation branding agency in facilitating and orchestrating marketing activities aiming at co-creation of the meanings and value of the nation brand of Viet Nam, and how the customers and other stakeholders join together in co-creating the brand, with or without the interactions with the nation branding agency. While traditional external interactions (involving the communication of value propositions) remain essential, internal interactions (enabling and facilitating the delivery of the promised value propositions) are also shown to be important in successfully establishing collective perceptions regarding a holistic umbrella brand. Within the setting of a book chapter, only one dimension of the nation brand – tourism, could be illustrated. Additional research on other dimensions of a nation brand, namely investment or education, could help further enlighten the framework.

The conceptual framework and analysis using the illustrative case suggested several implications for nation branding and avenues for future research. In today's business environment, where everyone and everything is connected, an integrative, co-creation view could help relate the fragmented research field of nation branding and provide a novel ground for future research that might work better for such a complex concept as a nation brand. The implications and suggestions for future research are presented in Table 13.3.

*Table 13.3*   *Implications of the co-creation perspective in nation branding and possible avenues for future research*

| Fundamental ideas of the co-creation perspective in nation branding | Managerial implications | Suggestions for future research |
| --- | --- | --- |
| The nation brand is constituted of the collective perceptions and contributions of different stakeholders | While traditional external interactions remain important, internal interactions are also shown to be crucial in successfully establishing collective perceptions regarding a holistic umbrella brand | The factors and actors influence the perceptions of consumers regarding a nation brand<br><br>The relationship between the value propositions of the nation and the development of detailed value propositions of the local service providers |
| Customers and other stakeholders are operant resources that create value for the brand | It is essential to balance the interests of different stakeholders in the network, encouraging them to contribute their resources to develop the value propositions of the country<br><br>The branding activities of nation branding agency should aim at facilitating the sharing of positive information and perceptions toward the brand | The motivations for different stakeholders in participating in co-creation activities<br><br>The relationship between the competitiveness of a nation brand and the strength of its network<br><br>The measurement of a nation brand value based on its network of stakeholders (stakeholder-based nation brand equity)<br><br>The difference in attitude and behaviour of customers in nation branding agency's directed communications and other undirected communications in online platforms |
| The nation brand forms the interface for both internal and external interactions of stakeholders in the network of the nation brand | The nation branding agency and the country leaders should regard their nation as a service system, with the nation brand as the umbrella for other service brands of the country | The role of the nation brand in mediating the relationship between the local service providers and their customers<br><br>The influence of the meaning and experience with one dimension of the nation brand on the perceptions of other dimensions |
| Sharing of knowledge and information facilitate and activate the co-creation of the nation brand | Feedbacks and suggestions of customers and other stakeholders should be collected systematically from different sources and be studied seriously to develop innovation or novel value propositions of the country | The source of innovation idea for a nation brand's offering<br><br>The impact of customers' feedback on the innovation of value propositions of the nation brand |

# REFERENCES

Aaker, D.A. (1991). *Managing Brand Equity*. New York, NY: The Free Press.

Aaker, D.A. (1996). *Building Strong Brands*. New York, NY: The Free Press.

Aaker, J.L. (1997). Dimensions of brand personality. *Journal of Marketing Research, 34*(3), 347–356.

Ahn, M.J., & Wu, H.C. (2015). The art of nation branding: National branding value and the role of government and the arts and culture sector. *Journal of Public Organization Review, 15*(1), 157–173.

Anholt, S. (2005). *Brand New Justice: How Branding Places and Products can Help the Developing World* (Rev. ed). Oxford: Elsevier Butterworth-Heinemann.

Bitner, M.J. (1995). Building service relationships: It's all about promises. *Journal of Academy of Marketing Science, 23*(4), 246–251.

Bloom Consulting (2019). *Country Brand Ranking Tourism Edition 2019–2020.* Bloom Consulting. https://www.bloom-consulting.com/en/pdf/rankings/Bloom_Consulting_Country_Brand_Ranking _Tourism.pdf

Brand Finance (2019). *Brand Finance Nation Brand 2019.* Brand Finance. https://brandfinance.com/ knowledge-centre/reports/brand-finance-nation-brands-2019/

Brodie, R.J. (2009). From goods to service branding: An integrative perspective. *Marketing Theory, 9*(1), 103–107.

Brodie, R.J., Glynn, M.S., & Little, V. (2006). The service brand and the service-dominant logic: Missing fundamental premise or the need for stronger theory. *Marketing Theory, 6*(3), 363–379.

Caldwell, N., & Freire, J.R. (2004). The differences between branding a country, a region and a city: Applying the brand box model. *Journal of Brand Management, 12*(1), 50–61.

Calonius, H. (1986). A market behavior framework. *Marketing Theory, 6*(4), 419–428.

Caru, A., & Cova, B. (2003). Revisiting consumer culture experience: A more humble and complete view of the concept. *Marketing Theory, 3*(2), 267–286.

Casidy, R., Helmi, J., & Bridson, K. (2019). Drivers and inhibitors of national stakeholder engagement with place brand identity. *European Journal of Marketing, 53*(7), 1445–1465.

Chandler, J.D., & Lusch, R.F. (2015). Service systems: A broadened framework and research agenda on value propositions, engagement, and service experience. *Journal of Service Research, 18*(1), 6–22.

Chigora, F., & Hoque, M. (2018). Marketing of tourism destinations: A misapprehension between place and nation branding in Zimbabwe tourism. *African Journal of Hospitality, Tourism and Leisure, 7*(4), 1–13.

CNN Travel (2020). *Destination Vietnam.* CNN Travel. https://edition.cnn.com/travel/destinations/ vietnam

Da Silveira, C., Lages, C., & Simoes, C. (2013). Reconceptualizing brand identity in a dynamic environment. *Journal of Business Research, 66*, 28–36.

Das, K. (2019). Vietnam's tourism industry continues its growth in 2018. *Vietnam Briefing.* https://www .vietnam-briefing.com/news/vietnams-tourism-industry-continues-growth-2018.html/

Day, G.S., & Montgomery, D.B. (1999). Charting new directions for marketing. *Journal of Marketing, 63*(4), 3–13.

D'Astous, A., & Boujbel, L. (2007). Positioning countries on personality dimensions: Scale development and implications for country marketing. *Journal of Business Research, 60*(3), 231–239.

Diamantopoulos, A., Schelegelmilch, B., & Palihawadana, D. (2011). The relationship between country-of-origin image and brand image as drivers of purchase intentions: A test of alternative perspectives. *International Marketing Review, 28*(5), 508–524.

Dinnie, K. (2010). *Nation Branding: Concepts, Issues, Practice* (Rev. ed.). Abingdon, UK: Routledge.

Fan, Y. (2010). Branding the nation: Towards a better understanding. *Place Branding and Public Diplomacy, 6*, 97–103.

Fetscherin, M. (2010). The determinants and measurement of a country brand: The country brand strength index. *International Marketing Review, 27*(4), 466–479.

*Financial Times* (2020). Vietnam tourism: Better marketing? *Financial Times.* https://www.ft.com/ content/7e4e0454-3561-3b2f-9d6c-8907e1b39921

Future Brand (2019). *Future Brand Country Index 2019.* Future Brand. https://www.futurebrand.com/ futurebrand-country-index

Gilmore, F. (2002). A country – can it be repositioned? Spain – the success story of country branding. *Journal of Brand Management, 9*(4), 281–293.

Grönroos, C. (1996). Relationship marketing logic. *Asia-Australian Marketing Journal, 4*(1), 7–18.

Grönroos, C. (2006). On defining marketing: Finding a new roadmap. *Marketing Theory, 6*(4), 395–417.

Gwyther, M. (2020). *Vietnam Tourism: Past, Present and Future.* City Pass Guide. https://www .citypassguide.com/blog/vietnam-tourism-past-present-and-future

Hakala, U., & Lemmetyinen, A. (2011). Co-creating a nation brand 'bottom-up'. *Tourism Review, 66*(3), 14–24.

Hakala, U., Lemmetyinen, A., & Kantola, S.P. (2013). Country image as a nation-branding tool. *Marketing Intelligence and Planning, 31*(5), 538–556.

Hao, A.W., Paul, J., Trott, S., Guo, C., & Wu, H. (2021). Two decades of research on nation branding: A review and future research agenda. *International Marketing Review, 38*(1), 46–69.

Helmi, J., Bridson, K., & Casidy, R. (2019). A typology of organizational stakeholder engagement with place brand identity. *Journal of Strategic Marketing*, DOI 10.1080/0965254X.2019.1593224

Herrero-Crespo, A., Gutiérrez, H.S.M., & Garcia-Salmones, M.M. (2016). Influence of country image on country brand equity: Application to higher education services. *International Marketing Review*, *33*(5), 691–714.

Huongdanvien [Tourguides] (2020). *Online Database for Tour Guides*. Huongdanvien. http://huongdanvien.vn/

Ind, N., Iglesias, O., & Markovic, S. (2017). The co-creation continuum: From tactical market research tool to strategic collaborative innovation method. *Journal of Brand Management*, *24*(4), 310–321.

Jaffe, E.D., & Nebenzahl, I.D. (2006). *National Image and Competitiveness Advantage: The Theory and Practice of Place Branding* (2nd ed.). Copenhagen: Copenhagen Business School Press.

Keller, K.L. (1993). Conceptualizing, measuring and managing customer-based brand equity. *Journal of Marketing*, *57*(1), 1–22.

Keller, K.L. (2003). *Strategic Brand Management* (2nd ed.). Upper Saddle River, NJ: Pearson.

Konecnik Ruzzier, M., & de Chernatony, L. (2013). Developing and applying a place brand identity model: The case of Slovenia. *Journal of Business Research*, *66*(1), 45–52.

Kotler, P., & Gertner, D. (2002). Country as brand, product, and beyond: A place marketing and brand management perspective. *Journal of Brand Management*, *9*(4/5), 249–261.

Kotsi, F., Balakrishnan, M.S., Michael, I., & Ramsøy, T.Z. (2018). Place branding: Aligning multiple stakeholder perceptions of visual and auditory communication elements. *Journal of Destination Marketing and Management*, *7*, 112–130.

Lee, R., Klobas, J., Tezinde, T., & Murphy, J. (2010). The underlying social identities of a nation's nation's brand. *International Marketing Review*, *27*(4), 450–465.

Lonely Planet (2020). *Welcome to Vietnam*. Lonely Planet. https://www.lonelyplanet.com/vietnam

Merz, M.A., He, Y., & Vargo, S.L. (2009). The evolving brand logic: A service-dominant logic perspective. *Journal of the Academy of Marketing Science*, *37*(3), 328–344.

Nguyen, H. (2020). Vietnam's tourism sector: Opportunities for investors in 2020. *Vietnam Briefing*. https://www.vietnam-briefing.com/news/vietnams-tourism-sector-opportunities-investors-2020.html/

Papadopoulos, N., & Heslop, L. (2002). Country equity and country branding: Problems and prospects. *Journal of Brand Management*, *9*(4), 294–314.

Pappu, R., & Quester, P. (2010). Country equity: Conceptualization and empirical evidence. *International Business Review*, *19*, 276–291.

Pike, S., Bianchi, C., Kerr, G., & Patti, C. (2010). Consumer-based brand equity for Australia as a long-haul tourism destination in an emerging market. *International Marketing Review*, *27*(4), 434–449.

Prahalad, C.K., & Ramaswamy, V. (2000). Co-opting customer competence. *Harvard Business Review*, *78*(1), 79–87.

Prahalad, C.K., & Ramaswamy, V. (2003). The new frontier of experience innovation. *MIT Sloan Management Review*, *44*(4), 12–18.

Prahalad, C.K., & Ramaswamy, V. (2004). Co-creation experiences: The next practice in value creation. *Journal of Interactive Marketing*, *18*(3), 5–14.

Rojas-Méndez, J.I. (2013). The nation brand molecule. *Journal of Product and Brand Management*, *22*(7), 462–472.

Rojas-Méndez, J.I., Papadopoulos, N., & Alwan, M. (2015). Testing self-congruity theory in the context of nation brand personality. *Journal of Product and Brand Management*, *24*(1), 18–27.

Schau, H.J., Muñiz Jr, A.M., & Arnould, E.J. (2009). How brand community practices create value. *Journal of Marketing*, *73*(5), 30–51.

Schau, H.J., Muñiz Jr, A.M., & Arnould, E.J. (2019). The co-creation of brands. In S.L. Vargo, & R.F. Lusch (Eds.), *The Sage Handbook of Service-Dominant Logic* (pp. 97–117). Thousand Oaks, CA: SAGE Publishing.

Schühly, A., & Tenzer, H. (2017). A multi-dimensional approach to international market selection and nation branding in sub-Saharan Africa. *Africa Journal of Management*, *3*(3–4), 236–279.

Siggelkow, N. (2007). Persuasion with case studies. *Academy of Management Journal*, *50*(1), 20–24.

Skoko, B., Jakopovic, H., & Gluvacevic, D. (2018). Challenges of branding in post-conflict countries: The case of Bosnia and Herzegovina. *Tourism*, *66*(4), 411–427.

Starr, R.G., & Brodie, R.J. (2016). Certification and authentication of brand value propositions. *Journal of Brand Management, 23*(6), 716–731.

Sun, Q., & Paswan, A. (2011). Country branding using product quality. *Journal of Brand Management, 19*(2), 143–157.

Supphellen, M., & Nyaarsdvick, I. (2002). Testing country brand slogans: Conceptual development and empirical illustration of a simple normative model. *Journal of Brand Management, 9*(4/5), 385–395.

Trip Advisor (2020). *Explore Viet Nam.* Trip Advisor. https://www.tripadvisor.co.nz/Tourism-g293921 -Vietnam-Vacations.html

US News (2020). Best countries: Viet Nam. US News. https://www.usnews.com/news/best-countries/ vietnam

Vallaster, C., & von Wallpach, S. (2013). An online discursive inquiry into the social dynamics of multi-stakeholder brand meaning co-creation. *Journal of Business Research, 66*(9), 1505–1515.

Vargo, S.L., & Lusch, R.F. (2004). Evolving to a new dominant logic for marketing. *Journal of Marketing, 68*(1), 1–17.

Vargo, S.L., & Lusch, R.F. (2008). Service-dominant logic: Continuing the evolution. *Journal of the Academy of Marketing Science, 36,* 1–10.

Vargo, S.L., & Lusch, R.F. (2016). Institutions and axioms: An extension and update of service-dominant logic. *Journal of the Academy of Marketing Science, 44,* 5–23.

Vargo, S.L. & Lusch, R.F. (2017). Service-dominant logic 2025. *International Journal of Research in Marketing, 34,* 46–67.

*Vietnam Investment Review* [VIR] (2014). From 'hidden' to 'timeless charm': Vietnam unveils guide-lines on new tourism brand identity. *Vietnam Investment Review.* https://www.vir.com.vn/from -hidden-to-timeless-charm-vietnam-unveils-guideline-on-new-tourism-brand-identity-31915.html

*Vietnam Investment Review* [VIR] (2017). Promoting tourism – Lever to develop Vietnam tourism industry. *Vietnam Investment Review.* https://www.vir.com.vn/promoting-tourism-lever-to-develop -vietnam-tourism-industry-52661.html

Vietnam Travel (2018). 'Vietnam – Timeless Charm' writing & video contest. Vietnam Travel. https:// vietnam.travel/vietnam-writing-contest

Vietnam Travel (2020). *Viet Nam – Timeless Charm.* Vietnam Travel. https://vietnam.travel/

Vietnamtourism (2020). *Events – News.* Vietnamtourism. http://vietnamtourism.vn/en/index.php/news/ cat/05

Warnaby, G. (2009). Towards a service-dominant place marketing logic. *Marketing Theory, 9*(4), 403–423.

World Bank (2020). International tourism, number of arrivals. https://data.worldbank.org/indicator/ST .INT.ARVL

Yoo, B., & Donthu, N. (2001). Developing and validating a multi-dimensional consumer-based brand equity scale. *Journal of Business Research, 52*(1), 1–14.

# 14. The dark side of brand co-creation: a psychological ownership perspective

*Fabian Bartsch and Bart Claus*

In a society fueled by the need for self-expression, continuous and globalizing growth, rapidly progressing connectivity, and growing skepticism toward market constructed meanings, consumers increasingly want to become the narrators of their own brand-related behavior (Leigh et al., 2006; Swaminathan et al., 2020). For some time, brand managers have acknowledged these changes in consumer–brand relationships and increasingly adopt a service-dominant logic in the development and management of their brands (Merz et al., 2009; Vargo & Lusch, 2004). This approach includes integrating customers in a brand co-creation process (Loureiro et al., 2020; Prahalad & Ramaswamy, 2004). Brand co-creation is defined as "an active, creative and social process based on collaboration between organizations and participants that generates benefits for all and creates value for stakeholders" (Ind et al., 2013, p. 9). Negligence to understand and manage these dynamics in a co-creation context can have severe consequences for customer–firm relationships (Buhalis et al., 2020; Grégoire et al., 2009).

A likely consequence and facilitator of co-creations is consumers' perception of psychological ownership (Fuchs et al., 2010). Rooted in multiple theoretical streams related to possession (McCracken, 1986; Richins, 1994), self-identity (Belk, 1988), and organizational behavior (Pierce et al., 2003), psychological ownership is defined as a "state where an individual feels as though the target of ownership or a piece of that target is 'theirs'" (Pierce et al., 2003, p. 86). From a possession and identity theory standpoint, psychological ownership has positive bottom-line implications, such as higher purchase intentions and increased willingness to pay (Fuchs et al., 2010; Peck & Shu, 2009). From a consumer standpoint, findings are mixed, as psychological ownership amplifies consumer responses bi-directionally. It may lead to positive responses like improved self-worth or willingness to engage (Pierce et al., 2003). Contrariwise, co-creation failures or mismanagement between stakeholders can cause even greater negative responses. Because of hurt feelings of psychological ownership, co-creators may develop anger or frustration with the firm (Bendapudi & Leone, 2003; Gebauer et al., 2013). We showcase a sentiment analysis on LEGO's acquisition of a second-hand reseller market and highlight how territorial claims can divide a community (see Box 14.1). The LEGO community is concerned about intrusion on their creations, thus experiencing loss of control. However, they also see the firm's decision as an opportunity to strengthen customer–firm relationships.

## BOX 14.1 SHOWCASE: LEGO'S ACQUISITION OF BRICKLINK – SENTIMENT ANALYSIS

**Case Description**

On November 26, 2019, the Lego Group announces the acquisition of BrickLink (www .bricklink.com), a major second-hand retailer for "Adult Fans of LEGO" (AFOL). The reception of the announcement among AFOLs was mixed. As major contributors to the LEGO brand sphere (e.g., creative input for new products, promotion of LEGO, significant financial commitments, and forging of the LEGO identity throughout the brand community), AFOLs are concerned about the potential repercussions of the acquisition. The community appears to be divided concerning threats to their hobby compared to opportunities because of Lego's decision.* Following the immediate announcement, the upcoming changes were fiercely discussed across LEGO online communities. How divided was the community in their feelings toward this change?

**Data and Methodology**

Comments were made from 128 unique users across 396 discussion posts following the acquisition announcement on eurobricks.com (+150,000-member strong Lego community);** 55,213 words were subjected to sentiment analysis using the Bing lexicon (Hu & Liu, 2004); we excluded stop words using the SMART list (Lewis et al., 2004) and categorized words based on their overall positive or negative connotation.

**Negative Sentiments**
52.6%

34.2%
**Positive Sentiments**

**Findings**

Results of the sentiment analysis highlight the ambiguous feeling of the community about the intrusion of LEGO into their community: 52.6% of posts showed more negative sentiments compared to 34.2% positively worded posts, 13.2% of posts used a balance of positive and negative words in their discussions of the announcement. The comparative word cloud discloses major trigger words revealing the divide of the community (Top 100 most frequently mentioned sentiment words, font size is associated with their frequency). On the one hand, the community shows concerns about the potential infringement on their hobby, including a potential loss of control; on the other hand, they see it as an opportunity to forge a stronger relationship between LEGO and its community.

*Source:* *Original announcement: https://bit.ly/37HdDg0; **Data source https://bit.ly/2NdElmU

This brief example underlines the need to include the potential negative consequences of psychological ownership into a firm's deliberation of co-creation strategies, yet literature until now did not systematically explore these potential negative consequences. In this chapter we identify from literature possessiveness, resistance to change, and unhelpful word-of-mouth (WOM) behavior, as most imminent potential negative consequences of psychological ownership. We map these out to what is commonly known as the three routes to ownership – control, knowledge, and investment of self (Pierce et al., 2001) on the one hand, and to common negative downstream consequences to co-creation processes gone bad on the other hand. Thus, our conceptual framework paints a more comprehensive picture of the central role of psychological ownership in co-creation processes, allowing for a better understanding of consumers' ambiguous responses to co-creation. In turn, this better understanding helps firms to take the appropriate managerial action to attenuate or even avoid potential negative outcomes of co-creation, while capitalizing on the benefits that these processes can yield.

This chapter focuses on consumers as stakeholders in developing co-created brands (Merz et al., 2009). It establishes and discusses a conceptual model along with a set of research propositions that highlights the potential "dark side" of brand co-creation driven by consumers' psychological ownership over the co-created brand (see Figure 14.1). We follow up by placing the negative consequences of perceived ownership into a brand co-creation setting alongside a set of actionable moderators that attenuate or amplify such effects. Finally, we offer managerial guidance on reducing the likelihood of negative feedback loops hampering future co-creation initiatives.

## 1.    THE CO-CREATED PATHWAY TO PSYCHOLOGICAL OWNERSHIP

Research on brand co-creation is prolific and includes strategies related to the co-creation of innovation (Prahalad & Ramaswamy, 2004), brand identity (e.g., da Silveira et al., 2013), brand value (Ramaswamy & Ozcan, 2016), and brand meaning (Muñiz & O'Guinn, 2001; Tierney et al., 2016). Likewise, from a firm perspective, brand co-creation has various benefits and serves a myriad of purposes in developing brand value. Co-creation helps firms to identify novel ideas (Poetz & Schreier, 2012; Steenkamp, 2020), understand their customers better (Ind et al., 2013), reduce costs (Ramaswamy & Gouillart, 2010), foster consumer–firm relationships (Hajli et al., 2017; Jones, 2005), and promotes creativity (Rouse, 2020). However, co-creation may also require managing tensions between various stakeholders (Kornum et al., 2017) and anticipating failures (Heidenreich et al., 2015). Firms' adoption of co-creation processes ranges from their use as a market research tool to in-depth strategic collaboration (Ind et al., 2017). In the former, brand value results from customer input at some stages of the brand development process. In the latter, brand value results from continuous long-term cooperation between the customer and the firm. From a consumer perspective, taking part in the co-creation process often results in the experience of intrinsic benefits of the process.[1] These benefits include feelings of enjoyment, a boost of personal integrity, expanding social ties with the (brand) community, and increasing product knowledge (Nambisan & Baron, 2007). Co-creation also leads to higher levels of brand engagement (Hsieh & Chang, 2016), and a series of other related functional, emotional, and self-expressive benefits (Ind et al., 2013; Schau et al., 2009). However, failure to manage co-creation or brand transgressions could cause dissatisfaction, negative word-of-mouth, brand avoidance, or even brand activism (Gebauer et al., 2013; Weijo et al., 2019).

Different from a pure transactional standpoint, co-creation creates brand value through direct interaction between a brand and its customers (Payne et al., 2008). Firms have pursued a myriad of co-creation strategies contributing to the value promises of their brands (Ind et al., 2017; Ramaswamy & Ozcan, 2016). Prominent examples include LEGO's idea-creation community[2] asking their most loyal consumers to create and vote on new product ideas, Harley Davidson's owner groups (HOG)[3] promoting their brand identity at approximately 80,000 community organized charity events worldwide, or Sephora's Beauty Insider community[4] offering personalized beauty advice to its members. These strategies even include the full-fledged envisioning and development of the video game Star Citizen[5] by 2.5 million supporters funding a $300 million investment. Central to these co-creation processes is the importance that brands place on community interactions (e.g., Harley Davidson chapter presidents, Sephora pro artist, LEGO staff picks), the identification of key contributors (e.g., contribution-based merits thorough voting, donating, badges, etc.), and the frequency of exchanges between the firm and its most loyal customers (e.g., LEGO contests, Star Citizen's weekly Roadmap Roundup, etc.). The more prominence is given to these brand–customer interactions, the greater are the derived benefits for brand value creation (Schau et al., 2009).

From a consumer standpoint, beyond the aforementioned benefits (e.g., Ind et al., 2013; Nambisan & Baron, 2007), co-creation processes empower customers to take an active part in brand- and product-related decisions. Thus, co-creation increases the likelihood that consumers develop feelings of ownership about the brand (Fuchs et al., 2010). Interestingly, research has shown that the positive bias in evaluative processes driven by feelings of psychological ownership (Franke et al., 2010; Fuchs et al., 2010), is also present in consumers' evaluations of co-created outcomes (Norton et al., 2012). Importantly, consumers' feelings of ownership are not limited to physical goods. Psychological ownership can be felt over a variety of targets, including job-related roles, product/brand-related ideas (Brown & Robinson, 2011; Pierce et al., 2003), services (Chen et al., 2020a), and the co-creation of brand identities and meaning.

Psychological ownership typically follows from a person's belief to (a) have control about the process–outcome relationship, (b) have intimate knowledge about the object, and (c) have invested energy, time, and effort in the object coming to be (Pierce et al., 2001). Consumers taking part in co-creation fulfill a duality in the customer–firm relationship. On the one hand, they are the revenue-generating targets of marketing activities. On the other hand, their participation includes them as "partial employees" in the development process (Bitner et al., 1997; Bowen, 1986). Accordingly, we draw on marketing (Belk, 1988) and human resource literature (Pierce et al., 2001) to delineate the relationship between consumers' feelings of control of, knowledge about, and investment in the co-creation process as antecedents to psychological ownership.

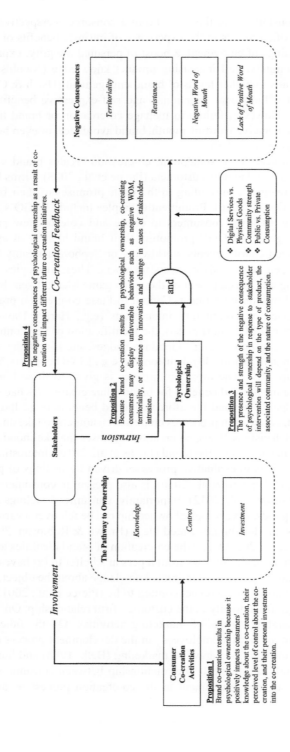

*Figure 14.1   The dark side of brand co-creation: a conceptual framework*

Consumers involved in co-creation processes, by definition, have some control over the co-created experience (Prahalad & Ramaswamy, 2004). Depending on co-creation's integration into marketing strategy (Ind et al., 2017) consumers' control about the outcome may include submitting new product ideas (e.g., LEGO), expressing interest for brand-related topics (e.g., Sephora), or even financial contributions to developing new game features (e.g., Star Citizen). Naturally, such participation requires at least a minimal involvement in the brand, the industry, and the (brand) community. Consumers taking part in co-creation will possess and develop better knowledge and perceive some control about the co-created brand and its products (Bowers & Martin, 2007; Hsieh et al., 2004). This intimate knowledge – difficult to access by the general audience – about the co-created brand differs from general product and brand knowledge. Participation in co-creation implies that participants are self-selected based on their interest in the brand (e.g., LEGO ideas) or on their history with the brand (e.g., Sephora's "very important beauty insider" [VIB] requires a $300 product investment, HOG requires owning a Harley motorcycle). Co-creation includes consumers into the (brand) ingroup. Moreover, "having a seat at the table" increases consumers' perceived feelings of control about the outcome and should, therefore, amplify a consumer's sense of psychological ownership (O'Hern & Rindfleisch, 2010).

Finally, participation in the co-creation process results in feelings of personal investment of time, energy, or labor in the co-created brand or product, which will further stimulate a sense of ownership for what consumers have shaped, created, or produced (Kirk et al., 2018; Norton et al., 2012; Pierce et al., 2003). Naturally, co-creation requires a significant time and energy commitment to the process and the brand. Co-creation can involve the design of new product ideas (e.g., Lego), the nurturing of community questions (e.g., Sephora), the organization of events (e.g., Harley Davidson), or the participation in quality assurance (e.g., Star Citizen). The more consumers invest in these processes, the more likely they will develop a sense of psychological ownership and feeling that their involvement with the brand results in them having a stake in the conversation about its direction, value, and identity. Thus, consumers' perceived level of control, knowledge, and investment determines consumers' sense of psychological ownership.

*Proposition 1: Brand co-creation results in psychological ownership because it positively impacts consumers' knowledge about the co-creation, their perceived level of control about the co-creation, and their personal investment into the co-creation.*

## 2.   NEGATIVE RESPONSES TO CO-CREATED "OWNED" BRANDS

Psychological ownership creates a strong association between its target (the co-creation) and the self (Belk, 1988; Ye & Gawronski, 2016). These associations form fast and automatically (LeBarr & Shedden, 2017), but strengthen over time (Strahilevitz & Loewenstein, 1998), repeated exposure, and interaction with the brand (Kirby & Greenwald, 2017). The association between the self and the ownership target creates a mindset that compares the target of ownership to the same standards as the self (Weiss & Johar, 2013). Much like self-enhancement theory puts forward that people are positively biased in evaluating their own importance and worth (Sedikides, 1993; von Hippel & Trivers, 2011), positive bias occurs in processing and assessing targets of psychological ownership. Consistent with findings of prospect theory and the endowment effect (Kahneman et al., 1990; Thaler, 1980), consumers' feelings of psychological ownership favorably affect memory, attitude, and valuation of the "owned" objects (e.g., Beggan, 1992; Dommer & Swaminathan, 2013; Morewedge & Giblin, 2015; van den Bos et al., 2010). In a co-creation context, these positive downstream effects (i.e., increases in brand awareness, attitude, and valuation) are important marketing outcomes. Among others, studies have emphasized the positive effects of co-creation on the value of brand offerings (Fang et al., 2008), customer engagement and brand relations (Füller, 2010; Hsieh & Chang, 2016), the credibility of brand communications (Acar & Puntoni, 2016), product demand (Fuchs et al., 2010), and financial performance (Nishikawa et al., 2013).

Co-creation also entails some risk. Self-enhancement theory supports that when the results of a co-creation process are positive, consumers might attribute these to their own efforts entirely. Thus, in the perception of these consumers, the company does not reciprocate their efforts, which might leave them disappointed in the firm's contribution (Bendapudi & Leone, 2003). Inversely, consumers might perceive unfairness or be overall dissatisfied with the co-creation outcome, triggering disruptive behavior and negative WOM (Gebauer et al., 2013). They may even cannibalize on an offer by taking the skill and experience they developed over the co-creation process to become competitors of – part of – the offer they contributed to earlier (Fodness et al., 1993).

Under the assumption that psychological ownership is an important facilitator between co-creation and consumers' responses to co-created outcomes, literature shows there is at least some ambiguity concerning whether co-creation always yields positive responses (Bendapudi & Leone, 2003; Heidenreich et al. 2015; Gebauer et al., 2013). Questions remain about the circumstances that support positive or negative (long-term) consequences of brand co-creation. The observation that psychological ownership is an important intervening variable in the co-creation–consumer relationship allows us to take a novel view on the potential drawbacks of co-creation for consumers and companies alike. In doing so, we will focus on territoriality, resistance to change, and negative effects related to WOM, building on the positive bias of consumers in evaluating themselves and evaluating co-created brands (Beggan, 1992; Huang et al., 2009).

## 2.1    This is My Brand – It Belongs to Me!

A first potential negative long-term outcome of psychological ownership is territorial behavior (Brown et al., 2005) or possessiveness. Territoriality is contingent on psychological ownership (Kirk et al., 2018). Literature defines territoriality as a need for exclusive control and an unwillingness to share (as in sharing ownership) or collaborate with others (Pierce et al., 2003). When co-creation contexts depend on multiple consumers creating a joint outcome, such territorial behavior will no doubt compromise the outcome of the co-creation process. Territorial behavior is triggered by another party's intrusion on a target of psychological ownership (e.g., community members "copying" ideas, companies not acknowledging co-creation efforts, etc.). The literature discusses territorial behavior in reaction to intrusion on mundane objects like a chair, but also in co-creation-related contexts such as product designs (Kirk et al., 2018). Territoriality is driven by the connection between self and the "owned" object, both positively biased in their perception. Psychological ownership constitutes an association between the self and something valuable. Another party's claim may compromise this association and, therefore, constitute a potential loss with strong emotional and behavioral responses as a result (Kahneman & Tversky, 1979; Kahneman et al., 1990; Shu & Peck, 2011).

Ample opportunities for the perception of intrusion exist in co-creation processes. First, other stakeholders can see a co-creating firm as a third-party entity or even a competitor in the process (Bendapudi & Leone, 2003). Thus, actions by the firm aimed at claiming or maintaining (e.g., legal) ownership over the co-creation can be perceived as intrusion (e.g., LEGO not crediting any follow-up products originating from LEGO Ideas). Second, co-creation often involves consumers collaborating toward an outcome together. Especially when a single or a few co-creations remain at the end (e.g., any form of community contest), growing feelings of ownership might lead to territorial claims by co-creation participants about who contributed what to the outcome. Intrusion can consist of displaying antecedent or actual conditions to ownership (Kirk et al., 2018). Consistent with the pathways to psychological ownership, these can involve displays of control over the co-creation (e.g., leading the discussion on a forum, rejecting ideas, exclusive access to resources, limiting the scope of the process, etc.), of knowledge (e.g., answering questions from others, adding new topics to the discussion, etc.), or of investment of self (e.g., experience with previous co-creation rounds, seniority on discussion boards, etc.). Evidently, these antecedents also involve explicit claims to ownership or lack of recognition of ownership by either the firm (launching the brand or communicating about it without acknowledging contributing stakeholders; Kazadi et al., 2015) or by other consumers contributing to the co-creation process.

*Proposition 2.1: Because brand co-creation results in psychological ownership, co-creating consumers may display with regard to the co-creation process and outcomes in cases of (perceived) stakeholder intrusion.*

## 2.2    This is My Brand – I Don't Want You to Change It!

A second negative potential consequence of psychological ownership is consumers' resistance to change (Pierce et al., 2003). A company might introduce an updated version of an earlier co-creation, introduce adaptations by in-house engineers or design experts to consumer co-creations, or abandon a product line altogether (see also Muñiz & Schau, 2005). Similar to consumers' feelings of territoriality, it is easy to imagine how positively biased perceptions of the self and targets of psychological ownership would yield resistance to change. A change could mean either consumers questioning the value of their perceived ownership or their association with the co-created brand. Consumers want to keep intact what is valuable to them. Owners selectively attend to perceived value increasing attributes of an object relative to perceived value decreasing attributes (Ashby et al., 2012). Moreover, evidence shows asymmetric resistance to change depending on whether a change leaves a contribution to an idea intact (additive change), or rather substitutes a previous contribution (subtractive change) (Baer & Brown, 2012). Evidently, a subtractive change is far more severe than an additive change. Regardless, even additive change can evoke territorial responses if changes interfere with the routes to ownership (i.e., giving up control or (relative) knowledge, or if consumers' investment of self becomes reduced relative to others).

The notion that psychological ownership is interwoven with resistance to change is also visible in findings that relate ownership to maintaining a sense of the past (Belk, 1990). Ownership cements objects, ideas, events, achievements, and other targets in relation to the owner but also in relation to time. This often entails powerful feelings of nostalgia toward the focal object (Zhou et al., 2012), which in case of brand updates or changes, may cause a decrease in consumer brand valuation (Shields & Johnson, 2016). Earlier, we discussed that ownership markers (e.g., recognition of a contribution to the co-creation process) could compromise further development of the process (which comprises change). This can happen based on other participants inhibiting their creative contributions to the process (Brown & Baer, 2015), but also by active opposition of idea owners (Pierce et al., 2009). Thus, psychological ownership about a co-created outcome might make consumers lose sight of "the bigger picture". Consequently, they might be less open to the ideas of others (intrusion by other consumers), might oppose making the co-creation fit the long-term strategy of the firm (intrusion by the firm), and might generally favor the status quo. Thus, we propose:

*Proposition 2.2: Because brand co-creation results in psychological ownership, co-creating consumers may display resistance to change in cases of (perceived) stakeholder intrusion.*

### 2.3    This is My Brand – I Will Tell Everyone You Are Doing It Wrong!

A third negative consequence of psychological ownership addresses how "owners" of co-created brands communicate about the brand to others. A common finding is that co-creation processes lead to positive WOM intentions (e.g., Acar & Puntoni, 2016; Schreier et al., 2012). However, assuming feelings of psychological ownership, there is a risk of passive or even disruptive WOM behavior. We distinguish among two potential adverse outcomes: (a) negative WOM as a reaction to a negative co-creation outcome and (b) absent positive WOM about a positive co-creation outcome.

Negative WOM resulting from co-creation can follow consumers' negative perception of the creation (e.g., a firm over-promising on features). Consumers' engagement in the co-creation process and experience of psychological ownership exacerbates these negative emotions (Sembada, 2018). Such negative perceptions are commonly based on the contributions of other stakeholders in the co-creation process – often the firm. In such situations, consumers might voice their dissatisfaction through negative WOM (Gebauer et al., 2013). Importantly, in cases of outcomes being worse than expected, consumers often attribute the negative result to the firm's intrusion into the process (Bendapudi & Leone, 2003). Thus, negative WOM likely targets the firm facilitating the co-creation process.

Less malign, but still harmful, is the absence of positive WOM when consumers' feelings of ownership lead them to hoard information – regardless or even because of consumers' positive evaluation of the co-creation. The consensus in the literature is that favorable consumer attitudes lead to positive WOM (Anderson, 1998). This is particularly true under high consumer involvement (Wangenheim & Bayón, 2007) – the latter facilitated by co-creation. However, psychological ownership can motivate consumers to hide and hoard information (Webster et al., 2008). Indeed, consumers often ponder on the fact that spreading positive WOM would increase the adoption of their possessions. In particular, to consumers with a high need for uniqueness (amplified by feelings of ownership), the latter is not a desirable outcome (Cheema & Kaikati, 2010). Thus, they prefer to stay silent about their "precious" belongings, which might also apply to outcomes of co-creation. Moreover, some early adopters of innovations engage in "share and scare" tactics – flaunting their involvement in the innovation while scaring potential customers about the innovation's price, complexity, or availability to ward off potential intrusion on what they consider "their" domain. Thus, they protect the uniqueness and exclusivity of their involvement with the focal object (Moldovan et al., 2015). In conclusion, psychological ownership could lead to negative WOM when contributors perceive co-creation outcomes as negative, or it could inhibit positive WOM as a protection mechanism when contributors perceive outcomes as positive. Thus, we propose:

*Proposition 2.3: Because brand co-creation results in psychological ownership, co-creating consumers may display negative or lack of positive WOM in cases of (perceived) stakeholder intrusion.*

In sum, despite the ample benefits of co-creation for brands, marketers need to acknowledge the potential drawbacks of co-creation strategies due to psychological ownership among participating customers, such as territoriality, resistance to change, or even negative WOM. In addition, society's proliferating connectivity only amplifies the number of potential channels consumers may voice their concerns (Arvidsson & Caliandro, 2016).

## 3.   CONTEXTUALIZING THE DARK SIDE OF CO-CREATION

The previous section identified the potential negative outcomes of co-creation processes driven by psychological ownership. The current section highlights some important moderators that may condition these effects. These moderators are, to some extent, intrinsic to the brand and its offerings, but their nature and impact are also, to some extent, manageable by the firm. While our discussion is certainly not comprehensive, we identify three primary moderators: the size and density of the brand community, the product type, and the type of consumption.

### 3.1   The Nature of the Community: Size and Density

Conflict based on feelings of ownership and its transgressions is probably a prime source of negative outcomes of co-creation. The size, structure, and nature of interactions in the community of co-creating consumers (or brand communities at large) determine how these conflicts occur, develop, and settle. Brand community size and density of links between members are often considered a positive force for the brand (Kumar & Nayak, 2019; Muñiz & O'Guinn, 2001). However, the entropy in larger and more interactive communities contributes to the probability of conflict over ownership. The more an individual member of the co-creation community is in touch with others, the more likely it is that territorial behavior and resistance to change manifest itself as defensive mechanisms against these interactions. On the other hand, strong ties within the community can also lead to a strong and unified response. Such a response can, for example, be provoked when a firm tries to seize control (thus intruding on ownership) over co-creation efforts over which consumers feel strong psychological ownership (e.g., IKEA's attempt to cease and desist over Ikeahackers.net, Weijo et al., 2019). In these cases of conflict with the firm, group size and group ties likely affect how the co-creation community will respond, for example, in terms of WOM.

Co-creation not only increases consumers' identification with the brand but also with the co-creation community (Gebauer et al., 2013). Identification with the co-creation community facilitates adherence to descriptive social norms in the group (e.g., on attitudes and behaviors toward the brand; Albrecht et al., 2017), but also facilitates emotional contagion among its members (Chen et al., 2020b). With anger over conflict, any individual member is more likely to copy anger from other members as the group is more familiar, and group size amplifies the strength of emotions (Du et al., 2014). Facilitated by today's ubiquitous possibilities for communicating, the latter can cause behavior harmful to the brand, including brand sabotage (Kähr et al., 2016). Moreover, brand communities can become consumer tribes, ganging up on the brand (e.g., #activism, boycotts, public protest, etc.), and plundering brand meaning and value (Cova et al., 2012), often leading the brand to retreat and apologize (Weijo et al., 2019). Thus, we propose that in co-creation settings, community size, and density of internal ties will moderate the outcomes of conflicts based on psychological ownership.

*Proposition 3.1: The presence and strength of the negative consequence of psychological ownership will increase with the size and density of the co-creation community.*

### 3.2   The Nature of the Product: Physical vs. Digital Goods

Co-creation can be implemented around both material goods (e.g., designing your own T shirt through a mass-customization toolkit, Franke et al., 2010) or digital services (e.g., contributing to the code of Red Hat Linux). Even though a contribution to a digital service might not be tangible, literature shows that consumers might feel ownership over completely intangible assets like ideas (Baer & Brown, 2012; Brown & Baer, 2015). However, some evidence suggests that psychological ownership of non-material co-creations might be more short-lived than that of material ones.

For instance, today, consumers have ubiquitous means of taking digital snapshots and store these in safe, quality preserving, and at-will available digital environments. Nonetheless, physical printed photographs never went out of vogue, evident by recent ventures of Amazon and Google into physical photo printing (Barret, 2017; Perez, 2016). Furthermore, worldwide Google Trends data for the last 15 years show that consumers prefer physical evidence of their creations. Interestingly, over this period, steady increases are noticeable for searches for "photo print" (+13.64%) and "photo book" (+17.78%), while searches went down for digital alternatives like "web album" (−90.41%) and "digital album" (−73.91%). Likewise, in that same period, consumers increasingly searched for "diary books" (+32.65%) in favor of a "digital diary" (−93.18%). The latter decline resonates with that of "e-book" (−89.77%) in the same period. Moreover, searches for "digital drawing" today are dominated by those for "canvas paint" with more than 300% and by those for "pencil drawing" even by almost 800%.

Literature attributes these differences to physical goods' ability to yield feelings of psychological ownership, their tangibility, and consumers' ability to exercise physical control, compared to digital services (Atasoy & Morewedge, 2018). Psychological ownership is facilitated by touch (Peck & Shu, 2009) and mental imagery of physical interaction (Peck et al., 2013). Moreover, material possessions are used to condense and store immaterial assets like ideas, events, and achievements to cement them in reality, rather than that they evaporate with time passing (Belk, 1988, 1990). Likewise, the negative effects of giving up ownership on identity loss can be mitigated by a physical representation of the ownership relation − for example, in a photograph (Winterich et al., 2017). Thus, we propose that without a tangible outcome of the co-creation process, effects of psychological ownership might dwindle quicker than when such evidence − for example, in the form of a physical product prototype − is available.

With tangibility a core distinguishing feature between physical goods and digital services, we propose:

*Proposition 3.2: The presence and strength of the negative consequence of psychological ownership will depend on whether the co-creation involves a physical good or a digital service.*

### 3.3 The Nature of Consumption: Public vs. Private

The strength of the potential consequences of co-creation through psychological ownership may also vary according to whether the co-created brand/product is publicly or privately consumed. Differences in consumption behavior depend on the likelihood that product consumption is subject to public scrutiny (Ratner & Kahn, 2002; Rodas & John, 2020). Public consumption refers to "situations in which individuals are aware of the fact that a decision will be observed and evaluated by others" (Zhang et al., 2006, p. 794). Private consumption refers to situations where individuals know that they will not be observed or evaluated by others.

A long-lasting premise of consumer culture theory argues for consumption as a vehicle of motivations like self-expression, identity-validation, and ingroup confirmation (e.g., Arnould & Thompson, 2005; Bearden & Etzel, 1982; Belk, 1988). This implies that when consuming brands or products visible to others, consumers are more likely to make choices that serve an underlying agenda supporting these motivations. Public consumption also elevates levels of variety-seeking behavior (Ratner & Kahn, 2002), increases social status (Griskevicius et al., 2010), and adherence to group norms (Berger & Heath, 2007).

In a co-creation context, we posit that consumers are more likely to voice their opinion for publicly consumed goods for self-validation, signaling, or groupthink reasons. Co-created brands that are publicly consumed (e.g., fashion) will be subject to more scrutiny from members of the co-creation community and other consumers community compared to privately consumed goods. This increases the likelihood that consumers voice concerns with co-creation, shifting blame from the individual to the brand as an identity protection mechanism (White & Argo, 2009). Likewise, publicly consumed goods are more effective vehicles to signal group membership to others (Kulviwat et al., 2009). Hence, any disrupting effects may also be amplified for these types of goods or settings as negative behavior can naturally be shared in the consumption context (e.g., public displays of discontent of fan communities). Finally, negativity and discontent with a brand are subject to community dynamics. Vocal and/ or senior members may hold opinion leadership over the co-creation. Since consumption is observable, group behavior is likely to be influenced by mechanisms of opinion leadership and groupthink (Watts & Dodds, 2007). In sum, we expect that the strength of consumers' negative responses to co-creation driven by psychological ownership will vary according to whether a brand/product is consumed in private or in public.

*Proposition 3.3: The presence and strength of the negative consequence of psychological ownership will depend on whether the product is consumed in private or public.*

## 4. ADDRESSING THE NEGATIVE FEEDBACK LOOP

The value-enhancing role of co-creation for brand management and the customer–firm relationships is grounded in the continuous engagement of stakeholders in defining brand identity and meaning (Ramaswamy & Ozcan, 2016). Above, we argue that psychological ownership is an important facilitator for understanding the meaning creation process (cf. Fuchs et al., 2010). In this chapter, we focus on consumers' negative responses to co-creation driven by psychological ownership. One can envision that territoriality, resistance to change, and consumer engagement in negative WOM impact future consumer–firm relationships and co-creation efforts. In fact, "relationships govern value-creation mechanisms in an exchange (i.e., communicating, adapting, and investing). Events that alter this governance structure often have strong and lasting effects on the behaviors that drive exchange performance" (Harmeling et al., 2015, p. 41). Progressing inter-connectivity will only strengthen such negative feedback effects, exposing brands to collective brand activism online (Arvidsson & Caliandro, 2016; Romani et al., 2015). Consequently, we propose and follow up with a discussion on possible managerial remedies:

*Proposition 4: The negative consequences of psychological ownership as a result of co-creation will affect different future co-creation initiatives.*

A recurring theme in the identified negative consequences of psychological ownership in contexts of co-creation is the potential for loss, conflict, and retaliation based on individual feelings of ownership. Territorial responses and other sources of negative outcomes are conditional on conflicting perspectives on who is entitled to feeling ownership over what – either between co-creating consumers or between consumers and the firm (Harwood & Garry, 2014). These conflicts comprise a perspective on ownership as an individual, exclusive, and sequential dyadic relationship between consumer and target. At any point in time, ownership claims established by one consumer infringe on claims of another. Although ownership can shift, both psychological owners (Pierce et al., 2009) and third parties (Brown & Baer, 2015) contribute to maintaining this status quo. However, contributions to co-creation can be collective, interactive, additive, and simultaneous. At any point in time, different co-creating consumers will simultaneously have various levels of control, knowledge, and investment of self with regard to the co-creation, thus experiencing various degrees of psychological ownership. For firms, it thus becomes important to shift focus away from individual contributions to co-creation. Instead, they should focus on crediting joint contribution by acknowledging the inherent value of the community as a co-creation force. Practical examples include democracy in decision making, consolidation of individuals' inputs, or collective community rewards.

Counter to their potential to amplify the negative effects of psychological ownership, brand communities fostering strong psychological ownership can also be a force for good. Different from the individual perspective on ownership, recent literature focuses on collective psychological ownership as an impetus to involvement, stewardship, and care for the collective target (i.e., the brand) of psychological ownership (Peck & Shu, 2015; Suessenbach & Kamleitner, 2018). As collective psychological ownership is equally created through control, knowledge, and investment of self (Shu & Peck, 2018), co-creation is likely to support collective psychological ownership in the same way as it supports individual psychological ownership. Crucially, collective psychological ownership will promote a group identity (Pierce & Jussila, 2010), part of which can be constructed by the co-creation process itself (Rouse, 2020). To avoid runaway consumer tribes, the firm should align its interests to the co-creation community and its group identity (Cova et al., 2012). This implies that the acknowledgment of collective identities is crucial in managing dysfunctional co-creation processes characterized by individual psychological ownership, territoriality, reluctance to change and progress, loss experiences, and negative WOM. Successful co-creation creates a shared sense of ownership aimed at supporting, building, and protecting the co-created brand. In promoting unprecedented levels of transparency in its development, Star Citizen has excelled in promoting such a sense of shared community. Despite several setbacks in the development of the video game, community contributions are growing and most members continue to defend "their" game.

Another possible remedy to offset the adverse consequences of psychological ownership in co-creation is a formal recognition of consumers' investment in co-creation. For instance, across any forms of communication, firms should acknowledge co-creation, underline the value of the brand community, and emphasize the joint efforts that went into creating the product and defining the brand. Ultimately, brand communication should be a strategic tool that bridges interests among diverse stakeholders of the brand. Several examples exist: LEGO crediting contributors to the success of their LEGO ideas (explicitly through profit sharing, implicitly through acknowledgment such as the 10K Club Interview series), Xiaomi crediting focal community members with exclusive access and discounts, or DHL leveraging and publicly crediting co-creation activities (Crandell, 2016).

Finally, territorial reactions can be anticipatory (e.g., withholding or misrepresenting information for fear of infringement, leaving the co-creation process, abandoning the brand or offer) or reactionary (e.g., reclaiming, anger, revenge, complaining, etc.) (Brown et al., 2005; Brown & Robinson, 2011; Griffiths & Gilly, 2012; Kirk et al., 2018). These territorial markings of co-creation outcomes (i.e., claims or signs of ownership) could discourage creative contributions to those same ideas from other participants (Brown & Baer, 2015). In all cases, these reactions are not conducive to a functional co-creation process, where a smooth exchange of information between various stakeholders is paramount to any potential positive outcomes (Fang et al., 2008). Literature indicates that failed co-creation episodes are best addressed by offering co-created service recovery (e.g., working with a service employee to find an alternative itinerary after a canceled flight; Roggeveen et al., 2012) and co-creation is, in general, an effective approach to service recovery (Dong et al., 2008). We endorse this position, as co-created recovery restores control and knowledge of the outcome and facilitates the investment of self, thus restoring psychological ownership that earlier transgressions might have upset.

## 5. CONCLUSIONS AND DIRECTIONS FOR FUTURE RESEARCH

In this chapter, we summarize current insights into co-creation and psychology ownership. Moreover, we integrate both literature streams into a conceptual framework that highlights the potential negative consequences of psychological ownership in a co-creation setting. Furthermore, we propose a set of contextualizing factors pertaining to the type of product, the community, and the nature of consumption. Despite advancing knowledge on brand co-creation and psychological ownership, both streams have seldom been considered in contributing jointly to co-creation outcomes. The few sources that do integrate co-creation and psychological ownership focus on immediate bottom-line consequences (e.g., Fuchs et al., 2010), but neglect potential disruptors to the customer–firm relationship over time. We propose that through elevated levels of product and process knowledge, perceived level of control, and investment, (brand) co-creation promotes feelings of psychological ownership among contributors. This, in turn, increases consumers' susceptibility to territorial claims, increases their resistance to change, and may provoke adverse WOM behavior.

This chapter further shows that the current progression of the literature on co-creation is prolific but not exhaustive (as also evident by the many contributions to this book). We observe that the theoretical understanding and empirical findings related to (brand) co-creation are fragmented. Similar co-creation elements use overlapping terminologies without a strict delineation from each other. Findings are often difficult to generalize to a larger context. Moreover, literature predominantly focuses on the "positive side" of co-creation, while scarcely considering its "dark side". This chapter presents a stepping stone and lays theoretical foundations for examining the "dark side" of co-creation.

We can envision several future research directions that could further develop our conceptual thoughts and offer empirical investigations into the topic at hand. First, despite the carefully delineated theoretical foundations of the proposed conceptual framework, empirical work is required to validate the established relationships in a co-creation setting as well as the potential inter-relationship among proposed outcomes with likely positive outcomes.

Second, in our conceptual discussion on the "dark side" of co-creation, we position psychological ownership as a key mediating process in the co-creation–(adverse) outcome relationship. We deliberately focused on negative responses that have an empirical foundation in the psychological ownership literature (e.g., Gebauer et al., 2013; Kirk et al., 2018; Shields & Johnson, 2016) and disrupt the brand on a large scale by easily spilling over to the extant brand community. We can further envision other negative responses because of increased feelings of ownership worthwhile investigating in future research. These include potential harmful behaviors such as boycott (i.e., refusing to buy the brand), temporal short-sightedness (i.e., a lack of understanding of how changes may benefit other consumers), or losing sight of the big picture (i.e., increased feelings of nostalgia resulting in a lack of understanding for a brand's need to progress and innovate to stay relevant). They also could lead to disruptions in the management of (future) co-creation processes.

Third, both for negative and lack of positive WOM, the literature shows that apart from situational variables such as the exclusive nature of the co-creation (Moldovan et al., 2015; Schreier et al., 2012), individual differences among contributors may shape outcomes (Cheema & Kaikati, 2010). It is likely that only a fraction of consumers involved in the co-creation process drive positive WOM, an often observed consequence of co-creation processes (e.g., von Wallpach et al., 2017). This heterogeneity is worth investigating to better understand how co-creation should take place in a multi-stakeholder setting. Similarly, previous works have focused on examining effects on those consumers that were part of the co-creation process (Schreier et al., 2012). These are often so-called "lead users" (von Hippel, 2007). This small group of lead users differs from "observing" consumers, who, in fact, represent the mass of potential buyers of a product (Fuchs & Schreier, 2011). Insights in the effects of various types of co-creation on this important group of "passive" consumers is also of crucial value for practice.

Fourth, we observe a limited understanding of how additional community dynamics shape responses to co-creation, brand value creation, and consumer responses to brand transgressions (Kumar, 2019). Worthy research questions relate to the optimal size of brand communities, the number of interactions taking place, and the network's density. Positive effects of psychological ownership may follow a diminishing rate of return in relation to community size. Once a community becomes too large, co-creation communities become difficult to manage. Larger communities develop their own dynamics, which increases risks associated with negative brand activism through online media channels. Moreover, it might be difficult to maintain a coherent sense of community across larger groups of consumers. This difficulty might, in turn, compromise opportunities to benefit from these groups' feelings of collective ownership over co-creations. The conditions under which this collective feeling of ownership emerges constitute another promising avenue for future research.

Finally, in addressing resistance to change, it is striking how literature identified that ambiguity of (legal) ownership of co-creations helps the creative process (Harwood & Garry, 2014). We would like to extend this notion and claim the important benefits of keeping ownership ambiguous – not only to what concerns the firm but also to what concerns individual contributing consumers. Doing so is likely at least a partial remedy to resistance to change as resulting from psychological ownership, making this an important avenue for future research.

## NOTES

1. Notwithstanding potential extrinsic benefits (e.g., potential compensation or discounts), which mostly serve as a self-rationalization mechanism to justify customers' involvement in the co-creation process.
2. See https://ideas.lego.com/.
3. See https://www.harley-davidson.com/us/en/owners/hog.html.
4. See https://www.sephora.com/community.
5. See https://robertsspaceindustries.com/.

## REFERENCES

Acar, O. A., & Puntoni, S. (2016). Customer empowerment in the digital age. *Journal of Advertising Research*, *56*(1), 4–8.

Albrecht, A. K., Walsh, G., Brach, S., Gremler, D. D., & van Herpen, E. (2017). The influence of service employees and other customers on customer unfriendliness: A social norms perspective. *Journal of the Academy of Marketing Science*, *45*(6), 827–847.

Anderson, E. W. (1998). Customer satisfaction and word of mouth. *Journal of Service Research*, *1*(1), 5–17.

Arnould, E. J., & Thompson, C. J. (2005). Consumer culture theory (CCT): Twenty years of research. *Journal of Consumer Research*, *31*(4), 868–882.

Arvidsson, A., & Caliandro, A. (2016). Brand public. *Journal of Consumer Research*, *42*(5), 727–748.

Ashby, N. J. S., Dickert, S., & Glockner, A. (2012). Focusing on what you own: Biased information uptake due to ownership. *Judgment and Decision Making*, *7*(3), 254–267.

Atasoy, O., & Morewedge, C. K. (2018). Digital goods are valued less than physical goods. *Journal of Consumer Research*, *44*(6), 1343–1357.

Baer, M., & Brown, G. (2012). Blind in one eye: How psychological ownership of ideas affects the types of suggestions people adopt. *Organizational Behavior and Human Decision Processes*, *118*(1), 60–71.

Barret, B. (2017). Review: Google Photo Books. Retrieved from https://www.wired.com/story/google-photo-books-review/.

Bearden, W. O., & Etzel, M. J. (1982). Reference group influence on product and brand purchase decisions. *Journal of Consumer Research*, 9(2), 183–194.

Beggan, J. K. (1992). On the social nature of nonsocial perception: The mere ownership effect. *Journal of Personality and Social Psychology*, 62(2), 229–237.

Belk, R. W. (1988). Possessions and the extended self. *Journal of Consumer Research*, 15(2), 139–168.

Belk, R. W. (1990). The role of possessions in constructing and maintaining a sense of past. *Advances in Consumer Research*, 17(1), 669–676.

Bendapudi, N., & Leone, R. P. (2003). Psychological implications of customer participation in co-production. *Journal of Marketing*, 67(1), 14–28.

Berger, J., & Heath, C. (2007). Where consumers diverge from others: Identity signaling and product domains. *Journal of Consumer Research*, 34(2), 121–134.

Bitner, M. J., Faranda, W. T., Hubbert, A. R., & Zeithaml, V. A. (1997). Customer contributions and roles in service delivery. *International Journal of Service Industry Management*, 8(3), 193–205.

Bowen, D. E. (1986). Managing customers as human resources in service organizations. *Human Resource Management*, 25(3), 371–383.

Bowers, M. R., & Martin, C. L. (2007). Trading places redux: Employees as customers, customers as employees. *Journal of Services Marketing*, 21(2), 88–98.

Brown, G., & Baer, M. (2015). Protecting the turf: The effect of territorial marking on others' creativity. *Journal of Applied Psychology*, 100(6), 1785–1797.

Brown, G., & Robinson, S. L. (2011). Reactions to territorial infringement. *Organization Science*, 22(1), 210–224.

Brown, G., Lawrence, T. B., & Robinson, S. L. (2005). Territoriality in organizations. *Academy of Management Review*, 30(3), 577–594.

Buhalis, D., Andreu, L., & Gnoth, J. (2020). The dark side of the sharing economy: Balancing value co-creation and value co-destruction. *Psychology & Marketing*, 37(5), 689–704.

Cheema, A., & Kaikati, A. M. (2010). The effect of need for uniqueness on word of mouth. *Journal of Marketing Research*, 47(3), 553–563.

Chen, K., Chen, J., Zhan, W., & Sharma, P. (2020a). When in Rome! Complaint contagion effect in multi-actor service ecosystems. *Journal of Business Research*. 121, 628–641.

Chen, T., Dodds, S., Finsterwalder, J., Witell, L., Cheung, L., Falter, M., Garry, T., Snyder, H., & McColl-Kennedy, J. R. (2020b). Dynamics of wellbeing co-creation: A psychological ownership perspective. *Journal of Service Management*, 121(December), 628–641.

Cova, B., Kozinets, R. V., & Shankar, A. (2012). Tribes, Inc.: The new world of tribalism. In B. Cova, R. V. Kozinets, & A. Shankar (eds), *Consumer Tribes* (pp. 19–42). Abingdon, UK: Routledge.

Crandell, C. (2016, June). Customer co-creation is the secret sauce to success. *Forbes.com*, Retrieved from https://www.forbes.com/sites/christinecrandell/2016/06/10/customer_cocreation_secret_sauce/#155f70825b6d.

da Silveira, C., Lages, C., & Simões, C. (2013). Reconceptualizing brand identity in a dynamic environment. *Journal of Business Research*, 66(1), 28–36.

Dommer, S. L., & Swaminathan, V. (2013). Explaining the endowment effect through ownership: The role of identity, gender, and self-threat. *Journal of Consumer Research*, 39(5), 1034–1050.

Dong, B., Evans, K. R., & Zou, S. (2008). The effects of customer participation in co-created service recovery. *Journal of the Academy of Marketing Science*, 36(1), 123–137.

Du, J., Fan, X., & Feng, T. (2014). Group emotional contagion and complaint intentions in group service failure: The role of group size and group familiarity. *Journal of Service Research*, 17(3), 326–338.

Fang, E., Palmatier, R. W., & Evans, K. R. (2008). Influence of customer participation on creating and sharing of new product value. *Journal of the Academy of Marketing Science*, 36(3), 322–336.

Fodness, D., Pitegoff, B. E., & Truly Sautter, E. (1993). From customer to competitor: Consumer cooption in the service sector. *Journal of Services Marketing*, 7(3), 18–25.

Franke, N., Schreier, M., & Kaiser, U. (2010). The "I designed it myself" effect in mass customization. *Management Science*, 56(1), 125–140.

Fuchs, C., & Schreier, M. (2011). Customer empowerment in new product development. *Journal of Product Innovation Management, 28*(1), 17–32.

Fuchs, C., Prandelli, E., & Schreier, M. (2010). The psychological effects of empowerment strategies on consumers' product demand. *Journal of Marketing, 74*(1), 65–79.

Füller, J. (2010). Refining virtual co-creation from a consumer perspective. *California Management Review, 52*(2), 98–122.

Gebauer, J., Füller, J., & Pezzei, R. (2013). The dark and the bright side of co-creation: Triggers of member behavior in online innovation communities. *Journal of Business Research, 66*(9), 1516–1527.

Grégoire, Y., Tripp, T. M., & Legoux, R. (2009). When customer love turns into lasting hate: The effects of relationship strength and time on customer revenge and avoidance. *Journal of Marketing, 73*(6), 18–32.

Griffiths, M. A., & Gilly, M. C. (2012). Dibs! Customer territorial behaviors. *Journal of Service Research, 15*(2), 131–149.

Griskevicius, V., Tybur, J. M., & Van den Bergh, B. (2010). Going green to be seen: Status, reputation, and conspicuous conservation. *Journal of Personality and Social Psychology, 98*(3), 392–404.

Hajli, N., Shanmugam, M., Papagiannidis, S., Zahay, D., & Richard, M. O. (2017). Branding co-creation with members of online brand communities. *Journal of Business Research, 70*(January), 136–144.

Harmeling, C. M., Palmatier, R. W., Houston, M. B., Arnold, M. J., & Samaha, S. A. (2015). Transformational relationship events. *Journal of Marketing, 79*(5), 39–62.

Harwood, T., & Garry, T. (2014). Co-creation and ambiguous ownership within virtual communities: The case of the Machinima community. *Journal of Consumer Behaviour, 13*(2), 148–156.

Heidenreich, S., Wittkowski, K., Handrich, M., & Falk, T. (2015). The dark side of customer co-creation: Exploring the consequences of failed co-created services. *Journal of the Academy of Marketing Science, 43*(3), 279–296.

Hsieh, A., Yen, C., & Chin, K. (2004). Participative customers as partial employees and service provider workload. *International Journal of Service Industry Management, 15*(2), 187–199.

Hsieh, S. H., & Chang, A. (2016). The psychological mechanism of brand co-creation engagement. *Journal of Interactive Marketing, 33*(February), 13–26.

Hu, M., & Liu, B. (2004, August). Mining and summarizing customer reviews. In *Proceedings of the Tenth ACM SIGKDD International Conference on Knowledge Discovery and Data Mining* (pp. 168–177).

Huang, Y. H., Wang, L., & Shi, J. Q. (2009). When do objects become more attractive? The individual and interactive effects of choice and ownership on object evaluation. *Personality and Social Psychology Bulletin, 35*(6), 713–722.

Ind, N., Iglesias, O., & Markovic, S. (2017). The co-creation continuum: From tactical market research tool to strategic collaborative innovation method. *Journal of Brand Management, 24*(4), 310–321.

Ind, N., Iglesias, O., & Schultz, M. (2013). Building brands together: Emergence and outcomes of co-creation. *California Management Review, 55*(3), 5–26.

Jones, R. (2005). Finding sources of brand value: Developing a stakeholder model of brand equity. *Journal of Brand Management, 13*(1), 10–32.

Kahneman, D., & Tversky, A. (1979). Prospect theory: An analysis of decision under risk. *Econometrica, 47*(2), 263–291.

Kahneman, D., Knetsch, J. L., & Thaler, R. H. (1990). Experimental tests of the endowment effect and the Coase theorem. *Journal of Political Economy, 98*(6), 1325–1348.

Kähr, A., Nyffenegger, B., Krohmer, H., & Hoyer, W. D. (2016). When hostile consumers wreak havoc on your brand: The phenomenon of consumer brand sabotage. *Journal of Marketing, 80*(3), 25–41.

Kazadi, K., Lievens, A., & Mahr, D. (2015). "Does it pay off to introduce my partner?" The role of stakeholder cocreation in consumers' willingness to pay. In I. Banks, P. De Pelsmacker, & S. Okazaki (eds), *Advances in Advertising Research (Vol. V)* (pp. 321–330). Weisbaden: Springer.

Kirby, T. A., & Greenwald, A. G. (2017). Mental ownership: Does mental rehearsal transform novel stimuli into mental possessions? *Journal of Experimental Social Psychology*, *73*(November), 125–135.

Kirk, C. P., Peck, J., & Swain, S. D. (2018). Property lines in the mind: Consumers' psychological ownership and their territorial responses. *Journal of Consumer Research*, *45*(1), 148–168.

Kornum, N., Gyrd-Jones, R., Al Zagir, N., & Brandis, K. A. (2017). Interplay between intended brand identity and identities in a Nike related brand community: Co-existing synergies and tensions in a nested system. *Journal of Business Research*, *70*(January), 432–440.

Kulviwat, S., Bruner, G. C., & Al-Shuridah, O. (2009). The role of social influence on adoption of high tech innovations: The moderating effect of public/private consumption. *Journal of Business Research*, *62*(7), 706–712.

Kumar, J. (2019). How psychological ownership stimulates participation in online brand communities? The moderating role of member type. *Journal of Business Research*, *105*(December), 243–257.

Kumar, J., & Nayak, J. K. (2019). Consumer psychological motivations to customer brand engagement: A case of brand community. *Journal of Consumer Marketing*, *36*(1), 168–177.

LeBarr, A. N., & Shedden, J. M. (2017). Psychological ownership: The implicit association between self and already-owned versus newly-owned objects. *Consciousness and Cognition*, *48*(February), 190–197.

Leigh, T. W., Peters, C., & Shelton, J. (2006). The consumer quest for authenticity: The multiplicity of meanings within the MG subculture of consumption. *Journal of the Academy of Marketing Science*, *34*(4), 481–493.

Lewis, D. D., Yang, Y., Rose, T. G., & Li, F. (2004). Rcv1: A new benchmark collection for text categorization research. *Journal of Machine Learning Research*, *5*(April), 361–397.

Loureiro, S. M. C., Romero, J., & Bilro, R. G. (2020). Stakeholder engagement in co-creation processes for innovation: A systematic literature review and case study. *Journal of Business Research*, *119*(December), 388–409.

McCracken, G. (1986). Culture and consumption: A theoretical account of the structure and movement of the cultural meaning of consumer goods. *Journal of Consumer Research*, *13*(1), 71–84.

Merz, M. A., He, Y., & Vargo, S. L. (2009). The evolving brand logic: A service-dominant logic perspective. *Journal of the Academy of Marketing Science*, *37*(3), 328–344.

Moldovan, S., Steinhart, Y., & Ofen, S. (2015). "Share and scare": Solving the communication dilemma of early adopters with a high need for uniqueness. *Journal of Consumer Psychology*, *25*(1), 1–14.

Morewedge, C., & Giblin, C. (2015). Explanations of the endowment effect: An integrative review. *Trends in Cognitive Sciences*, *19*(6), 339–348.

Muñiz Jr., A. M., & O'Guinn, T. C. (2001). Brand community. *Journal of Consumer Research*, *27*(4), 412–432.

Muñiz Jr., A. M., & Schau, H. J. (2005). Religiosity in the abandoned Apple Newton brand community. *Journal of Consumer Research*, *31*(4), 737–747.

Nambisan, S., & Baron, R. A. (2007). Interactions in virtual customer environments: Implications for product support and customer relationship management. *Journal of Interactive Marketing*, *21*(2), 42–62.

Nishikawa, H., Schreier, M., & Ogawa, S. (2013). User-generated versus designer-generated products: A performance assessment at Muji. *International Journal of Research in Marketing*, *30*(2), 160–167.

Norton, M. I., Mochon, D., & Ariely, D. (2012). The IKEA effect: When labor leads to love. *Journal of Consumer Psychology*, *22*(3), 453–460.

O'Hern, M. S., & Rindfleisch, A. (2010). Customer co-creation: A typology and research agenda. *Review of Marketing Research*, *6*(1), 84–106.

Payne, A. F., Storbacka, K., & Frow, P. (2008). Managing the co-creation of value. *Journal of the Academy of Marketing Science*, *36*(1), 83–96.

Peck, J., & Shu, S. B. (2009). The effect of mere touch on perceived ownership. *Journal of Consumer Research*, *36*(3), 434–447.

Peck, J., & Shu, S. (2015). From tragedy to benefit of the commons: Increasing shared psychological ownership. In Kristin Diehl & Carolyn Yoon (eds), *Advances in Consumer Research Volume 43* (pp. 40–44). Duluth, MN: Association for Consumer Research.

Peck, J., Barger, V. A., & Webb, A. (2013). In search of a surrogate for touch: The effect of haptic imagery on perceived ownership. *Journal of Consumer Psychology, 23*(2), 189–196.

Perez, S. (2016). Amazon undercuts rivals with launch of new photo printing service, Amazon Prints. Retrieved from https://techcrunch.com/2016/09/22/amazon-undercuts-rivals-with-launch -of-new-photo-printing-service-amazon-prints/.

Pierce, J. L., & Jussila, I. (2010). Collective psychological ownership within the work and organizational context: Construct introduction and elaboration. *Journal of Organizational Behavior, 31*(6), 810–834.

Pierce, J. L., Jussila, I., & Cummings, A. (2009). Psychological ownership within the job design context: Revision of the job characteristics model. *Journal of Organizational Behavior, 30*(4), 477–496.

Pierce, J. L., Kostova, T., & Dirks, K. T. (2001). Toward a theory of psychological ownership in organizations. *Academy of Management Review, 26*(2), 298–310.

Pierce, J. L., Kostova, T., & Dirks, K. T. (2003). The state of psychological ownership: Integrating and extending a century of research. *Review of General Psychology, 7*(1), 84–107.

Poetz, M. K., & Schreier, M. (2012). The value of crowdsourcing: Can users really compete with professionals in generating new product ideas? *Journal of Product Innovation Management, 29*(2), 245–256.

Prahalad, C. K., & Ramaswamy, V. (2004). Co-creation experiences: The next practice in value creation. *Journal of Interactive Marketing, 18*(3), 5–14.

Ramaswamy, V., & Gouillart, F. (2010). Building the co-creative enterprise. *Harvard Business Review, 88*(October), 100–109.

Ramaswamy, V., & Ozcan, K. (2016). Brand value co-creation in a digitalized world: An integrative framework and research implications. *International Journal of Research in Marketing, 33*(1), 93–106.

Ratner, R. K., & Kahn, B. E. (2002). The impact of private versus public consumption on variety-seeking behavior. *Journal of Consumer Research, 29*(2), 246–257.

Richins, M. L. (1994). Valuing things: The public and private meanings of possessions. *Journal of Consumer Research, 21*(3), 504–521.

Rodas, M. A., & John, D. R. (2020). The secrecy effect: Secret consumption increases women's product evaluations and choice. *Journal of Consumer Research, 46*(6), 1093–1109.

Roggeveen, A. L., Tsiros, M., & Grewal, D. (2012). Understanding the co-creation effect: When does collaborating with customers provide a lift to service recovery? *Journal of the Academy of Marketing Science, 40*(6), 771–790.

Romani, S., Grappi, S., Zarantonello, L., & Bagozzi, R. P. (2015). The revenge of the consumer: How brand moral violations lead to consumer anti-brand activism. *Journal of Brand Management, 22*(8), 658–672.

Rouse, E. D. (2020). Where you end and I begin: Understanding intimate co-creation. *Academy of Management Review, 45*(1), 181–204.

Schau, H. J., Muñiz, A. M., & Arnould, E. J. (2009). How brand community practices create value. *Journal of Marketing, 73*(5), 30–51.

Schreier, M., Fuchs, C., & Dahl, D. W. (2012). The innovation effect of user design: Exploring consumers' innovation perceptions of firms selling products designed by users. *Journal of Marketing, 76*(5), 18–32.

Sedikides, C. (1993). Assessment, enhancement, and verification determinants of the self-evaluation process. *Journal of Personality and Social Psychology, 65*(2), 317–338.

Sembada, A. (2018). The two sides of empowering consumers to co-design innovations. *Journal of Services Marketing, 32*(1), 8–18.

Shields, A. B., & Johnson, J. W. (2016). What did you do to my brand? The moderating effect of brand nostalgia on consumer responses to changes in a brand. *Psychology & Marketing, 33*(9), 713–728.

Shu, S. B., & Peck, J. (2011). Psychological ownership and affective reaction: Emotional attachment process variables and the endowment effect. *Journal of Consumer Psychology, 21*(4), 439–452.

Shu, S. B., & Peck, J. (2018). Solving stewardship problems with increased psychological ownership. In J. Peck & S. Shu (eds), *Psychological Ownership and Consumer Behavior* (pp. 227–237). New York: Springer.

Steenkamp, J. B. E. M. (2020). Global brand building and management in the digital age. *Journal of International Marketing, 28*(1), 13–27.

Strahilevitz, M. A., & Loewenstein, G. (1998). The effect of ownership history on the valuation of objects. *Journal of Consumer Research, 25*(3), 276–289.

Suessenbach, S., & Kamleitner, B. (2018). Psychological ownership as a facilitator of sustainable behaviors. In J. Peck & S. Shu (eds), *Psychological Ownership and Consumer Behavior*. New York: Springer, pp. 211–225.

Swaminathan, V., Sorescu, A., Steenkamp, J.-B. E. M., O'Guinn, T. C. G., & Schmitt, B. (2020). Branding in a hyperconnected world: Refocusing theories and rethinking boundaries. *Journal of Marketing, 84*(2), 24–46.

Thaler, R. H. (1980). Toward a positive theory of consumer choice. *Journal of Economic Behavior & Organization, 1*(1), 39–60.

Tierney, K. D., Karpen, I. O., & Westberg, K. (2016). Brand meaning cocreation: Toward a conceptualization and research implications. *Journal of Service Theory and Practice, 26*(6), 911–932.

van den Bos, M., Cunningham, S. J., Conway, M. A., & Turk, D. J. (2010). Mine to remember: The impact of ownership on recollective experience. *Quarterly Journal of Experimental Psychology, 63*(6), 1065–1071.

Vargo, S. L., & Lusch, R. F. (2004). Evolving to a new dominant logic for marketing. *Journal of Marketing, 68*(1), 1–17.

von Hippel, E. (2007). Horizontal innovation networks—By and for users. *Industrial and Corporate Change, 16*(2), 293–315.

von Hippel, W., & Trivers, R. (2011). The evolution and psychology of self-deception. *Behavioral and Brain Sciences, 34*(1), 1–16.

von Wallpach, S., Hemetsberger, A., & Espersen, P. (2017). Performing identities: Processes of brand and stakeholder identity co-construction. *Journal of Business Research, 70*(January), 443–452.

Wangenheim, F. v., & Bayón, T. (2007). The chain from customer satisfaction via word-of-mouth referrals to new customer acquisition. *Journal of the Academy of Marketing Science, 35*(2), 233–249.

Watts, D. J., & Dodds, P. S. (2007). Influentials, networks, and public opinion formation. *Journal of Consumer Research, 34*(4), 441–458.

Webster, J., Brown, G., Zweig, D., Connelly, C. E., Brodt, S., & Sitkin, S. (2008). Beyond knowledge sharing: Withholding knowledge at work. In J. M. Joseph (ed.), *Research in Personnel and Human Resources Management* (Vol. 27, pp. 1–37). Bingley, UK: Emerald Group Publishing Limited.

Weijo, H., Bean, J., & Rintamäki, J. (2019). Brand community coping. *Journal of Business Research, 94*(January), 128–136.

Weiss, L., & Johar, G. V. (2013). Egocentric categorization and product judgment: Seeing your traits in what you own (and their opposite in what you don't). *Journal of Consumer Research, 40*(1), 185–201.

White, K., & Argo, J. J. (2009). Social identity threat and consumer preferences. *Journal of Consumer Psychology, 19*(3), 313–325.

Winterich, K. P., Reczek, R. W., & Irwin, J. R. (2017). Keeping the memory but not the possession: Memory preservation mitigates identity loss from product disposition. *Journal of Marketing, 81*(5), 104–120.

Ye, Y., & Gawronski, B. (2016). When possessions become part of the self: Ownership and implicit self-object linking. *Journal of Experimental Social Psychology, 64*(May), 72–87.

Zhang, Y., Feick, L., & Price, L. J. (2006). The impact of self-construal on aesthetic preference for angular versus rounded shapes. *Personality and Social Psychology Bulletin, 32*(6), 794–805.

Zhou, X., Wildschut, T., Sedikides, C., Shi, K., & Feng, C. (2012). Nostalgia: The gift that keeps on giving. *Journal of Consumer Research*, *39*(1), 39–50.

# PART IV

# ETHICAL IMPLICATIONS OF BRAND CO-CREATION

# 15. The universal moral standards and the ethics of co-creation[1]

*Sumire Stanislawski*

## 1. INTRODUCTION

With the internet's evolution "from simple information retrieval to interactivity, interoperability, and collaboration" (Campbell et al., 2011, p. 87), relationships between brands and consumers have changed irrevocably. Consumers are increasingly participating in the value creation process in previously unimaginable ways (Hoyer et al., 2010), ranging from submitting design ideas for new products to creating viral hashtags to punish "bad" brands. Consumers now have increased access to means of production and distribution—blurring conventional boundaries between producers and consumers (Cova et al., 2011; Kotler, 1986; Prahalad & Ramaswamy, 2000). Consumer participation in brand co-creation is now a reality that all brands must learn to navigate.

Co-creation brings unique ethical challenges, especially as it is often practiced on digital platforms where consumers' ethical concerns are highly common (Nadeem et al., 2019). Though co-creation is becoming more widespread, its ethical issues have yet to be sufficiently addressed as will be seen throughout this chapter. This chapter investigates the ethics of co-creation by applying Schwartz's "universal moral standards for corporate codes of ethics" (2002) to examine current practices in the marketplace and make recommendations toward ethically navigating the complexities of brand co-creation.

## 2. BACKGROUND

### 2.1 Marketing Ethics

Marketing ethics is defined as "the systematic study of how moral standards are applied to marketing decisions, behaviours, and institutions" (Murphy et al., 2005, p. 17). Areas covered by marketing ethics research are wide-ranging, including: functional areas (such as product-related issues), subdisciplines of marketing (such as internet-related issues), and specific ethics-related topics (such as vulnerable consumer-related issues) (Nill & Schibrowsky, 2007). Laczniak and Murphy (2019) argue for the importance of including both positive and normative thinking in marketing ethics and customer–brand relationships. To this end, this chapter will not only describe what is occurring in today's marketplace (positive), but will also apply ethical values and make recommendations on how co-creation ought to work (normative).

There are various approaches to analyzing marketing ethics, including: stakeholder-oriented, process-oriented (e.g., advertising), and value-oriented (Brenkert, 2008; Maignan et al., 2005). Though each approach is useful, no one approach is comprehensive due to the variety and complexity of ethical issues. As such, this chapter will use aspects from all three approaches, but will be organized under a value-based framework: Schwartz's "universal moral standards for corporate codes of ethics." This code of ethics was developed based on extensive review of: (1) employees; (2) company codes of ethics; (3) global codes of ethics; and (4) the business ethics literature (Schwartz, 2002), and aimed to identify moral values that "retain their significance despite differences in culture, religion, time, and circumstance" (Schwartz, 2005, p. 31). Areas of convergence of these four sources were articulated into six universal moral standards: trustworthiness, respect, responsibility, fairness, caring, and citizenship. Note that responsibility, fairness, respect, and citizenship are found in the "Statement of Ethics" of the American Marketing Association (AMA). AMA also mentions honesty and transparency, encompassed by trustworthiness in Schwartz's standards. In addition, AMA's stated goal to "do no harm" points toward their embracement of caring (AMA, n.d.). This indicates the appropriateness of using Schwartz's universal moral standards in a marketing context.

## 2.2    Co-creation

As indicated by Ramaswamy and Ozcan (2018), there is little consensus on the definition of "co-creation" in literature as seen through multiple reviews. For example, Lusch and Vargo (2006) recognize two components to value co-creation: co-creation of value and co-production. In terms of co-creation of value, they contend that "value can only be created with and determined by the user in the 'consumption' process and through use or what is referred to as value-in-use. Thus, it occurs at the intersection of the offerer and the customer over time" (p. 284). Co-production is seen as subordinate to this and is defined as "participation in the creation of the core offering itself. It can occur through shared inventiveness, co-design, or shared production of related goods, and can occur with customers and any other partners in the value network" (p. 284). Yet, it is common in the literature to use the term "co-creation" for what Lusch and Vargo call "co-production" (O'Hern & Rindfleisch, 2009; Prahalad & Ramaswamy, 2004), and some use "co-production" and "co-creation" interchangeably (Gebauer et al., 2010).

Though the term "co-creation" is used throughout this chapter, it is used primarily to discuss "co-production" as Lusch and Vargo conceptualize it. Additionally, the focus will be on co-creation that utilizes digital platforms where the intensity of consumer participation is relatively high (Kalaignanam & Varadarajan, 2006). This is counter to a broader concept of participation where passive involvement is included (Voorberg et al., 2015), and follows the view of Schau et al. (2018) that "the creation of value by consumers needs to be more thoroughly investigated, including the extremes and the enablers of coproduction" (p. 98). Also, it is thought that choosing more "tangible" instances of co-creation will help readers envision "fuzzy" ethical issues more concretely.

To further narrow the scope of inquiry, the actors studied are brands and their consumers, as they are the most visible co-creation actors in the marketplace and have been focused on in the marketing ethics literature (Schlegelmilch & Öberseder, 2010). While acknowledging the limits of the term "consumer" under co-creation where there is a blurring of roles between consumers and producers, this chapter will use it for simplicity's sake and also because of the lack of a suitable alternative to denote this actor in a practical way. This is in line with Schau et al. (2018) where "consumer" is used "to represent an individual actor (e.g., a person) who integrates resources to create value for him/herself, beyond a person who makes purchase decisions (e.g., customer)" (p. 111).

# 3. UNIVERSAL MORAL STANDARDS IN CO-CREATION

The following sections combine past literature and marketplace examples of co-creation to investigate Schwartz's six universal moral standards in the context of co-creation. The purpose here is not to create an exhaustive list, but rather to raise awareness by exploring key issues. Though many of the raised issues can be studied against multiple moral standards, they have been simplified here in the interest of brevity.

## 3.1 Trustworthiness

Trust includes notions of honesty and reliability (Schwartz, 2002), and can be conceptualized as "existing when one party has confidence in an exchange partner's reliability and integrity" (Morgan & Hunt, 1994, p. 23). According to Brenkert (1997), trust was "discovered" by marketing in the 1960s and has become increasingly prominent. Discussions of trust in marketing tend to revolve around two key issues. One is the role of trust in various areas of marketing (e.g., in advertising). The second looks at trust as "something that is itself to be marketed," both explicitly and implicitly, to attract partners and consumers (e.g., offers of warranties) (Brenkert, 1997, p. 77).

From an ethical perspective, a key issue in co-creation is its creation of mutual dependency between brands and consumers. Because such deeper inter-dependency is still relatively new, norms surrounding how to navigate this complex relationship are still solidifying. Research has indicated that brands often must give up some degree of control when undertaking co-creation, particularly in new product development (NPD) (O'Hern & Rindfleisch, 2009; von Hippel, 2005). Thus, trust is indispensable in co-creation because brands and consumers need to be able to rely on each other to act with integrity.

To this end, co-creation platforms typically manage brand–user relationships through end-user agreements. However, such agreements tend to be overly long, complex, and written in legal terminology that most consumers do not understand (Pitta et al., 2003). This creates the "no-reading problem" where consumers "expect more favorable terms than they actually receive" (Ayres & Schwartz, 2014, p. 545). Moreover, such agreements often include language that agreements are "subject to change without notice." This is highly questionable in terms of trustworthiness, especially since many co-creation platforms have high switching costs and lock-in effects (Farrell & Klemperer, 2007; Haucap & Heimeshoff, 2014). Users of co-creation platforms often invest significant time and effort into building their presence and generating content, which leaves them vulnerable to any unilateral changes in user agreements.

Facebook,[2] a social networking site, has been accused of violating trust by changing privacy settings and terms of service without notice. In 2009, there was a public outcry when its terms were changed in a way that seemed to grant Facebook the right to user content perpetually and irrevocably—even after deletion (Walters, 2009). In 2019, US regulators approved a record $5 billion fine to settle an investigation into data privacy violations related to whether Facebook had violated a 2011 agreement under which it was required to clearly notify users and gain "express consent" to share data (Michaelidou et al., 2020). Though many are dissatisfied with such practices, people hesitate to terminate their relationship with Facebook because it dominates globally.[3] Such practices are problematic, and many are calling for changes in current practices related to end-user agreements (Ayres & Schwartz, 2014). Some recommendations include engaging in sincere stakeholder dialogue, making agreements more easily understandable, and stricter monitoring and punishment for violations.

The abovementioned recommendations are, in many regards, a call for increased transparency. Indeed, literature indicates trust is related to transparency, where more transparency leads to more trust (Kang & Hustvedt, 2014; Rawlins, 2008). Transparency can counter undermining of trust, and opens up "working procedures not immediately visible to those not directly involved in order to demonstrate the good working of an institution" (Moser, 2001, p. 3). Today, the internet and other digital systems play a key role in transparency (Meijer, 2009). As these systems enable companies to share information easily, consumers are demanding that companies do so in meaningful ways (Einwiller & Will, 2008).

One area where a lack of transparency can cause issues is electronic word of mouth (eWOM). As eWOM has become increasingly ubiquitous and influential in consumer decision-making (Chu & Kim, 2011), various ethically questionable practices have been observed. Some have obvious manipulative intent such as fake reviews (Luca & Zervas, 2016), while others' motives and credibility are more difficult to judge. One factor is that paid advertisements and eWOM can become hard to distinguish under co-creation. Though co-creators may not be paid directly for positive reviews, they are not neutral parties—feelings of pride or other such intrinsic motivations can influence them. While this is not necessarily an issue on its own, transparent disclosure of any such potential conflict of interest is crucial.

Today, there are growing questions regarding eWOM in the area of social media influencers. Generally, brands have often embraced influencers' ability to promote the brand and provide services to other consumers by freely sharing knowledge and advice (Smith et al., 2018). Yet, at the same time, brands can also struggle to manage influencers with the "growing trend for social media users to flex their social media muscle by labelling themselves brand ambassadors on social media … without explicit organizational recognition" (Smith et al., 2018, p. 7). Influencers wield influence because they are perceived as more real, relatable, approachable, and compelling to imitate (Jin et al., 2019, p. 568); yet, the "billion-dollar influencer marketing industry is largely uncharted territory" (Childers et al., 2019, p. 258). In response to such trends, the US Federal Trade Commission has created "Disclosures 101 for Social Media Influencers," which clarifies requirements to "make it obvious when you have a relationship ('material connection') with the brand. A 'material connection' to the brand includes a personal, family, or employment relationship or a financial relationship—such as the brand paying you or giving you free or discounted products or services" (Federal Trade Commission, 2019, p. 2). While this takes a step in the right direction toward developing appropriate norms of behavior, its narrow definition of "material connection" may not cover the various ways co-creation can create relationships with a brand.

## 3.2    Respect

Human rights are a central concern of respect (Schwartz, 2002), and labor rights are a major area of ethical concern in co-creation (Cova et al., 2011; Ritzer & Jurgenson, 2010). Dujarier (2016) identified three ways consumers are being put to work in today's marketplace: (1) directed self-production (an extension of self-service), (2) collaborative co-production (unpaid profit-making work), and (3) organization work (resolving contradictions of consumption), and demonstrated that consumers are assuming increasing share in productive and profitable tasks.

Cova and Dalli (2009) criticize the "extreme optimism" of some views of co-creation, and contend that while consumers participate in the value creation process through "immaterial labour and primary (direct) social relationships," it is the producer, and not the consumer, who receives revenue derived from the market (p. 316). Moreover, they argue that consumers pay "a 'price premium' for the fruits of their labour, as the use value provided by co-created commodities is said to be higher than that which can be achieved through standardised production's rationalised systems" leading to "double exploitation" (p. 327). However, Pongsakornrungsilp and Schroeder (2011) are critical of this view and contend that such double exploitation is "not necessarily a threat to consumers because it may instead enable them to play active roles in value co-creation and gain power against brand owners" (p. 303). Cochoy (2015) also challenges notions of naive and passively exploited consumers and argues that "presenting the opportunistic use of consumers' 'playful' or 'free' activities by market actors in terms of labor raises serious issues" (p. 149). While there is room for debate on whether consumers are exploited by—or are enjoying—co-creation, more discussion is needed on what obligations, if any, brands have to those whose labor they benefit from. Brands must consider how they can respectfully engage with consumers who "work" for them, but are not employees—especially as they increasingly capture value from co-created outcomes.

Another human right that must be respected in co-creation is the right to privacy (United Nations General Assembly, 1949). Goodwin (1991) defines consumers' right to privacy as "the consumer's ability to control (a) presence of other people in the environment during a market transaction or consumption behavior and (b) dissemination of information related to or provided during such transactions or behaviors to those who were not present" (p. 152). Of particular concern in co-creation is the safeguarding of confidential information obtained through the co-creation relationship.

Often, consumers are given access to co-creation platforms free of charge because profits are obtained by selling user data, especially for advertising (Ritzer & Jurgenson, 2010). This gives rise to a "privacy paradox" where "most users indicate they are concerned about their privacy, yet they share personal information widely" (Zurbriggen et al., 2016, p. 248). Users may feel it is impractical or impossible to opt out of the mass surveillance of these sites, and the inherent "power imbalance between the surveillor and the surveilled" exacerbates these issues (p. 258). Governments are becoming more sensitive to such matters, and Google's proposed takeover of Fitbit, a fitness tracking smartwatch, was probed by EU regulators due to concerns of whether this would give Google access to too much personal data (BBC News, 2020a). While some data sharing may be acceptable, transparency and good end-user agreements that comply with acceptable privacy norms and allow users to "manage privacy boundaries to achieve a balance between accessibility and retreat" are needed (Baruh et al., 2017, p. 26).

## 3.3    Responsibility

Responsibility includes notions of accountability (Schwartz, 2002). According to Mascarenhas (1995), morally responsible actors "commit themselves to a task and readily accept accountability for its success and failure. They enter into decisions and actions aware of their risk and potential, willing to be blamed if they are performed faultily, and rightfully claiming credit for their probity" (p. 45). Marketing literature on responsibility has focused on product safety with debate over the "scope, content, and limits of that duty" and how to manage tradeoffs between safety and price (Curlo, 1999, p. 38). When factoring in co-creation, the issue of product safety becomes even more complex. Who is responsible if co-created outcomes fail or cause harm? Can non-professional (and usually unpaid) co-creators be held responsible when their ability to make decisions with awareness of all associated risks and potentials is highly questionable? The balance of responsibility for co-created outcomes is an area that merits further delibera-tion. At the least, it is clear that brands ought to have discussions with co-creators regarding possible risks and potentials related to co-creation and its outcomes. This may include: edu-cating co-creators on product safety standards, rigorously testing co-designed offerings, and creating industry norms surrounding inclusion of co-creators in the value chain.

At the same time, one must acknowledge that consumers may not only be at fault through ignorance or negligence. Consumers are known to engage in ethically questionable—or even outright illegal—behaviors at times (Fukukawa, 2002; Fullerton & Punj, 2004; Reynolds & Harris, 2005). This gives rise to the question of how much onus can be placed on a brand to monitor and prevent unethical or illegal behaviors by their co-creators. For example, Google allows developers to build and sell custom watch faces for smartwatches using the Android mobile operating system (Google, n.d.). Though many use this platform to create original designs, there have also been issues with "pirated" smartwatch faces that mimic iconic face designs from established watch brands (Trademarks and Brands Online, 2015). While obvious infringements are taken down once reported, it can be difficult to judge designs that are not exact copies of the original, but which obviously take "inspiration" from them. While brands are clearly responsible to respond to stolen designs, it is questionable whether they can (or even ought to) take on the responsibility of determining the line between homage and copying.

Though consumers who engage in ethically questionable and illegal activities would be morally (and likely legally) responsible for any losses the firm or others may suffer, brands may be hesitant to pursue any legal claims against culpable co-creators. This is a thorny issue as the global nature of co-creation platforms makes it difficult and costly to prosecute across jurisdictions, and such pursuit may further damage the brand's reputation through negative press coverage.

Issues related to responsibility have also been playing out on social media platforms related to the idea of "fake news." Many strongly criticized Facebook for potentially influencing the outcome of the 2016 US presidential election by allowing fake news to proliferate (Allcott & Gentzkow, 2017). In response, Facebook updated their Facebook Audience Network adver-tisement policy, and Google also said it would ban websites that peddle fake news from using its online advertising service (*New York Times*, 2016). However, both platforms have been reluctant to take on the responsibility (and added costs) for monitoring all available content on its platforms. Additionally, monitoring opens these platforms up to accusations of censorship and bias, and questions continue on how such platforms can ethically conduct themselves.

Thus, questions remain on who is responsible for co-created outcomes and how this respon-sibility should be managed. A major point of consideration is balancing the feasibility (both in terms of time and cost) of reviewing co-created content—especially as co-creation tools and expressions multiply—against the necessity for due diligence and proactive monitoring of co-creator activities to prevent harm. Of note here is the argument that onerous burdens would unduly hamper brands from engaging in co-creation and stifle expression and innovation.

Brands must be aware of these issues and create codes of conduct to address such situations in ways that balance often-contradictory responsibilities.

## 3.4    Fairness

Fairness includes notions of process, impartiality, and equity (Schwartz, 2002), and consumer perceptions of fairness are based on "the seller and buyer receiv[ing] roughly proportional maximum outcomes relative to their minimal inputs" (Ingram et al., 2005, p. 240). An issue here is that relative inputs are often unclear in co-creation, while also requiring relatively higher inputs from consumers, including "monetary and non-monetary costs of time, resources, physical and psychological effort to learn and participate in the co-creation process" (Hoyer et al., 2010, p. 288).

Even as brands increasingly profit from co-creation, they commonly claim exclusive and royalty-free license to co-created content (Banks & Humphreys, 2008), while only offering "exposure" instead of monetary compensation to co-creators. For example, the Big Bang Racing video game had over eight million user-generated levels within two years of launch, while less than 0.0002 percent of levels in the game were created by the brand's employees (Pocket Gamer Biz, 2018). While the brand profits, users merely "receive social validation for their work in the form of likes and follows" (Pocket Gamer Biz, 2018). The ethicality of brands using their stronger market position to enforce such terms may be viewed as questionable from the stance of fairness, and is likely to see more debate as co-creation becomes increasingly common. In fact, brands are also beginning to raise questions related to the idea of "exposure" as a replacement for monetary payment due to incidences of social media influencers demanding "freebies" in exchange for positive reviews—or even to withhold negative ones—as their power in the marketplace increases (BusinessVibes, 2016).

At the same time, it needs to be recognized that various consumers have differing perceptions of fairness, and thus, varying expectations for the distribution of benefits of co-created outcomes (Banks & Humphreys, 2008; Gebauer et al., 2013). In fact, not all consumers wish to retain intellectual property rights, and some may prefer free revealing and creation of public goods (Alexy, 2009; von Hippel, 2005). To cater to such varied desires of co-creators, some brands offer different types of co-creation opportunities. For example, Threadless, a t-shirt co-creation platform where users submit designs for voting and commercialization, went from only having an "exposure" plus cash prize contest model to creating an option for artists to retain rights and receive royalties on each sale instead (Threadless, 2014). Another example is LEGO[4] and its Ideas website which allows customers to join "activities" (to show off LEGO builds for likes and feedback from the community), "contests" (to submit LEGO build ideas for a prize), and "product ideas" (to submit design ideas for potential commercialization and 1 percent of net sales) (LEGO Ideas, n.d.). Each of these categories of participation has differing levels of required inputs and potential outcomes, which consumers can choose based on their preferences. In order to create the right mix of such options, brands ought to have sustained dialogue with their co-creators to address fair allocation of value captured from co-created outcomes, as "a lack of consistency in intellectual property policies might create perceptions of unfairness among consumer contributors ... [and] create legal entanglements" (Hoyer et al., 2010, p. 289).

## 3.5    Caring

Caring involves avoiding unnecessary harm and helping others in need (Schwartz, 2002). The ethics of care stresses responding to others' needs, and emphasizes that the vulnerable require more care (Held, 2006). In this context, research in marketing has focused on targeting vulnerable consumers such as children, the elderly, and the poor (Schlegelmilch & Öberseder, 2010). When marketing to vulnerable populations, tensions can arise "when there is a question of whether the product is serving the distinct needs of a market or taking advantage of their particular vulnerability" (Abela & Murphy, 2008, p. 43). For example, people question whether children ought to be included in co-creation as they lack the capacity to make judgments regarding economic exchanges and are often unaware of legal rights (Brenkert, 1998), and cannot understand the full implications of end-user agreements, nor be able to make sound judgments to protect their privacy (Noyes, 2011). In fact, many brands have minimum age requirements or separate platforms for children, such as YouTube Kids that caters to children under 13 and "provides a more contained environment for kids to explore YouTube and makes it easier for parents and caregivers to guide their journey" (YouTube, n.d.).

Brenkert (1998) asserts, "Marketing to the vulnerable cannot simply look to consumer injury as the measure of unfair treatment of the vulnerable" (p. 7). Therefore, the ethical implications of access to co-creation platforms by vulnerable groups must be considered. Though there may not be direct injury from such exclusion, one can posit that the needs of the vulnerable will be unfairly overlooked if they lack access to co-creation opportunities—especially as NPD co-creation grows. In fact, it is known that co-creation can play a significant role in inclusive business models. For example, co-creation can help alleviate poverty by including the poor in the value chain (such as last-mile distribution), and by making goods and services accessible at an affordable price that reflect their unique needs (Goyal et al., 2015). This requires brands to demonstrate care as they engage with people, as "dignity can be (and sometimes already is) assured and promoted by deliberately including the poor into relevant value-added business processes" (Hahn, 2012, p. 47). As co-creation increasingly permeates the marketplace and influences available offerings, brands are likely to come under pressure to engage with vulnerable groups that have historically been underserved by offering co-creation opportunities as a form of corporate social responsibility.

This relates to the idea of treating consumers equally and without discrimination. Though co-creation may require some form of quality control or curation of content, brands must be respectful of all people and avoid making biased decisions regarding limiting access to co-creation opportunities—especially if this capitalizes on any lock-in effects. A recent case for concern is TikTok, a popular video-sharing app from China, which reportedly "instructed moderators to suppress posts created by users deemed too ugly, poor, or disabled for the platform ... [and] moderators were also told to censor political speech" (Biddle et al., 2020). From an ethical perspective, decisions to include or exclude users or content should be made in an unbiased manner without favoritism or prejudice—in essence maintaining impartiality of decisions. Furthermore, any criteria for inclusion or exclusion should be set forth in a clear manner. It is desirable that brands avoid even the appearance of using their position of advantage in a discriminatory manner.

## 3.6   Citizenship

Citizenship includes notions of obeying laws and positive contribution to society (Schwartz, 2002). In terms of obeying the law, intellectual property is again an area of contention (Grimes, 2006; Herman et al., 2006; O'Hern & Rindfleisch, 2009). Advancements in technologies have made it easy for people to pirate or reverse engineer brand offerings and share them widely across the globe. Though there have been some legal actions taken to counter this trend, it has been largely difficult for rights holders to track and sue individuals. For example, the U.S. music industry's strategy of suing individual consumers was highly controversial and did little to combat music piracy (McBride & Smith, 2008). Therefore, rights holders have shifted their target to co-creation platforms such as YouTube, an online video-sharing platform. In response to multiple lawsuits, YouTube enhanced their pages informing users about intellectual property and developed a Content ID system to check uploaded videos against a database of copyrighted materials (YouTube Help, n.d.). Social expectations are growing for brands engaging in co-creation to actively inform co-creators about pertaining laws and to structure their platforms in ways to curtail illegal acts. Yet, YouTube's Content ID system is not without controversy, with accusations that it allows for false or unfair claims that penalize innocent parties and stifle creativity (Boroughf, 2015).

Legal ambiguity also results from the borderless nature of co-creation platforms. As people from various countries access global platforms, differences in laws and customs can lead to ethical tensions. It may even be difficult for brands to recognize "illegal" behavior, as laws and their interpretation can differ significantly by country. Further complexity arises when particular laws are considered ethically questionable—such as those related to human rights. In such cases, brands may find themselves under pressure to not acquiesce to such laws on the one hand, and to respect national sovereignty on the other.

Twitter and other social media platforms are widely used across the globe to organize protests (Al-Jenaibi, 2016; Askanius & Uldam, 2011; Theocharis et al., 2015). Often protestors disobey laws as a form of civil disobedience, and governments may use this as a reason to restrict access to or to request information about "criminal" activities from platforms. Recently, various social media platforms announced that they will "pause" cooperation with police requests for user information in Hong Kong due to China's imposition of a new security law that is criticized as a breach of the 1985 Sino-British joint declaration treaty for transfer of sovereignty (BBC News, 2020b). How this will play out in the long term—especially considering the lucrativeness of the Chinese market—is yet to be seen. Though there is a strong argument that it is ethical for brands to support such "illegal" activities, they must carefully balance such support for human rights with respect for legal and cultural differences.

## 4.   CONCLUSION

Throughout this chapter, it has been illustrated that ethical issues in co-creation have yet to be sufficiently addressed, and that ethically questionable conduct by both brands and consumers is seen in today's marketplace. Table 15.1 summarizes these issues and the suggested recommendations raised in this chapter.

*Table 15.1    Universal moral standards and co-creation*

| Universal Moral Standards | Description | Issues in Co-Creation | Recommendations |
|---|---|---|---|
| Trustworthiness | Including notions of honesty, integrity, reliability, and loyalty | • Managing interdependent relationships<br>• Potential conflicts of interest | • Clear end-user agreements<br>• Transparent disclosures |
| Respect | Including notions of respect for human rights | • Use of "free" labor<br>• Right to privacy | • Discerning playful vs. exploitative work<br>• Meaningful options to manage privacy |
| Responsibility | Including notions of accountability | • Safety of co-created offering<br>• Unethical/illegal conduct by co-creators | • Creating industry norms for standards and practices<br>• Balancing monitoring vs. stifling expression and innovation |
| Fairness | Including notions of process, impartiality, and equity | • Fair distribution of benefits from co-creation | • Offering various options for benefit-sharing |
| Caring | Including notions of avoiding unnecessary harm | • Protecting children<br>• Access to co-creation by vulnerable populations<br>• Equal treatment without discrimination | • Age limits and "safe" spaces for children<br>• Providing access as CSR<br>• Clear inclusion/exclusion standards |
| Citizenship | Including notions of obeying laws and protecting the environment | • Intellectual property<br>• Legal and cultural differences | • Structuring platforms to curtail illegal acts<br>• Educating and monitoring co-creators<br>• Balancing moral stances vs. respecting national sovereignty |

*Source:* Adapted from Schwartz (2002, pp. 29–30).

Across the various given recommendations, it is seen that preventing ethical issues from arising is preferable to costly and time-consuming policing—especially as this is difficult to pursue across jurisdictions and can cause accusations of censorship or bias. To improve prevention, all actors engaged in co-creation must be made aware of its inherent ethical issues. However, awareness is only part of the solution, as ways to address these various complex issues are not always self-evident, especially to non-professional participants in co-creation. To this end, it is desirable that brands establish and implement clear guidelines and codes of conduct that go beyond general terms and conditions—which often are not even read as discussed earlier. When ethical issues do arise, brands should be transparent about such issues and immediately act to rectify the situation. High standards of ethical behavior and self-regulation by brands may also prevent the passage of overly burdensome laws that may not be flexible or adaptable enough to capture the dynamic nature of co-creation and rapidly changing technologies. Also, brands should keep in mind that they are in competition with other brands to attract the best co-creators. Thus, investing in building a reputation as a trustworthy and fair partner that treats co-creators with care and respect is likely to pay dividends in the long term. Proactive engagement in ethics will help create a positive environment for brands and consumers to engage in co-creation in a manner that increases well-being for themselves and for society at large.

This study is limited by its theoretical nature and its focus on particular actors (brands and consumers) and digital co-creation platforms. This, in turn, restricted the scope of ethical issues considered. It is also readily acknowledged that the various issues raised in this chapter were simplified for the sake of analysis, and, in reality, could have been analyzed against multiple moral standards. Additionally, given recommendations did not comprehensively address all raised issues, and continuous development of appropriate solutions by researchers and practitioners is desired. For future research, more empirical evidence on how brands and consumers perceive and react to various ethical issues in co-creation is also sought.

## NOTES

1.  This chapter is a substantially rewritten and updated version of a previously published article by the author. The first version of this paper appeared as: Stanislawski, S. (2011), "The Service-Dominant Logic of Marketing and the Ethics of Co-Creation," *The Bulletin of the Graduate School of Commerce, Waseda University*, Vol. 73, pp. 109–133.
2.  While Facebook enables other brands to participate in co-creation through its platform, Facebook itself is a brand that is heavily reliant on co-creation by its users. Facebook benefits its users by allowing them to easily create, disseminate, share, and follow content, while it captures the value created from such user-generated content. In this sense, the value of many social media brands can be understood as being derived from consumer co-creation activities where user participation in the platform comprises the core value proposition.
3.  Various alternatives to Facebook have been launched, but have had limited success despite their commitment to privacy. As Facebook has acquired Instagram, a photo and video-sharing app, in 2012, and WhatsApp, a messaging and voice over IP app, in 2014, their dominance has only increased.
4.  The author would like to acknowledge the reviewer for suggesting inclusion of this case.

## REFERENCES

Abela, A. V., & Murphy, P. E. (2008). Marketing with integrity: Ethics and the service-dominant logic for marketing. *Journal of the Academy of Marketing Science, 36*(1), 39–53.

Alexy, O. (2009). *Free Revealing: How Firms can Profit from Being Open.* Springer Science & Business Media.

Al-Jenaibi, B. (2016). The Twitter revolution in the Gulf countries. *Journal of Creative Communications, 11*(1), 61–83.

Allcott, H., & Gentzkow, M. (2017). Social media and fake news in the 2016 election. *Journal of Economic Perspectives, 31*(2), 211–236.

American Marketing Association. (n.d.). *Codes of Conduct | AMA Statement of Ethics.* https://www.ama.org/codes-of-conduct/ (accessed April 13, 2020).

Askanius, T., & Uldam, J. (2011). Online social media for radical politics: Climate change activism on YouTube. *International Journal of Electronic Governance, 4*(1/2), 69–84.

Ayres, I., & Schwartz, A. (2014). The no-reading problem in consumer contract law. *Stanford Law Review, 66*, 545–610.

Banks, J., & Humphreys, S. (2008). The labour of user co-creators: Emergent social network markets? *Convergence, 14*(4), 401–418.

Baruh, L., Secinti, E., & Cemalcilar, Z. (2017). Online privacy concerns and privacy management: A meta-analytical review. *Journal of Communication, 67*(1), 26–53.

BBC News (2020a, July 2). Google's Fitbit takeover probed by EU regulators. *BBC News Technology.* https://www.bbc.com/news/technology-53264058 (accessed July 3, 2020).

BBC News (2020b, July 8). Hong Kong: Facebook, Google and Twitter among firms "pausing" police help. *BBC News Technology*. https://www.bbc.com/news/technology-53308582 (accessed July 8, 2020).

Biddle, S., Ribeiro, P. V. & Dias, T. (2020, March 16). Invisible censorship: TikTok told moderators to suppress posts by "ugly" people and the poor to attract new users. *The Intercept*. https://theintercept .com/2020/03/16/tiktok-app-moderators-users-discrimination/ (accessed June 23, 2020).

Boroughf, B. (2015). The next great YouTube: Improving content ID to foster creativity, cooperation, and fair compensation. *Albany Law Journal of Science and Technology*, *25*(1), 95–127.

Brenkert, G. G. (1997). Marketing trust: Barriers and bridges. *Business & Professional Ethics Journal*, *16*(1/3), 77–98.

Brenkert, G. G. (1998). Marketing and the vulnerable. *The Ruffin Series of the Society for Business Ethics*, *1*, 7–20.

Brenkert, G. G. (2008). *Marketing Ethics*. Blackwell Publishing.

BusinessVibes (2016, March 7). 7 ways to save your brand from influencer blackmail. *Business 2 Community*. https://www.business2community.com/strategy/7-ways-save-brand-influencer -blackmail-01473242 (accessed June 28, 2020).

Campbell, C., Pitt, L. F., Parent, M., & Berthon, P. R. (2011). Understanding consumer conversations around ads in a Web 2.0 world. *Journal of Advertising*, *40*(1), 87–102.

Childers, C. C., Lemon, L. L. & Hoy, M. G. (2019). #Sponsored #Ad: Agency perspective on influencer marketing campaigns. *Journal of Current Issues & Research in Advertising*, *40*(3), 258–274.

Chu, S. C., & Kim, Y. (2011). Determinants of consumer engagement in electronic word-of-mouth (eWOM) in social networking sites. *International Journal of Advertising*, *30*(1), 47–75.

Cochoy, F. (2015). Consumers at work, or curiosity at play? Revisiting the presumption/value cocreation debate with smartphones and two-dimensional bar codes. *Marketing Theory*, *15*(2), 133–153.

Cova, B., & Dalli, D. (2009). Working consumers: The next step in marketing theory? *Marketing Theory*, *9*(3), 315–339.

Cova, B., Dalli, D., & Zwick, D. (2011). Critical perspectives on consumers' role as "producers": Broadening the debate on value co-creation in marketing processes. *Marketing Theory*, *11*(3), 231–241.

Curlo, E. (1999). Marketing strategy, product safety, and ethical factors in consumer choice. *Journal of Business Ethics*, *21*(1), 37–48.

Dujarier, M. A. (2016). The three sociological types of consumer work. *Journal of Consumer Culture*, *16*(2), 555–571.

Einwiller, S., & Will, M. (2008). Towards an integrated approach to corporate branding – Findings from an empirical study. *Corporate Communications: An International Journal*, *7*(2), 100–109.

Farrell, J., & Klemperer, P. (2007). Coordination and lock-in: Competition with switching costs and network effects. *Handbook of Industrial Organization*, *3*, 1967–2072.

Federal Trade Commission. (2019, November). *Disclosures 101 for Social Media Influencers*. FTC Guidance. https://www.ftc.gov/tips-advice/business-center/guidance/disclosures-101-social-media -influencers (accessed June 13, 2020).

Fukukawa, K. (2002). Developing a framework for ethically questionable behavior in consumption. *Journal of Business Ethics*, *41*, 99–119.

Fullerton, R. A., & Punj, G. (2004). Repercussions of promoting an ideology of consumption: Consumer misbehavior. *Journal of Business Research*, *57*(11), 1239–1249.

Gebauer, H., Johnson, M., & Enquist, B. (2010). Value co-creation as a determinant of success in public transport services. *Managing Service Quality: An International Journal*, *20*(6), 511–530.

Gebauer, J., Füller, J., & Pezzei, R. (2013). The dark and the bright side of co-creation: Triggers of member behavior in online innovation communities. *Journal of Business Research*, *66*(9), 1516–1527.

Goodwin, C. (1991). Privacy: Recognition of a consumer right. *Journal of Public Policy & Marketing*, *10*(1), 149–166.

Google (n.d.). *Build Watch Faces*. Android Developers Documentation Device Guides Overview. https://developer.android.com/training/wearables/watch-faces.

Goyal, S., Sergi, B. S., & Jaiswal, M. (2015). How to design and implement social business models for base-of-the-pyramid (BoP) markets? *European Journal of Development Research*, *27*(5), 850–867.

Grimes, S. M. (2006). Online multiplayer games: A virtual space for intellectual property debates? *New Media & Society, 8*(6), 969–990.

Hahn, R. (2012). Inclusive business, human rights and the dignity of the poor: A glance beyond economic impacts of adapted business models. *Business Ethics: A European Review, 21*(1), 47–63.

Haucap, J., & Heimeshoff, U. (2014). Google, Facebook, Amazon, eBay: Is the internet driving competition or market monopolization? *International Economics and Economic Policy, 11*(1/2), 49–61.

Held, V. (2006). *The Ethics of Care: Personal, Political, and Global.* Oxford University Press on Demand.

Herman, A., Coombe, R. J., & Kaye, L. (2006). Your second life? Goodwill and the performativity of intellectual property in online digital gaming. *Cultural Studies, 20*(2/3), 184–210.

Hoyer, W. D., Chandy, R., Dorotic, M., Krafft, M., & Singh, S. S. (2010). Consumer cocreation in new product development. *Journal of Service Research, 13*(3), 283–296.

Ingram, R., Skinner, S. J., & Taylor, V. A. (2005). Consumers' evaluation of unethical marketing behaviors: The role of customer commitment. *Journal of Business Ethics, 62*(3), 237–252.

Jin, S. V., Muqaddam, A., & Ryu, E. (2019). Instafamous and social media influencer marketing. *Marketing Intelligence & Planning, 37*(5), 567–579.

Kalaignanam, K., & Varadarajan, R. (2006). Customers as co-producers. In R. F. Lusch & S. L. Vargo (Eds.), *The Service-Dominant Logic of Marketing: Dialog, Debate, and Directions* (pp. 166–179). M. E. Sharpe.

Kang, J., & Hustvedt, G. (2014). Building trust between consumers and corporations: The role of consumer perceptions of transparency and social responsibility. *Journal of Business Ethics, 125*(2), 253–265.

Kotler, P. (1986). Prosumers: A new type of consumer. *The Futurist, 20*, 24–28.

Laczniak, G. R., & Murphy, P. E. (2019). The role of normative marketing ethics. *Journal of Business Research, 95*, 401–407.

LEGO Ideas (n.d.). *How It Works.* Lego Ideas Website. https://ideas.lego.com/howitworks (accessed November 6, 2020).

Luca, M., & Zervas, G. (2016). Fake it till you make it: Reputation, competition, and Yelp review fraud. *Management Science, 62*(12), 3412–3427.

Lusch, R. F., & Vargo, S. L. (2006). Service-dominant logic: Reactions, reflections and refinements. *Marketing Theory, 6*(3), 281–288.

Maignan, I., Ferrell, O. C., & Ferrell, L. (2005). A stakeholder model for implementing social responsibility in marketing. *European Journal of Marketing, 39*(9/10), 956–977.

Mascarenhas, O. A. (1995). Exonerating unethical marketing executive behaviors: A diagnostic framework. *Journal of Marketing, 59*(2), 43–57.

McBride, S., & Smith, E. (2008, December 19). Music industry to abandon mass suits. *Wall Street Journal, 19.*

Meijer, A. (2009). Understanding modern transparency. *International Review of Administrative Sciences, 75*(2), 255–269.

Michaelidou, N., Micevski, M., & Cadogan, J. W. (2020). Users' ethical perceptions of social media research: Conceptualisation and measurement. *Journal of Business Research*, https://doi.org/10.1016/j.jbusres.2020.03.005.

Morgan, R. M., & Hunt, S. D. (1994). The commitment–trust theory of relationship marketing. *Journal of Marketing, 58*(3), 20–38.

Moser, C. (2001). How open is "open as possible"? Three different approaches to transparency and openness in regulating access to EU documents. *HIS Political Science Series, 80*, 1–24.

Murphy, P. E., Laczniak, G. R., Bowie, N. E., & Klein, T. A. (2005). *Ethical Marketing: Basic Ethics in Action.* Prentice Hall.

Nadeem, W., Juntunen, M., Hajli, N., & Tajvidi, M. (2019). The role of ethical perceptions in consumers' participation and value co-creation on sharing economy platforms. *Journal of Business Ethics*, 1–21. https://doi.org/10.1007/s10551-019-04314-5.

*New York Times* (2016, November 14). Google and Facebook take aim at fake news sites. *New York Times.* http://nyti.ms/2ezMPpS (accessed April 16, 2020).

Nill, A., & Schibrowsky, J. A. (2007). Research on marketing ethics: A systematic review of the literature. *Journal of Macromarketing, 27*(3), 256–273.

Noyes, K. (2011, May 16). Nintendo 3DS targeted in anti-DRM campaign. *PC World.* https://www
.pcworld.com/article/227957/nintendo_3ds_targeted_in_anti_DRM_campaign.html (accessed June
23, 2020).

O'Hern, M. S., & Rindfleisch, A. (2009). Customer co-creation: A typology and research agenda. In N.
K. Malholtra (Ed.), *Review of Marketing Research, Vol. 6.* (pp. 84–106). M. E. Sharpe.

Pitta, D. A., Franzak, F., & Laric, M. (2003). Privacy and one-to-one marketing: Resolving the conflict.
*Journal of Consumer Marketing, 20*(7), 616–628.

Pocket Gamer Biz (2018, April 17). Why you should consider developing user-generated content-based
mobile games. *Pocket Gamer Biz Comment & Opinion.* https://www.pocketgamer.biz/comment
-and-opinion/67934/why-you-should-consider-developing-ugc-mobile-games/ (accessed November
6, 2020).

Pongsakornrungsilp, S., & Schroeder, J. E. (2011). Understanding value co-creation in a co-consuming
brand community. *Marketing Theory, 11*(3), 303–324.

Prahalad, C. K., & Ramaswamy, V. (2000). Co-opting customer competence. *Harvard Business Review,
78*(1), 79–87.

Prahalad, C. K., & Ramaswamy, V. (2004). Co-creation experiences: The next practice in value creation.
*Journal of Interactive Marketing, 18*(3), 5–14.

Ramaswamy, V., & Ozcan, K. (2018). What is co-creation? An interactional creation framework and its
implications for value creation. *Journal of Business Research, 84,* 196–205.

Rawlins, B. R. (2008). Measuring the relationship between organizational transparency and employee
trust. *Public Relations Journal, 2*(2), 1–21.

Reynolds, K. L., & Harris, L. C. (2005). When service failure is not service failure: An exploration of
the forms and motives of "illegitimate" customer complaining. *Journal of Services Marketing, 19*(5),
321–335.

Ritzer, G., & Jurgenson, N. (2010). Production, consumption, prosumption: The nature of capitalism in
the age of the digital "prosumer". *Journal of Consumer Culture, 10*(1), 13–36.

Schau, H. J., Muñiz, A. M., Jr., & Akaka, M. A. (2018). The cocreation of brands. In S. L. Vargo & R. F.
Lusch (Eds.), *The SAGE Handbook of Service-Dominant Logic* (pp. 97–117). Sage.

Schlegelmilch, B. B., & Öberseder, M. (2010). Half a century of marketing ethics: Shifting perspectives
and emerging trends. *Journal of Business Ethics, 93*(1), 1–19.

Schwartz, M. S. (2002). A code of ethics for corporate code of ethics. *Journal of Business Ethics,
41*(1/2), 27–43.

Schwartz, M. S. (2005). Universal moral values for corporate codes of ethics. *Journal of Business Ethics,
59*(1/2), 27–44.

Smith, B. G., Kendall, M. C., Knighton, D., & Wright, T. (2018). Rise of the brand ambassador:
Social stake, corporate social responsibility and influence among the social media influencers.
*Communication Management Review, 3*(1), 6–29.

Theocharis, Y., Lowe, W., Van Deth, J. W., & García-Albacete, G. (2015). Using Twitter to
mobilize protest action: Online mobilization patterns and action repertoires in the Occupy Wall
Street, Indignados, and Aganaktismenoi movements. *Information, Communication & Society, 18*(2),
202–220.

Threadless (2014, March 4). *Design Challenge Submission Legal Terms & Conditions.* Threadless Legal.
https://www.threadless.com/geekchic/legal/ (accessed June 13, 2020).

Trademarks and Brands Online (2015, February 27). Time to wise up: Watch face designs and IP
infringement. *Trademarks and Brands Online.* https://www.trademarksandbrandsonline.com/article/
luxury-brands-keeping-a-close-watch (accessed November 6, 2020).

United Nations General Assembly (1949). *Universal Declaration of Human Rights* (Vol. 3381).
Department of State, United States of America.

von Hippel, E. (2005). *Democratizing Innovation.* The MIT Press.

Voorberg, W. H., Bekkers, V. J., & Tummers, L. G. (2015). A systematic review of co-creation and
co-production: Embarking on the social innovation journey. *Public Management Review, 17*(9),
1333–1357.

Walters, C. (2009, February 15). Facebook's new terms of service: "We can do anything we want
with your content. Forever." *Consumerist.* http://consumerist.com/2009/02/facebooks-new-terms-of
-service-we-can-do-anything-we-want-with-your-content-forever.html (accessed June 23, 2020).

YouTube (n.d.). An app made just for kids. *YouTube Kids*. https://www.youtube.com/kids/ (accessed November 7, 2020).

YouTube Help (n.d.). Copyright and rights management. *YouTube Help Center*. https://support.google.com/youtube/topic/2676339 (accessed June 1, 2020).

Zurbriggen, E. L., Ben Hagai, E., & Leon, G. (2016). Negotiating privacy and intimacy on social media: Review and recommendations. *Translational Issues in Psychological Science, 2*(3), 248–262.

# 16. Co-creation of conscientious corporate brands – facilitating societal change towards sustainability: a structured literature analysis

*Christine Vallaster and Philip Lechner*

## 1. INTRODUCTION

Society is facing increasing pressure to address major issues including climate change, biodiversity loss, limited resources, and social inequality (Beltramello et al., 2013; European Commission, 2019). During the Covid-19 pandemic, an increasing number of corporate brands have made it their task to contribute to solving social and ecological problems like these.

Companies that tackle these challenges have been found to have higher levels of customer loyalty, resulting in increased brand equity and reputation (Naidoo and Abratt, 2018; Pritchard and Wilson, 2018). Although companies are not legally bound to operate within the parameters of responsible brand positioning, there appears to be an increasing amount of them that not only focus on maximizing profits, but on social and/or ecological value creation as well. Examples of these kinds of corporate brands include the B-Corp (https://bcorporation.net[1]) certified outdoor clothing company Patagonia Inc. In addition to fair and resource-saving production methods, as well as the use of recycling and upcycling, Patagonia sees itself as an ambassador of social change and protector of the planet, pursuing these values through publicity and political activity (Patagonia, 2020). These activities – along with many other actions coordinated with several stakeholders – result in strong associations with the corporate brand Patagonia (Kemming and Mattias, 2019). The idea that corporate brands are the continuous product of socially interactive and therefore co-creative processes is based on the service-dominant logic developed by Vargo and Lusch (2006, 2008, 2016). Interactive and communicative processes with a corporate brand are "strategic" in the sense that they shape a corporate brand's mission, vision, goals, and objectives (cf. Bhattacharya et al., 2009), allowing branded organizations and their stakeholders to jointly decide on what they want to achieve and how (cf. Biraghi and Gambetti, 2013; Hillebrand et al., 2015; Merz et al., 2009).

Authors like Iglesias and Ind (2020) or Rindell et al. (2011) define corporate brands that want to live out sustainability and strong ethics as *conscientious corporate brands* (see also the expression "brands that do good" by Naidoo and Abratt, 2018 and Roper et al., 2018). Through their actions and communication, conscientious corporate brands (CCBs) communicate their responsible orientation and make their defined conscious brand identity visible and experienceable (Mast, 2016). At the core of the corporate brand is its identity which is co-created

via four different, yet interrelated performances: communicating; internalizing; contesting; and elucidating. *Communicating* involves the activities performed by stakeholders in transmitting the corporate brand identity; *internalizing* concerns the activities performed to bring the brand identity to life; *contesting* is a comparative process by which stakeholders confront the corporate brand identity with their perceptions; *elucidating* involves activities performed by stakeholders to develop an evolved shared understanding of the corporate brand. (Iglesias and Ind, 2020, p. 711)

In this chapter we argue that these co-creative corporate branding processes have the power to facilitate a societal transformation towards increased/better sustainability. Sustainability in this context refers to achieving the triple bottom line, that is addressing people, planet, and profit objectives (Jonker et al., 2011). These goals are, however, at least partially in contradiction to how marketing and corporate branding are commonly perceived as primary drivers of over-consumption, that is they encourage people to consume products they do not really need (Schaefer and Crane, 2005). Here, brands are often depicted as attempting to (mis-)use the sustainability idea to generate profit, undermining sustainability as a result (Moisander et al., 2010). Therefore, there is reason to contest that if CCBs are perceived as agents working towards increased sustainability, then this process requires a delicate and effective handling of the four above-mentioned co-creative corporate branding processes. It is widely unclear how these co-creative processes actually contribute to facilitating a societal transformation that achieves real sustainability. Based on a structured literature analysis, we discuss the challenges that CCBs face in their role when managing co-creative processes, and as agents towards a more sustainable society.

## 2.    SETTING THE STAGE: CONSCIENTIOUS CORPORATE BRANDS (CCBS) AND CO-CREATION PROCESSES

Conscientious corporate brands (CCBs) define and embrace a transformative purpose through a set of guiding principles that relate to the triple bottom line of profit–people–planet (Iglesias and Ind, 2016; Iglesias et al., 2020). By meeting these objectives, CCBs are faced with the paradoxical effort to maneuver between value protection (i.e. generating profit) and value generation (i.e. creating social and/or ecological value). The understanding that brands and their meanings emerge through continuous social interactions and practices among multiple, networked stakeholders (Hatch and Schultz, 2010; Merz et al., 2009) has evolved in the relevant literature. Adopted from the service-dominant logic developed by Vargo and Lusch (2006, 2008, 2016), corporate brands are defined as dynamic social interactive processes involving a multiplicity of stakeholders (Hillebrand et al., 2015; Merz et al., 2009), that is, "any individual or group inside or outside the organization that shows an interest in a brand and actively participates in brand-related discourse" (Vallaster and von Wallpach, 2013, pp. 1506–1507). In line with recent branding literature, these interactive branding processes are "co-creative" in the sense that they consist of ongoing discourses among multiple stakeholders (also termed "multi-log" (Vallaster and von Wallpach, 2013, p. 1506)). This kind of co-creation requires access to and transparency of information regarding company-internal processes and structures (Hatch and Schultz, 2010). Interactive branding processes shape a corporate brand's vision and objectives (Bhattacharya et al., 2009), and allow organizations and their stakeholders to jointly agree on what they want to achieve and how (Biraghi and Gambetti, 2013; see also Vallaster and von Wallpach, 2018).

Strong corporate brands like Patagonia or other certified B-corps (www.bcorporation.net) aim to facilitate a societal and economic change towards (among many things) operating within the planet's finite resources, and leveraging social inequality. Authors that discuss branding have come up with the terminology of *conscientious brands* (Iglesias and Ind, 2020), a term which we use in the following. Claims or missions such as "Tastes good, does good" by the B-corp-certified company Innocent Drinks are rooted (so to speak) in their corporate DNA, and align their internal capabilities and operations with a strong ethical strategic positioning, all of which is manifested by the organization's distinctive capabilities (Rindell et al., 2011). Achieving this means that the purpose and principles need to be lived out by the corporate brand's employees, that is internal stakeholders, they are also ideally adopted by its external stakeholders as well (Iglesias and Ind, 2020). One notable pitfall here is how it is these kinds of communicative actions and stories connected to the idea of sustainability that can potentially evoke cynical reactions by the people attempting to live out these values. In other words, if sustainability is at the core of a corporate brand, and the identity of the organization is not consistent with what they promise, this can cause misperceptions and mistrust on behalf of the stakeholders and in the eyes of consumers (Iglesias et al., 2020). For instance, the ice cream company Ben and Jerry's uses fair trade and organic ingredients along its entire value chain, and contributes part of its profits to support local groups or those in need (Ben and Jerry's, 2020). What many consumers might not know, however, is that they also are in the hands of Unilever, a large British multinational consumer goods company. Consumers here might question how sustainability can be lived out and implemented into operational processes within a corporation of this size. After all, and at least from the consumers' perspective, this retail business model aims at optimal efficiency, perhaps with no room for extra costs arising from fair trade raw materials or sustainable packaging. Perhaps their supply chains are perceived as too complex, with any number of additional boundaries that might achieve only semi-sustainable actions, or business practices that are not sustainable at all (Parguel et al., 2011). This kind of critical questioning and reflection by stakeholders is part of the co-creational branding processes, potentially hindering the sustainability efforts by corporate brands.

The context of conscientious corporate brands (CCBs) is special because they follow three, partly competitive objectives: protecting value (profit-oriented) while at the same time generating social and/or ecological value creation. This tripartite arrangement increases the complexity and dynamics of co-creational processes, leaving much room to discuss whether CCBs have a role to play in fostering changes towards a society that understands the urgency of protecting limited planetary resources. In this chapter we provide a structured literature analysis with the aim to better understand the mechanisms and specifics that drive co-creational processes of CCBs, helping to better understand their role in a changing society. Also, we aim to better understand the value that these co-creative processes offer in shifting a society towards one that is more in line with planetary resource limits.

## 3.    METHODOLOGY

This chapter is based on secondary research using a structured literature research method (Kornmeier, 2007). While research on the processes of co-creation of (corporate) brands is growing (e.g. Merz et al., 2009; Vallaster and von Wallpach, 2013), the context of CCBs is different, as is the case with the co-creative processes of *communication, internalizing, contesting,* and *elucidating.* This chapter therefore aims to provide a thorough overview of related topics and frameworks proposed in the academic literature. According to Pittaway et al. (2014), framing a question to guide the inclusion and exclusion of articles during the review process is a key aspect of a structured literature review. The selected articles aimed to answer: *What are the specifics of co-creative processes of CCBs (i.e. what are their characteristics, and how do they function?),* and *How do these co-creative processes contribute in shifting a society towards one that sustainably uses limited planetary resources?*

We followed the procedure developed by Tranfield et al. (2003), commencing with a thematically designed keyword search (Lamé, 2019). Along with branding literature that adopts a co-creative perspective (using keywords like "corporate (conscientious) brand" and "co-creation/co-creative"), we screened entrepreneurship literature referring specifically to "sustainable", "green", "social", "eco" or "impact" + "entrepreneur(ship)" in their respective titles. The initial search was intentionally kept broad to avoid skipping any relevant articles articulating the concept of CCBs and co-creation, but not containing any of the keywords. In a second step, we checked whether the content of the articles was related to issues within the area of sustainability. Hence, the main selection criteria were the context of the search terms and journal ranking. We then expanded into organizational literature dealing with a "hybridity" and "political" or "communicative" perspective. Box 16.1 shows the keywords we used for this literature review, as well as the research process.

## BOX 16.1 LITERATURE RESEARCH – PROCEDURE AND SELECTION CRITERIA

**Databases:**

ScienceDirect, Springer Gabler, EBSCOhost

**Keywords:**

"brand co-creation", "conscientious (corporate) brands", "corporate political action/activity", "ethical (corporate) brands", "greenwashing", "brand communication", "hybrid organization", "responsible (corporate) brands", "social enterprise", "sustainable enterprise", "social/eco/impact entrepreneurship"

**Language:**

English and German

**Publishing years:**

2005–2020

**Selection criteria:**

Journals listed in the VHB-JOURQUAL with C-Level or higher peer reviewed articles; books and e-books; works from the field of business administration

**Analysis procedure:**

Title → Abstract → Full text

Applying the keywords, 1,231 sources were identified in the first step. The titles were then used as a selection criterion, with 125 sources remaining as a result. Sixty-one sources were available for a full text analysis following a further examination of the abstracts. These 61 titles were used for conceptual explanations. The content was specifically examined with regard to the concepts of "communicating", "internalizing", "contesting", and "elucidating".

For our data collection, only journals with at least a C-Level on the VHB JOURQUAL were used (Bouncken et al., 2015). Moreover, to avoid already outdated literature in the literature analysis, the focus was set on sources published in 2005 and later, a timeframe matching the evolution of the brand co-creation concept. We conducted the literature research between July and September 2020, and were able to identify 1,231 resources in the manner described. To manage the identified sources, a reduction process was carried out by classifying the title, followed by reading the abstracts and an examination of the full texts to decide whether the source was suitable (Booth et al., 2016). A full-text analysis of the remaining 61 sources was carried out by reading paragraphs and aligning the content with the research question.

## 4.    FINDINGS: CO-CREATIONAL CCB PROCESSES

The co-creational processes of CCBs are laid out in the following, evaluating their potential to shift society towards greater sustainability. Table 16A.1 in the Appendix lists the academic contributions we chose, singling out the identified co-creational processes as they relate to *communicating, internalizing, contesting,* and *elucidating*.

### 4.1    Moving Beyond Communication: Political Statements and Their Co-creative Power

Brand communication and sustainability have become increasingly important in the public discourse (Ind and Horlings, 2016). CCBs have discovered their purpose, providing arguments about why they do what they do to emotionally reach their target groups and motivate them to act (Biraghi and Gambetti, 2013). Messages that address socially and ecologically relevant topics have the potential to emotionally capture a growing segment of the market (Berrone et al., 2017; Lundqvist et al., 2013). For instance, with its claim and related advertisements, the UK brand Innocent Drinks (of which Coca-Cola holds a 90% stake) reminds people that even with small everyday life actions, people can do something good for themselves as well as for the environment and society (www.innocent.com). In Innocent's promotional "Chain of Good" video, protagonist Mark is seen shopping in the supermarket, deciding whether to set off a chain reaction by buying an Innocent product and supporting a family in Peru as a result, or buying the beverage of a non-sustainable competitor. Such communicative activities should nudge co-creative brand behavior, which could include talking favorably about the brand, increasing brand loyalty, or finally in responsible consumer purchasing.

A major issue with this kind of communication is that some activities might appear very detached from how management really behaves towards and deals with stakeholders. This could result in consumers reacting with cynicism and distrust, especially if they determine that "green" or "social" are being promised and communicated but not lived up to (Vallaster et al., 2012). This kind of co-creation decreases a CCB's authenticity and damages their sustainability efforts. Some CCBs take it one step further by launching messages championing their ideologies in the marketplace (Holt, 2016). One example of this includes Patagonia. Known for its strong environmentalist stance, it has included a special "Vote the Assholes Out" message on the labels of its recent range of shorts. As they have confirmed on Twitter, this is in line with the company's positioning, and similar kinds of communication have been adopted by other companies. For instance, Siemens' CEO has repeatedly launched statements against racism, supporting German chancellor Angela Merkel's immigration policies as a pushback against some German media outlets' negative reporting (https://www.welt.de/wirtschaft/article178507992/Joe-Kaeser-Siemens-Chef-lobt-Merkels-Fluechtlings-Deal.html). While this kind of communication has received extensive co-creative support, a more recent public discussion between the Siemens CEO and a German climate activist about climate change and the role of corporations actually backfired: a few days after the discussion, Siemens confirmed a deal to help develop a major coal mine in Australia (https://www.bbc.com/news/world-europe-51089468). This is a good example of the juggling co-creative act between economic and social/ecological interests, which might generate unclear, inconsistent company and sustainability co-creation, most notably when viewed through the eyes of consumers and other stakeholders.

## 4.2    The Paradoxical Nature of Internalizing

CCBs shape their business models around improving social or ecological challenges as they combine non-profit and for-profit elements (Haigh et al., 2015b), internalizing and co-creating a hybrid brand identity as a result by employees, suppliers or other major stakeholders.

The literature review describes "hybridity" as the idea of combining different business logics (Boyd, 2009), or as Battilana and Lee (2014) explain in an often-quoted sentence: "we introduce and develop the idea of hybrid organizing, which we define as the activities, structures, processes and meanings by which organizations make sense of and combine aspects of multiple organizational forms" (p. 398). Different types of hybridity are possible. For example, hybridity can combine different legal forms, use varying organizational logics (such as pursuing profit maximization *and* public benefit), or join different institutional identities (Battilana and Lee, 2014; Battilana et al., 2012). Often described as social enterprises, hybrid organizations move between non-profit and for-profit operations, and therefore co-create added value on an ecological and/or social level (Achleitner and Block, 2018; Haigh et al., 2015a; Hoffman, 2009; Jay, 2013; Pache and Santos, 2013). One example of this is the company manomama from Augsburg, Germany. While the heyday of the textile industry in Augsburg is long over, manomama is a textile producer whose business model has a key focus on sustainability. Founded in 2011 by Sina Trinkwalder, manomama offers disadvantaged people such as the mentally disabled or long-term unemployed an opportunity to work under permanent employment conditions at a regular wage of at least 10 euros per hour. The company's textiles are made exclusively of ecologically and regionally produced raw materials (manomama GmbH, 2020). In 2019, manomama GmbH had 140 employees, generating around 9 million euros in revenue (www.manomama.de). Hybrid companies are market-oriented, with a strong focus on delivering societal and/or ecological benefits (Atiq and Karatas-Ozkan, 2013). Done successfully, this is manifested in increasing co-creative interaction between traditional market-oriented activities and generally beneficial outcomes, with for-profit companies increasingly engaging in socially responsible activities. Under these conditions, non-profit organizations furthermore co-create their brand identity through carrying out a growing number of commercial activities to supplement their sources of funding (Battilana et al., 2012).

*Internalizing* refers to organizing structures in a way that allows the hybrid brand identity of CCBs' promises to be lived by employees. In hybrid settings, managerial tensions can arise when walking the line between profit creation and value creation for society (Vallaster and von Wallpach, 2018; Vallaster et al., 2019). Tensions might occur as a result of mission drift (Ramus and Vaccaro, 2017), difficulties in recruiting or hiring staff, or funding issues. For instance, CCBs that depict accountability as their brand's core element are often less attractive to traditional financial institutions because their strategic focus is not primarily on profit generation (Davies and Chambers, 2018). In terms of balancing these tensions and paradoxes while managing hybrids, authors like Vallaster et al. (2019) identify actual sets of practices through which tensions can be leveraged, including the capability of paradoxical framing, systems thinking, or building resilience. One example of this can be seen with the story of entrepreneur Hans-Dietrich Reckhaus, the founder of the company Reckhaus (www.reckhaus.com) that for 60 years has specialized in the development and manufacture of insect control products. His company shows the importance of building up the right capabilities to better navigate the contradictions and paradoxes triggered by an organization's hybrid nature, that is how a CCB's business approach extends beyond mere profit (Reckhaus and Baumgarth, 2020). About eight years ago, Reckhaus was asked "How much is a fly worth?" Reckhaus's business was killing insects. As he had never thought about their value before, this co-creative question about the corporate brand caught him by surprise. Together with the conceptual artists Frank and Patrik Riklin, he kicked off the "Save flies in Deppendorf" campaign that came to symbolize his change in thinking (www.fliegenretten.de). An organizational transformation commenced that continues to this day, with Reckhaus transforming from exterminator to the first lobbyist for insects and their habitat. The founder has since initiated and launched many new innovations, in one instance explaining that what matters is attitude before profit. So in this case, it appears that the identity of a (social) entrepreneur and/or their organization plays a significant role in leveraging conflicting thinking and the process of internalizing (current research lacks in-depth knowledge of this issue; a wealth of insightful findings are very likely here with future research).

### 4.3   Contesting – Co-creation through Stakeholders

As pointed out in the theoretical review, we follow the understanding that a wide variety of stakeholders in the brand ecosystem enact and co-create the brand identity of CCBs (von Wallpach et al., 2016). Hence, brand management is no longer a completely controlled process of articulating defined values and artifacts, but is instead a social, interactive process in which stakeholders develop and articulate values in their own manner, enacting their brand identity at the same time (Vallaster and von Wallpach, 2018). Research shows that CCBs embracing a hybrid, responsible brand identity, are attractive to consumers and specific market segments, allowing them the potential to grow (Bhattacharya et al., 2009; Markovic et al., 2018). Because of the increasing attractiveness found in this kind of activity, many other not yet sustainably conscious organizations have participated in this as well, bringing up another key aspect in this entire issue: far too many companies engage in what is widely labeled as *greenwashing* (Chan and Orazi, 2020). Next to legal loopholes, factors like reward-driven incentives (such as bonus payments or higher dividends), or simply an overestimation of the sustainability performance may facilitate greenwashing, de-constructing responsible CCB positioning (Delmas and Burbano, 2011). A famous example of this is seen with automaker VW. Historically known for excellent, emission-reducing engine technology, in 2015 it was revealed that VW had manipulated the software of 11 million diesel vehicles to achieve low emission test results that in actuality were above emission regulation levels during normal driving conditions (Chan and Orazi, 2020). Nevertheless, the company's sustainability report cast VW as a sustainability-oriented company, and claimed environmental accountability as part of its corporate culture. The media supported this image, ranking the company 16th among the "best global green brands" (Brodmerkel, 2015). This kind of co-construction by stakeholder groups de-constructs the core of CCB. For CCBs, "doing good for society" legitimizes their business vis-à-vis their stakeholders (Berrone et al., 2017; Iglesias et al., 2020). The literature shows that greenwashing leads to "increasing consumer cynicism and mistrust" (Jahdi and Acikdilli, 2009, p. 103), with many consumers automatically assuming greenwashing efforts any time sustainability is communicated (Moisander et al., 2010; Parguel et al., 2011). This "halo effect" represents an existential threat to CCBs (Cordano et al., 2010). If the public reacts cynically, that is co-creates negative brand meaning, and diminishes the importance of a company's social and/ or sustainable activities, it will be even more difficult for authentic CCBs to gain visibility and attractiveness. And if overall stakeholder interest declines, CCBs may not be able to maintain their business models at all (Delmas and Burbano, 2011).

### 4.4   Elucidating as Co-creational Political Activity

CCB activity is often described as corporate political action, that is deliberate activities aimed at legislators or decision-makers in government or politics (den Hond et al., 2014) to drive the achievement of corporate goals (Baysinger, 1984; Lux et al., 2011). Activities such as lobbying, campaign contributions, support of certain political candidates, political donations, or building relationships with politically relevant people (Baron, 1995; Spurgin, 2015; Weber, 1997) can benefit in a financial, social, or ecological way (Nalick et al., 2016; Weber, 1997). Through participation on a political level (referred to as *political activism*, cf. Carrasco Monteagudo and Buendía-Martínez, 2020), CCBs become agents of change (Lyon et al., 2018). Just one example of this is seen with German companies like Vaude (www.vaude.com) or einhorn.org (www.einhorn.org) who campaign for the development of a legal framework found with, for example, the German company form gGmbH, a market-orientated limited liability company that maintains an additional focus on public benefits (Weidmann and Kohlhepp, 2020). Public attention can be a considerable issue, serving as a driving factor towards a co-creative social transformation, and changing the competitive conditions for all actors. Hence, CCBs use their political ecosystems to exert influence (Oliver and Holzinger, 2008), while their brand identity is at the same time co-created by the relevant stakeholders who have a role model function (Spurgin, 2015) and help facilitate development towards a sustainable society.

Elucidating involves activities performed by stakeholders aiming to develop an evolving, shared understanding of CCBs (Iglesias and Ind, 2020). They are often perceived as representatives of certain stakeholder groups or community interests, stand up for them, and can even be part of them. As such, CCBs try to preserve these interests through business activity, hoping to trigger social change towards the shared beliefs between a CCB and its participating communities or stakeholder groups (Jahdi and Acikdilli, 2009; Wells and Anasti, 2019). An attempt is made here by all stakeholders to try to meet societal needs that cannot be sufficiently met by governments (Nissan et al., 2012) or the market (Demirel et al., 2019).

## 5.    IMPLICATIONS AND FURTHER RESEARCH

Our structured literature analysis revealed that an integrated perspective of different research streams is effective in helping understand the extent to which conscientious corporate brands take on greater social accountability and work to achieve better sustainability by initiating processes of co-creation. In particular, we looked at the co-creative processes laid out by Iglesias and Ind (2020), describing relevant knowledge of state-of-the-art literature outlined in the methods section.

CCBs stand up for their convictions and become political actors (Scherer and Palazzo, 2011). They are driven by ethical and moral issues anchored in their corporate brand identity, influence other companies and institutions that operate within their business sphere, and are triggered into action by changing norms, property rights, and governmental legislation (Pacheco et al., 2010) or societal interests. Along with communicating political statements, and with the paradoxical nature of internalizing and challenges by stakeholders in mind, CCBs importantly *elucidate* their co-creational processes, hoping to emerge as proactive actors in a transformational process as a result. They do this with the aim of building up a certain amount of pressure on stakeholders (Seelos and Mair, 2005) as they pay increasing attention to sustainable companies (Berrone et al., 2017).

The interests of society and today's communication/media environment affect the way CCBs present themselves and behave. CCBs also take part in the transformation of societal and political aspects themselves, with societal transformation potentially leading to changed competitive conditions due to the shifting interests of stakeholders (Zimmer and Obuch, 2017). Put differently, since companies seek to gain approval from their stakeholders, they obviously position themselves in line with their interests (Berrone et al., 2017). Therefore, CCBs can be considered as having a role model function, specifically when, and only when, they act authentically. Just one example of this is how in 2020, the outdoor apparel retail co-op REI (www.rei.com/opt-outside) closed all of its US stores on "Black Friday", asking its customers to go outside and enjoy nature instead of consuming more products.

Future research could be arranged around the four co-creative processes addressed in this chapter in an effort to better understand them as they relate to CCBs. Our literature analysis reveals that there is little to no empirical research that investigates the co-creative processes of CCBs and their transformational effects on society. Co-constructive processes of CCBs make organizations more transparent and accessible than they have ever been as they attract stakeholder interest, remain alert to greenwashing, and work to maintain effective CCB political activity. Future empirical research should include the role of storytelling in the process of co-construction, or the role of ethics and morals as they relate to authentic marketing and branding communication.

Furthermore, the co-creational branding processes of CCBs in an international context might be primed by their specific socio-cultural environments or political contexts. In-depth analysis of existing CCBs in different countries or regions could achieve interesting insights that might be particularly relevant for global brand management.

The brand identity of CCBs appears to be driven by their management's and employees' attitudes. This means there is reason to assume that the process of co-creation is also – at least partially – influenced by how CCB's internal stakeholders (i.e. employees) facilitate co-creational branding and exchange processes with their external stakeholders. Future research should help generate in-depth knowledge of how individual attitudes or personal identity influence co-creative branding processes.

## NOTE

1. "Certified B Corps are enterprises that have successfully passed the voluntary and private certification process initiated by B Lab, a US-based non-profit organization. The certification covers the company's operations and measures its positive policies, practices and outputs in areas such as governance, workers, customers, community, the environment, and regarding the products and services which they sell" (Villela et al., 2019, p. 2).

## REFERENCES

Achleitner, A.K., Block, J. (2018). Hybride Organisationen an der Schnittstelle zwischen Gewinn- und Gemeinwohlorientierung. In Achleitner, A.K., Block, J., Strachwitz, R.G. (eds.), *Stiftungsunternehmen: Theorie und Praxis* (pp. 3–20). Band 8. Wiesbaden: Springer Fachmedien.

Atiq, M., Karatas-Ozkan, M. (2013). Sustainable corporate entrepreneurship from a strategic corporate social responsibility perspective: Current research and future opportunities. *International Journal of Entrepreneurship and Innovation*, 14(1), 5–14.

B Corporation (2020). About B Corps. https://bcorporation.net/about-b-corps. Accessed September 4, 2020.

Baron, D.P. (1995). Integrated strategy: Market and nonmarket components. *California Management Review*, 37, 47–65.

Battilana, J., Lee, M. (2014). Advancing research on hybrid organizing – Insights from the study of social enterprises. *Academy of Management Annals*, 8(1), 397–441.

Battilana, J., Lee, M., Walker, J., Dorsey, C. (2012). In search of the hybrid ideal. *Stanford Social Innovation Review*, 10(3), 51–55.

Baysinger, B.D. (1984). Domain maintenance as an objective of business political activity: An expanded typology. *Academy of Management Review*, 9(2), 248–258.

Beltramello, A., Haie-Fayle, L., Pilat, D. (2013). *Why New Business Models Matter for Green Growth*. Paris: OECD Publishing.

Ben and Jerry's (2020). How we do business. https://www.benandjerry.com.au/values/how-we-do-business#community. Accessed September 4, 2020.

Berrone, P., Fosfuri, A., Gelabert, L. (2017). Does greenwashing pay off? Understanding the relationship between environmental actions and environmental legitimacy. *Journal of Business Ethics*, 144(2), 363–379.

Bhattacharya, C.B., Korschun, D., Sen, S. (2009). Strengthening stakeholder–company relationships through mutually-beneficial corporate social responsibility initiatives. *Journal of Business Ethics*, 85, 257–272.

Biraghi, S., Gambetti, R.C. (2013). Corporate branding: Where are we? A systematic communication-based inquiry. *Journal of Marketing Communications*, 21, 260–283.

Booth, A., Sutton, A., Papaioannou, D. (2016). *Systematic Approaches to a Successful Literature Review*. Second edition. Los Angeles: Sage.

Bouncken, R.B., Gast, J., Kraus, S., Bogers, M. (2015). Coopetition: A systematic review, synthesis, and future research directions. *Review of Managerial Science*, 9(3), 577–601.

Boyd, B. (2009). *Hybrid Organizations: New Business Models for Environmental Leadership*. Sheffield, UK: Greenleaf Publishing.

Brodmerkel, F. (2015). VW Dieselgate: Greenwashing ist Betrug am Verbraucher. https://pr-journal .de/fragen-und-meinungen/autoren-beitraege-themen-der-zeit/16635-vw-dieselgate-greenwashing-ist -betrug-am-verbraucher.html. Accessed December 2, 2020.

Carrasco Monteagudo, I., Buendía-Martínez, I. (2020). Political activism as driver of cooperative sector. *VOLUNTAS: International Journal of Voluntary and Nonprofit Organizations*, 40(1), 1–13.

Chan, E.Y., Orazi, D.C. (2020). "They did not walk the green talk!": How information specificity influences consumer evaluations of disconfirmed environmental claims. *Journal of Business Ethics*, 163(1), 107–123.

Cordano, M., Marshall, R.S., Silverman, M. (2010). How do small and medium enterprises go "green"? A study of environmental management programs in the U.S. wine industry. *Journal of Business Ethics*, 92(3), 463–478.

Daub, C.-H. (2008). Nachhaltige Unternehmen unter Innovationsdruck. *Marketing Review St. Gallen*, (4), 18–22.

Davies, I.A., Chambers, L. (2018). Integrating hybridity and business model theory in sustainable entrepreneurship. *Journal of Cleaner Production*, 177, 378–386.

Delmas, M.A., Burbano, V.C. (2011). The drivers of greenwashing. *California Management Review*, 54(1), 64–87.

Demirel, P., Li, Q.C., Rentocchini, F., Tamvada, J.P. (2019). Born to be green: New insights into the economics and management of green entrepreneurship. *Small Business Economics*, 52(4), 759–771.

den Hond, F., Rehbein, K.A., Bakker, F.G.A. de, Lankveld, H.K.-v. (2014). Playing on two chessboards: Reputation effects between corporate social responsibility (CSR) and corporate political activity (CPA). *Journal of Management Studies*, 51(5), 790–813.

European Commission (2019). *Reflection Paper: Towards a Sustainable Europe by 2030*. Brussels: Publications Office of the European Union.

Haigh, N., Kennedy, E.D., Walker, J. (2015a). Hybrid organizations as shape-shifters: Altering legal structure for strategic gain. *California Management Review*, 57(3), 59–82.

Haigh, N., Walker, J., Bacq, S., Kickul, J. (2015b). Hybrid organizations: Origins, strategies, impacts, and implications. *California Management Review*, 57(3), 5–12.

Hatch, M.J., Schultz, M. (2010). Toward a theory of brand co-creation with implications for brand governance. *Journal of Brand Management*, 17(8), 590–604.

Hillebrand, B., Driessen, P., Koll, O. (2015). Stakeholder marketing: Theoretical foundations and consequences for marketing capabilities. *Journal of the Academy of Marketing Science*, 43, 411–428.

Hoffman, A.J. (2009). *Hybrid Organizations. New Business Models for Environmental Leadership*. Sheffield: Greenleaf Publishing.

Holt, D. (2016). Branding in the age of social media. *Harvard Business Review*, http://fleurwillemijn .com/wp-content/uploads/2019/09/Branding-in-the-Age-of-Social-Media.pdf. Accessed October 15, 2020.

Iglesias, O., Ind. N. (2016). How to build a brand with a conscience. In Ind, N., Horlings, S. (eds.), *Brands with a Conscience: How to Build a Successful and Responsible Brand* (pp. 204–211). London: Kogan Page.

Iglesias, O., Ind. N. (2020). Towards a theory of conscientious corporate brand co-creation: The next key challenge in brand management. *Journal of Brand Management*, 27, 710–720.

Iglesias, O., Markovic, S., Bagherzadeh, M., Singh, J. (2020). Co-creation: A key link between corporate social responsibility, customer trust, and customer loyalty, *Journal of Business Ethics*, 163(1), 151–166.

Ind, N., Horlings, S. (2016). *Brands with a Conscience: How to Build a Successful and Responsible Brand*. London: Kogan Page.

Jahdi, K.S., Acikdilli, G. (2009). Marketing communications and corporate social responsibility (CSR): Marriage of convenience or shotgun wedding? *Journal of Business Ethics*, 88(1), 103–113.

Jay, J. (2013). Navigating paradox as a mechanism of change and innovation in hybrid organizations. *Academy of Management Journal*, 56(1), 137–159.

Jonker, J., Stark, W., Tewes, S. (2011). *Corporate Social Responsibility und nachhaltige Entwicklung: Einführung, Strategie und Glossar*. Berlin Heidelberg: Springer Gabler.

Kemming, D., Mattias, C. (2019). Bestandsaufnahme 2: Fallbeispiele für Marken als politische Akteure. In Kemming, J.D., Rommerskirchen, J. (eds.), *Marken als politische Akteure* (pp. 21–48). Wiesbaden: Springer Gabler.

Kornmeier, M. (2007). *Wissenschaftstheorie und wissenschaftliches Arbeiten: Eine Einführung für Wirtschaftswissenschaftler*. Heidelberg: Physica-Verlag.

Lamé, G. (2019). Systematic literature reviews: An introduction. *Proceedings of the Design Society: International Conference on Engineering Design*, 1(1), 1633–1642.

Lundqvist, A., Liljander, V., Gummerus, J., Van Riel, A. (2013). The impact of storytelling on the consumer brand experience: The case of a firm-originated story. *Journal of Brand Management*, 20, 283–297.

Lux, S., Crook, T.R., Woehr, D.J. (2011). Mixing business with politics: A meta-analysis of the antecedents and outcomes of corporate political activity. *Journal of Management*, 37(1), 223–247.

Lyon, T.P., Delmas, M.A., Maxwell, J.W., Bansal, P., Chiroleu-Assouline, M., Crifo, P., Durand, R., Gond, J.-P., King, A., Lenox, M., Toffel, M., Vogel, D., Wijen, F. (2018). CSR needs CPR: Corporate sustainability and politics. *California Management Review*, 60(4), 5–24.

manomama GmbH (2020). Wir über uns. https://www.manomama.de/. Accessed October 15, 2020.

Markovic, S., Iglesias, O., Singh, J., Sierra, V. (2018). How does the perceived ethicality of corporate services brands influence loyalty and positive word-of-mouth? Analyzing the roles of empathy, affective commitment, and perceived quality. *Journal of Business Ethics*, 148(4), 721–740.

Mast, C. (2016). *Unternehmenskommunikation. Ein Leitfaden. 6. Überarbeitete und erwei-terte Auflage*. Konstanz, München: UKV.

Merz, M.A., He, Y., Vargo, S.L. (2009). The evolving brand logic: A service-dominant logic perspective. *Journal of the Academy of Marketing Science*, 37(3), 328–344.

Moisander, J., Markkula, A., Eräranta, K. (2010). Construction of consumer choice in the market: Challenges for environmental policy. *International IJC*, 34(1), 73–79.

Naidoo, C., Abratt, R. (2018). Brands that do good: Insight into social brand equity. *Journal of Brand Management*, 25, 3–13.

Nalick, M., Josefy, M., Zardkoohi, A., Bierman, L. (2016). Corporate sociopolitical involvement: A reflection of whose preferences? *Academy of Management Perspectives*, 30(4), 384–403.

Nissan, E., Castaño, M.-S., Carrasco, I. (2012). Drivers of non-profit activity: A cross-country analysis. *Small Business Economics*, 38(3), 303–320.

Oliver, C., Holzinger, I. (2008). The effectiveness of strategic political management: A dynamic capabilities framework. *Academy of Management Review*, 33(2), 496–520.

Pache, A.-C., Santos, F. (2013). Inside the hybrid organization: Selective coupling as a response to competing institutional logics. *Academy of Management Journal*, 56(4), 972–1001.

Pacheco, D.F., Dean, T.J., Payne, D.S. (2010). Escaping the green prison: Entrepreneurship and the creation of opportunities for sustainable development. *Journal of Business Venturing*, 25(5), 464–480.

Parguel, B., Benoît-Moreau, F., Larceneux, F. (2011). How sustainability ratings might deter "greenwashing": A closer look at ethical corporate communication. *Journal of Business Ethics*, 102(1), 15–28.

Patagonia (2020). Transforming trash into fleece. https://eu.patagonia.com/gb/en/home/. Accessed September 4, 2020.

Pittaway, L., Holt, R., Broad, J. (2014). Synthesising knowledge in entrepreneurship research – The role of systematic literature reviews. In Chell, E., Karataş-Özkan, M. (eds.), *Handbook of Research on Small Business and Entrepreneurship* (pp. 83–105). Cheltenham, UK and Northampton, MA, USA: Edward Elgar Publishing.

Pritchard, M., Wilson, T. (2018). Building corporate reputation through consumer responses to green new products. *Journal of Brand Management*, 25, 38–52.

Ramus, T., Vaccaro, A. (2017). Stakeholders matter: How social enterprises address mission drift. *Journal of Business Ethics*, 143(2), 307–322.

Reckhaus, H.-D., Baumgarth, C. (2020). Vom Kammerjäger zum Landschaftsgärtner – Wie die Fliege "Erika" die Firma Reckhaus transformierte! In Schmidt, H.J., Baumgarth, C. (eds.), *Forum Markenforschung* (pp. 125–137). Wiesbaden: Springer Gabler.

Rindell, A., Svensson, G., Mysen, T., Billström, A., Wilén, K. (2011). Towards a conceptual foundation of "conscientious corporate brands". *Journal of Brand Management*, 18(9), 709–719.

Roper, S., Lim, M., Iglesias, O. (2018). "Brands that do good" (11th global brand conference), University of Bradford School of Management. *Journal of Brand Management*, 25, 1–2.

Schaefer, A., Crane, A. (2005). Addressing sustainability and consumption. *Journal of Macromarketing*, 25(1), 76–92.

Scherer, A.G., Palazzo, G. (2011). The new political role of business in a globalized world: A review of a new perspective on CSR and its implications for the firm, governance, and democracy. *Journal of Management Studies*, 48(4), 899–931.

Seelos, C., Mair, J. (2005). Social entrepreneurship: Creating new business models to serve the poor. *Business Horizons*, 48(3), 241–246.

Sierra, V., Iglesias, O., Markovic, S., Singh, J. (2017). Does ethical image build equity in corporate services brands? The influence of customer perceived ethicality on affect, perceived quality, and equity. *Journal of Business Ethics*, 144(3), 661–676.

Spurgin, E. (2015). Do business leaders have role model obligations to be good political actors? *Business and Society Review*, 120(2), 277–301.

Tranfield, D., Denyer, D., Smart, P. (2003). Towards a methodology for developing evidence-informed management knowledge by means of systematic review. *British Journal of Management*, 14(3), 207–222.

Vallaster, C., von Wallpach, S. (2013). An online discursive inquiry into multi-stakeholder corporate brand meaning co-creation. *Journal of Business Research*, 66, 1505–1515.

Vallaster, C., von Wallpach, S. (2018). Brand strategy co-creation in a nonprofit context: A strategy-as-practice approach. *Nonprofit and Voluntary Sector Quarterly*, 47(5), 984–1006.

Vallaster, C., Lindgreen, A., Maon, F. (2012). Strategically leveraging corporate social responsibility to the benefit of company and society: A corporate branding perspective. *California Management Review*, 54(3), 34–60.

Vallaster, C., Maon, F., Lindgreen, A., Vanhamme, J. (2019). Serving multiple masters: Micro-foundations of dynamic capabilities in hybrid for-profit organizations. *Organization Studies*, https://doi.org/10.1177/0170840619856034.

Vargo, S., Lusch, R. (2006). Service-dominant logic: What it is, what it is not, what it might be. In Vargo, S., Lusch, R. (eds.), *The Service-Dominant Logic of Marketing: Dialog, Debate and Directions* (pp. 43–55). London; New York: Routledge.

Vargo, S., Lusch, R. (2008). Service-dominant logic: Continuing the evolution. *Journal of the Academy of Marketing Science*, 36, 1–10.

Vargo, S., Lusch, R. (2016). Service-dominant logic 2025. *Journal of Research in Marketing*, 34, 46–67.

Villela, M., Bulgacov, S., Morgan, G. (2019). B Corp certification and its impact on organizations over time. *Journal of Business Ethics*. https://doi.org/10.1007/s10551-019-04372-9.

von Wallpach, S., Voyer, B., Kastanakis, M., Mühlbacher, H. (2016). Co-creating stakeholder and brand identities: Introduction to the special section. *Journal of Business Research*, 70, 395–398.

Weber, L.J. (1997). Ethics and the political activity of business: Reviewing the agenda. *Business Ethics Quarterly*, 7(3), 71–79.

Weidmann, C., Kohlhepp, R. (2020). Die Besteuerung der gGmbH. In Weidmann, C., Kohlhepp, R. (eds.), *Die gemeinnützige GmbH: Errichtung, Geschäftstätigkeit und Besteuerung einer gGmbH* (pp. 107–140). Wiesbaden: Springer Gabler. https://doi.org/10.1007/978-3-658-20775-5_5.

Wells, R., Anasti, T. (2019). Hybrid models for social change: Legitimacy among community-based nonprofit organizations. *VOLUNTAS: International Journal of Voluntary and Nonprofit Organizations*, 31, 1134–1147.

Zimmer, A., Obuch, K. (2017). A matter of context? Understanding social enterprises in changing environments: The case of Germany. *VOLUNTAS: International Journal of Voluntary and Nonprofit Organizations*, 28(6), 2339–2359.

*Table 16A.1  Sources and focus of analysis*

| ° | Author | Title | Year | Journal/Book | Focus/Co-creational processes |
|---|--------|-------|------|--------------|-------------------------------|
| 1 | Berrone et al. | Does greenwashing pay off? Understanding the relationship between environmental actions and environmental legitimacy. | 2017 | *Journal of Business Ethics* | Communicating/Contesting |
| 2 | Biraghi and Gambetti | Corporate branding: Where are we? A systematic communication-based inquiry. | 2013 | *Journal of Marketing Communication* | Communicating/Contesting |
| 3 | Holt | Branding in the age of social media. | 2016 | *Harvard Business Review* | Communicating/Contesting |
| 4 | Jahdi and Acikdilli | Marketing communications and corporate social responsibility (CSR): Marriage of convenience or shotgun wedding? | 2009 | *Journal of Business Ethics* | Communicating/Contesting |
| 5 | Parguel et al. | How sustainability ratings might deter "greenwashing": A closer look at ethical corporate communication. | 2011 | *Journal of Business Ethics* | Communicating/Contesting |
| 6 | Schaefer and Crane | Addressing sustainability and consumption. | 2005 | *Journal of Macromarketing* | Communicating/Contesting |
| 7 | Chan and Orazi | "They did not walk the green talk!": How information specificity influences consumer evaluations of disconfirmed environmental claims. | 2020 | *Journal of Business Ethics* | Communicating/Contesting |
| 8 | Bhattacharya et al. | Strengthening stakeholder–company relationships through mutually-beneficial corporate social responsibility initiatives. | 2009 | *Journal of Business Ethics* | Communicating/Contesting/Elucidating |
| 9 | Iglesias and Ind | Towards a theory of conscientious corporate brand co-creation: The next key challenge in brand management. | 2020 | *Journal of Brand Management* | Communicating/Contesting/Elucidating/Internalizing |
| 10 | Iglesias et al. | Co-creation: A key link between corporate social responsibility, customer trust, and customer loyalty. | 2020 | *Journal of Business Ethics* | Communicating/Contesting/Elucidating/Internalizing |
| 11 | Ind and Horlings | *Brands with a Conscience: How to Build a Successful and Responsible Brand.* | 2016 | Kogan Page | Communicating/Contesting/Elucidating/Internalizing |

| | Author | Title | Year | Journal/Book | Focus/Co-creational processes |
|---|---|---|---|---|---|
| 12 | Markovic et al. | How does the perceived ethicality of corporate services brands influence loyalty and positive word-of-mouth? Analyzing the roles of empathy, affective commitment, and perceived quality. | 2018 | *Journal of Business Ethics* | Communicating/Contesting/Elucidating |
| 13 | Merz et al. | The evolving brand logic: A service-dominant logic perspective. | 2009 | *Journal of the Academy of Marketing Science* | Communicating/Contesting/Elucidating |
| 14 | Sierra et al. | Does ethical image build equity in corporate services brands? The influence of customer perceived ethicality on affect, perceived quality, and equity. | 2017 | *Journal of Business Ethics* | Communicating/Contesting/Elucidating |
| 15 | Vallaster and von Wallpach | Brand strategy co-creation in a nonprofit context: A strategy-as-practice approach. | 2018 | *Nonprofit and Voluntary Sector Quarterly* | Communicating/Contesting/Elucidating |
| 16 | Vallaster and von Wallpach | An online discursive inquiry into multi-stakeholder corporate brand meaning co-creation. | 2013 | *Journal of Business Research* | Communicating/Contesting/Elucidating |
| 17 | Cordano et al. | How do small and medium enterprises go "green"? A study of environmental management programs in the U.S. wine industry. | 2010 | *Journal of Business Ethics* | Communicating/Contesting/Internalizing |
| 18 | Delmas and Burbano | The drivers of greenwashing. | 2011 | *California Management Review* | Communicating/Contesting/Internalizing |
| 19 | Carrasco Monteagudo and Buendía-Martínez | Political activism as driver of cooperative sector. | 2020 | *VOLUNTAS* | Communicating/Elucidating |
| 20 | den Hond et al. | Playing on two chessboards: Reputation effects between corporate social responsibility (CSR) and corporate political activity (CPA). | 2014 | *Journal of Management Studies* | Communicating/Elucidating |
| 21 | Hatch and Schultz | Toward a theory of brand co-creation with implications for brand governance. | 2010 | *Journal of Brand Management* | Communicating/Elucidating |
| 22 | Hillebrand et al. | Stakeholder marketing: Theoretical foundations and consequences for marketing capabilities. | 2015 | *Journal of the Academy of Marketing Science* | Communicating/Elucidating |
| 23 | Lundqvist et al. | The impact of storytelling on the consumer brand experience: The case of a firm-originated story. | 2013 | *Journal of Brand Management* | Communicating/Elucidating |

| ° | Author | Title | Year | Journal/Book | Focus/Co-creational processes |
|---|--------|-------|------|--------------|-------------------------------|
| 24 | Roper et al. | "Brands that do good" (11th global brand conference). | 2018 | *Journal of Brand Management* | Communicating/Contesting/Elucidating/Internalizing |
| 25 | Wells and Anasti | Hybrid models for social change: Legitimacy among community-based nonprofit organizations. | 2019 | *VOLUNTAS* | Communicating/Contesting/Elucidating/Internalizing |
| 26 | Achleitner and Block | Hybride Organisationen an der Schnittstelle zwischen Gewinn- und Gemeinwohlorientierung | 2018 | Springer Gabler | Internalizing |
| 27 | Atiq and Karatas-Ozkan | Sustainable corporate entrepreneurship from a strategic corporate social responsibility perspective: Current research and future opportunities. | 2013 | *International Journal of Entrepreneurship and Innovation* | Internalizing |
| 28 | Battilana et al. | In search of the hybrid ideal. | 2012 | *Stanford Social Innovation Review* | Internalizing |
| 29 | Battilana and Lee | Advancing research on hybrid organizing – Insights from the study of social enterprises. | 2014 | *Academy of Management Annals* | Internalizing |
| 30 | Boyd | *Hybrid Organizations: New Business Models for Environmental Leadership.* | 2009 | Greenleaf Publishing | Internalizing |
| 31 | Davies and Chambers | Integrating hybridity and business model theory in sustainable entrepreneurship. | 2018 | *Journal of Cleaner Production* | Internalizing |
| 32 | Haigh et al. | Hybrid organizations as shape-shifters: Altering legal structure for strategic gain. | 2015a | *California Management Review* | Internalizing |
| 33 | Haigh et al. | Hybrid organizations: Origins, strategies, impacts, and implications. | 2015b | *California Management Review* | Internalizing |
| 34 | Hoffman | *Hybrid Organizations: New Business Models for Environmental Leadership.* | 2009 | Greenleaf Publishing | Internalizing |
| 35 | Iglesias and Ind | How to build a brand with a conscience. | 2016 | Kogan Page | Internalizing |
| 36 | Jay | Navigating paradox as a mechanism of change and innovation in hybrid organizations. | 2013 | *Academy of Management Journal* | Internalizing |
| 37 | Jonker et al. | *Corporate Social Responsibility und nachhaltige Entwicklung: Einführung, Strategie und Glossar* | 2011 | Springer Gabler | Internalizing |
| 38 | Naidoo and Abratt | Brands that do good: Insight into social brand equity. | 2018 | *Journal of Brand Management* | Internalizing |
| 39 | Nissan et al. | Drivers of non-profit activity: A cross-country analysis. | 2012 | *Small Business Economics* | Internalizing |

| | Author | Title | Year | Journal/Book | Focus/Co-creational processes |
|---|---|---|---|---|---|
| 40 | Pache and Santos | Inside the hybrid organization: Selective coupling as a response to competing institutional logics. | 2013 | Academy of Management Journal | Internalizing |
| 41 | Pacheco et al. | Escaping the green prison: Entrepreneurship and the creation of opportunities for sustainable development. | 2010 | Journal of Business Venturing | Internalizing |
| 42 | Rindell et al. | Towards a conceptual foundation of "conscientious corporate brands". | 2011 | Journal of Brand Management | Internalizing |
| 43 | Vallaster et al. | Serving multiple masters: Micro-foundations of dynamic capabilities in hybrid for-profit organizations. | 2019 | Organization Studies | Internalizing |
| 44 | Weidmann and Kohlhepp | Die Besteuerung der gGmbH. | 2020 | Springer Gabler | Internalizing |
| 45 | Lux et al. | Mixing business with politics: A meta-analysis of the antecedents and outcomes of corporate political activity. | 2011 | Journal of Management | Internalizing/Elucidating |
| 46 | Seelos and Mair | Social entrepreneurship: Creating new business models to serve the poor. | 2005 | Business Horizons | Internalizing/Elucidating |
| 47 | Moisander et al. | Construction of consumer choice in the market: Challenges for environmental policy. | 2010 | International IJC | Contesting |
| 48 | Baron | Integrated strategy: Market and nonmarket components. | 1995 | California Management Review | Contesting/Elucidating/Internalizing |
| 49 | von Wallpach et al. | Co-creating stakeholder and brand identities: Introduction to the special section. | 2016 | Journal of Business Research | Contesting/Elucidating/Internalizing |
| 50 | Vallaster et al. | Strategically leveraging corporate social responsibility to the benefit of company and society: A corporate branding perspective. | 2012 | California Management Review | Contesting/Elucidating/Internalizing |
| 51 | Daub | Nachhaltige Unternehmen unter Innovationsdruck. | 2008 | Marketing Review St. Gallen | Contesting/Internalizing |
| 52 | Ramus and Vaccaro | Stakeholders matter: How social enterprises address mission drift. | 2017 | Journal of Business Ethics | Contesting/Internalizing |
| 53 | Baysinger | Domain maintenance as an objective of business political activity: An expanded typology. | 1984 | Academy of Management Review | Elucidating |

| o | Author | Title | Year | Journal/Book | Focus/Co-creational processes |
|---|--------|-------|------|--------------|-------------------------------|
| 54 | Lyon et al. | CSR needs CPR: Corporate sustainability and politics. | 2018 | *California Management Review* | Elucidating |
| 55 | Nalick et al. | Corporate sociopolitical involvement: A Reflection of whose preferences? | 2016 | *Academy of Management Perspectives* | Elucidating |
| 56 | Oliver and Holzinger | The effectiveness of strategic political management: A dynamic capabilities framework. | 2008 | *Academy of Management Review* | Elucidating |
| 57 | Scherer and Palazzo | The new political role of business in a globalized world: A review of a new perspective on CSR and its implications for the firm, governance, and democracy. | 2011 | *Journal of Management Studies* | Elucidating |
| 58 | Spurgin | Do business leaders have role model obligations to be good political actors? | 2015 | *Business and Society Review* | Elucidating |
| 59 | Weber | Ethics and the political activity of business: Reviewing the agenda. | 1997 | *Business Ethics Quarterly* | Elucidating |
| 60 | Zimmer and Obuch | A matter of context? Understanding social enterprises in changing environments: The case of Germany. | 2017 | *VOLUNTAS* | Elucidating |
| 61 | Demirel et al. | Born to be green: New insights into the economics and management of green entrepreneurship. | 2019 | *Small Business Economics* | Elucidating/Internalizing |

# 17. Organizational citizenship behaviour principles: a guide for employees and customers in the brand value co-creation journey

*Maja Arslanagić-Kalajdžić and Vesna Babić-Hodović*

## 1. INTRODUCTION

The traditional concept of branding is founded on the understanding of the organization as the creator of brand value proposition, brand meaning and brand communication. The organization is responsible for building the outward image to the public (Morrison & Crane, 2007). The essential idea is that the organization can control the entire branding process and build desirable brand elements through controlled communication channels if customers accept the messages and a brand identity that the organization wants to create (Kapferer, 2008).

The new way of doing business, the development of new trends in customer demand and the growing share of services in the global economy, have caused many changes in branding processes. Since the emergence of service-dominant logic and the assertion of Vargo and Lusch (2004) that "value is defined by and co-created with the consumer rather than embedded in output" (p. 6), the process of *co-creation* is gaining relevance for researchers and practitioners who are now exploring different ways in which co-creation can enhance brand identity and image. Building on these ideas, Prahalad and Ramaswamy (2004) suggest understanding a brand as an experience between employees and customers who collaborate in the process of creation. More generally, brand co-creation is a collaborative process between a company and its stakeholders, which can be used both strategically, as an innovation method, and tactically, as a marketing research tool (Ind et al., 2017). When embracing co-creation actions for their brands, companies apply a stakeholder-centric approach, considering the feedback and solutions from various groups of stakeholders (primarily customers, but also employees, partners, advisors, and other collaborators). However, what still lies unexplored are ethical considerations of such actions as well as the customer perceived ethicality of co-creation (Iglesias et al., 2019; Markovic et al., 2018).

New generations of brands refocused from an output (or product) conceptualization to the conceptualization of the brand as a social process and integrated experience that leads to brand value and brand image for target customers and the public (Merz et al., 2009; Prahalad & Ramaswamy, 2004). In this context, brand value implies the unique entity developed as the result of the interaction and cooperation of the most influential and most important organizational stakeholders – employees and customers. Moreover, brand value becomes one of the key factors for the development of the relationship between customers and organization, together with brand personality (Aaker, 1999) and brand trustworthiness (i.e., keeping promises delivered to customers).

Changes in branding processes also impact brand value. Iglesias et al. (2013) defined a concept of the organic value of the brand (OVB) to build an integrated brand value co-creation model (BVCC). Here, brand meaning, brand understanding, and brand image are the result of the interaction and relationship of employees as internal customers, and customers as external ones. OVB assumes that the influence of employees and customers on brand categories is much stronger than the organization's influence. BVCC argues that brand value is built at the point where the organization and the customer meet, which is labelled as "conversational space" (Iglesias et al., 2013). Therefore, organizations lose control over the process of brand value and brand image development; key roles belong to employees and customers whose engagement integrates with the process of brand value co-creation (Yi & Gong, 2013). Thus, employees become part of the branding process, humanizing the value proposition and motivating customers to participate in the value development process. The biggest challenge for the organization is how to ensure employees engage and manage these processes.

The BVCC concept, with its conversational space, relies on the premises of the service literature. The integration of employees responsible for creating services to customers and the value-in-use concept (Grönroos, 2011) are defined in the concept of interactive marketing (Babic-Hodovic, 2010), which determines the overall service experience and consequently the brand value and brand image of the service. A positive experience during the interaction process is a part of the three-dimensional understanding of service marketing (internal, external, and interactive marketing) and results with interactive branding where first-line employees and customers work together for service brand value creation. Here, brands have an important integrative role where the connection between customers and the organization is achieved through an interface between employees and customers (Dall'Olmo Riley & De Chernatony, 2000). Now, through the BVCC concept, this conversational and interactive moment has been expanded to all brands.

This study focuses on the role of employees and customers in brand value co-creation actions. We identify that the concept of citizenship, which is recognized as one of the six universal moral principles that should guide brand co-creation (Markovic et al., 2018; Stanislawski, 2011), is highly relevant both for employees and customers. All other moral principles, identified by the same authors, are strongly correlated with the citizenship concept, namely: trustworthiness, respect, responsibility, fairness, and care. We can consider citizenship in terms of corporate citizenship (Maignan et al., 1999) and organizational citizenship (Organ, 1988). Corporate citizenship is focused on the initiatives and actions of organizations with the intention to behave responsibly regarding societal problems, while organizational citizenship (behaviour) is focused on the behaviours of employees as good citizens in the organization they work for. In the field of business ethics, there is already evidence on the ethical implications of citizenship activities, such as organizational identification and turnover intention (Lin & Liu, 2019). The notion of citizenship is particularly relevant for employees, who are essential for building the brand (Iglesias et al., 2013), but it can be manifested towards customers in the co-creation process (Vargo & Lusch, 2004). In this study, we focus on organizational citizenship behaviour (OCB).

Against this background the following research questions are developed: what are the underlying theoretical principles of OCB; why should OCB practices be relevant to employees and customers in the brand co-creation process; and how can managers use already known OCB practices in implementing brand co-creation processes? Consequently, the intended contributions of this study are threefold. First, we aim to contribute to the literature on branding and

ethics by analysing ethical aspects of OCB through a bibliometric literature review and applying them in the context of brand value co-creation. Second, by deriving propositions based on
the theoretical principles of OCB, we discuss the implications of OCB practices for the process
of brand co-creation highlighting its role for employees on the one side and customers on the
other. Finally, we derive implications for managing brand co-creation processes and suggest
procedures businesses should adopt to ensure adequate application of the citizenship standard.

## 2.   BRAND VALUE CO-CREATION

In their organic value of the brand (OVB) proposal, Iglesias et al. (2013) argue that brand value
is a result of the "conversation" between consumers and the organization. This interactivity
(Vallaster & Lindgreen, 2011) can be related to the established service literature where the
concept of interactive marketing is recognized through the interaction between the organization (i.e., frontline employees) and customers (Grönroos, 2011). Merz and colleagues (2009)
propose a dual perspective of customers and organization, emphasizing that the interaction
between employees and customers is the most important feature in the BVCC process.

The organic view of the brand challenges the idea regarding the power of the organization
in defining a unique brand proposition for customers. The concept also challenges the notion
that control over the development of brand meaning and the way a brand operates (fulfilling
brand promises) belongs exclusively to the organization (Iglesias & Ind, 2020). Thanks to the
shift of power to customers and other stakeholders through participation and collaboration,
the desired brand identity can be steered in a different direction than the one the organization
wanted to achieve (Balmer, 2010).

Value co-creation occurs when customers already have relationships with the brand that
are characterized by strong emotions and value sharing (France et al., 2016; Kaufmann et al.,
2016), which means that customers need to have trust in the brand as reliable and transparent
(Hatch & Schultz, 2010; Prahalad & Ramaswamy, 2004) in order to feel committed to the
brand and the organization (Muniz & O'Guinn, 2001). In this context, the role of employees as
brand access points is emphasized (Hatch & Schultz, 2010), as the way they behave influences
the co-creation process.

Ind et al. (2017) developed a co-creation continuum in which co-creation covers a spectrum
ranging from a purely tactical tool (e.g., market research) to a strategic method (e.g., collaborative innovation). On the one hand, the tactical approach is applied within already developed
research methods in the organization. According to the co-creation continuum, tactical BVCC
occurs when organizations want to verify the relevance and acceptability of ideas and campaigns already created by the organization. This is a step forward from traditional research
methods that focus on studying customer preferences with the goal of improving organizational outcomes.

On the other hand, we believe that for the co-creation of brand value, the strategic approach
has much more potential than the tactical one. This approach requires more openness to customer suggestions and customer involvement at different stages of new idea development. To
make this happen, organizations change their systems and culture to get more benefits from the
process. The level of employee and customer involvement is important to the ultimate brand
image and value perceived by various stakeholders. Namely, employees' commitment and
contribution in creating and improving brand value is more obvious and evident in services

than in tangible products. Following this, Kaufmann and colleagues (2016) and Fetscherin and colleagues (2014) suggest that service brands should receive special attention when it comes to BVCC processes.

Employee and customer contribution to BVCC can manifest itself in a direct form when interaction and conversation between customers and brand/employees occur. This is the case with people-processing services where customers need to be present during the service process otherwise services cannot be delivered (Yi & Gong, 2013). Indirect brand value co-creation implies customers, but also employees' participation and "work" in advocating and promoting brand value through different channels and networks, brand or other communities, and other actions which are not directly related to the brand (France et al., 2016; Ind et al., 2013).

Since brand promises are based on the organizational perceptions of brand identity that are implemented through the decisions and actions of the employees, the role of employees in brand value co-creation is regarded as crucial (Burmann et al., 2009). Organizations are faced with challenging and limited options to develop, influence or control customers' perceptions of brand and brand value (ibid.). Thus, brand managers continuously orchestrate and coordinate employees' behaviour that directly or indirectly determines brand experience (Brakus et al., 2009) and brand value (Henkel et al., 2017).

BVCC is a result of emotional engagement with the brand and self-expressiveness (France et al., 2016) so the role and participation of brand representativeness (in most cases employees have that role) is essential (Yi & Gong, 2013). Namely, employees, especially frontline ones, humanize the brand, their actions and behaviour are focused on customer motivation to emotionally connect with brands and organization. This type of behaviour, which directly influences brand experience for the customers, but also for the employees themselves, is understood as behavioural branding and is directly related to high levels of quality (Dhiman & Arora, 2020). That means that the behavioural branding of employees (Kaufmann et al., 2016), or their effort to "live the brand" and work on aligning internal and external stakeholders (Gregory, 2007), and investing in more effort and actions than they are required to do, increases the relevance and importance of organizational culture and management practice for brand value co-creation (Hatch & Schultz, 2010).

In this process, employees are crucial, and so is their ethical behaviour. Ethics in a business context implies the application of general ethical ideas by management and employees, which on the one hand benefits society, and on the other hand increases employee commitment and productivity as well as organizational profitability (Harris, 1990). The ethical behaviour of employees is a result of their moral principles and the corporate culture developed around ethical principles. Employees have a positive attitude and a high level of commitment when they see a high level of ethical behaviour from managers and other employees, as well as the organization's efforts in ethical business development. In fact, employees are more motivated and empowered to work for a good cause when they work for "good companies" that use ethical business practices (Singh, 2011).

The ethical climate in the organization causes a strong alignment between the employees' values and the organization's values, the employees' confidence in values developed by leaders, and as a consequence their motivation and commitment to achieving the organization's goals (Cullen et al., 2003) and brand value co-creation (Nadeem et al., 2019). In this study, the focus is on the transactional ethical issues as a prerequisite for customer and employee involvement in BVCC. Namely, there is an active role for customers in value co-creation when ethical concerns arise (Nadeem et al., 2019). In the process of buying and connecting with the organization, ethical customers think about the impact of the buying process not just for them personally but also for society (Harrison et al., 2005). Therefore, ethical customers, similar to employees, are more likely to participate in the process of brand value co-creation (Cullen et al., 2003).

Consequently, OCB as a form of citizenship can help attract and engage ethical customers (Starr, 2009) and improve the BVCC processes. Namely, ethical customers try to make the world a better place while buying and using products or services (Maniates, 2001; Shamir, 2008). Therefore, they would be inclined to choose ethical companies and employees who accept OCB principles and to work with them in the process of increasing brand co-creation, brand value and image.

## 3.    ORGANIZATIONAL CITIZENSHIP BEHAVIOUR

The concept of responsible business to both an organization and individuals, and its importance for an organization's sustainability and competitiveness, is immanent to business and the markets of today. The responsible behaviours of individuals and organizations are strongly interrelated, and of high importance for a company's image as well as brand success. However, studies are more focused on organizational than individual responsibility, and different types of cause promotion, cause marketing, sponsorship and charitable actions are included in research about responsible initiatives of organizations and market reaction on that behaviour (Kotler & Lee, 2005).

In contrast, individual responsibility is related to individual behaviour in an organization and the impact of that behaviour towards achieving the organization's goals. Work position, motivation, but also the personal characteristics of an individual affects their work in an organization beyond their formal job requirements (Organ, 1988). This appears as their willingness to exceed the job's requirements in order to support other individuals or work for the organization's interests (Bolino & Turnley, 2003). Scholars explain this type of behaviour as organizational citizenship behaviour – OCB (Organ, 1988; Podsakoff et al., 2000).

Organ (1988) defined OCB as discretionary behaviours that were not monitored and rewarded by the organization, but which help organizational functioning. According to Organ (1997), organizational citizenship behaviour helps companies to achieve competitive advantages based on employees' knowledge, skills, and readiness to invest more time and effort to achieve organizational goals. Managers cannot request them to behave in that way, but also in many cases that additional work is not paid or rewarded (Motowidlo, 2000). In this context, others suggest that employees may decide to subordinate their individual interest for the good of other individuals or the organization (Bolino & Turnley, 2003). Similarly, Bolino (1999) states that this type of helping behaviour is directed to other individuals or the organization with a goal to create benefits and increase the wellbeing of others.

In Wang and Sung's (2014) work, OCB is also considered as a behaviour that is not in an employee's job description and which may or may not be rewarded by the organization. This means that OCB is not required from employees, but it may contribute directly to organizational goals and indirectly to an individual's job performance and possible reward. In the development of the OCB concept, a legitimate suggestion to monitor and reward such behaviour is created (Podsakoff et al., 2000). Consequently, the difference between in- and extra-role behaviours became blurred (Baker & Bulkley, 2014), as well as between intrinsic and extrinsic individual motivations.

OCB assessment is based on the reciprocity norm principle, which evolves from trade-offs in relationships between employees and the organization (Lester et al., 2008). Reciprocity is explained through Gouldner's idea (1960) that giving and receiving are mutually contingent and that reciprocity comprises of attitudes and actions. Two types of reciprocity are suggested, strategic reciprocity where future rewards are assumed (Axelrod, 1986) and altruistic reciprocity as an internalized norm that arises out of moral obligation with no future expectations. In the context of OCB and reciprocity, it is obvious that OCB evolves from altruistic reciprocity, since the efforts of individuals are discretionary and not motivated by future rewards (Organ, 1988).

Acceptance of the idea about the growing role of employees in organizations' mission achievement, individually (not only as part of the organization) and development of the theory of marketing multidimensionality (internal, external, and interactive marketing), affect OCB understanding. Namely, two different dimensions of OCB can be distinguished in the literature: interpersonal organizational citizenship behaviour (OCB-I) and organizational citizenship behaviour (OCB-O). In the case of OCB-I, the behaviour is directed at the co-workers and benefits may be created for individual and organizational performance (Organ & Paine, 1999; Williams & Anderson, 1991), while OCB-O represents behaviours that directly benefit the organization and is also known in the literature as compliance (Smith et al., 1983).

OCB-O is oriented towards the organization and its general success (Williams & Anderson, 1991). This type of behaviour encompasses following Organ's dimensions (1988): conscientiousness – going beyond minimum requirements in complying with organizational rules; sportsmanship – following organizational regulations and tolerating certain bad situations without a complaint; and civic virtue – being proactive when participating in organizational activities.

OCB-I is an interpersonal orientation towards co-workers and other individuals (Tourigny et al., 2019) and it can be further broken down to the person- and task-focused citizenship behaviour. Individual-focused behaviour provides for self-esteem maintenance and deals with problems of a more personal nature and, according to Van Dyne and LePine (1998), appears in the form of listening, counselling, being accessible and similar. Task-focused behaviour is oriented to the resolution of work-related problems and it is more related to organization-based issues. To conclude, OCB-I represents altruistic behaviours and assumes interactions aimed at other individuals, hence, we regard that it is of additional benefit for BVCC if such behaviour is nurtured in organizations.

Both OCB dimensions are associated with group performance (Podsakoff et al., 1997) and the financial and customer service performance of the organization (Walz & Niehoff, 1996). Empirical evidence found that both types of OCB-I are more strongly related to organizational and group performance than OCB-O (Podsakoff et al., 2000).

Citizenship behaviour is a viable tool for increasing productivity as well as coordinating activities between employees (Podsakoff et al., 1997) that will increase organizational performances. On the other hand, there are opposite attitudes regarding the time individuals spend supporting others. For example, Bergeron (2007) suggests that people may allocate working hours to OCB. In these cases, OCB may be at the expense of regular jobs and job performance, meaning that OCB has a detrimental impact on individuals through limits on their achievement and consequently extrinsic rewards in financial terms. Although the results of previous studies are somewhat inconclusive, the majority of previous findings illustrate that OCB has a positive impact on organizations and their goals and is beneficial for boosting the ethical climate in BVCC activities.

## 4.    BIBLIOMETRIC ANALYSIS OF THE OCB FIELD

### 4.1    Methodology

We started the bibliometric analysis by performing a Scopus database search in November 2020. Scopus is an abstract and indexing database with full-text links that is produced by Elsevier. It provides access to journal articles and the references included in those articles, allowing the searcher to search both forward and backward in time (Burnham, 2006). The keyword "organizational citizenship behaviour*" (where the asterisk sign allowed for any variations in the last word, e.g., behaviours) was searched in the title, abstract, and keywords of manuscripts. This query returned 3,647 unique results. We then limited the query to the subject area "Business, Management and Accounting" to narrow in on 2,247 results. No other limitations were made, capturing all types of documents, publication stages, source titles, keywords, affiliations, source types and any additional criteria in Scopus.

To grasp the structure of the field, we first described the resulting dataset in terms of the relevant information about the OCB field, such as timespan, first publication, interest in the topic, outlets that publish manuscripts, and most-cited manuscripts. The next step of the analysis was the co-citation analysis where we analysed references from the original manuscripts in the dataset in more depth. This analysis enabled the identification of manuscripts that are cited multiple times in the OCB dataset, as well as the co-citation of pairs and their co-occurrences enabling the recognition of the baseline structure of the OCB field in terms of theoretical grounds. Finally, in order to visualize and group the co-occurrences, we conducted the clustering of references. This process enabled us to get more in-depth with the structure of the field and recognize main groups of references and interconnection between the references within the cluster. Based on the findings generated from this process, we derived suggestions and propositions for the use of OCB premises to improve ethicality in BVCC processes.

### 4.2    Dataset Description

The resulting dataset covers a timespan from 1988 to 2020, with the first manuscript being published on the topic coming from *Personnel Psychology* and being a book review of Organ's (1988) book on the topic of organizational citizenship behaviour. Peak interest for the topic has occurred in the past five years, with as many as 261 papers published on the topic in 2019.

Topics related to organizational citizenship behaviour have been published in various outlets (91% as journal articles), and the following are the leading journals (with more than 50 manuscripts published) for the area: *Journal of Business Ethics* (73 published manuscripts), *International Journal of Human Resource Management* (66 published manuscripts), *Journal of Organizational Behaviour* (65 manuscripts), *Journal of Management* (52 manuscripts). We have narrowed down our search to the articles from outlets that have 30 or more articles on this topic, which resulted in 12 journals (see Table 17.1) and the subset of 555 documents for subsequent analysis. In this subset, Alexander Newman and Miao Qing are the most prolific authors, both having eight and seven publications in the area.

*Table 17.1    Journals that published 30+ articles in the OCB field*

| Journal Title | Number of Manuscripts |
| --- | --- |
| *Journal of Business Ethics* | 73 |
| *International Journal of Human Resource Management* | 66 |
| *Journal of Organizational Behaviour* | 65 |
| *Journal of Management* | 52 |
| *Journal of Business and Psychology* | 46 |
| *Journal of Managerial Psychology* | 45 |
| *Personnel Review* | 41 |
| *Leadership Quarterly* | 39 |
| *International Journal of Hospitality Management* | 33 |
| *Journal of Business Research* | 32 |
| *Journal of Occupational and Organizational Psychology* | 32 |
| *Journal of Vocational Behaviour* | 31 |

When it comes to the citations, the works have been cited in total by 25,472 other publications. The top 20 articles have 300 and more citations, and carry a total of 17,653 citations, and there are five articles with more than 1,000 citations (see Table 17.2), carrying a total of 11,566 citations. The top-cited manuscripts display meta-analyses of the field as well as reviews of the theoretical background and empirical literature of organizational citizenship behaviours (Meyer et al., 2002; Podsakoff et al., 2000). They are further related to transformational leadership (Podsakoff et al., 1990), organizational commitment (Meyer et al., 2002; Williams & Anderson, 1991), and employee engagement (Saks, 2006).

### 4.3    Co-citation Analysis

One of our main goals in this study was to better understand the underlying theoretical propositions of OCB and to assess their applicability to ethicality in BVCC. This can be achieved through the co-citation analysis procedure, which enables insights into the internal structure of the field (Mullins et al., 1977). Namely, the purpose of our co-citation analysis and subsequent clustering of co-cited references is to assess top-cited references in the field in terms of their theoretical rationale and contributions in terms of the common and most important themes in the OCB field that consequently have the potential to improve the ethicality of BVCC processes.

We continued with the analysis of the 555 selected manuscripts dataset by using BibExcel (Persson et al., 2009) with the aim to produce a co-citation analysis that deals with the relationships among the authors and publications themselves. A total of 40,725 references from the original manuscripts were analysed. We first calculated frequencies of appearance of individual references in the manuscript and identified eight publications that appeared 40 or more times in the manuscripts, which suggests that they are the most influential manuscripts in the field. These are presented in Table 17.3.

*Table 17.2    Most cited articles in the organizational citizenship behaviour field*

| Authors | Year | Title | Journal title | Citations |
|---|---|---|---|---|
| Meyer et al. | 2002 | Affective, continuance, and normative commitment to the organization: A meta-analysis of antecedents, correlates, and consequences | *Journal of Vocational Behaviour* | 2,908 |
| Podsakoff et al. | 1990 | Transformational leader behaviours and their effects on followers' trust in leader, satisfaction, and organizational citizenship behaviours | *Leadership Quarterly* | 2,509 |
| Podsakoff et al. | 2000 | Organizational citizenship behaviours: A critical review of the theoretical and empirical literature and suggestions for future research | *Journal of Management* | 2,488 |
| Williams & Anderson | 1991 | Job satisfaction and organizational commitment as predictors of organizational citizenship and in-role behaviours | *Journal of Management* | 2,000 |
| Saks | 2006 | Antecedents and consequences of employee engagement | *Journal of Managerial Psychology* | 1,661 |

*Table 17.3     List of top manuscripts by occurrence*

| Publication | Occurrence |
|---|---|
| Williams, L. J., & Anderson, S. E. (1991). Job satisfaction and organizational commitment as predictors of organizational citizenship and in-role behaviours. *Journal of Management, 17*(3), 601–617. | 143 |
| Organ, D. W. (1988). *Organizational Citizenship Behaviour: The Good Soldier Syndrome.* Lexington Books/DC Heath and Co. | 124 |
| Podsakoff, P. M., MacKenzie, S. B., Paine, J. B., & Bachrach, D. G. (2000). Organizational citizenship behaviours: A critical review of the theoretical and empirical literature and suggestions for future research. *Journal of Management, 26*(3), 513–563. | 72 |
| Smith, C. A., Organ, D. W., & Near, J. P. (1983). Organizational citizenship behaviour: Its nature and antecedents. *Journal of Applied Psychology, 68*(4), 653–663. | 61 |
| Organ, D. W., & Ryan, K. (1995). A meta-analytic review of attitudinal and dispositional predictors of organizational citizenship behaviour. *Personnel Psychology, 48*(4), 775–802. | 56 |
| Lee, K., & Allen, N. J. (2002). Organizational citizenship behaviour and workplace deviance: The role of affect and cognitions. *Journal of Applied Psychology, 87*(1), 131–142. | 47 |
| LePine, J., Erez, A., & Johnson, D. (2002). The nature and dimensionality of organizational citizenship behaviour: A critical review and meta-analysis. *Journal of Applied Psychology, 87*(1), 52–65. | 43 |
| Organ, D. W. (1997). Organizational citizenship behaviour: It's construct clean-up time. *Human Performance, 10*(2), 85–97. | 42 |

*Table 17.4     The co-citations in the organizational citizenship behaviour field*

| Co-occurrences | Co-citation Pairs | |
|---|---|---|
| 28 | Podsakoff et al., 2000 | Williams & Anderson, 1991 |
| 25 | Smith et al., 1983 | Williams & Anderson, 1991 |
| 23 | Organ, 1988 | Williams & Anderson, 1991 |
| 21 | Podsakoff et al., 2000 | Smith et al., 1983 |
| 21 | Moorman, 1991 | Williams & Anderson, 1991 |
| 20 | Organ & Ryan, 1995 | Williams & Anderson, 1991 |
| 20 | Organ, 1988 | Smith et al., 1983 |

It can be clearly seen that the works of Dennis Organ are seminal in the field, from his book about organizational citizenship behaviours in 1988, to two additional articles he co-authored, and which found their place on the list. Apart from Organ's work, and the work of Williams and Anderson (1991), which tried to explain OCB with job satisfaction and organizational commitment, it is interesting to note that there are three articles relevant from the field that tackle the domain of psychology and are published in the *Journal of Applied Psychology* (Smith et al., 1983; Lee & Allen, 2002; LePine et al., 2002).

Ultimately, we created co-occurrence pairs in a way that we selected only references with a frequency of 30 or higher. The resulting co-occurrence set was made with 116 unique pairs. In Table 17.4, the top co-citation pairs are presented – ones that appear together 20 and more times in the references. The resulting seven co-citation pairs are made of seven manuscripts that represent the theoretical basis of the OCB field.

### 4.4     Co-citations Clustering

We continued the analysis of co-citations by network visualization of the data, using VOS viewer (Van Eck & Waltman, 2010). Here, we aimed for visualization of the co-citation dataset produced above. The dataset of 40,725 cited references was analysed with a threshold of a minimum of 20 citations of a cited reference in the selected dataset. A total of 29 resulting manuscripts were analysed and grouped in three clusters (Figure 17.1) with an overall 374 links and a total link strength of 1,988 (minimum strength is set to 1 and normalization was conducted based on the association strength; attraction = 2, repulsion = 1). Weights of the circles on the figures represent the number of citations.

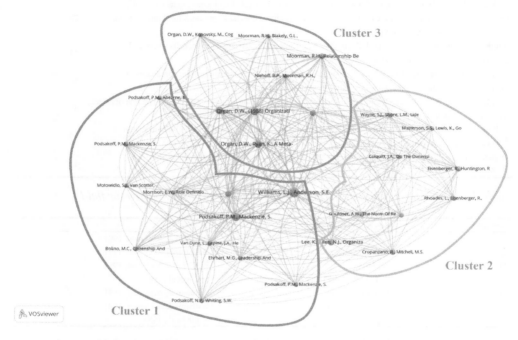

*Figure 17.1    Three cluster solution bibliometric co-citation network of organizational citizenship behaviour field*

In terms of their content and structure, three clusters explain different aspects of OCB. The first cluster deals with the dimensionality of OCB and its antecedents and consequences. The position of OCB in the firm is assessed and contrasted with other behavioural constructs. The second cluster of references sets up the theoretical stage for OCB with the norm of reciprocity and perceived organizational support in its focus. Furthermore, this cluster gathers references on affect and cognition and their role in OCB. The third cluster captures the OCB definition and organizational justice theoretical framework as a base for the OCB actions.

The first cluster consists of 12 references with Williams and Anderson (1991) being the lead reference with a total link strength of 352, followed by Podsakoff et al. (2000), with a total link strength of 263. Williams and Anderson's seminal work (1991) distinguishes two main dimensions of organizational citizenship behaviours: OCB-O – behaviours that benefit organizations in general (also labelled as generalized compliance); and OCB-I – behaviours that immediately benefit specific individuals and indirectly benefit the organization (also labelled as altruism). It shows they act as separate concepts in research practice, finding that OCB-O is better predicted by extrinsic components of job performance, while OCB-I is better predicted by intrinsic components of job performance. The second leading article (Podsakoff et al., 2000) presents a meta-analytic review study, analysing the substance of OCB and its distinctiveness from other forms of behaviours (such as in-role behaviours), its antecedents and consequences, and context. The third article in the first cluster (Leine et al., 2002) also discusses the nature of the OCB constructs in a meta-analytic way and finds that there is strong support for it to be an aggregate construct in terms of its measurement.

The second cluster consists of nine manuscripts, with the lead one (total link strength of 135) being Lee and Allen's (2002) work that assesses how affect and cognition shape OCB and workplace deviance. The study shows that OCB-O is correlated with job cognitions (fairness, recognition) and in this way it reflects planned and deliberate behaviours motivated by reciprocity needs. In terms of OCB-I, they show a slightly higher correlation with job affect than with job cognition. The second influential manuscript in this cluster (link strength of 127) is Gouldner's (1960) seminal piece that presents the norm of reciprocity and its theoretical bases. Finally, the third article in the ranking by link strength (link strength of 115) is by Eisenberger et al. (1986) that defines, and measures perceived organizational support.

The third cluster, with its eight manuscripts, presents the final piece of the definitional framework in the OCB literature, with Organ's book (1988) being the lead and the strongest piece of work (total link strength of 244). Mostly, studies use Organ's work to define the OCB. It is followed by Smith et al.'s (1983) work on the antecedents of OCB (total link strength of 243), and Organ and Ryan's (1995) meta-analytic review of attitudinal and dispositional predictors of OCB (total link strength of 221). This cluster predominantly includes theoretical aspects of organizational justice, with its dimensions of distributive, interactional and procedural justice, as an important driver of OCB (Niehoff & Moorman, 1993).

## 5.    DISCUSSION AND PROPOSITIONS

To better understand ethical considerations in BVCC, we explored OCB as a relevant ethical domain in management theory and practice. Since OCB is already a well-researched area, we conducted a bibliometric analysis to derive suggestions for improving the ethics of brand value co-creation. The final bibliometric analysis grouped the main references of the OCB field into three clusters. Our propositions are aligned with the structure of each cluster.

*Proposition 1: OCB can be used as a lever to introduce an ethical corporate culture into BVCC processes.*

Previous studies confirm the strong relationships in employee–customer collaboration in BVCC processes. The first cluster of our analysis clearly shows that OCB-I and OCB-O are distinct and relevant dimensions, and we regard that OCB-I is necessary for employees to ethically engage in BVCC processes. This dimension is better predicted by intrinsic components of job performance (Hunt et al., 1989; Podsakoff et al., 2000), so organizations need to work on creating and developing an ethical corporate culture (Schwartz, 2013). Schwartz (2013) defines ethical corporate culture as a composite of shared values, beliefs and assumptions based on core ethical values that permeate throughout the organization. Key culture elements are consistent with OCB-I and should positively impact the interactions that occur in the conversational place when co-creating brand value. Namely, OCB-I includes altruistic behaviours and commitment to others' wellbeing improvement that contributes to the ethical corporate culture and ethical values of the organization. Managers aiming at improving the ethicality of BVCC processes can remind their key employees of the corporate culture and values of the organization and aim at boosting their levels of OCB-I.

*Proposition 2: The norm of reciprocity that drives OCB has a spillover effect on interactions in BVCC processes.*

Employee commitment to the organization (OCB-O) and consequently to BVCC processes increases when employees perceive that the organization provides benefits to them. Gouldner (1960) emphasizes reciprocity as a source of social cohesion among employees, and between employees and the organization. The reciprocity norm refers to a set of socially accepted rules about a particular exchange in which one side gives a resource to another side who is obligated to return the favour. OCB research relies heavily on the norm of reciprocity in social exchanges between employees, between supervisors and subordinates, and in the workplace in general. Findings on the influence of OCB-I on employees' engagement and contributions in operational processes, confirm that management should support and enrich OCB-I. Moreover, employees continuously have strong relationships with customers who demand reciprocity between the value received and the value provided, that is, they behave within the framework of giving and returning the equivalence (Simmel, 1950). Therefore, social exchange and the reciprocity norm being embedded in OCB actions have the potential for a spillover effect on BVCC processes and can serve as a mechanism to explain ethical phenomena in interactions between customers and employees in value co-creation. Groth (2005) suggested that employee satisfaction results will spillover on customer satisfaction in the process of interaction with the organization. Their exchange is considered as a social exchange (Bowen, 1990) and consequently in cases when customers get benefits, they feel a moral obligation to respond and take reciprocal actions. Similarly, as this is illustrated with satisfaction, ethical behaviours driven by OCB can have a spillover effect from employees and organizations to consumers and vice versa.

Namely, positive spillover effects would be a consequence of social exchange, employees' behaviours and engagement, and caused primarily by the reciprocity norm, that is, positive internal relations between managers/supervisors and employees. Those employees are more committed and engaged in OCBs with both colleagues and also customers. Furthermore, employees' engagement can be recognized in OCB-O and OCB-I where employees with increased OCB have higher engagement in the process of BVCC. To improve ethicality in the BVCC processes, managers should consider how they define the reciprocity for employees engaged in the BVCC processes, as well as what are the give-and-take elements of reciprocity for involved customers.

*Proposition 3: For BVCC processes to become more strategic in the co-creation continuum, organizations should adhere to principles of organizational justice that also drive OCB.*

Co-creation as a process, and by that the brand value co-creation, is still searching for its place on a continuum between tactics and strategy (Ind et al., 2017). A strategic approach to BVCC would be more beneficial to the organization. The final proposition that emerged from our bibliometric analysis of the OCB field is the contributing effect of organizational justice embedded in OCB (Niehoff & Moorman, 1993) to the BVCC processes. Organ (1988) suggested that distributive justice is relevant for OCB because if employees perceive fair distribution at work, they are more likely to respond with an increase in their OCB input and vice versa. In addition, procedural justice, through its components of formal procedures and interactional justice, is also relevant for employees' attitudes and behaviours (Niehoff & Moorman, 1993). Through its effect on OCB, organizational justice dimensions can have important repercussions on BVCC processes. The organization can institutionalize BVCC processes and make them more strategic by detailing and defining formal procedures as well as the distribution of work for co-creation, and with that ensure better BVCC performance. Moreover, justice, especially in terms of formal procedures, benefits the consumers as well, since they can know in advance what is required from them as an input and what to expect in the process.

## 6.     CONCLUSION AND FUTURE RESEARCH

This manuscript identifies the origins of the OCB field by using a bibliometric co-citation analysis. These origins evolve around three clusters of the most relevant publications which contribute to the final shape of the field. Based on these clusters, we identify three concrete propositions for organizations to make their BVCC processes more ethical by relying on already known practices of OCB: (1) using OCB as a lever to introduce an ethical corporate culture; (2) relying on the norm of reciprocity in employee–consumer interactions (conversational space); and (3) practising organizational justice propositions to make BVCC more strategic. An ethical climate accepted and developed through OCB can lead to employees' readiness to participate in business processes and BVCC in particular, improving in that way organizational performance such as brand value, customer satisfaction and loyalty.

Further studies should empirically examine OCB perspectives and their relevance for BVCC, as additional ethical BVCC processes should be more beneficial to the final desired brand outcomes, such as brand value, loyalty, re-patronage intentions and brand love. Further research should examine other dimensions of citizenship – such as corporate citizenship – and its role in organizational ethical performance in the BVCC context (Maignan & Ferrell, 2001). In addition to citizenship, other aspects of transformational leadership and ethical change in corporate culture to accommodate co-creation processes should also be considered.

## REFERENCES

Aaker, J. L. (1999). The malleable self: The role of self-expression in persuasion. *Journal of Marketing Research, 36,* 45–57.
Axelrod, R. (1986). An evolutionary approach to norms. *American Political Science Review,* 80, 1095–1111.
Babic-Hodovic, V. (2010). *Marketing usluga: Koncept, strategije I implementacija.* [Services marketing: Concept, strategies and implementation]. Sarajevo: School of Economics and Business.
Baker, E. W., & Bulkley, N. (2014). Paying it forward vs. rewarding reputation: Mechanisms of generalized reciprocity. *Organization Science.* https://doi.org/10.1287/orsc.2014.0920
Balmer, J. M. T. (2010). Explicating corporate brands and their management: Reflections and directions from 1995. *Journal of Brand Management, 18*(3), 180–196.
Bergeron, D. M. (2007). The potential paradox of organizational citizenship behaviour: Good citizens at what cost? *Academy of Management Review, 32*(4), 1078–1095.

Bolino, M. C. (1999). Citizenship and impression management. Good soldiers or good actors? *Academy of Management Review, 24*, 82–98.

Bolino, M. C., & Turnley, W. H. (2003). Going the extra mile: Cultivating and managing employee citizenship behaviour. *Academy of Management Executive, 17*(3), 60–71.

Bowen, J. (1990). Development of a taxonomy of services to gain strategic marketing insights. *Journal of the Academy of Marketing Science, 18*(1), 43–49.

Brakus, J. J., Schmitt, B. H., & Zarantonello, L. (2009). Brand experience: What is it? How is it measured? Does it affect loyalty? *Journal of Marketing, 73*, 52–68.

Burmann, C., Zeplin, S., & Riley, N. (2009). Key determinants of brand management success: An exploratory empirical analysis. *Journal of Brand Management, 16*, 264–284.

Burnham, J. F. (2006). Scopus database: A review. *Biomedical Digital Libraries, 3*(1), 1–8.

Cullen, B. J., Parboteeah, P. K., & Victor, B. (2003). The effects of ethical climates on organizational commitment: A two-study analysis. *Journal of Business Ethics, 46*(2), 127–141.

Dall'Olmo Riley, F., & De Chernatony, L. (2000). The service brand as relationships builder. *British Journal of Management, 11*(2), 137–150.

Dhiman, P., & Arora, S. (2020). A conceptual framework for identifying key employee branding dimensions: A study of hospitality industry. *Journal of Innovation & Knowledge, 5*, 199–208.

Eisenberger, R., Huntington, R., Hutchison, S., & Sowa, D. (1986). Perceived organizational support. *Journal of Applied Psychology, 71*(3), 500–507.

Fetscherin, M., Boulanger, M., Filho, C. G., & Souki, G. Q. (2014). The effect of product category on consumer brand relationships. *Journal of Product & Brand Management, 23*(2), 78–89.

France, C., Merrilees, B., & Miller, D. (2016). An integrated model of customer–brand engagement: Drivers and consequences. *Journal of Brand Management, 23*(2), 119–136.

Gouldner, A. W. (1960). The norm of reciprocity: A preliminary statement. *American Sociological Review, 25*(2), 161–178.

Gregory, A. (2007). Involving stakeholders in developing corporate brands: The communication dimension. *Journal of Marketing Management, 23*(1–2), 59–73.

Grönroos, C. (2011). Value co-creation in service logic: A critical analysis. *Marketing Theory, 11*(3), 279–301.

Groth, M. (2005). Customers as good soldiers: Examining citizenship behaviours in internet service deliveries. *Journal of Management, 31*(1), 7–27.

Harris, J. R. (1990). Ethical values of individuals at different levels in the organizational hierarchy of a single firm. *Journal of Business Ethics, 9*(9), 741–750.

Harrison, R., Newholm, T., & Shaw, D. (2005). *The Ethical Consumer.* London: Sage.

Hatch, J. M., & Schultz, M. (2010). Toward a theory of brand co-creation with implications for brand governance. *Journal of Brand Management, 17*, 590–604.

Henkel, P. A., Boegershausen, J., Rafaeli, A., & Lemmink, J. (2017). The social dimension of service interactions: Observer reactions to customer incivility. *Journal of Service Research, 20*(2), 120–134.

Hunt, S. D., Wood, V. R., & Chonko, L. B. (1989). Corporate ethical values and organizational commitment in marketing. *Journal of Marketing, 53*, 79–90.

Iglesias, O., & Ind, N. (2020). Towards a theory of conscientious corporate brand co-creation: The next key challenge in brand management. *Journal of Brand Management, 27*(6), 710–720.

Iglesias, O., Ind, N., & Alfaro, M. (2013). The organic view of the brand: A brand value co-creation model. *Journal of Brand Management, 20*, 670–688.

Iglesias, O., Markovic, S., Singh, J. J., & Sierra, V. (2019). Do customer perceptions of corporate services brand ethicality improve brand equity? Considering the roles of brand heritage, brand image, and recognition benefits. *Journal of Business Ethics, 154*(2), 441–459.

Ind, N., Iglesias, O., & Schultz, M. (2013). Building brands together: Emergence and outcomes of co-creation. *California Management Review, 55*(3), 5–26.

Ind, N., Iglesias, O., & Markovic, S. (2017). The co-creation continuum: From tactical market research tool to strategic collaborative innovation method. *Journal of Brand Management, 24*(4), 310–321.

Kapferer, J. N. (2008). *The New Strategic Brand Management: Creating and Sustaining Brand Equity Long Term.* London: Kogan Page Publishers.

Kaufmann, H. R., Loureiro, S. M. C., & Agapi Manarioti, A. (2016). Exploring behavioural branding, brand love and brand co-creation. *Journal of Product & Brand Management, 25*(6), 516–526.

Kotler, P., & Lee, N. (2005). *Corporate Social Responsibility*. Hoboken, NJ: John Wiley and Sons, Inc.

Lee, K., & Allen, N. J. (2002). Organizational citizenship behaviour and workplace deviance: The role of affect and cognitions. *Journal of Applied Psychology*, *87*(1), 131–142.

LePine, J., Erez, A., & Johnson, D. (2002). The nature and dimensionality of organizational citizenship behaviour: A critical review and meta-analysis. *Journal of Applied Psychology*, *87*(1), 52–65.

Lester, S. W., Meglino, B. M., & Korsgaard, M. A. (2008). The role of other orientation in organizational citizenship behaviour. *Journal of Organizational Behaviour: The International Journal of Industrial, Occupational and Organizational Psychology and Behaviour*, *29*(6), 829–841.

Lin, Y. T., & Liu, N. C. (2019). Corporate citizenship and employee outcomes: Does a high-commitment work system matter? *Journal of Business Ethics*, *156*(4), 1079–1097.

Maignan, I., & Ferrell, O. C. (2001). Antecedents and benefits of corporate citizenship: An investigation of French businesses. *Journal of Business Research*, *51*(1), 37–51.

Maignan, I., Ferrell, O. C., & Hult, G. T. M. (1999). Corporate citizenship: Cultural antecedents and business benefits. *Journal of the Academy of Marketing Science*, *27*(4), 455–469.

Maniates, M. F. (2001). Individualization: Plant a tree, buy a bike, save the world? *Global Environmental Politics*, *1*(3), 31–52.

Markovic, S., von Wallpach, S., & Gyrd-Jones, R. (2018). Multi-stakeholder knowledge sharing and brand co-creation: Ethical considerations. In K. Hamilton, M. Alexander, S. Gounaris, M. Karampela, & E. Lacka (Eds.), *Proceedings of the European Marketing Academy (EMAC) Conference 2018: People Make Marketing*. Glasgow: European Marketing Academy.

Merz, M. A., He, Y., & Vargo, S. L. (2009). The evolving brand logic: A service-dominant logic perspective. *Journal of the Academy of Marketing Science*, *37*(3), 328–344.

Meyer, J. P., Stanley, D. J., Herscovitch, L., & Topolnytsky, L. (2002). Affective, continuance, and normative commitment to the organization: A meta-analysis of antecedents, correlates, and consequences. *Journal of Vocational Behaviour*, *61*(1), 20–52.

Moorman, R. H. (1991). Relationship between organizational justice and organizational citizenship behaviours: Do fairness perceptions influence employee citizenship? *Journal of Applied Psychology*, *76*(6), 845–855.

Morrison, S., & Crane, F. G. (2007). Building the service brand by creating and managing an emotional brand experience. *Journal of Brand Management*, *14*(5), 410–421.

Motowidlo, S. J. (2000). Some basic issues related to contextual performance and organizational citizenship behaviour in human resource management. *Human Resource Management Review*, *10*(1), 115–126.

Mullins, N. C., Hargens, L. L., Hecht, P. K., & Kick, E. L. (1977). The group structure of co-citation clusters: A comparative study. *American Sociological Review*, *42*, 552–562.

Muniz, A. Jr., & O'Guinn, T. (2001). Brand community. *Journal of Consumer Research*, *27*(4), 412–432.

Nadeem, W., Juntunen, M., Hajli, N., & Tajvidi, M. (2019). The role of ethical perceptions in consumers' participation and value co-creation on sharing economy platforms. *Journal of Business Ethics*, *169*, 421–441.

Niehoff, B. P., & Moorman, R. H. (1993). Justice as a mediator of the relationship between methods of monitoring and organizational citizenship behaviour. *Academy of Management Journal*, *36*(3), 527–556.

Organ, D. W. (1988). *Organizational Citizenship Behaviour: The Good Soldier Syndrome*. Lexington, MA: Lexington Books/DC Heath and Co.

Organ, D. W. (1997). Organizational citizenship behaviour: It's construct clean-up time. *Human Performance*, *10*(2), 85–97.

Organ, D. W., & Paine, J. B. (1999). A new kind of performance for industrial and organizational psychology: Recent contributions to the study of organizational citizenship behaviour. In C. L. Cooper & I. T. Robertson (Eds.), *International Review of Industrial and Organizational Psychology*, Vol. 14 (pp. 337–368). New York: John Wiley & Sons Ltd.

Organ, D. W., & Ryan, K. (1995). A meta-analytic review of attitudinal and dispositional predictors of organizational citizenship behaviour. *Personnel Psychology*, *48*(4), 775–802.

Persson, O., Danell, R., & Schneider, J. W. (2009). How to use Bibexcel for various types of bibliometric analysis. *Celebrating Scholarly Communication Studies: A Festschrift for Olle Persson at his 60th Birthday*, *5*, 9–24.

Podsakoff, P. M., Ahearne, M., & MacKenzie, S. B. (1997). Organizational citizenship behaviour and the quantity and quality of work group performance. *Journal of Applied Psychology, 82*, 262–270.

Podsakoff, P. M., MacKenzie, S. B., Moorman, R. H., & Fetter, R. (1990). Transformational leader behaviours and their effects on followers' trust in leader, satisfaction, and organizational citizenship behaviours. *Leadership Quarterly, 1*(2), 107–142.

Podsakoff, P. M., MacKenzie, S. B., Paine, J. B., & Bachrach, D. G. (2000). Organizational citizenship behaviours: A critical review of the theoretical and empirical literature and suggestions for future research. *Journal of Management, 26*(3), 513–563.

Prahalad, C. K., & Ramaswamy, V. (2004). Co-creation experiences: The next practice in value creation. *Journal of Interactive Marketing, 18*(3), 5–14.Saks, A. M. (2006). Antecedents and consequences of employee engagement. *Journal of Managerial Psychology, 21*(7), 600–619.

Schwartz, M. S. (2013). Developing and sustaining an ethical corporate culture: The core elements. *Business Horizons, 56*, 39–50.

Shamir, R. (2008). The age of responsibilization: On market-embedded morality. *Economy and Society, 37*(1), 1–19.

Simmel, G. (1950). *The Sociology.* Glencoe, IL: Free Press.

Singh, J. B. (2011). Determinants of the effectiveness of corporate codes of ethics: An empirical study. *Journal of Business Ethics, 101*(3), 385–395.

Smith, C. A., Organ, D. W., & Near, J. P. (1983). Organizational citizenship behaviour: Its nature and antecedents. *Journal of Applied Psychology, 68*(4), 653–663.

Stanislawski, S. (2011). The service-dominant logic of marketing and the ethics of co-creation. *Bulletin of the Graduate School of Commerce-Waseda University, 73*, 109–133.

Starr, M. A. (2009). The social economics of ethical consumption: Theoretical considerations and empirical evidence. *Journal of Socio-Economics, 38*(6), 916–925.

Tourigny, L., Han, J., Baba, V. V., & Pan, P. (2019). Ethical leadership and corporate social responsibility in China: A multilevel study of their effects on trust and organizational citizenship behavior. *Journal of Business Ethics, 158*(2), 427–440.

Vallaster, C., & Lindgreen, A. (2011). Corporate brand strategy formation: Brand actors and the situational context for a business-to-business brand. *Industrial Marketing Management, 40*(7), 1133–1143.

Van Dyne, L., & LePine, A. J. (1998). Predicting voice behaviour in work groups. *Journal of Applied Psychology, 83*(6), 853–868.

Van Eck, N. J., & Waltman, L. (2010). Software survey: VOSviewer, a computer program for bibliometric mapping. *Scientometrics, 84*(2), 523–538.

Vargo, S. L., & Lusch, R. F. (2004). Evolving to a new dominant logic for marketing. *Journal of Marketing, 68*(1), 1–17.

Walz, S. M., & Niehoff, B. P. (1996). Organizational citizenship behaviours and their effect on organizational effectiveness in limited-menu restaurants. In J. B. Keys & L. N. Dosier (Eds.), *Academy of Management Best Papers Proceedings* (pp. 307–311). Statesboro: Georgia Southern University, College of Business Administration, Office of Publications and Faculty Research Services.

Wang, Y.-D., & Sung, W.-C. (2014). Predictors of organizational citizenship behaviour: Ethical leadership and workplace jealousy. *Journal of Business Ethics, 135*, 1–12.

Williams, L. J., & Anderson, S. E. (1991). Job satisfaction and organizational commitment as predictors of organizational citizenship and in-role behaviours. *Journal of Management, 17*(3), 601–617.

Yi, Y., & Gong, T. (2013). Customer value co-creation behaviour: Scale development and validation. *Journal of Business Research, 66*(9), 1279–1284.

# 18. "We look within... So we can look up" – towards a nonviolent ethics of human brand co-creation

*Monica Porzionato and Cecilia Cassinger*

## 1.    INTRODUCTION

The way in which social media influencers (SMI) manage their human brands receives increasing attention in brand co-creation research (e.g. Centeno & Wang, 2017; Von Wallpach et al., 2017). SMIs have rapidly become important actors in the contemporary marketing landscape due to their ability to form intimate and authentic relationships with large numbers of followers (Centeno & Wang, 2017; Jin et al., 2019). By integrating paid content with pieces of their everyday life, SMI brands are viewed as able to influence consumption patterns on a deeper level (Khamis et al., 2017). Such pieces of everyday life are, however, often controversial in nature to attract maximum attention. SMI brands are performed in public and are typically loved as much as they are hated by consumers (Fournier & Eckhardt, 2019). In contrast to traditional celebrities, influencers monetise their public personas by means of exchanging private and intimate details about their everyday life, which is believed to make them more credible, authentic, and trustworthy (Jin et al., 2019).

Extant research on human brand co-creation predominantly adopts a stakeholder perspective to examine how identities of human brands are created and performed by diverse actors, such as consumers, media, and investors (Centeno & Wang, 2017; Vallaster & Von Wallpach, 2013; Von Wallpach et al., 2017). Previous studies demonstrate that human brand identities do not refer to intrinsic personal qualities, but are outcomes of interactions with various audiences (Abidin, 2016; Marwick, 2015, 2017; Zhang, 2017). A typical ethical dilemma arising from the relationship between the SMI brand and its followers concerns the reconciliation between sponsored content, influencer credibility, and consumer trust (Iglesias et al., 2020; Lou & Yuan, 2019; Wang et al., 2020). This dilemma is typically approached from the perspective of formal ethics, and concerns legal regulations and restrictions of marketing in terms of signposting paid content, as well as the moral responsibility of influencers towards their followers with reference to privacy and shared content (Dhanesh & Duthler, 2019). The relation between the influencer brand and followers is viewed as asymmetric in power where the individual influencer persuades or even manipulates followers to consume in certain ways (Abidin, 2016; Chae, 2018).

In this chapter, we argue that this way of viewing the relationship between influencer and follower rests on the idea of existing rational autonomous subjects, audiences, and economic structures. In particular, this view relies on the assumption that SMIs and their followers have separate and self-standing identities (e.g. victims, perpetrators, winners and losers, ethical and unethical individuals, etc.) able to fully act, or refuse to act, in an ethical manner. Hence, from this viewpoint, ethicality concerns the relationship between individuals, rather than the institutional environment in which the relationship is embedded, producing a reductionist understanding of human brand co-creation. By contrast, we propose an ethical approach to human brand co-creation that shifts focus from the relationship between the influencer and followers to the complex *relational constitution* of the human brand and its followers. To this end, we draw on an ethical approach inspired by Butler's (2020) work on nonviolent ethics, wherein the author aims at abandoning the prevalent individualistic conception of ethics as a matter of an individual faced with a moral choice. For Butler, this conceptualisation of ethics ends up in considering violence, and nonviolence, as individual acts, rather than acts embedded in a broader institutionalisation of violence. As such, Butler shows how the violent and the nonviolent are in an unavoidable relation to each other, a relation that precedes them and forms their very positions. We propose that approaching SMIs and their followers as co-constructed within the same economic logic, stressing their unavoidable dependency, allows us to abandon the asymmetric view of power in the understanding of influencers and followers, wherein one is considered to be able to rationally act either unethically/violently or ethically/nonviolently. A relational ethics approach enables understanding the relationship between followers and influencers in a nonviolent ethical manner.

The nonviolent ethical approach challenges key assumptions prevalent in the brand co-creation literature. First, it suggests that the relation between human brands and followers is non-oppositional and relational. Second, by contrast to critical research that points to the violent relationship between the publicly constructed brand persona and the individual self, it proposes that human brands are relationally constructed. Third, the approach challenges the idea of the autonomous human brand by suggesting that its existence depends on institutional arrangements and structural conditions. Fourth, it poses a critique against brand co-creation practices that rely on exploiting followers' need for recognition and provides means of how to resist the reproduction of norms of recognition according to market mediated claims of tolerance and interdependency (cf. Zembylas, 2019).

In what follows, we begin by outlining the problems with what we here refer to as a violent ethical approach to human brand co-creation. Thereafter, we propose a nonviolent approach based on bodily ontology, dependency and relationality. We illustrate the closeness and difference of the violent and nonviolent ethical approach by analysing the relationship between SMI and followers at the brand platforms of *goop* and *Yoga Girl*. We note that nonviolence follows on violence and that nonviolence should be understood as a discursive counter-practice to, or "undoing", acts of violence (Zembylas, 2019). Finally, we discuss the implications of our analysis for the ethics of human brand co-creation. We propose that a focus on a nonviolent ethics of relationality may help us capture the systemic and structural conditions of human brand co-creation.

## 2.    VIOLENT ETHICS OF HUMAN BRAND CO-CREATION

Self-branding is a central practice in the freelance labour market of the digital knowledge economy (Gandini, 2016; Hearn, 2008; Marwick, 2015). It refers to branding techniques that seek to turn the self into a commodity for sale in the labour market (Lair et al., 2005). The practice may be understood as a response to the need of white collar workers to stand out in an uncertain and flexible work life brought about by the shift to a post-Fordist economic order. Peters (1999) argued that self-branding would potentially revolutionise work by shifting attention from the mass of workers to the individual working subject. Social media facilitates integrating celebrity culture into self-presentation and individual subjectivity (Gandini, 2016). Celebrity culture may be defined as a particular embodied "mindset and a set of practices that courts attention through insights into its practitioners' private lives, and a sense of realness that renders their narratives, their branding, both accessible and intimate" (Khamis et al., 2017, pp. 202–203). Furthermore, in order to convey an authentic self, celebrities use strategic intimacy to craft a public persona that can be consumed by an audience (Abidin, 2016; Leban et al., 2020).

Critical examinations of human brands typically understand them as outcomes of an immaterial and often emotional form of labour enacted by individuals performing the brand (e.g. Abidin, 2016; Hearn & Schoenhoff, 2015). Wissinger (2009) approaches branding practices of self-commodification among fashion models as immaterial, aesthetic, and entrepreneurial labour. These forms of labour, she argues, commodify modelling into a fashionable lifestyle that is packaged and sold for consumption. The understanding of brands as deriving value from immaterial forms of labour resonates with research conceptualising brands as platforms that mediate social actions and relationships (e.g. Arvidsson, 2006). Brands organise communication in providing a comprehensible narrative for the individual according to which her or his public persona can be consumed. Self-branding is about constantly selling of the self, pitching one's dreams, relentlessly moving forward, and never being satisfied (Zwick et al., 2008). There are always new challenges and more to achieve. In this sense personal branding overlaps with governing techniques of liberal subjectivity, which is manifested in discourses of personal responsibility, individual success, and consumerism (Rose, 1999). As we will demonstrate through the examples of *goop* and *Yoga Girl*, human brands in the wellness industry are framed as being about individual self-empowerment. They thus perpetuate an idea that health and success are built on personal rational actions and choices, which consequently divide subjects into losers and winners, healthy and unhealthy.

One of the assumptions underpinning human brand co-creation in the context of SMIs is that the value of the brand is dependent on the extent to which the influencer is able to exert influence over followers (Audrezet et al., 2020). The relationship between influencer and followers is understood as asymmetrical in power where the influencer exercises authority over followers. Ethical considerations of this relationship, therefore, rely on individuality. They typically focus on the violent consequences of branding and influencing practices of SMIs, for instance, with reference to SMIs' authentic self, conflictual relationship with followers, prosumption patterns, and psychological wellbeing (Audrezet et al., 2020; Hearn & Schoenhoff, 2015; Zhang, 2017). Arguably, understanding their relationship on the basis of an individualist ethics reduces SMIs and followers to opposing parts neglecting that SMIs are also subjected to the same institutional power of liberal market forces as followers. In fact, in order to succeed, influencers need to be loved and supported by the public. In other words, the separation of SMIs and followers upholds a lack of recognition of the liberal market logic that they are both outcomes of.

Similarly, an individualist ethics may result in reducing violence to the act of an abstract entity, like the economic market, over both influencers and followers. For example, the valorisation of influencers and consumers' private spheres and everyday practices in brand co-creation (see e.g. Arvidsson, 2006; Cova & Dalli, 2009) may be seen as a violent outcome of an institutional system in which economic rewards are more important than privacy and intimacy. This view highlights how both influencers and followers risk becoming alienated from the end products of their immaterial forms of labour, that is to say, from one another. Alienation may lead to loss of subjectivity, meaning and purpose, which are constitutive features of violence (cf. Wieviorka, 2009). Experiences of not being compensated for the immaterial labour involved in the human branding process may lead to feelings of inadequacy and anxiety, since it means that the individual is tangled up in a form of self-improvement that never ends (Zwick et al., 2008). Feelings of not being good enough and a sense of meaninglessness may result in a violence that is directed towards the self. In view of the lack of a distinct conflict with an employer, and the influencer being the one who brands and becomes branded, the only direction for violence is inwards.

Thus, we argue that an ethics centred on individuality proposes a violent understanding of the relationship between influencer and followers according to which the individual becomes either the perpetrator of or victim of violence. We argue that this ethical stand is problematic if we want to grasp the structural and institutional conditions of human brands and how they contribute to perpetuate these conditions. In fact, violence should not be conceived of as an attribute of certain individualistic doings (i.e. of the influencers over the followers, of the market over the influencers) but as a concept guiding the doings of all the subjects involved. In other words, "violent" should be less considered as an adjective for the doings of self-standing entities and more for the doings these entities carry out according to a broader institutionalisation of violence they contribute to maintain. In the next section we consider human brand co-creation through a relational ethics of nonviolence as proposed by Butler (2020).

## 3.    NONVIOLENT ETHICS OF HUMAN BRAND CO-CREATION

Feminist philosophers and social theorists have rethought universalist notions of ethics, typically employed in the marketing literature, through concepts of vulnerability, recognition, interdependency, and suffering (Butler, 2004, 2012). At the centre of this thinking we find the idea that humans are ontologically connected through their bodily vulnerability. In her book *The Force of Nonviolence*, Butler (2020) argues against the binary of violence and nonviolence. By contrast, she invites us to rethink violence from ethical premises grounded on the individuality of human subjects to ones tied in subjects' unavoidable interconnectedness. In this regard, she underlines how both the actualisation and the negation of violence are commonly conceived of in terms of individual choices, wherein, for example, one refuses to use violence as a result of a rational decision. Such a tendency, she argues, reinstates the misleading belief that there exist in society pre-existing typologies of identity which can be either violent or nonviolent and that, therefore, nonviolence is a matter of choosing between these identities. In other words, nonviolent individuals are viewed as those who choose not to adopt violence as a means to achieve certain objectives, and which consequently recognise their own self according to this choice. Conversely, Butler urges us to focus on the structural aspect of violence where it is a structural phenomenon that cannot be tied to individual bodies and subjectivities, but to the daily functioning of social institutions. In other words, violence and nonviolence are not acts of free-standing individuals derived from a rational choice, but the result of structural and systemic practices which frame violence as a rational choice.

Institutional arrangements, economic systems and forms of governance, she claims, constantly reiterate meanings of power as standing on the presence of ontological entities called the Self and the Other, and responding to what she calls "an unequal distribution of grievability" (Butler, 2020, p. 93). As a result of this, violence is based on a division between grievable and non-grievable lives, which are perceived as worthy of preservation. For Butler, instead, the point is to recognise that both positions of Self and Other as grievable are themselves the result of a biopolitical landscape, meaning that they are socially constructed. Consequently, she denounces to societies and social institutions the adoption of an ethics tied to individualism – thus as a matter of an individual faced with a rational moral choice – and proposes instead to rethink that ethics in relational terms, as one based on the recognition of individuals' shared condition of vulnerability.

Therefore, to overcome violence, for Butler, the point is to recognise the social construction of both positions (of the violent and nonviolent) and to acknowledge that both positions are unavoidably interconnected. In other words, nonviolence is itself violence because it is by considering myself nonviolent that I consider another self as violent: I *am through* my making you different. Instead, Butler invites us to see how both selves exist within the same structural system which creates them either as violent or nonviolent. In this way, violent and nonviolent individuals are thought of being created through their pre-existing relationship. According to Butler, ethics should be based on this pre-exceeding of the relations between subjects rather than on individual subjects, since individual subjects do not exist as such outside of social bonds. As a result, preserving and grieving all lives is not a result of an ethical rational choice, but of an ethical recognition of our unavoidable interconnectedness, it is "because we are already tied together in a social bond that precedes and makes possible our lives" (Butler, 2020, p. 93). Overcoming violence is therefore less a matter of including/excluding violent bodies in the social realm, and more a question of redefining the very means through which violent bodies are constructed:

> My question is not just what we, as morally accountable subjects, do, or refuse to do, to preserve a life or set of lives, but how the world is built such that the infrastructural conditions for the preservation of life are reproduced and strengthened. (Butler, 2020, p. 72)

With Butler, then, it is possible to rethink the ethical view on human brands based on an individualist notion of rational subjects acting either unethically/violently or ethically/ nonviolently towards each other. The key insight that we take from Butler is that violence is constantly created through the doings of individuals according to a broader conceptualisation of violence. In other words, violence is institutionalised and does not belong to individual bodies alone.

In the following section, we examine the relationship between celebrity influencers and their followers at the Instagram accounts of *goop* and *Yoga Girl*. These brands perpetuate a certain idea of self-worthiness and wellbeing, which we argue is based on a problematic liberal idea of an individual self. The point of the next section is twofold. First, we attempt to show how both influencers and followers share ideas of individual wellbeing through narratives of self-empowerment gained through connection, empathy and vulnerability with the other. We argue that the advocacy of the unavoidable co-dependency with the other is here nevertheless used to promote self-standing identities. Second, we propose that an ethical approach based on individuality is unable to capture the fact that influencers and followers are part of the same system which decrees their existence.

## 4.    HUMAN BRAND CO-CREATION AT *GOOP* AND *YOGA GIRL*

In this section, two instances of human brand co-creation in the self-care industry are analysed through a study of posts by influencers and followers on the Instagram accounts of *goop* and *Yoga Girl*. Instagram posts containing notions related to relational ethicality were collected during a time period of one month between July and August in 2020. Because the posts were assembled during the COVID-19 pandemic crisis, they may be viewed as extreme cases of themes of suffering, loss, and interconnectedness. The brand platforms build on the brand personas of actress and celebrity, Gwyneth Paltrow, and micro-celebrity and yoga instructor Rachel Brathen. *goop* started in 2008 as Paltrow's weekly newsletter to her friends, and rapidly grew into a lifestyle brand encompassing e-commerce, pop-up stores, brand collaborations, and the private label G (Caulfield, 2015; Logan, 2017). Even though Paltrow has sought to distance herself from the corporate brand, her brand persona is central in social media and on the online brand site. The e-commerce company is built around Paltrow's exclusive lifestyle and controversial self-care practices. Her celebrity friends and family members regularly feature on *goop*'s Instagram account and e-commerce platform to create familiarity and intimacy with followers.

Brathen teaches yoga in her studio at Aruba and online under the brand *Yoga Girl. Yoga Girl* is also the name of Brathen's book – a *New York Times* bestseller – and Instagram account, which currently has 2.1 million followers (Porkoláb, 2017). The brand narrative of *Yoga Girl* is focused on Brathen's struggles to come to terms with depression, while juggling multiple roles of being mother to her 5-year-old daughter, wife, teacher, entrepreneur, and human. Brathen and Paltrow converge in that they present themselves as pioneers in wellness and often use political statements to stir attention. They are also similar in the way that they draw on a discourse of ethical relationality, albeit in an individualised and commoditised form. An example of this is the dissolution of mind and body, which is often stressed by Paltrow.

> *goop*: Vicky Vlachonis (an osteopath that I have the incredible good fortune to work with in London) has been instrumental in getting me to understand the importance of the mind body connection. A true healer, Vicky is one of a few very special practitioners who have taught me to take a more holistic approach, an approach which inextricably links our emotional state to our physical health. Below you will find her theory and some very practical, useful tips. Love, gp

Under headings such as "own your pain", "Letting go of the weight we are carrying", the message is by engaging in practices of fasting, exercising, dieting, and meditating, we can learn how to control the body through the mind, and vice versa. Over the years, Paltrow has created considerable attention in the media by talking about her personal experiences of orgasm, conscious uncoupling from her celebrity husband, vagina steaming, and detoxing diets. Logan (2017, p. 601) argues that *goop* represents an ascetic form of post-industrial consumerism by preaching "the gospels of minimalism". She further writes: "In the interplay between Gwyneth Paltrow's own body, the body of her corporation, and the implied bodies of the brand's audience, goop expands the possibilities of self-limitation" (2017, p. 601). In this way, *goop* promotes practices that reduce excess materiality in order to accumulate capital.

Influencers are often described as a mix of distant friends and micro-celebrities. Micro-celebrities are different from traditional celebrities in that they often feel obligations towards their followers and a responsibility to respond and recognise them which blurs the boundary between the performer and audience on social media platforms (Marwick, 2015).

The blurred boundary diminishes the distance between influencer and follower; public and private. An example of this is how Paltrow's followers know her by her nickname "gp" under which the content and products at *goop* are curated.

| | |
|---|---|
| *goop*: | Shelter-in-place started at the beginning of spring, and unbelievably, we're now closing out summer. The days feel long, but the seasons feel short. I've spent the last month near my mum on the East Coast, getting as much quality time together as possible (she also agreed to be our goop product tester). As remote life stretches on, our team has been swapping small indulgences and skin saviours, as well as the things keeping us sane and entertained. Here are some of mine. (And let us know what your hits are.) Love, GP |
| Joyconnector: | Sun, sauna, soak in salt water Cuddles, fresh oj, the best earl grey I can find, laughter til my face hurts Smiles and chats with neighbors Daily gratitude lists, journal prompts and moving my body to exhaustion and sweat to clear my heart, my mind, this gorgeous vessel in the flesh Connecting with inspiration team Dancing to heart sounds Dreaming my dreams every day xx |
| goop@joyconnector: | love that |
| gwynethpaltrow@joyconnector: | will you be my best friend |
| kazzielove2@joyconnector: | wonderful. You are a poet |
| elizabeth.foord@gwynethpaltrow: | this made me chuckle and realise how much I love the slower rhythm. I care more about the small things that make an enormous difference like 15 mins of yoga and counting all the different shades of green trees around our nearby lake. Reading rich intense books. Savoring the jigsaw puzzle with my daughter. Having long bonding conversations with the family. The hustle can bustle off |
| kimshook64@joyconnector: | yes, I concur! All of the above! To feed your soul&to look within with gratitude |
| joyconnector@gwynethpaltrow: | how much fun would that be?! Let's play! |

This post by gp, involving her personal relationship with her mother, received an unusual high number of comments, in total 264. The majority of comments were responses to gp; other comments touched upon things such as being in lock-down during the COVID-19 pandemic, BLM protests, and criticising gp's exclusive lifestyle and followers for "participating in the scam". This type of critique against gp is frequently occurring at *goop*'s Instagram account. Critics play an important role in co-creating *her* as an exclusive brand. Critics are those who cannot afford, or for other reasons, cannot participate in the luxurious asceticism promoted at *goop*. In relation to the successful, affluent, and "worthy" followers of gp, critics become the unworthy, the poor, the unhealthy, and the ugly.

Underpinning self-care brands is the ethical idea that in order to transform the world, one first needs to transform oneself (Rose, 1999). The embodiment of this idea in the personal narratives of Brathen and gp is key to create intimacy with followers and brand legitimacy (see also Abidin, 2016). This is displayed in the following posts on *Yoga Girl*:

| | |
|---|---|
| Yogagirlofficial: | You have the right to decide for yourself when you are grateful and when you are feeling pain. Yes, you can be grateful for the lessons but sometimes if there is something in your life that is just feeling painful, then chances are you need permission to sit with that to heal it. Give yourself permission to be with the pain, to sit with it, to complain, to talk about it, without rushing or trying to turn all around and get back to the positive. Give yourself permission to feel how you truly feel, no judgement, no shame, no trying to get back into a better place. (Yoga Girl) |
| Fidohanna: | you got me. I feel it. My sister got a baby last night in Sweden and I live in Thailand and can't get back home to see them and it really breaks my heart. So, Thanks for this post … I feel blessed but sad at the same time. |

The accounts of personal interactions between gp, Brathen and followers may be thought of as adhering to a market rhetoric typical for self-care brands focusing on recognition, interdependency and vulnerability. Recognition is accomplished in the responses of gp and Brathen to followers, but there are also moments of recognition among followers themselves. Recognition is enabled by addressing universal themes of pain, suffering, and bodily tensions, thus referring to a bodily ontology (Butler, 2015, 2020) suggesting that our vulnerable bodily condition – the awareness that I can cause you pain and vice versa – makes us dependent on one another. In the following interaction between *Yoga Girl* and her followers it is possible to trace articulations of brokenness, pain and suffering, which are central to relational ethics. Pain and suffering are central to relationships and human experiences and therefore concern us all.

"Hold on, pain ends #Beirut" (yoga_girl)
"YOU ARE SAFE YOU ARE SAFE YOU ARE SAFE YOU ARE SAFE YOU ARE SAFE YOU ARE SAFE YOU ARE SAFE YOU ARE SAFE YOU ARE SAFE YOU ARE SAFE…." (yoga_girl)

| | |
|---|---|
| Linda_sheridan: | We are strong we are love we are light we are well being |
| Amandasimplywell@linda_sheridan: | I love this! Such powerful affirmations! |
| Linda_sheridan@amandasimplywell: | love to you and to all |
| Annashilling: | I use this mantra daily "I am safe" it helps if you have a history of trauma which makes you feel unsafe no matter what the current environment. |
| Jen.loves.yoga: | When my son was little and had terrible night terrors, we started doing a night time meditation, drawing |

|  | a big bubble of flight around us that would protect him as he slept. We'd repeat the mantra, "I am safe and protected." "I am safe and protected". |
|---|---|
| Plainjayne111: | Thank you for your openness and honesty. |
| Laurahardynutrion: | Yessss to this. The mainstream media and all that is going on in the world is threatening our confidence to feel safe and secure. I really resonate with this. Thank you@yoga_girl. |

Interdependence means that we become aware of the ways in which our existence and our life are dependent on others' struggles, efforts, and burdens. This feature may be observed in the way that followers and influencers are tied to one another on the platform and the many posts and articles concerning unity and connecting with others. Ideas of interconnectedness and dependency are the core of the brand values and business models of *goop* and *Yoga Girl*. *goop* presents the company brand as "we operate from a place of curiosity and non-judgment, and we start hard conversations, crack open taboos, and look for connection and resonance everywhere we can find it" (goop.com). Yoga Girl describes her business as being a "community, a movement, a lifestyle ... We look within ... So we can look up." (yogagirl.com).

The relationship between the influencers of Paltrow and Brathen and their followers is marked by a highly individualised market mediated ethics of relationality. The use of ethics in this manner corresponds to Leban et al.'s (2020) argument that high-net-worth influencers display ethicality in conspicuous ways to mitigate the tension between being ethical and having an affluent lifestyle. It is noteworthy, however, that brand platforms like *goop* and *Yoga Girl* use concepts of interdependency and equal vulnerability to establish an intimate relationship with their community of followers although promoting the idea of individual wellbeing achieved through self-enhancement. Even though fundamentally dissimilar in expression, the empowering message of suffering and hard work at *goop* and *Yoga Girl*, echoes the beauty brand L'Oréal's 1990s individualist slogan "Because you are worth it". If L'Oréal tied self-worth to taking care of appearance, *goop* and *Yoga Girl* mobilise feminism, wellness, wellbeing, psychedelics, medicine, psychology, style/fashion, to improve the individual self. In other words, influencers acknowledge the unavoidable relationality between them, their followers, and everything else around them (e.g. nature, other cultures, etc.), in order to promote sovereign identities.

## 5.    DISCUSSION

The cases presented above show how through their doings *goop* and *Yoga girl* perpetuate the belief that there exists something like a Self which has the ability to choose to relate to others either for wellbeing (i.e. the message that influencers promote) or for economic purposes (i.e. the influencer brand). The point of interest for this chapter is that as long as there persists the belief in the existence of a self-standing individual, relationality can only be phrased as an act of will, and not as an unavoidable social condition. Co-dependency and vulnerability are here used as guiding ideas in the process of human brand co-creation, while at the same time exploiting people's need for recognition and interconnectedness. Butler's understanding of vulnerability within the framework of nonviolent ethics underscores this point:

> The relational understanding of vulnerability shows that we are not altogether separable from the conditions that make our lives possible or impossible. In other words, because we cannot exist liberated from such conditions, we are never fully individuated. (Butler, 2020, p. 46)

Following this reasoning, equality of success, beauty, health, wellbeing, achievement, are not best understood in individualistic terms, but in structural ones. Brands are institutions in which violent and nonviolent ethical relationships are embedded and thus co-existing. My wellbeing is dependent on the wellbeing of others, which is not the least the COVID-19 pandemic has shown us. I do not exist without you, and my achievement of wellbeing is not separate from your achievement of wellbeing. All lives are equally grievable, respected, important, not because I gain something out of your wellbeing, nor because I have the power to decide over your wellbeing, but because our wellbeing is interconnected. Celebrity culture and the perception of beauty, health, success and happiness, we argue, needs to be conceived of as structural phenomena. This is because being beautiful, successful, healthy are not a matter of personal strength, will and determination but a different allocation of opportunities which can be overcome by not only giving more opportunities to those who have none (although this is certainly helping), but in rethinking their very own aspiration, health institutions, and success ideals as co-dependent from others. It is not about me giving back to you, but in recognising our interdependence in a structural system and preventing the repetition of inequality. The achievement, whatever it might be, has to be rethought starting from an ethics of interconnection between people (and the Earth).

Therefore, looking at the relation between influencers and followers through an ethical lens, we claim, should not lead us to conclude that influencers promote certain values and ideas out of a rational ability to act either ethically or unethically. On the contrary, a relational ethics should highlight how individuals' rational actions are *also always* the mechanisms through which certain values are perpetuated at a larger scale in society. As such, an ethics based on relationality is one which is connected to a broader political struggle to highlight the construction of the idea of self-standing individuals and rational choices. We condemn that an ethics based on individuality fails to do so, and suggest that a relational ethical approach represents a more sustainable way for SMIs to relate to their community of followers in that it involves rethinking market mediated individualised claims of – for instance – success and wellbeing. The implications of this ethical approach are that human brands of SMIs and their followers are relationally constructed in and through social interaction, and that influencers and followers have institutional responsibilities towards one another and society. Their responsibilities are not defined in moral or legal terms, but by their relations on which their existence depends and which precedes them.

## ACKNOWLEDGEMENT

The research behind this contribution was funded by Formas, the Swedish research council for sustainable development, project 2018-02238.

# REFERENCES

Abidin, C. (2016). Visibility labour: Engaging with influencers' fashion brands and# OOTD advertorial campaigns on Instagram. *Media International Australia, 161*(1), 86–100.

Arvidsson, A. (2006). *Brands: Meaning and Value in Media Culture.* London: Routledge.

Audrezet, A., De Kerviler, G. & Moulard, J. G. (2020). Authenticity under threat: When social media influencers need to go beyond self-presentation. *Journal of Business Research, 117,* 557–569.

Butler, J. (2004). *Precarious Life: The Powers of Mourning and Violence.* London: Verso.

Butler, J. (2012). Precarious life, vulnerability, and the ethics of cohabitation. *Journal of Speculative Philosophy, 26*(2), 134–151.

Butler, J. (2015). *Notes Towards a Performative Theory of Assembly.* Cambridge, MA: Harvard University Press.

Butler, J. (2020). *The Force of Nonviolence: The Ethical in the Political.* London: Verso Books.

Caulfield, T. (2015). *Is Gwyneth Paltrow Wrong About Everything? How the Famous Sell Us Elixirs of Health, Beauty & Happiness.* Boston: Beacon Press.

Centeno, D. & Wang, J. J. (2017). Celebrities as human brands: An inquiry on stakeholder–actor co-creation of brand identities. *Journal of Business Research, 74,* 133–138.

Chae, J. (2018). Explaining females' envy toward social media influencers. *Media Psychology, 21*(2), 246–262.

Cova, B. & Dalli, D. (2009). Working consumers: The next step in marketing theory? *Marketing Theory, 9*(3), 315–339.

Dhanesh, G. S. & Duthler, G. (2019). Relationship management through social media influencers: Effects of followers' awareness of paid endorsement. *Public Relations Review, 45*(3), 101765.

Fournier, S. & Eckhardt, G. M. (2019). Putting the person back in person-brands: Understanding and managing the two-bodied brand. *Journal of Marketing Research, 56*(4), 602–619.

Gandini, A. (2016). Digital work: Self-branding and social capital in the freelance knowledge economy. *Marketing Theory, 16*(1), 123–141.

Hearn, A. (2008). Meat, mask, burden: Probing the contours of the branded self. *Journal of Consumer Culture, 8*(2), 197–217.

Hearn, A. & Schoenhoff, S. (2015). From celebrity to influencer: Tracing the diffusion of celebrity value across the data stream. In P. D. Marshall, & S. Redmond (Eds.). *A Companion to Celebrity* (pp. 194–211). Hoboken, NJ: John Wiley & Sons, Inc.

Iglesias, O., Markovic, S., Bagherzadeh, M. & Singh, J. J. (2020). Co-creation: A key link between corporate social responsibility, customer trust, and customer loyalty. *Journal of Business Ethics, 163*(1), 151–166.

Jin, S. V., Muqaddam, A. & Ryu, E. (2019). Instafamous and social media influencer marketing. *Marketing Intelligence & Planning, 37*(5), 567–579.

Khamis, S., Ang, L. & Welling, R. (2017). Self-branding, "micro-celebrity" and the rise of social media influencers. *Celebrity Studies, 8*(2), 191–208.

Lair, D. J., Sullivan, K. & Cheney, G. (2005). Marketization and the recasting of the professional self: The rhetoric and ethics of personal branding. *Management Communication Quarterly, 18*(3), 307–343.

Leban, M., Thomsen, T. U., von Wallpach, S. & Voyer, B. G. (2020). Constructing personas: How high-net-worth social media influencers reconcile ethicality and living a luxury lifestyle. *Journal of Business Ethics.* Available at https://doi.org/10.1007/s10551-020-04485-6.

Logan, D. W. (2017). The lean closet: Asceticism in postindustrial consumer culture. *Journal of the American Academy of Religion, 85*(3), 600–628.

Lou, C. & Yuan, S. (2019). Influencer marketing: How message value and credibility affect consumer trust of branded content on social media. *Journal of Interactive Advertising, 19*(1), 58–73.

Marwick, A. E. (2015). Instafame: Luxury selfies in the attention economy. *Public Culture, 27*(1), 137–160.

Marwick, A. E. (2017). Entrepreneurial subjects: Venturing from alley to valley. *International Journal of Communication, 11,* Forum, 2026–2029.

Peters, T. (1999). *The Brand You 50 (Reinventing Work): Fifty Ways to Transform Yourself from an "Employee" into a Brand That Shouts Distinction, Commitment, and Passion!* New York, NY: Knopf Doubleday Publishing.

Porkoláb, C. (2017). Nude yoga girl talks self-love and overcoming negative emotions. *Forbes*, November, 30. Available at https://www.forbes.com/sites/courtneyporkolab/2017/11/30/nude-yoga -girl-talks-self-love-and-overcoming-negative-emotions/#2f53ad513b6.

Rose, N. (1999). *Powers of Freedom: Reframing Political Thought*. Cambridge: Cambridge University Press.

Vallaster, C. & Von Wallpach, S. (2013). An online discursive inquiry into the social dynamics of multi-stakeholder brand meaning co-creation. *Journal of Business Research*, *66*(9), 1505–1515.

Von Wallpach, S., Voyer, B., Kastanakis, M. & Mühlbacher, H. (2017). Co-creating stakeholder and brand identities: Introduction to the special issue. *Journal of Business Research*, *70*, 395–398.

Wang, X., Tajvidi, M., Lin, X. & Hajli, N. (2020). Towards an ethical and trustworthy social commerce community for brand value co-creation: A trust–commitment perspective. *Journal of Business Ethics*, *167*(1), 137–152.

Wieviorka, M. (2009). *Violence: A New Approach*. London: Sage.

Wissinger, E. (2009). Modeling consumption: Fashion modeling work in contemporary society. *Journal of Consumer Culture*, *9*(2), 273–296.

Zembylas, M. (2019). A Butlerian perspective on inclusion: The importance of embodied ethics, recognition and relationality in inclusive education. *Cambridge Journal of Education*, *49*(6), 727–740.

Zhang, L. (2017). Fashioning the feminine self in "prosumer capitalism": Women's work and the transnational reselling of Western luxury online. *Journal of Consumer Culture*, *17*(2), 184–204.

Zwick, D., Bonsu, S. K. & Darmody, A. (2008). Putting consumers to work: Co-creation and new marketing governmentality. *Journal of Consumer Culture*, *8*(2), 163–196.

# 19. The ethics of conspicuous virtue signaling: when brand co-creation on social media turns negative
*Ulf Aagerup*

## 1. INTRODUCTION

The rapid evolution of information technologies has led to an amplified brand–stakeholder interconnectivity, which is changing the landscape for brands (Gyrd-Jones & Kornum, 2013; Swaminathan et al., 2020). Brand meaning is co-created through the interconnection of different social systems, across time and geographic space (Tierney et al., 2016). Social media is without a doubt the most ubiquitous system of this kind. Increased consumer-to-consumer brand communications on social media can be a mixed blessing for companies. On the positive side, it provides brands with the opportunity to involve their key stakeholders in brand co-creation processes, and as a result enjoy the fruits of their labor. On the negative side, there is no way to control what is said about the brand. In other words, to gain coveted resonance, the brand must relinquish control (Fournier & Avery, 2011). This in turn means that the boosted impact on brands that consumer-to-consumer communications can provide can turn negative, and the brand can be hurt by consumers (Christodoulides, 2009). Increased consumer power is a good thing if it allows consumers to complain about real transgressions, and thus improve conditions concerning the environment or social responsibility. In previous writings (e.g. Romani et al., 2015; Hershkovitz, 2017; Hansen et al., 2018) on consumers' negative online brand communications, brand protests have indeed been treated as sincere actions by genuinely dissatisfied individuals. There is, however, a less genuine type of behavior on social media in the form of virtue signaling. A virtue signaler is a person who claims to be deeply concerned with a moral issue but is in reality mostly concerned with how talking about it will make him or her look (Grubbs et al., 2019). Virtue signaling has so far predominately been a topic for philosophers (Tosi & Warmke, 2016; Levy, 2019), psychologists (Crockett, 2017; Jordan & Rand, 2019a), and for pundits in the media (e.g. Bartholomew, 2015; Haidt & Rose-Stockwell, 2019). Recently, Wallace et al. (2020), however, introduced the term conspicuous virtue signaling (CVS) to the business ethics literature and provided evidence that consumers communicate about brands with morally positive connotations on social media in order to make themselves appear virtuous. In addition to this, we know from psychology (Tosi & Warmke, 2016) that people publicly disassociate themselves from that which is unvirtuous for the sake of moral self-promotion. If this type of behavior is directed towards a brand it constitutes negative CVS. An example of negative CVS could be a situation where a person who holds no particular opinion on animal rights realizes that his or her friends on social media do, and therefore calls for a boycott of a fashion brand because it uses fur. It is safe to assume that such behavior exists, even if scholarly studies on the phenomenon are scarce.

Connecting to the work of Wallace et al. (2020), the purpose of this chapter is to discuss the ethics of negative CVS taking into consideration the perspectives of multiple stakeholders like brands, social media companies, social media users, and loyal brand users. The ethics of negative CVS are relevant for two reasons. The first regards whether it is morally defensible from a virtue standpoint to disingenuously spread negativity about others. The second reason is whether, from a utility perspective, negativity on social media can produce bad outcomes by hurting companies, jeopardizing the livelihoods of the attacked brands' employees, and by cyberbullying consumers who use a 'bad' brand. In this chapter it is argued that although negative CVS can promote prosocial behavior and deter transgressions, it overall constitutes an unethical practice by which perpetrators and social media companies gain different forms of rewards at the expense of the attacked brands and their users.

## 2. THEORETICAL FRAMEWORK

This chapter is based on the idea that people model their brand-related social media behaviors to make other people like them. A theoretical explanation of why this is plausible is presented below.

### 2.1 Self-enhancement and Virtue Signaling

To achieve self-enhancement, people manage their self-presentation so as to maximize social rewards and at the same time avoid social punishments (Schlenker, 1980, p. 91). One way to do so is to affiliate oneself with the right products and brands. Parker (2009, p. 176) states that 'self-enhancement occurs through associations with goods that have desirable social meaning that also bring favorable reactions from significant references'. A common technique to achieve this goal is to conform to social norms (Fiske & Taylor, 2013). This in turn places an emphasis on knowing the norms of one's reference group, because they determine how its members will react to self-enhancement attempts. For instance, ordering champagne whilst in the company of one group of people can boost a person's reputation (Ostberg, 2007) but have the opposite effect in the company of another group of people (Aagerup, 2020).

Self-enhancement comes in many guises. The champagne example is an illustration of conspicuous consumption. Veblen (1899) coined the term to denote how people consume visibly expensive products to show their wealth and thereby gain status. A similar mechanism called virtue signaling exists, where instead of money, people display moral virtues to gain social rewards (e.g. West, 2004; Grace & Griffin, 2009). It is common to communicate publicly about anything that has to do with right and wrong (Levy, 2019). The ability to discuss matters of moral concern with other people is an indispensable tool both for interpersonal dealing and promoting moral improvement (Tosi & Warmke, 2016). However, in practical use, the term virtue signaling has taken on a narrower and more negative meaning, similar to what Tosi and Warmke (2016) call moral grandstanding (the term virtue signaling will henceforth be used to describe the phenomenon). It is a use of moral communication that attempts to get others to make certain desired judgments about oneself, namely, that one is worthy of respect or admiration because one has some particular moral quality. This can take the form of virtual conspicuous consumption of products and brands with morally positive connotations in order to make the consumer appear virtuous (Wallace et al., 2020). This means that virtue signaling is commonly associated with some level of hypocrisy. The virtue signaler only claims to care about a moral issue but is in reality mostly concerned with how talking about it will make him or her look (Grubbs et al., 2019). It is thus driven by vanity and self-aggrandizement rather than by a concern for others (Bartholomew, 2015).

There is an argument to be made that accusations of virtue signaling is just an effective way to discredit people with better morals than yourself—if you make the claim that the accused virtue signaler does not mean what s/he says, you do not have to feel bad because you do not measure up to his or her standards (McCaffrey, 2017). However, there is one recurring finding that strongly suggests that people act morally to impress others rather than to enact positive change in the world; namely that people display higher morals if they believe that others can observe what they are up to and judge them for it. West (2004) describes via the term conspicuous compassion how people use visible cues like cancer bracelets to project their ego and inform others what deeply caring individuals they are. In a similar vein Grace and Griffin (2009) provide evidence for conspicuous donation behavior, which means that people become more generous if their charitable donations are made public. Another context for virtue signaling is that of conspicuous conservation, which relates to green consumer behavior. In this context, Sexton and Sexton (2011) show that consumers are willing to pay more for products if they signal 'greenness' to other people. People engage in conspicuous conservation either to stand out (Griskevicius et al., 2010) or to fit in (Aagerup & Nilsson, 2016), but either motive requires a prospect of social rewards. Regardless of the specific context, the pattern is thus that people care more about being good if they think there is an audience. People have a sub-conscious desire to signal their virtue. Even in private, people implicitly ask themselves, 'If I were being observed, how good would I look?' (Jordan & Rand, 2019b). This suggests that individuals are, at least partly, not just motivated by the positive effect their actions may have, but by the impression it will have on others' opinions of them.

In addition to seeming good because you align yourself with that which is virtuous, it is also possible to signal that you are good by distancing yourself from that which is bad. In a marketing context this is called moral brand avoidance (Lee et al., 2009) and it arises when a consumer makes an active choice to avoid or even attack a brand because his or her ideological beliefs clash with brand values or associations (Rindell et al., 2014). This can be a strong influence on behavior because consumers are even more motivated to avoid being associated with negative images than to be associated to positive ones (Banister & Hogg, 2004). The reason is that because in addition to an ideal self to which they aspire, consumers also have an undesired self. The undesired self encompasses everything consumers do not want to be (Bosnjak & Rudolph, 2008) and the standard that individuals use to assess their well-being is how distant they are from subjectively being like their most negative self-image (Ogilvy, 1987). For virtue signaling consumers this means that it would be very bad if their friends got the impression that they liked a morally reprehensible brand. It therefore becomes paramount to clearly communicate whatever reservations they may have.

## 2.2 Conspicuous Virtue Signaling: When Social Media Comes into Play

Wallace et al. (2020) coin the term 'conspicuous virtue signaling' (CVS) to describe how social media intensifies but also modifies virtue signaling so it becomes more negative in character. In addition to associating themselves with 'good' things, virtue signalers on social media disassociate themselves from 'bad' things for the sake of moral self-promotion (Tosi &

Warmke, 2016). This often takes the form of moral outrage, which is the expression of anger and disgust at the violation of a moral standard (Crockett, 2020). It is common that virtue signaling consists of saying you hate things. According to Bartholomew (2015) this is a form of camouflage. The emphasis on hate distracts from the fact you are really saying how good you are. The social media milieu plays a particular role in promoting this type of behavior. If a person constantly expresses negativity in his or her real-life conversations, his or her friends will likely find the person tiresome. However, when there is an audience, the payoffs are different; outrage can boost the person's status (Haidt & Rose-Stockwell, 2019). Negativity on moral issues is not just perceived more favorably on social media compared to real life, it also spreads more easily. Brady et al. (2017) measured the reach of half a million tweets and found that each moral or emotional word used in a tweet increased its virality by 20 percent on average. Another study (Pew Research Center, 2017) showed that posts exhibiting 'indignant disagreement' received nearly twice as much engagement—including likes and shares—as other types of content on Facebook. What is more, in face-to-face encounters, most people experience resistance towards attacking other people, and self-regulate accordingly (Wehr, 1979, chapter 4). However, as Crockett (2017) argues, the normal forces that might stop us from joining an outrage mob—such as time to reflect and cool off, or feelings of empathy for a person being humiliated—are attenuated when we cannot see the person's face, and when we are asked, many times a day, to take a side by publicly 'liking' the condemnation. All in all, for individuals, there is a bigger reward associated with displays of moral outrage on social media than there is in real life, and a smaller risk of backlash too. It is therefore easy to understand why negative conspicuous virtue signaling is so prevalent. Tosi and Warmke (2016) also describe an exacerbating factor, namely the one-upmanship of CVS. If someone is already outraged over a moral transgression, the only way for someone else to get credit on social media is to express even greater outrage. People therefore tend to trump up moral charges, pile on in cases of public shaming, announce that anyone who disagrees with them is obviously wrong, or exaggerate emotional displays. Social media companies on their part have a vested interest in promoting such negativity and outrage. Their business model is to keep as many people as possible active on their sites for as long as possible. This enables them to expose users to advertising while at the same time collecting valuable user data. Because nothing goes viral like morally outrageous content (Crockett, 2020) social media companies adapt their algorithms to disproportionally promote it (Flaxman et al., 2016; Meenakshi Sadagopan, 2019).

CVS does not just target brands that are perceived as lacking in moral fiber, but also the consumers who use such brands. We judge people by the brands they choose, which is why brands work so well as tools for self-expression (Chernev et al., 2011). In cases of hostility towards a brand, it is therefore understandable that the negative reactions will extend to the people who use the brand. Their usage is seen as endorsement of the brand, and their purchases are what allow the brand to thrive. Consequently, if the brand is perceived as bad, so are its users. According to Lukianoff and Haidt (2015) there are values and behaviors that are acceptable to a group, and there are those that are not. If someone displays unacceptable behavior, even accidentally, members of the group can score social points by calling them out. A person can thus signal his or her own virtue by pointing out when someone else fails to live up to moral standards (Miller, 2019).

## 2.3   Brand Co-creation on Social Media

The co-creation approach requires that we consider a brand as the result of a process that involves many actors rather than something that companies alone create via brand management (da Silveira et al., 2013). The co-creation of brands is therefore a collaborative effort between multiple stakeholders (Markovic & Bagherzadeh, 2018), where the stakeholders bring their equities together to co-create brand equity (Jones, 2005). For co-creation to occur each stakeholder must consequently find value in participating but they must also contribute something of value. This process takes place through the processes and relationships within a stakeholder ecosystem (Gyrd-Jones & Kornum, 2013). In the presented case, this ecosystem is comprised by brands, consumers, and social media companies. The social media ecosystem relies on the creation, exchange, and distribution of content between brands, consumers, and social media companies. This content is valuable to each stakeholder for different reasons. In the system, everyone contributes, and everyone benefits.

The social media ecosystem is an intricate web of actors, and their motivations vary. Although most brands exist to make money, there are exceptions, like not-for-profit brands that may prioritize other goals, for example affecting societal change. Although most social media platforms maximize their 'stickiness' and map user data, there are alternatives that do not collect or sell user data, or even show ads. Also, although most social media users log on to keep in touch with their friends, there are examples of people who use social media to make money (e.g. WeChat users affiliated with Alibaba etc.). The ambition of this text is, however, to describe the ecosystem of brand co-creation on social media focusing on the most typical types of brands, social media companies, and social media users.

One way to conceptualize value is as capital. Bourdieu (1984, p. 114) describes different types of capital: economic, social, and cultural capital. Economic capital refers to money, social capital refers to resources linked to the possession of a network of relationships of mutual acquaintance and recognition, and cultural capital relates mostly to social standing (Bourdieu, 1986, p. 56). The stakeholders in the ecosystem of brand co-creation on social media are motivated to participate in the process because they want to accrue capital.

Brand equity is the value of a brand based on its potential to make its owner money (Biel, 1992). A brand's potential to make its owner money is in turn determined by how well-known it is, and whether potential consumers have strong, unique, and positive associations of it (Keller, 1993). The reason for brands to engage consumers on social media is therefore to raise awareness and improve brand image, because that will increase profits. The main motivation for the brands to engage in co-creation on social media is thus to increase their economic capital. A necessary condition for this is that the brands find an audience on social media. To attract an audience, brands provide social media users with entertainment and information (Dolan et al., 2016). Users on their part employ social media to stay connected to their friends and acquaintances, but also in large part for reputation management. Social media platforms allow consumers to selectively self-present themselves (Durayappah, 2011) and they tend to showcase the most positive versions of their lives (Copeland, 2011). The main motivation for individuals to engage in co-creation on social media is thus to increase their social and cultural capital. In doing so, they provide value to social media companies in the form of content that attracts more users. Social media companies benefit from this, because they sell advertising to third parties, so their income goes up as the user base grows. The main motivation for social media companies to engage in brand co-creation on social media is thus to increase their economic capital. This ecosystem is delineated in Table 19.1.

*Table 19.1    The ecosystem of brand co-creation on social media*

| Stakeholders | Value sought | Type of capital primarily sought |
|---|---|---|
| Social media users | Reputation/self-enhancement | Cultural |
| | Network of relationships | Social |
| Brands | Brand awareness | Economic |
| | Brand image | |
| Social media companies | Content | Economic |
| | Audience for ads | |

## 2.4    Winners and Losers of Negative CVS

In the process of brand co-creation on social media described above, some stakeholders gain capital as a result of conspicuous virtue signaling at the expense of others. If successful, conspicuous virtue signalers increase their social media reach via re-tweets, likes, and shares. This extends their networks of relationships of mutual acquaintance and recognition, that is their social capital. What is more, as a result of conspicuous virtue signaling their social standing in their group of like-minded people is raised, which means that their cultural capital grows; they become persons of note. The conspicuous virtue signalers achieve these capital gains at the expense of the brands they attack. As their image is tarnished brands lose some of their ability to generate profits, which means they lose economic capital. Loyal brand users that are targeted by conspicuous virtue signalers risk losing social media friends if the attacks work as intended, because morally upstanding individuals do not want to be caught following a 'toxic' person on social media. In this way, they lose social and cultural capital commensurate to the conspicuous virtue signalers' gains in these areas. Lastly, by promoting outrage, social media companies gain new users to target with ads and whose user information they can sell. In doing so they gain economic capital. The distribution of different forms of capital as a result of conspicuous virtue signaling are summarized in Table 19.2.

*Table 19.2    The winners and losers of negative conspicuous virtue signaling*

| Winners | Losers | Type of capital |
|---|---|---|
| Conspicuous Virtue Signalers | Attacked brand users | Social |
| | | Cultural |
| Social media companies | Attacked brands | Economic |

## 2.5    The Ethics of Negative CVS

Phenomena are often deemed exceptionable because they are wrong for reasons of principle (Jeffreys, 2009), and/or because they do not work (O'Mara, 2015). Below, negative CVS is analyzed in relation to moral principles as well as the outcomes it is likely to produce.

## 2.6 Negative CVS in Relation to Moral Principles

Ethical evaluations of actions are based on whether a virtuous person would engage in them. It is generally accepted that generosity is a more virtuous trait than egotism. Conspicuous virtue signalers who use outrage to reap rewards at the expense of brands and brand users act egotistically. The same is true for social media companies who consciously promote outrage for financial gain even though they see that it hurts others.

On a related note, it is also generally accepted that courage is a more virtuous trait than cowardice. This reflects poorly on negative CVS. The personal costs and risks of punishing immoral behavior on digital platforms are considerably lower than they would be face-to-face. Options for punishing a wrongdoer in the real world may include things like verbal confrontation or even physical aggression, which involve conflict, effort, and risk of retaliation. In contrast, on social media attacks can be performed with the click of a button, and people can punish others from behind the protection of their screen and take refuge in the safety in the masses of other online participants (Crockett, 2020). If a person engages in CVS but shies away from conflicts when there is a risk of personal discomfort, that person is lacking in courage.

Lastly, from a perspective of virtue ethics, what determines the moral quality of an act is not simply the nature of the action, but also the motivation for it (Aristotle, 1985). The outrage that a person displays over a perceived transgression is oftentimes feigned (Jordan & Rand, 2019b), and virtue signaling is about how good we seem rather than how good we are (West, 2004). This is borne out by the findings of Wallace et al. (2020) which show that individuals who engage in CVS are actually likely to engage in unethical behaviors if they think it may impress others. This indicates that CVS is simply a version of conspicuous consumption and does not indicate prosocial intent; rather the opposite—if they must choose, conspicuous virtue signalers choose self-presentation over ethics, revealing some measure of vanity.

## 2.7 The Consequences of Negative CVS

The considerations presented above are evaluations of CVS against moral principles. Another way to evaluate the ethics of a phenomenon is to consider whether it leads to positive or negative outcomes. Although such utilitarian ethics are often criticized in the business ethics literature (Gustafson, 2013), expected outcomes are commonly the yardstick managers use to decide which course of action is right and which is wrong. From a consequentialist perspective of this kind, the morals are less clear than when negative CVS is viewed through the lens of virtue ethics. From this perspective it is possible to defend negative CVS, because even if conspicuous virtue signalers are disingenuous when they call out brands and brand users, their outrage can deter transgressions. Unfortunately, however, even from an outcome perspective negative CVS is questionable. The potential good and bad outcomes of negative CVS are presented below.

Being called out on social media for a moral transgression constitutes social punishment. Because all punishment is in itself evil, it is only acceptable if it promises to exclude some greater evil (Bentham, 1789, p. 13). From a consequentialist perspective, negative CVS is thus a moral practice if it prevents more harm than it causes, and this is oftentimes presented as its justification. The dominant framework for understanding why moral outrage evolved in human society has tended to focus on its ability to promote prosocial behavior, such as cooperation within groups, and identify other behaviors that need to be discouraged (Crockett, 2020). Moral outrage has historically been useful because it has acted as a deterrent against transgressions and has guided human behavior in a positive direction (Levy, 2019). This perspective does not require good intent or sincere motives on the part of the outraged. Even if negative CVS happens for the 'wrong' reasons, it is justified from a consequentialist perspective if it leads to positive outcomes. However, an unfortunate effect of negative CVS is that it attenuates the impact of outrage (Crockett, 2020). If digital mediums make it much easier to express outrage, or even encourages and exaggerates it, then it could become much more difficult to separate a prosocial signal from the noise. If the public nevertheless succeeds in picking up the message, another detrimental outcome of negative CVS is that it devalues the signal that moral anger can send. If it becomes too prevalent, and we therefore start interpreting all expressions of outrage as negative CVS, the reliability of outrage as a sign of injustice is undermined and will eventually be ignored. Excessive use of outrage thus leads to outrage exhaustion, making it more difficult to feel and express anger when it is required for purposes more important than self-enhancement (Tosi & Warmke, 2020).

Another problem with negative CVS is that it supplants good deeds, or even precludes them. From an existentialist perspective (see Sartre, 2007) actions rather than intentions determine if a person is good or bad. A big problem with CVS is that it does not require action. It is possible to be or at least to feel good without doing good, and CVS may therefore crowd out actual good deeds. This is apparent in the case of 'clicktivism' (White, 2010), which is a lazy form of activism that allows people to support or denounce something without actually doing anything. In a marketing context this translates into a situation where individuals do not even have to buy a brand to get social rewards, they just have to show their peers on social media that they like it (Wallace et al., 2020).

This passivity carries over into other realms of the conspicuous virtue signalers life. Individuals who engage in CVS are actually less likely to engage in prosocial behaviors in real-world settings (Wallace et al., 2020). A possible interpretation of this seemingly counterintuitive finding is that because these individuals already receive social rewards as a result of their communications on social media, their thirst for social affirmation is sated, and they therefore do not need to do good to feel good.

In today's world of social media, in which individuals have the power to hurt brands (Christodoulides, 2009), and in which the business climate is unusually challenging (Kost, 2020), the third bad outcome of negative CVS is that it can hurt vulnerable companies (van Den Broek et al., 2017). It is important that stakeholders believe that brands have a genuine commitment to ethics (Vallaster & Lindgreen, 2013; Aaker et al., 2004). When negative conspicuous virtue signalers accuse brands of ethical transgressions the accusations do not have to be real to cause damage; they just have to seem real to enough people. This damage to brands is exacerbated by the promotion of outrage by social media companies, and by the one-upmanship required to cut through the noise of negative CVS.

Last but not least, another unfortunate outcome of negative CVS is that it may hurt vulnerable people. To attack a person via social media is commonly referred to as cyberbullying (Kowalski et al., 2014). This can take the form of a consumer interaction process about a brand during which one consumer harasses another consumer (Breitsohl et al., 2018). Negative CVS fulfills these criteria. This is ethically problematic, because cyberbullying is related to a number of negative outcomes, like higher stress and lower job satisfaction (Snyman & Loh,

2015), absenteeism, depression, low grades in school (Giumetti & Kowalski, 2016), and even suicide (Messias et al., 2014).

## 3.    DISCUSSION

The conclusion is that negative CVS is unethical and should be avoided. The moral failings occur on two levels: the personal, and the structural. On the personal level, individuals who engage in negative CVS fail to act morally when they attack brands and individuals insincerely to gain social rewards. Although individuals bear some responsibility for their behavior, it is reasonable to assume that they do not realize the potential consequences. Social media has only existed for a little more than a decade, while human reward systems have evolved over millennia. When the environment has changed dramatically, like it has between village life a hundred years ago and life on social media today, it is hard to blame individuals. People with the same mental hardware as the villagers a hundred years ago now face opportunities to go after those they dislike and be rewarded for it, while at the same time risking very little in the way of consequences. What is more, studies show that littering public discourse with even more accusations and blame is unlikely to help people improve their behavior. Calling people virtue signalers in conversation is likely to make things worse (Kalla & Broockman, 2020). Therefore, it is hard to police the phenomenon on the individual level. Social media companies on the other hand deserve more of the blame for CVS. They know about, and even encourage, the use of outrage in order to make money. A damning piece of evidence against the morality of social media in its current form is that the people who invented it ban it from their own homes (Rudgard, 2018). Social media can thus be likened to tobacco—a lucrative product whose addictive properties keep consumers hooked for life, but one that has such detrimental effects that those who know what it does to humans keep it away from their children (Weller, 2018).

The ethics of negative CVS are especially harmful because CVS leads to such inequitable distribution of rewards with social media companies ending up with most of the money. However, even though culpability lies with the social media companies who profit from it, the responsibility to correct the situation will by necessity land elsewhere. At every major world change we have seen examples of people taking advantage. It happened when Europeans came to America and killed most of the bisons, it happened when factory owners during the Industrial Revolution had workers endure unsafe conditions, and it happened when the Berlin Wall came down and oligarchs got hold of public goods in the Eastern bloc. If there is money to be made some actors will adapt to new circumstances and exploit lack of regulations and loopholes. It would be nice if everyone took moral responsibility, but historical evidence does not provide many reasons to expect such behavior. What is more, there is no specific reason to believe that the tech firms of Silicon Valley would be more virtuous than firms in any other industry; quite the opposite. The tech world rewards being first to market, and companies therefore have a single-minded focus to gain a first-mover advantage, resulting in an attitude to 'move fast and break things' as Facebook founder Mark Zuckerberg famously put it.

What is required is therefore societal control to reign in the worst ethical violations brought on by the new structure of social media. It may be time to demand that some of the richest companies in history stop hoarding most of the profits while externalizing the costs of negative CVS to its victims. It is even possible to take the argument further. It is not the inequitable distribution of the spoils from negative CVS that is the most egregious issue; it is that social media companies knowingly promote hurtful behaviors in the first place. Sharing those profits with other brand co-creators would not make the practice moral. A possible remedy for this ill would be to make social media companies liable for the things that are published on their platforms. For obvious reasons, they are unwilling to make this change (it would cost a fortune to monitor what everyone posts). Instead, the companies like to compare themselves to utility companies who just distribute information, but who do not publish it. However, as they have gotten more and more into controlling which information goes to which user, this claim becomes harder to sustain.

In the research stream concerned with the ethical problems related to brand co-creation there has previously been an emphasis on the companies exploiting consumers in the brand co-creation process. By switching the perspective to the potential harm consumers can inflict on brands in the same context provides a new and interesting contribution.

While previous work on conspicuous virtue signaling have primarily focused on how social media users affiliate with brands that do good as a means for self-enhancement, the presented text instead concerns itself mainly with how social media users use outrage to distance themselves from brands which are perceived to lack morals to achieve the same goal. In the limited writings on the effects of consumers' negative online communication on brands, brand protests have been treated as sincere actions by genuinely dissatisfied individuals. Building on the emerging research stream of CVS and emphasizing negativity as a strategy for self-enhancement, an alternative understanding of the phenomenon is provided, which thereby extends literature.

This chapter is written from a perspective that assumes that online protests are always detrimental to brands. However, in today's polarized society in which individuals join 'teams' and build their self-image based on affiliation with those teams, it is possible that negative CVS could actually benefit brands. Social interactions might generate brand commitment and shared brand beliefs under certain conditions (Vallaster & Lindgreen, 2013). If a company, for example, comes under fire for opposing gay marriage, consumers who share its view may rally in defense of the brand. If the attack comes from people who are not the target market in the first place, online protests could create awareness and strong, positive, and unique associations for the brand in the minds of its intended customers and thus end up increasing brand equity. A situation of this kind would, in turn, place the ethics of negative CVS presented here on its head.

## REFERENCES

Aagerup, U. (2020). Building nightclub brand personality via guest selection. *International Journal of Hospitality Management, 85*(February). doi:https://doi.org/10.1016/j.ijhm.2019.102336

Aagerup, U., & Nilsson, J. (2016). Green consumer behavior: Being good or seeming good? *Journal of Product & Brand Management, 25*(3), 274–284.

Aaker, J., Fournier, S., & Brasel, S. A. (2004). When good brands do bad. *Journal of Consumer Research, 31*(1), 1–16. doi:10.1086/383419

Aristotle (1985). *Nicomachean Ethics*. Cambridge, MA: Hackett Publishing Company.

Banister, E. N., & Hogg, M. K. (2004). Negative symbolic consumption and consumers' drive for self-esteem. *European Journal of Marketing, 38*(7), 850–868. Retrieved from http://search.ebscohost.com/login.aspx?direct=true&db=buh&AN=14533888&site=bsi-live.

Bartholomew, J. (2015). Easy virtue. *Spectator*. Retrieved from https://www.spectator.co.uk/article/easy -virtue.

Bentham, J. (1789). *An Introduction to the Principles of Morals and Legislation*. Econlib.

Biel, A. L. (1992). How brand image drives brand equity. *Journal of Advertising Research, 32*(6), RC-6-RC-12. Retrieved from http://search.ebscohost.com/login.aspx?direct=true&db=buh&AN= 16967714&site=bsi-live.

Bosnjak, M., & Rudolph, N. (2008). Undesired self-image congruence in a low-involvement product context. *European Journal of Marketing, 42*(5/6), 702–712. Retrieved from 10.1108/03090560810862598 http://search.ebscohost.com/login.aspx?direct=true&db=buh&AN=32795422&site=bsi-live.

Bourdieu, P. (1984). *Distinction – A Social Critique of the Judgement of Taste*. Cambridge, MA: Harvard University Press.

Bourdieu, P. (1986). *The Forms of Capital*. New York: Greenwood Press.

Brady, W. J., Wills, J. A., Jost, J. T., Tucker, J. A., & Van Bavel, J. J. (2017). Emotion shapes the diffusion of moralized content in social networks. *Proceedings of the National Academy of Sciences, 114*(28), 7313–7318. doi:10.1073/pnas.1618923114.

Breitsohl, J., Roschk, H., & Feyertag, C. (2018). Consumer brand bullying behaviour in online communities of service firms. In M. Bruhn & K. Hadwich (Eds.), *Service Business Development: Band 2. Methoden – Erlösmodelle – Marketinginstrumente* (pp. 289–312). Wiesbaden: Springer Fachmedien Wiesbaden.

Chernev, A., Hamilton, R., & Gal, D. (2011). Competing for consumer identity: Limits to self-expression and the perils of lifestyle branding. *Journal of Marketing, 75*(3), 66–82. doi:10.1509/jmkg.75.3.66.

Christodoulides, G. (2009). Branding in the post-internet era. *Marketing Theory, 9*(1), 141–144. doi:10 .1177/1470593108100071.

Copeland, L. (2011, June 15, 2017). The anti-social network. *Slate*. Retrieved from http://www.slate .com/articles/double_x/doublex/2011/01/the_antisocial_network.html.

Crockett, M. J. (2017). Moral outrage in the digital age. *Nature Human Behaviour, 1*(11), 769–771. doi: 10.1038/s41562-017-0213-3.

Crockett, M. J. (2020). Molly Crockett: How social media amplifies moral outrage. *The Eudemonic Project*. Retrieved from https://www.eudemonicproject.org/ideas/how-social-media-amplifies-moral -outrage.

da Silveira, C., Lages, C., & Simões, C. (2013). Reconceptualizing brand identity in a dynamic environment. *Journal of Business Research, 66*(1), 28–36. doi:https://doi.org/10.1016/j.jbusres.2011.07.020.

Dolan, R., Conduit, J., Fahy, J., & Goodman, S. (2016). Social media engagement behaviour: A uses and gratifications perspective. *Journal of Strategic Marketing, 24*(3–4), 261–277. doi:10.1080/0965254X .2015.1095222.

Durayappah, A. (2011). Facebook enhances self-esteem, study finds. *Psychology Today*. Retrieved from http://www.psychologytoday.com/blog/thriving101/201103/facebook-enhances-self-esteem-study -finds.

Fiske, S. T., & Taylor, S. E. (2013). *Social Cognition: From Brains to Culture*: Thousand Oaks, CA: SAGE Publications.

Flaxman, S., Goel, S., & Rao, J. M. (2016). Filter bubbles, echo chambers, and online news consumption. *Public Opinion Quarterly, 80*(S1), 298–320. doi:10.1093/poq/nfw006.

Fournier, S., & Avery, J. (2011). The uninvited brand. *Business Horizons, 54*(3), 193–207.

Giumetti, G. W., & Kowalski, R. M. (2016). Cyberbullying matters: Examining the incremental impact of cyberbullying on outcomes over and above traditional bullying in North America. In R. Navarro, S. Yubero, & E. Larrañaga (Eds.), *Cyberbullying Across the Globe: Gender, Family, and Mental Health* (pp. 117–130). Cham: Springer International Publishing.

Grace, D., & Griffin, D. (2009). Conspicuous donation behaviour: Scale development and validation. *Journal of Consumer Behaviour, 8*(1), 14–25. doi:10.1002/cb.270.

Griskevicius, V., Tybur, J. M., & Van den Bergh, B. (2010). Going green to be seen: Status, reputation, and conspicuous conservation. *Journal of Personality & Social Psychology, 98*(3), 392–404. Retrieved from http://search.ebscohost.com/login.aspx?direct=true&db=buh&AN=50255036&site= ehost-live.

Grubbs, J. B., Warmke, B., Tosi, J., James, A. S., & Campbell, W. K. (2019). Moral grandstanding in public discourse: Status-seeking motives as a potential explanatory mechanism in predicting conflict. *PLOS One, 14*(10), e0223749. doi:10.1371/journal.pone.0223749.

Gustafson, A. (2013). In defense of a utilitarian business ethic. *Business and Society Review, 118*(3), 325–360. doi:10.1111/basr.12013.

Gyrd-Jones, R. I., & Kornum, N. (2013). Managing the co-created brand: Value and cultural complementarity in online and offline multi-stakeholder ecosystems. *Journal of Business Research, 66*(9), 1484–1493.

Haidt, J., & Rose-Stockwell, T. (2019). The dark psychology of social networks. Why it feels like everything is going haywire. *The Atlantic* (December). Retrieved from https://www.theatlantic.com/magazine/archive/2019/12/social-media-democracy/600763/.

Hansen, N., Kupfer, A.-K., & Hennig-Thurau, T. (2018). Brand crises in the digital age: The short- and long-term effects of social media firestorms on consumers and brands. *International Journal of Research in Marketing, 35*(4), 557–574.

Hershkovitz, S. (2017). 'Not buying cottage cheese': Motivations for consumer protest—the case of the 2011 protest in Israel. *Journal of Consumer Policy, 40*(4), 473–484.

Jeffreys, D. S. (2009). *Spirituality and the Ethics of Torture.* New York: Palgrave Macmillan.

Jones, R. (2005). Finding sources of brand value: Developing a stakeholder model of brand equity. *Journal of Brand Management, 13*(1), 10–32. doi:10.1057/palgrave.bm.2540243.

Jordan, J., & Rand, D. G. (2019a). Signaling when no one is watching: A reputation heuristics account of outrage and punishment in one-shot anonymous interactions. *PsyArXiv.* Retrieved from https://doi.org/10.31234/osf.io/qf7e3.

Jordan, J., & Rand, D. (2019b). Are you 'virtue signaling'? *New York Times.* Retrieved from https://www.nytimes.com/2019/03/30/opinion/sunday/virtue-signaling.html.

Kalla, J. L., & Broockman, D. E. (2020). Reducing exclusionary attitudes through interpersonal conversation: Evidence from three field experiments. *American Political Science Review, 114*(2), 410–425. Retrieved from https://www.ocf.berkeley.edu/~broockma/kalla_broockman_reducing_exclusionary_attitudes.pdf.

Keller, K. L. (1993). Conceptualizing, measuring, managing customer-based brand equity. *Journal of Marketing, 57*(1), 1–22. Retrieved from http://search.ebscohost.com/login.aspx?direct=true&db=buh&AN=9308118328&site=bsi-live.

Kost, D. (2020). How small businesses can survive the coronavirus outbreak. *Working Knowledge.* Retrieved from https://hbswk.hbs.edu/item/how-small-businesses-can-survive-the-coronavirus-outbreak.

Kowalski, R. M., Giumetti, G. W., Schroeder, A. N., & Lattanner, M. R. (2014). Bullying in the digital age – A critical review and meta-analysis of cyberbullying research among youth. *Psychological Bulletin, 140*(4), 1073–1137.

Lee, M. S. W., Motion, J., & Conroy, D. (2009). Anti-consumption and brand avoidance. *Journal of Business Research, 62*(2), 169–180. doi:http://dx.doi.org/10.1016/j.jbusres.2008.01.024.

Levy, N. (2019). Is virtue signalling a perversion of morality? *Aeon Magazine.* Retrieved from https://aeon.co/ideas/is-virtue-signalling-a-perversion-of-morality.

Lukianoff, G., & Haidt, J. (2015). The coddling of the American mind. *The Atlantic,* (September). Retrieved from https://www.theatlantic.com/magazine/archive/2015/09/the-coddling-of-the-american-mind/399356/.

Markovic, S., & Bagherzadeh, M. (2018). How does breadth of external stakeholder co-creation influence innovation performance? Analyzing the mediating roles of knowledge sharing and product innovation. *Journal of Business Research, 88*(7), 173–186.

McCaffrey, M. (2017). In praise of virtue signaling. Retrieved from https://fee.org/articles/in-praise-of-virtue-signaling/.

Meenakshi Sadagopan, S. (2019). Feedback loops and echo chambers: How algorithms amplify viewpoints. *The Conversation.* Retrieved from https://theconversation.com/feedback-loops-and-echo-chambers-how-algorithms-amplify-viewpoints-107935.

Messias, E., Kindrick, K., & Castro, J. (2014). School bullying, cyberbullying, or both: Correlates of teen suicidality in the 2011 CDC youth risk behavior survey. *Comprehensive Psychiatry, 55*(5), 1063–1068. https://doi.org/10.1016/j.comppsych.2014.02.005.

Miller, G. (2019). *Virtue Signaling: Essays on Darwinian Politics & Free Speech*. Cambrian Moon.

Ogilvy, D. (1987). The undesired self: A neglected variable in personality research. *Journal of Personality and Social Psychology*, *52*(2), 379–385.

O'Mara, S. (2015). *Why Torture Doesn't Work: The Neuroscience of Interrogation*. Cambridge, MA: Harvard University Press.

Ostberg, J. (2007). The linking value of subcultural capital: Constructing the Stockholm Brat enclave. In R. V. K. a. A. S. Bernard Cova (Ed.), *Consumer Tribes: Theory, Practice, and Prospects* (pp. 93–107). Oxford, UK: Elsevier/Butterworth-Heinemann.

Parker, B. T. (2009). A comparison of brand personality and brand user–imagery congruence. *Journal of Consumer Marketing*, *26*(3), 175–184. doi:10.1108/07363760910954118.

Pew Research Center (2017). *Critical Posts Get More Likes, Comments, and Shares than Other Posts*. Retrieved from Washington DC: https://www.people-press.org/2017/02/23/partisan-conflict-and -congressional-outreach/pdl-02-23-17_antipathy-new-00-02/.

Rindell, A., Strandvik, T., & Wilén, K. (2014). Ethical consumers' brand avoidance. *Journal of Product & Brand Management*, *23*(2), 114–120. doi:10.1108/JPBM-09-2013-0391.

Romani, S., Grappi, S., Zarantonello, L., & Bagozzi, R. P. (2015). The revenge of the consumer! How brand moral violations lead to consumer anti-brand activism. *Journal of Brand Management*, *22*(8), 658–672.

Rudgard, O. (2018). The tech moguls who invented social media have banned their children from it. *Irish Independent* [Online]. Retrieved from: https://www.independent.ie/life/family/parenting/the -tech-moguls-who-invented-social-media-have-banned-their-children-from-it-37494367.html.

Sartre, J.-P. (2007). *Existentialism is a Humanism*. London: Yale University Press.

Schlenker, B. R. (1980). *Impression Management: The Self-concept, Social Identity, and Interpersonal Relations*. Monterey, CA: Brooks/Cole Publishing Company.

Sexton, S. E., & Sexton, A. L. (2011). *Conspicuous Conservation: The Prius Halo and Willingness to Pay for Environmental Bona Fides*. Paper presented at the UCE, Berkeley, California.

Snyman, R., & Loh, J. (2015). Cyberbullying at work: The mediating role of optimism between cyber-bullying and job outcomes. *Computers in Human Behavior*, *53*, 161–168. doi:https://doi.org/10.1016/j.chb.2015.06.050.

Swaminathan, V., Sorescu, A., Steenkamp, J.-B. E. M., O'Guinn T. C. G., & Schmitt, B. (2020). Branding in a hyperconnected world: Refocusing theories and rethinking boundaries. *Journal of Marketing*, *84*(2), 24–46.

Tierney, K. D., Karpen, I. O., & Westberg, K. (2016). Brand meaning cocreation: Toward a conceptualization and research implications. *Journal of Service Theory and Practice*, *26*(6), 911–932.

Tosi, J., & Warmke, B. (2016). Moral grandstanding. *Philosophy & Public Affairs*, *44*(3), 197–217.

Tosi, J., & Warmke, B. (2020). Oscar acceptance speeches: When moral outrage verges on grand-standing [Opinion piece]. Retrieved from https://edition.cnn.com/2020/02/10/opinions/award-show -grandstanding-warmke-tosi/index.html.

Vallaster, C., & Lindgreen, A. (2013). The role of social interactions in building internal corporate brands: Implications for sustainability. *Journal of World Business*, *48*(3), 297–310.

van Den Broek, T., Langley, D., & Hornig, T. (2017). The effect of online protests and firm responses on shareholder and consumer evaluation. *Journal of Business Ethics*, *146*(2), 279–294.

Veblen, T. (1899). *The Theory of the Leisure Class*. New York: MacMillan.

Wallace, E., Buil, I., & de Chernatony, L. (2020). 'Consuming good' on social media: What can con-spicuous virtue signalling on Facebook tell us about prosocial and unethical intentions? *Journal of Business Ethics*, *162*(3), 577–592. doi:10.1007/s10551-018-3999-7.

Wehr, P. (1979). *Conflict Regulation*. New York: Routledge.

Weller, C. (2018). Silicon Valley parents are raising their kids tech-free—and it should be a red flag. *Business Insider* [Online]. Retrieved from: https://www.businessinsider.com/silicon-valley-parents -raising-their-kids-tech-free-red-flag-2018-2?r=US&IR=T.

West, P. (2004). *Conspicuous Compassion: Why Sometimes it Really is Cruel to be Kind*. Civitas, Institute for the Study of Civil Society.

White, M. (2010). Clicktivism is ruining leftist activism. *The Guardian*. Retrieved from https://www .theguardian.com/commentisfree/2010/aug/12/clicktivism-ruining-leftist-activism.

# PART V

# CRITICAL REFLECTIONS ON THE FUTURE OF BRAND CO-CREATION

# 20. Brand co-creation and degrowth: merging the odd couple

*Feyza Ağlargöz*

## 1.    INTRODUCTION

As vividly experienced globally during the recent pandemic, threats to sustainability are intensifying. Contemporary consumers' mindsets have shifted, and they are turning to alternative and more sustainable modes of consumption. Even companies located at the edge of the capitalist spectrum now feel pressures from today's empowered customers and hence try to understand and integrate degrowth fundamentals to varying degrees by questioning their search for endless growth. Fast fashion brand H&M is working on developing more sustainable solutions. Flygskam, which can be translated as flight shaming, started in the travel industry in Sweden and has since spread to other industries (Hoikkala, 2019). Consequently, it is becoming indispensable for brands to bear responsibility for sustainable development goals in collaboration with consumers as value co-creators.

Today, degrowth is viewed as a path towards a more sustainable future. Without consumer support, degrowth's potential has yet to be realized. In this chapter, it is argued that brand co-creation has the ontological capability to embrace these two phenomena; thus, the purpose of this chapter is to bridge the gap between brand co-creation and degrowth ideals. The chapter will challenge assumptions that brand co-creation and degrowth cannot occur in tandem. Having its roots in the empowered consumer discourse, insights on brand co-creation will be transferred to the context of degrowth, fueling discussions on the practical applicability of various alternatives. The chapter starts by delineating the empowerment of consumers in terms of brand co-creation and then highlights global macroscale conditions emphasizing sustainability and brand co-creation, providing a brief introduction to the degrowth literature, and the chapter concludes by discussing degrowth ideals with brand co-creation efforts by identifying various alternatives.

## 2.    EMPOWERMENT OF CONSUMERS AND BRAND CO-CREATION

From a strategic point of view, the bargaining power of consumers from past to present has changed considerably. Under past conditions, consumers had to settle for what was available, their needs and wants were underappreciated, and it was difficult for them to communicate with brands. Recently, there has been a trend towards more empowered consumers who have the opportunity to choose between many alternatives, whose needs and wants are taken into account and who can easily interact with brands. Today's consumers are more informed, more connected, and more potent against brands than ever before.

What is empowerment? How are consumers empowered today? Increased competition among companies, an abundance of alternatives in post-affluent societies, and recently the Internet and social media have helped shift power from businesses to consumers in markets. It is straightforward to think that empowerment involves the sharing of power with subordinates. For those at the lower end of the power equilibrium, empowerment denotes an increase in self-determination and self-efficacy and a decrease in feelings of powerlessness (Füller et al., 2009). Rezabakhsh et al. (2006) modified the power concept developed by French and Raven (1959) into three categories. First, expert power comes from knowledge about the quality and prices of products in the market. Before the development of social media, expertise was predominantly in the hands of businesses. Another significant force is sanctioning power, from which the consumer can discipline or punish businesses in two different ways. Consumers can abandon the businesses that they are not satisfied with and prefer another business or brand. Alternatively, consumers can express their dissatisfaction, complain, and convey negative experiences to other consumers around them and on social media. The third type is legitimate power. Even with consumer-oriented marketing approaches, businesses asked consumers about their demands and needs but later decided on the design and pricing of products themselves. With this process, the consumer has had a passive role by accepting or rejecting the offer. With the development of new virtual business models and social media platforms, consumers can now play an essential role in determining prices and other marketing elements. Virtual auction systems, group buying sites, and dynamic pricing practices strengthen the role of consumers as price determiners. On the other hand, the Internet and social media also strengthen the role of consumers in product design. Many brands today allow their consumers to create their designs over the Internet (Rezabakhsh et al., 2006).

However, this process of empowerment did not emerge overnight. Lipovetsky (2011, pp. 25–31) divided the development of consumer capitalism into three phases. Phase I started around the 1880s and ended with the Second World War. Fundamental features of this phase include standardized goods at low prices, mass production, the invention of mass marketing, and modern consumers. The modern consumer in this phase is typically bourgeois or even elite. Packaging, advertising, and brand names were the innovations of this phase. Phase II ran from 1950 to the end of the 1970s. This phase is associated with the mass consumption society, democratization, and the availability of consumer goods for all members of society. This phase marked the start of buying for pleasure. Consumerism of this phase is related to individualism and mass psychology. Luxuries, fashion, leisure, holidays, hedonism, and individual tastes, behaviors, and attitudes are prominent features. However, in this phase, consumers were passive. Lipovetsky (2011) characterized the third phase as involving the formation of a hyper-consumption society beginning in the 1980s. A new type of consumer can be described as erratic, nomadic, volatile, unpredictable, fragmented, and deregulated. Medical awareness and obsessions with health issues have increased. In this phase, the symbolic power of the brand has thrived. Above all, consumers have transformed into prosumers.

Positioning the empowerment process within a historical perspective opens up a discussion of its sources. Denegri-Knott et al. (2006, pp. 963–964) classify consumer power into three broad domains. From the perspective of the consumer sovereignty model, consumer empowerment occurs when the consumer is free to act as a rational and self-interested actor. In this model, consumers are assumed to be well informed and autonomous. On the other hand, the cultural model of power distinguishes between consumer resistance and consumer empowerment. Here, consumers are caught up in political and cultural forces. Consumer resistance is defined as the artisan-like creativity, deception, and cunning of the consumer in market areas designed by the power of the marketer. In addition, consumer empowerment requires a consumer who is capable of manipulating and even producing these spaces. The discursive model of power defines power as the ability to construct discourse as a system in which certain knowledge is possible, while other knowledge is not. The discursive power model attempts to reconcile these two approaches to consumer power by focusing on the question of how consumers co-create markets, power, and knowledge. Overall, Denegri-Knott et al. (2006) reject a universal and generalizable definition of power and suggest a more inclusive, cross-border and multidimensional understanding of power. The authors argue that this understanding of power may generate a view of consumer empowerment as complementary to a company's power, resulting in value co-creation.

Let us see how Denegri-Knott et al.'s (2006) discursive model of power functions in real life. For instance, in commercial online communities, customers can potentially play a different role than that of a mere passive user; they can act as product marketers, product testers, product designers, or product conceptualizers (Rossi & De Chiara, 2009). Web 2.0 is defined by sites with content produced wholly or in part by consumers who also consume them (Ritzer, 2010, p. 75). With Web 2.0, the participation and interaction capabilities of users have developed and resulted in various forms of user-generated content. Consumers express themselves through user-generated content such as text, novels, poetry, photos/images, music, audio, videos, films, citizen journalism, educational content, mobile content, and virtual content in different platforms. It is self-evident that consumers can play a more active and collaborative role in content creation and consumption (OECD, 2007). Empowered consumers can use their power in different ways by, for instance, posting online consumer reviews and mobilizing consumer activism/movements, social movements, buycotts, boycotts, protests, and brand co-creation. With the notion of empowered consumers in mind, brand co-creation is a novel, constructive and collaborative way of using consumer power.

Consumers are no longer just the targets of companies, and they are no longer located at the dead end of the production value chain. Consumers are at the very heart of consumption and production processes with a highly productive role (Cova et al., 2015, p. 467). They are also co-marketers who share their experiences, opinions, and stories of products with others. When a brand creates strong connections with its customers by providing opportunities to gather and share positive and brand-relevant experiences, the relationship between the brand and its customers can reach another level. Consumers can add this relationship to their labor and expertise; these consumers are called co-producers by Martin and Schouten (2015, p. 74). For example, consumers are involved in the marketing process and supply chain when they assemble or recycle IKEA furniture. As noted above, prosumers, a concept generally attributed to Alvin Toffler (1980), engage in many production activities, such as providing word-of-mouth communication, generating new product ideas, contributing product designs, defining meaning for brands and affecting other consumers' decisions in addition to consuming (Cova et al., 2015).

Toffler (1980) defines three societies. The first wave is characterized by people consuming what they produce. They are not solely producers or consumers; they might be called prosumers. The Industrial Revolution separated these two functions into producers and consumers. The second wave involved an industrial society based on production for exchange. In the postindustrial age, a synthesis of first- and second-wave societies comprised the third wave, which brought prosumers back into economic life but this time with high technology (Toffler,

1980). Prosumers prefer to produce some of the goods and services they consume instead of purchasing these goods and services from others. This kind of production is for use rather than for exchange (Kotler, 2010, p. 52). Toffler presents arguments for more prosumption activities that involve the combination of production and consumption (Strähle & Grünewald, 2017, p. 95), such as decreasing work hours after the Industrial Revolution, larger proportions of highly educated people, rising costs of skilled labor, a need for more physical activity, an ability to produce better goods and services independently, and seeking individuation (Kotler, 2010, p. 54). Prosumption is a highly liquid phenomenon involving a very permeable relationship between production and consumption. Prosumption has always been involved in both production and consumption and always exists. Over time, trends of putting the consumer to work, co-creating a variety of experiences, and do-it-yourself technologies have accelerated from pumping one's own gasoline at the gas station to acting as an audience or long-term performer in reality. Social changes such as the rise of Web 2.0 have expanded both the practice of prosumption and attention to it (Ritzer, 2010, pp. 72–75; Strähle & Grünewald, 2017, p. 95). Consumers generally prefer prosumption activities that provide high cost savings, require minimal skill, require little time and effort, and provide high levels of personal satisfaction. Consumers seek a favorable combination of these characteristics through prosumption activities (Kotler, 2010, p. 55). Consumers like to be involved in product design and production. Marketers should look for opportunities to facilitate prosumption activities. Kotler (2010, p. 58) identifies two main prosumer profiles: avid hobbyists who spend most of their time producing for exchange but who fill their leisure time with one or a few main hobbies and archprosumers who practice a lifestyle of voluntary simplicity.

There has been a rapid shift towards personalized consumer experiences from a product/company-focused view on the meaning of value and the process of value creation. Informed, networked, empowered, and active consumers are increasingly co-creating value with companies (Prahalad & Ramaswamy, 2004a, p. 5). Consumers are increasingly likely to produce what they consume, to act as prosumers (Ritzer, 2010, p. 77). Consumers can participate in all facets of new product creation, such as idea generation and evaluation; product concept elaboration, evaluation and challenge; new product tests and experience (Füller et al., 2009, p. 72). Since we cannot avoid this, we should acknowledge this. The smartest marketers today bow to the empowered, entrepreneurial, and free consumer who now rules the digital, globally networked marketplaces in search of open-ended value propositions (Zwick et al., 2008, p. 184).

Brand co-creation[1] enters the scene as a powerful tool for marketing both for practitioners and scholars. An enormous number of articles open with statements denoting the power shift between companies and consumers; needless to say, brand co-creation is a reflection of the reconfiguration of power dynamics in today's contemporary societies. Brand co-creation can be viewed as generally unpaid creative contributions from consumers for consumer labor and value production (Schroeder, 2011, p. 146; Zwick et al., 2008). Brand co-creation refers to customers' voluntary resource contributions to a company's brand building activities. It is self-evident that consumers must obtain some form of benefit from their co-creation behavior (Schroeder, 2011, p. 147). Denegri-Knott et al. (2006, p. 965) state that the success of a new product may no longer be determined by its added value but rather by the range of manipulations it allows the customer to make. The meaning of value has changed, transitioning from value enclosed in the product to value that empowers the customer to customize. Brands are co-produced through the ongoing relationship between consumers and such brands (Ritzer, 2010, p. 75).

To clarify this concept, we should also discuss its contradictions. Value co-creation is a way of sharing, combining, and renewing the resources and capabilities of companies and active consumers to create value (Arnold, 2017, p. 180). Co-creation, as a set of organizational strategies and discursive procedures aimed at reconfiguring social relations of production, works through the freedom of the consumer subject to encourage and capture the know-how of this creative commons (Zwick et al., 2008, p. 184). Enlisting customers as producers and charging them for their work constitutes an interesting contradiction that points to the importance of promoting a discourse of empowerment and self-actualization in conjunction with that of co-creation (Zwick et al., 2008, p. 185).

Moreover, co-creation can be applied to almost any type of innovation: operational, product, service, business strategy, and management innovation (Ramaswamy & Özcan, 2014, p. 280). Value co-creation can be extended to a larger spectrum: co-conception (military and defense contracts), co-design (Boeing and United Airlines), co-production (IKEA), co-promotion (word of mouth), co-pricing (eBay and, negotiated pricing), co-distribution (magazines), co-consumption (utility), co-maintenance (patient–doctor), co-disposal (self-serve), and even co-outsourcing (captive business process outsourcing) (Sheth & Uslay, 2007, p. 305). Needless to say, within the co-creation paradigm, customers are central and vital participants in the new product development process. For instance, self-organizing communities of volunteer programmers (O'Hern & Rindfleisch, 2010) develop computer applications such as Apache, Linux, and Firefox.

Every stakeholder of a company, namely, customers, employees, managers, financiers, partners, or citizens in communities, can bring capital to the value creation process through their value creation capacities by becoming co-creators (Ramaswamy & Özcan, 2014, p. 222). This participation of stakeholders, specifically consumers, can reach a level called brand co-creation. In brand co-creation, brand value is co-created through network relationships and social interactions within the ecosystem of stakeholders such as consumers, employees, not-for-profit organizations, and business partners (Hatch & Schultz, 2010, p. 592). It appears that the promise of creating a mutually beneficial relationship can now be fulfilled. Management and marketing thinkers celebrate the new logic of collaborative value creation as an indication of consumer empowerment and the transfiguration of marketing to a model of equal, satisfying, and mutually beneficial relationships between producers and consumers (Zwick et al., 2008, p. 186).

Empowered consumers, prosumption and brand co-creation are complementary and indispensable notion of today's trends. Brand co-creation emerges as a new form of collaboration between consumers and companies. Strähle and Grünewald (2017, p. 96) define co-creation as an evolving form of prosumption through which consumers collaborate with companies or with other consumers to produce goods or services. Bonsu and Darmody (2008, p. 355) define co-creation as a means of consumer empowerment in a world where market powers still largely remain capital. The consumer empowerment construct can be used to describe consumers' involvement in brand co-creation. In contrast, co-creation helps consumers feel more empowered (Bonsu & Darmody, 2008; Füller et al., 2009). Füller et al. (2009) found that levels of perceived empowerment and enjoyment have a strong impact on successful consumer co-creation.

To provide a full picture of what brand co-creation is we should underline the enablers of brand co-creation. Priharsari et al. (2020) studied the enablers of value co-creation in sponsored online communities and identified four categories. Firm-related enablers include participatory leadership, reward systems and transparency, which require listening and pro-actively responding to online communities. Individual-related enablers include motivation, personal and personal evaluation. Technological enablers include individuals' interpretations of technology such as its associations, interactivity, persistence, and visibility. Finally, social enablers are related to the community in terms of content quality; equality; and a sense of community, similarity and trust.

To conclude this discussion of consumer empowerment to brand co-creation, the DART (dialog, access, risks–benefits, and transparency) model introduced by Prahalad and Ramaswamy (2004a, p. 9) should be underlined. Prahalad and Ramaswamy (2004a, p. 9) offered building blocks of consumer–company interaction for value co-creation. The model paves the way for effective interaction between consumers and brands. Long-lasting interactions can be achieved by competing for customers' business. Today, it is easier to copy and enhance products or services than it was in the past. However, it is difficult to copy what one does and how people work and engage with stakeholders (Padhi, 2018, p. 147). Last, the idea of brand co-creation also embraces the concept that consumers know what they want better than brands (Hankammer & Kleer, 2018, p. 1712). Brand co-creation shows excellent poten-tial to address the social and individual needs of customers. Today, people need to feel that they are valued and appreciated. Regardless of how small the contribution, consumers need to see that they are making a difference. In the next section, how brand co-creation can connect micro- and macro-level societal changes is elaborated.

## 3.　MACROSCALE CHANGES LEADING TO INDIVIDUAL TRANSFORMATIONS: SUSTAINABILITY, ALTERNATIVES, AND BRAND CO-CREATION

In addition to the aforementioned power shift in favor of consumers, the world is riddled with macro-level problems. While writing this chapter, I believe that in no other time has this been more self-evident. In her newly published book, Henderson (2020) pictures capitalism as an order destroying the planet and destabilizing society as wealth reaches its peak, and she further states that time is running out to solve the already delayed contemporary problems. The world is running out of options, and alarm signals are stronger than ever before. As an umbrella term, sustainability in almost every facet of life has been seen as a means of salvation. As a Janusian phenomenon, the abundance, prosperity, and peace promised by globalization and growth has gradually been replaced with persistent and growing poverty and inequality, resource depletion, climate change, biodiversity loss, a reduced sense of well-being and an accelerated occurrence of environmental disasters and industrial accidents (Azam, 2017, p. 63). Due to recent economic, financial, environmental, and climate crises, alternative types of economies are on the rise today. Even the global COVID-19 pandemic has revealed the need for change and underscored the merits of alternatives. Haase et al. (2018, p. 57) define alternative econ-omies in which actors pursue value creation in a way that expresses relationships between human beings and nature that differ from those characteristics of "regular" or nonalternative economies. Alternatives are more sustainable, less materialistic practices (Eden, 2017, p. 274). Business-as-usual logic seems to be eradicated sooner or later.

The collaborative and sharing economy (Atsushi, 2014; Botsman & Rogers, 2011; Buczynski, 2013; Gansky, 2010), gig work and the gig economy (Ağlargöz & Ağlargöz,

2020; De Stefano, 2016), the do-it-yourself movement (Fox, 2014; Wolf & McQuitty, 2011), community gardens (Crossan et al., 2016; Parker et al., 2007), urban homesteading (Kaplan & Blume, 2011; Parker & Morrow, 2017), localization and self-sufficiency (Parker et al., 2007; Shuman, 2000), voluntary simplicity (Elgin, 2010; McDonald, 2014), the circular economy (Camacho-Otero et al., 2020), freecycling (Eden, 2017), slow food, smallness, the social economy, community currencies, and cooperatives (Parker et al., 2007) are just versions of alternatives for the economy, business, and customers. These alternatives are creating different ways of life, although some of them may overlap with and compensate for each other. Above all, degrowth is one of the most discussed alternatives. Azam (2017, p. 64) argues that degrowth is not an alternative but a matrix of alternatives.

Within this context, today's changing and empowered consumers are not satisfied with just meeting their needs. They expect sustainable options in fulfilling their needs. Consumers have begun demanding more from businesses. Natural, nontoxic or organic food and textiles, fair trade products, green housing/building options, vegan and cruelty-free cosmetics, and green and sustainable products are in higher demand. Consumers prefer brands offering better working conditions to their employees. Responsible consumers' purchasing decisions place more emphasis on positive impacts than negative impacts for the overall well-being of themselves and society (Martin & Schouten, 2015, p. 48). The role of consumers has changed from isolated to connected, from unaware to informed, and from passive to active. Consumers display these transformations in many ways and forms, such as through information access, worldviews, networking, experimentation, and activism. Consumers try to exercise their influence in every part of the business system. Hence, co-creation experience can be viewed as the basis for providing unique value for each individual (Prahalad & Ramasway, 2004b, pp. 4–5).

A global shift in consumer attitudes towards social and environmental sustainability drives brands to become more sustainable. In this sense, a brand must gain and retain stakeholder trust to be respected as sustainable (Martin & Schouten, 2015, p. 157). Bemporad and Baranowski (2008) offer some principles for sustainable branding by embracing sustainability and brand co-creation. In their proposition, brands are positioned to engage with their stakeholders in value creation. These brands are co-owned by employees, consumers, suppliers, investors, etc. who provide ideas, insights and peer-to-peer influence to brands. Here, being a sustainable brand requires utilizing brand co-creation. Moreover, co-creation is seen as the central factor of a circular economy in identifying sustainable alternatives (Walcher & Leube, 2017).

There have been several attempts to bridge sustainability and brand co-creation. Fadeeva (2004, p. 166) states that a collaborative approach has been denoted as a principal approach to environmental sustainability. Grekova et al. (2016) found that environmental collaboration with customers affects performance indirectly by stimulating food and beverage processors to implement sustainable process improvements that subsequently bring about cost savings and market gains. Verran (2010) argued that solutions encouraging sustainable consumption could be co-created between businesses and consumers. Systematic solutions to problems such as climate change and environmental degradation will have to be identified by all stakeholders via value co-creation. Hankammer and Kleer (2018) evaluated the sustainability potential of mass customization, which is a particular example of collaborative value co-creation for the specific case of degrowth business models. Build-to-order ideas, potential upgradability, and the stronger involvement of customers help foster sustainability through mass customization. Arnold (2017, pp. 186–187) claims that co-creation with consumers can initiate incremental shifts towards more sustainable activities and offers that co-creation processes should focus on the whole value chain and thus involve different stakeholders (at least consumers and suppliers) to minimize negative social and environmental impacts and foster sustainable development. Verran (2010) found that consumers believe they have a role to play in influencing the sustainability practices of grocery retailers.

From a multistakeholder perspective, sustainable value co-creation by customers and producers collectively considering environmental and societal implications is essential to increase value to all stakeholders (Badurdeen & Liyanege, 2011, p. 180). A co-creation-based view of the economy and society involves expanding collective self-interest based on the notion that "we do even better for ourselves by doing well for others, too" (Ramaswamy & Özcan, 2014, p. 236). The co-creative enterprise can cut costs and improve efficiency by drawing innovative ideas from customers, employees, and stakeholders at large. Co-creation enables a more efficient discovery and development of sustainable growth opportunities (Ramaswamy & Özcan, 2014, p. 289). Value co-creation represents an opportunity for businesses and consumers to find a new source of value creation in the services of sustainable consumption (Verran, 2010, p. 114). The quality of people's lives, regardless of the nature of the economic system in which businesses operate, is at the core of the co-creation vision (Ramaswamy & Özcan, 2014, p. 248). This view shows that brand co-creation and the quality of people's lives are to be considered together. Eventually, brand co-creation serves as an opportunity to realize these ideals by generating degrowth.

## 4.    DEGROWTH: AN OXYMORON OR A REAL PANACEA?

The concept of degrowth (fr. *decroissance*) was first coined in France. The concept has since expanded across Europe, Canada, Australia, the UK, and the US (Cohen, 2011). Degrowth questions the ways of life linked to growth by asking: what makes life and people prosperous? (Bauhardt, 2014, p. 60). Azam (2017, p. 64) called degrowth postgrowth or breaking the addiction to growth. The idea that endless growth and consumption are unsustainable is the underlying logic of degrowth. Advocates of degrowth argue that the solution is not to make growth greener or more socially equitable but to produce and consume less, which is the opposite of growth. Proponents of degrowth champion localization, smallness, and simplicity, which are becoming popular among post-affluent societies (Parker et al., 2007, pp. 69–70). Degrowth is based on the premise of reducing consumption for the good of society and the natural environment (Helm et al., 2012, p. 4). While macroeconomics of limitless growth imply lifestyles of insatiable consumption, macroeconomics of degrowth imply lifestyles of voluntary simplicity (Alexander, 2012).

The degrowth movement has proposed the attainment of autonomous, self-sufficient, and environmentally respectful companies with sufficient potential to guarantee the well-being of all citizens utilizing locally available resources (Plaza-Úbeda et al., 2020, p. 71). According to Azam (2017, p. 64), degrowth involves reducing the consumption of natural resources and energy for the balance of nature, inventing a new political and social form running contrary to ideologies of growth and development, building a pluralistic and diverse social movement and employing diverse ways to move beyond growth and reject immoderation. According to Fournier (2008, p. 532), degrowth is not just a quantitative concept of producing and consuming less but a tool proposed to initiate a more radical break with dominant economic thinking. Degrowth ideals emphasize a paradigmatic reorganization of values, in particular the (re) verification of social and ecological values and (re)politicization of the economy. Removing actors from the economy asks fundamental questions about the nature, distribution, use, and abuse of wealth.

Carbo et al. (2018) argue that as expected from degrowth, reducing consumption does not require individual sacrifice or a decrease in well-being. Instead, the degrowth mindset aims to maximize happiness and well-being through nonconsumptive means such as sharing work and consuming less. Martin and Schouten (2015) stress that living sustainably does not necessarily require sacrificing current needs and caring only about the future. Overall, the purpose of degrowth is to facilitate the development of people and society by changing the ways that we live and consume resources. In the degrowth literature, some scholars tend to use the concept of sustainable degrowth. "Sustainable degrowth" is both a concept and a social-grassroots movement with its origins in the fields of ecological economics, social ecology, economic anthropology, and environmental and social activist group studies (Martínez-Alier et al., 2010, p. 1741). Schneider et al. (2010, p. 512) define sustainable degrowth as an equitable downscaling of production and consumption that increases human well-being and enhances ecological conditions at the local and global levels in the short and long term.

Degrowth proposes that human progress is possible without growth. Degrowth may cause a decrease in GDP, but the ultimate goal is the pursuit of well-being, ecological sustainability, and social equity (Kallis, 2011; Schneider et al., 2010). However, Chertkovskaya et al. (2017, pp. 189–190) state that since growth cannot be negative, degrowth is not the opposite of what the economy is doing. From their perspective, degrowth can be seen as a critique of the growth ideology as a hypothesis for something new, which includes ecological demand with less output, material, and energy use. They argue that less is different; it is about changing our social organization so that we can also live with producing and consuming less.

No discussion of growth is complete without touching on GDP. There is also a growing view around the world that GDP is a poor measure of progress and an increasing desire to do something about this (O'Neill, 2015). Victor (2015) expresses that in pursuing economic growth goals, economies may fail to meet other objectives that would directly contribute to well-being and prosperity, such as full employment, more leisure, richer social lives, greater democratic participation, and a resilient environment. Additionally, economic growth in rich countries is likely to occur at the expense of economic growth in developing countries. Victor (2015) concludes that post-affluent societies should think about managing without growth or even with degrowth. Considering sustainability as a critical endeavor for long-term competitive advantage for brands (Martin & Schouten, 2015), Helm et al. (2012, pp. 4–5) argue that even though the potential negative implications of economic degrowth for marketing practices may seem overwhelming, degrowth as a marketing strategy can conceivably be economically viable or offer new and creative opportunities to gain competitive advantages. As has been preached in economics courses, a recession involves a shrinkage of the existing economy, an economy that requires growth to remain stable, while degrowth calls for a shift to a different kind of economy altogether that does not require growth in the first place. It is possible to reduce aggregate economic activity in high-income nations while at the same time maintaining and even improving indicators of human development and well-being (Hickel, 2019, p. 57). Overall, degrowth can be seen as an understanding of means of compensating today's economic, environmental, and societal deficiencies.

From a macroscale perspective, Europe's GDP per capita is 40 percent lower than that of the US, yet Europe performs better in virtually every social category, as European countries tend to be more equal and more committed to public goods (Hickel, 2019, p. 58). Some degrowth supporters propose using the genuine progress indicator (GPI) instead of GDP as a metric of the well-being of a nation. The GPI is composed of 26 indicators of three main focuses: economic, social, and environmental. Moreover, some states in the US are moving towards the use of the GPI; the Organisation for Economic Co-operation and Development (OECD) provides the Better Life Index, and Canada has developed the Canadian Index of Well-Being (https://uwaterloo.ca/canadian-index-wellbeing/).

By restoring public services and expanding commons, people's access to the goods that they need to live well without high levels of income is one of the core claims of degrowth. The objective of degrowth is to scale down materials and energy consumed by the global economy by focusing on high-income nations with high levels of per capita consumption. The idea is to achieve this objective by reducing waste and shrinking sectors of economic activity that are ecologically destructive and offer little if any social benefit (Hickel, 2019, pp. 56–57). The solution is not to make growth greener or more socially equitable but rather to challenge the very principle of growth: to produce and consume less, especially in more developed countries (Parker et al., 2007, p. 69). To trigger a degrowth process that will be peaceful, convivial, and sustainable, there are eight interdependent goals, namely, reevaluation, reconceptualization, restructuring, redistribution, relocalization, reduction, reuse and recycling (Latouche, 2009, p. 32). Degrowth proposes that economic growth is not sustainable and that human progress without growth is possible. Degrowth demands a strong democracy, defends ecosystems, and proposes an equal distribution of wealth. Sustainable degrowth involves a voluntary, smooth and equitable transition towards a regime of less production and consumption (Yolles, 2018, p. 282). Degrowth is focused on the relocalization of activities, the redistribution of wealth, recovering the meaning of work, convivial and soft technologies, slowing down, and giving power back to grassroots communities (Azam, 2017).

Finally, one naturally asks how to bridge degrowth ideals with brand co-creation. Degrowth transformation must be intentional and democratic. It requires a long-term commitment to the downscaling of production and consumption and to the reorganization of society in a different way and has justice and equality at its core (Degrowth.info, 2020). Pollex and Lenschow (2018, p. 1870) expect that for the European Union as a region with advanced human resources and a long legacy of welfare states but poor natural resources, a moderate degrowth discourse will continue to provoke policymakers and encourage scientists and researchers to develop ideas and solutions for well-being that extend beyond GDP growth. Bonaiuti (2018, p. 1800) claims that advanced capitalist societies have entered a phase of involuntary degrowth with possible major effects on the system's capacity to maintain its present institutional framework. Cohen (2011, pp. 176–178) categorizes sustainable consumption as either weak or strong. In weak consumption, the "sustainable" option becomes just another product on a supermarket shelf among the other options. In contrast, strong sustainable consumption seeks to foster transformational changes in both the quantity and quality of resource use. Degrowth is classified as a mode of strong sustainable consumption that calls for large-scale reductions in the volume of resources appropriated by wealthy countries. With the changes expressed in the previous section, consumers drive degrowth by changing their consumption patterns (Roulet & Bothello, 2020).

## 5.   DEBATE BETWEEN DEGROWTH AND BRAND CO-CREATION: CONSTRUCTING NEW AVENUES FOR SUSTAINABLE BRANDING

Even Philip Kotler believes that consumer attitudes and behaviors towards today's capitalism will change after the recent pandemic. According to Kotler (2020), people will carefully examine what they consume, how much they consume, and how all of this is influenced by class issues and inequality. The anti-consuming movement is growing. Kotler (2020) categorizes five types of anti-consumerists. The first group of consumers is composed of "life simplifiers" who want to eat and buy less and downsize their possessions and who prefer renting to buying and owning. The second group consists of "degrowth activists" who feel that too much time and effort are spent on consumption. They call for conservation and reducing material needs. The third group includes "climate activists" who are concerned about carbon footprints that pollute air and water indirectly as a result of consumption. Fourth, there are "sane food choosers" who have turned to vegetarianism and veganism and who are upset with how we kill animals for food. The last group includes "conservation activists" who call not to destroy existing goods but to reuse, repair, redecorate them or give them to the needy. These individuals oppose any acts of planned obsolescence and luxury goods. The line between these groups is not clear. They all share common concerns about the future of the world. The pandemic has become an indicator that degrowth is possible and needed, demonstrating the unsustainability and fragility of our current lives. A sustainable alternative political-economic system that prioritizes human well-being over economic growth is needed (Degrowth.info, 2020). When the pandemic is over, capitalism will have moved to a new stage. Consumers will be more thoughtful about what they consume and how much they need to consume. They will become producers of their food needs, choose quality and healthy foods, buy sensible clothing and other goods, look for responsible brands and become more conscious of the planet (Kotler, 2020).

Scholars have started to see great potential in integrating degrowth ideals with brand co-creation. Dubuisson-Quellier (2015, p. 410) states that consumers are not only buyers with economic power but also citizens with political power to affect the market and brands. At the more radical end of the collective action spectrum are degrowth debates. Especially in the digital age, prosumers who both consume and produce value transform consumption patterns. Fuster Morell (2015) claims that digital commons realize degrowth's call for decommodification. The Internet provides an atmosphere for being nonprofit- and community-oriented, which is fundamental to degrowth. Similarly, brand co-creation by consumers and other stakeholders at some level facilitates degrowth goals. Vandevoort (2018) states that collaborative value creation is a business model criterion for a degrowth company. Hankammer and Kleer (2018) argue that several elements of collaborative value creation and its enabling technologies coincide with degrowth ideals. Transforming consumers into prosumers who co-create products, co-fund production, and contribute to challenges with their ideas could support the transition from sufficient consumption to degrowth understandings. Hankammer (2018) points out that collaborative value creation models can be a mainstay for the design of alternative sustainable business models due to the collaborative character of the concept of degrowth. Plaza-Úbeda et al. (2020, p. 73) argue that in line with degrowth, stakeholder integration requires directing business activity towards value creation for the production of goods and services. This value is not only economic, as stakeholders' concerns are not always economic. This concept emphasizes the importance of collaborative processes and wealth co-creation.

Numerous alternatives exist. Wiedenhoft Murphy (2017) includes co-creation, prosumers, and prosumption among the alternative forms of consumption that individuals and communities turn to. Problems related to mass consumer society require structural change, such as degrowth policies by planned economic contraction, reducing the use of raw materials, and decreasing air and water pollution and economic inequality. This structural change may come about with the help of alternative forms of consumption that Wiedenhoft Murphy (2017) identified. Another point that can serve as an indicator of the degrowth and brand co-creation relationship is based on Parrique's (2019, p. 285) work. Degrowth suggests artisanship and self-production/vernacular production. The vernacular is do-it-yourself, self-taught, often unpaid, made-at-home production or self-production, which is used by sensitive consumers. Degrowth blurs the division by discussing co-production or prosumption (Parrique, 2019, p. 285). Hankammer (2018) found five areas in which collaborative value creation could contribute to the objectives of degrowth: reducing overproduction, extending product lifetimes, promoting sufficient consumption, increasing local resilience, and enabling the downscaling of production in a democratized way. Kostakis et al. (2018) studied commons-based peer production and offered the "design global, manufacture local" (DGML) approach as a new form of value creation by fulfilling the localization conditions of degrowth.

Demaria et al. (2013, pp. 201–205) classified degrowth strategies. Oppositional activism may include demonstrations, boycotts, campaigning, civil disobedience, direct action and protest songs. Building local, decentralized, small-scale and participatory alternatives such as cycling, reuse, sharing economies/collaborative consumption, vegetarianism and veganism, cohousing, agroecology, ecolabeling, ecovillages, solidarity economies, consumer cooperatives, alternative banks or credit cooperatives, time baking, and decentralized renewable energy cooperatives involves the creation of new institutions. Reformism involves actions adopted within existing institutions to create conditions for societal transformation. For example, while challenging capitalism through certain actions, many radical organic farmers still organize their lives around cars and computers that can be considered "reformist". Degrowth action strategies of reformism, building alternatives, and opposition activism are very suitable for collaborative approaches (Haucke, 2018, p. 1721). Degrowth promoters/actors can be activists engaged in opposition and practitioners who develop alternatives. Some actors call for a complete revision of the existing institution, while others call for transformation or partial conservation. These actors can include consumers and companies.

Roulet and Bothello (2020) identify three strategies of consumer-driven degrowth for large companies by examining companies at the forefront of the degrowth movement. First, companies can pursue degrowth-adapted product design by producing products that have longer lifespans, are modular, and are locally produced. Such companies must move away from planned obsolescence. Second, companies can engage in value chain repositioning where they exit certain stages of the value chain and delegate certain tasks to other stakeholders. For instance, Local Motors company crowdsources designs and crowdfunds projects from its potential consumers. In this way, the company offers different avenues to consumers despite production limits. With stakeholder engagement in their operations, companies can act faster to adapt degrowth. Finally, companies can lead through a degrowth-oriented standard setting to standardize a practice or technological platform. For example, the apparel company Patagonia follows an antigrowth strategy. Nike, Walmart, and H&M are taking advice from

Patagonia and benchmarking the strategy. Tesla released all of its patents in 2014 to increase the diffusion of electric vehicles.

To reach degrowth ideals, systems and companies should strengthen their interactions with customers. For a behavioral change towards degrowth, customer participation is of the utmost importance. Communication strategies helping to increase the level of customer participation and brand co-creation are one of the crucial links between the company and customers. For Hatch and Schultz (2010), this engagement can be accomplished through social networking, information sharing, and structuring relationships with the company supporting the brand as the organizer of community activities, which in turn serves as a basis for brand co-creation. For example, Tomassini (2019, p. 367) focuses on how co-creation approaches help develop and explore new knowledge by encouraging a process of thinking in an interdisciplinary and participative way with a network of collaborators, vendors, and customers. The co-creational dimension of such firms constructs diverse values and paradigms together with a network of collaborators, vendors and customers. Tomassini (2019) found that small value-based tourism firms perceive smallness and degrowth concepts as a way to control firms' outcomes and quality through a selective approach valuing human relationships, inclusiveness, participation, and conviviality and not as a rejection of growth and business opportunities.

Let us now review some exemplary cases bridging degrowth ideals and brand co-creation. Bike Kitchens are do-it-yourself bicycle repair studios in which citizens can borrow tools and space to repair or build their bikes. Additionally, they serve as recycling centers for unwanted bikes, enabling citizens to access spare parts or build entirely new bikes from old parts, and they are generally run on a nonprofit basis through some form of volunteering system (Bradley, 2018, p. 1676). Bike Kitchens as a part of sharing and do-it-yourself culture can be seen as a mode of degrowth. Fairphone, a social enterprise company developing smartphones with minimal environmental impact, meets the criteria of degrowth and sustainable consumption. Fairphone smartphones are codeveloped by designers and consumers under principles of fairness, which was realized by crowdsourcing. Fairphone might allow individuals to express their attendance to a degrowth-oriented consumption movement (Haucke, 2018). Degrowth-motivated co-creation can also be applied in agriculture. Savarese et al. (2020) found that community-supported agriculture is based on the active participation of consumers as stewards of economic, social, and environmental value. Some scholars have studied community-supported agriculture as an example of microeconomic models and degrowth. This approach to co-creation could become an alternative mode for food companies and networks to collaborate with and involve consumers. Plaza-Úbeda et al. (2020) offer Patagonia as an example of a business with a degrowth position. Patagonia's mission statement reveals its degrowth position clearly by stating "Build the best product, cause no unnecessary harm, use business to inspire and implement solutions to the environmental crisis" (Patagonia, 2020). Patagonia seeks to motivate customers to consume less through its advertising messages and shift consumption patterns towards responsible consumption (Plaza-Úbeda et al., 2020, p. 76). Another example is the Swedish retailing giant IKEA. IKEA opened a pilot second-hand store in Stockholm that sells used furniture after repair to reach its 2030 climate targets. The used furniture comes from municipal recycling centers where people can donate furniture (Ringstrom, 2020). This initiative may reflect a new approach to brand co-creation with degrowth.

On a societal level, degrowth can also be viewed as an economic and social movement based on anti-consumerism and anti-productivism (Kallis, 2018, p. 6). Degrowth is an example of an activist-led science (Demaria et al., 2013, p. 210). Boycotts, buycotts, online consumer reviews, consumer activism, and social and consumer movements are ways of expressing consumers' choices and personal reactions. One of the most effective among these reactions are social movements. From a marketing point of view, Buechler (2000) describes social movements as collective efforts by individuals to transform consumer society. Social movements mediate the relationship between companies and individual ethical customers and positively influence their value perceptions (Sebastiani et al., 2013). The totality of these attempts to transform various elements of the social order surrounding consumption and marketing can also be called consumer movements, a specific subcategory of social movements (Chaney & Philippe, 2019; Hyman & Tohill, 2017, p. 4; Kozinets & Handelman, 2004, p. 691). As said above, consumers' potential power is increasing, and the rise of new technology, especially social media, offers a means to help realize this power. Consumer groups have launched many political actions in recent years; among them, attacks on multinational corporations' practices have been common (Zureik & Mowshowitz, 2005, p. 48). In this vein, social movements can influence businesses' environmental practices through several distinct pressures. One form of influence is indirect: by changing the general operating environment of all firms in an industry or economy. Another path is realized by the diffusion of cultural change in public sentiment that alters businesses' social environments (e.g., in the form of consumer preferences). Another form of influence is more direct where movements interact with organizations. A prominent direct pathway includes pressure campaigns launched against specific target firms for their environmental practices. Such campaigns use familiar protest repertoires such as boycotts, lawsuits, media and street protests to threaten a company's reputation and even disrupt its operations (Weber & Soderstrom, 2012, pp. 255–256). Consumer movements are also combined with offline actions (Chaney & Philippe, 2019). Other than these traditional modes, digital and social media have caused an interesting shift in communication in social movements. Consumers now play more active roles than the mere spectators or bystanders of the mass media era (Bennett & Segerberg, 2016, p. 368). Social movements have challenged and transformed the markets. King and Pearce (2010, p. 251) identify three prominent ways in which movements have instigated change. According to these, challenging corporations directly, creating transnational systems of private regulation and creating market alternatives through institutional entrepreneurship have been the main interrelated means used to fulfill this purpose (King & Pearce, 2010). McInerney (2014) also researched social movements' constitution of markets. Some movements have fundamentally contested economic systems. Therefore, it can be claimed that these movements have played a creative, destructive, and regulative role.

Sebastiani et al. (2013) found that companies and social movements could interact to codesign new business models. Eataly is a retail chain that offers a new food distribution paradigm inspired by sustainability, sharing, and responsibility. The slow food movement and Eataly interacted dialectically during the initiation of a new business venture. This format aimed to present quality products from local farmers and create a better environment. The interaction between Eataly and the slow food movement influences the company's acceptance from consumers who wish to find new ways to actively participate in transforming the market into a more ethical one. In another example, the social movement against overtourism in Barcelona has emerged as a degrowth campaign that calls for alternative governance and management measures (Milano et al., 2019). Demaria et al. (2013, p. 194) stated that anti-car and anti-advertising activists, cyclist and pedestrian rights campaigners, partisans of organic agriculture, critics of urban sprawl, and promoters of solar energy and local currencies have started seeing degrowth as an appropriate common representative frame for their worldview. It is now claimed that degrowth has evolved into an interpretative frame for various social movements (Demaria et al., 2013, p. 194), providing fertile ground for brand co-creation.

## 6.  CONCLUSION: THE END IS THE NEW BEGINNING!

Ontologically, brand co-creation plays a unique role in creating both the individual and society concurrently. By challenging the notion of "power over" to Mary Parker Follett's notion of "power with", brand co-creation opens up new horizons for empowered contemporary consumers seeking sustainable alternatives. The end of this debate has to be viewed as a new beginning. With bee death, environmental pollution, global warming, radioactive contamination, the effect of base stations, and the misuse of pesticides, as the consumers of this world humans always take, but once they remember that they need to give back, nothing is left. Capitalism's assumption of people's unlimited desire for goods and for the earth's unlimited resources to support unlimited growth is now being questioned (Kotler, 2020). After the pandemic, companies will first respond and recover and then most will be expected to realize that they need to renew themselves. Statements such as "postpandemic manufacturing will seek ways of balancing efficiency and resilience and creating trust by transparency, logic, empathy, and sustainability" (HBR Türkiye, 2020) can be read in *Harvard Business Review*'s Turkish version. When and how fast this transformation will occur remains unknown, but one can be sure that it has already begun.

Most new products fail because they do not fully address real customer needs and wants. Therefore, an increasing number of companies are empowering customers and allowing them to actively participate in value co-creation (O'Hern & Rindfleisch, 2010, p. 101). Customers are the ones who know the products and services of companies best, and they have specific ideas about how to improve. Moreover, radical changes require stakeholders to take part in value co-creation. Therefore, companies should be supportive of a co-creative approach. As stated above, close customer–firm relationships enable a company to face the market's needs and save money for ongoing customer acquisition (Arnold, 2017, p. 186). The creative potential of consumer co-creation heralds a new era of consumer empowerment. Ramaswamy and Özcan (2014, p. 247) argue that the co-creation paradigm bridges human experience with the economy by returning human experiences to the economy in a meaningful way. Value co-creation is not aimed at disciplining consumers and shaping actions according to a given norm; it is about working with and through the freedom of the consumer (Zwick et al., 2008, p. 163).

There is great synergy potential for degrowth and brand value co-creation. Degrowth is not only a critique of the current world order but also proposes alternatives to it. Degrowth requires less use of nonrenewable resources through the use of various methods such as downshifting and/or reuse, the repair and sharing of resources, the relocalization of economies, democratization, and the cultivation of noncapitalist forms of economies and relations. Well-being, happiness, and equality are the essential conditions of degrowth when using different methods such as voluntary simplicity, downshifting, anti-consumption, and activism (Lloveras & Quinn, 2017). There may be criticisms of degrowth as of the other alternatives that are captured by marketing logic with the commercialization of lifestyles (Lipovetsky, 2011, p. 36). Degrowth as a relatively small but growing movement should not be ignored by companies. As illustrated in this chapter, companies should find innovative ways to achieve consumer-driven degrowth. Businesses that successfully implement degrowth will become more resilient and adaptable. In this way, companies will sell better instead of necessarily selling more, and while respecting the environment; hence, they can grow by satisfying contemporary consumers (Roulet & Bothello, 2020). Consumer-driven degrowth requires incorporating consumers into the value co-creation process. This chapter reveals that degrowth with all goals and features and brand value co-creation with its relationship to sustainability are intersected. To progress the debate, the upsides and downsides of specific elements of brand value co-creation from a degrowth perspective must be empirically measured in further studies.

## NOTE

1. In this chapter, brand co-creation and brand value co-creation are used interchangeably.

## REFERENCES

Ağlargöz, O., & Ağlargöz, F. (2020). The collaborative and sharing economy. In M. Parker, K. Stoborod, & T. Swann (Eds.), *Anarchism, organization and management critical perspectives for students* (pp. 157–168). Routledge.

Alexander, S. (2012). Degrowth implies voluntary simplicity: Overcoming barriers to sustainable consumption. Retrieved March 25, 2020, from https://ssrn.com/abstract=2009698 or http://dx.doi.org/10.2139/ssrn.2009698

Arnold, M. (2017). Fostering sustainability by linking co-creation and relationship management concepts. *Journal of Cleaner Production, 140*(1), 179–188. http://dx.doi.org/10.1016/j.jclepro.2015.03.059

Atsushi, M. (2014). *The rise of sharing: Fourth-stage consumer society in Japan*. International House of Japan.

Azam, G. (2017). Degrowth. In P. Solón (Ed.), *Systematic alternatives* (pp. 59–76). Fundación Solón/Attac France/Focus on the Global South.

Badurdeen, F., & Liyanage, J. P. (2011). Sustainable value co-creation through mass customisation: A framework. *International Journal of Sustainable Manufacturing, 2*(2/3), 180–203. https://doi.org/10.1504/IJSM.2011.042151

Bauhardt, C. (2014). Solutions to the crisis? The green new deal, degrowth, and the solidarity economy: Alternatives to the capitalist growth economy from an ecofeminist economics perspective. *Ecological Economics, 102*(2014), 60–68. http://dx.doi.org/10.1016/j.ecolecon.2014.03.015

Bemporad, R., & Baranowksi, M. (2008). Branding for sustainability: Five principles for leveraging brands to create shared value. Retrieved April 4, 2020, from https://www.csrwire.com/press_releases/14047-Branding-for-Sustainability-Five-Principles-for-Leveraging-Brands-to-Create-Shared-Value

Bennett, W. L., & Segerberg, A. (2016). Communication in movements. In D. della Porta, & M. Diani (Eds.), *The Oxford handbook of social movements* (pp. 367–382). Oxford, UK: Oxford University Press.

Bonaitui, M. (2018). Are we entering the age of involuntary degrowth? Promethean technologies and declining returns of innovation. *Journal of Cleaner Production, 197*(2), 1800–1809. http://dx.doi.org/10.1016/j.jclepro.2017.02.196

Bonsu, S. K., & Darmody, A. (2008). Co-creating second life. Market–consumer cooperation in contemporary economy. *Journal of Macromarketing, 28*(4), 355–368. https://doi.org/10.1177/0276146708325396

Botsman, R., & Rogers, R. (2011). *What's mine is yours: How collaborative consumption is changing the way we live*. Harper Collins Publishers.

Bradley, K. (2018). Bike Kitchens – Spaces for convivial tools. *Journal of Cleaner Production, 197*(2), 1676–1683. https://doi.org/10.1016/j.jclepro.2016.09.208

Buczynski, B. (2013). *Sharing is good*. New Society Publishers.

Buechler, S. M. (2000). *Social movements in advanced capitalism*. Oxford University Press.

Camacho-Otero, J., Tunn, V. S. C., Chamberlin, L., & Boks, C. (2020). Consumers in the circular economy. In M. Brandão, D. Lazarevic, & G. Finnveden (Eds.), *Handbook of the circular economy* (pp. 74–87). Cheltenham, UK and Northampton, MA, USA: Edward Elgar Publishing.

Carbo, J. A., Dao, V. T., Haase, S. J., Hargrove, M. B., & Langella, I. M. (2018). *Social sustainability for business*. Routledge.

Chaney, D., & Philippe, D. (2019). The power of speech: Consumer movements' discursive strategies in digital mobilization. In R. Bagchi, L. Block, & L. Lee (Eds.), *NA – Advances in Consumer Research*, Volume 47 (pp. 501–502). Duluth, MN: Association for Consumer Research.

Chertkovskaya, E., Paulsson, A., Kallis, G., Barca, S., & D'Alisa, G. (2017). The vocabulary of degrowth: A roundtable debate. *Ephemera Theory & Politics in Organization, 17*(1), 189–208.

Cohen, M. J. (2011). (Un)sustainable consumption and the new political economy of growth. In K. M. Ekström, & K. Glans (Eds.), *Beyond the consumption bubble* (pp. 174–190). Routledge.

Cova, B., Pace, S., & Skalen, P. (2015). Brand volunteering: Value co-creation with unpaid consumers. *Marketing Theory, 15*(4), 465–485.

Crossan, J., Cumbers, A., McMaster, R., & Shaw, D. (2016). Contesting neoliberal urbanism in Glasgow's community gardens: The practice of DIY citizenship. *Antipode, 48*(4), 937–955. https://doi.org/10.1111/anti.12220

De Stefano, V. (2016). The rise of the "just-in-time workforce": On-demand work, crowd work and labour protection in the "gig-economy". International Labour Office, Inclusive Labour Markets, Labour Relations and Working Conditions Branch. 2016 Conditions of Work and Employment Series: No. 71. Geneva: ILO.

Degrowth.info editorial team. (2020). A degrowth perspective on the coronavirus crisis. https://www.degrowth.info/en/2020/03/a-degrowth-perspective-on-the-coronavirus-crisis/

Demaria, F., Schneider, F., Sekulova, F., & Martinez-Alier, J. (2013). What is degrowth? From an activist slogan to a social movement. *Environmental Values, 22*(2), 191–215.

Denegri-Knott, J., Zwick, D., & Schroeder, J. E. (2006). Mapping consumer power: An integrative framework for marketing and consumer research. *European Journal of Marketing, 40*(9/10), 950–971. https://doi.org/10.1108/03090560610680952

Dubuisson-Quellier, S. (2015). From targets to recruits: The status of consumers within the political consumption movement. *International Journal of Consumer Studies, 39*(5), 404–412. https://doi.org/10.1111/ijcs.12200

Eden, S. (2017). Blurring the boundaries: Prosumption, circularity and online sustainable consumption through Freecycle. *Journal of Consumer Culture, 17*(2), 265–285. https://doi.org/10.1177/1469540515586871

Elgin, D. (2010). *Voluntary simplicity: Toward a way of life that is outwardly simple, inwardly rich* (2nd ed.). Harper Collins.

Fadeeva, Z. (2004). Promise of sustainability collaboration – potential fulfilled? *Journal of Cleaner Production, 13*(2), 165–174. https://doi.org/10.1016/S0959-6526(03)00125-2

Fournier, V. (2008). Escaping from the economy: The politics of degrowth. *International Journal of Sociology and Social Policy, 28*(11/12), 528–545. https:// 10.1108/01443330810915233

Fox, S. (2014). Third wave do-it-yourself (DIY): Potential for prosumption, innovation, and entrepreneurship by local populations in regions without industrial manufacturing infrastructure. *Technology in Society, 39*(2014), 18–30. https://doi.org/10.1016/j.techsoc.2014.07.001

French, Jr., J. R. P., & Raven, B. (1959). The bases of social power. In D. Cartwright (Ed.), *Studies in social power* (pp. 150–167). Ann Arbor: University of Michigan, Institute for Social Research.

Fuster Morell, M. (2015). Digital commons. In G. D'Alisa, F. Demaria, & G. Kallis (Eds.), *Degrowth: A vocabulary for a new era* (pp. 159–161). Routledge.

Füller, J., Mühlbacher, H., Matzler, K., & Jawecki, G. (2009). Consumer empowerment through internet-based co-creation. *Journal of Management Information Systems, 26*(3), 71–102. https://doi.org/10.2753/MIS0742-1222260303

Gansky, L. (2010). *The mesh: Why the future of business is sharing*. Portfolio Penguin.

Grekova, K., Calantone, R. J., Bremmers, H. J., Trienekens, J. H., & Omta, S. W. F. (2016). How environmental collaboration with suppliers and customers influences firm performance: Evidence from Dutch food and beverage processors. *Journal of Cleaner Production, 112*(3), 1861–1871. https://doi.org/10.1016/j.jclepro.2015.03.022

Haase, M., Becker, I., & Pick, D. (2018). Alternative economies as marketing systems? The role of value creation and the criticism of economic growth. *Journal of Macromarketing, 38*(1), 57–72. https://doi.org/10.1177/0276146717728776

Hankammer, S. M. (2018). Essays on customized and collaborative value creation from the perspective of sustainability [Doctoral dissertation, RWTH Aachen University]. https://publications.rwth-aachen.de/record/721475/files/721475.pdf

Hankammer, S., & Kleer, R. (2018). Degrowth and collaborative value creation: Reflections on concepts and technologies. *Journal of Cleaner Production, 197*(2), 1711–1718. https://doi.org/10.1016/j.jclepro.2017.03.046

*Harvard Business Review Türkiye* (HBR Türkiye) (2020, June 26). Üretimde yeni dönem, yeni perspektifle [Webinar]. https://webinar.hbrturkiye.com/live/uretimde-yeni-donem-yeni-perspektifler/8c5e6004587de6b1c99acf01ebf0efde

Hatch, M. J., & Schultz, M. (2010). Toward a theory of brand co-creation with implications for brand governance. *Brand Management, 17*(8), 590–604. https://doi.org/10.1057/bm.2010.14

Haucke, F. V. (2018). Smartphone-enabled social change: Evidence from the Fairphone case? *Journal of Cleaner Production, 197*(2), 1719–1730. http://dx.doi.org/10.1016/j.jclepro.2017.07.014

Helm, S. V., Wooliscroft, B., &. Rahtz, D. R. (2012). The role of marketing in degrowth. In M. Haase, & M. Kleinaltenkamp (Eds.), Proceedings of the 37th Annual Macromarketing Conference 2012, Berlin, Germany: Freie Universitat Berlin, 4–6.

Henderson, R. (2020). *Reimagining capitalism in a world on fire*. Penguin.

Hickel, J. (2019). Degrowth: A theory of radical abundance. *Real-World Economics Review, 87*(19 March), 54–68.

Hoikkala, H. (2019, October 27). H&M CEO sees "terrible" fallout as consumer shaming spreads. BNN Bloomberg. https://www.bnnbloomberg.ca/h-m-ceo-sees-terrible-fallout-as-consumer-shaming-spreads-1.1338212

Hyman, L., & Tohill, J. (2017). Shopping for change: Consumer activism and the possibilities of purchasing power. In L. Hyman, & J. Tohill (Eds.), *Shopping for change* (pp. 1–16). Cornell University Press.

Kallis, G. (2011). In defence of degrowth. *Ecological Economics, 70*(5), 873–880. https://doi.org/10.1016/j.ecolecon.2010.12.007

Kallis, G. (2018). *Degrowth*. Agenda Publishing.

Kaplan, R., & Blume, K. R. (2011). *Urban homesteading-heirloom skills for sustainable living*. Skyhorse Publishing.

King, B. G., & Pearce, N. A. (2010). The contentiousness of markets: Politics, social movements, and institutional change in markets. *Annual Review of Sociology, 36*(2010), 249–267.

Kostakis, V., Latoufis, K., Liarokapis, M., & Bauwens, M. (2018). The convergence of digital commons with local manufacturing from a degrowth perspective: Two illustrative cases. *Journal of Cleaner Production, 197*(Part 2), 1684–1693. http://dx.doi.org/10.1016/j.jclepro.2016.09.077

Kotler, P. (2010). The prosumer movement. A new challenge for marketers. In B. Blättel-Mink, & K. Hellmann (Eds.), *Prosumer revisited* (pp. 51–60). VS Verlag für Sozialwissenschaften.

Kotler, P. (2020). The consumer in the age of coronavirus. *Journal of Creating Value, 6*(1), 12–15. https://www.linkedin.com/pulse/consumer-age-coronavirus-philip-kotler-world-marketing-summit

Kozinets, R. V., & Handelman, J. M. (2004). Adversaries of consumption: Consumer movements, activism, and ideology. *Journal of Consumer Research, 31*(3), 691–704. https://doi.org/10.1086/425104

Latouche, S. (2009). *Farewell to growth* (D. Macey, Trans.). Polity Press (original work published 2007).

Lipovetsky, G. (2011). The hyperconsumption society. In K. M. Ekström, & K. Glans (Eds.), *Beyond the consumption bubble* (pp. 25–36). Routledge.

Lloveras, J., & Quinn, L. (2017). Growth and its discontents: Paving the way for a more productive engagement with alternative economic practices. *Journal of Macromarketing, 37*(2), 131–142. https://doi.org/10.1177/0276146716670213

Martin, D., & Schouten, J. (2015). *Sustainable marketing*. Pearson Education Limited.

Martínez-Alier, J., Pascual, U., Vivien, Franck-D., & Zaccai, E. (2010). Sustainable de-growth: Mapping the context, criticisms and future prospects of an emergent paradigm. *Ecological Economics, 69*(9), 1741–1747. https://doi.org/10.1016/j.ecolecon.2010.04.017

McDonald, S. (2014). Voluntary simplicity. In M. Parker, G. Cheney, V. Fournier, & C. Land (Eds.), *The Routledge companion to alternative organization* (pp. 210–219). Routledge.

McInerney, P. (2014). *From social movement to moral market: How the circuit riders sparked an IT revolution and created a technology market.* Stanford University Press.

Milano, C., Novelli, M., & Cheer, J. M. (2019). Overtourism and degrowth: A social movements perspective. *Journal of Sustainable Tourism, 27*(12), 1857–1875.

OECD (2007). Participative web: User-created content. Retrieved April 2, 2020, from https://www.oecd.org/sti/ieconomy/participativewebanduser-createdcontentweb20wikisandsocialnetworking.htm

O'Hern, M. S., & Rindfleisch, A. (2010). Customer co-creation. A typology and research agenda. In N. K. Malhotra (Ed.), *Review of marketing research* (Vol. 6) (pp. 84–106). Emerald Group Publishing Limited. https://doi.org/10.1108/S1548-6435(2009)0000006008

O'Neill, D. (2015). Gross domestic product. In G. D'Alisa, F. Demaria, & G. Kallis (Eds.), *Degrowth: A vocabulary for a new era* (pp. 103–106). Routledge.

Padhi, P. K. (2018). Towards a sustainable value co-creation framework: Ethical cognitive couture, cognitive system, and sustainability. *International Journal of Engineering and Management Research, 8*(4), 135–149. https://doi.org/10.31033/ijemr.8.4.17

Parker, B., & Morrow, O. (2017). Urban homesteading and intensive mothering: (Re) gendering care and environmental responsibility in Boston and Chicago. *Gender, Place & Culture, 24*(2), 247–259. https://doi.org/10.1080/0966369X.2016.1277186

Parker, M., Fourneir, V., & Reedy, P. (2007). *The dictionary of alternatives.* Zed Books.

Parrique, T. (2019). The political economy of degrowth [Doctoral dissertation, Université Clermont Auvergne; Stockholms Universitet]. https://tel.archives-ouvertes.fr/tel-02499463/document

Patagonia (2020). https://www.patagonia.com.au/pages/our-business-and-climate-change

Plaza-Úbeda, J., Pérez-Valls, M., & Céspedes-Lorente, J. J. (2020). The contribution of systems theory to sustainability in degrowth contexts: The role of subsystems. *Systems Research and Behavioral Science, 37*(1), 68–81. https://doi.org/10.1002/sres.2600

Pollex, J., & Lenschow, A. (2018). Surrendering to growth? The European Union's goals for research and technology in the Horizon 2020 framework. *Journal of Cleaner Production, 197*(2), 1863–1871. http://dx.doi.org/10.1016/j.jclepro.2016.10.195

Prahalad, C. K., & Ramaswamy, V. (2004a). Co-creation experiences: The next practice in value creation. *Journal of Interactive Marketing, 18*(3), 5–14. 10.1002/dir.20015

Prahalad, C. K., & Ramaswamy, V. (2004b). Co-creating unique value with customers. *Strategy & Leadership, 32*(3), 4–9. https://doi.org/10.1108/10878570410699249

Priharsari, D., Abedin, B., & Mastio, E. (2020). Value co-creation in firm sponsored online communities: What enables, constrains, and shapes value. *Internet Research, 30*(3), 763–788.

Ramaswamy, V., & Özcan, K. (2014). *The co-creation paradigm.* Stanford University Press.

Rezabakhsh, B., Bornemann, D., Hansen, U., & Schrader, U. (2006). Consumer power: A comparison of the old economy and the internet economy. *Journal of Consumer Policy, 29*(1), 3–36. https://doi.org/10.1007/s10603-005-3307-7

Ringstrom, A. (2020, October 29). IKEA opens pilot second-hand store in Sweden. https://uk.reuters.com/article/uk-ikea-second-hand/ikea-opens-pilot-second-hand-store-in-sweden-idUKKBN27E3GO?il=0

Ritzer, G. (2010). Focusing on the prosumer on correcting an error in the history of social theory. In B. Blättel-Mink, & K. Hellmann (Eds.), *Prosumer revisited* (pp. 61–79). VS Verlag für Sozialwissenschaften.

Rossi, C., & De Chiara, A. (2009). The challenge of co-creation: Corporate blogs and collaborative product innovation. *SSRN Electronic Journal.* http://dx.doi.org/10.2139/ssrn

Roulet, T., & Bothello, J. (2020, February 14). Why "de-growth" shouldn't scare businesses. *Harvard Business Review.* https://hbr.org/2020/02/why-de-growth-shouldnt-scare-businesses

Savarese, M., Chamberlain, K., & Graffigna, G. (2020). Co-creating value in sustainable and alternative food networks: The case of community supported agriculture in New Zealand. *Sustainability, 12*(3), 1252. https://doi.org/10.3390/su12031252

Schneider, F., Kallis, G., & Martinez-Alier, J. (2010). Crisis or opportunity? Economic degrowth for social equity and ecological sustainability. *Journal of Cleaner Production, 18*(6), 511–518. https://doi .org/10.1016/j.jclepro.2010.01.014

Schroeder, J. E. (2011). Value creation and the visual consumer. In K. M. Ekström, & K. Glans (Eds.), *Beyond the consumption bubble* (pp. 137–148). Routledge.

Sebastiani, R., Montagnini, F., & Dalli, D. (2013). Ethical consumption and new business models in the food industry. Evidence from the Eataly case. *Journal of Business Ethics, 114*(3), 473–488. https://doi .org/10.1007/s 10551-012-1343-1

Sheth, J. N., & Uslay, C. (2007). Implications of the revised definition of marketing: From exchange to value creation. *Journal of Public Policy & Marketing, 26*(2), 302–307.

Shuman, M. H. (2000). *Going local – Creating self-reliant communities in a global age*. Routledge.

Strähle, J., & Grünewald, A. (2017). The prosumer concept in fashion retail: Potentials and limitations. In J. Strähle (Ed.), *Green fashion retail* (pp. 95–117). Springer.

Toffler, A. (1980). *Third wave*. Bantam Books.

Tomassini, L. (2019). The co-creation of diverse values and paradigms in small values-based tourism firms. *Tourism Recreation Research, 44*(3), 359–369. https://doi.org/10.1080/02508281.2019 .1576376

Vandevoort, M. (2018). Degrowth: A viable business model? [Master's thesis, Gent University]. https:// www.scriptieprijs.be/sites/default/files/thesis/2018-09/Masters%20dissertation%20-%20Degrowth %20a%20viable%20business%20model%3F.pdf

Verran, G. B. (2010). The application of value co-creation in advancing solutions to sustainable consumption [Master's thesis, Gordon Institute of Business Science, University of Pretoria]. https:// repository.up.ac.za/bitstream/handle/2263/26575/dissertation.pdf?sequence=1&isAllowed=y

Victor, P. A. (2015). Growth. In G. D'Alisa, F. Demaria, & G. Kallis (Eds.), *Degrowth: A vocabulary for a new era* (pp. 109–112). Routledge.

Walcher, D., & Leube, M. (2017). Circular economy by co-creation. Retrieved March 25, 2020, from https://www.researchgate.net/publication/318463015_Circular_Economy_by_Co-Creation

Weber, K., & Soderstrom, S. B. (2012). Social movements, business, and the environment. In P. Bansal, & A. J. Hoffman (Eds.), *The Oxford handbook of business and the natural environment* (pp. 248–265). Oxford University Press.

Wiedenhoft Murphy, W. (2017). *Consumer culture and society*. Sage.

Wolf, M., & McQuitty, S. (2011). Understanding the do-it-yourself consumer: DIY motivations and outcomes. *AMS Review, 1*(3–4), 154–170. https://doi.org/10.1007/s13162-011-0021-2

Yolles, M. (2018). Sustainability development: Part 3 – the cybernetics of co-evolution through amenity. *International Journal of Markets and Business Systems, 3*(3), 276–296.

Zureik, E., & Mowshowitz, A. (2005). Consumer power in the digital society. *Communications of the ACM, 48*(10), 46–51.

Zwick, D., Bonsu, S. K., & Darmody, A. (2008). Putting consumers to work "co-creation" and new marketing govern-mentality. *Journal of Consumer Culture, 8*(2), 163–196. https://doi.org/10.1177/ 1469540508090089

# 21. Brand co-creation management in the light of the social-materiality approach

*Géraldine Michel and Valérie Zeitoun*

## 1. INTRODUCTION

For the past 20 years, co-creation has motivated a large number of studies with a variety of approaches and propositions (Gyrd-Jones & Kornum, 2013; Vallaster & Von Wallpach, 2013; Von Wallpach et al., 2017). From an economic or financial standpoint, value co-creation is defined as "the phenomenon of corporations creating goods, services and experiences in close cooperation with experienced and creative consumers" (Foster, 2007, p. 715). In this context, the consumer is consciously and willingly working for the brand and can be considered a co-producer of economic value (Cova et al., 2011). In this chapter, we consider the brand as a commercial brand with which consumers and other stakeholders can interact through their experiences, consumption or uses. From a cultural perspective, co-creation is mostly understood as the immaterial value generated by consumers' consumption practices. In this case, the appropriation by consumers generates an immaterial value that can modify and enrich the brand meaning (Cova et al., 2011) which is understood to be the result of the interaction between brand communication and consumer perception (Berthon et al., 2009). In this chapter, we consider co-creation as a process not only related to consumers but also to other interested groups like co-workers, opinion leaders, and even non-users (Diamond et al., 2009; Von Wallpach et al., 2017). We focus on the immaterial value that consumers or other stakeholders co-create, as well as the effect it has on the brand's meaning and identity. This immaterial value comes from stakeholders' adoption and appropriation of the brand. While this appropriation has always existed through the consumption and/or the use of the goods, it has recently undergone a major shift with the emergence of Web 2.0, which has largely encouraged user-generated content and, thus, has stimulated brand co-creation (Cova et al., 2011).

If we can consider that people have always co-produced the value of goods by using them and attributing meanings and values to them (Arvidsson, 2008; Prahalad & Ramaswamy, 2000), the brand co-creation process still raises major questions. How does co-creation happen? How does the immaterial value co-created by stakeholders enrich the brand? What is the dark side of brand co-creation? And how does improving brand management ensure a constructive co-creation process? To address these questions, we adopted a comprehensive position. We explore brand co-creation dynamics and we suggest considering a new perspective on brand co-creation management through the social-materiality approach. The chapter is organized in six parts. First, we define brand co-creation as an integration of the stakeholders' brand appropriations (1), we explain how brand co-creation enriches the brand, filling an empty space within the brand identity (2), and we highlight the dark side of brand co-creation as a loss of brand identity (3). Second, based on the social-materiality approach, we propose a new perspective to gain a better understanding of brand management within the co-creation context (4, 5). Finally, we propose a new co-creation framework for a constructive brand co-creation (6).

## 2.    THE BRAND CO-CREATION PROCESS: FROM THE STAKEHOLDERS' APPROPRIATION TO THE TRANSFORMATION OF BRAND MEANING

Co-creation can be conceived as a cultural process implying the production of an immaterial resource that results from stakeholders' appropriation and transfiguration of the brand meaning. In this regard, co-creation has been investigated from two major angles. The first angle focuses on the narratives (stories or images) about a brand that consumers or other stakeholders produce and share. It has led to a large amount of research into online or offline word of mouth (Baker et al., 2016; Hennig-Thurau et al., 2004) and the influence of user-generated brand content (Ashley & Tuten, 2015; Christodoulides et al., 2012). This perspective is based on an information-processing approach where stakeholders make a brand judgment based on a real or projected experience (Payne et al., 2008). The second angle takes a more experiential point of view, ranging from Holbrook (1996), who defines consumer value as an "interactive relativistic preference experience," to a more recent stream of research focusing on stakeholders' performance of brand identity (Von Wallpach et al., 2017).

In these two contexts, research on brand co-creation has taken a comprehensive and holistic look at how not only customers but also various other stakeholders find and create brand meaning and value (Batey, 2008; Cova et al., 2011; McCracken, 1986). According to the more experiential approach, people bring and add meaning to a brand because they make it theirs. In so doing, through experience, stakeholders appropriate the brand, which implies personalization and engenders a transformation (Cova & Dalli, 2009). In this perspective, brands adopt multiple new appropriations (Diamond et al., 2009; Von Wallpach et al., 2017). The brand becomes the product of a dynamic interaction between the stakeholders. It continually evolves and consists of heterogeneous but interplaying components that, taken as a whole, are better understood as a gestalt (Diamond et al., 2009; Wider et al., 2018) or an assemblage (Lury, 2009; Parmentier & Fischer, 2015; Wider et al., 2018). Consequently, the brand incorporates different pieces of meaning, which leads to an amazing plasticity of its identity.

## 3.    WHEN CO-CREATION ENRICHES AN EMPTY SPACE IN BRAND IDENTITY

Stakeholders' brand appropriations have the potential to take part in the construction of a new brand meaning and constitute a distinctive competitive advantage for the brand (Thompson et al., 2006). Indeed, stakeholders' brand appropriations generate immaterial value that can be incorporated into the brand and can constitute a source for enriching the brand identity. This co-creation process is also a way to forge a deep affective bond between stakeholders and the brand (Thompson et al., 2006). However, a brand can only be enriched by stakeholders if they find the brand sufficiently involving (Brown et al., 2003; Fournier, 1998). Stimulating brand enrichment through co-creation requires an inspirational brand to trigger brand appropriation and deliver immaterial value which will be incorporated in the brand identity. Besides, we can consider that brand enrichment through co-creation needs the right equilibrium between stability and flexibility. In this sense, co-creation requires strong brand values. These values are the foundations needed to structure the potential modifications brought by stakeholders' appropriation (Michel, 2017; Payne et al., 2008) and to drive the nonnegotiable brand consistency (Matthiesen & Phau, 2005). Despite the required solid foundation, a certain openness is also needed. Indeed, when the brand offers an empty space the stakeholders are able to invest in, this openness appears as a support for the evolution of meaning (Pitt et al., 2006). Brand co-creation implies that the brand implicitly gives some room for input from the stakeholders, or for any change that might be due to an unexpected demand from the stakeholders.

This is typically the case with the adult Lego consumers who generate renewed brand meaning based on the initial strong brand value of creativity (Von Wallpach et al., 2017). Whether adults can adopt (or re-adopt) the toys has never been a topic for brand managers – no message is given about the supposed age range, and in that sense Lego as a company left an empty space that was naturally filled by its older customers. Nespresso's change towards a more environmentally friendly attitude was mainly guided by the expectations of stakeholders. Nespresso not having ruled on the subject had left space for such a specific request. Ultimately, brand co-creation constitutes a way to enrich brand identity and stretch the brand capacity. However, as explicitly described by Cova and Dalli (2009), stakeholders are not partners, they do not co-produce but perform immaterial work instead. They engender a new brand form independent of the producer's objectives and strategy, irremediably questioning the brand identity status, its essence and more importantly its consistency and coherence through times and spaces.

## 4.   THE DARK SIDE OF CO-CREATION: DAMAGING THE BRAND IDENTITY

As highlighted in the literature, brand co-creation can also involve some risks and it presents two major threats: confusion and dilution. Brands can become the location where disparate or even antinomic components aggregate in a chaotic form, disfiguring the brand and, thus, creating the doppelgänger brand image (Thompson et al., 2006). The brand is then deeply harmed because of disparaging images and stories that circulate through shared popular culture media, thereby making it easy to launch brand attacks (ibid.). In such cases, the potential richness of co-creation becomes chaos, and the brand's internal consistency and coherence can be compromised or even damaged. Dilution, which entails the weakening of important brand value perceptions (Bambauer-Sachse & Mangold, 2011), is the other major risk. Dilution can take two forms: tarnishing or blurring (Pullig et al., 2006). Tarnishing happens when the brand is directly attacked. Blurring is more insidious and is a process that weakens the brand's associations and distinctive characteristics, such as unique benefits or attributes. The multiplicity and diversity of interpretations coming from various sources generate numerous new and disparate associations that make the brand quite fuzzy and generate a loss of idiosyncrasy. For instance, with a variety of products (books, airlines, clothes, trains, mobile phones, etc.), the Virgin brand acts in different markets, with a multiplicity of stakeholders (different kinds of retailers, business-to-business and business-to-customer activities, etc.) without a clear red line, generating a loss of meaning for the employees and clients. The symbolic capital and the significance of the brand end up being irreversibly altered. These two major threats (confusion and dilution) reveal that co-creation can induce a major risk of value loss for the brand. In this perspective (as said before), strong brand values and a solid brand identity foundation are important to limit the risks of the co-creation dilution or confusion. Indeed, the core brand values constitute a useful foundation to ensure stability within the dynamic co-creation context (Michel, 2017). Also, in this context, the manager is no longer a "guardian" but more a "conductor" able at the same time to retain a significant degree of control and to choreograph the stakeholders' inputs (Diamond et al., 2009). Based on this idea, that brand management has a major role to play in modeling brand co-creation, a new paradigm for brand management emerges with one major question arising: How can brand managers regulate and administer the brand while acknowledging stakeholder participation? A question that immediately echoes the call for more research to "guide brand managers in their understanding of brands as complex processes and support them in finding their role as orchestrators in the continuous becoming of brands" (Wider et al., 2018, p. 304). To address this goal, we introduce the social-materiality framework.

## 5.    THE SOCIAL-MATERIALITY FRAMEWORK

Only a few studies have offered empirical insights into how to handle brand co-creation processes. In this regard, Essamri et al. (2019) have proposed a model for managing brand co-creation based on managing the brand relationships with stakeholders. Given the scarcity of research on brand co-creation management, their contribution is a valuable first step. However, in order to better understand the arrangement of the meanings and the condition of a constructive co-creation process, we recommend shifting from an experiential and socio-cultural perspective to a social-material one. First, we will briefly review the cultural co-creation anchorage, then succinctly expose the theoretical framework referring to the theory of practices (Schatzki, 2002), before proposing that brand materiality (expression through tangible action and doings) can be a new perspective to better understand how to orchestrate brand co-creation.

### 5.1    From a Socio-Cultural Co-Creation Anchorage to a Social-Material Perspective

From the very beginning, co-creation has introduced a distinctive customer status: being active and part of a social and cultural fabric (Prahalad & Ramaswamy, 2000). Value is no longer generated by the goods or services that a firm provides but is inextricably based on the user's experience (Prahalad & Ramaswamy, 2004). From there, co-creation has led to a new brand vision. Embedded in service-dominant logic theory, it "views brand in terms of collaborative, value co-creation activities of firms and all of their stakeholders and brand value in terms of the stakeholders' collectively perceived value-in-use" (Merz et al., 2009, p. 328). The definition stipulates that the co-created value is a "value-in-use," which directly implies a focus on how, beyond functionality, the consumer or any other stakeholder assigns cultural, symbolic or affective meaning to a product or a brand. In this context, most of the research has been done within a socio-cultural perspective (Cova & Dalli, 2009), where meaning is mostly attributed and explored through the lens of the consumers' experience and primarily based on the experiential, symbolic, or ideological aspects of consumption. This meaning is imbued and is ascribed to objects by subjects who undermine the object's capacity to play a role in generating meaning (Bettany, 2007). Investigating the status of an object in consumer culture theory, Bettany (2007) shows the need to reconsider the object's status and materiality in order to open the field of exploration and look not only at how "'consumers consume,' but also at how objects 'object', where 'object' is taken as a verb" (Bettany, 2007, p. 54). This view supports the idea that objects can be considered as "actants" capable of situating, influencing, or modifying social practices. In this regard, the theory of practices, and especially Theodore Schatzki's (1990) work, can help to better understand how an object can object, that is to say how an object such as a brand can materially act and change a set of practices.

### 5.2    The Theory of Practices: A Set of Doings and Sayings to Produce Meaning

The classical dualism opposing the symbolic to the factual and the cultural to the material has generated a long tradition of asymmetric sociology (Reckwitz, 2002). One of the first attempts to solve this dichotomy was Bruno Latour's (1990, 1991) proposal of "symmetrical anthropology." According to his notion of social networks and social practices, human beings and non-human actants (things) are considered equal components (Latour, 1991). This redesigns the status of the material object by conferring on it a capacity to act (Reckwitz, 2002). This analytical framework treats human and non-human participants equally as active participants in a social practice (Bettany, 2007). Although this consideration of the object as an actant has been somewhat contested, it has also inspired a great number of researchers (Butler, 1993; Haraway, 1989; Schatzki, 1990, 2003, 2011). Based on the theory of practices, Schatzki has developed what he calls a site ontology (Schatzki, 2002) – a theoretical framework to analyze interactions between human activity and social environment. Following Latour, Schatzki considers only one level of social reality (no distinction between micro and macro levels), and all activities are situated within intertwined practices – a practice being defined as a "temporally evolving, open-ended set of doings and sayings" (Schatzki, 2002, p. 87). In this configuration, subject and object are no longer distinct, and both produce meaning and materiality (Bettany, 2007). Social-materiality recognizes that non-human entities (things or objects) play a role within the practices. Things belong to the sphere of activities that, in Schatzki's model, imply sayings and doings. Activities set up a social arrangement and deliver a consistent meaning to action as much as words do (Schatzki, 2011). On this basis, we can consider and analyze brand materiality as a new paradigm for brand management, especially within the context of co-creation.

## 6.    BRAND MATERIALITY AS A NEW PERSPECTIVE FOR ORCHESTRATING BRAND CO-CREATION

As discussed earlier in this chapter, co-creation is mainly about the spontaneous generation of a renewed meaning that can modify brand identity. Based on Schatzki's approach, significance and meaning are to be understood as the result of an activity, including sayings and doings. In this direction the brand, as a non-human entity able to generate, influence, or modify social practices, needs to enact its narrative in order to build and deliver its significance. The construction of a meaning needs to go through enactment to be delivered and this question of enactment or actualization leads to the question of performativity (Goffman, 1959, 1967; Tumbat & Belk, 2013).

## 6.1   Brand Performativity and the Co-Construction of Brand Identity

Most of the research considers brand performativity from a cultural and/or symbolic perspective, through which brands act to perform individuals' self-identity rather than the brand identity (Von Wallpach et al., 2017). If, in line with Butler (1993), we consider identity as being performed rather than said or discursively expressed, then brands might reaffirm their identities in a structured way through performativity. In other words, by taking actions, brands can reorganize their identities while respecting stakeholder inputs. These performative actions can go from simply enacting their missions to taking social or political stands. In concrete terms, it ranges from 7-Eleven shops that do not need to say that they are open 24 hours a day, seven days a week, as these are their opening hours; to Starbucks announcing the company's plans to hire 10,000 refugees over the next five years in response to US President Trump's Muslim ban. More and more brands are manifesting their identities through their actions: Molson beer renovating local grocery stores in Quebec, LVMH producing and freely distributing hand sanitizer during the COVID-19 outbreak in France, Burger King supporting small restaurants during the lock down, and so on. Brands take actions, and by doing so express and develop their identities.

Within the co-creation paradigm, where goods no longer differentiate themselves (Prahalad & Ramaswamy, 2004), actions constitute a new way for brands to make their identities more tangible. Some earlier research proved the relevance of brands' performativity within the context of building (Lucarelli & Hallin, 2015) or strengthening (Von Wallpach et al., 2017) their identities. For instance, we can mention the American Girl brand, which builds its dynamic and moving identity through multiple sources such as "the culture at large, the founder's brand creation myth, the company's stewards, adult women, and the girls who represent the brand's primary target market" (Diamond et al., 2009, p. 122). Interestingly, the brand has succeeded in developing such a rich identity by showing evidence of its narrative not only thanks to the dolls but also through its conversation cards, musical revue, movies for TV and even a café (Diamond et al., 2009). By enacting their narratives based on their foundational values, while incorporating the different meanings that emanate from stakeholders, brands adapt their significance and perform their enriched or renewed identities in a tangible and consistent way through times and spaces.

## 6.2   Brand Materiality as a Guardian of Identity within the Brand Co-Creation Process

Despite the importance of brand actions and brand commitments in society, the role of brand actions in the construction of brand identity remains poorly explored. In the context of co-creation, we argue that brand actions and brand materiality can constitute a concrete expression of the brand values that protect the brand from dilution due to stakeholder inputs. This proposition can be illustrated through various examples of brand co-creation and the role of brand materiality as a support to ensure continuity with the brand's roots.

Lacoste can be seen as a prototypical example. In the mid-1990s, the brand was known to target posh youngsters, but its famous crocodile logo has been seen more and more in rap music videos, becoming a symbol of hip hop subculture. Young people from suburban areas appropriated the brand, which irremediably deflected the elegance and discretion codes of the brand (especially since they showcased themselves wearing total Lacoste looks from head to toe). For a few years, the brand seemed unable to manage the situation, and seemed paralyzed, fearing that this new image would just drive away its chic clientele. Lacoste, which is traditionally associated with status symbols, could definitely have been strongly eroded by the appropriation and meaning distortion operated by these hip hop communities. However, in the early 2000s, Lacoste took a new turn. The newly arrived artistic director, Christophe Lemaire, capitalized on the urban and trendy youth and launched a very colorful range of polo shirts to expand its target audience; Lacoste created "Lacoste Live," which picks up aesthetic codes from urban culture. The integration of this trend into the brand's actions allowed Lacoste to enrich the brand and reinvent itself while remaining coherent with its identity.

Fred Perry is another notable example. Originally associated with the 1960s' cosmopolitan and anti-traditionalist British Mods subculture, the brand has been appropriated by various and sometimes antinomic communities. Associated with the racist skinhead movement, the brand is also strongly represented in the gay community. The brand has not tried to fight against the skinhead appropriation, but by opening a shop in Paris's gay area the brand has showed the world that as a brand they do not endorse political or homophobic exploitation. Today, no fewer than four or five different communities are associated with the Fred Perry brand. Thus, its actions show a certain ability to integrate and absorb various and numerous cultures, which makes it possible to call Fred Perry a polysemous brand (Michel, 2017). By contrast, some brands have been captured and remain exploited by particular communities, such as Helly Hansen or Lonsdale, whose names are being hijacked by far-right youth. They have been unable to maintain their identities through concrete actions that would allow them to reaffirm their values while distancing themselves from those communities, which are sometimes very remote from their original commercial target. To the extent that brands are not the only ones to produce signs, these examples show the importance of doings and beings to control their meanings as much as they can.

## 7. MANAGING BRAND MATERIALITY TO ENSURE BRAND LEGITIMACY AND ENCOURAGE CONSTRUCTIVE BRAND CO-CREATION

From a social-material perspective, by expressing its identity through doings as much as through sayings, a brand can build legitimacy in the eye of stakeholders. This legitimacy rests on the organization's ability to make its doings understandable and to connect its values with facts (Suchman, 1995). In the context of co-creation, exerting brand identity through concrete actions is a key to remaining a legitimate brand for the stakeholders (Zeitoun, 2016). In this regard, as underlined by Holt (2002), when speeches and acts (or sayings and doings) are manifest and consistent with the perceived or intended identity, the brand becomes a relevant cultural resource for the audience. In other words, the construction of brand legitimacy provides an opportunity to stimulate brand enrichment through co-creation, while ensuring sufficient stability to prevent the side effects of co-creation.

For instance, the Nike brand evinces a certain balance and consistency between, on the one hand, its discourses (saying) regarding sport, innovation and collectivist values and, on the other hand, its actions (doings) through avant-garde products, social initiatives to foster sport in deprived areas and its social actions against racism, like its support of athlete Colin Kaepernick. This consistency and equilibrium between the brand's values and its acts are central to Nike's legitimacy in the eyes of its consumers and this motivates them to participate in the brand's life. At the same time, Nike knows how to listen to its clients and incorporate their ideas into its products. This is what happened in 2006 when the use of the iPod by Nike joggers gave Nike the idea of collaborating with Apple to launch Nike+, an intelligent sensor incorporated in the shoes that communicates with Apple devices (iPhone or iPod) and records the duration of the run, the number of kilometers jogged and all kinds of other information. More recently, Nike launched "Nike by you," a customization tool allowing consumers to design the performance (barefoot feeling, better cushioning, etc.) and style (colors, laces, etc.) of their running shoes. The Nike case illustrates the idea that brand materiality, as a tangible, concrete expression of a brand's values, can build brand legitimacy in the consumers' eyes and serve as a source of inspiration for them to appropriate the brand themselves. In turn, this brand appropriation can become a source of inspiration for managers that can incorporate the newly produced meanings and values. According to our brand co-creation framework (Figure 21.1), we suggest a constructive brand co-creation process with five steps: (1) the brand provides consistent sayings and doings, (2) this participates in the construction of brand legitimacy for consumers and other stakeholders, (3) further it stimulates the brand appropriation by stakeholders, (4) that is incorporated in an empty space of brand identity, (5) these four steps completed, a new constructive co-creation process can occur again. This constructive brand co-creation process is based on the brand materiality allowing both stability and plasticity of the brand identity that is a key to the brand longevity.

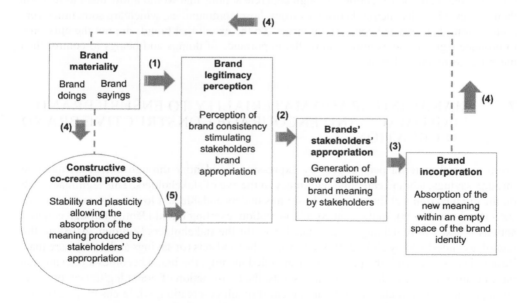

*Figure 21.1    Brand co-creation process based on the brand social-materiality approach*

## 8. CONCLUSION

Our research contributes to the literature of brand co-creation on two major points. First, beyond the definition of co-creation as an immaterial value co-created and a creation of meaning (Cova et al., 2011), this chapter presents the immaterial value co-created by stakeholders as an integration process of the stakeholders' brand appropriations. This analysis contributes to better understand how co-creation enriches the brand by filling an empty space of its identity. Second, beyond the idea that brands act to perform individuals' self-identity (Von Wallpach et al., 2017), this chapter enlarges the vision and considers brand materiality as a new framework to analyze how brands perform their own identities including and absorbing the stakeholders' inputs. The brand materiality conception allows orchestration of stability and flexibility for a constructive brand co-creation, thus enriching the previous research on brand co-creation management (Essamri et al., 2019).

Brand co-creation offers a potential opportunity for a brand to grow and develop over time. To this end, co-creation requires a sufficiently anchored brand identity that has a strong backbone and empty spaces allowing the co-creation process to enrich the brand identity without disfiguring or transfiguring it. To take advantage of co-creation, which is the positive signal of an inspiring and aspirational brand, managers need to find a way to absorb the new meaning and adapt to it while maintaining the permanence that makes their brand reliable and relevant. Looking at the brand through the lens of the social-materiality approach offers new insights when considering the issue of brand management within the context of co-creation. We suggest thinking of a brand's doings, its materiality, as a relevant way to enact brand identity and sustain the solid foundations required to manage a brand in the long term. Directly linked to co-creation and the necessary dynamic identity within stability, the social-materiality perspective presents a chance to reflect on the issue of brand legitimacy, understood as the right connection between the brand's sayings and doings. This new framework offers a different comprehensive approach to the co-creation and opens up new avenues for research that integrates brand materiality as the perspective to stimulating positive co-creation.

## REFERENCES

Arvidsson, A. (2008). The ethical economy of customer coproduction. *Journal of Macromarketing, 28*(4), 326–338.

Ashley, C., & Tuten, T. (2015). Creative strategies in social media marketing: An exploratory study of branded social content and consumer engagement. *Psychology & Marketing, 32*(1), 15–27.

Baker, A. M., Donthu, N., & Kumar, V. (2016). Investigating how word-of-mouth conversations about brands influence purchase and retransmission intentions. *Journal of Marketing Research, 53*(2), 225–239.

Bambauer-Sachse, S., & Mangold, S. (2011). Brand equity dilution through negative online word-of-mouth communication. *Journal of Retailing and Consumer Services, 18*(1), 38–45.

Batey, M. (2008). *Brand Meaning*. New York: Routledge.

Berthon, P., Pitt, L. F., & Campbell, C. (2009). Does brand meaning exist in similarity or singularity? *Journal of Business Research, 62*(3), 356–361.

Bettany, S. (2007). The material semiotics of consumption or where (and what) are the objects in consumer culture theory? In W. Russell & J. F. Sherry, (Eds.), *Research in Consumer Behavior, 11*, Bingley, UK: Emerald Group Publishing Limited, 41–56.

Brown, S., Kozinets, R. V., & Sherry Jr., J. F. (2003). Teaching old brands new tricks: Retro branding and the revival of brand meaning. *Journal of Marketing, 67*(July), 19–33.

Butler, J. (1993). *Bodies That Matter: On the Discursive Limits of "Sex"*. London: Routledge.

Christodoulides, G., Jevons, C., & Bonhomme, J. (2012). Memo to marketers: Quantitative evidence for change: How user-generated content really affects brands. *Journal of Advertising Research, 52*(1), 53–64.

Cova, B., & Dalli, D. (2009). Working consumers: The next step in marketing theory? *Marketing Theory, 9*(3), 315–339.

Cova, B., Dalli, D., & Zwick, D. (2011). Critical perspectives on consumers' role as "producers": Broadening the debate on value co-creation in marketing processes. *Marketing Theory, 11*(3), 231–241.

Diamond, N., Sherry Jr, J. F., Muñiz Jr, A. M., McGrath, M. A., Kozinets, R. V., & Borghini, S. (2009). American Girl and the brand gestalt: Closing the loop on sociocultural branding research. *Journal of Marketing, 73*(3), 118–134.

Essamri, A., McKechnie, S., & Winklhofer, H. (2019). Co-creating corporate brand identity with online brand communities: A managerial perspective. *Journal of Business Research, 96*, 366–375.

Foster, R. J. (2007). The work of the new economy: Consumers, brands, and value creation. *Cultural Anthropology, 22*(4), 707–731.

Fournier, S. (1998). Consumers and their brands: Developing relationship theory in consumer research. *Journal of Consumer Research, 24*, 343–373.

Goffman, E. (1959). *The Presentation of Self in Everyday Life*. New York: Doubleday.

Goffman, E. (1967). *Interaction Ritual: Essays on Face-to-Face Behavior*. Garden City, NY: Anchor Books.

Gyrd-Jones, R. I., & Kornum, N. (2013). Managing the co-created brand: Value and cultural complementarity in online and offline multi-stakeholder ecosystems. *Journal of Business Research, 66*(9), 1484–1493.

Haraway, D. J. (1989). Teddy bear patriarchy: Taxidermy in the Garden of Eden, New York City, 1908–1936. In *Primate Visions: Gender, Race, and Nature in the World of Modern Science* (pp. 26–58). New York: Routledge.

Hennig-Thurau, T., Gwinner, K. P., Walsh, G., & Gremler, D. D. (2004). Electronic word-of-mouth via consumer-opinion platforms: What motivates consumers to articulate themselves on the internet? *Journal of Interactive Marketing, 18*(1), 38–52.

Holbrook, M. B. (1996). Customer value: A framework for analysis and research. In K. P. Corfman & J. G. Lynch Jr. (Eds.), *Advances in Consumer Research*, vol. 23 (pp. 138–142). Provo, UT: Association for Consumer Research.

Holt, D. B. (2002). Why do brands cause trouble? A dialectical theory of consumer culture and branding. *Journal of Consumer Research, 29*(1), 70–90.

Latour, B. (1990). Postmodern? No, simply amodern! Steps towards an anthropology of science. *Studies in History and Philosophy of Science Part A, 21*(1), 145–171.

Latour, B. (1991, ed. 2012). *We Have Never Been Modern*. Cambridge, MA: Harvard University Press.

Lucarelli, A., & Hallin, A. (2015). Brand transformation: A performative approach to brand regeneration. *Journal of Marketing Management, 31*(1–2), 84–106.

Lury, C. (2009). Brand as assemblage: Assembling culture. *Journal of Cultural Economy, 2*(1–2), 67–82.

Matthiesen, I., & Phau, I. (2005). The "HUGO BOSS" connection: Achieving global brand consistency across countries. *Journal of Brand Management, 12*(5), 325–338.

McCracken, G. (1986). Culture and consumption: A theoretical account of the structure and movement of the cultural meaning of consumer goods, *Journal of Consumer Research, 13*(1), 71–84.

Merz, M. A., He, Y., & Vargo, S. L. (2009). The evolving brand logic: A service-dominant logic perspective. *Journal of the Academy of Marketing Science, 37*(3), 328–344.

Michel, G. (2017). From brand identity to polysemous brands: Commentary on "Performing identities: Processes of brand and stakeholder identity co-construction". *Journal of Business Research, 70*, 453–455.

Parmentier, M. A., & Fischer, E. (2015). Things fall apart: The dynamics of brand audience dissipation. *Journal of Consumer Research, 41*(5), 1228–1251.

Payne, A. F., Storbacka, K., & Frow, P. (2008). Managing the co-creation of value. *Journal of the Academy of Marketing Science, 36*(1), 83–96.

Pitt, L. F., Watson, R. T., Berthon, P., Wynn, D., & Zinkhan, G. (2006). The penguin's window: Corporate brands from an open-source perspective. *Journal of the Academy of Marketing Science, 34*(2), 115–127.

Prahalad, C. K., & Ramaswamy, V. (2000). Co-opting customer competence. *Harvard Business Review, 78*(1), 79–90.

Prahalad, C. K., & Ramaswamy, V. (2004). Co-creation experiences: The next practice in value creation. *Journal of Interactive Marketing, 18*(3), 5–14.

Pullig, C., Simmons, C. J., & Netemeyer, R. G. (2006). Brand dilution: When do new brands hurt existing brands? *Journal of Marketing, 70*(2), 52–66.

Reckwitz, A. (2002). The status of the "material" in theories of culture: From "social structure" to "artefacts". *Journal for the Theory of Social Behaviour, 32*(2), 195–217.

Schatzki, T. R. (1990). Do social structures govern action? *Midwest Studies in Philosophy, 15*, 280–295.

Schatzki, T. R. (2002). *The Site of the Social: A Philosophical Account of the Constitution of Social life and Change*. University Park, PA: Penn State Press.

Schatzki, T. R. (2003). A new societist social ontology. *Philosophy of the Social Sciences, 33*(2), 174–202.

Schatzki, T. R. (2011). Where the action is (on large social phenomena such as sociotechnical regimes). Sustainable Practices Research Group, Working Paper, 1, 1–31.

Suchman, M. C. (1995). Managing legitimacy: Strategic and institutional approaches. *Academy of Management Review, 20*(3), 571–610.

Thompson, C. J., Rindfleisch, A., & Arsel, Z. (2006). Emotional branding and the strategic value of the doppelgänger brand image. *Journal of Marketing, 70*(1), 50–64.

Tumbat, G., & Belk, R. W. (2013). Co-construction and performancescapes. *Journal of Consumer Behaviour, 12*(1), 49–59.

Vallaster, C., & Von Wallpach, S. (2013). An online discursive inquiry into the social dynamics of multi-stakeholder brand meaning co-creation. *Journal of Business Research, 66*(9), 1505–1515.

Von Wallpach, S., Hemetsberger, A., & Espersen, P. (2017). Performing identities: Processes of brand and stakeholder identity co-construction. *Journal of Business Research, 70*, 443–452.

Wider, S., Von Wallpach, S., & Mühlbacher, H. (2018). Brand management: Unveiling the delusion of control. *European Management Journal, 36*(3), 301–305.

Zeitoun, V. (2016), Nouvelle perspective sur la relation marque-consommateur: La mécanique relationnelle analysée à travers le prisme du théâtre, PhD dissertation, IAE Paris, Université Paris 1 Panthéon-Sorbonne.

# 22. Violent brands: from neoliberal vessels to far-right fantasies

*Sofia Ulver*

In her 2018 novel *The Perfect Life* Silvia Avallone writes "He had read a few pages by Marx and knew that human labour is contained in things, and that the time, the wrongs, and the suffering penetrate the veins of materia, even their atoms." The quote elucidates the young man Zeno's anxiety over how things and brands he surrounds himself with will be de-coded by his new girlfriend Dora. But, more importantly for this chapter, the quote also works as an apt illustration of how scholars in critical marketing studies have imagined brands over the last decades; that is, as fetishes or assemblages of (exploitative) social and cultural relations, and as entities in themselves assembling culture together with other institutional actors (e.g. Lury 2004, 2009). Following this logic, the brand can be said to be both co-crea*ted* and co-crea*ting*. Whereas brand managerial scholars would see this notion of co-creation in an adulatory sense as an opportunity to increase economic value (e.g. Ind et al. 2017), critical scholars would rather see this in a pejorative sense (e.g. Zwick et al. 2008) as the capitalist exploitation of consumers' free labour (Arvidsson 2005), or as a trojan horse of neoliberal ideology and its accompanying power relations (e.g. Klein 2000), just as did Zeno.

By brand *co-creation* I here refer to various kinds of meaning-making consumer activities that contribute to economic as well as social and cultural valorization of a specific brand. This chapter explores the established anti-capitalist idea of brand co-creation as a vessel for systemically violent relations (e.g. Ulver 2017), in the light of a radically changing political landscape in the Western world, namely the burgeoning populist far right. What happens with anti-capitalist brand co-creation critique typically targeting the neoliberal fantasy of free markets and responsible consumers (Carrington et al. 2016; Cronin & Fitchett 2020; Veresiu & Giesler 2018) through the systemic relations assembled into brands, when more brands come to embody far-right fantasies about authoritarian, systemic relations (Miller-Idriss 2017)? How are we to understand critique of neoliberal brand co-creation as a depoliticizing distraction (Dean 2014), if the very premise of critique evaporates?

This chapter will continue with a brief literature review of the critical literature on brand (co-creation) (Arvidsson 2005, 2008; Bradshaw et al. 2006; Cova et al. 2011; Entwistle & Slater 2014; Klein 2000; Lury 2004, 2009; Slater 2014; Zwick et al. 2008), ending in a synthesis of the core underpinnings of this critique. It will then move over to discussing how the premises of these underpinnings are, and are not, changing in choir with the rise of far-right politics and consumer culture in Europe, America and Asia (Daniels 2018; Gilroy 2019; Masood & Nisar 2020). Due to these large potential shifts I will, in line with others (Miller-Idriss 2017), argue that the systemic relations governed by authoritarian far-right movements will increasingly be assembled into brands and co-created in mainstream consumer culture. I will also illustrate how contemporary far-right imagination is visualized by contemporary brands as well as co-created in consumer culture, and discuss if and how this nascent movement may challenge the established critical perspective on brands as vessels of neoliberal relations, and force it to expand across other political ideologies.

# 1.   CORE UNDERPINNINGS OF ANTI-CAPITALIST BRAND CO-CREATION CRITIQUE

Somewhat simplified, in critical marketing and sociology, critique of brand co-creation rests upon two interrelated focal points; one that stresses the capitalist exploitation of consumers' free labour, and one that attends to how neoliberal ideology is abstracted through the brand but concretized when *in use*.

## 1.1   Brand Co-Creation as Exploitation of Free Labour

Drawing on "autonomist Marxism," valorization of brands through co-creation has been explained by Arvidsson (2005) as an *ethical surplus* emerging out of consumers' immaterial labour. In the sense that the brand value is sustained by consumers (for "free" for the companies), it can also be seen as an unethical exploitation of these consumers. In the unstable and reflexive co-productive era, consumers' identity production is subsumed as a source of surplus value by the controlling and exploitative aspects of brands. Leaning on the same neo-Marxist theories on value, Zwick et al. (2008) echo Arvidsson in terms of seeing co-creation as a new marketing technique and as an exploitation of creative and valuable forms of consumer labour. Moreover, they add Foucault's theoretical concept of *governmentality* and suggest that this is a move away from the market disciplining consumers directly and instead managing them indirectly with and through their (coerced) "freedom." This, they say, is often expressed by the popular business neologism *prosumer* which holds that the consumer nowadays is unmanageable but fortunately a source of great creativity to leverage on. From this perspective control and exploitation didn't end with the Fordist era, but has in "the complex machinations of global information capitalism" just transformed into a new sort of consumer government, operating in everyday life and everyday spaces, that *requires* a "free consumer subject" (ibid. p. 168).

Also, the influential idea labelled by Vargo and Lusch (2004) as the *service-dominant logic* (SDL), assumes that marketing now always should see its role as a mere moderator and partner of consumers' creativity, and most importantly that the value of products and brands, not just services, are only realized when consumers integrate them into their own creation process of value, hence, co-creation of value. This, Zwick et al. (2008) argue, has altered the imagination of the fundamental marketer–consumer relationship. The firm is now not only relying on its own operations but on consumers' (free) labour power to co-innovate shared meanings, community and trust, but also the actual use-value of products and services. This is "one of the most advanced strategies for capitalist accumulation and consumer control" (ibid. p. 177) where consumers' labour is expropriated as surplus value and their voluntary activities are channelled into raw material for companies' commodity production. Here the post-Marxian equation is as follows: Income − Labour into production = "Dead labour" from commodity < Value produced from their brand work. Hence, the capitalist profit may now be even higher than before when consumers were not seen as co-producers. On this, Hietanen, Andéhn and Bradshaw (2018) take a post-Marxist (and Baudrillardian) perspective, and criticize the value co-creation propositions in SDL precisely for failing to include the critical politico-economical aspects of capitalism. Because, as part of the commodity exchange, through the mystification of both use-value and social relations, consumption is "the moment in which we lose sights of the means of production and move inside an ideology of capitalist reproduction" (ibid. p. 107). This happens through the process of *fetishization,* a concept based on Marx's *commodity fetishism*, where the use-value is abstracted (mystified) into exchange-value. As a fetish, the brand is able to distract the human from seeing the exploitative relations embedded in the means of production required for that commodity to exist in the first place.

In relation to this, Cova et al. (2011) take a semantically somewhat less critical stance. Although they agree with the general point that 21st-century information capitalism has forged the production of use- and exchange-value to increasingly depend on the participation of formerly passivated consumers, they question the use of the labour and (therefore also) the exploitation concepts in all cases, and suggest to *sometimes* replace "work" for labour depending on the experience of the consumer. This is quite different from previous articles where the criterion is that, despite a joyful experience, it should be called exploitation as the company nevertheless profits more because of premium price-setting and the unpaid production made by the consumer. Hence, although agreeing in principle, the difference lies in whether one should consider consumer experience as a criterion or not; hence a consumer-centric versus consumer de-centric approach.

All in all, from a Marxian perspective, the exploitation of consumers could be seen as a sort of technological progress in extracting more relative surplus value when it no longer can be extracted from anywhere else, as for example natural resources of wage workers. Capitalism can sustain itself only by extracting more and more relative surplus value, not least by reducing socially necessary labour time, where the exploitation of wage workers must not exceed the means for workers to reproduce themselves. Or, as Marx (1980, p.275) put it;

> The owner of labour power is mortal. If then his appearance in the market is to be continuous; and the continuous transformation of money into capital assumes this, the seller of labour power must perpetuate himself "in the way that every living individual perpetuates himself, by procreation". The labour-power withdrawn from the market by wear and tear, and by death, must continually be replaced by, at the very least, an equal amount of fresh labour-power.

Extracting surplus value from consumers' work is of course an intelligible capitalist strategy—a strategy which Arvidsson (2020) argues transforms, as principle, throughout history. Accordingly, in contemporary digital capitalism, it is concentrated more and more around the production of consumer-generated (big) data at digital platforms.

### 1.2    Brand Co-Creation as Concretizing Neoliberal Ideology

The other critical perspective on brand co-creation frames the critique more metaphorically. Here the brand is seen as a vessel of neoliberal ideology, hence an ideal-typical de-regulated version of capitalism (Dean 2014; Harvey 2005), which abstracts ethically problematic social relations, and unfolds through consumer co-creation and integration of the brand into the consumer's value creation process. That is, neoliberal capitalism reproduces itself.

Celia Lury, a sociologist, explicates this ideological reproduction particularly well. She writes about the brand as a "set of relations between products or services" (2004, p.1), and as a "platform for the patterning of activity, a mode of organizing activities in time and space." Like a car consists of parts, the brand, too, emerges in parts but *implicates*, as she expresses it, social relations. Each part on its own does not make a car, or a brand, but the proper unification of the parts does. This requires particular ways of relating them, and these relations are set by the specific economic system at hand. For example, in car factory X, preset financial ratios will determine how fast each unification of car parts must be made at the assembly line, in what order this should be made, in co-operation with whom or which robot, and as a result, how much time (if any) the worker has at her or his disposal to take a needed break (but also how much (or little) money there will be on his or her pay check at the end of the month). In addition, each unification requires the presence of parts that perhaps must be shipped from other parts of the world, in order for the cost to remain as low as possible for the brand owner in the end. Hence, other cost-minimizing ratios must be enforced upon workers on the ships, in the harbours, at the warehouses and in the terminals of ground transport. This chain of social relational events continues backwards through workers at factories supplying factory X's assembly line with parts, and moves through the car brand's outsourced or in-house innovation, product, research and development department employees, the brand managers, their managing chief directors, their executive board, and the capital owners whose investments must give sufficient dividends to continue investing in the car company for *growth*; any company's main objective in neoliberal economy. Hence, in the factory production of goods the capital owners organize the social relationships between workers and the technical relationship between machines, and as another layer on top of this, through the brand production they calibrate also the social relations between all products and services governed by that brand. All the social relations accounted for above, and of course plenty more (just think of all distributers, service workers, marketing people, consumers, waste-workers, etc.), are unified and mobilized according to the capital owners' demand for monetary growth, and embodied by the specific car brand.

To theoretically understand this embodiment, we can look at brands as *assemblages* and branding as a process of *assembling culture* (Lury 2009). This branding is not only involving multiple forms of technologies, proceeding in various institutional contexts and making use of strategic relations, but also as assembling culture itself. From that perspective, the brand is not only the visual brand itself, but all social relations involved in forming the (brand) assemblage itself (Slater 2014). For example, Onyas and Ryan (2015) were able to show how coffee brand owners enacted the brand vision by assembling upstream and downstream actors into actualizing the brand's social mission, and thereby unbundled the brand as a market-shaping device, and its own machine. The journalist Naomi Klein (2000) famously detailed such a Trojan horse-like relationship in her world-wide best seller *No Logo*, and argued that the neoliberal system demands exploitation of workers and environmental resources preferably in other parts of the world than where the brand is consumed, so that the mystifying brand veneer is not scratched.

Unlike in pre-industrial times where the production of goods could be self-sufficiently governed by one and the same family over generations, industrialization's factory organization squeezed time and space together and each wage worker became more of a machine than a creator, as she would typically repeat one isolated activity with only one of the product's parts. Therefore, the complexities of social relations are inherent in the product. And the brand, as an extra layer of mystification through communication and logotypes, hides these relations that, according to the critics, are systemically exploitative of wage workers and reproduces a stratified class system.

Thus, from the "vessel" perspective, when consumers take part in co-creating brand value through various activities—for example by creating communities, engaging in open innovation, and producing online data in social media—they not only become part of the globalized social relations complex themselves but they also become part of actively reproducing this system.

## 2.   AUTHORITARIAN RELATIONS ASSEMBLED INTO BRANDS

Over the last two decades social scientists, journalists, authors, and indeed citizens themselves, have witnessed a growing divide in the public's oppositional ideological stances, often referred to as political polarization (Pew Research Center 2014, 2016). Although all extremes gain from polarization (McCarty 2019; Prior 2013), it is especially the populist right that has been able to convert this into actual political power, not only in Pan America, Europe, Russia and China (Berman 2019; Krastev & Holmes 2019), but also in other parts of Asia (Masood & Nasir 2020). In general, social scientists see this growth in popularity for the populist right as a threat to democracy, as it risks normalizing the rise of the more extreme and radical far-right ideology which in turn supports an authoritarian and anti-democratic political system (Mounk 2018). But what does this have to do with brands and the co-creation of brands?

### 2.1   Brands' Valorization of Violence

If far-right ideologies, inherently protectionist, nationalistic and against the globalization processes of neoliberalism, are gaining ground (Krastev & Holmes 2019), we may want to begin reflecting upon what social (and/or cultural) relations the brand would be a vessel of, and what social relations consumers then would be a part in reproducing. To approach this re-thinking we can start by looking into a consumer culture where brands already act as vessels of far-right ideologies. Although they often sell their goods internationally in their web shops, they are typically commercial extensions of neo-fascist movements in specific countries, for example the Italian neo-fascist movement *CasaPound*, the American neo-fascist movement *Proud Boys* (whose webshop was closed down 9th of October 2020 by their web host after President Trump had not condemned them in the pre-election debate) or *Det Fria Sverige* and *Nordisk Ungdom* in Sweden. All these sell various kinds of merchandise and clothing representing their movement. But there are also specialized fashion brands that are not officially associated with a specific political party, albeit discursively and visually rooted in far-right ideology, such as *Svastone* and *MilitantZone* in Ukraine, *White Rex* in Russia, and *Ansgar Aryan* and *Thor Steinar* in Germany. The clothing (or merchandise) sold by these brands is symbolically loaded with political codes and messages. In her academic book, *The Extreme Gone Mainstream – Commercialization and Far Right Youth Culture in Germany*, the sociologist Cynthia Miller-Idriss (2017) studies the codes and iconographic strategies of such brands from inside contemporary far-right consumer culture. Looking at how these groups historically have tried (and partly succeeded) to transform from extreme to mainstream by way of consumer culture, she describes how far-right extremists have left the hard-edged skinhead style behind and, instead, started to produce and consume sophisticated, commercial and fashionable brands that deploy coded symbols. For example, when worn under half-zipped bomber jackets the brand names of *Consdaple* and *Lonsdale* visually appear as the abbreviations (in *Consdaple*'s case fully but in *Lonsdale*'s case the first four letters) of the Nazi party NSDAP. The consumer culture of these coded symbols, entangled in its own market system, work as an important gateway for young people into the extremist scenes where the normalization of the aesthetic styles and their accompanying brands work to simplify recruitment and radicalization of new political members and activists. Milller-Idriss reports from within the youth culture of the far right drawing on interviews with these brand consumers, who describe in detail how emotionally fascinated they are by these brands and how strongly they identify both with the brands themselves and with the ideology they imply. In relation to strong affects of fascination, Miller-Idriss manages to show how the far-right brands' iconography often directly evoke death and violence. Such symbols of death are deployed in three main ways; through abstract death (e.g. the skull-and-crossbones symbol or *Totenkopf,* the "death's head"), specific deaths (e.g. straightforward death images of lynching), and death threats (e.g. sweatshirt with the print "Born yellow, born red, born black, born dead"). Miller-Idriss (ibid. p.21) argues that "symbols of death are thus a performative strategy to demonstrate fearlessness and suggest violence as a means to achieve nationalist or extremist goals". In terms of co-creation, the consumers of these brands are inviting others (and themsleves) to co-create the far-right brand's valorization of violence. From that perspective, these are not only "violent" brands by way of inherently exploitative social relations (Ulver 2017), but *literally* violent in their very existence.

Although information about the ownership of overtly far-right brands is very difficult (if not close to impossible) to find, some brands (like *Thor Steinar* and *Lonsdale*) are owned by large, multinational, seemingly "unpolitical" brand groups, which in terms of ownership makes them no different from most other brands in the global economy. Some high-profile brands (e.g. *Yakuzu* or *Erik and Sons*) do not communicate anywhere who are their owners, whereas others are openly owned by political far-right groups (e.g. *Det Fria Sverige* (*DFS*) or *Nordisk Ungdom*). In any case, as uncovered by Miller-Idriss, far-right supporters stay very loyal to these brands in which they actively invest their social, cultural and political identities. But these brands must be used in social contexts to work as political markers and community. If Miller-Idriss is right about the brands' power to lure consumers into a far-right political engagement, then the co-productive aspect is especially practised through community-making around the brands and the very active social display of the brand as a "linking value" (Cova 1997). By forming such tight communities around the brands, and using them as literal codes to (often secretly) make communication possible with each other in public spaces, they are indeed co-creating value for these brands for free.

In that way, in terms of extracting free labour from their consumers, these far-right brands are not different from any other co-created brands; in fact they may be better at it than the lion's share of brands out there. But if we look at the brand co-creation critique I have accounted for previously—the assumption that brands implicate the social relations of the ruling global economic system (Lury 2004), and that this system in turn thrives on the ideas of neoliberalism—then the issue becomes more complicated.

## 2.2    Brands as Vessels of *any* Ideology

Structurally, neoliberalism is generally said to prosper on *de*-regulated global flows of finance, goods and services (Dean 2014). Hence, in an ideal-typical neoliberal global economic system the social relations implicated by the brand would be calibrated by capital owners among multinational corporations, individual and intermediary investors (such as banks) and other financial intermediaries, who all accumulate capital based on the economic surplus value expropriated through consumers' free labour. But far-right ideology does not support that kind of system. Looking at the historical legacy of the contemporary far right, in its authoritarian vision of civilization, fascism did not include free capitalism but a nationalist, state-controlled economy (Blamires & Jackson 2006). Hence, far-right ideology may support a sort of state capitalism (for example, the Nazi party's tight control of and collaboration with brands like *Volkswagen* and *Hugo Boss* before and during the Second World War, using the prisoners in the concentration camps as slaves for free labour), not free trade and globalization which neoliberal capitalism builds upon, but a nationalist, protectionist and strictly authoritarian economy. A potential far-right systemic web of social relations implicated in the brand would then be quite different from the web imagined by contemporary brand critics.

Although many contemporary intellectuals bring forth the crisis of capitalism, for example that it is in "critical condition" (Streeck 2014, p. 61) and the "crisis of digital capitalism looks very much like the crisis of European feudalism in the 14th century" (Arvidsson 2020, p.18), very few believe there is a threat to the capitalist hegemony, as it is known to absorb all political movements into marketizable commodities. For example, Krastev and Holmes' (2019) narrative of the East's revenge for having been taken for granted to obediently mimic the West in post-Cold War politics, at the same time tells the story that it is now precisely the West's strategies in the market economy that are imitated by the East to promote nationalist, populist (and in some places far) right ideologies on a global scale. However, if such an imitation of free capitalism would be kept by the populist (and in some places far) right once in power, or if a more traditional far-right ideology of state capitalism would be enforced, is of course difficult to know. In any case, brand co-creation critics focusing specifically on Marx's premises on value would perhaps have to re-think in terms of who ultimately would accumulate the capital emerging from (potential) surplus value; the state, the political class, the capitalists, or someone/something else? Also, the brand assemblage critics may have to re-focus if the co-production of brands comes to be integrated with another politico-economic system. Finally, the critique of neoliberal co-optation (by brands) as *de*-politicizing would lose relevance. Branding and co-creation of brands would be techniques to finance the capital streams towards the local, authoritarian state (when in government) and not globally, and is hence strongly politicizing. While some consumer culture researchers have argued that politicized marketing and consumption is nothing but a de-politicization in its distraction from real politics (Brunk et al. 2017; Veresiu & Giesler 2018), others have argued that consumer resistance can, indeed, be partly successful in its politizication of consumption (e.g. Thompson & Kumar 2016). However, we may suspect that the ongoing political polarization encourages brands to be more openly ideological, not least because citizens from all political camps are now using the techniques of consumer resistance to gain political capital (Ulver & Laurell 2020). Accordingly, they would encode ideological movements into branded merchandise and openly sponsor or be owned by specific political parties, but not distract consumers from voting. Quite the opposite. Consumers' politically polarized activism, voting, and civilian engagement would give fodder to the extremes, which would spill over to the mainstream, and ultimately into the pockets of brand owners. Then, if (co)owners increasingly would be far-right political organizations, the capital would not only flow into a complex which promotes neoliberal globally free trade but also into an authoritarian, protectionist and nationalist system. And indeed, any system may hide behind the brand veneer. For instance, consumer researcher Elif Izberk-Bilgin (2012) unveiled how Turkish Islamist consumers engage in a "consumer jihad" against western "infidel" brands by only buying brands that according to them support a market "based on Islamic principles" (p.680). Even centrally planned socialist economies such as the Eastern bloc states during the Cold War period (1949–1990) used branding to differentiate between products, among which many are now of course absorbed by the neoliberal economy as part of the "Ostalgie" marketplace (Brunk et al. 2017). At the time, those brands were state-owned and subsequently supported a socialist, political system. But if such brands often are called generic, not in terms of brand name but in terms of lack of competition, there are contemporary examples of non-generic, global brands that support communist economies. For example, through the controversies around Chinese state-owned global brands like *Huawei* and *TikTok*, we have come to learn that far-left state capitalism has succeeded with this endeavour for a long time.

## 3.    REFLECTIONS ON FUTURE RESEARCH

From the reflections I have made in this short chapter, the reader can hopefully see the need for future research that engages with the co-creation of political brand narratives and the indirect co-production of political systems, in a more empirical and detailed fashion. First, we need to know more about the ownership of brands, and in what ways, and how, their capital flows move. In terms of extremist brands, capital flows to the political sphere is of extra importance. But also, from a more "mainstream" critical marketing perspective, the larger ownership of brands with liberal political narratives ought to be paid more attention, especially if the purpose is for researchers to begin to "imagine opportunities for resistance and emancipatory change" (e.g. Lambert 2019, p.329). Overall, ownership structures are seldom the focus of attention in research on brands, even though the ownership structure often clashes with what is communicated to consumers about the brand, and therefore may reveal serious hypocrisy. For example, the "Swedish" oat drink brand *Oatly*'s communicated system criticism clashes with their ownership structure where both the heavily criticized, global private equity company *Blackstone* and Chinese state-owned *China Resources* are large owners. Subsequently, brands' ownership could potentially become the next territory for organized consumer resistance groups, whose co-creation of brand narratives may influence not only mainstream consumers, but also journalists and politicians.

Second, we need to know more about the culture of extremist fantasies and their relationship to the market. As found by Miller-Idriss (2017), if brands are strategically used to lure youth into political extremes where violence is encouraged, then the detrimental effect of cultural branding strategies has reached new levels for society. But in order for public policy makers to know how to handle this we need to ask questions like: What is it about the co-creation of these brand narratives that strikes a chord with consumers? What makes the co-created narratives so appealing and how are they spread? What about these consumer cultures is so alluring that violence seems to become an acceptable, even preferred, form of societal participation? Here, the case of political extremist brands provides fodder both for research on public policy and for research on brand co-creation, as the particularities of consumer engagement in these extreme cases may stand out more than consumer engagement in mainstream cases would.

Third, we need to explore how brand co-creation not only can reproduce one version of the economic system, but also others. We need to know more about how other economic and political ideologies leverage from consumer brands to finance their systems. As argued in this chapter, brands can work as fetishes of many kinds of political systems, whether Islamist, socialist, fascist or neoliberal. So far consumers have known relatively little about the actual structures behind brands and what kind of system they are co-producing by supporting them. This is something critical researchers ought to engage with.

Finally, the topic of this chapter paradoxically implies that critical researchers' focus on brands can in itself be considered to be a sort of fetishization. The focus on brands among critical researchers' in marketing studies, organization studies or sociology, is framed as a critique of brands and branding when it actually is meant to be much more radical and political than that. The brand is only one layer of manipulation and veneer seen from the perspective of the entire political system it is part of. Emphasizing the brand as its own conceptual stream of research consecrates it into Brand with capital B instead of only as one small part of a larger criticism of System (with capital S). It may indeed work as a legitimizer among, for example, marketing scholars, to do system-critical research and still be able to publish in marketing journals. Yet, the extraction and highlighting of Brand does little to de-fetishize its lure on consumers, or on researchers for that matter.

As for Zeno, he can safely continue to read his Marx. But, he should probably not be too sure about whose pockets get thick from his "value-creative" brand consumption.

## REFERENCES

Arvidsson, A. (2005) Brands: A critical perspective. *Journal of Consumer Culture*, 5(2), 235–258.
Arvidsson, A. (2008) The ethical economy of customer coproduction. *Journal of Macromarketing*, 28(4), 326–338.
Arvidsson, A. (2020) Capitalism and the commons. *Theory, Culture & Society*, 37(2), 3–30.
Berman, S. (2019) *Democracy and Dictatorship in Europe – From the Ancien Régime to the Present Day*. Oxford, UK: Oxford University Press.
Blamires, C. P., & P. Jackson (2006) *World Fascism – A Historical Encyclopedia*. Santa Barbara: ABC-CLIO.
Bradshaw, A., McDonagh, P., & D. Marshall (2006) No space – New blood and the production of brand culture colonies. *Journal of Marketing Management*, 22, 579–599.
Brunk, K. H., Giesler, M., & B. J. Hartmann (2017) Creating a consumable past: How memory making shapes marketization. *Journal of Consumer Research*, 44(3), 1325–1342.
Carrington, M. J., Neville, B., & D. Zwick (2016) The ideology of the ethical consumption gap. *Marketing Theory*, 16(1), 21–38.
Cova, B. (1997) Community and consumption: Towards a definition of the "linking value" of product or services. *European Journal of Marketing*, 31(3/4), 297–316.
Cova, B., Dalli, D., & D. Zwick (2011) Critical perspectives on consumers' role as "producers": Broadening the debate on value co-creation in marketing processes. *Marketing Theory*, 11(3), 231–241.
Cronin, J., & J. Fitchett (2020) Lunch of the last human: Nutritionally complete food and the fantasies of market-based progress. *Marketing Theory*, April, 1–21.
Daniels, J. (2018) The algorithmic rise of the "alt-right". *Contexts*, 1, 60–65.
Dean, M. (2014) Rethinking neoliberalism. *Journal of Sociology*, 50(2), 150–163.
Entwistle, J., & D. Slater (2014) Reassembling the cultural. *Journal of Cultural Economy*, 7(2), 161–177.
Gilroy, P. (2019) Agonistic belonging: The banality of good, the "alt right" and the need for sympathy. *Open Cultural Studies*, 3, 1–14.
Harvey, D. (2005) *A Brief History of Neoliberalism*. Oxford: Oxford University Press.

Hietanen, J., Andéhn, M., & A. Bradshaw (2018) Against the implicit politics of service-dominant logic. *Marketing Theory*, 18(1), 101–119.

Ind, N., Iglesias, O., & S. Markovic (2017) The co-creation continuum: From tactical market research tool to strategic collaborative innovation method. *Journal of Brand Management*, 24(4), 310–321.

Izberk-Bilgin, Elif (2012) Infidel brands: Unveiling alternative meanings of global brands at the nexus of globalization, consumer culture, and Islamism. *Journal of Consumer Research*, 39, 663-687.

Klein, N. (2000), *No Logo*. London: Fire and Water

Krastev, I., & S. Holmes (2019) *The Light that Failed: A Reckoning*. UK: Allan Lane

Lambert, A. (2019). Psychotic, acritical and precarious? A Lacanian exploration of the neoliberal consumer subject. *Marketing Theory*, 19(3), 329–346.

Lury, C. (2004) *Brands: The Logos of the Global Economy*. New York: Routledge.

Lury, C. (2009) Brand as assemblages: Assembling culture. *Journal of Cultural Economy*, 2, 67–82.

Marx, K. (1980) *Capital*, Vol. 1, translated by Ben Fowkes. New York: Penguin Classics.

Masood, A., & M. A. Nisar (2020) Speaking out: A postcolonial critique of the academic discourse on far-right populism. *Organization*, 27(1), 162–173.

McCarty, N. (2019) *Polarization – What Everyone Needs to Know*. New York, NY: Oxford University Press.

Miller-Idriss, C. (2017) *Extreme Gone Mainstream – Commercialization and Far Right Youth Culture in Germany*. Princeton, NJ: Princeton University Press.

Mounk, Y. (2018) *The People vs. Democracy – Why Our Freedom is in Danger and How to Save It*. Boston, MA: Harvard University Press.

Onyas, W. I., & A. Ryan (2015) Exploring the brand's world-as-assemblage: The brand as a market shaping device. *Journal of Marketing Management*, 31(1–2), 141–166.

Pew Research Center (2014) Political Polarization in the American Public.

Pew Research Center (2016) *The Modern News Consumer*, Amy Mitchell, Jeffrey Gottfried, Michael Barthel, and Elisa Shearer (authors), *Pew Research Center*, 7.

Prior, M. (2013) Media and political polarization. *Annual Review of Political Science*, 16, 101–127.

Slater, D. (2014) Ambiguous goods and nebulous things. *Journal of Consumer Behaviour*, 13, 99–107.

Streeck, W. (2014) How will capitalism end? *The New Left Review*, 87, 35–64.

Thompson, C. J., & A. Kumar (2016) Political consumerism as neoliberal therapy: How an actually existing neoliberalism produces entrepreneurial passion. In P. Moreau & S. Puntoni (Eds), *NA Advances in Consumer Research*, Volume 44. Duluth: Association for Consumer Research,.

Ulver, S. (2017) Brand as violence. In V. Tarnovskaya & J. Bertilsson (Eds), *Brand Theories*. Lund: Studentlitteratur.

Ulver, S., & C. Laurell (2020) Political ideology in consumer resistance – Analyzing far right opposition to multicultural marketing. *Journal of Public Policy and Marketing*, 39(4), 477–493.

Vargo, S. L., & R. F. Lusch (2004) Evolving to a new dominant logic for marketing. *Journal of Marketing*, 68(January), 1–17.

Veresiu, E., & M. Giesler (2018) Beyond acculturation: Multiculturalism and the institutional shaping of an ethnic consumer subject. *Journal of Consumer Research*, 45(3), 553–570.

Zwick, D., Bonsu, S. K., & A. Darmody (2008). Putting consumers to work: Co-creation and new marketing governmentality. *Journal of Consumer Culture*, 8(2), 163–196.

# PART VI

# CASE STUDIES ON BRAND CO-CREATION

# 23. Alternative methods to study affective information processing in brand co-creation
## *Monika Koller and Peter Walla*

## 1. INTRODUCTION

The process of brand co-creation involves emotions (Mingione et al., 2020). This applies to positive emotions in terms of attitude towards the brand (Kaufmann et al., 2016), as well as to negative emotions due to a failure in co-creation (Sugathan et al., 2017). Moreover, there has been considerable research on consumers' emotional connectedness with brands (Ramaswamy & Ozcan, 2016). Especially when consumers are involved in brand co-creation, it is likely that a shared sense of emotional ownership of the brand will be established (Hsieh & Chang, 2016). Hence, when studying brand co-creation from a consumer perspective, it is important to have a closer look at the emotional processes involved. However, studying emotions has proven to be a challenge per se, which is largely due to the still existing lack of a clear definition (Walla, 2018; vom Brocke et al., 2020). Many scholars use the terms feeling and emotion interchangeably, which causes great confusion and hinders further progress in our understanding of anything around emotion. To support a more detailed understanding regarding those two different terms we first want to suggest a distinct solution to this problem. The grounds for both emotions and feelings are best understood as being based on Affective Neuroscience, a field founded by Jaak Panksepp (1998). On the basis of Panksepp's understanding, Walla (2018) proposed a distinct model separating and defining the terms emotion and feeling while grounding both in basic neural activation labeled as affective processing. Human behavior is guided by both cognitive and affective processing. While cognitive processing deals with semantic content, affective processing is about valence, which means approach- and withdraw-related content. In other words, there is neural activation that codes for the grade of pleasantness or unpleasantness of any stimulus and provides output to decision making centers that control and guide behavior. While affective processing is the very basis, feelings arise when bodily responses occur that are mostly chemical releases of some sort. Finally, emotions are there to communicate those feelings. Thus, according to this model, emotions are what one can observe in another person. Fear, for instance, is a feeling and the emotion linked to it is a respective facial expression plus other behaviors that reflect the feeling of fear. In summary, affective processing guides behavior and emotions communicate feelings (Walla, 2018).

Strikingly, most often, authors who write about emotion usually have a much more complex understanding of it than emotion simply being understood as observable behavior. In fact, it turns out that what other authors mean by emotion, even though they usually don't elaborate on some definitions in the first place, often comes close to the abovementioned affective processing concept. This is important, because the current chapter aims at proposing a method that is known for its particular sensitivity to affective processing. For the purpose of this chapter though, we use the term affective processing straight away, referring to it as neural activation coding for valence.

Besides suggesting a clear understanding and definition of emotion and feeling, this chapter focuses on the emergence of consumer neuroscience about two decades ago. Consumer neuroscience is an interdisciplinary endeavor to investigate the biological roots of consumer behavior. Doing so, it also predominantly contributes to the difficulties involved in the measurement of "emotions".

In this chapter we outline how selected psychophysiological methods can help to study affective processing in brand co-creation. First, as a basis for further methodological suggestions, we elaborate on "emotions" and affective processing from an evolutionary perspective including further elaboration on the mentioned emotion model. Second, we provide an overview of which methods in contemporary consumer neuroscience may contribute to a better understanding and measurement of affective processing. Third and finally, we provide two examples of how to apply selected psychophysiological methods to study attitudes towards brands. This provides fundamental knowledge, which can be translated into further research on attitudes in brand co-creation.

## 2.    A BRIEF NOTE ON CONSUMER NEUROSCIENCE

About two decades ago, marketing started to use knowledge gained within the area of biological psychology and neuroscience. The main questions aimed to get a better understanding of consumer behavior, for example how consumers perceive brands and make purchase decisions (Lee et al., 2018). One promising advantage of consumer neuroscience is to overcome different types of biases, which are usually associated with traditional methods of marketing research, such as self-report data. First, applying psychophysiological and neuroscientific methods may help to overcome the bias of social desirability in answering. Second, measuring physiological data might help to measure information that respondents are partly or even completely unaware of. Measuring implicit attitudes is one key application within consumer neuroscience. This includes the measurement of affective processing and emotions. Affective processing-related information is not easy to put into words at a specific moment in time. Therefore, psychophysiological and neuroscientific methods are especially promising when it comes to measuring it.

Our brain knows more than we are capable of putting into words or images. A majority of information rests in a sub- or even unconscious sphere. This information guides our behavior, but we are unable to talk about it consciously. One potential way to access this treasure is brain imaging techniques, such as fMRI (functional magnetic resonance imaging), electroencephalography (EEG) and magnetencephalography (MEG). With the technological innovation to make use of fMRI for applied settings in the early 1990s, a new era in explaining human (consumption) behavior began (Bandettini, 2007; Senior et al., 2007). Researchers had the opportunity to look inside the "black-box" (the human brain) and monitor its activities associated with marketing- or consumption-related stimuli in a more comprehensive manner. Neuroscientific techniques such as fMRI can contribute to our understanding of what brain areas are activated when being confronted with particular stimuli (see, e.g., Plassmann et al., 2012). The interpretation of this data allows conclusions to be drawn on whether we like something or not. It may help to gather another piece of the puzzle in understanding cognitive and affective processes underlying observed consumption behavior. However, along with this groundbreaking opportunity, fMRI also has its limitations. This is especially the case when the topic of interest relates to field applications and when high temporal resolution is demanded. FMRI is still very resource intensive and the participant must lie in a narrow tube, which is a very unrealistic setting, significantly limiting the external validity of the obtained results. Therefore, other neuroscientific (e.g., EEG) and psychophysiological methods (e.g., skin conductance, heart rate, or startle reflex modulation) have also been introduced to the field of consumer neuroscience (Bosshard et al., 2016; Walla et al., 2017).

Next to the methodological advancements it is important that after almost 20 years of experience, the field of consumer neuroscience research also further developed its relevance and potentially new topical applications in the field. It is important to know which method lends itself to being the most appropriate for measuring cognitive and/or affective information processing. Moreover, together with selecting the appropriate method, discussions focusing on ethical aspects with the different involved stakeholders are necessary (see, e.g., Willingham & Dunn, 2003).

## 3.    THE EVOLUTION OF EMOTION

To better understand the added value of consumer neuroscience to traditional marketing research methods, we draw on knowledge from evolutionary biology and psychology. Every time the human brain determines behavior, it is tailoring its activity to best cope with the external environment: for example, if it is cold outside, we choose warm clothes. The evolution of mammals has established a neural network, which is essential to survival; making decisions to understand external stimuli – for example, is an animal approaching us wild or tame, is this fruit edible or fatal? This type of mental activity is called affective information processing. It deals with the question of "HOW" stimuli are that one is exposed to rather than "WHAT" they are. The latter, in terms of understanding which type of particular animal or fruit it is, what their names are, and so on, refers to cognitive information processing. This type of very complex cognitive information processing (including semantic processing) predominantly happens in the cortex and developed later in evolution. For pure survival, affective information processing has always been much more important. Avoiding a potentially harmful snake is much more essential than knowing what type of snake it is, let alone its scientific name. As can be seen, affective processing is the essential neural information source that feeds into like, dislike and any further kind of preference-related decision making. As mentioned above, Walla (2018) comes to the conclusion that affective processing (neural activity) guides behavior and proposes that an "emotion" should simply be understood as behavioral output to communicate feelings. To dig a bit deeper into the history of all this, in their chapter, Walla and Panksepp (2013) already highlighted that "emotion" is used by different authors as if one would call the wheels of a car "car", somebody else would call its engine "car", while a further one would call the entire car "car" and yet another one would call driving "car". This analogy was meant to describe the interchangeable use of the term emotion, which obviously creates unnecessary confusion hindering further progress in emotion research (see also vom Brocke et al., 2020). Only recently, within the NeuroIS community (also Society), has it been established that an emotion is a behavioral response (e.g., a facial expression) to affective processing. In other words, an emotion is simply behavior (see Walla, 2018, and Figure 23.1). Perhaps, it seems too easy and even a reductionist approach, but easy solutions should be seen as good solutions if they still help to sort out a clear definition problem. In this chapter, it is suggested to follow this notion for any future activities in the field of brand co-creation.

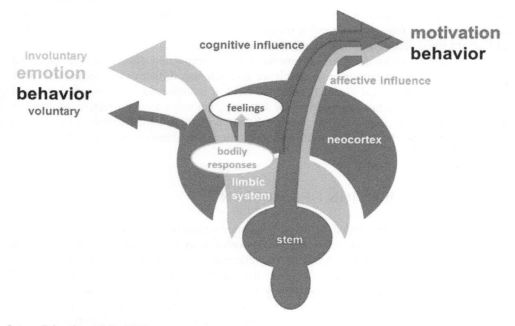

*Source:* Taken from Walla (2018).

*Figure 23.1    Emotion model*

Figure 23.1 visualizes the emotion model introduced by Walla (2018). According to this model any behavior is initially triggered deep inside the brain by old neural structures belonging to the brain stem. Before actual execution of any behavior (i.e., muscle contraction) it is adapted through affective and cognitive information processing that influence and thus modify the way we behave (arrows pointing right: motivation behavior). If affective processing crosses a certain threshold then bodily responses occur that are felt via conscious experience. Simultaneously, involuntary emotion behavior occurs (i.e., muscle contractions that display affective responses) that can be observed by conspecifics (lighter arrow pointing to the left). In addition, voluntary emotion can be elicited fully intentionally (darker arrow pointing to the left). Note that according to this model, emotion is not information processing, but it is behavior (emotions are behavioral output). Also, according to this model, fear is not an emotion, it is a feeling. One feels fear and fearful behavior showing a conspecific that one feels fear is what this model calls an emotion.

Talking about potentially harmful snakes and affective processing sounds like evolutionary aspects thousands of years old; however, affective information processing as well as decisions made by this system still guide our brain in everyday life today. Pure affective evaluations of our brain happen at an unconscious level, but they are very efficient. From a neuroanatomy perspective, the core location of affective information processing is the limbic system, particularly the amygdalae and the nucleus accumbens (see, e.g., LeDoux, 1995). They serve as a kind of intrinsic evaluation system checking whether a stimulus from the external environment is potentially dangerous or not. It is important to note that subjective feeling is neither critical nor necessary for the brain to determine affective information processing for decision making. For instance, experienced fear might be accompanied by bodily reactions such as sweating or shivering. These bodily reactions are then consciously recognized by the individuals as feelings. Emotions are then communicating that feeling to conspecifics (see also Walla & Panksepp, 2013).

# 4. METHODS TO MEASURE AFFECTIVE INFORMATION PROCESSING

Next to the aforementioned methods, for example fMRI, there are also other, more cost-efficient psychophysiological methods that are beneficial in this regard. Startle reflex modulation (SRM) is one such method that is capable of measuring raw affective information processing procession at an unconscious level. SRM includes using electromyography (EMG). Modulation of the startle reflex was initially found in animal studies on rodents. After that, it was found that humans also demonstrate a modulated startle reflex as a reaction to their current affective state (Vrana et al., 1988; Mallan & Lipp, 2007). When studying startle reflex modulation in humans, the magnitude of an eye-blink response to loud and short acoustic white noise is taken as a measure of startle reflex magnitude. The startle reflex is an automated response, being hard-wired at a basic level. What makes it interesting for studying affective processing is the fact that the eye-blink amplitude is reduced in the case of positive affective processing, and increased in the case of negative affective processing in relation to a so-called lead stimulus – a foreground stimulus to which a participant is exposed (Lang et al., 1998). The beauty of SRM is that it is objective in nature as well as independent from cognitive information processing. Hence, it is ideally sensitive to affective processing (i.e., pleasant versus unpleasant). It lends itself as an alternative method to measure the valence of affective content on a fine-graded scale. Moreover, it can be perfectly combined with other physiological methods, such as skin conductance, to also capture the level of arousal and thus the intensity of the engagement of the sympathetic nervous system (Bradley et al., 1993).

# 5. ATTITUDE TOWARDS BRANDS – SELECTED CASE STUDIES

In the following, we want to outline two selected examples on how consumer neuroscience may help to better measure affective aspects related to brands. These insights might also provide further guidance for the design of empirical studies in the area of brand co-creation. In our first example, we show that SRM is indeed promising to capture attitudes towards brands, because attitudes include a large involvement of affective processing (see Walla et al., 2011). In our second example, we build on the findings of our first example and show how psycho-physiological methods can help to better understand a change in attitude towards brands, for instance through the impact of evaluative conditioning (see Walla et al., 2017).

## 5.1 Case Study 1 – Startle Reflex Modulation and Brand Attitude

In 2011, Walla, Brenner, and Koller applied startle reflex modulation to assess the affective (formerly called emotional) facets of brand attitude. One goal of their study was to test whether SRM lends itself to being an appropriate tool in this regard. Twenty-one subjects participated in their lab experiment. Prior to the startle experiment, participants rated 300 common international brands in an online questionnaire, according to their liking or disliking of the respective brands. One unique feature of the study was that the stimulus material for the actual startle experiment was created specifically for each individual participant, significantly enhancing both internal and external validity. During the actual startle experiment, a list of individually ranked brand names, together with some filler brands, was presented to each participant. Results showed that SRM does indeed seem to be capable of capturing the affective part of brand attitudes. Significantly reduced eye-blink amplitudes were found for the liked brand names compared to the disliked brand names. In other words, reading the disliked brand names evoked a significantly stronger startle reflex (as they produced a negative affective state) than reading the liked brand names (which produced a positive affect).

## 5.2 Case Study 2 – Startle Reflex Modulation, Brand Attitude and Evaluative Conditioning

Walla et al. (2017) investigated the different aspects of implicit versus explicit measures of brand attitude. Attitudes towards brands are learned evaluations and, as such, can be modified (Dainton & Zelley, 2011). They are composed of at least three different components, which are knowledge, affective content and behavior tendencies (see, e.g., Banyte et al., 2007). Of interest in their study were the means by which our already established attitudes concerning specific brands are modified via evaluative conditioning (EC) and how these changes vary across explicit and implicit measures, which may be differently sensitive to the abovementioned components. In their paper (Walla et al., 2017), they test the hypothesis that there is more to brand attitude than what is in a self-report and that different measures demonstrate this through their varying sensitivity related to EC effects. Data was collected via self-report, startle reflex modulation (SRM), skin conductance (SC) and heart rate (HR) as well as the implicit association test (IAT) from 21 participants. Similar to the study presented in Case 1, individually liked/disliked brands were identified for each participant via an online survey (participant's ten most liked and ten most disliked brands – individual extreme attitude ratings – out of a set of 300 common brands). These 20 target items, specifically chosen for each participant, were combined with 180 non-target brand names (filler items). Stimuli for each participant were shown in a random order. All brand names were presented in white letters (same font type for all brand names) on a black background (no logos were presented during this study). The pictures for the EC procedures were taken from the IAPS (international affective picture system; Lang et al., 2008). The major finding of this study was that different measures testing whether or not EC had an effect on established brand attitude reveal different results. The IAT is known to reveal non-conscious attitudes particularly with respect to their underlying cognitive aspects. In their study, IAT-based findings showed a significant conditioning effect after one, ten and 16 conditioning procedures in the case of disliked brand names conditioned with positive images. They could also show that the attitude towards a comparison brand that was not subject to conditioning did not show any change as a function of time. The

IAT results, very similar to the SRM findings, indicate a change in attitude in one direction, namely from disliked to liked. SRM, known to be sensitive to raw affective processing, turned out to be sensitive to evaluative conditioning effects on established brand attitude too, though demonstrating that more than just one conditioning procedure is needed to manipulate the attitude component SRM is most sensitive to. Raw affective processing, as in reading brand names, is assumed to be related to implicit brand attitude. Based on that, Walla et al. (2017) interpret that implicit brand attitude seems to be more sensitive and vulnerable to evaluative conditioning effects than explicit attitude. Implicit attitudes may be particularly interesting in situations where consumers make their purchase decisions not so much based on cognitive information processing, but rather as a result of their so called "gut feeling", which is said to be associated with raw affective processing. This might also become relevant in the process of brand co-creation.

## 6.    CONCLUSION

Our two selected case studies show that SRM indeed represents a promising tool to measure affective components of brand attitude. Even though methods such as fMRI are also able to capture affective responses, it is their poor temporal resolution and the high related costs that make SRM an attractive alternative. Since affective aspects are predominantly important in brand co-creation, we suggest that co-creation research should also have a closer look at alternative methods to measure them. Next to traditional methods already used, such as exploratory qualitative approaches or quantitative methods, SRM could be an especially promising candidate to capture the affective elements arising within brand co-creation, especially as previous research suggests that SRM is particularly sensible to measure implicit attitudes towards brands. Disentangling explicit from implicit attitudes towards brands in brand co-creation as well as studying their respective consequences might be a relevant step towards a more in-depth understanding of psychological phenomena going on during the process of brand co-creation. The suggested solution is not to replace traditional methods with SRM, but to complete them with it. In addition to this methodological suggestion we also propose following the idea that affective processing guides behavior (and is thus most interesting to brand co-creation) while emotions communicate feelings (they do so in that they are behavioral responses that can be observed by conspecifics). We hope that our ideas stimulate further research on different methods to capture affective information processing in brand co-creation and to study information processing in brand co-creation on a broader basis.

## REFERENCES

Bandettini, P. (2007). Functional MRI today. *International Journal of Psychophysiology*, *63*, 138–145.

Banyte, J., Joksaite, E., & Virvilaite, R. (2007). Relationship of consumer attitude and brand: Emotional aspect. *Engineering Economics*, *2*(52), 65–77.

Bosshard, S.S., Bourke, J.D., Kunaharan, S., Koller, M., & Walla, P. (2016). Established liked versus disliked brands: Brain activity, implicit associations and explicit responses. *Cogent Psychology*, *3*, DOI: 10.1080/23311908.2016.117669.

Bradley, M.M., Lang, P.J., & Cuthbert, B.N. (1993). Emotion, novelty, and startle reflex: Habituation in humans. *Behavioral Neuroscience*, *107*, 970–980.

Dainton, M., & Zelley, E. D. (2011). *Applying Communication Theory for Professional Life: A Practical Introduction*. Thousand Oaks, CA: SAGE Publications.

Hsieh, S.H., & Chang, A. (2016). The psychological mechanism of brand co-creation engagement. *Journal of Interactive Marketing, 33*, 13–26.

Kaufmann, H.R., Loureiro, S.M.C., & Manarioti, A. (2016). Exploring behavioral branding, brand love and brand co-creation. *Journal of Product & Brand Management, 25/6*, 516–526.

Lang, P.J., Bradley, M.M., & Cuthbert, B.N. (1998). Emotion, motivation, and anxiety: Brain mechanisms and psychophysiology. *Biological Psychiatry, 44*, 1248–1263.

Lang, P.J., Bradley, M.M., & Cuthbert, B.N. (2008). International affective picture system (IAPS): Affective ratings of pictures and instruction manual. Technical Report A-8. University of Florida, Gainesville, FL.

LeDoux, J. E. (1995). Emotion: Clues from the brain. *Annual Review of Psychology, 46*, 209–235.

Lee, N., Chamberlain, L., & Brandes, L. (2018). Welcome to the jungle! The neuromarketing literature through the eyes of a newcomer. *European Journal of Marketing, 52*, 4–38.

Mallan, K.M., & Lipp, O.V. (2007). Does emotion modulate the blink reflex in human conditioning? Startle potentiation during pleasant and unpleasant cues in the picture–picture paradigm. *Psychophysiology, 44*, 737–748.

Mingione, M., Cristofaro, M., & Mondi, D. (2020). 'If I give you my emotion, what do I get?' Conceptualizing and measuring the co-created emotional value of the brand. *Journal of Business Research, 109*, 310–320.

Panksepp, J. (1998). *Affective Neuroscience: The Foundations of Human and Animal Emotions*. New York: Oxford University Press.

Plassmann, H., Ramsoy, T.Z., & Milosavljevic, M. (2012). Branding the brain: A critical review and outlook. *Journal of Consumer Psychology, 22*(1), 18–36.

Ramaswamy, V., & Ozcan, K. (2016). Brand value co-creation in a digitalized world: An integrative framework and research implications. *International Journal of Research in Marketing, 33*, 93–106.

Senior, C., Smyth, H., Cooke, R., Shaw, R.L., & Peel, E. (2007). Mapping the mind for the modern market researcher. *Qualitative Market Research: An International Journal, 10*, 153–167.

Sugathan, P., Ranjan, K.R., & Mulky, A.G. (2017). An examination of the emotions that follow a failure of co-creation. *Journal of Business Research, 78*, 43–52.

vom Brocke, J., Hevner, A., Léger, P.M., Walla, P., & Riedl, R. (2020). Advancing a NeuroIS research agenda with four areas of societal contributions. *European Journal of Information Systems, 29*, 9–24, DOI: 10.1080/0960085X.2019.1708218.

Vrana, S.R., Spence, E.L., & Lang, P.J. (1988). The startle probe response: A new measure of emotion? *Journal of Abnormal Psychology, 97*, 487–491.

Walla, P. (2018). Affective processing guides behavior and emotions communicate feelings: Towards a guideline for the NeuroIS community. In Davis, F., Riedl, R., vom Brocke, J., Léger, P.M., & Randolph, A. (Eds.), *Information Systems and Neuroscience. Lecture Notes in Information Systems and Organisation*, vol 25. Cham: Springer. https://doi.org/10.1007/978-3-319-67431-5_16

Walla, P., & Panksepp, J. (2013). Neuroimaging helps to clarify brain affective processing without necessarily clarifying emotions. In Fountas, K.N. (Ed.), *Novel Frontiers in Advanced Neuroimaging*. Rijeka: InTech.

Walla, P., Brenner, G., & Koller, M. (2011). Objective measures of emotion related to brand attitude: A new way to quantify emotion-related aspects relevant to marketing. *PLoS ONE, 6*, 1–7.

Walla, P., Koller, M., Brenner, G., & Bosshard, S. (2017). Evaluative conditioning of established brands: Implicit measures reveal other effects than explicit measures. *Journal of Neuroscience, Psychology, and Economics, 10*, 24–41.

Willingham, D.T., & Dunn, E.W. (2003). What neuroimaging and brain localization can do, cannot do and should not do for social psychology. *Journal of Personality and Social Psychology, 85*(4), 662–671.

# 24. Prolonging the shared project value of surplus co-creation

*Yun Mi Antorini and Gry Høngsmark Knudsen*

## 1.    INTRODUCTION

Product co-creation is often characterized as an endeavor that individual consumers take on in collaboration with a company, in which the company receives added value from the partnership (Prahalad & Ramaswamy, 2000, 2004). Accordingly, much co-creation activity takes place in company-hosted co-creation communities, in which companies initiate and provide digital space for co-creation projects. Besides contributing solutions that address their consumption needs, consumers benefit from the enjoyment of undertaking the co-creation task (Lakhani & Panetta, 2007) and from receiving recognition from professionals in the co-creation process (Jeppesen & Frederiksen, 2006). The known outcomes for consumers who partake in co-creation communities are social status (Mathwick et al., 2008), social affirmation (Hartmann et al., 2015), and consumer empowerment through its influence on product design (Füller et al., 2009). Consequently, ideas often work to mobilize consumers socially when they encounter others who share an interest in seeing their ideas brought to life. Furthermore, research has shown that co-creation communities play a significant role in co-creation processes, for example, by distributing work tasks to alleviate the individual co-creator (Knudsen & Antorini, 2021).

## 2.    SURPLUS CO-CREATION

As there is generally a surplus of ideas provided by consumers compared with the ideas that companies and organizations can absorb or need, many co-creation projects remain at the idea stage and are not realized as products. For example, an early co-creation initiative by BMW had 497 consumers submitting 300 ideas, of which only three ideas were considered for realization (BMW, 2010). In situations in which only a fraction of the consumer-suggested ideas are realized, we suggest that the unproduced co-creation attempts can be characterized as *potentials* that demonstrate both effort and emotional investment by the co-creator and the larger group of consumers who became invested in the idea. We argue that this situation can be described as surplus co-creation, which leaves traces of co-creation activities, emotional investment, and shared consumer passion but lacks final approval—the production by the company or organization. We point out that these surplus ideas represent untapped resources of community and consumer engagement, and we contend that companies can explore these resources more to maintain consumer interest in co-creation activities. To further unpack this overlooked aspect of co-creation, we present a case of surplus co-creation in which users collaborate on an idea for a LEGO product. We propose that a shared sense of project value motivates consumers to collaborate and drive an idea toward completion. We observe that the shared sense of project value lives on when a co-creation project is completed, even when the co-creation project is not successful. As observed by Arvidsson (2011, p. 269), co-creation relies on this shared sense of project value. As co-creation projects are often subject to given timeframes after which they cease to exist, the shared project value lives a perilous life given the uncertainty of a project outcome.

## 3.   PROLONGING PROJECT VALUE LIFE

Similar to Arvidsson (2011), we suggest that the shared sense of project value established among supporting consumers in a co-creation community holds value to them even if the project is not accepted by the company. However, this sense of shared value is often over-looked both in theoretical perspectives and in managerial practice. In this case, we recommend that companies find ways to sustain and support this sense of shared project value even after they might have rejected the project idea itself. Building on Arvidsson, we assert that a shared sense of project value leaves an ethical conundrum for companies facilitating co-creation communities. We propose that companies could work with more realization and engagement routes when it comes to the afterlife for discarded projects, such as providing prolonged engagement opportunities, letting third parties develop projects, and facilitating the sharing of building instructions, among others.

The takeaway from this case is developing perspectives on how to create a positive contin-uation with consumers when surplus ideas are rejected for production. First, we build on the insight that co-creation activities represent strong emotional brand engagement (Hollenbeek, 2011), which can be characterized as a high-risk investment on the consumer part that calls for some form of reciprocal recognition from the company. Second, co-creation communities build social and project value among consumers, which provides additional opportunities for commitment and brand loyalty building. Thus, companies can sustain co-creation through heightened support of forms of project realization other than the ones currently offered. Finally, through a shared sense of project value in surplus ideas, new and additional innova-tions might emerge that could benefit not just the consumers but also the company.

## 4.   LEGO IDEAS

We build a case based on a rejected project from the LEGO Ideas platform. The project in that sense represents a case of surplus co-creation because the company decided not to pursue the idea, even after large numbers of consumers convened around the idea to support its realiza-tion. The LEGO Ideas platform is a co-creation community in which users can upload ideas for new products. Other users vote on the ideas with the aim of reaching 10,000 votes, which will enable the idea to be reviewed by the LEGO Group. During the voting process, other users comment on the idea and suggest improvements; they help spread the word of the idea and recruit more voters. Thus, like-minded passions meet and thrive around particular ideas. For this case, we deal with an example of an idea that reached the 10,000 votes necessary for production but was rejected as a result of the LEGO Ideas review process. The data for the case are sourced from the publicly accessible project page on the LEGO Ideas platform. The data consisted of text, such as project descriptions, timelines, and user comments on the project idea and the project owner. It also consisted of images and videos of the project. We collected the data manually and analyzed them from a traditional qualitative perspective. Using an ethnographic approach, we analyzed the data thematically, focusing on terms of commitment and supporting activities, such as sharing the project outside of the LEGO Ideas platform. The point of the analysis was to understand the ways in which consumers express their commitment and investment in the project and develop a shared sense of project value. The data for this case are part of a larger study that included ten cases encompassing both approved and rejected project ideas.

## 5. THE CASE

The project idea for a new LEGO Ideas set, *Plum Creek – The Little House on the Prairie*, was submitted by a young French LEGO fan. It is based on the TV show and novels by Laura Ingalls Wilder, *Little House on the Prairie*. The project consists of several buildings and other parts, such as a cart and animals. It is the first project that the user has ever uploaded. A majority of the comments from other LEGO Ideas members focus on the impressive level of detail, authenticity, and creative design of the project idea. An example can be seen in the following user comment:

> Amazing job! This looks almost exactly like the house and the barn in the TV series. You have included a tremendous amount of detail and have a very nice project! I agree with you that it is probably too big as is to be a set, but I would love to see the house become a set (and maybe the barn as a second set?) Best of luck on 10,000 supporters!

Beyond merely commenting on the level of detail and authenticity, the above user also critically evaluates the market potential with comments on the set size and how the idea can be split up to be more marketable. Through critical engagement with the idea, the user helps qualify and negotiate the possibilities of the idea.

The project was updated three times and received 838 comments over the course of gathering 10,000 votes. Along the way, the project provides opportunities for other users to share their enthusiasm for both the TV show and the novels. Some even confess that the project inspires them to reengage with both the TV show and the novels. Furthermore, several users discuss the project in the more general context of pioneer and Western themes. To advance the project, many users share—and encourage others to share—the project on other sites, particularly themed social media sites outside of the LEGO Ideas platform, where fans of the TV show and the novel meet. An example is the following, written by a user:

> Every year my oldest daughter has me re-read all the entire set to her. We would really love a set like this. In fact, I've started pushing for support on Twitter with the hashtag #LittleHouseLego. This is one of the most unique pop-culture related sets I have seen in a long time and I know my family would get a ton of use out of it.

In the above comment, the user uses their interest in the original narrative and TV show to help drive attention for the project. Thus, on their own initiative, the user creates a hashtag for Twitter to raise awareness of the project. Because the user shares a commitment to the narrative, they go the extra mile to promote the project outside the LEGO Ideas platform. The community's engagement with the project ebbs and flows throughout the different phases. In total, the voting process went on for one and a half years. During the process, one particular user was especially committed to the project and the idea.

The user takes a username related to the project, and throughout the voting spends considerable time urging other users to help attract voters. This user also works to keep up the spirit when voting is less prolific. Already in their first comment, the user shares their commitment to the project: This is excellent! needs to get approved I've shared the link on many pages hopefully we can get those numbers we need :).

From the beginning, this user identifies a "we" who cares about the project and works to get the votes. In a later comment, the user writes,

> We're gonna make this happen! Sharing and voting there must be a billion Little House Fans.

The user keeps invoking the "we" that emerges from sharing a passion for the Little House TV show and novel.

However, whereas the project successfully raised the 10,000 votes needed to enter the review process, the set was not selected for production. Upon meeting the goal of gathering 10,000 votes, the project is considered completed and enters a phase in which the project owner can no longer update the project, nor can users vote. However, the comments and the project are still visible and serve as a clear reminder of the passion and commitment many users felt and shared around the idea. With the closing of the voting process, consumer passion and engagement become *homeless*. That is, the voting and commentary provided an opportunity for the users to meet and engage with one another, but they now lacked their previously shared purpose and their reason for coming together.

## 6.    DISCUSSION

The above case is an example of surplus co-creation, in which an idea was not pursued by the company, but it raised sufficient votes for it to be considered for production. In this case, it becomes evident that users share an understanding of the value that the project holds. Below, we discuss the case as an extension of current theory that primarily focuses on the company–consumer nexus when it comes to the value derived from co-creation (Pralahad & Ramaswamy, 2000, 2004). On the other hand, theory that focuses solely on consumers primarily emphasizes brand attachment or social outcomes (Schau et al., 2009). Building on Skålén et al. (2015), we suggest that this focus on consumers and brand or company attachment provides a too limited co-creation perspective.

### 6.1    Redeeming Disappointed Users

As our case suggests, project value is also important to consumers on many different levels. Thus, the project owner is but one member of a larger group of users who come together to realize the potential of an idea. The group is driven by its shared fandom relationship (Knudsen et al., 2019) with the TV show and the novel, but it also has wider interest in adjacent themes, such as Western and pioneer toys. They express their enthusiasm through voting, making comments, encouraging participation, sharing ideas and suggestions for improvements, and offering to buy the building instructions should the project not be selected for realization. As in the case of most co-creation projects, in which users come together for a specific period to complete a particular task, shared engagement and enthusiasm for the project develop. These create a sense of subcommunity, but when the voting process is complete, this subcommunity dissolves because of the lack of an active project to unite them.

The lack of emotional connection to a subcommunity is especially tough in cases in which the product idea is rejected for production. Previous research has examined interaction in communities as a matter of community ties and knowledge about brands/products, community practices, and roles (Kozinets et al., 2008). We argue that a shared sense of project value in cases of co-creation can be an equally important driver for subcommunities. In the case at hand, the specific narrative of the *Little House on the Prairie* is an additional factor in gathering project supporters, that is, a means through which voters often recognize a good build, a creative idea, and an authentic project rendering; a further reason to support a project is the fandom it represents (Knudsen et al., 2019) to large groups of users. Thus, where research hitherto has looked at value creation for companies in co-creation processes (Pralahad & Ramaswamy, 2000, 2004) or the alliances between a community and a brand or company (Skålén et al., 2015), we suggest that the extended engagement in particular co-creation processes holds emotional value and represents the extended collaboration between co-creators and the surrounding community.

## 6.2   Creating an Afterlife for Rejected Ideas

Thus, the above case illustrates the conceptualization of value that consumers get from community practices by demonstrating "community engagement practices" (Schau et al., 2009, p. 34) in cases in which ideas are not chosen for production. The emotional and practical investment and efforts that a project represents to the users result in surplus co-creation ideas; however, these are lost with the rejection of the idea. Given the strong investment and considerable time that some users demonstrate, we build on the work of Arvidsson (2011) and suggest that there is an ethical obligation to reward consumers' engagement even when their ideas are not chosen for production.

Thus, we suggest that companies engaged in consumer co-creation develop ways to facilitate an afterlife for consumers' sense of shared project value. Companies can use this afterlife to understand more about consumer interests and build stronger relationships with consumers. In the above case, LEGO Ideas' process for getting an idea into review creates a commitment that goes beyond the temporal and spatial restrictions set up through the platform. Finding ways to nurture surplus co-creation ideas can be a way to maintain community engagement. An example of such an initiative is the currently ongoing BrickLink Designer Program. Here, the LEGO-owned platform, BrickLink, aims to realize some otherwise rejected project ideas through crowdfunding.

## 6.3   Acknowledging Collective Co-Creation

We further point out that the shared sense of project value that consumers develop around ideas comes from their shared efforts to get the idea to the review stage. Therefore, we propose finding ways of letting users acknowledge one another's collaborative efforts because this is where the shared sense of value is most visible to the subcommunity. That is, when users help promote a project or in other ways help develop the idea, the project owners often express their gratitude in comments and acknowledge the skills of the assisting users. Implementing structures of acknowledgment and gratification can enable users to build more strongly on the collective aspects of co-creation. These structures could *live on* with the idea even when it is rejected for production to help consumers manifest and maintain their sense of shared value and commitment. Through mobilization of the community, more aspects of the project are developed and vocalized in comments. Thus, building on the community interest even if the specific project does not go on to be produced renders more avenues for further co-creation and aspects of why consumers decide to engage in co-creation projects. Finally, we argue that companies could benefit from extending their collaborations with consumers. While we expect that users will initially be disappointed that their shared passion (in this case) is not selected for realization, their activities and interactions offer the possibility of obtaining a better understanding of what their passion is about and how to accommodate it or work with it in the future, thereby creating more opportunities for new co-creation avenues.

On a practical level, acknowledging consumer efforts in a variety of ways, especially when an idea is rejected for production, could be a way to recognize surplus co-creation as valuable to the engaged consumers. For example, a simple suggestion is to allow comment sections to remain open so that consumers can maintain their shared relationship based on a specific idea or theme. Another suggestion could be to facilitate themes that can gather subgroups and unite groups with similar thematic interests. That way, co-creation projects become the focal activity and the driver of social activity.

## REFERENCES

Arvidsson, A. (2011). Ethics and value in customer co-production. *Marketing Theory*, *11*(3), 261–78.
BMW. (2010). *BMW Group co-creation lab.* https://www.press.bmwgroup.com/global/article/detail/T0082655EN/bmw-group-co-creation-lab?language=en
Füller, J., Mühlbacher, H., Matzler, K., & Jawecki, G. (2009). Consumer empowerment through internet-based co-creation. *Journal of Management Information Systems*, *26*(3), 71–102.
Hartmann, B. J., Wiertz, C., & Arnould, E. J. (2015). Exploring consumptive moments of value-creating practice in online community. *Psychology and Marketing*, *32*(3), 319–40.
Hollenbeek, L. (2011). Demystifying customer brand engagement: Exploring the loyalty nexus. *Journal of Marketing Management*, *27*(7/8), 785–807.
Jeppesen, L., & Frederiksen, L. (2006). Why do users contribute to firm-hosted user communities? The case of computer-controlled music instruments. *Organization Science*, *17*(1), 45–63.
Knudsen, G. H., & Antorini, Y. M. (2021). Hard work: Unanticipated collaboration in co-creation processes. *Journal of Association of Consumer Research*, *6*(4), 435–46.
Knudsen, G. H., Hjort, M. F., & Blaser, L. J. (2019). Playing with fandom. *MedieKultur*, *35*(66), 18–36.
Kozinets, R. V., Hemetsberger, A., & Schau, H. J. (2008). The wisdom of consumer crowds: Collective innovation in the age of networked marketing. *Journal of Macromarketing*, *28*(4), 339–54.
Lakhani, Karim R., & Panetta, J. A. (2007). The principles of distributed innovation. *Innovations*, Summer, 97–112. https://www.mitpressjournals.org/doi/pdf/10.1162/itgg.2007.2.3.97
Mathwick, C., Wiertz, C., & De Ruyter, K. (2008). Social capital production in a virtual P3 community. *Journal of Consumer Research*, *34*(6), 832–49.
Prahalad, C. K., & Ramaswamy, V. (2000). Co-opting customer competence. *Harvard Business Review*, *78*(January–February), 79–87.
Prahalad, C. K., & Ramaswamy, V. (2004). Co-creation experiences: The next practice in value creation. *Journal of Interactive Marketing*, *18*(3), 5–14.

Schau, H. J., Muniz, A. M., & Arnould, A. J. (2009). How brand community practices create value. *Journal of Marketing, 73*(September), 30–51.

Skålén, P., Pace, S., & Cova, B. (2015). Firm-brand community value co-creation as alignment of practices. *European Journal of Marketing, 49*(3/4), 596–620.

# 25. The iconization of Greta Thunberg: the role of myths in co-creating a person brand

*Teresa Brugger and Verena E. Wieser*

## 1. GRETA THUNBERG AND THE FRIDAYS FOR FUTURE SUSTAINABILITY MOVEMENT

In summer 2018, Sweden went through a massive heatwave that broke temperature records and affected nature seriously by causing wildfires (Jung et al., 2020; *The Local*, 2018). In August of that same year, the 15-year-old Swedish teenager Greta Thunberg decided to stop attending school on Fridays in order to raise awareness of the consequences of climate change and to call for political change (Crouch, 2018). On her first school strike day, Greta sat lonely in front of the Swedish parliament, holding a white paper sign saying "Scholstreijk for klimatet" (School Strike for Climate) (BBC, 2020).

Two years later, a lot has changed in Greta's life—besides that she still strikes every Friday with a white paper sign, reading the same words. Her school strike soon gained attention all over the world, and she has managed to move millions of followers worldwide to join the sustainability movement called "Fridays For Future" on the streets and online (Ramzy, 2019). On 20th of September 2019 approximately four million people in 161 countries participated in the largest climate change strike in history (Woodward & De Luce, 2019). In September 2020 the hashtags #climatestrike and #FridaysForFuture showed 634k and 839k results on the social media platform Instagram (accessed on 16/09/20). Greta held speeches at the UN climate change conference and at other political events, met with powerful leaders and activists, like Barack Obama, the Pope, or Malala, and earned honors and awards, like the "TIME's person of the year award" in 2019. With simple but pointed messages Greta continues urging politicians and the world's citizens to finally take climate protection action for the next generations to come, to fully implement the 2015 Paris Agreement within the United Nations Framework Convention on Climate Change (Zeit Online, n.d.), and to stop a climate catastrophe as long as there is still time (Thunberg, 2018).

## 2. THE GRETA THUNBERG PERSON BRAND

Over the last two years the young Swedish teenager Greta Thunberg has not only become the face of a global climate movement, but she herself has also become an iconic person brand attracting manifold brand associations. According to Parmentier and Fischer (2012) a person brand is defined by several associations linked to a specific person that consumers have in mind. When briefly screening Social Media for the keyword "Greta Thunberg," it appears that her name stands for dominant shared consumer associations, like sustainability and social change. Greta's yellow rain jacket, her serious face expression, and the white paper sign in her hands have become visual brand associations. At the same time Greta also attracts contradictory emotional brand associations, like hope for a better future and hate against herself and the movement she stands for.

A peculiarity of a person brand is that it has numerous competitors who might have the same potential, while a product or service brand mostly has a few direct competitors (Parmentier & Fischer, 2012). Many other teenagers or adults with a virtuous mission and a brave personality could have raised awareness for climate change; but Greta is the one who is known all over the world. So, how has Greta Thunberg become the iconic person brand she is today?

## 3.   THE CO-CREATION OF A PERSON BRAND: A CULTURAL BRANDING PERSPECTIVE

In this case study we propose that the reach and relevance of the Greta Thunberg person brand in such a global dimension cannot solely be attributed to her own branding means and actions. Instead it can be understood as the result of a multi-stakeholder brand co-creation process. The case study aims to understand how different brand stakeholders co-create a person brand like Greta Thunberg from a cultural branding perspective. Such a perspective suggests that myths—understood as shared stories that address latent societal tensions and convey culturally shared beliefs—are at the core of building an iconic brand (Holt, 2004; Holt & Cameron, 2010). In the context of person branding, cultural branding can be understood as a process by which mythic narratives are created, shared, and spread around a person, which ultimately connect the person brand with larger societal discourses. Together, these narratives form a mythic persona (Dion & Arnould, 2016; Stern, 1994); a socially constructed character of the human being, whose brand image can either become strongly associated with aspects linked to the person (Fournier & Eckhardt, 2019), or can become disassociated from the person throughout the brand co-creation process (Dion & Arnould, 2011, 2016).

While consumer and brand research has dominantly focused on studying brand managers' role in (person) brand building, recent research conveys that stakeholders like consumers and the media take an important role in brand co-creation (Centeno & Wang, 2017; Fournier & Alvarez, 2019; Humphreys & Thompson, 2014). In the case of Greta Thunberg, one can assume that consumers and the media actively take part in her person brand co-creation process: 10.5 million people follow Greta's Instagram profile and her most commented post counts 142,956 comments (accessed 08/10/2020), and newspapers regularly feature Greta Thunberg when journalists report about her activism, or comment on her life and personality. In the following, this case study will hence investigate how Greta herself, consumers, and the media contribute to the co-creation of the mythic persona Greta Thunberg.

## 4.   CO-CREATED MYTHIC NARRATIVES AROUND GRETA THUNBERG

Our person brand co-creation analysis draws on a vast pool of netnographic data which captures written and visual communication material of the person, consumers, and the media in the year 2019. We chose to sample Greta Thunberg's Instagram posts, consumers' Instagram comments that respond to her posts (retrieved in March 2020), and newspaper articles from four international online newspaper outlets (*CNN*, *Sueddeutsche Zeitung*, *The Guardian*, *USA*

*Today*). For the sake of data organization and reduction we identified the most resonant five key events in 2019, sampled Greta's respective Instagram posts, 1,600 Instagram comments per event, and one newspaper article per event of each outlet. The final data set encompasses nine Instagram posts of Greta Thunberg, 24 newspaper articles, and 893 Instagram comments (as we stopped analyzing comments when new comments did not lead to new analytic patterns). For data analysis, we adopted the lens of French philosopher Roland Barthes on myth to the data set (Barthes, 1973). In this perspective myth is not the same as a fictionalized story, but a means to communicate. Barthes describes myth via a semiological system, which explains the relation between the *signifier* (a word or image) and a *signified* expressing the message behind. Together they build a sign and communicate a meaning. According to Barthes, myth forms a second-order semiological system, whereas the sign of a first-order system functions as the signifier in the second. Via metalanguage (the signified of the second layer) an alternative, fundamental signification is transmitted. Hence, through mythical communication, any word or image can transform into the terminology of a mythical system. In our data analysis, we identified metalanguage in stakeholder communications (e.g., inferring the ascriptions of heroic personality traits from consumer comments) to reveal the major co-created mythic narratives that build the Greta Thunberg person brand. Furthermore, we distinguished between communication myths and action myths; while communication myths evolve around what and how is communicated, action myths convey how goals are reached.

### 4.1    The Heroic Greta Thunberg

The most dominant communication myth contributing to the Greta Thunberg persona is the *hero* myth. Rooting in mythology, the hero myth highlights the heroic personality traits of the person brand Greta Thunberg. One example is the attribute of *being strong*. In their comments consumers repeatedly praised and admired Greta for her bravery and strength and ascribed the label of a savior to her:

> You are an absolute inspiration and a savior! And remember, whilst these bullies who have no life are actively choosing to put you down (how unbelievably sad), YOU ARE SAVING THE WORLD! (Instagram user 1, 2019)

Greta herself contributed to such heroic ascriptions, for instance, by describing her diagnosis of the Asperger syndrome as a "superpower", rather than a potential challenge. However, Greta not only created myth via the topics she talked about, or the language she used, but also via the metalanguage her pictures conveyed. Consider, for instance, her Instagram post showing the cover page of the *TIME* magazine issue of December 23rd, 2019 (gretathunberg, 2019a). The cover featured Greta Thunberg as person of the year 2019, standing on the shore in Lisbon in casual clothing, and gazing towards the rough sea with her serious facial expression. Such imagery transferred a heroic image of a brave girl rising up to challenges and potential dangers which lie outside the picture's frame.

The hero myth is accompanied and supported by a strong action myth—*the discovery trip*. This myth emerges from Greta Thunberg's sailing trip to the US in summer 2019. When Greta took a year off from school to focus on campaigning she intendedly chose to travel to the UN climate change conference by sailing boat in order to set a signal against more polluting travel options (Behrmann, 2019; Woodward & De Luce, 2019). Amongst consumers and the media, the sailing trip evoked metalanguage of a discovery trip. Journalists, for instance, extensively covered the departure scene of the sailing trip, using vivid visual language to describe the gripping atmosphere of a hero starting an adventurous mission: "On white-crested swells under leaden skies, the teenage climate activist Greta Thunberg has set sail from Plymouth on arguably her most daunting challenge yet" (Reuters, 2019). At the same time they pointed out the risks and uncertainties she put up with when entering unknown terrain: "This leaves the crossing with a sailboat. However, sailors rarely travel across the Atlantic in August because of the danger of hurricanes" (Fridays for Future, 2019). As journalists chose to portray a rather challenging journey (e.g., featuring a rough sea and dark skies), they steered images of a brave girl facing these challenges. Consumers picked up on the story of a challenging journey, for instance, through congratulating her when she arrived in America. One consumer wrote: "As so many millions have done. Welcome to America G.!" (Instagram user 2, 2019).

With such statements, consumers connected Greta with the long history of settlers passing the famous but challenging route across the Atlantic Ocean to arrive in New York in the hope for a better life.

### 4.2    The End of the World and Revolution Myths

Another prominent communication myth in the data set is the *end of the world myth*. On her Instagram account Greta pushed an image of the world facing a climate catastrophe and mass extinction. Via verbalizing emotions like fear of resource shortage, and anger about a stolen future of the young generation, she transmitted the metalanguage of the end of the world. One famous example was her speech at the UN climate change conference, which she also posted on her Instagram account (gretathunberg, 2019b). Her speech portrayed an apocalyptic scenario, emphasizing a stolen future for her and all other young people in case we continue to live like we do now. The tears in her eyes demonstrated her fear of this dystopian scenario, and her anger about missing political action to avoid this scenario becoming real. While Greta initiated this mythic narrative, other stakeholders joined in with their own words. Consumers contributed to this narrative by confirming her perspective and repeating it: "it is obvious our planet is being ruined by human civilization" (Instagram user 3, 2019). Journalists added scientific facts to their reports about an imminent climate catastrophe: "The world is currently on track to warm by as much as 3.4C by the end of the century, the UN warned, a situation that would escalate disastrous heatwaves, flooding, droughts and societal unrest. Major coral reefs and many other species face extinction" (Milmann, 2019). Via such detailed factual reports the myth got embedded in science, and the frightening future scenario became more immediate and tangible.

Linked to this communication myth is the action myth of the *revolution*. A revolution commonly refers to a rapid change in the given political, social, or economic conditions, whereas the aim is to tackle social problems and to reframe power structures with a new political beginning (Schubert & Klein, 2018). Although Greta herself did not directly use the rhetoric of revolution, she called on society—from citizens to politicians—to stand up and strike against the status quo. She posted pictures of much frequented climate change strikes to demonstrate that the people, and especially the young generation, blamed failing authorities, and were ready to initiate change. One example is the caption of her post about the speech at the UN Climate Change Conference:

You are failing us. But the young people are starting to understand your betrayal. The eyes of all future generations are upon you. And if you chose to fail us I say we will never forgive you. We will not let you get away with this. Right here, right now is where we draw the line. The world is waking up. And change is coming, whether you like it or not. (gretathunberg, 2019b)

Several newspapers added a sense of revolution via reporting about the global reach and actions of the "Fridays for Future" movement. The global climate strike was, for example, described as the "largest in history" (Zaschke, 2019), and a peaceful revolution of the young: "Hundreds of thousands of young people have taken to the streets from Manila to Copenhagen as part of the latest student climate strikes to demand radical action on the unfolding ecological emergency" (Taylor et al., 2019). Again, although revolution is not directly called out, meta-language conveys the impression of a relevant societal tension in need for radical solutions. As the name Greta Thunberg was often mentioned in connection with the movement, she was put in the middle of the revolution myth, and was endowed with a leadership role: "The Swedish teenager has become the figurehead of a burgeoning movement of youth climate activists" (Picheta, 2019).

### 4.3    Demystification

A third prominent theme in our consumer data is the *demystification* of the Greta Thunberg persona. As a response to dominant communication and action myths, stakeholders created myths that contradicted myths, or eliminated "the mystifying features of" a myth (see Merriam Webster for definition of "demystification"). Demystifying language was most evident in consumer data whereas consumers demystified the hero myth by employing emotional language. Commenters used expressions of hate, personal attack, and provocation, when, for instance, blaming Greta that she posts "shit" (Instagram user 4, 2020), when promoting hashtags like #fuckgreta on Instagram, or when celebrating environment-polluting consumption practices, like driving cars with a large environmental footprint. These critical statements not only undermined the credibility of the heroine, but also of her followers; they set a direct and stark contrast to supporters idolizing Greta Thunberg as "hero" (Instagram user 5, 2019), or to slogans like "Make the world Greta again." As another example of demystification, consumers contradict the end of the world myth with statements like "except it's not science you are promoting but instead lies" (Instagram user 6, 2019). Others undermined action myths, like the revolution myth, when blaming Greta Thunberg for not doing enough. Consumers demanded that she should be taking more direct action (like planting trees herself), instead of restricting herself to holding speeches and raising awareness.

## 5.    THEORETICAL AND MANAGERIAL IMPLICATIONS

After an intense year of campaigning in 2019, the name "Greta Thunberg" no longer just stands for a Swedish teenager refusing going to school on Fridays to strike for a change in global climate policy. Instead, Greta Thunberg has become a heroine fighting for climate protection, breaking moorings for a challenging discovery trip, and initiating what some call a historical climate change revolution. Although Greta has become a symbol of hope for those who long for change, she has also attracted controversial debate; stakeholders engaging in demystification and emotional language added contradictive meanings to the person brand.

The results of this case study support the view of cultural branding that myth-making is crucial to establish an iconic person brand. The case, however, also adds to a cultural branding perspective that research needs to take into account how multiple stakeholders co-create versatile myths through metalanguage in different ways. On one hand, some mythic narratives may thrive when the person brand (consciously or not) taps into a prevalent social disruption (Holt & Cameron, 2010). When Greta fueled the *end of the world myth*, for instance, she connected her persona to the booming but complex global sustainability discourse of the 21st century, which was in search for new solutions and leaders—or icons, respectively. On the other hand some more person-centered myths, like the *hero myth*, were considerably carried on and expanded by brand stakeholders, like consumers and the media. In Greta Thunberg's case stakeholders' metalanguage contributed to establish a strong *mythic core* of the person brand. However, we also found *demystification* tendencies on its periphery, which conveyed an oppositional image of the same person brand. In extreme and prolonged cases of demystification, these tendencies may lead to the evolution of a contradictory "doppelgänger" (Thompson et al., 2006) persona, which originates in a parallel ideological domain, yet competes with the initial person brand for public relevance. In Greta's year of campaigning in 2019, however, such a push of meanings into opposite directions did not hinder the mythic core persona from growing in reach and relevance, but rather sparked further brand interest, and ultimately myth-making. Nevertheless, future research on person branding needs to investigate how core and periphery myths evolve and interrelate over time.

For brand managers this case study suggests that myth-making is a relevant communication tool for successful person branding. Brand managers need to engage with myths through screening the public discourse around a person for metalanguage, and through entering into a conversation with stakeholders on this level. For instance, nourishing a revolution myth can attract the attention of consumers who are sharing the same vision of change (even if they are not fully sharing the passion for the exact same cause), or can attract media attention, which is likely to add further mythic visual language or facts to person brand communications.

## REFERENCES

Barthes, R. (1973). *Mythologies*. Frogmore: Paladin.

BBC (2020). Greta Thunberg: Who is she and what does she want? Retrieved September 15, 2020, from: https://www.bbc.com/news/world-europe-49918719.

Behrmann, S. (2019). 9 things to know about the teenage climate change activist Greta Thunberg. *USA Today*. Retrieved September 15, 2020, from: https://eu.usatoday.com/story/news/politics/2019/09/18/greta-thunberg-6-things-know-climate-change-activist/2358463001/.

Centeno, D., & Wang, J. J. (2017). Celebrities as human brands: An inquiry on stakeholder–actor co-creation of brand identities. *Journal of Business Research*, *74*, 133–138.

Crouch, D. (2018). The Swedish 15-year-old who's cutting class to fight the climate crisis. *The Guardian*. Retrieved September 15, 2020, from: https://www.theguardian.com/science/2018/sep/01/swedish-15-year-old-cutting-class-to-fight-the-climate-crisis.

Dion, D., & Arnould, E. (2011). Retail luxury strategy: Assembling charisma through art and magic. *Journal of Retailing*, *87*(4), 502–520.

Dion, D., & Arnould, E. (2016). Persona-fied brands: Managing branded persons through persona. *Journal of Marketing Management*, *32*(1–2), 121–148.

Fournier, S., & Alvarez, C. (2019). How brands acquire cultural meaning. *Journal of Consumer Psychology*, *29*(3), 519–534.

Fournier, S., & Eckhardt, G. M. (2019). Putting the person back in person-brands: Understanding and managing the two-bodied brand. *Journal of Marketing Research*, *56*(4), 602–619.

Fridays for Future (2019). Greta Thunberg segelt nach Amerika [Greta Thunberg sails to America]. *Sueddeutsche Zeitung*. Retrieved March 27, 2020, from: https://www.sueddeutsche.de/panorama/ thunberg-friday-for-future-klima-1.4545338.

gretathunberg (2019a). "Wow this is unbelievable…" [Instagram post]. Retrieved March 26, 2020, from: https://www.instagram.com/p/B58C1l8JLox/.

gretathunberg (2019b). "Right here, right now…" [Instagram post]. Retrieved March 26, 2020, from: https://www.instagram.com/p/B2w-0NsCkXp/.

Holt, D. B. (2004). *How brands become icons: The principles of cultural branding* (1st ed.). Boston: Harvard Business School Press.

Holt, D. B., & Cameron, D. (2010). *Cultural strategy: Using innovative ideologies to build breakthrough brands* (1st ed.). Oxford: Oxford University Press.

Humphreys, A., & Thompson, C. J. (2014). Branding disaster: Reestablishing trust systemic risk anxieties. *Journal of Consumer Research*, *41*(4), 877–910.

Jung, J., Petkanic, P., Nan, D., & Kim, J. H. (2020). When a girl awakened the world: A user and social message analysis of Greta Thunberg. *Sustainability* (Switzerland), *12*(7), 1–17.

Milmann, O. (2019). Greta Thunberg condemns world leaders in emotional speech at UN. *The Guardian*. Retrieved March 27, 2020, from: https://www.theguardian.com/environment/2019/sep/23/ greta-thunberg-speech-un-2019-address.

Parmentier, M. A., & Fischer, E. (2012). How athletes build their brands. *International Journal of Sport Management and Marketing*, *11*(1–2), 106–124.

Picheta, R. (2019). Greta Thunberg reaches New York after 15-day yacht journey. *CNN*. Retrieved March 27, 2020, from: https://edition.cnn.com/2019/08/28/us/greta-thunberg-new-york-landfall-scli -intl/index.html.

Ramzy, A. (2019). Students across the world are protesting on Friday. Why? *New York Times*. Retrieved March 12, 2020, from: https://www.nytimes.com/2019/03/14/world/europe/climate-action-strikes -youth.html.

Reuters (2019). Greta Thunberg sets sail for New York on zero-carbon yacht. *The Guardian*. Retrieved March 27, 2020, from: https://www.theguardian.com/media/2019/dec/11/greta-thunberg -time-magazine-person-of-the-year-2019.

Schubert, K., & Klein, M. (2018). *Das Politiklexikon* (7th ed.). Bonn: Dietz.

Stern, B. (1994). Authenticity and the textual persona: Postmodern paradoxes in advertising narrative. *International Journal of Research in Marketing*, *11*(4), 387–400.

Taylor, M., Pidd, H., & Murray, J. (2019). Hundreds of thousands of students join global climate strikes. *The Guardian*. Retrieved March 27, 2020, from: https://www.theguardian.com/environment/2019/ nov/29/hundreds-of-thousands-of-students-join-global-climate-strikes.

*The Local* (2018). Sweden heatwave: Hottest July in (at least) 260 years. Retrieved September 15, 2020, from: https://www.thelocal.se/20180723/sweden-heatwave-hottest-july-in-at-least-260-years.

Thompson, C. J., Rindfleisch, A., & Arsel, Z. (2006). Emotional branding and the strategic value of the doppelgänger brand image. *Journal of Marketing*, *70*(1), 50–64.

Thunberg, G. (2018). The disarming case to act right now on climate change [Video file]. Retrieved September 12, 2020, from: https://www.ted.com/talks/greta_thunberg_the_disarming_case_to_act _right_now_on_climate_change?language=de.

Woodward, A., & De Luce, I. (2019). How Greta Thunberg started a new climate change movement. *Business Insider*. Retrieved September 15, 2020, from: https://www.businessinsider.de/international/ greta-thunberg-bio-climate-change-activist-2019-9/?r=US&IR=T.

Zaschke, C. (2019). Greta Thunberg: Besser sachlich als laut. *Sueddeutsche Zeitung*. Retrieved March 27, 2020, from: https://www.sueddeutsche.de/politik/greta-thunberg-klimaschutz-un-1.4613675.

Zeit Online (n.d.). Greta Thunberg: Die Klimakämpferin. Retrieved September 15, 2020, from: https:// www.zeit.de/thema/greta-thunberg.

# 26. Finding new product ideas at Eisenbeiss: integrating non-frontline employees into co-creation processes

*Oliver Koll*

## 1. THE COMPANY

Eisenbeiss is a manufacturer of specialized gear solutions. The family-controlled company is headquartered in Enns in Austria and owns a subsidiary in Sacramento in the United States. The company sells gear equipment to customers in various industries: special machinery manufacturers (for example, extrusion of plastic waste, PVC compounding, or cereal), large power supply players (like Caterpillar or GE) as well as developers of plants for steel and aluminum production. Note that most of Eisenbeiss's customers are plant manufacturers who integrate Eisenbeiss gears as one of many components into the equipment they sell. In addition, Eisenbeiss provides services (repair, maintenance, problem detection) for its own gears, but also users of machinery involving competitive gear technology.

In most of these markets, Eisenbeiss and its customers have collaborated for decades and both sides have an in-depth understanding of each other's capabilities and requirements. New product ideas usually result either from new technical requirements put forward by customers or product enhancements suggested by Eisenbeiss to increase the efficiency of processes or the durability of their components. In each case, the engineers of both parties work closely to ensure that new components (i.e. the gears produced by Eisenbeiss) can be easily integrated into the machinery manufactured by its customers.

Eisenbeiss has a reputation to provide specialized gearing solutions which typically are not available as off-the-shelf products and which prove their value (and justify their price premium) in particularly tough settings, like extreme temperatures, complicated construction settings, challenging materials or engine-wearing processes. In such circumstances, only a handful of companies globally can meet the technical requirements of gear customers.

However, Eisenbeiss has limited exposure to the actual users of the machinery which feature their gearing solutions. They do not sell gears to PVC manufacturers, food producers, steel mills or power plants, but to the suppliers of machinery to these industries. The service unit is the only part of the organization that regularly gets in touch with companies using the machinery equipped with Eisenbeiss gears (see Figure 26.1 for an example of a gear solution and Figure 26.2 for an Eisenbeiss gear in use).

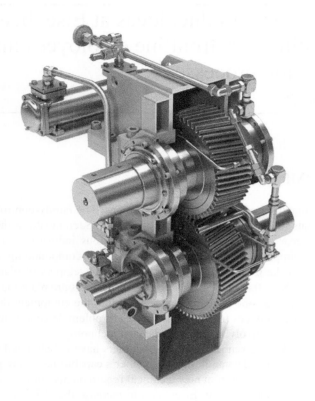

*Figure 26.1     Gears for gas engine power generators*

## 2.     THE CHALLENGE

Given the close relationship with customers, but limited access to the actual users of their gear solutions, management was wondering whether the company might miss out on opportunities for new products: "It is always the same people (i.e. client-facing personnel) interacting with the same set of clients (i.e. machinery producers) from which we derive ideas for development projects" was a commonly stated concern. Whether true or not, there was concern that the company did not take a broad enough perspective in its search for new ideas.

Amongst various plans to take a broader perspective (e.g. visiting fairs of industries not yet served, hiring people with different educational backgrounds), the CEO of the company decided to initiate a new format for the detection of new product ideas during the COVID summer of 2020. In close collaboration with a consulting company that has worked with the company on strategy and positioning projects for the past two years, the ambition was to leverage the intellectual and creative capabilities of a wider selection of employees (especially non-client-facing staff) in the organization to come up with new product ideas. The consultancy was tasked with developing an efficient and effective framework for this co-creation process with a duration of less than four weeks in total (see Figure 26.3).

The goal was simple: identify three to five ideas for new products with substantial market potential which also strengthen the Eisenbeiss brand reputation as one of the most innovative players in the industry. Ideally the exercise should only take a few weeks to exploit the slack available in some parts of the organization during the first pandemic wave in 2020.

*Figure 26.2      Bridge in Rotterdam harbor equipped with Eisenbeiss lifting gears*

## 3.      THE CO-CREATION PROCESS

The first task was to choose participants among the company's workforce. Instead of putting all responsibility on the leadership team, the CEO decided that the innovation taskforce was to consist of a mixture of people from various functions, for example construction, services, operations, manufacturing and sales. Some people in this team were in regular contact with customers and users, while others had an in-depth understanding of quality control, supply chain issues, or construction demands. Overall 14 persons were nominated to participate – with leadership choosing mostly relatively new and rather young people in the organization to avoid a "been there, done that" mentality. This selection, while deliberate, was not without risk: the lack of experience and client interaction might prevent a customer-driven search for new ideas, and limit the acceptance of findings by higher management.

First, all participants took part in an online briefing session, for cost reasons, but also because this was the first COVID summer (2020) and options for physical meetings were limited. This session included setting the goal for the group, outlining expectations regarding the involvement of everyone, defining roles and presenting nine case studies of successful innovations by comparable companies. Three of the case studies focused on product or service improvement (e.g. a tractor company adding four-wheel steering for better handling in tight spaces), three on developing completely new markets (e.g. a cable car company moving from alpine markets to urban passenger transport) and three on new business models (a machinery manufacturer renting out its assortment instead of selling it). None of these examples was sup-

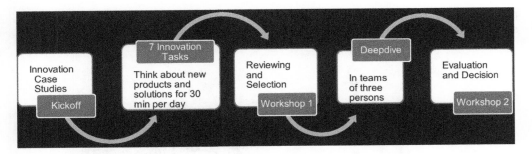

*Figure 26.3    Project outline*

posed to be a perfect role model for Eisenbeiss, but reflecting about these ideas was supposed to broaden the mindset of the participants to help uncover new ideas for the brand.

Second, for seven days in a row, each of the participants had to come up with three ideas per day. These ideas were a response to a task shared by email and had to be submitted anonymously to an online "diary". The task contained a different stimulus every day to help the creative thinking of the participants. These stimuli ranged from reading an article covering the most successful innovations in the industry over the past year, to interviewing a customer about their most pressing challenges regarding user requirements, to studying the websites of competitors. After the seven days more than 200 different ideas were generated (after removing double entries).

Third, these ideas were evaluated and pruned through an iterative process in two (live, not virtual) workshops. During the first one, seven two-person groups "visited" seven flipcharts which contained all ideas identified via the online diaries, but structured by similarity of topics. Each team, consisting of one more client-facing and one less client-facing member, was tasked to return with three ideas that in their opinion showed the most potential for the Eisenbeiss brand. Teams were encouraged to think beyond the ideas shown on the flipcharts. More specifically, if during the discussion about these ideas a new or an improved one emerged then that idea would make the team's shortlist. The three favorites had to be summarized and presented to the whole group with an emphasis on customer benefits provided, potential clients and their fit with the desired Eisenbeiss brand reputation (i.e. the gear producer that provides the best solution to any challenging condition: extreme heat or cold, extreme demands on machinery, difficult construction settings, etc.). The likely market success (e.g. in terms of sales) was not a factor at this stage. After the 21 ideas were presented and amended with additional ideas of the remaining participants (for example regarding potential users, synergies with existing technologies, sales activities or product offerings), 12 unique ideas remained since many of the favorites were too similar to treat them as distinct. The group then voted for their favorites by individually choosing three of these ideas and ranking them. Three, two and one points were allocated to each #1, #2, and #3 choice respectively.

The seven ideas that received the most points made it to the shortlist and were respectively allocated based on interest and enthusiasm for the idea to teams of two or three persons. Each team had the responsibility of preparing a short business case (based on the *business model canvas* logic) for the idea over the next ten days. Each group therefore carefully reviewed the benefits provided, potential customers, internal requirements, or barriers to a successful development. The seven ideas ranged from service-dominant (like online trainings) to sales-focused (like a webshop) to business-model based (pay for use) concepts. After intensive discussions, three ideas were chosen to be pitched to the management team of the company as candidates for the company's innovation funnel in 2021.

## 4.   THE LEARNINGS

New product ideas in B2B settings come from many sources: commercially savvy people in the R&D department, attentive sales people willing to listen to customer comments, analyses of complaints, competitive intelligence, technological break-throughs in one's own or a neighboring industry, or ideas brought up by other partners in the stakeholder system. Irrespective of the source, fostering the motivation and ability of stakeholders involved in co-creation processes is an important organizational capability and one for which most organizations willingly admit room for improvement. While all of these approaches can be fruitful, none guarantees success. It therefore comes as no big surprise that most organizations engage more in trial-and-error approaches to come up with the next "big thing" rather than a structured process.

The project initiated by Eisenbeiss followed a structured process, but still serves as an example of an experiment with an uncertain outcome – both in terms of the actual marketplace success the ideas will deliver (which is unknown at this stage), but also with respect to the organizational evaluation of the approach. Its success can be evaluated on three different levels: individually, structurally and procedurally.

Regarding the individual perspective, participants reported being extremely motivated throughout the four weeks, with many interviewing and seeking feedback for their ideas with multiple people inside and outside the organization. It was obvious that participants enjoyed being part of an atypical task and did not mind moving beyond their usual assignments.

From a structural perspective the process assigned responsibility to a team which had (in this particular setup) never worked together, consisted of people from multiple organizational layers and functions, and triggered sharing between organizational members that usually do not interact. As such, the project did certainly help develop and deepen personal relationships and increase the understanding of staff for specific challenges of other organizational teams.

From a procedural perspective, participants went far beyond the minimum requirements set out by the organizers which resulted in more information being collected, more internal stakeholders being integrated, and more customer feedback sought. Hence the stakeholders involved in the process turned out to extend beyond the core team and the results reflected the ideas of a large portion of the company's workforce and a small selection of the company's total stakeholder system.

So, is this an approach that should be adopted by other organizations? Probably – but only if top management shows a strong commitment for the initiative and signals appreciation for participants' efforts throughout the whole process. Without that appreciation organizational members are unlikely to engage in some necessary steps for co-creation: (a) move beyond their own personal network and functional team in searching for useful innovation stimuli; (b) test and learn from the reaction of peers and other stakeholders; and (c) evaluate each idea not only with respect to its sales potential, but also with respect to its fit with the brand's desired reputation.

# 27. Turning lead into gold: from weighty consumer feedback to co-creation

*Peter Espersen*

## 1. INTRODUCTION

Co-creation is not a new concept; it has been done tacitly for centuries: from farmers who've jointly improved their farming equipment (Ruggles, 2000) to organized co-creation as the basis for business model generation and achievement of competitive advantage (Ramaswamy & Gouillart, 2010). Co-creation differs from traditional user research and consumer feedback, by letting consumers actively build and take part in the process, and not just submit ideas and give input. Therefore, value co-creation represents a departure from the classic value creation model, where the company creates value and the consumer then consumes value. Thus, co-creation is a new way of thinking about how value is generated (Prahalad & Ramaswamy, 2004).

This chapter aims to share insights based on experiences of implementing co-creation projects in different contexts. For more than 15 years, the author applied co-creation in various contexts, such as Danish TV2 and Pixable, in MMO gaming world at Habbo Hotel and as an entrepreneur in the digital community space around voting, among others. This chapter will discuss co-creation in the context of three organizations: Habbo Hotel, Pixable and jovoto. It will present ways of creating opportunities for co-creation, co-creation outcomes and general learnings derived from the methods and processes that have been adopted.

## CASE 1: HABBO HOTEL – SETTING THE STAGE FOR CREATORS

### Background

Habbo (www.habbo.com) is an online virtual community targeted towards teens and young adults where members create their own avatars, make friends, chat, build rooms, design and play games. Founded in 2000 in Finland, Habbo now operates nine language communities (or "hotels"), with users in more than 150 countries and "over 120 million user-generated rooms in the 9 Habbo language communities" (https://www.sulake.com/habbo).

### Particularities of the Co-Creation Context

Value co-creation in a virtual world is different to classical co-creation of products or tangible assets. In massively multiplayer online games (MMOG), storytelling and meaning is being co-created as part of users' role-play experience. Thus, being an only user or "single player" is not part of the core experience. The task for Habbo's management was to set up the virtual world to stimulate time on site, engagement, virtual activities and ultimately increase spending among the users.

**Methods and Process**

The team at Habbo originally worked within the community by controlling the online environment and scheduling activities for the users. They controlled consumer requests and tried to align activities with offline events and popular culture. Over time, the task of Habbo's staff moved from producing original content and curated experiences to providing story starters, support and orchestration – and making sure that the Habbo software supported users in the co-creation efforts (which was unfortunately not always the case). Co-creation in Habbo's universe relates the meaning, activities between avatars/users in the game. Examples include creating homemade avatar football games with rules based on an honor system, avatar dance competitions, suggestions for actual assets and manifestations outside of the game platform, popular fan-sites and even an online radio station by users for users (https://www.radio.net/s/lautfm-habbo-hotel). These on-platform co-creation activities, that included activities across territories and language barriers, were the most successful. Enthusiastic users interested in a certain theme or activity that was not supported by the original software (such as avatar football) created user-generated content (UGC), which allowed them to pursue their interest, and encouraged others to join them. Over time, fans took ownership for their own events, recruiting user-moderators to help them run the events as well as running them with regular intervals (e.g., a yearly football tournament with winners, prizes and even player trades between the teams). In addition, off-platform co-creation activities, such as meet-ups, tutorials, fan-created sites and radio webcasts were initiated.

Co-creation within Habbo often led to revenue opportunities for the company. Users requested sponsored content, like branded content as well as unique items that could have a viral effect. One prime example is a fan wanting their avatar to mimic real-life activities, such as using an Apple iPod leading to an in-Habbo version.

**Conclusion**

The key learning from Habbo's co-creation efforts is that managerial actions can affect spending and stimulate creativity. Habbo's management learned to provide the tools for the users to create their own meaning, activities and content. The greatest successes were achieved when focus switched from leading activities to creating play starters and options for the users to self-organize. The economic outcome of the switch was immediate and led to an increase in both direct spending on virtual goods for their hotel room, called "furni" and indirect forms of consumer loyalty and retention.

# CASE 2: PIXABLE – COMMUNITY AS A WAY OF SCALING

## Background

Founded in 2008, Pixable was a media product focused on 18–14-year-old millennials in the U.S. to deliver news; user-generated content and sponsored content. Pixable was a top 100 mobile website in the U.S. measured on traffic in 2014.

## Particularities of the Co-Creation Context

In early 2015, Pixable (http://www.pixable.com/) had a need to build a platform where content could be sourced from partners and users. Citizen journalism was already gaining popularity at the time, and the blogosphere created many sustainable companies such as Huffington Post and Mic. For Pixable it was an easy way to scale, but also it hit on a number of other value points for the company, such as authenticity and meeting consumer demand. Scaling content in the fast-moving world of online news proved to be a challenge for a small editorial staff. Niche content provided value, but would need to be scaled significantly to be profitable. Experiments with syndication of content from large news outlets such as Huffington Post and Mic.com had proved successful, but this content was geared towards mainstream audiences.

## Methods and Process

The team at Pixable knew that the solution to "more and better" content was to generate content that would be (1) cost-effective and (2) cater to their niche market. The solution was to create a contributor platform, where Pixable users could submit content for editorial consideration. This method of submission for possible publication created a forum for young, aspiring journalists to get published by a reputable media outlet and gain recognition beyond their own social channels. To further scale content, a co-creation initiative was created to leverage user-generated journalism in niche areas, such as cooking, local news and various hobby/passion areas that drew large numbers of followers. A process was developed that made it possible for users to submit articles for editorial review, they were then bounced back and forth between the editorial team and the writer so as to ensure quality, and then ultimately published on the platform. Brand partnerships with major outlets such as Huffington Post, UrbanSpoon and Mic.com added value for the Pixable community, resulting in a faster process and higher perceived value and prestige for citizen journalists.

## Conclusion

The Pixable contributor network resulted in fast scaling of niche content as well as value for the company and users. Pixable received direct value in the form of increased time on site and ultimately added revenue. Indirect value was created through Pixable's ability to create content in areas where the team did not have expertise (e.g., tapping into niche cultures). The users got the experience of becoming published on a leading news site and were able to use it to strengthen their digital presence.

## CASE 3: JOVOTO – HIGH-END DESIGN BY PRACTICE COMMUNITY

### Background

jovoto (www.jovoto.com) is a co-creation and open innovation platform helping organizations gain access to customer-centric solutions. It is a global community of over 100,000 creative professionals that help organizations by co-creating design solutions. jovoto has been around for more than ten years and has worked with global brands like Greenpeace, Coca-Cola and Adidas.

### Particularities of the Co-Creation Context

Clients look to jovoto to increase their innovation capabilities and seek input on design problems where they lack core capabilities or internal expertise. Companies turn to jovoto when the task is limited in scope and can be seen as an add-on to current strategy. jovoto has the opportunity to create closed, by invitation only, challenges to its community. Company partners need to understand the risks of disclosing proprietary information to external parties but need to share enough information to generate results. The risk/reward is usually worth it for them.

### Methods and Process

jovoto is an attractive partner for brands who seek to create unexpected outcomes in a pay-as-you-go consultancy model. While jovoto's infrastructure, technology platform and process are developed and maintained by jovoto, the core value lies in "the community", in terms of community size and capabilities. The distribution of roles is as follows: jovoto staff and client frame, set target and rewards, and launch a design challenge on the digital platform. It then falls to the community to interpret the brief and deliver towards the objectives. Finally it falls to the client to implement and move the design forward and internalize it. During this process, jovoto experienced several challenges in relation to running co-creation:
Client-related challenges

- Business development and sales is a constant challenge for the jovoto team. The sales cycle and proof of concept can take time. That, along with the company's pay-as-you-go model to support smaller clients and projects leads to smaller growth.
- Conclusions from independent external parties may be vastly different than original client expectations. Integrating said results may also be a challenge as the project owner/client might not have the agency or structure to implement all changes suggested by the community.
- Further, jovoto has had a challenge, as all co-creation and crowd sourcing platforms, with their output being too divergent in nature, and not as spot on as clients desire.

Community-related challenges

- Project acceptance by the community is highly dependent on the specific challenge as well as the prize offered.

- As the community works on more difficult challenges, output quality is not always on par with the client's expectation and integration and transfer of ownership from the community producers to the client can be difficult. There is competition for the right talent. The talent can be distracted as they use other platforms as well, such as 99designs, Designhill or Upwork.
- The core value of jovoto lies in its community and this is hard to claim ownership of.

## Conclusion

Building an engaged community takes time and maintenance is cumbersome. jovoto takes care of this for clients and has the knowledge and skills to ensure the right users are triggered to enter client challenges. Finally, a general challenge for jovoto is to ensure quality of output. jovoto has attempted to solve this issue in the following ways:

- Reducing size of the cohorts who gain access to a challenge as well as implementing qualifications for it; slimming down the cohort and qualifying it (from 100,000 to 10,000 active users).
- Creating bespoke cohorts for specific clients to work continuously on in-depth problems. This results in the selected community learning about the client's product as well as about what is expected and how to optimize output for effect. It also allows the company to learn what the community is capable of and in turn how to better utilize their skills.
- jovoto built a sizeable case repository, which can act as inspiration to both clients and the community. This has been a successful way of sharing best practice and continuous learning.

## 2.    LESSONS LEARNED ON CO-CREATION

### 2.1    Prepare Well

Do your homework before engaging the crowd. You create anticipation and you have partners and users spend time and sometimes work based on you starting the process. This, along with the emotional energy users and partners are going to invest can create tension and disappointment.

Some good questions to ask yourself are:

- What tools are you going to use to manage the process?
- What timeline are you aiming for?
- Does the group that you are engaging have the skill set that matches the challenge?

### 2.2    Set Your Rules of Engagement

Make sure that you create solid engagement principles for the process. These shouldn't be difficult to remember and they should act as guiding stars for all employees and participants in the process. Part of the engagement principles is creating a "sample space" in which you are able to in-source/act on the outcome of the co-creation process. This ensures that the process does not grind to a halt and that the outcome is something that the company is able to use.

## 2.3   Always Create Win–Win

If the process and outcome is not a win–win, disappointment can happen on both sides. This closes the door for future co-creation and can result in tension and dissatisfaction.

## 2.4   The Users are Smarter than You, More than You and Never Sleep

Keep in mind, that users and partners, especially if they are numerous, are creative and can attempt to take advantage of missteps and loopholes in the co-creation process. Therefore, it is incredibly difficult to change and amend a process once it is running and it is not recommended making it up on the go.

## REFERENCES

Prahalad, C. K., & Ramaswamy, V. (2004). Co-creation experiences: The next practice in value creation. *Journal of Interactive Marketing*, 18(3), 5–14.

Ramaswamy, V., & Gouillart, F. (2010). Building the co-creative enterprise. *Harvard Business Review*, October 2010, 1–9.

Ruggles, D. F. (2000). *Gardens, landscape, and vision in the palaces of Islamic Spain*. Penn State Press.

# Closing remarks

We extend a special thanks to Edward Elgar and its staff, who have been most helpful throughout this entire process. Equally, we warmly thank our contributors, with whom we have worked closely. They have exhibited the desire to share their knowledge and experience with this book's readers—and a willingness to put forward their views for possible challenge by their peers. We hope that this compendium of chapters and themes stimulates and supports colleagues in their teaching, learning and leadership development.

Stefan Markovic, Copenhagen, Denmark
Richard Gyrd-Jones, Copenhagen, Denmark
Sylvia von Wallpach, Copenhagen, Denmark
Adam Lindgreen, Copenhagen, Denmark, and Pretoria, South Africa

# Index

Printed and bound by CPI Group (UK) Ltd, Croydon, CR0 4YY

16/04/2025